Birth of the Republic
The Origin of the United States

Birth of the Republic
The Origin of the United States

by
Warren L. McFerran

PELICAN PUBLISHING COMPANY
Gretna 2009

*The word "Pelican" and the depiction of a pelican are trademarks
of Pelican Publishing Company, Inc., and are registered in the
U.S. Patent and Trademark Office.*

ISBN 9781589807273

Printed in the United States of America

Published by Pelican Publishing Company, Inc.
1000 Burmaster Street, Gretna, Louisiana 70053

Birth of the Republic

The Origin of the United States

Dedicated to my wife, Susan

Contents

"The States can never lose their powers till the whole people of America are robbed of their liberties. These must go together; they must support each other, or meet one common fate."

    – Alexander Hamilton
    (New York State Ratifying Convention, 1788)

"I hope that no gentleman will think that a State will be called at the bar of the federal court...It is not rational to suppose that the sovereign power should be dragged before a court."

    – John Marshall
    (Virginia State Ratifying Convention, 1788)

"View the system then as resulting from a spirit of Accommodation to different Interests....It is a great Extent of Territory to be under One free Government; the manners and modes of thinking of the Inhabitants, differing nearly as much as in different Nations of Europe....We have, as you will see, taken a portion of power from the Individual States, to form a General Government for the whole to preserve the Union....The powers of the General Government are so defined as not to destroy the Sovereignty of the Individual States."

    – Pierce Butler
    (Letter to Weedon Butler, October 8, 1787)

Key Influences and Commentators on the American Constitutional Period

First Row: John Locke, George Washington, Thomas Jefferson, John Taylor of Caroline, and Patrick Henry. *Second Row:* Benjamin Franklin, James Madison, Alexander Hamilton, Edmund Randolph, and John Dickinson. *Third Row:* Gouverneur Morris, James Wilson, Oliver Ellsworth, William Paterson, and Pierce Butler. *Fourth Row:* Gunning Bedford, Luther Martin, and Roger Sherman.

Chapter One
The Rise of American Civilization

There are few modern textbooks which accurately portray the historical rise of American civilization, and even fewer that accurately relate the true principles of the American political system as established by our Founding Fathers. Ever since the time of the War Between the States, most of what we regard as historical scholarship has been employed, not to accurately portray our constitutional system as one founded on proper divisions of authority and wise limitations of power, but to celebrate the triumph of the Federal Government over the sovereignty of the States and the inalienable rights of the American people.

Shortly after that tragic and historically significant war, an earnest effort was made to rewrite American history and to reinterpret the Federal Constitution. Ignoring completely all the plain facts to the contrary, it was widely proclaimed that the United States of America was a single, consolidated Nation, ruled by a supremely sovereign National Government, and that this had always been the intention of those who wrote and adopted the supreme law of the land! The existence of the States was deemed an historical mistake or a political oversight that could no longer be tolerated by an intolerant Federal Government, and if allowed to survive at all, the States could exist only as local divisions or branches of the centralized national authority. Accompanying the introduction of this novel and radical concept was the inauguration of the alarming growth – both in terms of its scope of authority and its powers – of the Government of the United States.

The growth of Big Government in the United States will undoubtedly stand as the greatest tragedy of the Twentieth Century. Its powers have grown so enormous over the years that there is no activity currently undertaken by any citizen which does not fall within its claimed jurisdiction and authority, as it seeks to regulate everything and dominate everyone. So draconian is its influence and authority, in fact, that it has categorized all people by sex, race, and age, and no man can avoid its discriminating practices. It has also literally catalogued each and every citizen by number, an incredible feat which no other totalitarian government in history has ever been able to accomplish.

With the advent of the Twenty-First Century, much of the mythology that has been relied upon to sustain the Leviathan State is being replaced by newer, more radical interpretations of American history and constitutionalism. This new *politically correct* revisionism goes far beyond anything ever before employed to ostensibly justify the existence of Big Brother, as it seeks to disparage our social and cultural heritage and to totally condemn the very foundations of our civilization.

A Politically Correct View of American Civilization

According to this newest "politically correct" mode of historical interpretation, when Christopher Columbus discovered the New World in 1492, it was a dark day in history. His chief accomplishment was not the spread of enlightened European civilization to the Western Hemisphere, but the destruction of indigenous civilizations in Middle America. The early settlers in North America, we are informed, were not courageous men and women who planted the seeds of a great civilization on wild, untamed shores. Rather, they were thieves and swindlers who stole the land from the native Indians.

Nor do the Founding Fathers of the American Republic escape the blanket condemnation. They were hypocrites who owned slaves while boldly proclaiming that all men are created equal. The Declaration of Independence they published to a candid world completely failed to liberate women from oppressive patriarchal bondage, and the Constitution they wrote and ratified did not loosen the chains of a single slave until amended some three-fourths of a century later. The new politically correct pseudo-scholarship also asserts that, when the hardy pioneers first pushed westward across the Appalachians toward the Pacific coast, this did not represent a divinely inspired Manifest Destiny for a young Republic. To the contrary, it foretold the doom of the noble civilizations established by the Indian savages, to say nothing of the majestic bison herds, and inaugurated the ever-accelerating destruction of the continent's delicate eco-system.

In their frenzy to force such distorted views on a resisting populace, history textbooks have been completely rewritten, academic courses have been thoroughly revised, and every form of mass communications has been utilized to trash our heritage and display an utter contempt for all things in American society that reflect the traditional influences of Christianity, the male sex, and the White race in general. The message being delivered by the new revisionists cannot be mistaken. Those forces traditionally credited with settling an uncharted continent, taming a wilderness, and giving rise to the greatest Republic the world has ever known should no longer be regarded as the noble *builders* of culture and civilization, but as the great *destroyers* of savage cultures and primitive civilizations. The world, in essence, would be a better place today had the New World never been discovered, and guilt-ridden modern Americans should be willing to atone for the grievous sins of their forefathers by forsaking their heritage and surrendering their country to those forces determined to build a new society on the ruins of the old civilization.

Common sense, to say nothing of a basic instinct for self-preservation, compels us to reject the absurdities of the new revisionism. While the new "politically correct" ideology is certainly correct in contending that the forces that have shaped modern America have been a mixture of good and evil, it fails miserably in identifying which of those forces were good and which were evil. The foundations of the American Republic – our traditional social, economic, and cultural heritage, as well as the political principles on which our civilization was founded – all of which the new radicals so bitterly condemn, are the very things that should forever merit the praise and admiration of all mankind. These are the things about America which are good. What deserves universal condemnation are those forces and ideologies, both past and present, that have worked to undermine our heritage and subvert our political system – those forces that have worked to transform our system of constitutionally limited government into a system of unconstitutionally unlimited government.

One of the greatest challenges we face today is to understand and differentiate between those forces and ideologies, both good and bad, that have shaped modern America. The challenge is made especially difficult by the fact that much of academia has long been devoted to obscuring the true principles of our social, economic, and political system. Yet the challenge must be met. The very survival of our civilization, which all honest observers now acknowledge is in decline, is at stake.

The great and noble principles upon which a civilization is built clearly transcend political considerations. The *religious beliefs* of its people, their *social habits* and *customs*, their *family structures*, their *ethics* and *moral value systems*, and their *economic practices*, all contribute greatly toward defining the character and nature of their civilization. Yet the focal point where all these values, customs, and habits are fused together to shape the destiny of a civilization is its *political system*. As long as it remains true to its original principles, the civilization will thrive. When its principles are subverted and corrupted beyond redemption, however, the civilization is doomed.

All of the good moral principles upon which American civilization was founded are enshrined in the Constitution of the United States. The social, cultural, economic, and political views of the Founding Fathers were, in fact, the *driving forces* that dictated the type of constitutional system they created for America. The political system of strictly limited government they bequeathed to us was deliberately designed to nurture and sustain a hardy civilization of God-fearing, Christian, self-reliant individuals.

For these reasons, the American political system has always served as the *focal point* for the contending forces that have shaped our destiny. Even the newest of the assaults upon our civilization – the current counter-culture conspiracy aimed at undermining the American way of life – is audaciously promoted under the telling label of *political correctness*. Yet, whether the attack on our liberties has come from the new revisionists, the environmental zealots, the "civil rights" crusaders of yesteryear, or those merely seeking to plunder the public treasury, the distinctive cry has ever been the same, "*More laws, more government, more centralization!*" How else can they force their corrupt and unpopular views on an unwilling people, except through the auspices of a highly centralized government that is no longer confined by constitutional restraints?

Perhaps now, more than at any other time in our history, a serious inquiry into the principles of constitutional government is needed – an inquiry into the sound principles on which our political system was founded. And there is no better starting point for this great inquiry than to examine, in exacting detail, the origin of the United States of America and the creation of its system of constitutionally limited government. If such an investigation serves no other purpose than to prove that the founders of the American Republic built wisely, then it will have served its purpose. But if our inquiry should happen to illustrate the proper remedy for the present distresses of the American people, as they battle against Leviathan, then it will prove itself to be an invaluable blessing.

During the first segment of our great inquiry we will discover how and why American civilization was born, why our revolutionary forefathers rebelled against the British Empire, the economic and political principles that guided the thinking of the Founding Fathers of the Republic, the great principles within the remarkable Declaration of Independence that asserted the birth of the sovereign States, and how these newly independent States were united under the Articles of Confederation. Particular emphasis in this segment of our quest for the truth will be placed on the origin of five fundamental political entities – the sovereign States, the United States of America, the Federal Union, the Federal Republic, and the Federal Government – that, when considered together, define our political system.

After ascertaining the origins of these key pillars of our political fabric, we will direct our attention to the Philadelphia Convention of 1787 which drafted our present Federal Constitution. Considering the great significance of the Constitutional Convention, we will examine its proceedings in considerable detail, to determine with precision the exact nature of the plan of government adopted by it. Since our objective is only to ascertain the truth, we will refrain from the practice of superficial historians to portray the Convention's delegates as an all-wise and all-patriotic body of men. Instead, we shall examine the records of the Grand Convention with a critical and discerning eye and with a determination to accurately and candidly analyze the various concepts therein presented by the delegates.

We will next direct our attention to the highly significant Ratification Period to determine the general understanding of the States at the time they adopted our present Constitution. Our inquiry will then take into consideration some of the more pertinent legacies that have endured from the Constitutional Era, including a critical analysis of the widely renowned *Federalist Papers*. Finally, we will complete our great inquiry into the origin of the United States by examining the text of our present Federal Constitution and by analyzing its main provisions.

Our purpose in examining the origin of the United States of America, it should be mentioned at the outset, is not to glorify the men who built our Republic. Many, but not all, of those who are popularly referred to as the *Founding Fathers* of the United States were indeed great and patriotic men whose contributions merit the praise and admiration of succeeding generations of Americans. But freedom cannot be established on the glorification of *men*. Liberty, if it is to survive, must be built on the glorification of *principles*. For this reason, our inquiry seeks only the glorification of the great principles on which the American constitutional system is founded.

As we examine our constitutional system in its pristine, original form, we will discover that it truly is a thing of great majesty and wondrous beauty, a marvelous system that reconciles power and liberty. And by the time we have finished our inquiry, it will be readily apparent that there can be only one genuine set of *politically correct* principles in our Republic – the principles of constitutionally limited government!

The Birth of American Civilization

Although Christopher Columbus had discovered the New World as early as 1492, progress toward settlement of the vast wilderness of North America did not really commence until nearly a century later. In 1585, a rugged group of hardy pioneers, sailing from England in seven ships, reached Roanoke Island with the intention of establishing in Virginia the first English settlement in the New World. When the ships that had carried the colonists to America sailed back to England, they were expected to return with fresh provisions for the colony within a year. But the war with Spain and her great

Spanish Armada prevented the return of the English ships for nearly three years.

When the ships finally returned to the New World settlement, the English sailors were stunned. Roanoke Island was completely deserted! The houses that the colonists had built had been dismantled, and a *fortress* had been erected. But it, too, showed signs of being deserted for a considerable length of time.

The only clue as to the fate of the courageous men, women, and children of the Roanoke Island Colony were the large letters – CROATAN – which had been carved on a tree. Thinking that the letters referred to Croatan Island, and that the colonists had sought refuge there, the British thoroughly searched the island but found no trace of the *Lost Colony of Virginia*.

The mysterious and tragic disappearance of the Roanoke Island Colony retarded, but did not discourage, the further advancement of the colonization movement among the English-speaking peoples. On April 10, 1606, King James I renewed interest in colonizing the New World by granting the First Charter of Virginia. Within this fundamental act, the *godly* and *Christian* purposes of the colonization effort were set forth in plain terms:

> We, greatly commending, and graciously accepting of, their Desires for the Furtherance of so noble a Work, which may, by the Providence of Almighty God, hereafter tend to the Glory of his Divine Majesty, in propagating of *Christian* Religion to such People, as yet live in Darkness and miserable Ignorance of the true Knowledge and Worship of God, and may in time bring the Infidels and Savages, living in those Parts, to human Civility, and to a settled and quiet Government; DO by these our Letters Patents, graciously accept of, and agree to, their humble and well-intended Desires;... [1]

Within the First Charter of Virginia, provision was also made for the establishment of local government within the proposed settlements:

> And we do also ordain, establish, and agree,...that each of the said Colonies shall have a Council, which shall govern and order all Matters and Causes, which shall arise, grow, or happen, to or within the same several Colonies, according to such Laws, Ordinances, and Instructions, as shall be, in that behalf, given and signed with Our Hand or Sign Manual, and pass under the Privy Seal of our Realm of *England*;... [2]

Further provision was made within this Charter for the formal ac-

---

[1] Harold C. Syrett (ed.), *American Historical Documents*, Barnes & Noble, Inc., New York, 1960, p. 2.
[2] *Ibid.*, p. 3.

knowledgement that the colonists in the New World settlements would be entitled to the very same *rights of Englishmen* as those actually living on the British Isles. Considering that this matter was destined to become a major issue during the American Revolution, we should carefully note this particular provision, which was expressed in the following language:

> Also we do...Declare...that all and every the Persons, being our Subjects, which shall dwell and inhabit within every or any of the said several Colonies and Plantations, and every of their children, which shall happen to be born within any of the Limits and Precincts of the said several Colonies and Plantations shall HAVE and enjoy all Liberties, Franchises, and Immunities, within any of our other Dominions, to all Intents and Purposes, as if they had been abiding and born, within this our Realm of *England*, or any other of our said Dominions. [3]

Based on these assurances as to the purpose of the colonization effort and as to the rights they would enjoy in the New World, a courageous band of settlers, sponsored as a private commercial venture by the London Company, set sail for the untamed wilderness of North America in December of 1606. Five months later – in May of 1607 – these brave souls landed at Jamestown in what would later become the State of Virginia, established the first *permanent* English settlement in the New World, and thereby planted the seeds of American civilization.

Some thirteen years after the founding of Jamestown, a hardy band of Separatists, seeking asylum from religious persecution, set sail from Holland to establish a new colony in the northern part of Virginia. But the new settlers, often referred to as Pilgrims, never reached their intended destination, landing instead at Plymouth Rock in what would later become the State of Massachusetts on a bleak day in December of 1620. Before disembarking from the *Mayflower*, the Pilgrim Fathers, realizing that they were outside the jurisdiction of any existing government, performed a solemn deed unparalleled in history. By mutual consent, they drew up a compact, that was signed by the adult males, which formally created a political society, or *body politic*, among themselves and their families.

Within the Mayflower Compact, they solemnly made this pledge:

> In the name of God, Amen. We, whose names are underwritten, the Loyal Subjects of our dread Sovereign Lord King *James*, by the Grace of God, of *Great Britain*, *France*, and *Ireland*, King, *Defender of the Faith*, &c. Having undertaken for the Glory of God, and Advancement of the Christian Faith, and the Honour of our King and Country, a Voyage to plant

---

[3] *Ibid.*, p. 3.

the first colony in the northern Parts of Virginia; Do by these presents, solemnly and mutually in the Presence of God and one another, covenant and combine ourselves together into a civil Body Politick, for our better Ordering and Preservation, and Furtherance of the Ends aforesaid; And by Virtue hereof do enact, constitute, and frame, such just and equal Laws, Ordinances, Acts, Constitutions, and Offices, from time to time, as shall be thought most meet and convenient for the general Good of the Colony; unto which we promise all due Submission and Obedience. [4]

The significance of the Mayflower Compact can never be overemphasized. Within this short political compact, God is mentioned no less than four times, and it is plain to discern, from both the Mayflower Compact and the First Charter of Virginia, that American civilization was founded on godly, Christian principles. The arduous sea voyage aboard the *Mayflower*, the Pilgrims stated in plain words, had been "undertaken for the Glory of God, and the Advancement of the Christian Faith," as well as for the honor of King and country. And the creation of a political society in the New World was undertaken "in the name of God."

The *Christian* foundations of American civilization were so plainly evident to later generations of Americans that Felicia D. Hemans was moved to pen a glowing tribute to the faith of the Pilgrim Fathers:

> Aye, call it holy ground,
>   The soil where first they trod!
> They have left unstained what there they found —
>   Freedom to worship God! [5]

The Mayflower Compact contains two other political principles that form a cornerstone of the American constitutional system. Prior to the pact, the notion of government-by-the-consent-of-the-governed had been little more than a theoretical concept, often urged by poets and philosophers, yet rarely if ever realized. Within the Mayflower Compact, however, the theory became a political reality. All forty-one adult males among the Pilgrims formally consented to the compact, thereby creating a political system genuinely founded on the consent of the governed.

The other significant political concept contained in the Mayflower Compact is the theory of *limited* government. The signers did not pledge submission and obedience to all laws that might be enacted, but only to "just and equal" laws. Nor was submission pledged to laws enacted for any reason

---

[4] Richard N. Current, Harry Williams, and Frank Freidel, *American History: A Survey*, Second Edition, Alfred A. Knopf, New York, 1966, quoted on p. 19.
[5] Thomas A. Bailey and David M. Kennedy, *The American Pageant: A History of the Republic*, Sixth Edition, D.C. Heath and Company, Lexington, 1979, quoted on p. 23.

whatsoever, but only to laws created "for the general Good of the Colony." As the authors of *The American Pageant: A History of the Republic* have correctly noted, the Mayflower Compact set "an invaluable precedent for later written constitutions." [6] It also represented a very significant step toward ensuring that a great civilization would blossom in the New World. "The pact was a promising step toward genuine self-government," historians Thomas A. Bailey and David M. Kennedy observed, "for soon the adult male settlers were assembling to make their own laws in open-discussion town meetings – a great laboratory of liberty." [7]

In the Jamestown Colony, genuine self-government was realized for the first time in 1619, when the first *House of Burgesses* convened on July 30th of that year. To this first session of the Virginia colonial legislature, which lasted until August 4, 1619, some eleven geographic constituencies sent a total of twenty-two representatives. Meeting in a church with Governor George Yeardley, the first democratic legislature in the New World passed acts "to regulate Indian trade, to govern personal conduct, to encourage silk production and a storage minimum of corn for each person, to discourage enticement of tenants and servants away from their masters, to establish a public 'magazine,' or warehouse, for tobacco, and other like measures affecting the daily life of the settlers." [8] As Professors Clarence L. Ver Steeg and Richard Hofstadter noted, "The precedent set by the establishment of a self-governing assembly in colonial Virginia was one of the most important and enduring political actions in American history." [9]

Despite the political accomplishments represented by the Virginia House of Burgesses and the Mayflower Compact, two great obstacles still had to be overcome before Plymouth Plantation and the Jamestown Colony could prosper and thus ensure the survival of the settlements in the New World. One was the harsh conditions faced by the settlers who had left the comforts of the Old World for the stark wilderness of North America. As Thomas A. Bailey and David M. Kennedy write in their book, *The American Pageant: A History of the Republic*, the first winter – cold, bitter, and harsh – faced by the newly arrived Pilgrims nearly annihilated their fledgling colony:

> The winter of 1620-1621 was a bone-chilling one, with cold and disease taking a grisly toll. Only 44 out of the 102 [original settlers] survived. At one time only seven were well enough to lay the dead in their frosty graves. Yet when the *Mayflower* sailed back to England in the spring,

---

[6] *Ibid.*, p. 22.
[7] *Ibid.*, p. 22.
[8] Clarence L. Ver Steeg and Richard Hofstadter (ed.), *Great Issues in American History: From Settlement to Revolution, 1584-1776*, Vintage Books, New York, 1969, p. 70.
[9] *Ibid.*, p. 70.

not a single one of the courageous band of Separatists left. As one of them wrote, "It is not with us as with other men, whom small things can discourage." The Pilgrim Mothers endured the same hardships as the Pilgrim Fathers, plus others, including childbearing. [10]

The other obstacle proved more ominous than the harsh winter wind. It was the specter of socialism. This specter haunted not only the Pilgrims, but also the original settlers in Jamestown Colony. The early colonial experience with collectivism, and the early rejection of the socialist system by the colonists, offer a stark lesson for all mankind.

The Colonial Rejection of Socialism

The settlers of Plymouth Plantation, like those who had settled in Jamestown some thirteen years earlier, had been persuaded to establish a collectivist economic system in the belief that socialism is more conducive to material prosperity than a system based on private property and individual responsibility. And both settlements discovered through practical experience that collectivism results in poverty, starvation, and death, and that rugged individualism, private property, and free enterprise are essential to the preservation of mankind and the advancement of civilization.

At the Jamestown Colony, the economic policy first adopted by the settlers was based on joint cultivation efforts with sustenance derived from a common storehouse. The good will, charity, and spirit of "togetherness" shared by the settlers, it was fondly believed, would be sufficient inducement to ensure the full devotion of all members of the society to the common cause. The fact that the hardest working and most productive members of the community would receive no greater reward for their efforts than the laziest among the group, it was thought, would not adversely affect either overall production or morale.

Such utopian thinking, however, was very quickly dispelled. Socialism and human nature, the colonists quickly discovered, do not mix well. The system had scarcely been inaugurated when a streak of laziness swept over the colony. Not surprisingly, morale dropped dramatically and productivity within the collectivist system was found insufficient to sustain the settlement. Hundreds of colonists perished from disease and lethal starvation during "the starving time," 1609-1610, in spite of the fact that the nearby woods rustled with plentiful game and the rivers teemed with fish. Captain John Smith, who had taken over as governor of the settlement in 1608, realized that the colony

---

[10] Thomas A. Bailey and David M. Kennedy, *Ibid.*, p. 22.

could only be saved by replacing the collectivist system with one based on private property and individual responsibility. Quoting Scripture, he issued the proclamation, "He who will not work shall not eat." [11] The rejection of socialism saved the Jamestown Colony.

The disastrous effects of socialism at Jamestown Colony and the relief experienced by the settlers after its rejection were related by Ralph Hamor, the first Secretary of the colony, in his *A True Discourse of the Present State of Virginia and the Successe of the Affaires There Till the 18 of June 1614*. In his discourse, published in 1615, Mr. Hamor compared and contrasted colonial conditions in 1614 with conditions existent under the earlier collectivist system, stating that production had been increased *ten-fold* after the rejection of socialism:

> [T]here is [now] plenty of foode, which every man by his own in-dustry may easily and doth procure....Formerly, when our people were fed out of the common store and laboured jointly in manuring [cultivation] and planting corne, glad was the man that could slippe from his la-bour....He would not take so much faithful and true paines in a week as now he will do in a day....We reaped not so much corne from the labour of 30 men as three men have done for themselves....The lives of many shall not onley be preserved, but also themselves kept in strength and heart.... [12]

The Pilgrims in Massachusetts learned a similar lesson. In his work, *Of Plymouth Plantation*, William Bradford chronicled the rapid deterioration of Plymouth Plantation and its approach toward starvation under a collectivist system of production, and noted its remarkable recovery after the rejection of socialism and the introduction of individual responsibility. In an entry dated "Early 1623," Governor Bradford related the rejection of socialism by the Pilgrims in these words:

> So they begane to think how they might raise as much corne as they could, and obtain a beter crop that they might not still languish in miserie. At length the Govr (with ye advise of ye cheefest amongst them) gave way that they should set corne every man for his own perticuler, and in that re-gard trust to themselves.
>
> And so [the Governor] assigned to every family a parcell of land. This had very good success; for it made all hands very industrious, so as much more corne was planted than other waise would have bene by any means ye Govr or any other could use, and saved him a great deal of trou-ble, and gave farr better contente. The women now wente willingly into ye

---

[11] *Ibid.*, quoted on p. 12.
[12] Gilbert M. Tucker, *Common-Sense Economics*, The Stackpole Company, Harrisburg, 1957, quoted on p. 243.

field, and took their little-ones with them to set corne, which before would aledg weakness, and disabilitie. The experience that was had in this common course and condition, tried sundrie years, and that amongst godly and sober men, may well evince the vanitie of that conceit, that ye taking away of property, and bringing in communitie into a common wealth, would make them happy and florishing; as if they were wiser than God.

For this communitie was found to breed much confusion and discontent, and retard much employment that would have been to their benefite and comforte. For ye yong-men did repine that they should spend their time and streingth to worke for other mens wives and children. The strong had no more in devission of victails and cloaths, then he that was not able to doe a quarter ye other could; this was thought injustice. And for mens wives to be commanded to doe service for other men, as dressing their meate, washing their cloaths, &c., they deemed it a kind of slaverie, neither could many husbands well brooke it. [13]

As this remarkable journal entry indicates, the socialist system first established at Plymouth Plantation necessitated an expansive, coercive type of political system that threatened to undermine the earlier political accomplishments made at the settlement. In accordance with the collectivist economic policy established there, Governor Bradford found himself – much to his discomfort – compelled to force able-bodied men to feed other men's families. And, in compliance with the socialist principle, the women had to be "commanded" to provide domestic labors for men other than their husbands. The Governor, whose honesty and integrity would not permit him to continue such a state indefinitely, noted that the collectivist system of production bred confusion, discontent, and "a great deal of trouble." Such an unnatural system came to be correctly viewed by the colonists as "injustice" and as "a kind of slaverie."

In the selection from *Of Plymouth Plantation* quoted above, special attention should be given to those passages where Governor Bradford comments on the folly of the belief that collectivism could ever produce, *under any circumstances*, anything but starvation and misery. Socialism did not fail in the colony because the Pilgrims refused to give it a chance to succeed. On the contrary, the socialist experience had been "tried sundrie years" and found seriously defective. Nor did socialism fail because of deficiencies in the character of the Pilgrims, for it had been practiced "amongst godly and sober men." Following the failure of collectivism at Plymouth Plantation, only the vain and conceited, who fancy themselves "wiser than God," could ever advocate such a system.

Because the early settlers of America quickly realized the disastrous

---

[13] *Ibid.*, quoted on p. 248-249.

folly of socialism and rejected it in favor of private property and free enterprise, both Jamestown Colony and Plymouth Plantation grew and prospered. Encouraged by the success attained by the early settlers, others began leaving the tired Old World for the vigorous New World. Those who arrived in North America to join existing settlements or to establish new settlements were not motivated by expectations or desires of receiving charity, welfare handouts, or social security. They sought only the opportunity to be free from political and religious persecution and the opportunity to forge a new life for themselves through their own industry. It was from these hardy, adventurous souls, who saw in the New World a new beginning for mankind, that a new civilization would arise.

The Separate Origins of the Thirteen Colonies

From the early settlements along the Atlantic seaboard of North America, thirteen separate and distinct colonies emerged. Although not all of the colonies originated as possessions of Great Britain, eventually all thirteen were in the British Empire. Virginia, which could trace her founding back to the establishment of Jamestown in 1607, was the oldest and most populous of the colonies. Chartered in 1606, 1609, and 1612, Virginia became a Royal Colony in 1624. New Hampshire, founded by John Mason in 1623, received its charter and became a Royal Colony 1679. Massachusetts, which had been founded by the Puritans in 1628, purchased the Maine territory in 1677 and was made a Royal Colony in 1679. Twelve years later, Plymouth Colony merged with Massachusetts.

The colony founded by Lord Baltimore in 1634 as a haven for persecuted Roman Catholics – Maryland – was chartered in 1632 as a Proprietary Colony. In 1635, emigrants from Massachusetts founded Connecticut, which was merged with the New Haven Colony and officially chartered as a Self-Governing Colony in 1662. Rhode Island, founded by Roger Williams in 1636, was chartered in 1644 and again in 1663 as the only other Self-Governing Colony. In 1653, Virginian emigrants founded North Carolina, which was chartered ten years later and which was made a Royal Colony in 1691. Although New York was originally founded by the Dutch in 1613, the colony was destined to become a British possession. In 1685, the colony, together with the Duke of York, founded twenty-one years earlier, was made a Royal Colony. Neighboring New Jersey, which was founded by Berkeley and Carteret in 1664, was never formally chartered but became a Royal Colony in 1702.

South Carolina was officially chartered in 1663, and seven years later the colony was founded. By 1729, she had been made a Royal Colony. In 1681, William Penn founded Pennsylvania, which was chartered as a Proprietary Colony in the same year. Although never chartered, the Proprietary Colony of Delaware was founded by Swedes in 1638. Forty-four years later, Delaware merged with Pennsylvania, but the separate autonomy of the former was granted in 1703 when Delaware was allowed to have its own assembly. The last of the thirteen colonies to be founded was Georgia, which was chartered in 1732 and founded by Oglethorpe a year later. In 1752, Georgia was made a Royal Colony.

There are five points of significance regarding the origin and development of the thirteen American colonies that merit the attention of the student of constitutional government. The first significant fact is that American civilization resulted not from the planning of some centralized government bureaucracy or planning board, but from the free will of countless individuals, each one seeking his own place in a new land. Had it been otherwise – had the authorities in London been inclined or even able to plan and control the colonies from their founding days – it is doubtful that American civilization would have survived.

As noted by the authors of *The American Pageant: A History of the Republic*:

> Not one of the original thirteen colonies, except Georgia, was formally planted by the British Government. The actual founding was done haphazardly by trading companies, religious groups, land speculators, and others. Authorities in London did not even dream that a new nation was being born. [14]

The second point of significance regarding the origin and development of the colonies that merits attention is the fact that they evolved *separately* and *independently* from one another. Although all the colonies were members of the British Empire and owed allegiance to the same British King, there was no direct political connection between the colonies themselves. There was no more direct political connection between Massachusetts and Virginia, for example, than there was between Britain and France.

Commenting on the nature of the colonial political structure, Dr. Jabez L.M. Curry, a political theorist and historian of the Old South, made these observations in his 1895 book, *The Southern States of the American Union*:

> In the colonial period there were thirteen commonwealths, with thirteen local governments. Each colony, distinct in origin, was separate

---

[14] Thomas A. Bailey and David M. Kennedy, *Op. cit.*, p. 81.

from, and independent of, the others; each was a dependency, and an integral part of the British Empire; each was a creature of the British state, and legally subject to its sovereignty. The common bond of union was through the allegiance to the British Crown....In all that pertained to the regulation of their respective affairs, they acted singly....Each colony had its legislative assembly, elected by its own people, and its separate judiciary. The basis of representation was different. In Massachusetts townships were the unit; in Virginia, counties; but in each the assembly was a representative body. The laws enacted had force, authority, sanction, only within the limits of the colony, and had no extra-territorial validity. What Massachusetts did had no civil efficacy, no government sanction, over Connecticut or Rhode Island. [15]

Dr. Curry's description introduces us to the third significant feature that characterized the origin and development of the thirteen American colonies. The relationship between the colonies and the mother country, as well as their relationship with one another, bears a striking resemblance to a *federal* system of government. Undoubtedly owing more to the relative remoteness of the colonies than to any desire to foster a spirit of independence in the colonies, the British Government allowed the colonial legislatures to exercise a wide latitude of autonomy over domestic affairs. One a day-to-day basis, each colony was a genuine self-governing body within the Empire, and the significance of this federal principle in the colonial mind can never be over-emphasized. One of the chief causes that would later compel the colonists to revolt, in fact, would be Britain's decision to suddenly deny this right of local self-government to the colonies.

The fourth point of significance is the remarkable fact that, within the American colonies, the local governments were the most pure, uncorrupted, republican institutions in the world. The colonial assemblies, which would later prove to be thorns in the side of King George III in the years just prior to the American Revolution, were models of popular government. To these colonial legislatures were elected the most eloquent orators, honest statesmen, and patriotic citizens within the colonies. It was only natural that, when the time came to defend the rights of America against the oppressions of Great Britain, the colonial assemblies would be in the forefront of the struggle for liberty.

Finally, it must be noted that colonial civilization was built upon godly foundations by a Christian people. We have already noted the strong professions made on behalf of Christianity within such important documents as the First Charter of Virginia and the Mayflower Compact. Other colonies were

---

[15] J.L.M. Curry, *The Southern States of the American Union*, G.P. Putnam's Son, New York, 1895, pp. 10-11.

also established on openly professed Christian principles, as illustrated by the introductory words of the Fundamental Orders of Connecticut, which was adopted on January 14, 1638:

> Forasmuch as it hath pleased the *Almighty God* by the wise disposition of his *divyne providence* so to Order and dispose of things that we the Inhabitants and Residents of Windsor, Harteford and Wethersfield are now cohabiting and dwelling in and uppon the River of Conececotte and the Lands thereunto adjoyneing; And well knowing where a people are gathered togather *the word of God* requires that to mayntayne the peace and union of such a people there should be an orderly and decent *Government established according to God*, to order and dispose of the affayres of the people at all seasons as occation shall require; doe therefore assotiate and conjoyne our selves to be as one Publike State or Commonwelth; and doe, for our selves and our Successors and such as shall be adjoyned to us att any tyme hereafter, enter into Combination and Confederation togather, to mayntayne and preserve the liberty and purity of the *gospell of our Lord Jesus* which *we now professe*, as also the disciplyne of the *Churches*, which according to *the truth of the said gospell is now practised amongst us*; As also in our Civell Affaires to be guided and governed according to such Lawes, Rules, Orders and decrees as shall be made, ordered and decreed, as followeth:... [Emphasis added] [16]

From the very beginning, American civilization was thus founded on godly principles. Colonial governments, like that of Connecticut, were "established according to God" and by "the word of God," and with the undisguised intention of promoting the Gospel "of our Lord Jesus." Great educational institutions, such as Harvard University in Cambridge, Massachusetts, were also established for the express purpose of promoting Christianity. And many of the colonial governments required that its officers take an oath of allegiance to the Holy Bible and to affirm a belief in Christian principles, a practice that continued even after the Declaration of Independence had bestowed sovereignty and independence on the colonies. At the time the Constitutional Convention assembled in the State House in Philadelphia in 1787, for instance, the Constitution of the State of Pennsylvania required the members of the State legislature to declare:

> I do believe in one God, the Creator and Governor of the Universe, the Rewarder of Good and Punisher of the Wicked. And I do acknowledge the Scriptures of the Old and New Testament to be given by Divine Inspiration. [17]

---

[16] Clarence L. Ver Steeg and Richard Hofstadter (ed.), *Op. cit.*, pp. 81-82.
[17] *1787: The Day-to-Day Story of the Constitutional Convention*, Exeter Books, New York, 1787, quoted on p. 162.

Early Colonial Attempts at Unification

Although the thirteen American colonies, as previously noted, were politically independent of one another, there did exist a natural spirit of community among them. Commenting on this spirit of unity among the colonies, Dr. Jabez L.M. Curry has noted:

> This common dependence, this amenability to British law, juxtaposition on a remote continent, sense of common danger from neighboring Indian tribes, the community of origin, language, literature, religion, and civil rights, naturally drew the Colonies into relationships of fraternity and friendship. Diversity of climate and productions and interposed mountains sectionalize peoples, raise international problems, and provoke alienations. The economic history of the Colonies, if thoroughly explored, would throw much needful light on their final union. This influence lessened colonial isolation, broadened the horizon of mutual interests, drew toward trade centres, and tended to develop a national character. Intercommunication, also, softened prejudices, promoted social intercourse, expanded trade, created a trend toward colonial fellowship and co-operation. The coast trade supplemented the work and influence of the interior highways, and brought colonial interests into closer unity. [18]

Recognizing that they shared much in common, several early attempts at political unification or confederation were made by some of the colonies. Although all of these early attempts ultimately failed to produce any lasting inter-colonial unity, they did reveal the strong bias throughout the colonies in favor of the *federal system of government.* The goal of the various colonial unity movements, in other words, was not to consolidate or merge the colonies into a single political body or to weaken the local authorities of the separate colonial legislatures. On the contrary, the objective of the unity movements was to unite the colonies for purposes of common defense, while leaving to each colony full autonomy over its own internal affairs. Especially significant in this regard were the two Confederations established among the New England colonies and Benjamin Franklin's Albany Plan of Union. Through these early attempts at colonial unity, the colonists learned valuable lessons in federalism that would later serve as invaluable guides in helping to foster unity during the American Revolution and during the subsequent Constitutional Era.

In 1643, four New England colonies – Massachusetts, Plymouth, Connecticut, and New Haven – formed the *New England Confederation*, which was created by a formal compact that declared:

---

[18] J.L.M. Curry, *Op. cit.* p. 11.

> The said United Colonies for themselves and their posterities do jointly and severally hereby enter into a firm and perpetual league of friendship and amity for offence and defence, mutual advice and succor upon all just occasions both for preserving and propagating the truth and liberties of the Gospel and for their own mutual safety and welfare. [19]

These "United Colonies" further agreed to proportionally share the burdens of their common defense, to immediately come to the aid of any member of their Federal Union that might be invaded or in danger of invasion, to appoint two commissioners each to manage their common concerns, and to refrain from beginning a war without the consent of at least six of the commissioners. Although the New England Confederation ceased to exist after 1684, due to a lack of interest in continuing the Union, this early attempt at colonial unity clearly demonstrated the desire of the colonists to utilize the federal concept as a means of sustaining, preserving, and strengthening the individual colonies.

It is of interest to note that the New England Confederation was formally proclaimed to be "perpetual" in nature. Yet, as we have observed, this Union that was intended to last forever survived only forty-one years. Those who created the Federal Union clearly understood that the purpose of a political association is to serve the interests of the members of the Union, and that whensoever the league ceases to fulfill that objective, it can and should be abolished, despite the fact that, when originally conceived, it was intended to endure forever. A final feature of the New England Confederation which merits our attention is the stated *purpose* of the political Union. Among the reasons given for creating a Federal Union was the colonial desire "for preserving and propagating the truth and liberties of the Gospel." This Federal Union, like the civilization it was created to serve, was thus founded upon Christian principles.

In 1686, just two years after the New England Confederation was abolished, seven New England colonies agreed to form a new Federal Union among themselves styled the *Dominion of New England*. Like its predecessor, this political Union was also founded in accordance with federal principles, wherein each member retained exclusive control over its own internal or domestic affairs. Due to a lack of interest among the member colonies in continuing the Confederation, the Union survived only three years.

Following these two New England attempts at unity, interest in unification remained at a low ebb for a number of years. It was not until 1754 that a Federal Union among the colonies was again seriously attempted. In that year, at the request of the British Government, seven colonies sent delegates

---

[19] Richard N. Current, Harry Williams, and Frank Freidel, *Op. cit.*, quoted on p. 60.

to an inter-colonial conference to consider ways of dealing with the perennial Indian danger. At the time, war with France was imminent, and many were convinced that only through political unification could the colonies adequately defend themselves. Among those delegates who were convinced of the necessity for colonial unity was Benjamin Franklin of Pennsylvania. With the aid of other delegates, he drew up a plan of inter-colonial government that would provide for the common defense of the colonies. Like the other Unions that had preceded it, Mr. Franklin's Albany Plan of Union was decidedly federal in nature. Unlike the previous Confederacies, however, which had been regional in scope, the Albany Plan represented the first serious attempt to unite *all thirteen colonies* into a single Confederation.

Under the Albany Plan of Union, a "general government" would be created to serve the common interests of the colonies. The British King would appoint a President-General for the general government, while the colonial legislatures would elect representatives to a Grand Council. With the advice of the Grand Council, the President-General would have sufficient powers to manage Indian relations and foreign affairs for the colonies, and to make such laws and raise such taxes as would be necessary to execute the delegated powers. All powers not yielded to the general government would remain with the colonies, which would each retain exclusive control over its own internal affairs.

When the Albany Plan of Union was submitted to the colonial assemblies for ratification, the result was a solid defeat of the unification plan. *With a unanimous voice, all of the colonies rejected the Albany Plan.* It was abundantly evident that it would take more than the dangers posed by the Indians and the threat of war with France to induce the colonies to surrender even a fraction of their powers to any general government. Sufficient inducement to seek unified action, in fact, would not be provided until after the French and Indian War, when the colonies, much to their horror and dismay, found themselves pitted against what was then the most formidable power in the world.

Confronted by a suddenly hostile British Government after the French and Indian War, the desire for closer unity among the colonies was quickly propelled to unprecedented levels. In 1765, some nine colonies would send delegates to the Stamp Act Congress. By 1772, all thirteen colonial legislatures would be informally united through the auspices of the Committees of Correspondence. Two years later, twelve of the colonies would dispatch representatives to the First Continental Congress. And by 1775, all thirteen of the colonies would send representatives to the Second Continental Congress. It would be this august body of American patriots that would publish the Declaration of Independence, wage the Revolutionary War against Great

Britain, and propose the Articles of Confederation to the newly independent and sovereign States.

Chapter Two
The American Revolution

The noted historian Charles A. Beard once observed that there are as many differing explanations for the cause of the American Revolution as there are historians. Although historical revisionism and reinterpretation can have positive benefits by bringing to light facts and truths that would not have been otherwise known, they can also be employed to suppress facts and obscure truth. And the latter effects are invariably realized whenever historical interpretations are molded to fit the needs of modern political movements.

By the end of the First World War, when politicians launched America down the path of internationalism, the traditional view of the Revolution as an inevitable revolt against British oppression and tyranny by a people determined to live as free men rather than as slaves, became somewhat of an embarrassment to the internationalists. So the process of rewriting the history of the American Revolution was inaugurated, in an effort to bend the historical record to conform to the new political agenda. The American Revolution, it was suddenly discovered, was nothing more than the result of a big misunderstanding between civilized, English-speaking peoples who, if allowed to cool their passions, could have easily worked out their few differences and saved the benevolent British Empire.

The honest student of constitutional government, however, has no ulterior motives, no axes to grind, and no contemporary political schemes to justify when interpreting history. The sole objective of the honest interpreter of the American Revolution is to ascertain the truth, and only the truth. And as we shall discover, the truth is that the British policy toward the American colonies was calculated to reduce American civilization to slavery, leaving the colonial patriots only two options – either to submit to tyranny or to fight for their rights as free men.

When the early settlers who planted the seeds of American civilization in the New World resolved, at an early date, to reject socialism in favor of private property and individual responsibility, their decision foretold an inevitable conflict with the British Government, whose mercantile colonial policy was based on socialistic exploitation of the colonies. As the thirteen American colonies grew to maturity, their sense of economic and political self-reliance also matured. It was only natural, therefore, that the British policy of regulating colonial affairs solely for the benefit of certain monied interests in the British Isles – while tolerated by the early North American settlements when the policy was in its infancy – was increasingly perceived as intolerable by the emerging civilization on the American continent.

British policy makers, evidently aware of the growing spirit of independence and self-reliance in the American colonies, initially sought to minimize the conflict and forestall the inevitable by resorting to a lax, half-hearted enforcement of the mercantile system. In addition, those policy makers sought to appease the growing desire among the colonists to control their own destiny by allowing the thirteen colonies to exercise a high degree of local autonomy over their own affairs. In all of the colonies, the democratically elected legislative assemblies thus functioned as virtually independent political units within the Empire.

Despite these initial British efforts to minimize the growing rift between colony and Crown, the existence of such a rift became clearly manifest during the French and Indian War. As historians Richard N. Current, T. Harry Williams, and Frank Freidel note in their book, *American History: A Survey*:

> So strong had grown the colonial feeling against direct legislation by Parliament that, during the French and Indian War, the English government did not attempt to tax or draft the colonists directly but called upon the assemblies to provide quotas of soldiers and supplies. This requisition system, itself a concession to provincial prejudice, heightened the self-importance of the [colonial] assemblies, and most of them further asserted their autonomy by complying in a slow and niggardly way. Some of them, unwilling to be taxed by Parliament, also refused to tax themselves; they issued paper money instead.
>
> In Virginia the legislature not only issued paper money but, when the resulting inflation raised the price of tobacco, also passed a law to deprive the Anglican clergy (who were paid in tobacco) of the benefits of the price rise. When this law was disallowed (1760), one of the ministers sued his vestrymen for his full pay. At the trial of the "parson's cause" the young lawyer Patrick Henry, defending the vestrymen, denounced the Privy Council for its tyranny and told his fellow Virginians to ignore its action. Roused by Henry's oratory, the jurors awarded the parson damages of only one penny. Thus did they defy the authority of the British government.
>
> In Massachusetts the merchants disregarded the laws of the empire even more flagrantly than did the planters in Virginia. Throughout the war these merchants persisted in trading with the enemy in Canada and in the French West Indies. British officials resorted to general search warrants – "writs of assistance" – for discovering smuggled goods and stamping out the illegal and unpatriotic trade. As attorney for the Massachusetts merchants, James Otis maintained that these searches violated the ancient

rights of Englishmen and that the law of Parliament authorizing the warrants was therefore null and void. With eloquence as stirring as Henry's, Otis insisted that Parliament had only a limited power of legislating for the colonies. [1]

As a result of the British-American victory in the French and Indian War, Great Britain ascended to new heights in terms of power, prestige, and glory. Especially significant in this regard was the acquisition by the Empire of the vast territorial regions of Canada. The London policy makers could then dream of the day when the entire North American continent would belong to them. In terms of martial power, Great Britain stood virtually unchallenged as the supreme power in the world.

But if the war had significantly increased the power and prestige of the Empire, it had likewise increased the British debts to staggering new heights. Imperialism proved to be a costly undertaking, and new sources of revenue had to be found to finance the imperial ventures. Accordingly, the British Government cast a greedy and calculating eye on the thirteen American colonies and began to reconsider its lax enforcement of the mercantile system.

As the authors of *American History: A Survey* note:

> As the war ended, the London policy makers faced a dilemma....On the one hand, they could revert to the old colonial system with its half-hearted enforcement of the mercantilist program, but that would mean virtual independence for the colonies. On the other hand, the men in London could renew their efforts to reform the Empire and enforce the laws, but that would lead to revolt and absolute independence. [2]

The decision made by the London policy makers was significantly influenced by a change of government in Britain that occurred when a new monarch came to the throne in 1760. Through patronage and bribes, the new monarch – George III – succeeded in taking control of Parliament away from the Whigs, thereby effectively negating the gains won by Englishmen in the Glorious Revolution of the previous century.

This conquest of the Legislative Branch by the Executive Branch paved the way for an unobstructed assault against the liberties of the American colonists. It was no surprise, therefore, that when the notorious Stamp Act – one of the first attacks made against the colonies by the new Tory government – was introduced in Parliament, it sailed through both houses, in the words of

---

[1] Richard N. Current, T. Harry Williams, and Frank Freidel, *American History: A Survey*, Second Edition, Alfred A. Knopf, New York, 1966, pp. 69-70.
[2] *Ibid.*, p. 70.

one commentator, "with less opposition than a turnpike bill." [3] The transformation of the government was made complete when the young King made George Grenville the Prime Minister in 1763.

With the Tories firmly in control in London, the decision was made to fully exploit the colonies by a vigorous enforcement of mercantilism. The policy makers clearly understood that, in adopting this course, they would be essentially robbing the American people of many of the rights and liberties of Englishmen that the colonists already possessed. And the policy makers, who clearly anticipated colonial opposition, were prepared to forcefully respond to any opposition that might be offered by the colonies. Following the French and Indian War, the British troops were ordered to remain stationed on American soil, one of the first indications that a new and more menacing colonial policy was about to commence.

Although strategies and tactics changed as frequently as did ministers during the critical years from 1763 to 1776, the overall policy and determination of the British Government remained remarkably consistent. The colonists must be forced to fund the imperial ventures of London by surrendering their property. And should the colonists refuse to tamely submit to exploitation, the Crown was firmly resolved to use whatever degree of force was necessary to compel them to surrender their rights.

The Mercantile System

To adequately understand why the colonies rebelled against the Empire, we must have a thorough and complete understanding of the British Government's exploitative policy toward those colonies. Although historians have generally been reluctant to apply the term *socialism* when describing the economic and political policy established by London for the colonies, there is no other word that more accurately describes the mercantile system. At its core, this system was based on economic exploitation of the colonies for the benefit of a monied aristocracy in England.

The hallmarks of mercantilism consisted of edicts emanating from a highly centralized and bureaucratic government, subversion of local political authority, heavy taxation and indebtedness, disregard for private property rights, draconian rules to regulate vast sections of the colonial economy, monopolies protected and nurtured by government policy, population control through restrictions on westward migration, and the use of military force

---

[3] Charles A. Beard and Mary R. Beard, *The Rise of American Civilization*, The Macmillan Company, New York, 1930, quoted on p. 207.

against civilian populations to enforce its mandates. Characteristic of the degree of control wielded over the colonial economy under this policy, the British Government imperially decreed that not so much as a single hobnail could be made in the colonies without its consent.

As historians Thomas A. Bailey and David M. Kennedy explain in their textbook, *The American Pageant: A History of the Republic*:

> The theory that shaped and justified English exploitation of the American colonies was mercantilism. According to this doctrine the colonies existed for the benefit of the Mother Country; they should add to its wealth, prosperity, and self-sufficiency. Otherwise why go to all the trouble and expense of governing and protecting them? The settlers were regarded more or less as tenants. They were expected to produce tobacco and other products needed in England, and not to bother their heads with dangerous experiments in agriculture or self-government. [4]

The mercantile system, ironically, could never have succeeded in accomplishing what its designers and promoters had envisioned. Like all other forms of socialistic exploitation, mercantilism was based on the false notion that a civilization can be progressively and heavily taxed to support the imperial objectives of a centralized government while, at the same time, its trade and commerce are progressively hindered and suffocated by restrictive barriers.

The internal contradictions in the policy thus doomed it to failure from the start. Over an extended period of time, such exploitation could only have resulted in the ruination of American civilization and, ultimately, of the whole British Empire. As the authors of *American History: A Survey* have correctly observed, "The long-run effect [on the colonies] would be to confine the enterprising spirit of the colonists and condemn them to a fixed or even a declining level of living." [5]

The seeds of this socialist policy were actually planted long before George III ascended to the throne. Some one hundred and twenty-five years before the Declaration of Independence, in 1651, the British Parliament gave birth to the mercantile system by enacting the Navigation Act. This law gave a monopoly to British shipping interests by requiring that all colonial goods bound for England must be carried on British ships manned by British sailors. "It was the first step," noted Samuel B. Pettengill, "in a program designed to restrict the commercial development of one part of the Empire for the

---

[4] Thomas A. Bailey and David M. Kennedy, *The American Pageant: A History of the Republic*, Sixth Edition, D.C. Heath and Company, Lexington, 1979, p. 81.
[5] Richard N. Current, T. Harry Williams, and Frank Freidel, *Op. cit.*, p. 77.

benefit of another part." [6]

This was followed nine years later by the Navigation Act of 1660, which required that all colonial exports to foreign nations must be routed through English ports. Also in 1660, in an effort to protect English fishermen from competition, Parliament barred New England fish from British markets. This represented the first step in the establishment of harmful and restrictive *trade barriers* designed to retard American economic development for the benefit of English merchants. Before long, Parliament extended the ban to encompass a wide range of New England products, including wheat, flour, corn, and meat.

In addition to controlling colonial exports, mercantilism was also extended to regulating colonial imports. Goods imported by the colonies from foreign nations were required to first pass through British ports. The effect of this trade restriction was increased profits for English manufacturers and ship owners, as well as artificially inflated prices in the colonies. Specific acts of Parliament also barred outright the importation by the colonies of a number of goods from European nations, and with the Colonial Duty Act of 1673, British insurers were awarded a monopoly in the colonial cargo insurance business.

Mercantilism even extended to the development of manufacturing within the colonies. In an effort to inhibit the industrialization of America and to prevent the colonies from becoming anything other than the suppliers of key raw materials needed by English manufacturers, Parliament enacted a number of laws designed to either retard or, in some instances, prohibit altogether, the production of commodities that were also produced in Great Britain, including wool, yarn, and cloth.

At the demand of ever-vigilant and greedy English monopolists, the weight of the British Government was used to crush every semblance of self-sufficiency and independence in the American colonies. When it was discovered, for instance, that New England hat makers had managed to develop a lucrative trade with Spain, Portugal, and the West Indies, English hat makers complained and demanded that Parliament outlaw the colonial trade. Parliament promptly awarded to the English manufacturers the monopoly in the foreign market they had demanded.

Further efforts to curtail economic development in the colonies extended to restrictive labor regulations. In an effort to limit the number of hat makers in America, for example, English law set a maximum limit of only two apprentices to a master hat maker, and a staggering seven years of apprenticeship was required. The effect of such policies as this was to stifle economic

---

[6] Samuel B. Pettengill, *Jefferson: The Forgotten Man*, America's Future, Inc., New York, 1938, p. 18.

development in America while steadily transferring the wealth of the colonies into the coffers of favored interest groups on the British Isles.

When, in 1717, certain iron and steel manufacturing interests in England petitioned Parliament for relief from colonial competition, the British Government responded by outlawing the construction in the colonies of any mills or machinery to process iron. Parliament also awarded a monopoly in the colonial molasses trade to certain British interests by enacting the Molasses Act of 1733. By this law, only molasses originating in the British West Indies could be lawfully imported by the colonies.

To protect the Hudson Bay Company and other English fur traders, the British Government, by royal proclamation in 1763, forbade fur trading west of the Alleghenies except by royal license. And the Sugar Act of 1764 further increased the draconian web of rules and regulations over the colonial economy by increasing the duty on colonial imports of foreign sugar and by prohibiting the importation of spirits.

Colonial patriots clearly recognized the tyrannical nature of the oppressive mercantile system. "The trade of the Colonies was laid under such restrictions," Thomas Jefferson reflected in later years, "as show what hopes they might form from the justice of a British Parliament were its uncontrolled power admitted over these States." [7] To the credit of the freedom-loving colonial patriots, they steadfastly refused to submit to such an uncontrolled power. And to the credit of that great people on the British Isles, it must be noted that not all of them approved of the policy of exploiting Americans.

Within Great Britain, a number of courageous voices were raised in defense of American rights and for equal justice for all members of the Empire. Chief among those who dared to challenge the whole theory of mercantilism was the brilliant Scottish economist and great champion of free enterprise, Adam Smith, whose monumental masterpiece, *The Wealth of Nations*, was published in 1776. "To prohibit a great people...," he solemnly concluded, "from making all that they can of every part of their own produce, or from employing their stock and industry in the way that they judge most advantageous to themselves, is a manifest violation of the most sacred rights of mankind." [8] Those who controlled the British Government, however, were too interested in pursuing their schemes of plunder to listen to such voices of truth and reason.

True to its socialistic nature, the mercantile system gave rise to centralized bureaucracies in London, whose purpose was to formulate plans and strategies calculated to maximize the exploitation of the colonies. In his book,

---

[7] *Ibid.*, quoted on p. 23.
[8] Thomas A. Bailey and David M. Kennedy, *Op. cit.*, quoted on p. 81.

The Rise of American Civilization, historian Charles A. Beard commented on
the growth of bureaucratic government resulting from the mercantile system:

> Whatever their source and purpose, these measures did not execute
> themselves. It was necessary to create or adapt agencies to enforce British
> law on the one hand and restrain colonial legislatures on the other. Chief
> among these institutions was a central board of administrative control
> known by different names at different times. The idea came from two mer-
> chants who had large investments in the colonies and in overseas trade. It
> took definite form in 1660 in the establishment of a committee of the
> king's council, charged with the duty of meeting twice a week to consider
> petitions, memorials, and addresses respecting the colonies. Thirty-six years
> later a regular body, known as the Board of Trade and Plantations, was or-
> ganized for the purpose of drawing under one high authority every branch
> of colonial economy and every transaction of consequence effected by His
> Majesty's governments beyond the sea.
>
> Until the eve of the Revolution, this Board kept all American affairs
> drawn tightly within its dragnet, holding five meetings a week during most
> of its career, and, in periods of relaxation, eight or ten sessions a month. If
> an English merchant or manufacturer had a complaint or suggestion to
> make about the acts of any colonial assembly, about the doings of any co-
> lonial authority, or about methods of controlling American industry, he
> could find a sympathetic hearing before the Board of Trade....In fact all
> acts of the colonial assemblies, with few exceptions, went before it for con-
> sideration, and on its recommendation were referred to the Crown for veto
> or disallowance. [9]

If ever there was a "power behind the throne," it was the Board of
Trade and Plantations. Through this bureaucracy, the aristocratic monopolists in the British Isles dictated colonial policy to the British Government,
both to King and to Parliament. The very existence of the Board of Trade at-
tested to the deep level of corruption with which the English government had
become infected.

Commenting on the wide latitude of power wielded by the Board of
Trade and Plantations, Professor Beard noted:

> Thousands of letters preserved in the English archives bear witness
> to the range, precision, multiplicity, and minuteness of the Board's grasp-
> ing activities. From its inception to the accession of George II, it held a
> tight rein, scrutinizing colonial economy with an eagle eye and recom-
> mending with firm insistence the annulment of objectionable bills passed
> by colonial legislatures. While, under the genial sway of Robert Walpole,
> whose motto for domestic and foreign statecraft was "let sleeping dogs
> alone," there was a period of mild administration, it meant no abandon-

---

[9] Charles A. Beard and Mary R. Beard, *Op. cit.*, pp. 197-198.

ment of established policy. At all events, there opened after the downfall of Walpole an epoch of thoroughness which continued until the stormy prelude of the Revolution was announced. Day after day, year in and year out, this engine of control kept pounding away on colonial affairs. Only to the eye of the superficial observer were the guardians of English imperialism asleep. [10]

In his book, *Jefferson: The Forgotten Man*, Samuel B. Pettengill summarized the sweeping scope of the economic consequences of mercantilism in these words:

> And so a long series of Acts of Parliament and edicts from the Board of Trade and Plantations, growing cumulatively, and beginning with fish in 1651, went on to include corn, flour, meat, wool, yarn, woolen, cloth, hats, bar and pig iron, sugar, molasses..., rum, spirits, tobacco, cotton, indigo, ginger, tar, pitch, hemp, turpentine, ship masts and yards, rye, beaver skins, copper and iron ore, hides, whale fins, silk, lumber, dye woods, finally winding up with tea, then the Tea Party in Boston Harbor and the shot heard 'round the world!...
>
> By July 4, 1776, the colonists had had all they wanted of economic planning by their competitors. On that day they tore those throttling hands from the throat of American commerce, industry and agriculture. "A long train of abuses" borne with "patient sufferings" and all "having in direct object the establishment of an absolute Tyranny over these States" were "submitted to a candid world." [11]

The harshness of the mercantile system, as previously noted, had been tempered only by the unwillingness of the British Government to fully enforce its mandates on the colonies. The Molasses Act, for example, was openly flouted in the colonies, and British authorities had long found it more convenient to politely look the other way as mercantile economic laws were routinely violated by the colonists. As long as the exploitative laws could be largely evaded by the Americans, the inevitable day of rebellion could be postponed indefinitely.

Following the French and Indian War, however, the new Tory government in London was determined to breathe new life into mercantilism. During the course of fifteen critical years, from 1760 to 1775, in which the oppressive policy was vigorously enforced, a lucrative, golden stream of wealth flowed from the pockets of Americans into British hands. The revenue obtained from the colonists by taxation alone increased by more than *tenfold* after the year 1763, and the economic impact on the colonies was staggering.

---

[10] *Ibid.*, p. 198.
[11] Samuel B. Pettengill, *Op. cit.*, pp. 21-22.

In New England, colonists who relied heavily on trade and commerce for their livelihoods soon found their businesses teetering on the brink of bankruptcy. Due to British policy, specie was in short supply, paper money was declared illegal, and many merchants were reduced to barter. In Virginia, planters found themselves rapidly slipping farther into debt at an accelerating rate. A cruel joke in wide circulation among the Southern States was that Patrick Henry's famous "Give me liberty, or give me death" oration should have been phrased as "Give me liberty, or give me debt." Economic stagnation, depression, and misery devastated all of the American colonies.

That the colonists were doomed to lives of poverty and misery, unless they rebelled, became apparent when the British Government issued a proclamation in 1763 that effectively prohibited the migration of settlers beyond the Allegheny Mountains. Constituting a form of population control, this royal proclamation was designed to ensure that the peopling of the rest of the North American continent would be done only in accordance with the dictates of the monopolistic interests that controlled the British Government. With the decree of the Proclamation Line of 1763, it was made manifest that the true advancement of American civilization in the New World would no longer be tolerated by the London bureaucrats.

The Subversion of the British Constitution

The oppressive nature of the mercantile system was not confined to its economic effects, pernicious as they were. Even more alarming, in the minds of many Americans, were its disastrous effects on the British Constitution and on the democratic system of free government established in the colonies. To effectively enforce an observance of the mandates of the mercantile system required that the British Government undermine popular government in America and subvert the principles of the British Constitution, that unwritten body of law on which the preservation of the rights of all Englishmen depended. In this regard, it might be questioned who were the real revolutionaries – those who sought to undermine the English constitutional system, or those who strove to maintain it.

When the British Government launched its new policy of vigorously enforcing the mercantile system on the American colonies, Parliament entertained no delusions that the colonial leaders would not recognize and understand the constitutional significance of the new policy. As Edmund Burke reminded his fellow Britons, a substantial number of the colonial leaders were either practicing lawyers or at least students of the law. As such, they had read the writings of John Locke and were well versed in the principles of the Glorious Revolution, which had witnessed the ascendancy of the dual concepts that the people have certain inalienable rights which are beyond the reach of government and that the powers of government are therefore limited in nature, especially in regard to private property. And as Edmund Burke had foreseen, when the crisis came, the American leaders turned invariably to the principles of constitutionally limited government and to the theory of the natural rights of man on which those principles were founded, as justification for their opposition to Parliament.

It was this great constitutional struggle during the critical years of 1760 to 1775, and not the War of Independence fought subsequent to it, that constituted the *real* American Revolution. As John Adams of Massachusetts recollected in 1815:

> What do we mean by the Revolution? The war? That was no part of the Revolution: it was only an effect and consequence of it. The Revolution was in the minds of the people, and this was effected, from 1760 to 1775, in the course of fifteen years before a drop of blood was shed at Lexington. [12]

The great constitutional crisis was inaugurated in earnest when Parliament enacted the Stamp Act in 1765. This act constituted the first *direct* tax ever levied by Parliament on the colonists, who, for the first time, witnessed a new form of life swarming among them – British tax collectors. The explosive reaction this act generated in America was due more to its political significance than to its economic consequences. Throughout the colonies arose the cry, "No taxation without representation!" The power to tax, the colonists well understood, was the power to destroy. Such power could only be trusted to those directly responsible to the people. Not only did simple justice require this; so, too, did the British Constitution.

In their book, *American History: A Survey*, historians Richard N. Current, T. Harry Williams, and Frank Freidel highlight the tremendous political significance of the British Government's move to directly tax the colonists:

> Grievous as were the economic consequences of George III's program, its political consequences would be as bad or worse. While colonial democracy was far from all-inclusive, the colonists were used to a remarkably wide latitude in self-government. Nowhere else in the world at that time did so large a proportion of the people take an active interest in public affairs. The chief centers of American political activity were the provincial assemblies, and here the people (through their elected representatives) were

---

[12] The Peoples Bicentennial Commission, *Voices of the American Revolution*, Bantam Books, Inc., New York, 1974, quoted on p. 97.

able to assert themselves because the assemblies had established the right to give or withhold appropriations for the costs of government within the colonies. If, now, the British authorities should succeed in raising extensive revenue directly from America, the colonial voters and their representatives would lose control over public finance, and without such control their participation in politics would be very nearly meaningless.

Home rule was not something new and different that these Americans were striving to get. It was something old and familiar that they desired to keep. They would lose it if the London authorities were allowed to carry out the program of raising revenues from colonial taxation and providing unconditional salaries for royal officials. The discontented Americans eventually prepared themselves to lay down their lives for a movement that was both democratic and conservative – a movement to conserve the liberties they already possessed. [13]

Hostile reaction to the Stamp Act was widespread in the colonies, although Virginia and Massachusetts took the lead in offering resistance to the alarming act of British aggression. The reaction in Virginia to the Stamp Act reached a climax in the House of Burgesses, where a young Patrick Henry boldly denounced the tax in a fiery speech and dramatically concluded by hinting that King George III , like other tyrants in history, might lose his head. In response to the shocked cries of "Treason!" that arose from some of those present, Mr. Henry defiantly replied, "If *this* be treason, make the most of it." [14] And in Massachusetts, Samuel Adams and other patriots organized the Sons of Liberty to oppose the British assault on colonial rights. Through their concerted actions of resistance, enforcement of the Stamp Act was made virtually impossible.

At the urging of James Otis, the Massachusetts legislature issued a call to the other colonies for an inter-colonial congress to demonstrate a united response against the new tax. In October of 1765, the Stamp Act Congress convened in New York, with representatives from nine colonies in attendance. Never before had so many colonies been represented in a united cause.

The delegates to the Stamp Act Congress drew up a formal list of resolutions that were dispatched to London. Within this document, the colonial representatives formally resolved:

> I. That His Majesty's subjects in these colonies owe the same allegiance to the Crown of Great Britain that is owing from his subjects born within the realm, and all due subordination to that august body the Parliament of Great Britain.
> II. That His Majesty's liege subjects in these colonies are intitled to

---

[13] Richard N. Current, T. Harry Williams, and Frank Freidel, *Op. cit.*, pp. 77-78.
[14] *Ibid.*, quoted on p. 78.

all the inherent rights and liberties of his natural born subjects within the kingdom of Great Britain.

III. That it is inseparably essential to the freedom of a people and the undoubted right of Englishmen, that no taxes be imposed on them but with their own consent, given personally or by their representatives.

IV. That the people of these colonies are not, and from their local circumstances cannot be, represented in the House of Commons in Great Britain.

V. That the only representatives of the people of these colonies are persons chosen therein by themselves, and that no taxes ever have been, or can be constitutionally imposed on them, but by their respective legislatures.... [15]

There are several very significant items within these resolutions that merit careful attention. Within the first resolution, the nine colonies represented at the Stamp Act Congress asserted that the American people, possessing all the rights of Englishmen, owed the same loyalty and allegiance to the Crown as did other Englishmen in the Empire, *but no more than that.* This was further stressed by the fifth resolution, which asserted that, in opposing the Stamp Act, the colonists were merely defending the British Constitution. In the second resolution, the colonies again sought refuge in the British Constitution, by asserting the rights of the colonists to all liberties guaranteed by that Constitution to all Englishmen.

What is especially interesting is the fourth resolution of the Stamp Act Congress. This resolution, like a number of other official statements issued by colonial political bodies in the same vein, clearly reveals that the colonial leaders were well aware of a plot then brewing in London to trick the colonies into accepting the subversion of the British Constitution and the centralization of all power in London. According this clever scheme, the British Government would offer to the colonies, in exchange for their acquiescence to the power grab, a token form of representation in Parliament.

Such trickery, the originators of the plan had hoped, would quiet the justifiable American concern that taxation without representation is inherently unjust. As the fourth resolution indicates, however, the Stamp Act Congress clearly understood that local interests could never be truly represented in a centralized government that is distant and remote from the people. Centralization of power and the continued preservation of the rights of man, they therefore deduced, were incompatible. In presenting such views, the colonial patriots were advancing arguments that were strikingly similar to those that would later be used by the champions of States' Rights to oppose the Federal Government's unconstitutional centralization of power.

---

[15] *Ibid.*, quoted on p. 79.

Although the British Government eventually repealed the hated Stamp Act, it also issued a formal declaration, styled the Declaratory Act of 1766, asserting its right to exercise *unlimited power* over the American people, including the right to take their property with or without representation. By insisting that it could enact legislation "to bind the colonies and people of America...in all cases whatsoever," [16] Parliament was, in effect, annulling the British Constitution.

Having asserted its totalitarian nature in word, Parliament proceeded to follow its words with deeds. With alarming swiftness, it moved to rob the American people of one liberty after another. Armed British soldiers were pressed into service to police the colonies and enforce the mercantile policy. And by act of Parliament, Americans were even required to provide quarter for these instruments of oppression. Perhaps most alarming of all, however, was the denial to the colonists of the right to a trial by a jury of their peers when accused of violating key mercantile acts. Under the new British policy, Americans accused of violating the Sugar and Stamp Acts were to be tried in admiralty courts. Not only was the right to a trial by jury unknown in these courts, but, in addition, the burden of proof was placed on the defendant. The assumption, in other words, was that the accused was guilty unless he could prove himself innocent of the charges levied against him.

When Governor Thomas Hutchinson addressed the Council and House of Representatives of Massachusetts in 1773, he announced what many had long suspected, that the British Government no longer recognized the existence of inalienable rights. The thesis presented to the stunned assemblymen amounted to nothing less than the repeal of all the political gains made by Englishmen since the Enlightenment. "They who claim exemption from acts of Parliament by virtue of their rights as Englishmen," he explained, "should consider that it is impossible the rights of English subjects should be the same, in every respect, in all parts of the dominions." [17] According to the revolutionary new theory of government, the American people were entitled to only those rights that the British Government, in its infinite wisdom, saw fit to grant to them. And as the supposed *source* of all rights enjoyed by Englishmen, the government in London could, at its discretion, withdraw those rights whenever if chose to do so.

If there had been any doubts as to the meaning of Governor Hutchinson's message, they were quickly removed when Parliament passed a series of "Intolerable" Acts in 1774. This bundle of legislation was calculated to rob Americans of some of their most basic liberties, chief among them their right

---

[16] *Ibid.*, quoted on p. 80.
[17] John M. Blum, *et al.*, *The National Experience* , Harcourt, Brace & World, Inc., New York, 1963, quoted on p. 83.

to government-by-the-consent-of-the-governed. In addition to undermining local authority, these laws also sought to subvert the colonial justice system.

Although the Intolerable Acts were specifically aimed at Massachusetts, they signified an attack on the rights of all Americans. Determined to starve the people of Massachusetts into submission, Britain closed the port of Boston to all shipping with the Boston Port Act. The Quartering Act extended the provisions of the earlier Mutiny and Quartering Acts by requiring the local authorities of Boston to find quarters for British soldiers within the limits of the city. In an effort to undermine the colonial system of justice, the Administration of Justice Act required that British soldiers and officials could not be tried in the same colony in which they were accused of crimes by local authorities.

The most ominous of the Intolerable Acts was the Massachusetts Government Act, which constituted an undisguised assault upon popularly elected, democratic government in that American colony. By its provisions, the prerogative of appointing members of the council was removed from the General Assembly and vested in the royal Governor. Furthermore, the act required that town meetings could no longer be held without the Governor's permission, and that juries would be selected only by sheriffs appointed by the Governor. This assault on local government in Massachusetts was soon being repeated throughout the colonies. It was only a matter of time before many of the colonial legislatures, officially prohibited from convening by royal edict, were forced to meet clandestinely as extralegal provincial congresses.

That conditions between the colonies and the mother country had been reduced to the level of undisguised warfare could no longer be denied by men of integrity. In the House of Burgesses, Patrick Henry arose to chastise those who entertained notions that peace with Britain was still possible. In a speech that would make him immortal, Mr. Henry addressed his fellow Virginians in these stirring words:

> Gentlemen may cry peace, peace – but there is no peace. The war is actually begun! The next gale that sweeps from the North will bring to our ears the clash of resounding arms! Our brethren are already in the field! Why stand we here idle? What is it that gentlemen wish? What would they have? Is life so dear or peace so sweet as to be purchased at the price of slavery? Forbid it, Almighty God – I know not what course others may take; but as for me, give me liberty or give me death! [18]

---

[18] Clarence B. Carson, *A Basic History of the United States*, Book II, American Textbook Committee, Wadley, 1984, quoted on pp. 12-13.

A month after Patrick Henry spoke these words, the warfare between Crown and colony became an armed conflict. The decisive event that transformed a colonial protest movement into a shooting war occurred on April 14, 1775. On that fateful day, British troops stationed in Boston were secretly ordered to advance on Lexington and Concord and confiscate the munitions depot belonging to the local Massachusetts militia.

This maneuver to disarm the colonists, however, did not go unnoticed. Thanks to the famous midnight ride of Paul Revere, the militiamen were forewarned. When the Redcoats arrived at Lexington, they found the Minutemen prepared to meet them, determined to resist force with force. On that site the embattled farmer of legendary fame stood his ground and fired the famous shot heard 'round the world; the Revolutionary War had begun.

Secession From the Empire

Confronted with an invigorated enforcement of the mercantile system following the French and Indian War, and with the growing destruction of local self-government in America, the American people resolved at an early date to defend themselves and their rights. Initially, the goal had been to direct the opposition toward Parliament and the various ministers in London. As long as the colonists officially maintained loyalty to the King, it was hoped, eventual reconciliation with the mother country was possible. The fact that King George III had already captured control of Parliament, of course, had doomed such hopes from the very start.

But if the colonies wished to defend their rights, it was clear that no one colony could ever hope to effectively oppose the power of Great Britain by itself. A significant step in the direction of realizing a united front against British tyranny was made by the Stamp Act Congress of 1765, in which representatives from nine colonies participated in the deliberations. Never before had so many colonies participated in such an inter-colonial council.

Leadership in the struggle against British aggression fell to two of the more populous colonies, Massachusetts and Virginia. The former colony bore the brunt of many hostile British actions in the years immediately preceding the outbreak of the Revolutionary War, and the patriotic stance taken by her citizens earned Massachusetts the exalted reputation as the *Cradle of Liberty*. Virginia, meanwhile, took the lead in unifying the spirit of the colonies into a common cause and in leading the colonies down the path to independence. For such leadership, the Old Dominion has aptly earned the honorary title of the *Cradle of Independence*.

That Massachusetts and Virginia should work so closely together, united in a common cause, during this time of trial and tribulation is especially remarkable in light of later historical developments. During this brief time, common cause united the greatest patriots of the North – men like John Hancock, John Adams, James Otis, and Samuel Adams – with the greatest minds in the South – great champions of liberty like Thomas Jefferson, James Madison, James Monroe, and Patrick Henry. What these great men, and others like them, accomplished by working together was nothing short of a miracle. Following the adoption of the Federal Constitution years later, the Spirit of '76 quickly faded away, never to return. Never again would America witness such wonderful harmony and collaboration between the leading men of the Southern and Northern sections of the American Union.

The next milestone in colonial unity came in 1772, when Samuel Adams suggested that the colonial legislatures throughout the thirteen colonies should establish and maintain an organized network of communications. Only through communications could ideas be freely exchanged and acted upon in an organized and united effort. Heeding this suggestion, the Virginia legislature established a Committee of Correspondence, and other colonial legislatures quickly followed suit. These Committees of Correspondence allowed all thirteen colonies, for the first time, to work in harmony for a common cause.

Two years later, in 1774, all of the colonies, save Georgia, sought to demonstrate their solidarity in opposing the British Government by sending representatives to the First Continental Congress, whose chief accomplishment was to draft a formal Declaration and Resolves that was published on October 14th of that year. Within these resolutions, the colonial representatives accused the British Government of exercising "unconstitutional powers" and claimed that the "unconstitutional" measures of that government were "illegal," "against law," "subversive of American rights," and "dangerous and destructive of American rights." [19] Resorting to a form of *interposition and nullification* that would later be used by the States to protect themselves from illegal actions by the Federal Government, the First Continental Congress asserted that "Americans cannot submit" to such "grievous acts and measures."[20]

Within the Declaration and Resolves of the First Continental Congress, the colonies emphatically rejected the novel and dangerous theory that some citizens in the British Empire were entitled to more rights than others. They formally resolved, "That our ancestors, who first settled these colonies, were at the time of their emigration from the mother country, entitled to all

---

[19] Charles Callan Tansill (ed.), *The Making of the American Republic: The Great Documents, 1774-1789*, Arlington House, New Rochelle, pp. 1-5.
[20] *Ibid.*, p. 5.

the rights, liberties, and immunities of free and natural-born subjects, within the realm of England." [21] In asserting the concept of inalienable rights, they further resolved, "That by such emigration they by no means forfeited, surrendered, or lost any of those rights, but that they were, and their descendants now are, entitled to the exercise and enjoyment of all such" natural rights. [22]

The colonies also asserted that "the foundation of English liberty, and of all free government, is a right in the people to participate in their legislative council." [23] To thwart any plot to trick them into accepting representation in Parliament as justification for the centralization of all power in London, the colonies, within the Declaration and Resolves of the First Continental Congress, summarily rejected the notion that their local interests could ever be represented in a central government. For this reason, the colonies were "entitled to a free and exclusive power of legislation in their several provincial legislatures," especially in regard to the power of the purse. If this principle were acknowledged – *if the British would agree to refrain from interfering with the colonial right of local self-government* – the colonies would "cheerfully consent" to the other oppressive operations of the mercantile system. [24]

The British Government, as previously noted, showed no restraint in its assault on the right of the colonists to local self-government, and by May of 1775, the colonies were more determined than ever to present a strong and unified voice of opposition against the mother country. When the Second Continental Congress convened in Philadelphia, a highly significant milestone in colonial unity had been reached. For the first time, *all thirteen of the colonies were formally represented in an inter-colonial council*, and the long-awaited unanimity of sentiment had come none too soon. By the time this body convened, the Revolutionary War had already started and colonial militiamen were already bleeding and dying on the field of battle in defense of liberty.

Acting in accordance with the wishes of the colonial assemblies they represented, the members of the Second Continental Congress moved swiftly to organize and coordinate the colonial efforts against the British. Under their direction, the colonial militias were brought together to constitute a Continental Army, and General George Washington was appointed commander of the Army. True to his patriotism and noble character, he refused to accept any monetary compensation or reward for his services.

In defense of the American cause, the Second Continental Congress issued an official policy statement styled the Declaration of the Causes and Ne-

---

[21] *Ibid.*, p. 2.
[22] *Ibid.*, pp. 2-3.
[23] Richard N. Current, T. Harry Williams, and Frank Freidel, *Op. cit.*, quoted on p. 91.
[24] *Ibid.*, quoted on p. 91.

cessity of Taking Up Arms. Within this document, issued on July 6, 1775, the colonies, still hoping for reconciliation with England, did not place the blame for the war directly on King George III. Instead, they *appealed* directly to that Monarch, placing the blame for the Revolutionary War on Parliament and on the King's ministers, "those artful and cruel enemies who abuse your royal confidence and authority for the purpose of effecting our destruction."[25]

Referring to themselves as the "Representatives of the United Colonies of North-America" within this Declaration – the forerunner of the Declaration of Independence – the members of the Second Continental Congress boldly asserted that the members of Parliament were blinded "by their intemperate rage for unlimited domination" and were "stimulated by an inordinate passion for a power not only unjustifiable," but also used for the "purpose of enslaving these colonies by violence." [26] The strident language employed was tempered only by the fact that the colonial accusations were directed at Parliament, and not directly at the Crown itself.

Within this remarkable Declaration, the Founding Fathers concisely related the historical rise of American civilization and the crisis of the British Empire:

> Our forefathers, inhabitants of the island of Great-Britain, left their native land, to seek on these shores a residence for civil and religious freedom. At the expense of their blood, at the hazard of their fortunes, without the least charge to the country from which they removed, by unceasing labour, and an unconquerable spirit, they effected settlements in the distant and inhospitable wilds of America, then filled with numerous and warlike nations of barbarians. – Societies or governments, vested with perfect legislatures, were formed under charters from the Crown, and an harmonious intercourse was established between the colonies and the kingdom from which they derived their origin. The mutual benefits of this union became in a short time so extraordinary, as to excite astonishment. It is universally confessed, that the amazing increase of the wealth, strength, and navigation of the realm, arose from this source; and the minister, who so wisely and successfully directed the measures of Great-Britain in the late war, publicly declared, that these colonies enabled her to triumph over her enemies. – Towards the conclusion of that war, it pleased our sovereign to make a change in his counsels. – From that fatal moment, the affairs of the British Empire began to fall into confusion, and gradually sliding from the summit of glorious prosperity, to which they had been advanced by the virtues and abilities of one man, are at length distracted by the convulsions, that now shake it to its deepest foundations. [27]

---

[25] John M. Blum, *et al.*, *Op. cit.*, quoted on p. 100.
[26] Charles Callan Tansill (ed.), *Op. cit.*, p. 10.
[27] *Ibid.*, pp. 10-11.

"But why should we enumerate our injuries in detail?" the representatives of the United Colonies asked. "By one statute it is declared, that Parliament can 'of right make laws to bind us in all cases whatsoever.' What is to defend us against so enormous, so unlimited a power?" In and of itself, they asserted, such a claim was cause for deep concern among a people that cherished freedom. "We saw the misery to which such despotism would reduce us." [28]

The last twenty-five percent of the Declaration on the Causes and Necessity of Taking Up Arms was penned by Thomas Jefferson, the talented and patriotic Virginian who would, twelve months later, write an even more famous Declaration. As Mr. Jefferson wrote in this notable 1775 Declaration, the Revolutionary War was being waged for a just cause:

> We are reduced to the alternative of chusing an unconditional submission to the tyranny of irritated ministers, or resistance by force. – The latter is our choice. – We have counted the cost of this contest, and find nothing so dreadful as voluntary slavery. – Honour, justice, and humanity, forbid us tamely to surrender that freedom which we received from our gallant ancestors, and which our innocent posterity have a right to receive from us. We cannot endure the infamy and guilt of resigning succeeding generations to that wretchedness which inevitably awaits them, if we basely entail hereditary bondage upon them.
>
> Our cause is just. Our union is perfect. Our internal resources are great, and, if necessary, foreign assistance is undoubtedly attainable. – We gratefully acknowledge, as signal instances of the Divine favour towards us, that his Providence would not permit us to be called into this severe controversy, until we were grown up to our present strength, had been previously exercised in warlike operation, and possessed of the means of defending ourselves. With hearts fortified with these animating reflections, we most solemnly, before God and the world, *declare*, that, exerting the utmost energy of those powers, which our beneficent Creator hath graciously bestowed upon us, the arms we have been compelled by our enemies to assume, we will, in defiance of every hazard, with unabating firmness and perseverance, employ for the preservation of our liberties; being with one mind resolved to die freemen rather than to live slaves. [29]

Thomas Jefferson further asserted that the war to defend America would continue for as long as necessary to resist the British aggressions:

> In our own native land, in defence of the freedom that is our birthright, and which we ever enjoyed till the late violation of it – for the protection of our property, acquired solely by the honest industry of our fore-

---

[28] *Ibid.*, p. 12.
[29] *Ibid.*, pp. 15-16.

fathers and ourselves, against violence actually offered, we have taken up arms. We shall lay them down when hostilities shall cease on the part of the aggressors, and all danger of their being renewed shall be removed, and not before. [30]

The Revolutionary War, stated Thomas Jefferson within this Declaration, was waged only to resist force with force, and it should not be construed as a War of Independence. When the rights and liberties of the American people were once again secure, and the British Government had ceased its hostility, he stressed, the colonies could once again resume their peaceful positions within the Empire.

This point was stressed by Mr. Jefferson in these words:

> Lest this declaration should disquiet the minds of our friends and fellow-subjects in any part of the Empire, we assure them that we mean not to dissolve that union which has so long and so happily subsisted between us, and which we sincerely wish to see restored. – Necessity has not yet driven us into that desperate measure, or induced us to excite any other nation to war against them. – We have not raised armies with ambitious designs of separating from Great-Britain, and establishing independent States. [31]

But if any members of the Second Continental Congress had hoped that such consoling words would facilitate reconciliation, those hopes were quickly dashed. King George III pompously and arrogantly refused to respond to the Declaration, and from Parliament the only response was a vote to dispatch *an additional twenty-five thousand troops* to suppress freedom in America. In February, 1775, both houses of Parliament presented an address to the King that pronounced the colonies to be in a *state of rebellion*. By August, the British King endorsed this view with his own official proclamation to that effect; and in December, Parliament enacted legislation that forbade all colonial trade and subjected all American ships and cargo to confiscation. Thus, by the end 1775, all reasonable hope for reconciliation with the mother country had completely vanished.

In an effort to sustain their rights *within* the Empire, the colonies were forced to increasingly rely on the doctrine of *interposition and nullification*. On May 31, 1775, for example, a set of resolutions was adopted by Charlotte Town, North Carolina, which "annulled" the authority of the King and Parliament and declared all royal commissions to be "null and void." The purpose was not to destroy the British Government or to secede from the Em-

---

[30] *Ibid.*, p. 16.
[31] *Ibid.*, p. 16.

pire, but only to prevent the destruction of colonial rights. Accordingly, it was resolved within the same act of nullification, "That these Resolves be in full Force and Virtue until...the legislative Body of *Great-Britain* resign its unjust and arbitrary Pretensions with Respect to *America.*" [32]

Until the British Government was brought once again within the limits of the British Constitution, the Charlotte Town committee resolved, the colonies could rightfully defend their rights within the Empire. It was thus resolved, "That the several Militia Companies in this county do provide themselves with proper Arms and Accoutrements, and hold themselves in Readiness to execute the commands and Directions of the Provincial Congress, and of this committee." [33]

As 1775 gave way to 1776, however, the emphasis shifted from interposition and nullification to *secession* from the British Empire. In January of 1776, a pamphlet entitled *Common Sense* suddenly appeared and significantly changed the colonial strategy and outlook. Its author, a recent emigrant from England named Thomas Paine, boldly asserted that reconciliation with Great Britain should *not* be the goal of those waging the Revolutionary War. The argument presented by this talented author was remarkably simple and very persuasive. Both in terms of blood and treasure that Americans were being forced to pay for the defense of their liberties, Mr. Paine noted, the cost was much too high for mere reconciliation. "The object contended for," he argued, "ought always to bear some just proportion to the expence....Dearly, dearly, do we pay for the repeal of the acts, if that is all we fight for." [34] Common sense dictated, he contended, that for such a high price, the American people should expect nothing less than *independence* for the thirteen colonies.

Common Sense was widely circulated throughout the colonies and George Washington even had it distributed among his soldiers to boost their morale. Its bold message seemed to strike a responsive chord in the American breast, and for the next six months the resisting colonial patriots began thinking more and more in terms of political independence from Great Britain. Beginning in March of 1776 and acting on their own accord, the colonies began establishing *republican* Constitutions for themselves, symbolizing not only a rejection of British control over them but also a rejection of monarchy as a form of government.

The movement toward independence was further propelled in April, one year after the Revolutionary War had begun, when North Carolina officially instructed its representatives in the Second Continental Congress to

---

[32] *Ibid.*, pp. 6 and 9.
[33] *Ibid.*, p. 9.
[34] John M. Blum, *Op. cit.*, quoted on p. 100.

seek political independence for the colonies. The following month, Virginia formally issued the same instructions to her representatives in the Congress. Also in May, at the urging of John Adams, the Second Continental Congress recommended that all colonies which had not already established republican governments for themselves should quickly do so. As May gave way to June, it was apparent that the Northern and Southern colonies were firmly united in the conviction that secession from the Empire was the only course left for the American people. And the more hesitant middle colonies were beginning to agree.

On June 7, 1776, in accordance with instructions from the legislature of the colony he represented, Richard Henry Lee of Virginia arose in the Second Continental Congress and moved that, "These United Colonies are, and of right ought to be, free and independent States." [35] For nearly a month, Congress debated the merits of the proposition and finally adopted the motion on July 2, 1776. With the adoption of Mr. Lee's resolution, the thirteen American colonies became sovereign and independent States.

While debating the merits of Richard Henry Lee's resolution, and in anticipation that the motion for independence would be adopted, Congress had appointed a committee to draft an appropriate statement that would both announce the independence of the States and justify their secession from the British Empire to a candid world. Although this august committee consisted of five men of distinction, the actual task of penning the famous Declaration of Independence fell to Thomas Jefferson of Virginia. Already famous for his ardent defense of the American Revolution, published in 1774 under the title of *A Summary View of the Rights of British America*, no other patriot leader was more suited to the task of explaining the American cause to the world than Mr. Jefferson. From his bold pen came a great document of liberty destined to stir the hearts of all men.

In eloquent style, Thomas Jefferson stated that all men are endowed by God with inalienable rights, that governments exist solely to protect these rights, and that, whensoever government fails to achieve this legitimate end, the people have a right to replace it with new government. This introduction was followed by a long list of the crimes committed against America by the British Government, including the imposition of taxes without consent, the abolition of trial by jury, the subversion of local self-government, the establishment of a military dictatorship, the burning of towns, the attempts to starve Americans into submission, the hiring mercenaries, and the incitement of savage Indians to ruthlessly slaughter White Americans.

Nor were these atrocities against America the result of a mere misun-

---

[35] Thomas A. Bailey and David M. Kennedy, *Op. cit.*, quoted on p. 102.

derstanding between colony and Crown, Mr. Jefferson asserted. They were the consequences of a sinister conspiracy against the American people, as he had boldly asserted two years earlier:

> Single acts of tyranny may be ascribed to the accidental opinion of a day; but a series of oppressions, begun at a distinguished period and pursued unalterably through every change of ministers, too plainly proves a deliberate, systematic plan of reducing us to slavery. [36]

Following a long list of grievances in the Declaration of Independence came the dramatic conclusion, wherein the secession of the colonies from Great Britain was formally asserted. In plain and unmistakable language, the thirteen American colonies unilaterally announced to a candid world that they had become independent and sovereign States! After a brief debate and some minor alterations in Mr. Jefferson's original draft, the Declaration of Independence was formally approved by the Second Continental Congress on July 4, 1776.

Thus was born the original thirteen sovereign States of the United States of America, conceived in a great struggle for constitutional government and baptized in the crucible of war. And with their Declaration of Independence, the thirteen colonies – now sovereign and independent States – transformed the Revolutionary War into a *War of Independence*.

The High Cost of Freedom

Prior to the issuance of the Declaration of Independence, the colonies had paid dearly for daring to assert and defend their rights under the British Constitution. After the Declaration was published, the American people were forced to pay considerably more – in blood, treasure, and tears – in defense of their newly acquired sovereignty and independence. General Washington's troops were forced to march barefoot through the snow, and American soldiers captured by the British were thrown into dungeons aboard ships where disease and famine took a heavy toll. Some 11,000 American captives were destined to die aboard the cruel prison ship *Jersey* alone. Even the noncombatant patriots were required to make personal sacrifices for the cause of freedom, and King George III made clear his intention of meting out harsh punishment on American "rebels" and "traitors" should England win the war.

When Benjamin Franklin grimly remarked to his fellow patriots that, if

---

[36] The Peoples Bicentennial Commission, *Op. cit.*, quoted on p. 139.

they failed to hang together, they would assuredly all hang separately, he may well have underestimated the fiery temperament of the British King. We may obtain an idea of what the fate of the American patriots would have been, had they lost the war, from the fate of some Irish patriots who were punished for their rebellion against the British Crown some twenty-eight years later.

In 1802, King George III approved the following death sentence for the Irish rebels:

> You are to be hanged by the neck, but not until you are dead; for while you are still living your bodies are to be taken down, your bowels torn out and burned before your faces, your heads then cut off, and your bodies divided each into four quarters, and your heads and quarters to be then at the King's disposal; and may the Almighty God have mercy on your souls. [37]

Such was the "mercy" of the English King against which America revolted. Against this foe, Americans marched into battle, always short of supplies and provisions, but never short of determination or steadfast resolve to live free or die. At one point, when General Washington's Army was severely crippled due to lack of munitions, American patriots seriously considered Benjamin Franklin's proposal that, if required by necessity, they should continue to wage war with bows and arrows. Such was the unfaltering determination of those willing to defend the liberties of America.

To derive some estimate of the steadfast willingness of our Founding Fathers to make whatever personal sacrifices were necessary to secure the blessings of liberty to the United States, we may turn to the fates of those fifty-six courageous souls who bravely signed the Declaration of Independence. In signing that document, they had each made a solemn pledge to one another: "We mutually pledge to each other our lives, our fortunes and our sacred honor." [38] Although many of the signers were hounded by the British and suffered greatly, not one defected. To the very end, each man remained true to his pledge.

A big prize in the eyes of the British was undoubtedly Thomas Jefferson, the wartime Governor of Virginia and the author of the Declaration of Independence. And British forces almost succeeded in capturing him, when they attempted to stealthily approach his residence and take him by surprise. Fortunately, Mr. Jefferson was alerted to the approach of the Redcoats, but only minutes before their arrival. After hastily seizing an armful of important papers, Governor Jefferson fled into the nearby woods just in the nick of

---

[37] Thomas A. Bailey and David M. Kennedy, *Op. cit.*, quoted on p. 103.
[38] *Ibid.*, quoted on p. 103.

time. One signer had thus managed to elude his persistent pursuers. Other signers would not be as fortunate.

British and Hessian soldiers plundered the home of signer Francis Lewis, set it ablaze, and kidnapped his wife. The extensive properties of William Floyd were also overrun by British troops. His wife and children were forced to flee to Connecticut and to live for the next seven years without any income. When the Floyd family returned home after the war, they found their beloved estate "despoiled of almost everything but the naked soil." [39] All property in New York City belonging to signer Philip Livingston was seized by British forces. His town house on Duke Street and his country estate in Brooklyn Heights were also confiscated. He died in 1778, penniless, yet still a member of the Second Continental Congress and still laboring on behalf of freedom's cause.

Another signer of the Declaration, Lewis Morris, who served as a Brigadier General in the New York militia, watched from a hiding place as British forces overran his farm, destroying timber and crops and stealing his livestock. The British also burned the library at the College of New Jersey — later renamed Princeton University — most of which had been brought from Scotland by the college's president and signer of the Declaration of Independence, Dr. John Witherspoon. Another signer, Francis Hopkinson, had his home in Bordentown, New Jersey, looted by avenging Redcoats. And two sons of signer Abraham Clark were captured by the British and imprisoned aboard the dreaded *Jersey*.

Another signer, John Hart, who had successfully managed to elude his pursuers for some time, received word one day that his wife lay dying at their home. Deciding to risk capture, he hastened to her bedside. But a traitor among the colonists betrayed him, and Mr. Hart was forced to flee. As Mr. Hart's wife lay dying in her bed, Hessian troops scoured the woods in search of his trail, and others ransacked the house. Although this brave signer of the Declaration managed to elude capture, he was not able to return home again for several months. What John Hart found on his return home broke his heart. His wife had already been buried, and his thirteen children had scattered. He died in 1779 without ever seeing any of his children again.

Another signer who paid dearly for his patriotism was Richard Stockton, a New Jersey State Supreme Court Justice. Although Judge Stockton and his family were able to find refuge with friends, he was betrayed by a Tory sympathizer. In the middle of night, troops raided the Judge's place of refuge, pulled him out of bed, and beat him. Judge Stockton was then imprisoned and deliberately starved. After his release, Judge Stockton returned home,

---

[39] Melvin Mund, "The Establishment - 1776," Freedom Talk, No. 85, Life Line, Dallas, 1969, p. 3.

only to discover that the British had looted and demolished it, including his library, the finest private one in America. Exhausted from his ordeal, he died soon thereafter, and his family was forced to live in poverty.

Reflecting on the many heroic sacrifices made by the signers of the Declaration of Independence, radio commentator Melvin Mund noted:

> Of the 56 men who signed the Declaration of Independence, nine died of wounds or hardships during the war. Five were captured and imprisoned, in each case with brutal treatment. Several lost wives, sons, or family. One lost his thirteen children. All were victims of manhunts and driven from their homes. Twelve signers had their homes burned, and seventeen lost everything they owned. [40]

Truly, freedom did not come cheaply. But the gallant efforts and noble sacrifices made by the Founding Fathers did not go unrewarded. With the surrender of General Cornwallis in 1781, the American cause was crowned with victory, a victory that was assured two years later by the terms of the Treaty of Paris, wherein the British Government formally acknowledged the independence of the thirteen sovereign States. The War of Independence had been won.

The Conservative Nature of the Revolution

Despite the overwhelming odds against which the thirteen States fought, they emerged victorious from the War of Independence. There are a number of factors that may be credited for their victory. One reason for the success of the American cause, quite clearly, was the willingness of the American patriots to make whatever sacrifices were necessary to ensure victory. And divine intervention certainly contributed to the American victory, as did the remarkable unanimity achieved by the American patriots.

Foreign assistance also played a significant role in influencing the outcome of the War of Independence. During the course of the war, Great Britain found herself battling not only the Continental Army, but also the armed forces of France, Spain, and The Netherlands. The assistance of France was especially valuable to the American cause, and many of the French officers dispatched to the United States to assist in our war effort came to admire the principles of which the war was based. Most notable in this regard was General Marquis de Lafayette, who succeeded in establishing a lifelong friendship with George Washington and Thomas Jefferson.

---

[40] *Ibid.*, p. 4.

One of the most important reasons accounting for the success of the American Revolution, however, is the one most often overlooked by students of history. Such oversight is undoubtedly owing to the *terminology* used to describe the events surrounding the War of Independence. Although numerous accounts of that time in our history have invariably applied the term *revolution* to describe those events, the name can be misleading, especially in light of the many other upheavals in history that also bear that label.

In many respects, the real *revolutionaries* during the American Revolution were the Tories, whose subversion of the British Constitution and assaults upon the liberties long enjoyed by the colonists constituted the real revolution. By this reckoning, those who resisted such aggressions were, to use a modern term, the *counter-revolutionaries*. But even if the term "revolution" can be applied to the American cause, a distinction must be made between the American Revolution and most other revolutions that have stained the pages of history with blood.

From start to finish, the American Revolution was *conservative* in nature. Its goal was not to overthrow the existing social order, to subvert the foundations of civil society, or to introduce radically new theories of economics, sociology, and politics. On the contrary, its purpose was merely to *preserve* the liberties already possessed by the colonial people, to *defend* the existing social and political order within the colonies, and to *maintain* the basic foundations of the British Constitution. Only when reconciliation with the mother country was impossible did the American patriots convert a war to defend their rights as Englishmen into a war to obtain independence from Great Britain.

The American patriots who masterminded the American Revolution were staunchly *middle class* in their origins and values. They were not anarchists bent on undermining law and order. On the contrary, they were the defenders of the law who sought only to maintain its supremacy over government as well as citizen. They did not seek to redistribute wealth, but only to preserve the right in property. And the movement they led was not an attempt to seize all power, but was instead a movement to prevent a power grab on the part of their enemies.

Stated differently, the American Revolution was exclusively a *political* revolution, standing in sharp contrast with the numerous leftist revolutions that are also *social* in nature. Admittedly, there were some occasions when it appeared as though the American Revolution might degenerate into an uncontrollable social upheaval, as when a mob of Bostonians assaulted some British soldiers, resulting in the historic "Boston Massacre." Mobocracy, however, was generally discouraged by the colonial leaders, who sought to oppose the illegal acts of Britain in an orderly, lawful manner. Even Thomas

Jefferson, widely regarded as the most broad-minded of the patriot leaders, frowned upon such acts as the Boston Tea Party.

At no time was it ever the intent of the American patriots to overthrow the existing social order. Even when the decision was made to seek independence by throwing off the authority of the British Government, a sharp distinction was made by the Founding Fathers between replacing an old government with a new one and replacing an existing social structure with a new society. Throughout the entire period – from the time of the Stamp Act Congress in 1765, through the War of Independence, and even to the adoption of our present Federal Constitution – great and profound changes in government were made, and yet *the existing social structure remained intact*. Those in American society who were most prominent – socially and politically – prior to the revolution retained such status after the revolution.

That the American Revolution differed sharply from the sundry radical revolutions that have plagued history has not escaped the notice of the Marxist historians. In the *Great Soviet Encyclopedia*, for example, which was published before the dissolution of the Soviet Union, the authors, while paying lip service to the American Revolution simply because it was a "revolution," acknowledged that, "The War for Independence was a bourgeois revolution." [41] This, of course, is the communist way of saying that the American Revolution was precisely the opposite of a socialist revolution.

The main objectives of the American Revolution were indeed contrary to and opposite of the objectives of modern-day socialist revolutions. The latter have as their goal the establishment of an all-powerful government that will regulate everything and control everyone. That is precisely the type of political system the American Revolution was designed to *eliminate*. This explains why the *result* of the American Revolution was such a great blessing, and why the *result* of socialistic revolutions is invariably a great curse to suffering mankind.

Commenting on the true character of the American Revolution in his book, *Jefferson: The Forgotten Man*, Samuel B. Pettengill wrote:

> [The American Revolution] was a War of Independence against too much government. It was an armed protest against a distant government that tried to build up one industry, or one part of the empire, or one class of people, at the expense of some other. No doubt it was justified in debate as "for the good of the Empire," or for the "general welfare" or other sonorous phrases with which legislation is decorated by pressure groups....
>
> It was an age which challenged the mercantilism of the Middle

---

[41] *A Soviet View of the American Past*, Annotated Translation on the Section on American History in the Great Soviet Encyclopedia, Scott, Foresman and Company, Glenville, 1960, p. 17.

Ages. This was a philosophy of a planned economy in which government, and government officials, undertook to tell men not only what they could *not* do but what they *must* do. It was to free themselves from the restrictions placed upon them and upon their business and commerce by the government of England that our fathers declared their independence....

The Declaration declared war against these restrictions. And the Constitution which followed thirteen years later, furnished safeguards against their return. These two documents dedicated America to private enterprise, and freed it from collectivism. Those, therefore, who would today control the most minute affairs of our people would turn the clock back to pre-Revolutionary time. Believing the Constitution antiquated, they want something still more antiquated. [42]

This was the great cause and the consequence of the American Revolution. When judged by the fruit it has borne, no other action ever undertaken by mortals can compare with it in either majesty or greatness. The American Revolution gave birth to the thirteen original sovereign States and paved the way for the creation of the greatest citadel of liberty in the history of the world – the United States of America.

---

[42] Samuel B. Pettengill, *Op. cit.*, pp. 17-18.

Chapter Three
The Declaration of Independence

The Declaration of Independence was popular among the American people the moment it was publicly read, then quickly became famous throughout the world as a result of the successful outcome of the American Revolution, and eventually became semi-sacred. Today, the great document is stored within closely guarded confines in the National Archives Building in Washington, D.C. However, for a time after it had been delivered to King George III of England, the Declaration was treated very casually – so casually, in fact, that it is nothing short of a miracle that it survived at all.

Following the American Revolution, the government of Great Britain returned the Declaration of Independence to the United States, for the document was obviously much more highly valued by America than by England. For years thereafter, that document was treated as any other state paper. During the War of 1812, for instance, when British forces invaded Washington, D.C., state papers – including the Declaration – had to be hidden to prevent their falling into the hands of the enemy. Accordingly, the Declaration of Independence was hidden under the front steps of a clergyman's house. British soldiers, fortunately, never knew what was directly beneath their feet as they tramped up and down those steps.

Scholars have estimated that, in the early years of our Republic, the Declaration of Independence was haphazardly transferred from one location to another no less than twenty-six times. Even in 1876, the centennial celebration year in the United States, the document was treated so casually that it was almost destroyed. In that year, the Declaration was sent to Philadelphia, where it was placed on display during a great celebration, and was then sent on to the Centennial Exposition, where it was nearly consumed in a fire. Afterwards, the document was housed in a room with an open fireplace, where it sustained heat and smoke damage.

It was finally decided that the Declaration of Independence should be better protected from the elements. The document was accordingly placed in a hermetically sealed case inside the Library of Congress from 1924 to 1952, except during the years of World War II, when it was stored in Fort Knox for safekeeping. It was not until 1952 that the Declaration found its present home in the National Archives Building. The document itself resides in a special glass case, filled with a preservative gas, and is stored in a bombproof, underground vault. The document and its protective case daily rise to ground-floor level to allow spectators to view the original copy of the great charter of freedom.

Although the Declaration of Independence is now more than two hundred years old, it is a document that is still extensively studied, analyzed, and interpreted. Such re-examinations of the Declaration are to be encouraged and welcomed by all honest advocates of constitutional government who seek inspiration by studying the words that created the sovereign American States. However, it must be noted that many of the newer reappraisals of the Declaration are, unfortunately, merely attempts to read into that document something which is not really there, something which would condone egalitarian schemes or justify socialist revolutions. Every generation of Americans should indeed study and evaluate the Declaration, not in an attempt to discover a way to use the instrument to supposedly justify modern schemes and designs, but in a sincere effort to ascertain the true foundations of our Federal Republic.

Evolution of the Declaration

Throughout the thirteen American colonies, as 1775 gave way to 1776, there arose a growing desire to turn the already existing armed conflict with Great Britain into a War of Independence. But if the colonies should decide to declare American independence from the mother country, exactly *who* should be declared independent? Should the colonies be merged into a single political society and assert independence as a *single* sovereign nation? Or should they maintain their separate political societies, yet work in concert with one another, and declare their independence as thirteen *separate* sovereign nations?

There actually was some sentiment expressed – from New Hampshire – in preference for the creation of a single American nation. The vast majority of sentiment throughout the colonies, however, was decidedly in favor of the creation of *separate* sovereignty for each colony. Should the decision be made to assert independence, therefore, it was agreed that such independence would convert each colony into a State.

Virginia was, at this time, the most populous, opulent, and influential of all the colonies. When the Old Dominion State resolved that political independence should be the goal of the American Revolution, the other colonies quickly adopted her sentiments. The tide turned in the direction of secession from the British Empire on May 15, 1776, when a convention in Virginia unanimously voted to instruct the colony's representatives in the Second Continental Congress to work for an inter-colonial statement that would jointly proclaim the independence of each of the colonies.

"In this state of extreme danger," the Virginia Convention declared, "we have no alternative left but an abject submission to the will of those overbearing tyrants, or a total separation from the Crown and Government of *Great Britain*." Considering the martial strength of the British Government, secession would necessitate military alliances, including "uniting and exerting the strength of all *America* for defence, and forming alliances with foreign Powers for commerce and aid in war." Compelled to act by "the external law of self-preservation," the Convention unanimously adopted two resolutions. [1]

These two resolutions declared:

> *Resolved, unanimously*, That the Delegates appointed to represent this Colony in General Congress be instructed to propose to that respectable body to declare the United Colonies free and independent States, absolved from all allegiance to, or dependence upon, the Crown or Parliament of *Great Britain*; and that they give the assent of this Colony to such declaration, and to whatever measures may be thought proper and necessary by the Congress for forming foreign alliances, and a Confederation of the Colonies, at such time and in the manner as to them shall seem best: Provided, That the power of forming Government for, and the regulations of the internal concerns of each Colony, be left to the respective Colonial Legislatures.

> *Resolved, unanimously*, That a Committee be appointed to prepare a Declaration of Rights, and such a plan of Government as will be most likely to maintain peace and order in this Colony, and secure substantial and equal liberty to the people. [2]

On June 7, 1776, in accordance with the instructions of the colony he represented, Richard Henry Lee of Virginia introduced the following resolution in the Second Continental Congress:

> *Resolved*, That these United Colonies are, and of right ought to be, free and independent States, that they are absolved from all allegiance to the British Crown, and that all political connection between them and the State of Great Britain is, and ought to be, totally dissolved.

> That it is expedient forthwith to take the most effectual measures for forming foreign Alliances.

> That a plan of confederation be prepared and transmitted to the re-

---

[1] Charles Callan Tansill (ed.), *The Making of the American Republic: The Great Documents, 1774-1789*, Arlington House, New Rochelle, p. 19.
[2] *Ibid.*, p. 20.

spective Colonies for their consideration and approbation. [3]

For nearly one month, the Second Continental Congress debated the merits of the Virginia proposal, which called upon them to issue a joint statement of independence for each colony, to solicit foreign aid for the War of Independence, and to draft and submit to the newly independent States a plan of government in a Federal Union. To avoid unnecessary delay, while the Congress debated Mr. Lee's resolution, a committee of distinguished men was appointed to draft a declaration that would formally assert the independence of the American States. On this committee were John Adams, Benjamin Franklin, Robert Livingston, Roger Sherman, and Thomas Jefferson. As all history books attest, the task of actually writing the Declaration of Independence was given to just one individual on the committee – Thomas Jefferson.

On June 28, 1776, the five-man drafting committee presented Mr. Jefferson's version of the Declaration of Independence to the Second Continental Congress, which read it and then set it aside to await the outcome of the great debate over Richard Henry Lee's resolution. Four days later, on July 2, 1776, the members of Congress – acting in accordance with instructions received from the their respective colonial legislatures – formally adopted Mr. Lee's resolution. The representatives in Congress assembled then painstakingly reviewed the draft of the Declaration submitted by Mr. Jefferson and, after making a few minor alterations, approved the final draft two days later.

Satisfied with the final version of the Declaration of Independence, the Second Continental Congress officially approved it on July 4, 1776, and it was signed by John Hancock of Massachusetts, the presiding officer of the Congress. Four days later, the Declaration was publicly read for the first time and was received by the people with great joy. Finally, on August 2, 1776, a formal signing ceremony was staged, when fifty-five members of the Second Continental Congress added their signatures below John Hancock's.

The fifty-six signers of the Declaration of Independence certainly realized that a date of great historical significance had arrived, a date that would be remembered and honored by generations of Americans yet unborn. However, which date would be honored? Would America commemorate Independence Day on July 2nd, in honor of the day when the colonies officially became sovereign States? Would it be July 4th, in honor of the day on which the Congress approved the Declaration of Independence? Would Americans choose July 8th, in remembrance of the day the Declaration was first read publicly? Or would American independence be commemorated on August 2nd, in observance of the day the signing ceremony was held?

---

[3] *Ibid.*, p. 21.

One of the signers of the Declaration of Independence – John Adams of Massachusetts – believed that America would always commemorate Independence Day on July 2nd. Writing to his wife, Abigail, on July 3, 1776, Mr. Adams stated:

> Yesterday the greatest question was decided which ever was debated in America, and a greater, perhaps, never was nor will be decided among men. A resolution was passed without one dissenting colony, "that these United Colonies are, and of right ought to be, free and independent States, and as such they have, and of right ought to have, full power to make war, conclude peace, establish commerce, and to do all other acts and things which other States may rightfully do."
>
> You will see in a few days a Declaration setting forth the causes which have impelled us to this mighty resolution, and the reasons which will justify it in the sight of God and man. A plan of confederation [the Articles of Confederation] will be taken up in a few days.
>
> When I look back to the year 1761, and recollect the argument concerning writs of assistance in the superior court, which I have hitherto considered as the commencement of this controversy between Great Britain and America, and run through the whole period, from that time to this, and recollect the series of political events, the chain of causes and effects, I am surprised at the suddenness as well as greatness of this resolution. Britain has been filled with folly, and America with wisdom. At least, this is my judgment. Time must determine.
>
> It is the will of Heaven that the two countries should be sundered forever. It may be the will of Heaven that America shall suffer calamities still more wasting, and distresses yet more dreadful. If this is to be the case, it will have this good effect at least. It will inspire us with many virtues which we have not and correct many errors, follies, and vices which threaten to disturb, dishonor, and destroy us.
>
> The furnace of affliction produces refinement, in States as well as individuals. And the new governments we are assuming in every part will require a purification from our vices, and an augmentation of our virtues, or they will be no blessings. The people will have unbounded power and the people are extremely addicted to corruption and venality, as well as the great. But I must submit all my hopes and fears to an overruling Providence, in which, unfashionable as the faith may be, I firmly believe....
>
> The second day of July 1776 will be the most memorable epocha in the history of America. I am apt to believe that it will be celebrated by succeeding generations as the great anniversary festival. It ought to be commemorated, as the day of deliverance, by solemn acts of devotion to God Almighty. It ought to be solemnized with pomp and parade, with shows, games, sports, guns, bells, bonfires, and illuminations, from one end of this continent to the other, from this time forward, forevermore.
>
> You will think me transported with enthusiasm, but I am not. I am well aware of the toil, and blood, and treasure that it will cost us to maintain this Declaration, and support and defend these States. Yet I can see

that the end is more than worth all the means, and that posterity will triumph in that day's transaction, even although we should rue it which I trust in God we shall not. [4]

John Adams was correct in believing that succeeding generations of Americans would annually celebrate Independence Day. Yet, rather than celebrate Independence Day on July 2nd, the prerogative of America has been to commemorate our separation from Great Britain on the 4th of July, in observance of the day when the Second Continental Congress adopted the final draft of the Declaration of Independence.

The Philosopher of the Revolution

To properly understand the principles of the Declaration of Independence, we must understand the mind of the great American patriot who wrote it. Although its basic principles were familiar to the generation of Americans then living, no other colonial leader could have hoped to match the grand style and eloquence displayed by its author in defense of the American cause. Due to the many contributions made by Mr. Jefferson to the success of the American Revolution, not the least of which was writing the famous Declaration, he has earned the enduring title of *Philosopher of the Revolution*.

Born April 13, 1743, at the Shadwell plantation in Virginia, Thomas Jefferson was a man of remarkable ability and brilliant intellect. This exceptional man was not only fluent in a number of languages, but he was also a scientist of distinction, an inventor, an architect, a musician, a lawyer, a chemist, as well as a statesman and patriot. His copious notes on the natural vegetation and terrain of Virginia revealed his keen interest in botany and natural history. And in later years, his home at Monticello was filled with scientific innovations and more resembled a museum of technology than a private residence. He was truly a scholar's scholar, and his devotion to scholarship led him to found the University of Virginia.

The man destined to become the Philosopher of the Revolution attended the College of William and Mary at Williamsburg and became a student of the Enlightenment. He diligently studied the principles of England's Glorious Revolution and read John Locke's *Second Treatise of Government* with great care and attention. From that great English philosopher, Mr. Jefferson learned that the legitimate powers of government are limited to the protection of the natural rights of man, and that government should be the

---

[4] John Adams, "The Mighty Resolution That Set America Free," *The Miami Herald*, Miami, July 4, 1972, p. 6-A.

servant in the political system and the people should be the masters. It was only natural, that, from the very start of the American Revolution, the young Virginian should align himself on the side of the colonial patriots, and that his natural talents and keen intellect should mark him as one of the key colonial leaders in the confrontation with the British Government.

Commenting on the crucial role played by Mr. Jefferson in the American Revolution, Caleb Perry Patterson made the following observations in his brilliant book, *The Constitutional Principles of Thomas Jefferson*:

> Jefferson, if not the key figure in the American Revolution, was one of three or four masterminds which determined its program and its results. The publication in 1774 of his *A Summary View of the Rights of British America*, in which he maintained that the colonies were under the Crown but legislatively independent of Parliament, contributed to the crystallization of political opinion in favor of a federalist form of government. In the *Summary View* is laid the foundation of States' rights. It is one of the greatest state papers of the Revolutionary Period and with some modifications was used by Edmund Burke in his great speech in the House of Commons on Conciliation with America. It was largely the source of the Declaration of Independence. Its relation to American federalism, however, lies in the fact that it was predicated on the thesis that American States already existed. States constitute one wing of our federalism and were the basis of the confederation; and there is still, constitutionally speaking, the Union of States. As long as the American States exist, Thomas Jefferson, their father, will live. [5]

The whole history of mankind, including the trials and tribulations of the American Revolution, taught Thomas Jefferson that infringements of liberty were due less to misunderstandings among men than to sinister conspiracies. It was not an honest difference of opinion that characterized the great struggles of mankind. Rather, the epoch struggle of the human race was between good and evil, between those who were honest and those who were not. "The whole art of government," he had stressed in *A Summary View of the Rights of British America*, "consists in the art of being honest." [6] In the Declaration of Independence, he would expand on this theme by asserting that the American Revolution was not caused by misunderstandings between Crown and colony or by British blundering, but was, in fact, caused by a ruthless conspiracy to rob Americans of their liberties.

To Mr. Jefferson, the measure of a government – whether it be good or

---

[5] Caleb Perry Patterson, *The Constitutional Principles of Thomas Jefferson*, Peter Smith, Gloucester, 1967, p. 27.

[6] The Peoples Bicentennial Commission, *Voices of the American Revolution*, Bantam Books, Inc., New York, 1974, quoted on p.129.

bad — was how closely it adhered to its true end of securing every man's right to life, liberty, and property. He understood that the more power a government exercised, the less rights the people could enjoy. Therefore, the fundamental maxim that, "That government is best that governs least," was always his guiding credo.

This maxim, he was convinced, applied equally to democratically elected governments as well as to monarchies and unrepresentative governments. He certainly never subscribed to the absurd notion that the powers of democratic governments do not require limitation since such governments are elective in nature, nor to the equally absurd fallacy that the more power a democratic government possesses the more power the people possess. He rejected such absurdities because he knew that the people could never be equated with their government. The key to controlling *all* forms of government, without exception, he therefore concluded, was to limit their powers.

The ideal government, in his mind, would be decidedly republican in nature, administered by only a relatively few public servants periodically elected by the people, and limited in power to the simple and plain duty of protecting society from common criminals and from the aggressions of foreign powers. "Restrain men from injuring one another," he indicated, "but leave them otherwise free to follow their own pursuits of industry and employment." [7]

Such a government, Mr. Jefferson thought, should have no power or authority to regulate the social and economic activities of the people. With government thus strictly limited in its powers, the people would have little to fear from their rulers, and the financial burden of supporting such a political system would be negligible. Should a government exceed these legitimate boundaries of power, he was convinced, it would invariably become venal and oppressive. "I own I am not a friend of a very energetic government," wrote the Philosopher of the Revolution. "It is always oppressive." [8]

"The trade of the Colonies was laid under such restrictions," Mr. Jefferson wrote of the mercantile system, "as show what hopes they might find from the justice of a British Parliament were its uncontrolled power admitted over these States." [9] A key objective of the American Revolution, therefore, should be to replace the mercantile economy with a free enterprise system based on *laissez-faire*. "The system into which the United States wished to go," he noted, "was that of freeing commerce from every shackle." [10] "What

---

[7] Samuel B. Pettengill, *Jefferson: The Forgotten Man*, America's Future, Inc., New York, 1938, quoted on p. 17.

[8] *Ibid.*, quoted on p. 23.

[9] *Ibid.*, quoted on p. 23.

[10] *Ibid.*, quoted on p. 23.

more is necessary to make us a happy and prosperous people; still one thing more, a wise and frugal government... which shall not take from the mouth of labor the bread it has earned." [11]

Collectivism, he was convinced, could only result in poverty and starvation. "Were we to be directed from Washington when to sow and when to reap," he soberly observed, "we should soon want bread." [12] The collectivist ideology of a Welfare State also struck Mr. Jefferson as being inherently dishonesty. For this reason, he stated that, "If we can prevent the government from wasting the labors of the people under the pretense of taking care of them, they must become happy." [13]

As long as government remained essentially local in character, he believed, the government could be kept within its proper limits. Centralization of power, therefore, was viewed as the greatest evil that could ever befall the American people. "What has destroyed liberty and the rights of man in every government which has existed under the sun?" Thomas Jefferson could ask. The self-evident answer was "the generalizing and concentrating all cares and powers into one body." [14] States' Rights, therefore, represented the chief means of preserving human rights in the United States. It was always his belief that, should the States ever lose their reserved powers to the Federal Government, it would become the most corrupt and wicked government on the earth.

"Our country is too large to have all of its affairs directed by a single government," [15] he insisted. "When all government, domestic and foreign, in little as in great things, shall be drawn to Washington as the centre of all power," he warned, "it will render powerless the checks provided of one government on another, and will become as venal and oppressive as the government from which we separated."

Those who administer government, he was firmly convinced, should always identify with the people, particularly those of the middle class who labor day in and day out to sustain themselves. The concept of government outlined in Plato's *Republic* was thoroughly repugnant to him. The American people, he asserted, did not need government administrators who fancied that they were wiser than those they governed and who regarded the people they ruled as little more than a flock of sheep. Despite the many accomplishments and distinctions to which he could boast, Mr. Jefferson always identified himself in spirit with the most humble of the middle class and preferred the title

[11] *Ibid.*, quoted on p. 7.
[12] *Ibid.*, quoted on p. 56.
[13] *Ibid.*, quoted on p. 88.
[14] *Ibid.*, quoted on p. 187.
[15] *Ibid.*, quoted on p. 56.

of "farmer" to any other. This preference is all the more remarkable when we consider his other titles – President of the United States, Vice President, Secretary of State, Governor of Virginia, Congressman, Founder of the University of Virginia, Author of the Declaration of Independence, and Minister to France!

Had Thomas Jefferson's services to America been limited to those he rendered during the trying days of the American Revolution, history would have recognized him as one of America's greatest philosophers and statesmen. His service to the cause of freedom, however, did not end when the War of Independence was successfully concluded. Even greater challenges and accomplishments lay ahead for the Philosopher of the Revolution.

The Constitution of the United States was to Mr. Jefferson the embodiment of the principles of good government – the embodiment of the principles of the Declaration of Independence. Preserving that Constitution in the true spirit in which it had been adopted by the States, therefore, was viewed as the only means of ensuring the survival of liberty in America. "Our peculiar security is in the possession of a written Constitution," he soberly wrote. "Let us not make it a blank paper by construction." [16]

What especially alarmed the author of the Declaration of Independence was that, once the Federal Government was allowed to escape from the confining chains of the Constitution, there would nothing left to limit its powers. The Federal Constitution was the only thing that protected the people from totalitarianism. "To take a single step beyond the boundaries thus specifically drawn" by the Constitution, he noted with concern, "is to take possession of a boundless field of power, no longer susceptible of any definition." [17]

Following the adoption of the Federal Constitution of 1787, the author of the Declaration of Independence became alarmed by the eagerness of some politicians to ignore the limits of the Constitution in an effort to establish a monied aristocracy, to subvert States' Rights, and to centralize power in the United States. Commenting on this alarming trend, Mr. Jefferson wrote:

> I see with the deepest affliction the rapid strides with which the Federal branch of our government is advancing towards the usurpation of all the rights reserved to the States, and the consolidation in itself of all powers, domestic and foreign; and that, too, by constructions which, if legitimate, leave no limits to their power. [18]

Standing in opposition of these forces of subversion, Thomas Jefferson soon found himself at the head of a political party dedicated to the preserva-

---

[16] *Ibid.*, quoted on p. 124.
[17] *Ibid.*, quoted on p. 124.
[18] *Ibid.*, quoted on p. 83.

tion of the true principles of constitutionally limited government. It was out of this great struggle of principles in the years immediately following the adoption of the Constitution of 1787 that gave rise to the American two-party system. And in opposing the unconstitutional and corrupt policies of the Federalist Party, Mr. Jefferson laid the foundations of American *conservatism*.

When presenting his opposition opinion on the First Bank of the United States – that great engine of the monied aristocracy – Thomas Jefferson set forth principles of constitutional construction that have since become famous as one of the most penetrating arguments ever written for a *strict interpretation* of the Constitution. And at a time when the unconstitutional actions of the Federal Government threatened to violate the basic liberties of Americans – in the form of the Alien and Sedition Laws – Thomas Jefferson turned to the State governments to lead the fight for freedom and became, thereby, the father of *State interposition and nullification*.

Following the election of 1800 – termed the "Revolution of 1800" by Mr. Jefferson – in which the invectiveness of his political enemies knew no limits, the principles of constitutional government in America were saved, at least for a time, from destruction. The Administration of Thomas Jefferson, our third President, served as a *model of republican government* in all its simplicity and proved to all doubters that a strictly limited government can indeed serve the true interests of the United States. Under President Jefferson's limited-government Administration, America geographically increased in size at a rate never before or since realized. From the addition of a vast new territory – the Louisiana Purchase – to the abolition of internal taxes and the reduction of the federal debt, the results of his two terms in offices constituted an unqualified blessing to the United States.

Upon leaving office, ex-President Jefferson received a letter of praise from the General Assembly of Virginia, dated February 7, 1809, thanking him for his many services to his country:

> We have to thank you for the model of an administration conducted on the purest principles of Republicanism; for pomp and state laid aside; patronage discarded; internal taxes abolished; a host of superfluous officers disbanded; the monarchic maxim "that a national debt is a national blessing," renounced and more than thirty-three millions of our debt discharged; the native right to nearly one hundred millions of acres of our national domain extinguished; and, without the guilt or calamities of conquest, a vast and fertile region added to our country, far more extensive than her original possessions, bringing along with it the Mississippi and the port of Orleans, the trade of the West to the Pacific Ocean, and in the intrinsic value of the land itself, a source of permanent and almost inex-

haustible revenue. These are points in your administration which the historian will not fail to seize, to expand, and teach posterity to dwell upon with
delight. [19]

Retiring from politics, the ex-President yearned to return to his farm,
his books, and his family, and to spend his remaining years living happily as
the "hermit of Monticello." His services to the cause of freedom, however,
were not yet over. As the *Sage of Monticello*, his advice was continuously
sought by younger statesmen, ever eager to learn from the Philosopher of the
Revolution. And when certain Northern politicians sought to agitate the slavery question in the federal arena, Thomas Jefferson was once again compelled
to act in defense of States' Rights and constitutionally limited government.

The great pretensions to humanitarianism put forth by the New England slavery agitators were especially displeasing to the author of the Declaration of Independence. Although himself a Southern slaveholder, Mr. Jefferson
had inserted within the original draft of the Declaration a strong condemnation of the British Government for allowing the slave trade to continue. Yet
this grievance had been stricken out of the final Declaration by the Second
Continental Congress, chiefly due to objections from the representatives from
the New England colonies, whose shipping interests had been so heavily involved in the profitable slave trade. To see the same section of the Union so
bitterly condemn the Southern States for the institution of slavery at a later
date, he thought, was sheer hypocrisy.

Those Northern politicians agitating against slavery, he concluded,
were not sincere. It was not genuine concern for another race of people that
motivated them, but only a desire to expand the power of the Federal Government and to trample upon the rights reserved by the Constitution to the
States. Mr. Jefferson never doubted for a moment the ultimate consequence
that would result from agitation of the slavery issue – a breakup of the Union.
Fearful for the future of the United States, he candidly confessed that the
machinations of these pseudo-humanitarians filled him with alarm, like a fire
bell in the night.

Equally alarming to the Sage of Monticello was the persistent trend to
unconstitutionally misuse the taxation powers of the Federal Government to
artificially establish a monied aristocracy in the United States. Although Mr.
Jefferson did believe in aristocracy – a *natural* aristocracy based on talent and
virtue – he was steadfastly opposed to any and all attempts to use the powers
of government to create an artificial aristocracy in the United States based on
wealth. Such an unnatural monied aristocracy could only be created by
wrongfully using the powers of government to create a sweeping system of

[19] Richard S. Poppen (ed.), *Thomas Jefferson*, St. Louis, 1904, p. 87.

plunder and redistribution of wealth.

In 1825, less than a year before his death, Mr. Jefferson penned a stern protest on behalf of the State of Virginia to demand the cessation of such illegal acts of plunder, redistribution of wealth, and centralization of power. If the pattern of plunder and centralization did not end, the author of the Declaration of Independence boldly asserted, the sovereign State of Virginia would consider seceding from the Federal Union.

Writing to William Short on January 8, 1825, Mr. Jefferson noted that those seeking the subversion of States' Rights were trying to impose upon the United States the very same type of government against which the American Revolution had been waged:

> Monarchy, to be sure, is now defeated....Yet the spirit is not done away. The same party takes now what they deem the next best ground, the consolidation of the government; the giving to the Federal member of the government, by unlimited constructions of the Constitution, a control over all the functions of the States, and the concentration of all power ultimately at Washington. [20]

And in a letter to William B. Giles, dated December 26, 1825, Thomas Jefferson wrote of his concerns for the American future:

> The younger generation having nothing in them of the feelings or principles of 1776, now look to a single and splendid government of an aristocracy, founded on banking institutions, and moneyed incorporations under the guise and cloak of their favored branches of manufactures, commerce and navigation, riding and ruling over the plundered ploughman and beggared yeomanry. This will be to them a next best blessing to the monarchy of their first aim, and perhaps the surest stepping stone to it. [21]

But these were questions that future generations would have to answer. Mr. Jefferson was firmly convinced that he and the other Founders of the Republic had performed an honest duty by giving to America a marvelous political system founded on constitutionally limited government. Yet, if future generations of Americans, in the enjoyment of material abundance and forgetful of the true sources of their happiness, should decide to throw away this wonderful heritage, the choice would be theirs. The dead, he realized, had neither the power nor the right to control them.

As the United States prepared to celebrate the fiftieth anniversary of the Declaration of Independence, its author lay on his deathbed at Monticello,

---

[20] *Ibid.*, p. 147.
[21] *Ibid.*, p. 148.

sustained only by a determination to live long enough to see the dawning of the 4th of July. On the evening of July 3rd, Mr. Jefferson awoke from his slumber, and, thinking that it was morning, said with apparent satisfaction, "This is the fourth of July." [22]

The remainder of the night was spent in fitful slumber, and Mr. Jefferson's mind wandered back through the years to those trying days of the American Revolution. At one point during the night, he sat up in bed, went through the motions of writing a letter, and, speaking of the Committee of Safety, said that it ought to be warned. The author of the Declaration of Independence died fifty minutes past noon on July 4, 1826, with his last wish fulfilled. He had lived long enough to see the fiftieth anniversary of American independence.

In Massachusetts, the last surviving signer of the Declaration of Independence – John Adams – also lay on his deathbed. He, too, died on July 4, 1826, never realizing that Mr. Jefferson had preceded him in death. Thinking that the Philosopher of the Revolution was still alive, Mr. Adams uttered his famous last words: "Thomas Jefferson still survives." [23] And truly, as long as the principles of constitutional government – *the principles of Jeffersonian government* – survive in America, the spirit of their father and chief defender, Thomas Jefferson, will indeed continue to live.

As we have previously indicated, no other American was more qualified to succinctly and boldly state the cause of liberty within the pages of the Declaration of Independence than Thomas Jefferson. Reflecting on the valuable contribution to freedom's cause made by Mr. Jefferson within the Declaration, Caleb Perry Patterson has noted:

> The basis of self-government set out in the Declaration of Independence was later incorporated in our national and State constitutions. Jefferson as chief author of the Declaration thus became a chief contributor to our constitutional system of government.....
>
> Without attempting to be original, Jefferson in the Declaration of Independence reduced the philosophy of the natural rights of man to a "common sense" basis and made it an "expression of the American mind." While this philosophy was revolutionary in all its aspects, it was soon to be incorporated into American constitutional law. Our bills of rights are only a more detailed statement of its principles. The doctrine that government derives its powers from the consent of the people is the basis of popular sovereignty, of delegated powers, and of a fundamental law enacted by the people in their original sovereignty. These principles are found in all our constitutions, both State and Federal....In other words, it announced the

---

[22] Andrew M. Allison, *The Real Thomas Jefferson*, Second Edition, National Center for Constitutional Studies, Washington, 1983, quoted on p. 333.
[23] Richard S. Poppen (ed.), *Op. cit.*, p. 20.

doctrine of a limited government, which [James] Madison said was the foundation principle of our constitutional system and without which constitutions are of little meaning. "The right of the people to alter or abolish" their constitutions is provided by the amendment process of our constitutions and, again, makes the people the master, government the servant. If these Jeffersonian principles were to be taken from our constitutions, only the structural features of our government would remain and totalitarianism would be invited. [24]

The Rights of Man

The Declaration of Independence can be divided logically into three basic sections. Within the first or introductory section, Thomas Jefferson sought to explain the purpose of the Declaration itself and to expound the theory of government on which the American Revolution was founded. This is the section of that great document that stirs the hearts of men and has made the Declaration famous throughout the world. The middle section of the Declaration of Independence is by far the largest of the three, and it is devoted to enumerating the long list of crimes against America committed by the British Government. Within this large section, Mr. Jefferson provides the *justification* for the American Revolution to a candid world. This section is then followed by the actual announcement of the birth of the thirteen sovereign and independent American States. Within this last section, it is made clear that independence is being declared on behalf of the thirteen States individually and separately.

Within the very first sentence, the purpose of the Declaration is explained:

> When in the course of human events, it becomes necessary for one people to dissolve the political bands which have connected them with another, and to assume among the powers of the earth, the separate and equal station, to which the Laws of Nature and of Nature's God entitle them, a decent respect to the opinions of mankind requires that they should declare the causes which impel them to the separation. [25]

The purpose of the Declaration of Independence, as indicated within this first sentence, was to explain to all mankind why the former colonies were declaring their independence from Great Britain. And within this first sentence are a number of points that merit our careful attention. The term "one

---

[24] Caleb Perry Patterson, *Op. cit.*, pp. 29-30.
[25] Richard Hofstadter, William Miller, and Daniel Aaron, *The United States: The History of a Republic*, Prentice-Hall, Inc., Englewood Cliffs, 1967, p. 870.

people," for instance, as used within this opening sentence, has been misconstrued over the years to falsely concoct a notion that, *by this expression*, the thirteen colonies were indicating their intention to merge into a single political body. Such a false interpretation, needless to say, can only be sustained by violating the basic rules of English grammar and syntax, not to mention common sense. The syntax of the sentence leaves no doubt as to the true meaning of the rhetorical expression "one people," which simply means *any* people.

Another significant point worth noting is that, within this first sentence, the American Revolution is defined as a revolution *political*, not social, in nature. It was the "political bands" between the colonies and the Empire that were broken by the Revolution, not the *social bonds* that connected together the individual citizens within each of the States. The action taken was proclaimed to be a "separation" or *secession* from the British Empire on the part of the former colonies, not an overthrow of their existing social order.

We should also note that the existence of God is expressly acknowledged within this first sentence of the Declaration, as is the existence of *natural law*. In asserting their sovereignty and independence, the thirteen States were assuming their places in a *State of Nature* governed only by the "Laws of Nature" and "Nature's God." Although it has become popular in recent years to deny the existence of both God and natural law, we see within the Declaration that the theory which justified American independence was founded on both.

A final point to be considered is that, within this very first sentence of the Declaration can be seen the powerful influence of the ideology that gave rise to the Age of Reason, particularly the philosophy of the English political theorist, John Locke. Indeed, most of the philosophical principles espoused within the Declaration of Independence were derived by Mr. Jefferson largely from what may be termed the *Lockean Theory of Government*. In particular, the Declaration was essentially a reassertion of the basic concepts found within the last chapter of the *Second Treatise of Government*, which is entitled "Of the Dissolution of Government."

Within this book, John Locke had stated:

> He that will with any clearness speak of the *Dissolution of Government*, ought, in the first place to distinguish between the *Dissolution of the Society*, and the *Dissolution of the Government*. That which makes the Community, and brings Men out of the loose State of Nature, into *one Politick Society*, is the Agreement which every one has with the rest to incorporate, and act as one Body, and so be one distinct Commonwealth. The usual, and almost only way whereby *this Union is dissolved*, is the Inroad of Foreign Force making a Conquest upon them. For in that Case,

(not being able to maintain and support themselves, as *one intire* and *independent body*) the Union belonging to that Body which consisted therein, must necessarily cease, and so every one return to the state he was in before, with a liberty to shift for himself, and provide for his own Safety as he thinks fit in some other Society. Whenever the *Society is dissolved*, 'tis certain the Government of that Society cannot remain. Thus Conquerours Swords often cut up Governments by the Roots, and mangle Societies to pieces, separating the subdued or scattered Multitude from the Protection of, and Dependence on that Society which ought to have preserved them from violence. The World is too well instructed in, and too forward to allow this way of dissolving of Governments to need any more to be said of it: and there wants not much Argument to prove, that where the *Society is dissolved*, the Government cannot remain; that being as impossible, as for the Frame of an House to subsist when the Materials of it are scattered, and dissipated by a Whirl-wind, or jumbled into a confused heap by an Earthquake. [26]

As John Locke wrote, and as our Founding Fathers realized, there is a profound difference between *dissolving a government* and *dissolving a society* — between a *political revolution* and a *social revolution*. Undermining and subverting society, to be sure, will invariably undermine and subvert its government, and replacing existing social structures with a new society clearly results in a new form of government. Yet, John Locke was too conservative and too wise to ever advocate or justify *social* revolution, and America's Founding Fathers shared his sentiments. While the English philosopher advocated a change of government, whenever necessary, he was thus firmly opposed to anything that would weaken and destroy society itself.

Upon reflection, it will become obvious that the dissolution of society and the dissolution of government are actually *opposing* concepts and *opposing* actions. This fact becomes apparent when it is realized that the reason *why* a dissolution of government would ever be undertaken, would be *to preserve an existing society*. While a society certainly has a right to defend itself by dissolving its government whenever such action is required to ensure its preservation, there can never be justification for a society to commit suicide.

What John Locke had in mind, when penning the last chapter of his treatise, was something similar to the American Revolution of 1776, the adoption of the Federal Constitution of 1787, or the creation of the Confederate States of America in 1860-1861. Throughout each of these great *political* movements, the social structure remained intact, and each was characterized by its remarkable *lack* of anarchy, confusion, rioting, and civil turmoil. In each of these three American political revolutions, local government – on

---

[26] John Locke, *Two Treatises of Government*, New American Library, New York, 1963, pp. 454-455.

which the preservation of the social order depends – remained intact and un-altered. And in each of these cases, this fact, more than any other, is what has differentiated these great changes in government from any socialist revolution that has ever stained the pages of history with the blood of the innocent.

The American Revolution, to be more accurately and precisely named, was actually an American *secession* from the British Empire. The colonial governments, although reconstituted during that period, remained intact, and the existing colonies merely became sovereign States. These colonies, or States, simply withdrew from the Empire by unilaterally declaring their independence.

As John Locke explained in the *Second Treatise of Government*, the only legitimate foundation of government is the *consent of the governed*. Government, in other words, is the *servant*, and the people are the *masters* of the political system. Within a legitimately constituted political system, the powers of government are *delegated* to it by the people, and government holds such delegated powers as a *trust*. Government violates that trust by inadequately defending the rights of the people in their lives, liberties, and properties from criminals and foreign powers. Even worse, government violates that trust by becoming *itself* a threat to the lives, liberties, and properties of the people. Whenever government violates its trust, the people may rightfully withdraw the delegated powers, thereby effectively dissolving the government, and may then institute new government, delegating to it such powers as they deem necessary and proper.

Such a proper view of government, so forcefully and brilliantly advocated by John Locke and later by Thomas Jefferson in the Declaration of Independence, forms the cornerstone of the concept of *constitutionally limited government*. It was this ideology that justified the American Revolution, and it was upon this Lockean-Jeffersonian school of thought that our constitutional system of government was founded.

Within the *Second Treatise of Government*, the Philosopher of the Enlightenment indicated the true purpose of civil society and reason why government exists:

> The Reason why Men enter into Society, is the preservation of their Property; and the end why they chuse and authorize a Legislative, is, that there may be Laws made, and Rules set as Guards and Fences to the Properties of all the Members of the Society....For since it can never be supposed to be the Will of Society, that the Legislative should have a Power to destroy that, which everyone designs to secure, by entering into Society, and for which the People submitted themselves to the Legislators of their own making; whenever the *Legislators endeavour to take away, and destroy the Property of the People*, or to reduce them to Slavery under Arbitrary

Power, they put themselves into a state of War with the People, who are thereupon absolved from any further Obedience, and are left to the common Refuge, which God hath provided for all Men, against Force and Violence. Whensoever therefore the *Legislative* shall transgress this fundamental Rule of Society; and either by Ambition, Fear, Folly or Corruption, *endeavour to grasp* themselves, *or put into the hands of any other an Absolute Power* over the Lives, Liberties, and Estates of the People; By this breach of Trust they *forfeit the Power*, the People had put into their hands, for quite contrary ends, and it devolves to the People, who have a Right to resume their original Liberty, and, by the Establishment of a new Legislative (such as they shall think fit) provide for their own Safety and Security, which is the end for which they are in Society. What I have said here, concerning the Legislative, in general, holds true also concerning the *supreme Executor* [and the judiciary]. [27]

Whensoever a government acts contrary to its trust, and the people attempt to preserve their society by dissolving it, such a government may resist such efforts with force. Such a government, Mr. Locke noted, places itself in a *state of war* with the people, and such a government would undoubtedly label the people as "rebels" and "traitors." But in these circumstances, who would be the real *rebel* and *traitor* – the people who seek to dissolve their tyrannically corrupt government, or the government that attempts to maintain its authority without the consent of the governed? John Locke had no difficulty in answering the question. Nor did Thomas Jefferson and the Founders of the American Republic.

As John Locke wrote in the last chapter of the *Second Treatise of Government*:

> To conclude, The *Power that every individual gave the Society*, when he entered into it, can never revert to the Individuals again, as long as the Society lasts, but will always remain in the Community; because without this, there can be no Community, no Common-wealth, which is contrary to the original Agreement: So also when the Society hath placed the Legislative in any Assembly of Men, to continue in them and their Successors, with Direction and Authority for providing such Successors, *the Legislative can never revert to the People* whilst that Government lasts: Because having provided a Legislative with Power to continue for ever, they have given up their Political Power to the Legislative, and cannot resume it. But if they have set Limits to the Duration of their Legislative, and made this Supreme Power in any Person, or Assembly, only temporary: Or else when by the Miscarriages of those in Authority, it is forfeited; upon the Forfeiture of their Rulers, or at the Determination of the Time set, *it reverts to the Society*, and the People have a Right to act as Supreme, and continue the Legis-

---

[27] *Ibid.*, pp. 460-461.

lative in themselves, or erect a new Form, or under the old form place it in
new hands, as they think good. [28]

Within the first section of the Declaration of Independence, Thomas
Jefferson reasserted the basic truths espoused by John Locke a century earlier.
In matchless style and bold tone, Mr. Jefferson asserted that government rests
on the consent of the governed, and that whensoever government fails to protect the God-given rights of the people, they have a right to alter or abolish
such government.

Mr. Jefferson stated this concept in stirring words that ring like a great
bell of liberty:

> We hold these truths to be self-evident, that all men are created
> equal; that they are endowed by their Creator with certain unalienable
> rights; that among these, are life, liberty, and the pursuit of happiness.
> That, to secure these rights, governments are instituted among men, deriv-
> ing their just powers from the consent of the governed; that, whenever any
> form of government becomes destructive of these ends, it is the right of the
> people to alter or abolish it, and to institute a new government, laying its
> foundation on such principles, and organizing its powers in such form, as
> to them shall seem most likely to effect their safety and happiness. [29]

As indicated by its author, the basic principles set forth within the Declaration of Independence are "self-evident" in nature and concept. Even to
those who have never read the works of John Locke or have never before understood what the Age of Reason contributed to mankind, the principles set
forth by Mr. Jefferson require little in the way of explanation. Such principles
should be obvious to all *honest* men, the author of the Declaration asserted,
and only the dishonest would ever attempt to refute, deny, or distort the concepts presented.

Thomas Jefferson began his summary of the concept of legitimate government by stating that "all men are created equal." This phrase, so cleverly
misquoted by later day Marxists and other radicals, most assuredly was not
intended as an endorsement of an egalitarian society wherein everyone would
have an equal amount of life, liberty, and property. Nor was such a statement
ever intended to deny the existence of *natural* differences that exist among
mankind, inequalities that stem from such *God-given* characteristics and *natural* traits as age, sex, and race. The intention of the Declaration of Independence was to affirm the laws of nature, not to refute them.

The author of the Declaration clearly understood that, in terms of tal-

---

[28] *Ibid.*, p. 477.
[29] Richard Hofstadter, William Miller, and Daniel Aaron, *Op. cit.*, p. 870.

ent and skill, for example, all men are *not* created equal. Therefore, the rewards for their labors should *not* be equal. *This phrase states only that all men should be regarded as equal before the law, in that all men are created with equal rights to life, liberty, and property.* As Mr. Jefferson indicated, this meaning should be "self-evident" to all who exercise common sense.

The true meaning of the phrase, "that all men are created equal," is perhaps best understood when it is realized what concept this statement was intended to oppose. Prior to the Enlightenment, it was widely asserted that government was sovereign, that Kings were more than mere mortals and derived their authority and powers directly from God, and that the lowly people were born as *subjects* to these God-ordained rulers. This concept of government, historically referred to as the *Divine Rights of Kings*, was best articulated by such writers as Sir Robert Filmer.

With the dawn of the Age of Reason, wise philosophers began to challenge the Divine Rights Theory by asserting the sovereignty of the people, the concept of government-by-the-consent-of-the-governed, and the compact or contract nature of government. The basis of this new theory of government was that *all men are created equal*, meaning only that no one man is specially created by God to be the lord and master of the political kingdom. This is how John Locke utilized the concept in his great work, and this is how the concept is employed in the Declaration of Independence. *The phrase "all men are created equal" means only that the American Theory of Government is based on a rejection of the Divine Rights of Kings.*

After rejecting the Divine Rights Theory, the author of the Declaration of Independence indicated the true *source* of the rights of man. Government, he indicated, is most certainly *not* the source of human rights. The right to own private property, for example, like all other natural rights, comes from God. Acknowledgement of the existence of God is clearly a prerequisite to an acknowledgement of all the other concepts associated with the Lockean-Jeffersonian theory of government. Without God, there can be no inalienable human rights; and without inalienable rights, there can be no legitimate foundation for government.

Among the God-given rights listed by Thomas Jefferson in the Declaration were life, liberty, and the pursuit of happiness. This list of enumerated rights was certainly not intended to be exclusive, as Mr. Jefferson made clear in the Declaration. The right to private property, for instance, is undeniably a key natural right of man in which all of the Founding Fathers, including Mr. Jefferson, firmly believed.

The purpose of government, said Mr. Jefferson, is "to secure these rights" granted equally by God to all men. The "just powers" of government, he asserted, are derived "from the consent of the governed." If the government is subverted from its true end and uses its delegated powers to destroy what it was intended to protect, then the people have a right to alter or abolish it, and to institute new government, "laying its foundation on such principles."

By this last statement, it is clear that *the Founding Fathers intended to establish the American system of government on this Lockean-Jeffersonian political theory.* The American system, in other words, would rest on the concept that the powers of government are limited to those delegated to it, that such delegated powers must be used by the government to pursue the ends for they were delegated, and that those who created the government could, at their discretion, alter or abolish it. The enduring greatness of the American political system, therefore, would center on the persistent determination to preserve, not the government, but the inalienable rights of man. Preserving the individual's rights to life, liberty, and property would be the chief *end* of the American political system, while the political institutions – from the Federal Government to the local county governments – would be merely the *means* to attain that great end.

Never before in the history of man had any political system been *founded* on such noble principles of government. The British, it is true, had attempted, with temporary success, to force these principles upon an already established political system. But it was not until the American Revolution, when the thirteen States adopted these principles *at their inception*, that such principles formed the *foundation* of a political system. This feature of our political system, in itself, was sufficient to make the United States of America uniquely great in the world.

After summarizing the political principles on which the United States would be founded, Thomas Jefferson next indicated that the decision to dissolve government, though necessary at times to preserve human rights, should not be made without sufficient thought by the people. And as he indicated, experience has amply demonstrated that mankind is basically conservative by nature, in that people are more prone to suffer oppressions than they are to assert their rights. The danger to be apprehended, therefore, is not that a people will recklessly cast aside a good government, but that they will not have the courage to reform or cast off a bad government. Yet, whensoever the powers of government are utilized in a conspiracy to rob the people of their liberties, Mr. Jefferson indicated, it is more than merely the right of the people to throw off such a government – *it is their duty.*

As the Philosopher of the Revolution stated:

> Prudence, indeed, will dictate that governments long established,
> should not be changed for light and transient causes; and, accordingly, all

experience hath shown, that mankind are more disposed to suffer, while evils are sufferable, than to right themselves by abolishing the forms to which they are accustomed. But, when a long train of abuses and usurpations, pursuing invariably the same object, evinces a design to reduce them under absolute despotism, it is their right, it is their duty, to throw off such government and to provide new guards for their future security. [30]

The Crimes of the British Government

"Such has been the patient sufferance of these colonies," Thomas Jefferson wrote, turning his attention from general principles to their practical application, "and such is now the necessity which constrains them to alter their former systems of government." [31] Here we see the second reference to the fact that the colonies were dissolving their political connection with Great Britain. Unlike the first reference made in the first sentence, however, which referred to the dissolution as a "separation" from the mother country, this reference indicated a desire to establish within the United States a *system* of government different from that within Great Britain.

Having stated the general principles of government that guided the colonies to seek independence, Mr. Jefferson introduced the second logical section of the Declaration by proclaiming that, "The history of the present King of Great Britain is a history of repeated injuries and usurpations, all having, in direct object, the establishment of an absolute tyranny over these States." [32] The "repeated injuries and usurpations" that characterized the government of King George III could have only one result or consequence. And that consequence – "the establishment of an absolute tyranny over these States" – was the "direct object" of the British Government. The British Government, in other words, was engaged in an evil *conspiracy* to establish a tyrannical dictatorship over America. "To prove this," Mr. Jefferson wrote, "let facts be submitted to a candid world...." [33]

These words are followed by a long list of crimes committed by the British Government. In total, Mr. Jefferson listed eighteen heinous crimes, one of which was further divided into nine separate crimes. The fact that all of the accusations were directed against the head of the British Government – King George III – was a clear indication that all hope of reconciliation with Great Britain had evaporated. Mention was scarcely made of Parliament or of the King's ministers. *It was the King himself, and thus the whole British Gov-*

---

[30] *Ibid.*, p. 870.
[31] *Ibid.*, p. 870.
[32] *Ibid.*, p. 870.
[33] *Ibid.*, p. 870.

ernment, who was fully condemned in the Declaration of Independence.

The crimes listed in the Declaration, generally speaking, can be categorized as falling into one of seven basic categories according to their nature. The first set of crimes listed in the Declaration clearly showed that the British Government had abandoned and forfeited any rightful claim to continued authority over the colonies. Not only had that government refused to act in accordance with the legitimate needs of the people, but it had also undermined the efforts of other authorities to serve those needs. Furthermore, it had indicated its refusal to fulfill the legitimate role of government unless and until the American people consented to forfeit their basic rights. In general terms, these constituted the broadest and most far-reaching crimes of the British Government.

The first three crimes specified by Thomas Jefferson fall within this first category:

> He has refused his assent to laws the most wholesome and necessary for the public good.
> He has forbidden his governors to pass laws of immediate and pressing importance, unless suspended in their operation till his assent should be obtained; and, when so suspended, he has utterly neglected to attend to them.
> He has refused to pass other laws for the accommodation of large districts of people, unless those people would relinquish the right of representation in the legislature; a right inestimable to them, and formidable to tyrants only. [34]

The second set of crimes listed in the Declaration related to the subversion or complete destruction of the popularly based colonial system of government. These crimes directly involved the British attempts to destroy democratic government and home rule within the colonies, and to subvert federalism within the Empire. That the colonies considered these to be such serious crimes indicated their strong attachment to the federal system of government.

Within this category of crimes specified by Thomas Jefferson were the following:

> He has called together legislative bodies at places unusual, uncomfortable, and distant from the depository of their public records, for the sole purpose of fatiguing them into compliance with his measures.
> He has dissolved representative houses, repeatedly for opposing, with manly firmness, his invasions on the rights of the people.

---

[34] *Ibid.*, p. 870.

He has refused, for a long time after such dissolutions, to cause others to be elected; whereby the legislative powers, incapable of annihilation, have returned to the people at large for their exercise; the state remaining, in the meantime, exposed to all the danger of invasion from without, and convulsions within. [35]

The third category of crimes enumerated in the Declaration of Independence centered around the attempts of the British Government to suffocate the growth of American civilization through population control measures. This type of crime was expressed as follows by Mr. Jefferson:

He has endeavored to prevent the population of these States; for that purpose, obstructing the laws for naturalization of foreigners, refusing to pass others to encourage their migration hither, and raising the conditions of new appropriations of lands. [36]

Thomas Jefferson next turned his attention to enumerating crimes relating to the British attempts to undermine the American legal or judicial system:

He has obstructed the administration of justice, by refusing his assent to laws for establishing judiciary powers.
He has made judges dependent on his will alone, for the tenure of their offices, and the amount and payment of their salaries. [37]

But the British Government's attempts to subvert constitutionally limited government extended beyond the destruction of local self-government in the colonies and the conquest of the Legislative and Judicial Branches by the Executive Branch. That Executive Branch of government was also guilty of establishing centralized bureaucracies that sent hordes of agents to control, harass, and intimidate the people. And to enforce its tyrannical edicts at gunpoint, the British Government had maintained a standing army in America. The fifth category of crimes within the Declaration, thus, related to King George III's efforts to establish a dictatorship over the American people founded on bureaucratic strangulation of freedom and military despotism.

Among the crimes of this type enumerated by Mr. Jefferson were the following:

He has erected a multitude of new offices, and sent hither swarms of officers to harass our people, and eat out their substance.

---

[35] *Ibid.*, pp. 870-871.
[36] *Ibid.*, p. 871.
[37] *Ibid.*, p. 871.

He has kept among us, in time of peace, standing armies, without the consent of our legislatures.

He has affected to render the military independent of, and superior to, the civil power. [38]

The sixth category of crimes listed in the Declaration of Independent related to the destruction of the British Constitution by the King of England. Although many of the crimes contained in this category were of a nature similar to those listed in other categories, the purpose of this separate category of crimes was to emphasize the *subversion of constitutional government* within the Empire. Among the crimes "foreign to our Constitution" were the creation of a military dictatorship, the subversion of the legal system, taxation without representation, the annihilation of free trade, the subversion of local government, centralization of power, and the destruction of the federal system of government. Of particular significance in this regard were the attempts to fundamentally alter "the powers of our governments" and the claims of the British Government to unlimited power.

A point of significance that deserves careful attention is the manner in which Mr. Jefferson referred to the unconstitutional acts of the British Government. By referring to such illegal measures as "acts of *pretended* legislation," he was stating, in effect, that such laws were null, void, and of no force because they were not made in pursuance of the British Constitution. Whenever a government makes a law in an area beyond its jurisdiction, it acts without legitimate authority. Therefore, the law in question is no law at all. *Without this acknowledgement of the limits of government, it would have been difficult, if not impossible, to justify the American Revolution.* In later years, Thomas Jefferson would again use this type of reasoning in expounding the theory of State interposition and nullification with regard to the American Constitution.

The crimes of this nature were expressed in the following words:

He has combined with others, to subject us to a jurisdiction foreign to our Constitution, and unacknowledged by our laws; giving his assent to their acts of pretended legislation:

For quartering large bodies of armed troops among us:

For protecting them by a mock trial, from punishment, for any murders which they should commit on the inhabitants of these States:

For cutting off our trade with all parts of the world:

For imposing taxes on us without our consent:

For depriving us, in many cases, of the benefit of trial by jury:

For transporting us beyond seas to be tried for pretended offences:

---

[38] *Ibid.*, p. 871.

For abolishing the free system of English laws in a neighboring province, establishing therein an arbitrary government, and enlarging its boundaries, so as to render it at once an example and fit instrument for introducing the same absolute rule into these colonies:

For taking away our charters, abolishing our most valuable laws, and altering, fundamentally, the powers of our governments:

For suspending our own legislatures, and declaring themselves invested with power to legislate for us in all cases whatsoever. [39]

The last category of crimes enumerated in the Declaration of Independence stemmed from the *treasonous actions* of the British Government. Such treasonous conduct was manifested by waging war against the American colonies, destroying their towns and murdering their citizens. Further treasonous acts included fomenting "domestic insurrections" among the Negro slaves and inciting the "merciless Indian savages" to ruthlessly slaughter men, women, and children. Although the term *treason* was not used by Mr. Jefferson in describing these crimes, it is of interest to note that treason would later be defined in the Constitution of 1787 as waging war against one or more of the States.

Among the treasonous crimes committed against the American people, Thomas Jefferson listed the following:

He has abdicated government here, by declaring us out of his protection, and waging war against us.

He has plundered our seas, ravaged our coasts, burnt our towns, and destroyed the lives of our people.

He is, at this time, transporting large armies of foreign mercenaries to complete the works of death, desolation, and tyranny, already begun, with circumstances of cruelty and perfidy scarcely paralleled in the most barbarous ages, and totally unworthy the head of a civilized nation.

He has constrained our fellow citizens, taken captive on the high seas, to bear arms against their country, to become the executioners of their friends, and brethren, or to fall themselves by their hands.

He has excited domestic insurrections amongst us, and has endeavored to bring on the inhabitants of our frontiers, the merciless Indian savages, whose known rule of warfare is an undistinguished destruction of all ages, sexes, and conditions. [40]

After listing the specific crimes committed by the British Government against the thirteen States, Thomas Jefferson added that such crimes were compounded by the fact that the British Government had repeatedly ignored the pleas of the colonies for mercy. "In every stage of these oppressions," he

---

[39] *Ibid.*, p. 871.
[40] *Ibid.*, p. 871.

noted, "we have petitioned for redress, in the most humble terms; our repeated petitions have been answered only by repeated injury." The British Government, therefore, was unfit to rule the American States. "A prince, whose character is thus marked by every act which may define a tyrant, is unfit to be the ruler of a free people." [41]

Reference to "a free people" within this sentence, like reference to "one people" in the Declaration's first sentence, is, of course, rhetorical in nature, and in no sense did it imply or signify that the thirteen colonies intended to merge into a single nation of people. The expression "a free people" could be replaced by the words *any free people* without changing the meaning of the sentence.

The British people, stated the author of the Declaration of Independence, shared the guilt of their King by their failure to come to the defense of their American cousins. Their acquiescence in the crimes committed by the British Government was related as follows by Mr. Jefferson, where the colonial act of "separation" or secession from the Empire is *stated as a fact*:

> Nor have we been wanting in attention to our British brethren. We have warned them, from time to time, of attempts made by their legislature to extend an unwarrantable jurisdiction over us. We have reminded them of the circumstances of our emigration and settlement here. We have appealed to their native justice and magnanimity, and we have conjured them, by the ties of our common kindred, to disavow these usurpations, which would inevitably interrupt our connections and correspondence. They, too, have been deaf to the voice of justice and consanguinity. We must, therefore, acquiesce in the necessity which denounces our separation, and hold them, as we hold the rest of mankind, enemies in war, in peace, friends. [42]

The Formal Announcement of Secession

Following the statement of general political beliefs that guided the Founding Fathers and the long list of crimes against Great Britain, Thomas Jefferson reached the dramatic conclusion of the Declaration of Independence. Although a sufficient number of hints and indications had been sprinkled throughout the first two sections of the document, the actual *declaration of independence* was reserved for the last paragraph. It is within this paragraph that the formal announcement was made to the world that the former thirteen colonies had become thirteen sovereign and independent States.

---

[41] *Ibid.*, p. 871.
[42] *Ibid.*, p. 871.

Inasmuch as this section of the Declaration contains the official announcement of the secession from the British Empire, it should be scrutinized with care and attention to detail. How was the announcement phrased? Exactly who or what was attaining independence through this announcement? The answers to these questions will further clarify our understanding of the true organic nature of the United States.

Thomas Jefferson phrased the declaration of political independence in these words:

> We, therefore, the *representatives of the United States of America*, in general Congress assembled, appealing to the Supreme Judge of the world for the rectitude of our intentions, do, in the name, and by the authority of the good people of these colonies, solemnly publish and declare, that, these *United Colonies* are, and of right ought to be, *free and independent States*: that they are absolved from all allegiance to the British Crown, and that all political connection between them and the *State of Great Britain* is, and ought to be, totally dissolved; and that, as *free and independent States*, they have full power to levy war, conclude peace, contract alliances, establish commerce, and to do all other acts and things which *independent states* may of right do. And, for the support of this declaration, with a firm reliance on the protection of Divine Providence, we mutually pledge to each other our lives, our fortunes, and our sacred honor. [Emphasis added] [43]

By this announcement of political independence from Great Britain, two new terms were introduced into the American political vocabulary – the "United States of America" and the "States." The former term was introduced in that section of the paragraph that described the members of the Second Continental Congress as the "representatives of the United States of America." Prior to issuing the Declaration, of course, those same members of Congress had referred to themselves as the "Representatives of the United Colonies."

The *United States of America* was clearly an expression intended to describe the former *United Colonies* in Congress assembled. At most, the United Colonies had been only a military alliance among the colonies, which had united in the common objective of self-preservation. Within the Declaration of Independence, where the expression "United States of America" is used for the first time in our history, the term referred to that same *military alliance* between the same colonies, which were thenceforth States.

Although the Second Continental Congress had been forced to assume many of the functions of a *de facto* general government during the course of the War of Independence, it had never been formally inaugurated or consti-

---

[43] *Ibid.*, p. 871.

tuted as a *de jure* Federal Government. Even at the time the Declaration of Independence was adopted, no one pretended that the United States existed as a *de jure* political union between the newly independent States. To have made such an assumption, in fact, would have been to renounce the very principles of government espoused within the Declaration. Such a political union, according to the American Theory of Government, could only come about as the result of the explicit *consent* of the States who would be the members of such a Federal Union. At the time the Declaration was published, no such consent had yet been given by any State.

When the Virginia Convention had instructed that State's representatives in the Continental Congress to seek independence for the thirteen colonies, it had also instructed them to work for a plan of confederation among the States. These instructions would not have been given if Virginia had regarded the Second Continental Congress as a true general government. And in giving such instructions to the Virginia delegation in the Congress, the Virginia Convention placed a stipulation on the request for a confederation among the States by requiring that "the power of forming Government" must "be left to the respective Colonial Legislatures." [44]

When Richard Henry Lee introduced his resolution on June 7, 1776, that the colonies should declare their independence of Great Britain, he had, within the resolution, also proposed that "a plan of confederation" should "be prepared and transmitted to the respective Colonies [States] for their consideration and approbation." [45] Two separate committees were appointed by the Second Continental Congress to effect the goals put forth in Mr. Lee's resolution. One was tasked with the highly urgent assignment of drafting the Declaration of Independence. The other committee, which began its work at a later date, was charged with the task of drafting a *plan of union* for the States to ratify. The plan that emerged from this committee was styled the Articles of Confederation, and the proposed Federal Constitution was submitted to the newly independent States for their consideration. By March 1, 1781, the Articles had been duly ratified by all thirteen States, at which time a political union was officially established between those States – a Federal Union that was styled the "United States of America."

Prior to the adoption of the Articles of Confederation, the "United States of America" was no more than a military alliance between thirteen sovereign States. It was in this sense that the expression was used within the Declaration of Independence by Thomas Jefferson. This is further borne out by the fact that those who styled themselves the "representatives of the United

---

[44] Charles Callan Tansill (ed.), *Op. cit.*, p. 20.
[45] *Ibid.*, p. 21.

States" asserted that they were acting "*in the name, and by authority of the good people of these colonies.*"

Understanding the necessity of presenting a *united front* against Great Britain, the States asserted their individual independence *jointly*, waged their War of Independence *jointly*, and negotiated terms of peace with Great Britain *jointly*. By acting in concert, they presented only one alternative to their common enemy – either acknowledge the sovereignty and independence of each and every State, or face the combined strength of all thirteen on the field of battle. It was a prudent strategy on the part of the American States to act in concert, and it was the only manner in which their separate sovereignties could have been sustained against such a powerful foe.

Further evidence of the intentions of the States is the fact that, within the Second Continental Congress, each State had only one vote, regardless of the number of representatives it might have. When the assertion was made, therefore, that the Declaration of Independence had been adopted *unanimously* in that Congress, the proclamation of unanimity was made in reference to the fact each State had cast its vote in favor of adopting it.

Another point of significance in this regard that is often overlooked by students and historians alike is the very high degree of control and authority each State legislature wielded over its representatives in the Second Continental Congress. Those representatives, though at times motivated by personal convictions to act otherwise, were obligated to follow the instructions given to them by their respective State governments, making those representatives essentially *ambassadors* of the State governments.

The true meaning of the other term introduced by the Declaration of Independence is no less ambiguous, although many modern authorities have attempted to obscure its definition. The former colonies, as announced within the Declaration, had become *States*. The selection of this term to describe former provinces that had become independent is especially significant. *The term "State" implies a sovereign body politic.* While acknowledging this basic truth, however, many modern authorities claim that the term, when used to describe the American States, has a *special meaning*, a meaning that somehow excludes the attributes of sovereignty.

If the American States are *not* really States and were *not* ushered into the world as sovereign political societies, then the Founding Fathers were indeed quite reckless with terminology. In the very same sentence in the Declaration where the term "States" is used to describe the former thirteen colonies, that very same term is used in reference to the nation of Great Britain! Did Thomas Jefferson have in mind two different meanings for the term within that sentence, one meaning when referring to the "State of Great Britain," and a different or special meaning when referring to the thirteen American States?

If any doubt could exist on this subject, then the remainder of the Declaration's final paragraph should settle the matter conclusively. While the "representatives of the United States" were the ones who published the announcement of political independence, the *beneficiaries* of the announcement were the States, not a consolidated nation styled the United States. Through the Declaration of Independence, those representatives did *not* proclaim the United States to be a free and independent nation. On the contrary, they proclaimed that the thirteen colonies had become "free and independent States."

The plural usage of the term *States* in the Declaration – as in the phrase, "free and independent *States*" – was not the result of casual or negligent writing on the part of Thomas Jefferson. While the Second Continental Congress had been debating the merits of Mr. Lee's famous resolution, New Hampshire proposed, on June 15, 1776, that the colonies should be declared "a free and independent *State*," [46] with the term *State* used in its singular sense. This proposal to consolidate the colonies into a single nation, however, was *rejected* in favor of the Virginia proposal to declare the colonies to be "free and independent *States*."

Through the Declaration, therefore, each and every one of the thirteen colonies had become a "State," and each one was the equivalent of Great Britain and all other nations in terms of sovereignty. And "as free and independent States," each one had "full power to levy war, conclude peace, contract alliances, establish commerce, and all other acts and things which independent states may of right do." *The Declaration of Independence was the birth certificate for the American sovereign States!*

Vested with full sovereign authority, each of the newly independent States could have gone its own way, politically speaking, following the issuance of the Declaration of Independence. Confronted by grueling warfare with Great Britain, however, and drawn together by sentiments of friendship, the newly sovereign States were fully apprised of the benefits of unity in the face of a common enemy. For this reason, the ink had scarcely dried on the Declaration of Independence before the States initiated the process of instituting a Federal Union under the Articles of Confederation. Until such time as the Articles could be ratified, however, the "United States of America" would remain a military alliance, and the Second Continental Congress would continue to function as the only practical means of presenting a united front against the aggressions of the British Government.

---

[46] Edward A. Pollard, *The Lost Cause*, E.B. Treat & Co., Publishers, New York, 1867, quoted on p. 35.

Properly Interpreting the Declaration

From the detailed analysis of the Declaration of Independence presented, it is clear that no single *nation* styled the United States of America was created by the American Revolution. *The only nations created by the War of Independence were the thirteen States.* These States, it is true, were united in common defense of their newly acquired sovereignty against the British Government. They were also united by a common spirit of liberty that permeated all of the States, as well as by natural sentiments springing from their closeness on the North American continent, by trade, and by their common language. Nonetheless, these sovereign States were not *politically* united until the adoption of the Articles of Confederation in 1781.

As obvious as these truths may seem, there have been many, especially since the days of Abraham Lincoln, who have endeavored to obscure the true origins of our States and of our Federal Union. Utilizing false interpretations of the history of the American Revolution and of the Declaration of Independence and War of Independence, a dishonest theory has been espoused that the Federal Union preceded the States, that the Union is older than the States who created it! According to this perverted theory, the States did not create the Federal Union. It was the other way around – the Union created the States. This twisted theory was relied upon as supposed justification for the invasion and conquest of the Southern States by the Federal Government during the War Between the States. And this is the theory that has been relied upon ever since that time to justify the unending consolidation of power in Washington, D.C.

Properly interpreting the Declaration of Independence is clearly of paramount importance for a proper understanding of the principles of constitutional government in the United States. If the enemies of constitutionally limited government are determined to obscure the true origins of our political system, then the friends of constitutional liberty must be equally determined to clarify those origins in unmistakable terms.

To counter the false theories of the origins of our political system that sprouted as a result of the War Between the States, a number of scholarly Jeffersonians have stepped forward to ensure that the truth would not be totally buried under an avalanche of lies. Alexander H. Stephens – who had served as the Vice President of the Confederate States of America – in his 1868 masterpiece, *A Constitutional View of the Late War Between the States*, diligently documented the true origins of our political system like a lawyer presenting his case before the bar of public opinion. And in 1881, the scholarly work of Jefferson Davis – the former President of the Confederate States of America –

entitled *The Rise and Fall of the Confederate Government*, was published. Turning to the original documents and papers of the Founding Fathers to support his thesis, Jefferson Davis proved beyond doubt that the Declaration of Independence gave birth to the sovereign States, which in turn established the Federal Union for their mutual benefit.

Since the appearance of these two monumental works of great significance, others have added their voices to a refutation of sundry false theories regarding the origins of our political system. One of the most penetrating arguments on behalf of the truth to be offered to the public was *The Sovereign States*, written by James J. Kilpatrick and published in 1957. Within his book, this noted and highly respected political commentator expounded the true principles of our constitutional system in a manner which could be understood by all Americans.

Regarding the Declaration of Independence, Mr. Kilpatrick wrote:

> Let us inquire, What, precisely, was it that we declared ourselves to be that Fourth of July? Hitherto there had been colonies subject to the King. That form of government would now be abolished. We would now solemnly publish and declare to a candid world – what? That the people of the colonies had formed a free and independent *nation*? By no means. Or that they were henceforth a free and independent *people*? Still no.
>
> This was the declaration: "That these United Colonies are, and of Right ought to be, Free and Independent States." Not one State, or one nation, but in the plural — *States*; and again, in the next breadth, so this multiple birth could not be misunderstood, "that as Free and Independent States, they have full Power to levy War, conclude Peace, contract Alliances, establish Commerce, and do all other Acts and Things which Independent States may of right do."
>
> It had opened, this Declaration, as an enunciation of what often are termed the "human rights," but it concluded, in the plainest terms, as a pronouncement of political powers – the political powers of newly created States. And these powers of war and peace, these powers of alliance and commerce, were published not as the powers of a National Government, but as powers henceforth asserted by thirteen free and independent States.
>
> Certainly Jefferson so understood our creation. "The several States," he was to write much later, "were, from their first establishment, separate and distinct societies, dependent on no other society of men whatever."
>
> So Mr. Justice Samuel Chase comprehended it: He considered the Declaration of Independence, "as a declaration, not that the United Colonies jointly, in a collective capacity, were independent States, etc., but that *each* of them was a sovereign and independent State, that is, that each of them had a right to govern itself by its own authority, and its own laws without any control from any other power on earth." From the Fourth of July, said Chase, "the American States were *de facto* as well as *de jure* in the

possession and actual exercise of all the rights of independent governments....I have ever considered it as the established doctrine of the United States, that their independence originated from, and commenced with, the declaration of Congress, on the Fourth of July, 1776; and that no other period can be fixed on for its commencement; and that all laws made by the legislatures of the several States, after the Declaration of Independence, were the laws of sovereign and independent governments."

So, too, the sage and cool-minded Mr. Justice Cushing: "The several States which composed this Union...became entitled, from the time when they declared themselves independent, to all the rights and powers of sovereign States."

Even [John] Marshall himself had no doubts: In the beginning, "we were divided into independent States, united for some purposes, but in most respects sovereign." The lines which separate the States, he remarked, were too clear ever to be misunderstood.

And for a contemporary authority, it is necessary only to turn to Mr. Justice Frankfurter, who some years ago fell into discussing the dual powers of taxation preserved under the Constitution: "The States," he said, "after *they* formed the Union" – not the people, but the *States*, "continued to have the same range of taxing power which they had before, barring only duties affecting exports, imports, and on tonnage." Regrettably, Mr. Justice Frankfurter appears in more recent times to have lost his concept of States forming a Union.

It is no matter. Evidence of the States' individual sovereignty is abundantly available. Consider, for example, the powers asserted on the part of each State in the Declaration "to levy War, conclude Peace, and contract Alliances." Surely these are sovereign powers. The States exercised them, as States, in the Revolutionary War. But it is of value to note that New York also very nearly exercised her war powers to enter into formal hostilities with the State of Vermont. Tensions reached so grave a point that Massachusetts, in 1784, felt compelled to adopt a formal resolution of neutrality, enjoining her citizens to give "no aid or assistance to either party," and to send "no provisions, arms, or ammunition or other necessities to a fortress or garrison" besieged by either belligerent. When New York adopted a resolution avowing her readiness to "recur to force," Vermont's Governor Chittenden (whose son was to be heard from thirty years later in another row) observed that Vermont "does not wish to enter into a war with the State of New York." But should this unhappy contingency result, Vermont "expects that Congress and the twelve States will observe a strict neutrality, and let the contending States settle their own controversy."

They did settle it, of course. New York and Vermont concluded a peace. The point is that no one saw anything especially remarkable in two separate sovereignties arraying themselves against each other. Vermont was then an individual political entity, as remote at law as any France or Italy. And New York, though a member of the Confederation, and thence technically required to obtain the consent of Congress before waging war, had every right to maintain a standing army for her own defense. [47]

Thirteen Sovereign States

The goal, purpose, and effect of the Declaration of Independence were clearly to give birth to thirteen sovereign American States, each one a free and independent body politic. State sovereignty was thus born on July 4, 1776. The United States of America – *as a loose military alliance between sovereign nations* – was also born on that date. However, the United States of America – *as a politically constituted Federal Union between the States* – did not come into existence until the adoption by the States in 1781 of the Articles of Confederation.

As the Declaration of Independence clearly asserts, all the rights and attributes of sovereignty were assumed by the States separately, each State for itself. Consequently, each of the States, after declaring independence, assumed the rights to wage war, conclude peace, regulate commerce, and to do all other acts which sovereign nations may legitimately do. *These vast powers – the attributes of political sovereignty – belonged to the several States separately, not to the Second Continental Congress.*

Those sovereign States, needless to say, would officially retain all of the powers derived from their sovereignty until such time as they officially delegated some of their powers to a Federal Government under the Articles of Confederation. Since the compact required the unanimous assent of all the States for its adoption, had just a single State been disinclined to political union, the Federal Union would not have been created, and the States would then have been no more united with one another than Britain is today united with Greece.

Although the hostilities in the War of Independence terminated following the surrender of General Charles Cornwallis at Yorktown in 1781, the war was not formally concluded until 1783, when the belligerents involved successfully concluded peace negotiations and signed the Treaty of Paris. The terms agreed to within this peace treaty are highly significant. The Declaration of Independence, of course, had proclaimed that the *cause* for which the War of Independence was waged was to secure the individual sovereignty and independence of each of the thirteen States. It is not surprising, therefore, that the Treaty of Paris of 1783 *officially recognized the individual sovereignty of each American State.* By the terms of this treaty, the British Government formally acknowledged, not that the United States was a free and independ-

---

[47] James Jackson Kilpatrick, *The Sovereign States*, Henry Regnery Company, Chicago, 1957, pp. 5-7.

ent country, but that each of the States, specifically mentioned by name, was a sovereign and independent nation!

As the Treaty of Paris of 1783 declared:

> His Britannic Majesty acknowledges the said United States, viz., New Hampshire, Massachusetts Bay, Rhode Island and Providence Plantations, Connecticut, New York, New Jersey, Pennsylvania, Delaware, Maryland, Virginia, North Carolina, South Carolina and Georgia *to be free, sovereign and independent States*; that he treats with them as such. [48]

Once again, it must be stressed that this peace treaty of September 3, 1783, did not assert that Great Britain would acknowledge one nation called the United States or any other single political entity to be "free, sovereign and independent." Instead, it was the several States who were acknowledged as being "free, sovereign and independent." And this internationally recognized view of our political status was in complete accord with the realities of our political system.

As James J. Kilpatrick has noted, other foreign powers also recognized the American States as individual sovereign bodies:

> More than five years earlier, a treaty of amity and commerce with France had established the same sovereign status of contracting parties. Louis XIV treated with the thirteen American States, but he recognized each of them as a separate power. And it is interesting to note that Virginia, feeling some action desirable to complete the treaty, prior to action by Congress, on June 4, 1779, undertook solemnly to ratify this treaty with France on her own. By appropriate resolution, transmitted by Governor Jefferson to the French minister at Philadelphia, the sovereign Commonwealth of Virginia declared herself individually bound by the French treaty. In terms of international law, Virginia was a nation; in terms of domestic law, she was a sovereign State. [49]

These newly sovereign and independent nations of America clearly understood the value of unity in a hostile and dangerous world. No sooner had the Declaration of Independence been published than the thirteen States drafted a plan of political association. Finally, in 1781 – *five years after the sovereign States came into existence* – the Articles of Confederation were officially ratified by the States. The Articles, which constituted our first Federal Constitution, officially gave birth to the United States as a political entity, formally created the Federal Republic, and legally inaugurated the Federal Union. And no matter how great are the efforts to obscure the true origins of

---

[48] *Ibid.*, quoted on p. 7.
[49] *Ibid.*, p. 8.

our constitutional system of government, the indisputable truth is that all of these great American political institutions were created *by*, *of*, and *for* the sovereign States.

Chapter Four
The Articles of Confederation

With the publication of their Declaration of Independence, the thirteen American States each became sovereign and independent nations. The War of Independence was waged to defend that assertion of individual sovereignty and, within the Treaty of Paris of 1783, the several States secured recognition and acknowledgement from the British Government that each of them was a free, independent, and sovereign State. As Mr. Justice Iredell observed in 1795, had these newly independent States decided not to formally unite together, each one would have gone its own way, for each "possessed all the powers of sovereignty, internal and external...as completely as any of the ancient kingdoms or Republics of the world, which never yet had formed, or thought of forming, any sort of Federal Union whatsoever." [1]

The need for unity, however, was apparent to the American patriots even before the Declaration of Independence was published. When faced by imminent and grave danger, human nature will invariably induce those facing the common danger to pool their resources and join together against the common foe. The threats faced by the New England colonies from hostile Indians produced the New England Confederation and the Dominion of New England some one hundred years before the American Revolution. Although those Confederations had collapsed when the perceived external threat dissipated, the lessons learned from these early experiments with federation were not forgotten.

When Benjamin Franklin's Albany Plan of Union was presented to the colonies for consideration in 1754, the threat posed by the Indians and the French was deemed insufficient to justify such a union by all of the colonies, who rejected it unanimously. Following the French and Indian War, however, the colonies faced a much more ominous threat. Finding themselves in a protracted confrontation with the mother country, the sentiments of the colonies quickly became favorable toward some form of unity. Beginning with the Stamp Act Congress of 1765, the unity movement gathered momentum over the next decade, as the colonies participated with increasing cooperation in the Committees of Correspondence, the First Continental Con-

---

[1] James Jackson Kilpatrick, *The Sovereign States*, Henry Regnery Company, Chicago, 1957, p. 11.

gress, and then the Second Continental Congress.

The States were wise enough to understand that, although the goal was individual sovereignty, they must collaborate and work jointly in the war effort against Great Britain. Only through a united effort could such a war have been contemplated and hazarded. Without united action, the common sense of America dictated, defeat would have been inevitable. As Benjamin Franklin reminded his fellow patriots in 1776, "We must all hang together, or most assuredly, we will all hang separately." [2]

Acting upon this wise counsel, the States always confronted the common enemy as a united body. The States pooled their martial powers together in a Continental Army, and Britain found herself battling the combined strength of all thirteen States. Even at the negotiating table, the British found themselves facing a solid wall of unity. The States were wise enough not to give King George III the opportunity to negotiate separate terms of peace with each of them. The alternatives facing the British Crown, therefore, were reduced to either acknowledging the sovereignty of all of the States, or continuing the war effort to subdue all of the States. By this means of united action, the States managed to win the war and attain the object for which they had fought – their individual sovereignty and independence.

The experiences gained by the States during the American Revolution and its resulting War of Independence made a deep impression on the American mind. If the States could win their sovereignty by means of a *military* alliance amongst themselves, what better means could be found to ensure the continued survival of that sovereignty than a *political* alliance that would allow them to present a united front against the world?

Such unity, it was widely perceived, should extend beyond the immediate crisis then confronting the infant Republics. Even if the War of Independence should prove successful, there would always be foreign danger of one form or another. Hostile Indian tribes still menaced the States. A number of powerful foreign nations would welcome the opportunity to selectively target some of the newly independent American States for conquest. And Great Britain would certainly remain a bitter enemy of the States long after the war. Perhaps she might resume aggressions in the future and attempt to recapture some or all of her lost American colonies. Without unity among the States, she could easily target each State, one at a time, and rob each them of their victory in the War of Independence.

That such apprehensions were well founded is evidenced by the fact that Great Britain again attempted to subdue the American people some

---

[2] The Peoples Bicentennial Commission, *Voices of the American Revolution*, Bantam Books, Inc., New York, 1974, quoted on p. 113.

thirty years after signing the Treaty of Paris with the United States. During the War of 1812 – the "Second War of Independence" – British soldiers once again invaded American soil, burned Washington, D.C., and attempted to rob the American States of their independence. An integral part of the British plan of conquest was to persuade the New England States to secede from the United States and rejoin the British Empire. Only the smashing victory by General Andrew Jackson at New Orleans and the American victory in the war prevented the dismemberment plot from succeeding. Had the States not been united throughout the war, they would have been easy prey for the conqueror.

Fully comprehending the perils they faced, even should the War of Independence prove successful, those who resolved that the colonies should seek independence also resolved that the new States should seek the safety of political union. Accordingly, when Virginia instructed her delegates in the Second Continental Congress to work for independence, she also instructed them to work for a Confederation to unite the States. Following these instructions, Richard Henry Lee included within his famous resolution a proposal of Confederation that would be prepared by the Congress and then submitted to the newly independent States for their approval.

The Preference for a Federal Republic

But if the newly independent American States were to be united within a political union, what would be the character of the Union? What would be the nature of the Federal Government thus created by the Union? What form would it assume, and upon what type of system would it rest? In answering these questions, the American patriots turned to their own historical and successful experiences with federalism and republicanism.

As to the *form* of government that should be created, there was little debate. The struggle with Great Britain during the trying years of 1763 to 1776 had amply demonstrated the folly of monarchy and the virtue of republican government. Throughout those trying years, all the organs and institutions of government associated with the English monarchy had been solidly arrayed against the colonies, while all the democratically elected organs of government based on republican principles had been solidly united in defense of American rights. From this battle royal, which pitted the republican institutions of government against the monarchical organs, the American mind was firmly set in favor of the former and against the latter. After 1776, no American, except for the blatant and open Tory sympathizers, would ever dare to publicly assert a preference for monarchy.

The mood of America, during this time in our history, may be ascertained by the opinions expressed by Thomas Jefferson, who wrote in 1782:

> In every government on earth is some trace of human weakness, some germ of corruption and degeneracy, which cunning will discover, and wickedness insensibly open, cultivate and improve. Every government degenerates when trusted to the rulers of the people alone. The people themselves, therefore, are its only safe depositories. [3]

If monarchy was thoroughly detested, so too was unbridled democracy. Like monarchies, wherein a minority could rule in all cases whatsoever, democracies were viewed as totalitarian in nature, owing to the fact that the majority could make an equal claim to an unlimited power to rule in all cases whatsoever. Democracies were also deemed unstable. Under such governments, society tended to degenerate into mobocracy and rioting; and the government tended to become demagogic, fiscally irresponsible, and morally corrupt.

Between these two extremes in government was the republican form of government. Like monarchies, Republics were regarded as stable in nature. Yet, unlike monarchies, Republics are based on majority rule, the consent of the governed, and the sovereignty of the people. Although Republics share these virtues with democracies, this is where their similarities end. Unlike democracies, Republics are based on the rule of law and on the concept that the majority may rule *only within prescribed limits*. In selecting a *form of government*, the sentiment throughout the States was universal. When the States formed new governments for themselves, each acting independently of the others, all thirteen adopted the *republican form*, a clear indication that they would accept nothing less from any political union between them.

As to the *system* of government which should be established for the fledgling sovereign States, there was equally little debate during this trying time. The only experience the States, during their period of colonial dependency, had ever had – from the days of the New England Confederation to the proposed Albany Plan of Union – was with a *federal system of government*. By such a system, the States could pool their resources in foreign affairs and present themselves as a great, single, consolidated power when dealing with other nations. Yet, within such a federal system, each State could retain its exclusive jurisdiction over its own domestic affairs. The only alternative to federation was to adopt a national system of government, whereby a centralized government would assume supreme authority over all their political concerns, foreign and domestic.

---

[3] Richard S. Poppen (ed.), *Thomas Jefferson*, St. Louis, 1904, pp. 25-26.

The colonial system under which the thirteen colonies had matured had contained many of the elements of a federal system. Although the colonial system had not been officially established as a federation, the British Government had long allowed the colonies to govern themselves in all areas of internal or domestic concern. The firm attachment of the American people to this system of government was made manifest during the American Revolution. One of the leading causes of that Revolution, in fact, had been Britain's attempts to destroy the rights of the colonies to govern themselves. This ardent defense of colonial rights was the precursor of the ardent defense of States' Rights that arose after the adoption of our present Constitution.

After asserting their independence *as sovereign States*, it would have been highly contradictory and subversive of the efforts of all who fought in the American Revolution to have willfully and deliberately surrendered that sovereignty and independence by erecting a consolidated National Union. Had the States desired to exist as mere provinces within an Empire dominated by a centralized government, they would never have seceded from the British Empire. They fought the war to free themselves from the dictates of consolidated power, not to merely exchange one set of imperial rulers for another set of centralized dictators.

The importance of building our political institutions on an honest foundation of liberty was of paramount importance to those who built our Republic, as the following words, written by Thomas Jefferson in 1781, readily attest:

> It can never be too often repeated that the time for fixing every essential right on a legal basis is while our rulers are honest, and ourselves united. From the conclusion of this war we shall be going down hill. It will not then be necessary to resort every moment to the people for support. They will be forgotten, therefore, and their rights disregarded. They will forget themselves, but in the sole faculty of making money, and will never think of uniting to effect a due respect for their rights. The shackles, therefore, which shall not be knocked off at the conclusion of this war, will remain on us long, will be made heavier and heavier, till our rights shall revive or expire in a convulsion. [4]

In establishing a political union between themselves, the thirteen sovereign States – whose territories extended from Canada to Spanish-controlled Florida, and from the Atlantic Ocean to the Mississippi River – were cognizant of the great challenge they faced. Never before in history had a Republic been established over such a vast stretch of geography. But if the republican form of government could be successfully merged with a federal system,

---

[4] *Ibid.*, p. 24.

thereby dividing powers between independent levels of government and placing limitations on power at all levels, perhaps liberty could endure on the American continent. Under such a political system, the foreign affairs of the States would be conducted by the general Republic, while all domestic affairs would be conducted separately by the smaller Republics.

With these considerations in mind, it is not surprising that the American States, after asserting their independence, would settle for nothing less than a *Federal Republic*. By such a Federal Union, they could obtain the blessings of a common defense while retaining the blessings of local sovereignty. These were the motivations that produced the Articles of Confederation, the first Constitution of the United States of America.

The Evolution of the Articles

The movement to formally unite the fledgling States in a political union was initiated with the famous resolution introduced in the Second Continental Congress on June 7, 1776, by Richard Henry Lee of Virginia:

> *Resolved*, That these United Colonies are, and of right ought to be, free and independent States, that they are absolved from all allegiance to the British Crown, and that all political connection between them and the State of Great Britain is, and ought to be, totally dissolved.
>
> That it is expedient forthwith to take the most effectual measures for forming foreign Alliances.
>
> That a plan of Confederation be prepared and transmitted to the respective Colonies for their consideration and approbation. [5]

Although this resolution was debated for nearly month and was not officially approved by the Congress until July 2, 1776, the members of Congress understood the urgency of the situation faced by the colonies. Rather than wait until Mr. Lee's resolution was formally adopted, the Second Continental Congress decided to appoint two separate committees to begin work on the first and last proposals. One committee, on which Thomas Jefferson served, was tasked with the assignment of drafting the Declaration of Independence. The other committee, appointed on June 12th and chaired by John Dickinson of Delaware, was assigned the task of drafting a plan of Confederation to unite the States, should the decision be made to seek independence.

Inasmuch as the proclamation of independence was deemed more

---

[5] Charles Callan Tansill (ed.), *The Making of the American Republic: The Great Documents, 1774-1789*, Arlington House, New Rochelle, p. 21.

pressing than the plan of Union, it was given preference by the Congress. As soon as Mr. Lee's resolution was formally approved on July 2nd, the representatives immediately turned their attention to the draft of the Declaration of Independence that had been penned by Mr. Jefferson. Cognizant of the plans being made to confederate the States, the author of the Declaration had inserted within that proclamation a political term never before seen in any public document – the "United States of America." This term had, in fact, been borrowed from the then-evolving Articles of Confederation, in which the expression was used to describe the proposed Confederation of States. By deliberating inserting this new political phrase into the Declaration, Thomas Jefferson was conveying a message to the British Government that the States, determined to remain united in their common defense, were already drafting plans for a formal *political* alliance to replace their existing *military* alliance.

On July 12, 1776, eight days after the Second Continental Congress had approved the final version of the Declaration of Independence, John Dickinson presented his draft of the Articles of Confederation to that body. Due to the pressing exigencies of the War of Independence, however, the Congress could not afford to devote its full attention to the proposed plan of government. Debates on the Articles were therefore intermittent, and it was not until more than a year later, on October 7, 1777, that Congress finally approved the constitutional plan. Like all other voting done within that body, the vote was taken by States, with each State having one vote.

The vote of approval within the Congress gave no force or validity to the Articles of Confederation. According to the American Theory of Government, on which the Declaration of Independence was founded, no State could be bound to any Union without its own consent. The States, thus, would be required to give their individual assentions to the Articles before the Constitution could be declared officially ratified. The vote taken in the Congress signified only that the drafting phase had been successfully concluded, and that the "Articles of Confederation and Perpetual Union Between the States" could then be presented to the States for their consideration. And in submitting the compact to the States, the Congress recommended adoption of the Articles under the conviction that a political union was necessary "to confound our foreign enemies, support public credit, restore the value of our money, enable us to maintain our fleets and armies, and add weight and respect to our counsels at home and our treaties abroad." [6]

The prescribed conditions of ratification required that the Articles of Confederation be officially ratified *unanimously* by all thirteen State govern-

---

[6] J.L.M. Curry, *The Southern States of the American Union*, G.P. Putnam's Sons, New York, 1895, quoted on p. 67.

ments. Some States acted quickly and gave ready assent to the proposed Constitution; other States acted more slowly. Virginia became the first State to ratify the plan, giving her assent by unanimous vote. By the end of 1778, ten States had formally ratified the Articles. Another State assented in 1779, and another a year later. Maryland proved to be the most reluctant State, and it was not until March 1, 1781, that she ratified the first Constitution of the United States.

Maryland's reluctance to accede to the compact was due to her concern regarding the territorial possessions of some of the States. These territorial possessions stretched from the western boundaries of the thirteen States westward to the Mississippi River, and from the panhandle of Florida northward to the Canadian border. In terms of geographical size, the Territories equaled or surpassed the combined land mass of the thirteen States proper. States having claim to portions of this vast expanse included Georgia, South Carolina, North Carolina, Virginia, Connecticut, and Massachusetts. In many cases, more than one State had a claim to certain portions of Territories. Virginia, for example, claimed all of the Territory from the Canadian border southward to what is now the current border of Tennessee. Broad sections of this same land mass, however, were also claimed by Massachusetts and Connecticut.

Maryland and the other States lacking territorial claims insisted that such Territories be ceded to the proposed Confederation, so that the great land mass could be eventually divided into new States with "free, convenient, and independent governments." [7] In 1780, the Congress took up the cause of these States and implored the more richly endowed States to relinquish their claims to their territorial possessions. In urging that the Territories be ceded to the proposed Confederation, the Second Continental Congress adopted the following resolution:

> *Resolved,* That the unappropriated lands that may be ceded or relinquished to the United States by any particular State, pursuant to the recommendation of Congress of the sixth day of September last, shall be disposed of for the common benefit of the United States, and be settled and formed into distinct republican States, which shall become members of the Federal Union, and have the same rights of sovereignty, freedom, and independence as the other States. [8]

By this resolution, the Congress not only resolved the immediate problem at hand, but also established an extremely valuable *precedent* for the dis-

---

[7] *Ibid.*, quoted on p. 68.
[8] *Ibid.*, quoted on pp. 68-69.

position of future Territories acquired by the United States. The territorial possessions of the United States would belong to *all of the States* for the mutual benefit of *all of these States*. Accordingly, citizens from all of the States would enjoy the right to emigrant to and settle within such common Territories.

Moreover, whenever a parceled section of the Territories attained sufficient population and met the prescribed requirements, that Territory would then be allowed to become a State and enter into the Federal Union *on a footing equal to that of the other States*, having "the same rights of sovereignty, freedom, and independence as the other States." There was to be no *seniority* system among the States, and the original thirteen States could not claim to have more rights within the Union than the newly admitted States, in spite of the fact that the new States would be created by the Union. *The new States would have exactly the same status and sovereignty as those States who had issued the Declaration of Independence and waged the War of Independence.*

Another point of interest with the resolution of the Second Continental Congress is the usage of the term "Federal Union" to describe the proposed Confederation. This is but one example from among the many that could be cited from that period showing that the men of that day clearly recognized the Articles of Confederation as a Federal Constitution designed to formally establish a Federal Union between sovereign States.

A final point of significance in regard to this resolution of the Congress should be noted, especially in light of the subsequent development of antagonism over the territorial possessions of the United States that dominated our ante-bellum history. Had those States initially claiming territorial possessions not been willing to relinquish their claims, it is highly doubtful if the thirteen States would ever have agreed to confederate. In such an event, each of the thirteen States would have gone its own way, and the settlement of the remainder of the North American continent would have proceeded along very different lines than it actually did.

Especially significant, under this consideration, is that *all of the Territories lying to the west of the thirteen States was claimed by the Southern States.* Virginia alone claimed all of the Territory from Canada to the future northern border of Tennessee, while South Carolina, North Carolina, and Georgia claimed the remainder of the Territories that extended down to the border of Florida. Had the States not confederated under the Articles, the Southern States – Virginia, in particular – would have had a decided advantage in expanding their civilizations westward to the Pacific Ocean. In such a case, what we now regard as the continental United States would be today predominantly *Southern* in its cultural and political connections.

Virginia, however, the most populous and powerful of the thirteen original States, was eager for Confederation and was willing to make a noble sacrifice to effect such a goal. Not only was Virginia the first State to ratify the Articles of Confederation, she was also the first State to cede her vast territorial claims to the United States, an act accomplished by 1784. Massachusetts followed suit and ceded her territorial claim the following year. Connecticut ceded her Territory to the United States in 1786, and was followed by South Carolina in 1787. In 1790, North Carolina ceded her territorial lands, and Georgia, the last to act, ceded her Territories in 1802.

As noted previously, with regard to these territorial possessions ceded to the United States, the agreement among the thirteen original States was quite clear. By this agreement, all of the territorial possessions of the United States would belong to all of the States jointly, and all the peoples of all the States would have an equal right to settle in them. As soon as possible, such Territories would be organized into States and admitted into the Federal Union. Although such States, in a sense, would be ostensibly "created by the Union," they would assume a status within the Union equal to the original thirteen States who created the Union. Or, as the resolution of the Second Continental Congress stated, such new States "shall become members of the Federal Union, and have the same rights of sovereignty, freedom, and independence as the other States."

In spite of this clear understanding at the establishment of the Federal Union, however, certain scheming politicians of a later generation would arise and dare to assert that new States admitted to the Union could not possibly claim sovereignty because they had been *created by the Union*. The Union, they would haughtily claim, is therefore superior to the States; the Union, thus, was sovereign, not the States it created. As we have already observed, however, such a false concept cannot be sustained by the historical record of the founding of the Federal Republic.

Satisfied with the plans to properly dispose of the western lands, Maryland ratified the Articles of Confederation in 1781. With Maryland's assent to the plan of government, the Articles were declared officially adopted, and, in the same year, a Federal Government was formally created for the first time in the United States in pursuance of the new Federal Constitution.

Significance of the Articles

"The Articles," wrote James J. Kilpatrick, "merit examination with the utmost care; they are too little studied, and there is much to be learned from them." [9] The advocate of constitutional government can indeed learn much by studying the Articles of Confederation. Of paramount importance, when studying the Articles, is the understanding that they constituted the first *Federal Constitution* for the United States of America.

Over the years, and especially since the War Between the States, a concerted effort has been made by many historians and political theorists to deny and refute the sovereignty of the States. Especially significant in this effort has been the attempt to pervert and distort the true history of the formative years of the United States. An integral part of this campaign has been the effort to deny that the Articles of Confederation actually constituted the first Constitution of the United States. This absurd fallacy rests upon the contention that the Articles were not officially styled a "Constitution," and therefore should not be regarded as one.

The foolishness of this contention becomes apparent when this line of reasoning is applied to objects other than constitutions of government. By this line of reasoning, an automobile, for instance, could not be called such unless the word "automobile" is somewhere written on the body or on the engine. Other illustrations could be cited with equal ease. Nowhere in the *Iliad*, for example, does it call itself an epic poem. Does that prove that it is not an epic poem? If we look at the chairs we sit in, it is highly doubtful if they contain such an expression as, "This is a chair." Does such an omission prove that it is not chair? And what of the sky and the air we breathe. Do they bear appropriate labels to identify themselves to us? Why, then, do we persist on referring to the air and the sky by such terms?

The significance of ascertaining whether the Articles did or did not comprise our first Federal Constitution should be readily apparent to the student of American political theory. Only by acknowledging that the Articles of Confederation comprised our first Constitution – serving as the predecessor to our present Federal Constitution – can the true evolution of the organic structure of the United States, as a political organization, be correctly determined.

As Alexander H. Stephens noted in his great work, *A Constitutional View of the Late War Between the States*:

> To understand properly the present Supreme law, we must look into what was the Supreme law before. The present is not the first Constitution of the United States. "The Union" existed *under an old Constitution.* The main object of the present Constitution, as appears in its Preamble, was to make "the Union" then existing more perfect. It was not to make a new one, or to change the fundamental character of the one then existing;

---

[9] James J. Kilpatrick, *Op. cit.*, p. 10.

no such purpose at least is declared on the face of the instrument; it was only to make the previous "Union" more perfect, or better adapted to secure the great objects for which it had been originally formed. [10]

Yet, there arose a certain school of thought – greatly propagated initially by the nationalistic politician from Massachusetts, Daniel Webster – asserting that the Union under our present Constitution is fundamentally different than the Union under the Articles of Confederation. In support of such a view, this school found it necessary to negate the concept of the Articles being the first Constitution of the United States. The views of Senator Webster on this subject, unfortunately, have continued to find adherents throughout the years.

"If there is one word in the English language that the people of the United States understand, it is the word Constitution," Daniel Webster asserted in a famous debate in the Senate. "It means," said he, "the fundamental law," and nothing like league, or compact, or Articles of Confederation. [11] Those who referred to the Articles as America's first Federal Constitution did not know what they were talking about, he insisted, for even the Founding Fathers knew that the Articles never constituted a Constitution.

In reply to the false assertion put forth by Senator Webster and the consolidationist school of thought, Alexander H. Stephens made the following comments in his book:

> Mr. Webster did say [such words]....I remember it well....But were not the Articles of Confederation a Constitution even according to his own definition? Did they not constitute the fundamental law of the Union of the States under the Confederation...? Being the fundamental law for their government for the *time being*, is it not perfectly proper to style them a Constitution upon the authority of Mr. Webster himself? In so styling them, I use the same term that has been applied to them by the highest authority, not only of that day, but since. As you question its propriety, however, we had better settle all points of difference as we go along, especially as a great deal often depends upon words barely, which are frequently, as Mr. Webster says, much more than sounds, being real things within themselves. Let me therefore just here refer to some authorities which I think clearly justify the use of the term as made by me. Mr. Curtis, in his *History of the Constitution of the United States*, volume I, page 139, says these Articles of Confederation were "the first written *Constitution* of the United States." Here is *Marshall's Life of Washington*, volume ii, page 83. In it is Washington's letter to the Governors of the several States, dated 8th of June, 1783, in which he speaks of the Articles of the then existing Confed-

---

[10] Alexander H. Stephens, *A Constitutional View of the Late War Between the States*, Volume 1, Kraus Reprint Co., New York, (orig. pub. in 1868) 1970, p. 51.
[11] *Ibid.*, Volume 1, quoted on p. 51.

eration as "*the Constitution*" of the States. Here is the first volume of *Elliot's Debates*; on page 96, is given, in full, a letter from the then Congress to the several States, making several recommendations to them. It is dated 18th of April, 1783. In this letter, on page 98, these words occur: "The last object recommended is Constitutional change of the rule by which a partition of the common burthens is to be made." This shows that the men of that day understood the Articles of "the Union" then existing to be a *Constitution*. Changes in these Articles they characterized as *Constitutional* changes. Here is the ninth volume of *Spark's Writings of Washington*. In this are given quite a number of letters written by him in 1788, after what I call the new Constitution had been agreed to by a Convention of the States in 1787....In these letters, Washington called this instrument...the *new Constitution*. Here is a letter written on the 23d of February, 1789, to Mr. Monroe, in which Washington says: "I received, by last night's mail, your letter dated the fifteenth of this month, with your printed observations on the *new Constitution*," etc. Here is another letter written by Washington to Henry Lee, under date 22d September, 1788, in which he also calls it the *new Constitution*. Another to Benjamin Lincoln, on the 26th of October, 1788, in which he uses the same language. These letters (and I refer to but a few of them) show, beyond cavil, that Washington considered the old Articles of "Union," as much as the new, a *Constitution*. Besides this, the writers in the *Federalist* usually designated the paper then before the States for their consideration as the *new Constitution* in contradistinction to the old or the Articles of Confederation. I cite but a few of them: Numbers 22, 39, 41 and 44....Moreover, two of the States, at least, Massachusetts and New Hampshire, in their Ordinances adopting and ratifying the present Constitution, expressly style it a *new Constitution*. Is more authority needed on this point to justify my use of the term Constitution in applying it as I did to the Articles of Confederation, as well as to the Articles of the present "Union," whatever they may be. The first was a fundamental law as long as it lasted as much as the other....

Well, then, if the old Articles of Union were a Constitution, the new Constitution is but new Articles of Union between the same parties; unless the new Constitution changes fundamentally the character of "the Union" then existing between them. The bare change of name, of course, does not affect any change of substance. [12]

The key to answering the question – Were the Articles of Confederation a genuine Constitution of the United States? – is to properly define terminology. *Webster's II, New Riverside University Dictionary*, for instance, provides three definitions for the noun "constitution," as follows:

1. The act or process of composing, setting up, or establishing. 2. a. Structure or composition: MAKE-UP. b. The physical make-up of a person <a strong *constitution*> 3. a. The system of fundamental laws and principles

---

[12] *Ibid.*, Volume 1, pp. 52-54.

that prescribes the nature, functions, and limits of an institution, as a government. b. The document on which such a system is recorded. [13]

The Third Edition of *Roget's International Thesaurus* associates the *structural meaning* of the word "constitution" with such terms as "structure," "construction," "composition," "make-up," "frame," "framework," "skeleton," and "anatomy." That same thesaurus associates the *legal meaning* of "constitution" with such concepts as "legality," "legitimacy," "legalization," "law," "rule," "code," "digest," "body of law," "jurisprudence," "unwritten constitution," and "written constitution." The adjective form of the term – "constitutional" – is associated with such terms as ""legal," "legitimate," "licit," "lawful," "authorized," and "sanctioned." And the opposite of constitutional – "unconstitutional" – is associated with such terms as "illegal," "unlawful," "illegitimate," "illicit," "against the law," "lawless," "unauthorized," "unallowed," "unwarranted," "unofficial," "felonious," "outlawed," and "criminal." [14]

Using these definitions and word associations, we may derive our own definition of the term *constitution*. A political constitution is an official, formal set of written or unwritten rules that define a government, establish its departments and divisions, assign functions to the various governmental organs, and delegate specifically enumerated powers to the various organs of government. By performing these functions, a constitution does much more than merely erect the framework of a government. *It also establishes the limits of power of the government thus created.* Only in this regard can the acts of the government be viewed as authorize or unauthorized, as lawful or unlawful, as constitutional or unconstitutional.

Having thus established a reliable definition of the key term in question, it may be said without hesitation that the Articles of Confederation did indeed comprise a Constitution for the United States of America. Being our first Federal Constitution, it established the Federal Government and the Federal Republic. It also established a Union which existed, not *over the States*, but, in the words of the Articles, "between the States." The Union thus created was not a National Union, but a Federal Union.

To properly understand the evolution of constitutional government in the United States, we should study the Articles of Confederation in detail. For this objective, we will rely on the copy of the Articles found in the Library of Congress edition of the *Journals of the Continental Congress*, which has also been reproduced in Charles C. Tallan's work, *The Making of the*

---

[13] *Webster's II, New Riverside University Dictionary*, The Riverside Publishing Company, 1984, p. 302.
[14] *Roget's International Thesaurus*, Third Edition, Thomas Y. Crowell Company, New York, 1962, pp. 131 and 634-635.

American Republic: The Great Documents, 1774-1789. The only liberties we will take with this copy concern the style used to capitalize the first letters in the words "United States," "States," and "Congress." In the original version of the Articles, the United States appears as both "United States" and "united states," the States are referred to as "States" and as "states," and Congress is often referred to as "congress." For consistency, we will capitalize the first letters of each word in these three terms at all times. Aside from this stylistic change, however, we shall not alter the original text.

The Preamble

Our first Federal Constitution consisted of a Preamble or Introduction, a total of thirteen Articles, and a concluding paragraph. Within the introductory statements, the purposes and objectives of the Articles of Confederation are explained. In accomplishing this, the introductory remarks, although not officially styled a "Preamble," served the same purpose as the Preamble contained in the Constitution of 1787.

The Preamble or Introduction of the Articles reads as follows:

> *To all to whom these Presents shall come, we the under signed Delegates of the States affixed to our Names, send greeting.*
> Whereas the Delegates of the United States of America, in Congress assembled, did, on the 15th day of November, in the Year of our Lord One thousand Seven Hundred and Seventy seven, and in the Second Year of the Independence of America, agree to certain articles of Confederation and perpetual Union between the States of Newhampshire, Massachusetts-bay, Rhodeisland and Providence Plantations, Connecticut, New York, New Jersey, Pennsylvania, Delaware, Maryland, Virginia, North-Carolina, South-Carolina, and Georgia in the words following, viz. "Articles of Confederation and perpetual Union between the States of Newhampshire, Massachusetts-bay, Rhodeisland and Providence Plantations, Connecticut, New-York, New-Jersey, Pennsylvania, Delaware, Maryland, Virginia, North-Carolina, South-Carolina and Georgia. [15]

Within this Preamble, two sets of representatives, one representing the States jointly and the other representing the States individually, are mentioned. Those representatives "in Congress assembled," who thus represented the common or joint interests of the States, were referred to as the "Delegates of the United States," while those representatives who represented the indi-

---

[15] Charles Callan Tansill (ed.), *The Making of the American Republic: The Great Documents, 1774-1789*, Arlington House, New Rochelle, p. 27.

vidual interests of the States were termed the "Delegates of the States." The Articles had been drafted with the common interests of all the States in mind, and had afterward been ratified by each State with its own interests in mind.

The nature of the Union to be created by the Articles is defined within the Preamble or Introduction as being federal in character, not national. Each State comprising the Union was mentioned by name, and the Union thus established was to be *between the States*, not over them. That the Confederation to be established was intended to be permanent is evident from the expression, "Articles of Confederation and *Perpetual Union* Between the States."

Perpetuity, of course, had earlier been claimed for the New England Confederation of 1643 by the four New England colonies who comprised that early Union. The formal expression, however, had not saved that Union from dismemberment when, at a later date, the parties to the compact resolved to end it after some forty years. The Confederation under the Articles would prove to have an even shorter life span than the New England Confederation. Established in 1781, the Articles were destined to be replaced in 1789 by a new Constitution, which, wisely, contained no reference to a perpetual existence. In the case of the Articles of Confederation, *perpetuity* thus translated into a practical life span of only eight years.

Article I

Article I of the Articles of Confederation consists of a single sentence that prescribes the official name of the Confederation: "The stile of this confederacy shall be 'The United States of America.'" [16] Thus, the formal title of the Confederation was to be the same one used by Thomas Jefferson in the Declaration of Independence to describe the military alliance of the thirteen sovereign States which had waged the War of Independence.

The selection of the term used – *United States of America* – was logically dictated by the nature of the Union and the circumstances in which it was founded. The last two words, "of America," were purely geographic in origin, signifying the obvious fact that the States in the Union were located in that hemisphere of the world known as America. The term "United" was selected as being the adjective form of the word *Union*, and it signified the fact that the political association was formed by *compact* among certain parties. Yet, who were the parties to that pact? Were the American people the parties to the compact? If so, the style of the Confederation would have been, The United *People* of America.

---

[16] *Ibid.*, p. 27.

By selecting the word *States*, instead of the term People, to define the Confederacy, the Union was thus defined as being among the States *in their sovereign capacities*. It was the States who formed the Union, and not a single or consolidated nation of American people. Therefore, the style of the Confederation was the Union of American States, or, more properly, "The United States of America."

Article II

Article II of our first Federal Constitution also consists of a single sentence. Its purpose was to confirm the obvious fact that, in forming a Federal Union styled the United States of America, the States did not sacrifice the sovereignty they had proclaimed in the Declaration of Independence and won through the War of Independence. Even had this Article been omitted from the Constitution, the sovereignty of the parties to the compact could have been deduced from the fact that the Union was established "between the States." But it was not omitted, and its inclusion in the Articles served as a *precedent* for the Tenth Amendment to our present Federal Constitution.

This Article declares that, "Each State retains its sovereignty, freedom, and independence, and every Power, Jurisdiction and right, which is not by this confederation expressly delegated to the United States, in Congress assembled." [17]

The Declaration of Independence had established the principle that government, to be legitimate, must rest on the consent of the governed. This Article applies that principle to the Federal Government created by the Articles of Confederation. The powers that could be exercised by the Federal Government, it stipulates, were limited to those *delegated* to it by the States. Powers not delegated could not be exercised by the Federal Government, for such powers remained exclusively in the hands of the respective States.

It is of interest to note the manner in which this expression of limited power is made. The powers delegated to the Federal Government are spoken of as powers "delegated to the United States." All powers, jurisdictions, and rights delegated by the States to the Union, in other words, were vested in the *Federal Government*, and not in an imaginary American nation of people. The only real beneficiary of any reduction of the rights reserved to the States, therefore, would have been the Federal Government, not the people of any consolidated American nation.

A final point of significance regarding the Second Article should be

---

[17] *Ibid.*, p. 27.

noted. Although it may appear obvious, it must be stressed that, by this provision, the States were retaining *all* of their sovereignty. Sovereignty, by its nature, is an *all-or-none* attribute, and inherent in its meaning – *supreme authority* – is the concept that it cannot be limited, divided, or delegated. Political *supremacy* cannot be limited or divided, nor can a supreme authority "delegate" its supremacy.

It is of paramount importance, when considering the question of sovereignty, to always differentiate between *sovereignty* and the *powers of government*, for these two concepts are not equivalent. *Sovereignty is the supreme political authority within society and is the legitimate source of all the powers of government.* According to the American Theory of Government, sovereignty is vested in the *peoples of the several States*, who are the *masters* of the American political system and who are the sources of the powers of all levels of government, both State and federal. The power to declare war, for example, is an important governmental power, but it is *not* a sovereign power. The power to create a government, delegate powers to it, and establish the limits of its authority, on the other hand, *is* a sovereign power. With this proper understanding of the true nature of political supremacy, it may be stated that the *powers* of government may be *delegated* by a State, *but not the sovereignty of its people.* To assert otherwise would be to subvert the American Theory of Government and to raise government to the level of master and sink the people to the level of servants or subjects of that government.

A proper interpretation of Article II, therefore, requires dividing the sentence into its two separate logic sections, so that its true meaning becomes more obvious. "Each State retains it sovereignty, freedom, and independence" within the Federal Union. Furthermore, each State retains "every Power, Jurisdiction and right, which is not by this confederation expressly delegated to the United States, in Congress assembled." This represents the proper construction of Article II.

Article III

Like the two preceding Articles, Article III consists of one sentence. By its provisions, the purpose of the Federal Union is explained and reason is given for the creation of the United States of America by the sovereign States. The previous Article, as already noted, confirmed the fact that the States retained their sovereignty within the Union. The Third Article builds upon that concept and proclaims the purpose of the Union to be, among other things, *the preservation of the sovereignty of the States*. In stark opposition to those who insist that States can never create a Federal Union without surrendering their sovereignty, this Article boldly asserts that the very *reason* why the States created the Federal Republic was to secure and perpetuate their individual sovereign rights.

In announcing the reasons for the formation of the United States of America as a political union between the States, Article III merely states an obvious truth – obvious, at least, to the Founding Fathers. The States had previously asserted their sovereignty in the Declaration of Independence. They had then waged a War of Independence in defense of their State sovereignty and had secured acknowledgement of that sovereignty from Great Britain in the Treaty of Paris of 1783. Why, after going through the horrors of a grueling war, would those States voluntarily throw away their sovereignty and independence? The States obviously united together for purposes of common defense to enable them to provide greater security for their hard-won sovereignty and independence.

As Article III states:

> The said States hereby severally enter into a firm league of friendship with each other, for their common defence, the security of their Liberties, and their mutual and general welfare, binding themselves to assist each other, against all force offered to, or attacks made upon them, or any of them, on account of religion, sovereignty, trade, or any other pretence whatever. [18]

The *United States of America* is herein described as a "league of friendship" between the States, and the implications of such an expression are clear. The States were the parties to this compact; they were the masters of the federal system. The Federal Government created by that pact was intended to be their servant, and the Union thus established was to exist solely for their convenience and safety. The order of superiority within the Federal Union thus established was beyond dispute. The States were to be supreme – they created and breathed life into the Articles of Confederation. Those Articles, in turn, were to be superior to the Federal Government which they established. The order of superiority was, therefore, from highest to lowest in rank: the sovereign States, the Federal Constitution, and the Federal Government.

Article III also introduced a new expression into the American political vocabulary – "general welfare." The significance of this expression lies in the fact that the framers of our present Federal Constitution borrowed this term from the Articles and inserted it into the Constitution of 1787, and that soon thereafter the expression was seized upon by consolidationists as an excuse to

---

[18] *Ibid.*, p. 27.

enlarge the powers of the Federal Government. By twisted logic of interpretation, it was asserted that the Federal Government could assume whatever powers it pleased and do whatever acts it desired, so long as it cloaked its deeds under the guise of promoting the "general welfare."

The true meaning of this term, however, is best ascertained from the Constitution where it first appeared. As the Third Article of the Articles of Confederation makes abundantly plain, the legitimate "general welfare" of the United States dictates the preservation of the sovereignty of the States. Anything that undermines the "religion, sovereignty, trade," or other rights of the States is subversive of the true general welfare of the United States.

Article IV

Article IV is longer than the three preceding ones, serving to create uniformity among the several States with regard to the "privileges and immunities" of all their free inhabitants, excluding paupers, vagabonds, and fugitives from justice. This Article also makes provision for the free and unrestrained movements of citizens across State boundaries, and for the laying of duties by the States. Were it not for this specific agreement among the States, a citizen of one State traveling through another State would have been required to obtain a visa and to carry a passport. It is this provision, in fact, which first gave rise to the concept of the *citizens of the several States* also being *citizens of the United States*.

These provisions are made in the following language:

> The better to secure and perpetuate mutual friendship and intercourse among the people of the different States in this union, the free inhabitants of each of these States, paupers, vagabonds and fugitives from justice excepted, shall be entitled to all privileges and immunities of free citizens in the several States; and the people of each State shall have free ingress and regress to and from any other State, and shall enjoy therein all the privileges of trade and commerce, subject to the same duties, impositions and restrictions as the inhabitants thereof respectively, provided that such restriction shall not extend so far as to prevent the removal of property imported into any State, to any other State, of which the Owner is an inhabitant; provided also that no imposition, duties or restriction shall be laid by any State, on the property of the United States, or either of them. [19]

The remaining portion of Article IV provided for the extradition of fugitives from justice in a fashion still practiced under our present Federal Con-

---

[19] *Ibid.*, p. 28.

stitution:

> If any Person guilty of, or charged with treason, felony, or other high misdemeanor in any State, shall flee from Justice, and be found in any of the United States, he shall, upon demand of the Governor or executive power, of the State from which he fled, be delivered up and removed to the State having jurisdiction of his offence.
>
> Full faith and credit shall be given in each of these States to the records, acts and judicial proceedings of the courts and magistrates of every other State. [20]

Attention should be directed to the crime of *treason* herein listed. Loyalty and allegiance, of course, are owed to the *sovereign*. Thus, in monarchies, loyalty is owed to the King, who is sovereign; and treason is an act of disloyalty to the sovereign King. In Republics, loyalty is owed to the people, who alone are sovereign. Treason within a Republic is defined as an act of disloyalty to the sovereign people. By listing treason as among the crimes that can be committed against a State, this Article further illustrates that sovereignty within the United States resides with the peoples of the respective States. This concept of loyalty and disloyalty, incidentally, also appears in our present Federal Constitution, where treason against the United States is defined as disloyalty to all the States jointly or to any of the States individually.

We should also note the usage, within the Articles, of the term "United States" as a *plural* entity. Within Article IV, this plural usage occurs twice, in the phrase, "the property of the United States, *or either of them*," and in the phrase, "be found *in any of the United States*." It is clear from these phrases that the words "the several States within the Union" could be substituted for the term "the United States" in the Articles of Confederation without a change in meaning or import. It is of significance to note that this plural usage of the term "United States" also appears within the Constitution of 1787!

Article V

The Fifth Article in our first Federal Constitution provides for representation in the Federal Government created by the Articles for the United States. Two specific organs of government were to be established, a Congress and a Committee of the States. Although each State could send anywhere from two to seven representatives to the Congress, on all questions before that body *each State was to have only one vote*. The members of Congress were ac-

---

[20] *Ibid.*, p. 28.

corded a degree of immunity in a manner similar to that established by our present Federal Constitution. No member of Congress could be held liable for any speech made in Congress, and Congressmen would enjoy limited immunity from arrest for minor violations of law.

The provisions of Article V are in these words:

> For the more convenient management of the general interests of the United States, delegates shall be annually appointed in such manner as the legislature of each State shall direct, to meet in Congress on the first Monday in November, in every year, with a power reserved to each State, to recall its delegates, or any of them, at any time within the year, and to send others in their stead, for the remainder of the Year.
>
> No State shall be represented in Congress by less than two, nor more than seven Members; and no person shall be capable of being a delegate for more than three years in any term of six years; nor shall any person, being a delegate, be capable of holding any office under the United States, for which he, or another for his benefit receives any salary, fees or emolument of any kind.
>
> Each State shall maintain its own delegates in a meeting of the States, and while they act as members of the committee of the States.
>
> Freedom of speech and debate in Congress shall not be impeached or questioned in any Court, or place out of Congress, and the members of Congress shall be protected in their persons from arrests and imprisonments, during the time of their going to and from, and attendance on Congress, except for treason, felony, or breach of the peace. [21]

As this Article indicates, *term limitations* were an integral part of our first Federal Constitution. This concept sprang from a belief that, to prevent certain interests from becoming entrenched in government, no elected official should be allowed to serve in the government beyond a fixed number of terms. Although term limitations were omitted from our present Federal Constitution, Thomas Jefferson established a precedent when he declined to run for a third term as President of the United States. Not until Franklin D. Roosevelt broke that precedent and served as President for life was an amendment added to our present Constitution to impose term limitations on the office of the Presidency.

Article VI

Article VI is the second longest Article within the Articles of Confederation, and it served as an agreement among the thirteen sovereign States to

---

[21] *Ibid.*, pp. 28-29.

each refrain from doing certain specified acts. The necessity for voluntarily imposing these restraints on the exercise of their sovereignty was essential to the functioning of the Union. If the goal was to present a united front against the world, then the States would, for example, need to refrain from directly conducting foreign affairs, or at least refrain from doing so without coordinating such actions with the other States.

By means of the Sixth Article, the States also agreed not to form other smaller Confederations within the main Confederacy without first explaining the nature of such a new Union and obtaining the consent of the other States. Furthermore, the States agreed not to lay duties and imposts that would interfere with or violate any treaties into which the United States had already entered or would enter. Had the States been unwilling to voluntarily accept such limitations as these, needless to say, political union would have been impossible.

This Article begins with these provisions:

> No State, without the Consent of the United States in Congress assembled, shall send any embassy to, or receive any embassy from, or enter into any conference, agreement, alliance or treaty with any King prince or state; nor shall any person holding any office of profit or trust under the United States, or any of them, accept of any present, emolument, office or title of any kind whatever from any king, prince or foreign state; nor shall the United States in Congress assembled, or any of them, grant any title of nobility.
>
> No two or more States shall enter into any treaty, confederation or alliance whatever between them, without the consent of the United States in Congress assembled, specifying accurately the purposes for which the same is to be entered into, and how long it shall continue.
>
> No State shall lay any imposts or duties, which may interfere with any stipulations in treaties, entered into by the United States in Congress assembled, with any king, prince or state, in pursuance of any treaties already proposed by Congress, to the courts of France and Spain. [22]

The main purpose for creating the Federal Union was to allow the States to pool their resources and establish a common agent to conduct their foreign affairs and provide for their common defense. In accordance with this objective, Article VI made provision for the military preparedness of the States. By its terms, the States agreed to each maintain an active armed force in cooperation with the supervision of the Federal Government. The States further agreed to each maintain an ample stock of munitions and other military supplies. The State militias were to be relied upon as the *backbone* of the

---

[22] *Ibid.*, p. 29.

common defense efforts of the United States. It was accordingly stipulated that "every State shall always keep up a well regulated and disciplined militia, sufficiently armed and accoutred."

As Article VI provided:

> No vessels of war shall be kept up in time of peace by any State, except such number only, as shall be deemed necessary by the United States in Congress assembled, for the defence of such State, or its trade; nor shall any body of forces be kept up by any State, in time of peace, except such number only, as in the judgment of the United States, in Congress assembled, shall be deemed requisite to garrison the forts necessary for the defence of such State; but every State shall always keep up a well regulated and disciplined militia, sufficiently armed and accoutred, and shall provide and constantly have ready for use, in public stores, a due number of field pieces and tents, and a proper quantity of arms, ammunition and camp equipage. [23]

Although the purpose of creating the United States of America was to pool their resources for purposes of common defense, the States wisely realized that occasions might arise when *direct self-defense* would be required. Whenever possible, of course, the Federal Government would be relied upon to defend the rights of any State from invasion. Yet, what if conditions did not permit the required delay before such a common defense could be provided? Within the Articles, we see that no State would be required to passively await action by the Federal Government when its safety or survival was at stake.

In acknowledgement of this natural right of self-defense, the remaining section of Article VI made provision for the States to defend themselves when required by existing circumstances:

> No State shall engage in any war without the consent of the United States in Congress assembled, unless such State be actually invaded by enemies, or shall have received certain advice of a resolution being formed by some nation of Indians to invade such State, and the danger is so imminent as not to admit of a delay till the United States in Congress assembled can be consulted: nor shall any State grant commissions to any ships or vessels of war, nor letters of marquee or reprisal, except it be after a declaration of war by the United States in Congress assembled, and then only against the kingdom or state and the subjects thereof, against which war has been so declared, and under such regulations as shall be established by the United States in Congress assembled, unless such State be infested by pirates, in which case vessels of war may be fitted out for that occasion, and kept so long as the danger shall continue, or until the United States in

---

[23] *Ibid.*, pp. 29-30.

Congress assembled, shall determine otherwise. [24]

Article VII

This short Article provided for the appointment of army officers in the common defense forces of the United States. By the terms of Article VII, each State could appoint all officers of the rank of Colonel or lower for all land-based troops provided by the State for the defense of the United States:

> When land-forces are raised by any State for the common defence, all officers of or under the rank of colonel, shall be appointed by the legislature of each State respectively, by whom such forces shall be raised, or in such manner as such State shall direct, and all vacancies shall be filled up by the State which first made the appointment. [25]

Article VIII

If the States intended to establish a common agent to provide for their common defense, then the expenses incurred from that defense effort should be borne by the several States. For this purpose, a "common treasury" would exist, and each State would contribute its share of revenue to this general fund. The contributions from the States to the common treasury would be proportionally based, not on their respective populations, but on the value of their land and the improvements made thereupon. The system of federal taxation, in other words, was to be based on the concept that *land is the chief source and measure of wealth*.

Article VII contains the rules for apportionment of federal taxes in its first section:

> All charges of war, and all other expences that shall be incurred for the common defence or general welfare, and allowed by the United States in Congress assembled, shall be defrayed out of a common treasury, which shall be supplied by the several States in proportion to the value of all land within each State, granted to or surveyed for any Person, as such land and the buildings and improvements thereon shall be estimated according to the mode as the United States in Congress assembled, shall from time to time direct and appoint. [26]

---

[24] *Ibid.*, p. 30.
[25] *Ibid.*, p. 30.
[26] *Ibid.*, p. 30.

The phrase "common defence and general welfare" merits attention, for this expression is also found within our present Federal Constitution, where it is used in precisely the same manner as it is here used in the Articles. The term was, as noted previously, copied directly from the Articles by those who wrote our current Constitution; its meaning in the new compact, therefore, can be no different than its meaning within the Articles of Confederation. It most clearly was not intended as a sweeping grant of power to authorize the Federal Government to tax and spend for any purpose that could be proclaimed as promoting the general welfare of the United States. On the contrary, it was intended as a *restrictive* provision on the tax-and-spend powers of the Federal Government. Only to pay for the costs of militarily defending the United States and to defer the costs of exercising the specific powers delegated to the Federal Government – *defined as the common defense and general welfare* – could taxes be raised for common treasury.

Although the Federal Government under the Articles could make requisitions, it could not directly collect such taxes. Instead, according to the remaining terms of Article VIII, it was the responsibility of the State governments to raise the requested funds and to tender the funds to the common treasury: "The taxes for paying that proportion shall be laid and levied by the authority and direction of the legislatures of the several States within the time agreed upon by the United States in Congress assembled." [27]

The experience of the colonies during the American Revolution, when the British Government attempted to use taxation as a means of subverting local governments, taught the Founding Fathers to fear a Federal Government possessing the power to levy taxes. The power to tax, they understood, was also the power to destroy. No common government, it was widely believed, should possess that much power.

By forcing the Federal Government to rely on the State governments for necessary revenue, however, the Articles effectively crippled the former. All too often, requests for revenue made by the Federal Government under the Articles went unheeded among many of the States. This provision of the Articles, widely regarded as the greatest defect in our first Federal Constitution, demonstrated the folly of allowing one level of government to be dependent on the other level for its revenue. Although the Constitution of 1787 satisfactorily remedied this defect by conveying a concurrent power to levy taxes to the Federal Government, the disastrous effects of consolidation and centralization following the War Between the States succeeded in once again introducing this problem in the United States. This time, however, the prob-

---

[27] *Ibid.*, p. 31.

lem is reversed. It is now the State governments who are forced to rely upon the Federal Government for much of their needed revenue.

Article IX

Article IX is by far the largest one of all, accounting for approximately forty percent of the text within the Articles of Confederation. Within this Article, the powers delegated to the Federal Government are presented and defined. Inasmuch as the Federal Government was intended to handle the foreign affairs of the States, including their interstate affairs, the powers delegated to the Federal Government in this Article were chiefly ones relating to those duties. In addition to establishing a Legislative Branch, the Ninth Article also made provision for the *judicial authority* of the United States.

The first section of this Article delegated to the Congress the exclusive power of declaring war and determining peace for the United States. It also authorized the Federal Government to exchange ambassadors with foreign nations, negotiate treaties, and enter into alliances with other countries. Congress was further empowered to establish the rules for the capture of "prizes" from enemies of the United States, to grant letters of marquee and reprisal in peace time, to try pirates and others who committed crimes on the high seas, and to establish courts of appeal in all cases of capture.

These powers were delegated in the following words:

> The United States in Congress assembled, shall have the sole and exclusive right and power of determining on peace and war, except in the cases mentioned in the sixth article – of sending and receiving ambassadors – entering into treaties and alliances, provided that no treaty of commerce shall be made whereby the legislative power of the respective States shall be restrained from imposing such imposts and duties on foreigners as their own people are subjected to, or from prohibiting the exportation or importation of any species of goods or commodities, whatsoever – of establishing rules for deciding in all cases, what captures on land or water shall be legal, and in what manner prizes taken by land or naval forces in the service of the United States shall be divided or appropriated – of granting letters of marquee and reprisal in times of peace – appointing courts for the trial of piracies and felonies committed on the high seas and establishing courts for receiving and determining finally appeals in all cases of captures, provided that no member of Congress shall be appointed a judge of any of the said courts. [28]

---

[28] *Ibid.*, p. 31.

Article IX further defined the judicial power of the United States, delegating to the United States the authority to decide such interstate issues as boundary disputes. By the terms of this Article, the federal judiciary was to serve as the final resort of appeal on all cases concerning interstate cases. An explicit guarantee was made to the States, however, that no State could be deprived of any territory within its established boundaries for the benefit of the Union. Such a guarantee would, of course, serve as a precedent for incorporating a similar guarantee within our present Federal Constitution.

Article IX delegated this authority with the following provisions:

> The United States in Congress assembled shall also be the last resort on appeal in all disputes and differences now subsisting or that hereafter may arise between two or more States concerning boundary, jurisdiction or any other cause whatever; which authority shall always be exercised in the manner following. Whenever the legislative or executive authority or lawful agent of any State in controversy with another shall present a petition to Congress stating the matter in question and praying for a hearing, notice thereof shall be given by order of Congress to the legislative or executive authority of the other State in controversy, and a day assigned for the appearance of the parties by their lawful agents, who shall then be directed to appoint by joint consent, commissioners or judges to constitute a court for hearing and determining the matter in question: but if they cannot agree, Congress shall name three persons out of each of the United States, and from the list of such persons each party shall alternately strike out one, the petitioners beginning, until the number shall be reduced to thirteen; and from that number not less than seven, nor more than nine names as Congress shall direct, shall in the presence of Congress be drawn out by lot, and the persons whose names shall be so drawn or any five of them, shall be commissioners or judges, to hear and finally determine the controversy, so always as a major part of the judges who shall hear the cause shall agree in the determination: and if either party shall neglect to attend at the day appointed, without showing reasons, which Congress shall judge sufficient, or being present shall refuse to strike, the Congress shall proceed to nominate three persons out of each State, and the secretary of Congress shall strike in behalf of such party absent or refusing; and the judgment and sentence of the court to be appointed, in the manner before prescribed, shall be final and conclusive; and if any of the parties shall refuse to submit to the authority of such court, or to appear or defend their claim or cause, the court shall nevertheless proceed to pronounce sentence, or judgment, which shall in like manner be final and decisive, the judgment or sentence and other proceedings being in either case transmitted to Congress, and lodged among the acts of Congress for the security of the parties concerned: provided that every commissioner, before he sits in judgment, shall take an oath to be administered by one of the judges of the supreme or superior court of the State, where the cause shall be tried, "well and truly to hear and determine the matter in question, according to the best of his

judgment, without favour, affection or hope of reward:" provided also, that no State shall be deprived of territory for the benefit of the United States.

All controversies concerning the private right of soil claimed under different grants of two or more States, whose jurisdictions as they may respect such lands, and the States which passed such grants are adjusted, the said grants or either of them being at the same time claimed to have originated antecedent to such settlement of jurisdiction, shall on the petition of either party to the Congress of the United States, be finally determined as near as may be in the same manner as before prescribed for deciding disputes respecting territorial jurisdiction between different States. [29]

The Ninth Article also delegated to the Federal Government the power to coin money of gold and silver, to establish a uniform system of weights and measures, to regulate Indian affairs, to appoint military officers in the armed forces of the United States, to make laws necessary for maintaining the Federal Government and the armed forces, and to establish and regulate post offices throughout the Confederacy. It is of interest to note that the Post Office, under the Articles, was required to charge an amount of postage sufficient to pay for its operating expenses.

These powers were delegated in the following language:

> The United States in Congress assembled shall also have the sole and exclusive right and power of regulating the alloy and value of coin struck by their own authority, or by that of the respective States – fixing the standard of weights and measures throughout the United States – regulating the trade and managing all affairs with the Indians, not members of any of the States, provided that the legislative right of any State within its own limits be not infringed or violated – establishing or regulating post-offices from one State to another, throughout all the United States, and exacting such postage on the papers passing thro' the same as may be requisite to defray the expences of the said office – appointing all officers of the land forces, in the service of the United States, excepting regimental officers – appointing all the officers of the naval forces, and commissioning all officers whatever in the service of the United States – making rules for the government and regulation of the said land and naval forces, and directing their operations. [30]

Recognizing the need for some standing authority to exist when the Congress was in recess, provision was made in the Ninth Article for a *Committee of the States*, to consist of one delegate from each State, to carry on the basic functions of the Federal Government during such periods of recess. The Congress was also empowered to appoint other committees and civil officers

---

[29] *Ibid.*, pp. 31-33.
[30] *Ibid.*, p. 33.

to perform the requisite *executive functions* of government. Furthermore, Congress could designate one of its members to serve as the "President" or presiding officer; but no member of Congress could serve in such a capacity for more than one year within a three-year period.

By the provisions of this Article, Congress was to handle all financial budgets for the United States. That body was also empowered to borrow money and issue bills of credit, with the requirement that it inform the States of the amount borrowed or issued every half-year. The United States was authorized to maintain a navy and, in cooperation with the States, land forces. The Ninth Article further allowed Congress to require quotas from the States to provide adequate defense for the Confederacy.

These provisions were stated as follows:

> The United States in Congress assembled shall have authority to appoint a committee, to sit in the recess of Congress, to be denominated "A Committee of the States," and to consist of one delegate from each State; and to appoint such other committees and civil officers as may be necessary for managing the general affairs of the United States under their direction – to appoint one of their number to preside, provided that no person be allowed to serve in the office of president more than one year in any term of three years; to ascertain the necessary sums of money to be raised for the service of the United States, and to appropriate and apply the same for defraying the public expences – to borrow money, or emit bills on the credit of the United States, transmitting every half year to the respective States an account of the sums of money so borrowed or emitted, – to build and equip a navy – to agree upon the number of land forces, and to make requisitions from each State for its quota, in proportion to the number of white inhabitants in such State; which requisition shall be binding, and thereupon the legislature of each State shall appoint the regimental officers, raise the men and cloath, arm and equip them in a soldier like manner, at the expence of the United States; and the officers and men so cloathed, armed and equipped shall march to the place appointed, and within the time agreed on by the United States in Congress assembled: But if the United States in Congress assembled shall, on consideration of circumstances judge proper that any State should not raise men, or should raise a smaller number than its quota, and that any other State should raise a greater number of men than the quota thereof, such extra number shall be raised, officered, cloathed, armed and equipped in the same manner as the quota of such State, unless the legislature of such State shall judge that such extra number cannot be safely spared out of the same, in which case they shall raise officer, cloath, arm and equip as many of such extra number as they judge can be safely spared. And the officers and men so cloathed, armed and equipped, shall march to the place appointed, and within the time agreed on by the United States in Congress assembled. [31]

---

[31] *Ibid.*, pp. 33-34.

All decisions of consequence required a majority vote within the Congress, except in certain instances when a three-fourths majority was required. Those decisions requiring the assent of at least nine States in Congress assembled were the following: engaging in war, granting letters of marquee and reprisal in time of peace, entering into treaties and alliances, coining money, regulating the value of coins, determining the budget for the common defense, issuing bills of credit, borrowing money, appropriating funds, deciding the quantity of war ships needed and the number of land and sea forces required, and appointing a "Commander-in-Chief" of the Army or Navy. The only act of Congress that required less than a majority vote was daily adjournment.

Article IX made these provisions as follows:

> The United States in Congress assembled shall never engage in a war, nor grant letters of marquee and reprisal in time of peace, nor enter into any treaties or alliances, nor coin money, nor regulate the value thereof, nor ascertain the sums and expences necessary for the defence and welfare of the United States, or any of them, nor emit bills, nor borrow money on the credit of the United States, nor appropriate money, nor agree upon the number of vessels of war, to be built or purchased, or the number of land or sea forces to be raised, nor appoint a commander in chief of the army or navy, unless nine States assent to the same: nor shall a question on any other point, except for adjourning from day to day be determined, unless by the votes of a majority of the United States in Congress assembled. [32]

Finally, Article IX authorized the Congress to adjourn at any time and to hold sessions at any location within the United States. No recess was to be longer than six months, and the monthly proceedings of Congress were to be published in an official *Journal*, except those relating to treaties, alliances, and military operations which, in the opinion of the federal legislature, required secrecy. The votes of each delegate could be recorded in the Congressional *Journal* and, at the request of a State's delegates, a copy of the *Journal* would be furnished to the State legislature for review.

As the concluding section of Article IX states:

> The Congress of the United States shall have power to adjourn to any time within the year, and to any place within the United States, so that no period of adjournment be for a longer duration than the space of six Months, and shall publish the Journal of their proceedings monthly, except such parts thereof relating to treaties, alliances or military operations, as in their judgment require secrecy; and the yeas and nays of the delegates of

---

[32] *Ibid.*, p. 34.

each State on any question shall be entered on the Journal, when it is desired by any delegate; and the delegates of a State, or any of them, at his or their request shall be furnished with a transcript of the said Journal, except such parts as are above excepted, to lay before the legislatures of the several States. [33]

Although the long-established wisdom of mankind dictates that the legislative, executive, and judicial powers of a government should never be vested in a single body, the Founding Fathers did not believe that this general maxim should apply to the Federal Government established by the Articles of Confederation, considering that so few powers were actually delegated to that government and that the Federal Government was so heavily dependent upon the State governments. When the decision was made to institute a new Federal Government, vested with greater authority, however, the Constitutional Convention of 1787 wisely took the precaution of dividing the Federal Government into separate and distinct branches and of establishing a system of checks and balances.

Article X

The Tenth Article delegated authority to the Committee of the States, which was to serve as the Federal Government during the recess periods of Congress. The powers of this committee, however were severely restricted to only those powers of Congress that the legislature might deem proper to delegate. Authority was explicitly denied to the Committee of the States, however, to exercise any power that required a three-fourths majority vote in the Congress. The Committee of States, in essence, served as little more than a symbolic token of the Federal Government.

The Committee of the States was provided for in these words:

> The committee of the States, or any nine of them, shall be authorized to execute, in the recess of Congress, such of the powers of Congress as the United States in Congress assembled, by the consent of nine States, shall from time to time think expedient to vest them with; provided that no power be delegated to the said committee, for the exercise of which, by the articles of confederation, the voice of nine States in the Congress of the United States assembled is requisite. [34]

---

[33] *Ibid.*, pp. 34-35.
[34] *Ibid.*, p. 35.

Article XI

The possibility that other colonies or provinces might be added to the Federal Union was provided for within Article XI. Canada, in particular, was cited by name as a possible future State in the Union, and by the terms of this Article that province was essentially extended an *invitation* to join the United States of America. If Canada wished to join our political Union, this portion of the Articles of Confederation declared that she would definitely be admitted into the Federal Union. "Canada acceding to this confederation, and joining in the measures of the United States," it was provided, "shall be admitted into, and entitled to all the advantages of this Union." The admission of any other province or State, however, would first require the approval of three-fourths of the existing States in the Union: "but no other colony shall be admitted into the same, unless such admission be agreed to by nine States." [35]

Despite such provisions, no other colony or province was ever admitted into the Union under the Articles of Confederation. Canada refused to accept the invitation thus offered to her, and the western Territories originally claimed by some of the States were not admitted into the Federal Union as new States until after the adoption of our present U.S. Constitution. Throughout its eight-year existence, the Union under the Articles consisted of only the original thirteen States.

Article XII

The Twelfth Article made provision for the assumption by the Federal Government of all debts incurred by the Second Continental Congress "in pursuance of the present Confederation." Of particular interest is the phraseology used to describe the establishment of the Federal Union, which establishment is referred to as "*the assembling of the United States.*"

Article XII presents this provision in the following language:

> All bills of credit emitted, monies borrowed and debts contracted by, or under the authority of Congress, before the assembling of the United States, in pursuance of the present confederation, shall be deemed and considered as a charge against the United States, for payment and satisfaction whereof the said United States, and the public faith are hereby solemnly pledged. [36]

---

[35] *Ibid.*, p. 35.
[36] *Ibid.*, p. 35.

Article XIII

The last Article consists of two sections, one of which contains what amounts to a *Supremacy Clause*, which asserts that the Articles of Confederation and all laws to be made in pursuance of that Constitution would constitute the supreme law of the land. The other section made provision for amending the Articles by the States. This Article is of particular interest, inasmuch as it bears a relationship to certain provisions of our present Federal Constitution, and it therefore merits close attention.

As Article XIII states:

> Every State shall abide by the determinations of the United States in Congress assembled, on all questions which by this confederation are submitted to them. And the Articles of confederation shall be inviolably observed by every State, and the union shall be perpetual; nor shall any alteration at any time hereafter be made in any of them; unless such alteration be agreed to in a Congress of the United States, and be afterwards confirmed by the legislatures of every State. [37]

A constitution of government is the fundamental law, whether it be a constitution for a sovereign State or nation, or for a federation or league of States. As such, it should not be tampered with or altered for light and transient reasons. The requirement provided for amending the Articles, however, was especially stringent, in that *unanimity* of opinion among the States is a phenomenon that would occur only in the most rare of circumstances. For this reason, the amendment process incorporated into our present Federal Constitution, while borrowing heavily from the Articles, reduces the required number of States needed to ratify an amendment to a three-fourths majority.

Of even greater significance is the section of Article XIII dealing with the *supremacy of the Federal Constitution*. Here we see proof positive that sovereign States may voluntarily undertake obligations and make agreements among themselves without ceasing to be sovereign. The very fact that the States did undertake such obligations and commitments proves that they were sovereign. *Only sovereign bodies can create a supreme law or constitution of government.*

Exactly what is it that is declared to be supreme by this Article? The statement that the Federal Constitution shall be "inviolably observed by every State," indicates that the Articles of Confederation constituted the *source* of the supreme law in the United States during the time the Union under it endured. The acts of the United States, in Congress assembled, *"on all questions*

---

[37] *Ibid.*, p. 35.

which by this confederation are submitted to them," would, together with the Articles themselves, comprise *the supreme law of the land.*

The qualifying clause served as a *restriction* on the proclaimed supremacy of the Articles, *limiting* the authority of Congress to the terms of the compact. In other words, laws of Congress *made in pursuance of the Constitution*, together with the Constitution itself, would constitute the supreme law throughout the United States. Laws *not* made in pursuance of the Articles, of course, would not be supreme; nor would they even be laws. They would be simply unconstitutional, and hence, null, void, and of no force.

The student of constitutional government could learn much about the nature of supremacy within our current Federal Union by comparing this provision in the Articles of Confederation with what is termed the "Supremacy Clause" of our present Federal Constitution. Like the Articles of Confederation, the Constitution of 1787 proclaims only that the Constitution, treaties made under its authority, and all laws *made in pursuance of the Constitution* shall constitute the supreme law of the land.

Concluding Words

The Articles of Confederation close with a concluding paragraph that declares:

> And Whereas it hath pleased the Great Governor of the World to incline the hearts of the legislatures we respectively represent in Congress, to approve of, and to authorize us to ratify the said articles of confederation and perpetual union. Know Ye that we the undersigned delegates, by virtue of the power and authority to us given for that purpose, do by these presents, in the name and in behalf of our respective constituents, fully and entirely ratify and confirm each and every of the said articles of confederation and perpetual union, and all and singular the matters and things therein contained: And we do further solemnly plight and engage the faith of our respective constituents, that they shall abide by the determinations of the United States in Congress assembled, on all questions, which by the said confederation are submitted to them. And that the articles thereof shall be inviolably observed by the States we respectively represent, and that the union shall be perpetual. In Witness whereof we have hereunto set our hands in Congress. Done at Philadelphia in the State of Pennsylvania the ninth day of July, in the Year of our Lord one Thousand seven Hundred and Seventy-eight, and in the third year of the independence of America. [38]

---

[38] *Ibid.*, pp. 35-36.

These concluding words were followed by the signatures of the delegates, which were added to the document over a three-year period, from 1778 to 1781. The signers and the respective States they represented were Josiah Bartlett and John Wentworth, Jr. in behalf of New Hampshire; John Hancock, Samuel Adams, Elbridge Gerry, Francis Dana, James Lovell, and Samuel Holten for Massachusetts; William Ellery, Henry Marchant, and John Collins of Rhode Island; Roger Sherman, Samuel Huntington, Oliver Wolcott, Titus Hosmer, and Andrew Adams from Connecticut; James Duane, Francis Lewis, William Duer, and Gouverneur Morris for New York; and John Witherspoon and Nathaniel Scudder in behalf of New Jersey.

Other signers were Robert Morris, Daniel Roberdeau, Jonathan Bayard Smith, William Clingar, and Joseph Reed for Pennsylvania; Thomas McKean, John Dickinson, and Nicholas Van Dyke of Delaware; John Hanson and Daniel Carroll from Maryland; Richard Henry Lee, John Banister, Thomas Adams, Jonathan Harvie, and Francis Lightfoot Lee on the part of Virginia; John Penn, Cornelius Harnett, and Jonathan Williams for North Carolina; Henry Laurens, William Henry Drayton, Jonathan Mathews, Richard Hutson, and Thomas Heyward, Jr. of South Carolina; and Jonathan Walton, Edward Telfair, and Edward Langworthy in behalf of Georgia.

A Federation of Sovereign States

Prior to undertaking our examination of the provisions of the Articles of Confederation, we provided a definition for a *constitution* of government. That definition was in the following language:

> A political constitution is an official, formal set of written or unwritten rules that define a government, establish its departments and divisions, assign functions to the various governmental organs, and delegate specifically enumerated powers to the various organs of government. By performing these functions, a constitution does much more than merely erect the framework of a government. *It also establishes the limits of power of the government thus created.*

From our examination of the Articles, it should now be settled beyond doubt that the Articles of Confederation was indeed a written constitution of government. As has been demonstrated, it did establish and provide for the departments and divisions of a Federal Government, which included a Congress, a Committee of the States, judicial courts, and various agencies to administer the law. The Articles also assigned functions to the various organs of the Federal Government. The Congress was to perform the function of the

Legislative Branch, a function that would be assumed by a Committee of the States during recess periods. The courts to be appointed by Congress were assigned a judicial function, and the various administrative agencies were assigned an executive function. In support of this last function, the Articles also provided for the armed forces of the United States, including land and sea forces, as well as for use of the State militias in the common defense of the Union.

In addition, the Articles defined and described the powers delegated by the States to the Federal Government. These powers were defined at great length in Article IX, and the specific powers of the Committee of the States were defined in Article X. And like all good constitutions of government, the Articles of Confederation served to limit the powers of the Federal Government to those that were expressly delegated to it.

The Articles of Confederation, it is apparent, fulfilled every key requirement that defines a constitution of government. Those Articles thus comprised the first Constitution of the United States. This was the Federal Constitution that formally established the Federal Union under the style of "The United States of America," and that created the first Federal Government for the United States. The system on which the Union "between the States" was founded was decidedly federal in nature, resting on the foundation of the sovereignty of the States. And the form of government on which Union was based was republican in character, as distinguished from either democracy or monarchy. The political system established by the Articles of Confederation was clearly a Federal Republic.

The organic structure of the United States was unequivocally defined within the Articles of Confederation. Under its terms, sovereignty resided in the peoples of the respective States, and the States were united only in their foreign and interstate affairs. In all intrastate matters, or affairs internal or domestic, the States retained exclusive jurisdiction to govern themselves. The design of the political system established by the Articles reveals the intention of the Founding Fathers to reap the benefits of unity while preventing the rights of man from being exposed to potential invasions by a centralized government.

Commenting on the significance of the Articles of Confederation, Russell Hoover Quynn wrote in his book, *The Constitutions of Abraham Lincoln and Jefferson Davis*:

> Note the great effort to bring the sovereign States into an effective and perpetual Union; the many repetitions of the phrase "the United States, in Congress assembled." The intent was a Federal Union, the style of the Confederacy to be, as Article I gives it, "The United States of Amer-

ica." With Article 2 comes the emphatic declaration that each State would retain "its sovereignty, freedom, and independence, and every power, jurisdiction, and right, which is not by this Confederation expressly delegated to the United States, in Congress assembled."

...By declaring their freedom, each had become an independent, sovereign State....This we have seen was a fact, historically true, though many orators from Webster to Lincoln, and many "historians" have made other claims, most of which were meant to be justification for a cruel, needless, Civil War. Save for such functions facing without — better performed as a unit before the world — each State was sovereign over its own internal affairs. [39]

Perhaps the most remarkable lesson to be gleaned from our study of the Articles of Confederation is that the States could retain their "sovereignty, freedom, and independence" while yet united by means of a Federal Union under a Federal Constitution that was declared to be the supreme law of the land. Although many political theorists, since the days of Daniel Webster and Abraham Lincoln, have dared to assert that such a political system is theoretically impossible, the Articles stand as stark testimony that such a system of government is indeed possible, both in theory and in practice.

Not only were the States of the Union proclaimed to be sovereign in the second of the Articles, but in Article III the very purpose of the Federal Union – *the reason why the States created the United States of America* – was identified as being the preservation of the sovereignty of the States. "The said States hereby severally enter into a firm *league of friendship* with each other," a league styled the United States of America, "to assist each other against all force offered to, or attacks made upon them, or any of them, on account of religion, *sovereignty*, trade, or any other pretence whatever." Words could not be plainer than those used in the Third Article. The United States of America was created to secure and defend the sovereignty of the States.

---

[39] Russell Hoover Quynn, *The Constitutions of Abraham Lincoln and Jefferson Davis*, Exposition Press, New York, 1959, pp. 231-232.

Chapter Five
Review and Summary

Thus far in our inquiry into the origin of the United States of America, we have examined the rise of American civilization from the earliest settlements in North America and the evolution of those settlements into mature colonies of Great Britain. We have also traced the evolution of the federal system of government from the period of the colonial struggle with the British Government, through the American Revolution and the Declaration of Independence, through the Treaty of Paris of 1783, to the formation of a league of sovereign States under the Articles of Confederation.

To complete our analysis of the origin of the United States, we should direct our attention to the final evolutionary stages of our present Federal Constitution during the historical era of 1781 to 1789, a period of approximately eight years. Further investigations will take us through the "Critical Period," when the weaknesses within the Articles of Confederation became apparent to many, through the highly significant Constitutional Convention of 1787, to the final adoption of our present U.S. Constitution by the States and the addition of the Bill of Rights.

Before proceeding to an examination of the drafting and ratification of our current Federal Constitution, however, we should briefly review and summarize the main principles we have already raised. By way of summary, the following concepts and facts should be readily apparent to the student of constitutional government:

1. American civilization was born during the years 1608 to 1620, with the establishment of colonies at Jamestown and Plymouth Plantation. The two key factors that helped to ensure the future greatness of American civilization were the early colonial acceptance of government based on the consent of the governed and the early rejection of collectivism. The first of these significant milestones came with the creation of the Virginia House of Burgesses in 1619 and the signing of the Mayflower Compact by the Pilgrim Fathers a year later. The other came as a result of the discovery in both early settlements that collectivism results in death, starvation, and slavery. Only by embracing the concepts of limited government, free enterprise, and private property rights were the two fledgling colonies able to survive and prosper. The success of these early settlements inspired others to leave the Old World to make new

homes for themselves in North America, which represented a new beginning for mankind and a great asylum for those fleeing political tyranny and religious persecution. Self-reliance and rugged individualism quickly became the hallmarks of the young, but rapidly growing, American civilization.

2. The peoples migrating to North America from the Old World eventually became subjects of Great Britain, forming thirteen distinct and separate colonies within the British Empire, named Georgia, South Carolina, North Carolina, Virginia, Maryland, Pennsylvania, Delaware, New Jersey, New York, Connecticut, Rhode Island, Massachusetts, and New Hampshire. These colonies had much in common, including a common allegiance to the same mother country, a thriving inter-colonial trade, and a common language. Each colony, however, developed separately and was politically independent from the others. Two experiments with political unity were made by some of the Northern colonies, resulting in the temporary unions of the New England Confederation and the Dominion of New England. Although each of these political unions was of a temporary nature, this experience with inter-colonial unity clearly demonstrated the American preference for the federal system of government.

3. The American colonists enjoyed, generally, the rights of Englishmen and formed colonial legislatures for themselves, each democratically constituted. While all of the colonies were loyal to the British Crown, each one possessed rights to self-government and was allowed to exercise a very high degree of local autonomy over its own domestic affairs. Especially significant in this regard was the long-standing right of the colonies not to be taxed except by their own elected representatives in their respective assemblies.

4. British policy toward the colonies was founded on a socialist system of exploitation historically termed "mercantilism." Such a system was characterized by a bureaucratic, highly centralized government that sought to regulate and control the development of the colonies to the advantage of a monied aristocracy in England. Many of the measures of the mercantile system were, for a number of years, enforced with laxness and lack of vigor. Following the French and Indian War, however, a new Tory government in London attempted to invigorate the enforcement of mercantilism on the thirteen American colonies. The rights of the colonists as Englishmen were denied by the government of King George III, and that government laid claim to unlimited power, thus subverting the British Constitution.

5. The colonies were determined to defend their rights against the British assault, but their protests were to no avail. Their liberties were curtailed, their right to self-government was denied, and a design to reduce them to slavery was made manifest. When the British Government resorted to martial force to subdue the colonies, the colonies were determined to resist force with

force, resulting in the firing of the first shots of the Revolutionary War in April of 1775 at Lexington and Concord. For more than a year after the commencement of a shooting war, the sole objective of the colonies was merely to secure recognition of their rights within the British Empire.

6. As the conflict with Great Britain intensified, the need for colonial unity became apparent. In 1765, an unprecedented number of colonies cooperated in an inter-colonial meeting known as the Stamp Act Congress. By 1772, all thirteen colonies, for the first time, were informally united by means of Committees of Correspondence. Two years later, twelve of the colonies sent representatives to the First Continental Congress; and by 1775, all thirteen colonies were represented in the Second Continental Congress. True colonial unity for common defense was thus finally achieved, and none too soon. By the time the Second Continental Congress convened, the Revolutionary War had already started.

7. With the outbreak of warfare between the colonies and the Crown, the colonial hope of reconciliation quickly faded and was replaced by a growing desire to seek political independence from the mother country. By the summer of 1776, the colonial assemblies all shared this desire and accordingly dispatched appropriate instructions to their representatives in Congress assembled. On July 2nd, the Congress formally approved the resolution of Richard Henry Lee of Virginia that the colonies should be declared free and independent States. Two days later, that body approved the final draft of the unanimous Declaration of Independence. That document declared that the colonies had seceded from the British Empire and had become "free and independent States," or *sovereign States*. To justify such action, the Declaration presented the Lockean-Jeffersonian concept of natural rights and listed a number of serious crimes committed against the American States by the British Government. With the announcement of secession from the Empire, the Revolutionary War was transformed into a War of Independence.

8. The Continental Congress was not a *de jure* government, although it was forced, by military necessity, to assume some of the *de facto* functions of a general government. It would be required to assume this role until such time as the newly independent States could establish a lawfully constituted Federal Government under the Articles of Confederation. The Continental Congress, serving as the united front for the thirteen States, patriotically coordinated the successful war effort against Great Britain.

9. The objective of the War of Independence, as expressed within the Declaration of Independence, was to secure, preserve, and defend the sovereignty of the States. By the terms of the Treaty of Paris of 1783 —signed by the representatives of Great Britain, Spain, France, and the American States — the British Government specifically acknowledged the sovereignty of the

States, listing each State by name. Within the Articles of Confederation, which went into effect two years prior to the signing of the peace treaty, the several States expressly retained their sovereignty and asserted that the Federal Union created by them – styled "The United States of America" – was intended to preserve and protect their respective sovereign rights. Those Articles constituted the first Federal Constitution for the United States, and they established the Federal Republic and provided for our first Federal Government.

10. Finally, it should be noted as a point of significance that the order of superiority established by the organic structure of the United States is easily ascertained. The States created the Articles of Confederation, which in turn established the Union and the Federal Government. The general government and the Union were only what the Federal Constitution said they were, and that Constitution was only what the States said it was. The States created it, and only by the assent of those States could its provisions be changed through amendment. Supremacy within the political system clearly resided in the States, whose respective peoples were sovereign. All legitimate authority flowed from that seat of sovereignty, which was born on July 4, 1776, including the Federal Union, the Federal Constitution, the Federal Government, and the Federal Republic.

As has already been demonstrated, the States retained their sovereignty while in the Federal Union created by the Articles of Confederation. In forming a more perfect Union under the Constitution of 1787, did the States voluntarily consent to throw away the sovereignty to which they had previously clung as a priceless possession? Or was that sovereignty retained by the States in the new Union? Did the adoption of the Constitution of 1787 destroy the federal system and erect a National Union in its place? Or did it perpetuate the existing Federal Union? Stated differently, was there a *fundamental change* in the organic structure of the United States effected by the adoption of our present U.S. Constitution? Or did that Constitution merely enlarge the powers of the Federal Government and divide the functions of government into three separate branches, but otherwise leave the basic structure of the Union unaltered? Let us continue with our inquiry and discover the answers to these significant questions.

Chapter Six
The Movement for a New Constitution

Much has been written on the crucial years immediately following the War of Independence, and most of what has been written has portrayed that period of our history as years of bleakness and despair. The post-war economic depression and the indebtedness of the States, in particular, have long been cited as the characterizing features of the 1780's by historians determined to focus on the weaknesses of the Articles of Confederation. The picture generally portrayed is that the United States, during this "Critical Period," was stagnated by economic distress, that no progress was made under the Articles, and that the distressing situation was alleviated only when the Articles were supplanted with the Constitution of 1787. Such a view, however, can be sustained only by exaggerating the inefficiencies of the Articles and the distress then experienced by the United States.

Commenting on this exaggerated view of the our historical development under the Articles, Professors Richard N. Current, T. Harry Williams, and Frank Freidel observed:

> Historians used to refer to the 1780's as the "Critical Period" of American history – a period supposedly of impending chaos and collapse from which the nation was rescued only by the timely adoption of a new Constitution. Actually the 1780's were years of hopeful striving rather than black despair, of economic recovery and not merely depression, of governmental progress under the Articles of Confederation despite temporary failures. [1]

Despite some inherent weaknesses, the Articles of Confederation actually served as an ideal constitution of government for the infant United States, and a number of positive benefits resulted from our first Federal Constitution. Chief among those benefits was the unifying effect the Articles had on the newly independent States. Although desirous of some degree of unity after declaring their independence, the States were understandably distrustful of centralized power in general and were determined to voluntarily place as few restrictions on the exercise of their sovereignty as possible.

---

[1] Richard N. Current, T. Harry Williams, and Frank Freidel, *American History: A Survey*, Second Edition, Alfred A. Knopf, 1966, p. 120.

Representing a compromise between an efficient general government and widespread fears of centralized power, the Articles were the only plan of government that could have united the newly independent States. Indeed, had an attempt been made to unite the thirteen States in a closer Union at this period of time, it is highly doubtful if the States would ever have agreed to unite with one another. This is a point stressed by the authors of *The American Pageant: A History of the Republic*:

> Despite their defects, the Articles of Confederation were a significant steppingstone toward the present Constitution. They clearly outlined the general powers that were to be exercised by the central government, such as making treaties and establishing a postal service. As the first written Constitution of the Republic, the Articles kept alive the flickering ideal of Union and held the States together – until such time as they were ripe for a strong Constitution by peaceful, evolutionary methods. The anemic Articles represented what the States regarded as an alarming surrender of their power. Without this intermediary jump, they probably would never have consented to the breathtaking leap from the old boycott Association of 1774 to the [present] Constitution of the United States. [2]

By initially creating a Federal Government with weak powers and little independence of action, the Founding Fathers were acting upon the wise maxim that, to err on the side of caution is preferable to erring in the other extreme, and is also more easily remedied. They clearly understood that it is always easier to *enlarge* the powers of a general government than it is to *reduce* those powers. Their experiences with the British Government had taught them the folly of entrusting too much power to any central government.

Specific areas in which genuine progress was realized under the Articles of Confederation included relations with foreign powers, international trade, the U.S. territorial possessions, Indian relations, and the peopling of the frontier. The Congress under the Articles successfully negotiated the Treaty of Paris of 1783, for example, in which the sovereignty and independence of the thirteen States was formally acknowledged by the British Government. When that government refused to fully comply with all parts of the peace treaty, including the withdrawal of all of its troops from the U.S. territorial possessions, the Congress faithfully represented the interests of the States by demanding full compliance with the terms of peace.

Under the Articles of Confederation, a number of influential foreign powers exchanged ambassadors with the United States. The French Government, for instance, willingly received Thomas Jefferson as the American min-

---

[2] Thomas A. Bailey and David M. Kennedy, *The American Pageant: A History of the Republic*, Sixth Edition, D.C. Heath and Company, Lexington, 1979, pp. 123-124.

ister to that country. Even King George III was willing to at least *receive* an American ambassador. Although the British Government refused to reciprocate, it did receive John Adams, who served ably as the American minister to London under the Articles.

The Congress under the Articles also negotiated highly satisfactory commercial treaties with a number of European nations, including the Netherlands in 1782, Sweden in 1783, and Prussia in 1785. In addition, the Federal Government negotiated a commercial treaty with the Sultan of Morocco in 1786 that allowed American ships to sail the Mediterranean Sea free from the depredations of some of the Barbary pirates. The climax of U.S. commercial ventures overseas under the Articles came in 1784-1785, when the *Empress of China*, without benefit of treaty, opened highly profitable trade routes to the Orient.

Under the Articles of Confederation, significant progress was made in the area of crafting a policy toward a portion of the western Territories originally claimed by the several States. After several attempts to devise a satisfactory territorial policy, a solution was finally found in the Northwest Ordinance of 1787. By the provisions of this measure, from three to five States were to be created from the Northwestern Territories. And as soon as any of these Territories attained sufficient population, that Territory was to be admitted into the Union "on an equal footing with the original States." [3]

In 1785 and 1786, the Congress under the Articles successfully negotiated treaties with the Iroquois and other Indian tribes, whereby the Indians agreed to surrender all claims to a section of land north of the Ohio River. When a number of Indians attempted to repudiate the treaties, Congress instructed the armed forces of the United States to protect American soil and eventually dispatched Revolutionary War hero George Rogers Clark to battle the Indians.

The peopling of the western Territories was inaugurated under the Articles of Confederation, when hardy pioneers like Daniel Boone began leading settlers to the new frontiers that lay beyond the Appalachians. No longer restrained by the British-imposed Proclamation Line of 1763, the westward march of American civilization signaled the birth of *Manifest Destiny*. Even under the Articles, it was clear to one and all that the future held much promise for the United States.

Considering the many benefits bestowed upon the United States by the Articles of Confederation, it is not surprising that a large number of Americans held our first Federal Constitution in high regard. Thomas Jefferson, for one, hailed the Federal Union created by the Articles as the best one "existing

---

[3] Richard N. Current, T. Harry Williams, and Frank Freidel, *Op. cit.*, quoted on p. 125.

or that ever did exist." To compare the Federal Government under the Articles with the European governments, noted the Philosopher of the Revolution, was like comparing "heaven and hell." [4]

The Critical Period

Although the Articles of Confederation merited the praise it received from many quarters, the first Constitution of the United States was defective in several areas, *as even its strongest supporters willingly acknowledged*. Its defects, however, were greatly magnified by events that would have distressed the United States regardless of which type of constitutional system had been adopted by the States. The economic and fiscal woes that occurred during the Critical Period of the 1780's were caused, not by the Articles, but by the great struggle to win independence from Great Britain.

The price paid by the States to secure their independence from Great Britain had far exceeded the blood, sweat, and tears of American patriots. The War of Independence had also been a major financial burden on the States, and when the war was over they found themselves saddled with heavy debts. Adding to the financial and commercial difficulties caused by the heavy debts, the British Government, following the war, closed off its Empire to American exports. British merchants, however, were eager to sell their goods to American buyers, and cheap British imports tended to retard the development of manufacturing in the United States. All these factors combined to produce a general economic depression in the United States, a depression that did not bottom out until 1786, one year before the historical Grand Convention of the States was held in Philadelphia.

The post-war economic and financial woes faced by the young Republic meant that the States rarely, if ever, had sufficient revenue available to fund their own governments, let alone adequate revenue to fulfill the requisitions of the Federal Government. Requests for funds from the States, therefore, often went partially or wholly unfulfilled, and the Federal Government was often forced to rely upon only *a quarter of the revenue* it had requested from the States.

It must again be stressed that the fiscal problems suffered by the United States extended beyond any weaknesses within the Articles of Confederation. Even if the Federal Government had been delegated the power to levy taxes under the Articles, it would have encountered difficulty trying to collect those taxes. The peoples of the several States, at this period, simply did not have

---

[4] Thomas A. Bailey and David M. Kennedy, *Op. cit.*, quoted on p. 123.

sufficient wherewithal to adequately sustain two levels of government.

Within the States, revenue to fund government functions was derived chiefly from a direct tax on land and its improvements. This revenue was supplemented by harbor fees and customs duties in most States, and in Maryland additional revenue was raised by means of an income tax. Although the tariffs levied by the States were primarily aimed at imports from foreign countries, to a certain extent the tariffs formed trade barriers between the States themselves. Such *interstate tariffs* constituted significant infringements on free enterprise and free trade *within* the United States. Although all sectors of the American economy were adversely affected by these interstate trade restrictions, the commercial interests of the Republic were especially harmed by the interstate rivalry.

The agrarian sector of the American economy was especially hard hit during the Critical Period. The post-war deflation, coupled with the tax burden placed upon their land, caused many hard-pressed farmers to demand relief in the form of paper money. Seven of the States heeded their cries for relief and began issuing such currency, thereby inflating prices and reducing the value of the monetary standard. Under the Articles, the Federal Government was powerless to prevent the States from undermining the rights in private property through this pernicious practice.

Chief among the inflationists of this period was tiny Rhode Island, which went so far as to declare its cheap paper money *legal tender*. All creditors having claims within that State were thus required to either accept the paper money or lose the right to collect their debts. But if Rhode Island turned a callous ear to the creditors, who loudly protested against this fiscal maneuver, the other New England States turned a callous ear to the desperate cries of relief from their highly taxed but debt-ridden farmers. In various parts of New England, distressed mobs of farmers created civil unrest, and in Massachusetts a virtual civil war erupted. At a time when hard money was extremely scarce, Massachusetts required that its farmers pay in specie, not merely their land taxes, but also their private debts to mortgage holders and other creditors. And the punishment for failure to meet debt obligations was harsh. Indebted farmers found their mortgages foreclosed and their properties seized, and on occasion they were sent to debtor's prison.

Many of the hard-pressed farmers in Massachusetts were veterans of the War of Independence, and they were willing to resist with force any attempt to seize their possessions. Banding together in the summer of 1786 under the leadership of Daniel Shays, a former Captain in the Continental Army, the rebellious farmers began disrupting court sessions and sheriff's auctions in an attempt to suspend all debt collections in the central region of the State. They also issued demands for tax relief, a wholesale moratorium on debt collections, abolition of debtor's prison, and the relocation of the State capital from wealthy Boston to the interior of the State.

When the demands of the Shaysites were not met by the State authorities, the rebel troops marched on Springfield in January, 1787, to seize the federal arsenal located there. To put down the rebellion, an army of State militiamen was dispatched from Boston, and following a pitched battle the Shaysites were scattered. Although Shays' Rebellion proved to be a military disaster, the Massachusetts authorities eventually conceded to the cries for relief from the farmers, especially in regard to tax relief and postponement of debt payments. And Daniel Shays and other key leaders of the rebellion, though initially sentenced to death, were eventually pardoned by the authorities.

The economic and fiscal woes confronting the young Republic fortunately proved to be of only a temporary nature. As the authors of *The American Pageant: A History of the Republic* point out, after the depression bottomed out in 1786, the dark clouds over the economy began to quickly dissipate:

> The nationwide picture was actually brightening before the Constitution was drafted. Nearly half the States had not issued semi-worthless paper currency; and some of the monetary black sheep showed signs of returning to the sound-money fold. Congressional control of commerce was in sight, specifically by means of an amendment to the Articles of Confederation. Prosperity was beginning to emerge from the fog of depression. By 1789 overseas shipping had largely regained its place in the commercial world. If conditions had been as grim in 1787 as painted by foes of the Articles, the move for a new Constitution would hardly have encountered such heated opposition. [5]

The Plot to Establish a Military Dictatorship

Far more alarming than the economic and fiscal distress suffered by the United States during this period, however, were a number of sinister maneuvers that occurred within the Continental Army. The treason of Benedict Arnold during the War of Independence had served notice that not all the high-ranking officers within the Army were truly loyal to the great cause of individual freedom and republican government for which the war was being waged. Some officers of the Army thoroughly detested the republican form and the federal system of government, believing that the only government

---

[5] *Ibid.*, p. 128.

worthy of their support was a National Monarchy sufficiently strong enough to crush any State that resisted the will of a highly centralized regime.

The threat posed by these monarchists within the Army was compounded by the financial straits within which the Federal Government was required to act. Due to lack of sufficient funds, Congress had been unable to pay the soldiers who fought in the War of Independence. Although General George Washington had generously volunteered his services to the cause of independence at no charge to the United States, the great bulk of his Army could not afford such a charitable attitude. They were required by economic necessity, however, to accept *promissory notes* in lieu of payment for their services. As the war came to an end, the United States thus found itself with an idle, standing army of veterans impatiently waiting for Congress to pay its great debt to them, a debt that Congress could not pay.

That some scheming individuals tried to exploit this delicate situation in an attempt to use the Army to force a *Military Dictatorship* on the United States is a matter of record. In the *Anas*, for example, Thomas Jefferson made reference to such sinister schemes:

> Before the establishment of our present government a very extensive combination had taken place in New York and the Eastern States among that description of people who were partly monarchial in principle or frightened with Shays's Rebellion and the impotence of the old Congress. Delegates in different places had actually had consultations on the subject of seizing on the powers of a government and establish them by force; had corresponded with one another, and had sent a deputy to General Washington to solicit his co-operation. He refused to join them. [6]

In John Fiske's *Critical Period*, published in 1888, one particular incident within the Army to establish a Military Dictatorship in 1782 is fully presented. This particular incident occurred after peace had been established but before the British Redcoats had been completely withdrawn from New York. The fears of Congress quickly turned away from the British Army and toward the American Army, whose soldiers were still awaiting their promised pay. The concern in Congress was so great that some members proposed disbanding the Continental Army despite the fact some British forces were still on American soil.

While Congress debated this question, a number of high-ranking officers in the Army decided to make their move to forcibly replace the Articles of Confederation with a monarchy. Although all of those involved are not known, the conspirators undoubtedly included General Knox and General

---

[6] Richard S. Poppen (ed.), *Thomas Jefferson*, St. Louis, 1904, p. 13.

Steuben. The plot commenced with a letter sent to George Washington, wherein the distresses of the United States and the Army were blamed on the republican form of government, *which was equated with turbulent democracy*.

According to this appeal, the United States had no clear leadership, the States were aimlessly adrift in a sea of chaos, and anarchy and misery would surely be the fate of America – unless, of course, a monarchy could be established under a powerful King who could instill order and efficiency in the affairs of government. The letter then invited General Washington to come forward, save America from impending doom, and declare himself King of America with the assurance of support from his loyal Army.

It is testimony to the virtuous character of George Washington that he did not hesitate to decline the invitation. In no uncertain terms, the head of the Continental Army promptly informed the individuals behind the scheme that they could not have found anyone to whom such an invitation would have been more odious. He did not, however, publicly disclose the incident, lest it further contribute to the widespread fear of the Army already existing in the Congress and State legislatures.

The scheming did not end with this refusal by General Washington to accept a Crown. One General asserted that "the Army was verging to that state which we are told will make a wise man mad." [7] Creditors were deliberately led to believe that, if the Army seized the reins of government, sufficient funds could then be found to pay all the public debts, not merely those owed to the war veterans. Such sentiments were shared by a number of prominent individuals, both in and out of the Army, including Robert Morris, Gouverneur Morris, and General Nathaniel Greene. When the latter wrote a discreet letter to the South Carolina legislature, the legislators of that State indicated their fear of military interference in civil affairs by dispatching an angry reply to the effect that they would tolerate "no dictation by any Cromwell." [8]

Another alarming incident occurred among the troops stationed at Newburgh, New York. In this case, trouble began when an anonymous, inflammatory letter – possibly authored by General Gates – was widely circulated among the soldiers. This appeal declared:

> My friends, after seven long years your suffering and courage has conducted the USA through a doubtful and bloody war; and the peace returns to bless – whom? A country willing to redress your wrongs, cherish your worth, and reward your services? Or is it rather a country that tramples upon your rights, disdains your cries, and insults your distresses? If such be your treatment while the swords you wear are necessary for the de-

---

[7] Russell Hoover Quynn, *The Constitutions of Abraham Lincoln and Jefferson Davis*, Exposition Press, New York, 1959, quoted on p. 235.
[8] *Ibid.*, quoted on p. 235.

fence of America, what have you to expect when those very swords, the instruments and companions of your glory, shall be taken from your sides, and no mark of military distinction left but your wants, infirmities, and scars? If you have sense enough to discover, and spirit enough to oppose tyranny, whatever garb it may assume, *awake* to your situation. If the present moment be lost, your threats hereafter will be as empty as your entreaties now. Appeal from the justice to the fears of government, and suspect the man who would advise to more moderation and longer forbearance. [9]

The last sentence may have been written with George Washington specifically in mind. In any case, General Washington was once again compelled to intervene and crush a plot to use his Army to establish a Military Dictatorship in the United States. The day after the inflammatory manifesto was issued, he issued a military order that specifically referred to the anonymous appeal and set a date for a meeting. At the meeting, General Washington addressed his officers at considerable length. He acknowledged the sufferings of the soldiers, yet urged forbearance, reminding his audience that Congress itself was laboring under great financial strains. When the General had finished speaking, not a man present dared to defend the inflammatory manifesto, and the crisis was allowed to dissipate without further incident.

When it became apparent that George Washington would never allow the Army to be used to force a National Monarchy upon the United States, the proponents of elitist government decided to change their tactics, but not their aims, by creating the Society of the Cincinnati. This Society, which still exists, has evolved considerably over the years until now it is nothing more than a genuinely patriotic organization, similar in nature to the Sons of the American Revolution. But this was certainly not the nature of the Society at the time of its founding.

The Society was named in honor of the legendary Cincinnatus, a Roman farmer who left his fields to become a totalitarian dictator during a time of crisis in ancient Rome. Once the crisis had passed, the legendary Cincinnatus nobly relinquished his dictatorial powers and humbly returned to his farm. By naming the Society after such a legendary "hero," the motives of its founders were unmistakable. Not only were the chief founders the very conspirators who had attempted to persuade General Washington to overthrow the Articles of Confederation, but the Society itself served as a unifying front for anti-republican and anti-federal agitation.

Although the Society of the Cincinnati was officially promoted as only a fraternity of Revolutionary War officers, its political influence was extremely

---

[9] *Ibid.*, quoted on pp. 235-236.

great both before and after the adoption of the Constitution of 1787. Many of the leading political figures in the Union were members of it, and these men seemed to share a common political ideology that favored a very strong, consolidated, highly centralized government. At the Constitutional Convention of 1787, for instance, many of the Society's members in attendance favored either a monarchical dictatorship, such as Alexander Hamilton, or an energetic National Government that would crush States' Rights under its iron fist. Following the adoption of our present Federal Constitution, the Society provided a powerful organizational base for the Federalist Party. The unmistakable political nature of the Society became evident beyond doubt when Mr. Hamilton took control of it a few years after it was organized.

The Rise of Factions

The sinister maneuvers within the Continental Army prior to its disbandment signaled the beginnings of a rapidly growing and alarming trend among certain political leaders within the United States to openly denounce, not merely some weaknesses within the Articles, but more generally the cherished concepts of federalism, States' Rights, and republicanism. Although such criticism frequently took the form of attacks on "democracy," there was no mistaking the true nature of the attacks. The Federal Union and all of the States were constituted as Republics, not as democracies. Attacks on "democracy," thus, were really thinly veiled attacks on the republican form of government.

The greatest cause for concern during the 1780's, therefore, was not the weakness inherent in the Articles of Confederation, nor even the fiscal and economic distress of the United States. What made the "Critical Period" truly *critical* was the rise of political factions within the United States. Although these factions were never formally organized into political parties under the Articles, it had become evident by the middle of the decade that no less than three distinct factions existed within the Federal Union, each separated from the other by strong sentiments.

The most dangerous and un-American of the three factions was the one comprised of the **National Monarchists**. It had been this faction which had originally hoped to use the Continental Army to establish a Military Dictatorship in the United States. The very fact that they initially attempted to establish a National Monarchy by means of *force* illustrates that this faction understood, from the very beginning, that the vast majority of Americans could never be persuaded to voluntarily *consent* to such a form and system of government.

Support for a National Monarchy was derived, in large measure, from those Americans who, during the American Revolution, had sided with the British Government. These individuals had never wanted American independence in the first place, and they certainly did not want any type of government other than the all-powerful, morally corrupt British system. This faction also drew support from those like John Adams of Massachusetts, who had once been American patriots, but whose political sentiments honestly led them to support a British system for America. Mr. Adams perhaps best summarized the views of these individuals when he said that, if the British Government could be purged of its corruption, it would be the best model of government the world had ever produced.

The National Monarchists acquired significant support from men like Alexander Hamilton of New York and Gouverneur Morris of Pennsylvania, who had supported the American cause against Great Britain for reasons not entirely honest. It was not the socialist exploitation of America that such individuals objected to, but only the fact that the sole beneficiary of such exploitation was a *British* monied aristocracy. What America needed, they believed, was a government modeled after that of Great Britain – *corruption and all* – so that an all-powerful general government could create and sustain an *American* monied aristocracy by exploiting the States and their peoples. Mr. Hamilton perhaps best summarized the views of these individuals when he asserted that the British Government was the best model of government the world had ever produced, and that to purge that government of its immoral corruption would be to rob it of its wondrous beauty.

The goal of the National Monarchists was to replace the existing Federal Republic with a political system founded upon *aristocracy* and *elitism*. To them, any semblance of poplar government – including all of the democratic features of the republican form of government – was equivalent to mobocracy and turbulent "democracy," which they vigorously denounced. The American people, in their opinion, simply had too much freedom. If order and discipline were to be established in the United States, they proclaimed, the individual citizens of the Republic must be willing to sacrifice a number of their most cherished rights, including the right to government founded on consent. Although the National Monarchists pretended to be the firm and unwavering champions of private property, the measures they advocated clearly marked them as socialistic invaders of genuine property rights.

In this regard, it is of interest to note that Alexander Hamilton, a key leader of this faction, first came to the attention of the other National Monarchists by his ardent defense of a Tory who had blatantly violated the property rights of a war veteran's widow during the American Revolution. The case handled by this shrewd lawyer involved the Trespass Act, a bill that passed in the New York legislature and that required all Loyalists who had occupied the private property of American patriots during the war to pay back rent to the landlords. The war veteran's widow, who was virtually impoverished, was suing a Tory merchant for occupying her property during the war without ever paying rent.

In defense of his Tory client, Mr. Hamilton viciously attacked the Trespass Act, claiming that its principles were unjust. Although he lost the case in question – the two parties agreeing to settle out of court – Mr. Hamilton was quickly propelled to fame as the friend of the Tories, especially of the rich and powerful Tories. And in spite of the arguments he used to denounce the Trespass Act, the future leader of the Federalist Party was promoted as a great champion of private property rights who could save America from the ravages of turbulent "democracy."

In assessing the challenges they faced, the National Monarchists realized that any attempt to establish a King and a House of Lords in America stood little chance of success. Accordingly, many of them were willing to sacrifice some of the outward forms of monarchy in order to promote the *spirit* of the British Government in the United States. An elected President who would hold his office for life, for instance, might be as good as a King, and the American people might be tricked into accepting such a system as "republican" in nature.

In the eyes of the National Monarchists, the chief enemies were the various State governments, which stood as shields between the central authority of the Union and the individual citizens. If a National Government were to be used to exploit the citizenry and rob them of their liberties, effective opposition from the State governments would have to be eliminated or reduced to insignificance. The State governments already existed, so they could not be easily abolished altogether. But they might be made subservient to a National Government by giving to the latter a right to nullify acts of the various State authorities.

The very essence of the system of government desired by the National Monarchists required the concentration of *all power* in the hands of a general government. *The National Monarchists, therefore, became the foremost opponents of States' Rights and State sovereignty.* The only way to establish a National Government with totalitarian power, they realized, was to rob the States of their sovereignty and reduce their reserved rights to nothing. The *form* of government they advocated, thus, was either purely monarchical or a derivative thereof; and the *system* of government they promoted was decidedly national in character.

The National Monarchists actually began their attacks on the Articles of Confederation before the first Federal Constitution went into effect in 1781. *A year earlier*, Alexander Hamilton had spearheaded their attack by denouncing the Articles as weak and inefficient and by urging a more "energetic" government for the United States. Mr. Hamilton, who became the unofficial leader of this faction, went on to play a leading role in the movement for a new Constitution.

Although the National Monarchists drew support from some very powerful and influential individuals, their supporters were fortunately few in number. Their main source of strength was in the New England States, where commercial interests could be more easily persuaded to believe that, if the United States were to adopt the British system, it would be *good for business*. After the adoption of the Constitution of 1787, many die-hard supporters in New England still clung to the hope that the United States might be eventually converted into some form of a National Monarchy. The leader of the National Monarchists – Alexander Hamilton – even went so far as to become a British spy, and to secretly work within the Administration of President George Washington to reverse the results of the Declaration of Independence.

Commenting on the nature of Mr. Hamilton's disloyalty to the United States, historians Richard Hofstadter, William Miller, and Daniel Aaron noted the following in their book, *The United States: The History of a Republic*:

> For years, while serving as Washington's closest adviser, Hamilton had also served as a secret consultant – "No. 7" in the British cipher — with British secret agents in the United States....As early as October, 1789, Hamilton told Major George Beckwith, his secret contact reporting on American affairs: "I have always preferred a connexion with you, to that of any other country, *we think in English*, and have a similarity of prejudices and predilections." Thereafter, Hamilton let nothing pass to Britain's disadvantage. [10]

The second faction that surfaced during the 1780's consisted of the **National Republicans.** This faction shared one key trait in common with the National Monarchists, a fact which caused many Americans to question if there was any real difference of importance between the two. Like the National Monarchists, the National Republicans were convinced that the chief enemies of progress were the State governments. Their solution to this supposed problem was virtually identical to that of the National Monarchists. They, too, desired to rob the States of their sovereignty and to force the State

---

[10] Richard Hofstadter, William Miller, and Daniel Aaron, *The United States: The History of a Republic*, Prentice-Hall, Inc., Englewood Cliffs, 1967, pp. 193-194.

governments to bow to the dictates of an energetic and all-powerful National Government.

Although only a minority of the American people supported this faction, it was more popular than the National Monarchists and enjoyed more widespread support among the leading political leaders of that era, including Edmund Randolph, George Wilson, John Marshall, and James Madison. The views of these individuals was perhaps best revealed when Mr. Madison asserted the opinion that a National Government should be created with the power to veto or nullify any law enacted by any State legislature.

Unlike the National Monarchists, however, this faction willingly accepted the republican forms of government created within the individual States and for the Union as a whole. Although they favored a strong central regime, they acknowledged that such a government should be accountable to the people. They also readily acknowledged the inalienable rights of the American people and the concept of government-by-the-consent-of-the-governed.

The attachment of the National Republicans to the rights of the people, however, was confined within rather narrow limits. They could be heard denouncing the excesses of "democracy" in the United States just as loudly as the National Monarchists, and many of them were convinced that the distress then experienced by the United States stemmed, in large measure, from the fact that the American people had too much freedom. In their view, Shays' Rebellion was proof of this fact. Only a really strong general government – one sufficiently empowered to enforce unquestioned obedience and submission from State governments and citizens alike – could save America from anarchy. Thus, while they advocated a powerful but republican *form* of government, this faction was convinced that the United States needed to replace its federal *system* of government with a national system.

Following the adoption of our present Federal Constitution, the coalition of interests that held the National Republicans together was dissolved. Some individuals, still determined to somehow transform our system in a national one, joined with the National Monarchists to create the Federalist Party under the leadership of Alexander Hamilton. Others, such as James Madison, acquiesced to the peoples' preference for a federal system and committed themselves thereafter, at least partially, to supporting and sustaining the principles on which our Federal Republic is founded.

By far the largest faction to appear in the 1780's, and the one enthusiastically supported by an overwhelming majority of the American people, consisted of the **Federal Republicans**. This faction received its greatest support from those American patriots who had not only supported the American cause during the Revolutionary War, but had also supported all of the great principles on which that war was fought. Many of the greatest leaders of the American Revolution belonged to this faction, including Samuel Adams of Massachusetts, Benjamin Franklin of Pennsylvania, as well as Thomas Jefferson and Patrick Henry of Virginia. Other leaders included the eminent and distinguished Luther Martin of Maryland, William Paterson of New Jersey, George Clinton of New York, Oliver Ellsworth of Connecticut, and James Monroe and John Taylor of Virginia. Although this faction was widely supported throughout the Union, its stronghold was in the Southern States.

Considering that this faction stood squarely for the defense of the noble gains won by the American Revolution, it was perhaps only natural that its foremost advocate should be the Philosopher of the Revolution. "One of the most threatening tendencies in American politics to Jefferson was the anti-republican reaction in the period following the Revolution," noted historian Caleb Perry Patterson. "No American statesman so clearly divined the nature of this movement and its ultimate objective as Jefferson." [11]

Mr. Patterson added:

> Despite the attempts of historians to minimize the basis of Jefferson's apprehension and in some measure to question the honesty and sincerity of his defense of popular rights, from events of the fifteen or twenty years following the Revolution we now see that his solicitude for the future of the Republic was abundantly justified. [12]

As pointed out by Professors Thomas A. Bailey and David M. Kennedy of Stanford University, however, those Federal Republicans who advocated popular government – such as Thomas Jefferson – realized that only those citizens who were literate and responsible should be enfranchised:

> Above all, Jefferson advocated the rule of the people. But he did not propose thrusting the ballot into the hands of *every* adult white male. He favored government *for* the people, but not by *all* the people – only by those men who were literate enough to inform themselves and wear the mantle of American citizenship worthily....The ignorant, he argued, were incapable of self-government. [13]

Thus, although the Federal Republicans were advocates of popular government and the democratic features that characterize the republican form of government, *they were not advocates of democracy*. Like the other factions,

---

[11] Caleb Perry Patterson, *The Constitutional Principles of Thomas Jefferson*, Peter Smith, Gloucester, 1953, quoted on p. 30.
[12] *Ibid.*, p 31.
[13] Thomas A. Bailey and David M. Kennedy, *Op. cit.*, p. 148.

they realized that the people can be as tyrannical as any repressive, unrepresentative government, and they made a sharp distinction between a democracy and the republican form of government. The fact that they feared excessive government more than they feared excessive liberty merely indicates that they clearly understood the great lesson of history, which teaches that the only thing to be more feared than an uncontrollable, all-powerful mob of people is an uncontrollable, all-powerful Big Government.

The Federal Republicans acknowledged that the Articles of Confederation suffered from defects and required a remedy. The remedy needed, however, was not what either the National Monarchists or the National Republicans advocated. Subverting the rights of the States and destroying their sovereignty, they firmly believed, was no remedy at all – it was in itself a *disease* far worse than anything then afflicting the United States. Nor was robbing the American people of their liberty regarded as a remedy by the Federal Republicans. The proper remedy, they insisted, was to add a few amendments to the Articles, delegate a few additional powers to the then existing Federal Government, and let the States and their peoples continue to enjoy their reserved rights and liberties.

Commenting on the views of the leading authority within the Federal Republican faction, the noted historian Dumas Malone has written:

> Jefferson did not let exaggerated fears taint his republican faith, for his observations in Europe had served to quicken it. Certain comments of his on the existing Federal Government in the United States are in startling contrast with what his friend Madison was saying about the constitutional needs of the hour. Sending information to Demeunier, he said: "The Confederation is a wonderfully perfect instrument, considering the circumstances under which it was formed." He was not merely putting the best face on things American when addressing a European, for he spoke in even stronger language to his own countrymen.
>
> He wrote to one Virginian: "But with all the imperfections of our present government, it is without comparison the best existing or that ever did exist." To another, he said that "with all the defects of our Constitutions, whether general or particular, the comparison of our governments with those of Europe, are like a comparison of heaven & hell. England, like the earth, may be allowed to take the intermediate station." His words amounted to a plea for republican government, toward which he was looking back with nostalgia. To still another American he wrote: "If all the evils which can arise among us, from the republican form of government, from this day to the day of judgment, could be put into a scale against what this country [France] suffers from its monarchical form in a week, or England

in a month, the latter would preponderate." [14]

The goal of the Federal Republicans was perhaps best summarized by Mr. Jefferson, when he declared that the object should be to make the States united in foreign affairs, but to leave them free and independent in domestic affairs. In advocating such a political system for the United States, this faction was thus promoting a republican *form* and a federal *system* of government. The goal could be accomplished by enlarging the powers of the Federal Government and by dividing that government into three separate branches, while preserving the independence of the State governments. *This faction, by advocating such an objective, became the only one that sought to preserve the sovereignty of the States.*

The ultimate consequence of the formation of these factions was the inevitable doom of the Articles of Confederation. By the middle of the 1780's, the only ones interested in reforming, and thereby saving, the Federal Union under the Articles were the Federal Republicans. The National Monarchists and the National Republicans openly opposed such attempts to honestly remedy the defects in the existing Federal Constitution. They wished for conditions to grow even worse, so that their drastic proposals for radical change might have some chance of success.

The opposition encountered by the honest reformers of the Articles was duly noted by the authors of the textbook, *American History: A Survey*:

> The issue was not whether the Confederation should be changed but how drastic the changes should be. Even its defenders came reluctantly to agree that the government needed strengthening at its weakest point, its lack of power to tax. To save the Articles of Confederation, its friends backed the impost amendment of 1782, which would have authorized Congress to levy customs duties, and all the States ratified the amendment except Rhode Island, whose single veto was of course enough to kill it. The next year a similar amendment was accepted by Rhode Island but defeated by New York. Later the State-rights advocates proposed that the States make to Congress a temporary and qualified grant of taxing authority (not an amendment to the Articles), but most of the centralizers had begun to lose interest in such remedies. They insisted upon a much more thoroughgoing change. [15]

Regarding the strategies of the National Monarchists and the National Republicans, who were united by their common desire to replace the existing Federal Union with a national system, historian John C. Miller made the fol-

---

[14] Dumas Malone, *Jefferson and His Time*, Volume II, Little, Brown and Company, Boston, 1951, pp. 160-161.
[15] Richard N. Current, T. Harry Williams, and Frank Freidel, *Op. cit.*, pp. 128-129.

lowing comments in his biography, *Alexander Hamilton and the Growth of the New Nation*:

> The nationalists themselves were far from unanimous in believing that the hour had struck for summoning a Constitutional Convention. Because of their failure to achieve even a modest measure of reform, some nationalists had become firmly wedded to caution; others thought that the country must be allowed to drift into greater confusion, even to the point of anarchy, before the people could be brought to see the necessity of a strong central government. Therefore, ran their argument, let the friends of strong government hold their hand until the people, in terror and despair, turned to them for succor. Then a truly National Government might be erected: even a King and nobility were thought by some to be within the realm of possibility.
>
> This plan of plucking the flower of strong government from the nettle of anarchy did not find favor with Hamilton. His inclination was always to control events rather than to permit them to control him; and he knew that by waiting for time and catastrophe to force a settlement, there was no certainty that the final arrangements would be to his taste....
>
> Among the nationalists, Hamilton's prestige was steadily mounting; unquestionably he was the boldest and most active of the advocates of a strong National Government. It remained to be seen whether boldness would succeed any better than had caution; certainly, it seemed to Hamilton, it could not do less. [16]

The fact that the movement for a new Constitution was chiefly led by the nationalists constitutes one of the greatest ironies of the Constitutional Era. No one contributed more to that movement than James Madison and Alexander Hamilton, and yet no two Americans would be more surprised or disappointed than they by the ultimate results of the Philadelphia Convention of 1787. The National Republicans and the National Monarchists may have spearheaded the movement for a new Constitution, but when the time came to actually construct that new plan of Union, the Federal Republicans were destined to emerge triumphant. For a season, however, it appeared as though nothing could stop the nationalists in their quest to annihilate State sovereignty and the federal system of government.

The Annapolis Convention of 1786

The earliest interstate meeting of consequence to be held in an effort to

---

[16] John C. Miller, *Alexander Hamilton and the Growth of the New Nation*, Harper & Row, Publishers, New York, 1959, p. 141.

remedy the defects in the Articles of Confederation was convened in 1785 at Mount Vernon, the home of George Washington. The original purpose of the meeting had been to bring together delegates from the neighboring States of Maryland and Virginia, in an effort to resolve bi-State trade issues. But when delegates also arrived from Delaware and Pennsylvania, the discussion was quickly enlarged to encompass a wider range of issues. The meeting at General Washington's home ended with a formal appeal to the Virginia legislature to issue a statement to the other States of the Union, requesting them to send delegates to a major convention to be held in Annapolis, Maryland, in September of the following year.

In accordance with this appeal, the General Assembly of Virginia issued a resolution on January 21, 1786, proposing "A Joint Meeting of Commissioners from the States to Consider and Recommend a Federal Plan for Regulating Commerce." [17] In calling for a Convention to consider and propose measures for a "Federal Plan" for "Regulating Commerce," the objective was clearly to introduce a *laissez faire* economy to the United States by eliminating the internal trade barriers erected by some States, *without otherwise altering the existing federal system of government*. That the purpose of the Convention was limited to the consideration of ways to restore free enterprise within the Union is evident from the formal authorization given by Virginia to her delegates to that meeting.

Virginia's delegates were officially instructed:

> ...[T]o take into consideration the trade of the United States; to examine the relative situations and trade of the said States; to consider how far a uniform system in their commercial regulations may be necessary to their common interest and their permanent harmony; and to report to the several States, such an act relative to this great object, as, when unanimously ratified by them, will enable the United States in Congress, effectually to provide for the same. [18]

Although nine States expressed interest in the proposed Annapolis Convention and appointed commissioners to the proposed Convention, only five States – New York, New Jersey, Pennsylvania, Delaware, and Virginia – actually sent delegates. Representing New York were Alexander Hamilton and Egbert Benson. New Jersey sent Abraham Clarke, William C. Houston, and James Schuarman. George Read, John Dickinson, and Richard Bassett represented Delaware at the Convention. The Old Dominion commissioned James Madison, Edmund Randolph, and Saint George Tucker as its delegates.

---

[17] Charles Callan Tansill (ed.), *The Making of the American Republic: The Great Documents, 1774-1789*, Arlington House, New Rochelle, p. 38.
[18] *Ibid.*, p. 38.

Trench Coxe was the sole delegate from Pennsylvania. Mr. Dickinson was unanimously elected Chairman of the Convention.

If any of the States who had sent commissioners to the Annapolis Convention, which convened on September 11, 1786, were expecting any practical proposals related to interstate commerce to emerge from the meeting, they were soon to be disappointed. Three days after convening, the Convention ended in complete failure. Exactly why the Convention failed to seriously consider and propose even one amendment to the Articles of Confederation is open to speculation. Was the defective attendance of the States solely to blame for this failure? It is of interest to note the views of the American minister in Paris at the time.

Writing in the *Anas* years later, Thomas Jefferson duly noted the failure of the majority of the States to send delegates to the Annapolis Convention. Yet, he also wrote that some National Monarchists within the Annapolis Convention had attempted to disrupt the proceedings by advocating principles incompatible with republican government. Upon observing that the other delegates had no intention of subverting the Federal Republic, the monarchists then pursued a course of obstruction within the Convention. By Mr. Jefferson's reasoning, these individuals hoped to see anarchy develop within the United States to justify their violent measures.

Mr. Jefferson's analysis may well be true. But considering the fact that the delegates to the Annapolis Convention were able to draft and sign a joint Report to their respective State governments that expressed their "unanimous conviction," it seems more probable that the delegates were more firmly united in sentiment than Thomas Jefferson believed. And judging from the nature of that Report, *which was penned by Alexander Hamilton*, it is probably more accurate to assume that the destructive influence of the *spirit of nationalism* had a more powerful influence within the Annapolis Convention than did the *spirit of monarchism*. Unfortunately, the official record of the Convention provides no information on the debates or discussions that occurred. All that is officially known about this Convention, therefore, is that five States sent delegates to Annapolis, Maryland, to consider ways to save the Articles of Confederation, but upon convening the delegates promptly drafted a Report to their State governments to urge the calling of another Convention and then adjourned.

Within the Report to the States issued by the Annapolis Convention on September 14, 1786, Alexander Hamilton dwelled at length on the official authorizations given to the delegates by their respective States. In commissioning the delegates, he noted, all of the States except New Jersey had placed severe restrictions on what the delegates could consider, limiting them, in essence, *to consider only interstate trade issues*. New Jersey, Mr. Hamilton noted with favor, had commissioned its delegates with the broad authority to "consider how far an uniform system in their commercial regulations and *other important matters*, might be necessary to the common interest and permanent harmony of the several States." [19]

Alexander Hamilton next noted that the commissioners appointed by New Hampshire, Massachusetts, Rhode Island, and North Carolina had failed to attend the Convention. Furthermore, he wrote, the States of Georgia, South Carolina, Maryland, and Connecticut had failed to even appoint delegates for the meeting. The fact that so few States actually sent delegates, coupled with the fact that most of those who did send delegates placed strict limitations on what they could discuss, was *officially* blamed for the failure of the Convention. After offering this excuse for the Annapolis Convention, Mr. Hamilton then made a lengthy appeal for the calling of yet another interstate meeting, urging that the States impose *no limits* on what defects in the Articles the delegates could discuss in the new interstate Convention.

As Alexander Hamilton wrote:

> Deeply impressed...with the magnitude and importance of the object confided to them on this occasion, your Commissioners cannot forbear to indulge an expression of their earnest and unanimous wish, that speedy measures may be taken, to effect a general meeting, of the States, in a future Convention, for the same, and such other purposes, as the situation of public affairs, may be found to require....
>
> In this persuasion, your Commissioners submit an opinion, that the Idea of extending the powers of their Deputies, to other objects, than those of Commerce, which has been adopted by the State of New Jersey, was an improvement on the original plan, and will deserve to be incorporated into that of a future Convention; they are the more naturally led to this conclusion, as in the course of their reflections on the subject, they have been induced to think, that the power of regulating trade is of such comprehensive extent, and will enter so far into the general System of the Federal Government, that to give it efficacy, and to obviate questions and doubts concerning its precise nature and limits, may require a correspondent adjustment of other parts of the Federal System.
>
> That there are important defects in the system of the Federal Government is acknowledged by the Acts of all those States, which have concurred in the present Meeting; That the defects, upon a closer examination, may be found greater and more numerous, than even these acts imply, is at least so far probable, from the embarrassments which characterise the present state of our national affairs, foreign and domestic, as may reasonably be supposed to merit a deliberate and candid discussion, in some mode, which will unite the Sentiments and Councils of all the States. In the choice of the mode, your Commissioners are of opinion, that a Convention

---

[19] *Ibid.*, quoted on p. 41.

of Deputies from the different States, for the special and sole purpose of entering into this investigation, and digesting a plan for supplying such defects as may be discovered to exist, will be entitled to a preference from considerations, which will occur, without being particularised.

Your Commissioners decline an enumeration of those national circumstances on which their opinion respecting the propriety of a future Convention, with more enlarged powers, is founded; as it would be an useless intrusion of facts and observations, most of which have been frequently the subject of public discussion, and none of which can have escaped the penetration of those to whom they would in this instance be addressed. They are however of a nature so serious, as, in the view of your Commissioners to render the situation of the United States delicate and critical, calling for an exertion of the united virtue and wisdom of all the members of the Confederacy.

Under this impression, Your Commissioners, with the most respectful deference, beg leave to suggest their unanimous conviction, that it may essentially tend to advance the interests of the Union, if the States, by whom they have been respectively delegated, would themselves concur, and use their endeavours to procure the concurrence of the other States, in the appointment of Commissioners, to meet at Philadelphia on the second Monday in May next, to take into consideration the situation of the United States, to devise such further provisions as shall appear to them necessary to render the Constitution of the Federal Government adequate to the exigencies of the Union; and to report such an Act for that purpose to the United States in Congress assembled, as when agreed to, by them, and afterwards confirmed by the Legislatures of every State, will effectually provide for the same. [20]

Within this official Report of the Annapolis Convention to the States, several significant points merit close scrutiny. First of all, we see within this Report a confirmation that the Articles of Confederation was viewed by the men of that day as a "Constitution." Also, it may be noted that the Congress established by those Articles was commonly referred to by contemporary writers as the "Federal Government." What is even more interesting is the general tone of this appeal for a new Convention to be held in Philadelphia. Based on this appeal, one might assume that all those at the Annapolis Convention, Alexander Hamilton included, were firm advocates of preserving the federal system of government.

Aside from the request that the States place no restrictions on the issues to be considered by the delegates to the next Convention, which is the only hint given that federalism might be in danger, the purpose of the call for a Grand Convention of the States was made perfectly clear. The proposed Convention would use its broad powers only within the limits of considering "*the*

---

[20] *Ibid.*, pp. 41-43.

general System of the Federal Government," and would recommend adjustments to "parts of *the federal system*" in an effort to remedy "important defects in *the system of the Federal Government.*"

While the delegates to the next Convention, Mr. Hamilton stated, should be free of restrictions on the specific issues they could consider, the *purpose* of the new Convention would be *strictly limited* to the stated objective, specifically "*to advance the interests of the Union*" then existing, a Federal Union between the States. Such a Convention would be held, he indicated, "*for the special and sole purpose*" of devising such provisions "as shall appear to them necessary *to render the Constitution of the Federal Government adequate to the exigencies of the Union.*"

If Alexander Hamilton or any other commissioner at the Annapolis Convention harbored any desire to use the proposed Philadelphia Convention as a means of destroying the Federal Republic, that fact was certainly well concealed from view within the Convention's official Report. By its terms, the new Federal Convention would consider and propose only those measures consistent with the principles of federalism, republicanism, and State sovereignty. Indeed, it may be stated without hesitation that, had any suggestion been made that the recommended Convention might propose, *or even consider*, replacing the federal system with a national one, such a Convention would never have been approved by the States.

One final point of significance should be noted regarding the Report issued by the Annapolis Convention. As Alexander Hamilton correctly noted, the results of the proposed Philadelphia Convention would carry no binding authority on the several States *without their explicit consent.* Whatever revisions in the Articles that might be recommended by the future Convention, such revisions would be only *proposals* for consideration. Once the new Federal Convention had completed its work, its proposals would then be submitted to the various States, who could either approve or reject the propositions. Such a procedure was not only dictated by the Articles of Confederation, but was also dictated by the concept of government by consent on which the American system was founded.

The Call for a Grand Convention of the States

The recommendation of the Annapolis Convention of 1786 – that a Grand Convention of the States be held in 1787 in the City of Philadelphia to revise the Articles of Confederation – met with favor in the Congress. The Federal Government thus issued a resolution to the thirteen States on February 21, 1787, urging them to heed the call for such a Convention, for the *sole and express* purpose of *invigorating the powers of the Federal Government* and of *preserving the Federal Union.* It is of interest to note, however, that the Congress stated as its reason or motive for adopting such a resolution, the desire *to establish a firm National Government!*

The call issued by the Congress, thus, introduced *for the first time* a suggestion that the results of the Federal Convention might be a *National Government.* No explanation was given, though, as to how such a product – "a firm National Government" – could possibly result from a call for a Convention limited to the *sole and express* objective of strengthening a Federal Government and preserving a Federal Union between sovereign States.

The resolution issued by Congress was prefaced by these words:

> Whereas there is provision in the Articles of Confederation & perpetual Union for making alterations therein by the assent of a Congress of the United States and of the legislatures of the several States; And whereas experience hath evinced that there are defects in the present Confederation, as a mean to remedy which several of the States and particularly the State of New York by express instructions to their delegates in Congress have suggested a Convention *for the purposes expressed in the following resolution* and such a Convention appearing to be the most probable mean of establishing in these States *a firm National Government.* [Emphasis added] [21]

Although such a Convention was thus proclaimed to be, in the words of Congress, "*the most probable mean of establishing in these States a firm National Government,*" that was *not* given as the official *purpose* of the Philadelphia Convention of 1787. The Federal Convention was to be held, said Congress, "*for the purposes expressed in the following resolution.*" The official purposes or objectives of the Convention, therefore, were only those expressed *within the actual resolution,* which was in these words:

> Resolved, that, in the opinion of Congress, it is expedient that, on the second Monday in May next, a Convention of delegates, who shall have been appointed by the several States, be held at Philadelphia, *for the sole and express purpose of revising the Articles of Confederation,* and reporting to Congress and the several Legislatures such alterations and provisions therein as shall, when agreed to in Congress and confirmed by the States, *render the Federal Constitution adequate to the exigencies of Government and the preservation of the Union.* [Emphasis added] [22]

---

[21] *Ibid.,* pp. 45-46.
[22] Jefferson Davis, *The Rise and Fall of the Confederate Government,* Volume 1, Thomas Yoseloff, Cranbury, (orig. pub. in 1881) 1958, quoted on pp. 88-89.

Within the resolution proper, the true and official *purposes* of the Grand Convention were stated in terms that could not possibly be mistaken or misinterpreted. The objective of the proposed Convention was not to draft a new Constitution for the United States, but *only to revise the Articles of Confederation*, which is referred to as "the *Federal Constitution*." This objective was prefaced by the restrictive clause "*sole and express*," words that clearly rejected any other possible objective or purpose for the Grand Convention of the States. The results of the Convention were likewise placed under *strict limitation*. The proposed Convention would be required to concentrate solely on ways to "render the Federal Constitution adequate to the exigencies of Government and the preservation of the Union."

There could be mistaking the meaning of these plain statements as to the purpose and objectives of the Federal Convention. A *National Government* certainly could *not* render a "Federal Constitution" more adequate to those exigencies of government, and the erection of a consolidated *National Union* on the ruins of sovereign States certainly could *not* preserve a Federal Union between the States. *Only by disregarding the previously stated motive of establishing a "firm National Government" could the true purposes of the Philadelphia Convention be realized.*

In his book, *New Views of the Constitution of the United States*, which was originally published in 1823, John Taylor of Caroline focused his keen eye on the call for the Grand Convention issued by the Congress. Before we examine his comments on this issue, however, we should first briefly assess his impressive credentials – credentials which qualified him, perhaps more than any other American of his time, to analyze and assess the events that occurred during the Constitutional Era.

Beyond doubt, John Taylor of Caroline was the most clairvoyant political theorist in American history, an observation that is derived from his ability to accurately interpret historical events, his uncanny ability to predict the future, and his ability to analyze a public issue from every angle. As early as 1820, for instance, he was able to not only predict the future War Between the States, but to trace causes of that predicted war back to their roots in the corrupt Hamiltonian system. An ardent patriot in the American Revolution, this Virginian had served as an officer, attaining the rank of Colonel, in both the Continental Army and the State militia. Following the adoption of the Constitution of 1787, Mr. Taylor served as a key leader in Thomas Jefferson's Democratic-Republican Party, being elected to both the Virginia legislature and the U.S. Senate.

But it was as an author and political theorist that he earned his chief claim to fame. As America's foremost *Philosopher of Federalism*, John Taylor of Caroline did more than any other statesman to contribute to the States' Rights school of thought that arose in Virginia and the Southern States as whole during the ante-bellum days of the Republic. And following the practice of many other Virginians at that time, such as John Randolph of Roanoke, Mr. Taylor often attached the name of his home *county* to his name – hence, the name, John Taylor *of Caroline*.

Among his great literary works that contributed mightily to the political views of the American people in the early days of the Republic were *Arator, An Inquiry into the Principles and Policies of the Government of the United States, Tyranny Unmasked, Construction Construed and Constitutions Vindicated*, and *New Views of the Constitution of the United States*. The influence that his writings had on the public mind was profound. John Adams, for one, read his books, although he complained that he could not understand them. And Thomas Jefferson stated that he had been able to correct some errors in his own concepts by reading Mr. Taylor's books, which he heartily endorsed.

In his masterpiece, *New Views of the Constitution of the United States*, John Taylor of Caroline made these observations regarding the call for a Grand Convention of the States:

> A short history of the Convention itself will enable us to understand its proceedings. A meeting of deputies from several States, in 1786, at Annapolis, recommended the appointment of commissioners to devise such *further* provisions, as shall appear to them necessary to render *the Constitution of the Federal Government*, adequate to the exigencies of the *Union*; and Congress, 1787, recommended a Convention of delegates to be appointed by the several States, as the most probable means of establishing in these States a firm *National* Government; and resolved that a Convention of delegates, who shall have been appointed by the *several States*, be held at Philadelphia for the *sole and express purpose* of revising the Articles of Confederation, and reporting to Congress and the several legislatures, such alterations and provisions therein, as shall, when agreed to in Congress and *confirmed by the States*, render the *Federal Constitution* adequate to the exigencies of government and the preservation of the Union. In these proceedings the word Convention is used to describe the deputies of a State, and the word Constitution as equivalent to the word Confederation. It is very remarkable, that the Congress of 1787 introduced the word *National* into the resolve recommending a Convention. It expressed an opinion "that a Convention was the most probable mean of establishing in these States a firm *National Government*." So far it unequivocally advocated the exchange of a Federal for a National form of government; but an intimation so plain and positive, that the State governments ought to be destroyed, might not have been received with applause, and might have obstructed the removal of the defects of the existing Federal Union. The expedient of complexity was therefore practised to flatter the opinion of the

States, and yet to supply a text for the advocates of a National Government. After suggesting this form as one *propositum*, towards which the Convention might direct its attention, Congress subjoined another; namely, "that the Convention shall render the *Federal* Constitution adequate to the exigencies of government." Except for the restriction comprised in the word Federal, this part of the resolve would have been as capacious as the expression "National Government," because a limitation of power to the exigencies of government, of which the government itself must judge, is no limitation at all. But it adds, "and the preservation of the Union." The recommendation of Congress comprises "a *National* Government, a *Federal* Constitution, the *preservation of the Union*, and a Convention for the *sole purpose of revising the Articles of Confederation*." These recommendations are at discord with each other, as a National and a Federal form of government are not the same form. By planting the word *National* among them, as a scion to be watered up to a tree, a concert between individuals, unfriendly to the political existence of the States, appears at this period to have existed. [23]

All of the States save Rhode Island received the Congressional resolution favorably and proceeded to authorize commissioners or delegates to attend the Grand Convention of the States. **New Hampshire** officially appointed four delegates to the Federal Convention: John Langdon, Nicholas Gilman, John Pickering, and Benjamin West. Only the first two actually attended the Convention, however, and both representatives signed the resulting Constitution. **Massachusetts** did not appoint Samuel Adams and John Hancock as delegates, as might have been expected. Instead, it commissioned Caleb Strong, Elbridge Gerry, Rufus King, Nathaniel Gorham, and Francis Dana. All of these delegates, except Mr. Dana, attended the Convention. Mr. Strong, however, was not present at the end of Convention to sign the new Constitution, while Mr. Gerry, although present at the signing ceremony, *refused* to sign the new plan of government.

Connecticut appointed as delegates William Samuel Johnson, Roger Sherman, and Oliver Ellsworth, who all attended the Philadelphia Convention. The later, however, was not present at the concluding signing ceremony. Three commissioners were appointed by **New York**: Alexander Hamilton, Robert Yates, and John Lansing. Although all of them attended the Convention, Mr. Yates and Mr. Lansing walked out in early July, and Mr. Hamilton was the sole delegate from that State willing to sign the new Constitution. **New Jersey** appointed seven delegates, but two of them — John Neilson and Abraham Clark — never attended the Federal Convention. William Livingston, David Brearley, and William Paterson did attend the Convention

---

[23] John Taylor, *New Views of the Constitution of the United States*, Da Capo Press, New York, (orig. pub. in 1823) 1971, pp. 11 and 13-14.

and added their signatures to the final product. Although William C. Houston attended the Convention, he was not present at the end to sign the new compact.

All eight of the delegates appointed by **Pennsylvania** attended the Grand Convention and signed the new Constitution. They were Benjamin Franklin, Thomas Mifflin, Robert Morris, George Clymer, Thomas Fitzsimons, Jared Ingersoll, James Wilson, and Gouverneur Morris. Similarly, all of the delegates appointed by **Delaware** – George Read, Gunning Bedford, Jr., John Dickinson, Richard Basset, and Jacob Broom – attended the Convention and affixed their signatures to the new pact.

The five delegates appointed by **Maryland** attended the Grand Convention. But only James McHenry, Daniel of St. Thomas Jenifer, and Daniel Carroll signed the new Constitution. Luther Martin and John Francis Mercer left the Convention before the signing ceremony. **Virginia** officially commissioned eight delegates to attend the Philadelphia Convention. Patrick Henry, however, was deeply suspicious of the motives of certain individuals – claiming that he *smelt a rat* – and he refused to attend. George Washington, John Blair, and James Madison not only attended, but signed the new Constitution. George Wythe and Dr. James McClurg both left the Convention early. Virginia's other two delegates at the Convention – Edmund Randolph and George Mason – *refused* to sign the new instrument of government.

North Carolina appointed a total of seven commissioners. Willie Jones, however, refused to attend, and Richard Caswell resigned his commission. Alexander Martin and William R. Davie both attended, yet were not present at the conclusion to sign the Constitution of 1787. Three of the delegates in attendance from this State, however, did sign the new plan of government. They were William Blount, Richard D. Spaight, and Hugh Williamson. The four delegates commissioned by **South Carolina** – John Rutledge, Charles C. Pinckney, Charles Pinckney, and Pierce Butler – all attended the Federal Convention and signed the new Constitution.

A total of six delegates were appointed by **Georgia**. George Walton and Nathaniel Pendleton did not attend the Philadelphia Convention; William Houstoun and William Pierce attended, but were not present to sign the new plan of Union; and William Few and Abraham Baldwin both attended and signed the new Constitution. **Rhode Island**, as previously mentioned, appointed no delegates.

Of the 65 delegates thus formally commissioned by twelve of the thirteen States to attend the Philadelphia Convention, ten never set foot in Convention Hall, thirteen attended but were not present at the conclusion to sign the new Federal Constitution, and three participated in the Convention's proceedings but deliberately withheld their signatures from the compact. By the time the Convention ended, only eleven of the States were officially represented, New York having withdrawn when Robert Yates and John Lansing resigned from the proceedings. By the time the Grand Convention ended, only 39 delegates were present and willing to sign the new Articles of Union. Thirty-eight of these signers represented the States officially present, and one signer – Alexander Hamilton of New York – signed on behalf of a State that had officially withdrawn from the Convention.

A number of men who had been prominent leaders during the American Revolution were not present in the Federal Convention of 1787. Thomas Jefferson was in France, and John Adams was in England. Samuel Adams and John Hancock were not appointed by their State, and Patrick Henry, although appointed as a delegate by his State, refused to attend. Those who did attend were predominantly lawyers, and they represented a cross section of the three great factions of political ideology that then existed in the United States. It is of interest to note that, of the 55 delegates who actually attended the Grand Convention, 27 of them were members of the Society of the Cincinnati!

Whatever may have been the personal motives and desires of those who attended the Federal Convention, all of the delegates were fully cognizant of two key factors that served as *limitations* on what they could and could not do. One limitation was purely *practical* in nature. The Convention could only deliberate and propose; it could not ratify and adopt. The results of their labors, in other words, would ultimately be *judged by the sovereign States* after the Convention had concluded its work. The other limitation was *legal* in nature and was derived from the commissions officially conferred on the delegates by the States they represented in the Convention.

The Credentials of the Delegates

The deputies appointed by their respective States, as mentioned above, were not free and unrestrained agents vested with unlimited and sovereign power to do whatever they pleased within the Philadelphia Convention of 1787. *Their authority was derived from, and limited by, the commissions given to them by the States they represented.* Thus, even if the call for the Federal Convention by Congress could have been cleverly misconstrued as a proposal for the construction of a firm National Government, *such a recommendation would have carried no weight,* for the delegates to the Federal Convention derived their authority to act, not from Congress, but from their respective State governments. It is important, therefore, that we fully understand the instructions given to these delegates by the States who commissioned them.

As John Taylor of Caroline noted:

> Let us see how these recommendations [of Congress] were received by a concert of States, and by the concert of individuals. Twelve States appointed deputies to assemble at Philadelphia, and each gave its deputies credentials specifying their powers. *The idea that the recommendation of Congress was addressed to an American nation or people, no where appeared, and that of a National Government was rejected by every State.* [Emphasis added] [24]

The sovereign State of New Hampshire formally commissioned its delegates on June 27, 1787, in "An Act for Appointing Deputies from This State to the Convention, Proposed to Be Holden in the City of Philadelphia in May 1787 for the Purpose of Revising the Federal Constitution." Within this measure, the House of Representatives briefly cited the need to remedy the defects in the Articles of Confederation. It then enacted that its delegates could meet with similarly commissioned delegates from the other States, specifically vesting its deputies with three powers: 1. "to discuss and decide upon the most effectual means *to remedy the defects of our Federal Union,*" 2. "to procure, and secure, *the enlarged purposes which it [the Federal Union] was intended to effect,*" and 3. "to report such an Act, to the United States in Congress, as when agreed to by them, and duly confirmed by the several States, will *effectually provide for the same.*" [Emphasis added] [25]

On April 9, 1787, the Governor of the Commonwealth of Massachusetts, James Bowdoin, officially commissioned that State's delegates in a letter that named the deputies and delineated their authority as follows:

> Whereas Congress did on the twenty first day of February A.D. 1787, Resolve "that in the opinion of Congress it is expedient that on the second Monday in May next a Convention of Delegates who shall have been appointed by the several States to be held at Philadelphia *for the sole and express purpose of revising the Articles of Confederation* and reporting to Congress and the several Legislatures, *such alterations and provisions therein* as shall when agreed to in Congress, and confirmed by the States *render the Federal Constitution adequate to the exigencies of government and the preservation of the Union.*" And Whereas the General Court have constituted and appointed you their Delegates to attend and represent this Commonwealth in the said proposed Convention; and have by Resolution of theirs of the tenth of March last, requested me *to Commission you for that purpose.*
>
> Now therefore Know Ye, that *in pursuance of the resolutions afore-*

---

[24] *Ibid.*, p. 14.
[25] Charles Callan Tansill (ed.), *Op. cit.*, p. 56.

said, I do by these presents, commission you...to meet such Delegates as may be appointed by the other or any of the other States in the Union to meet in Convention at Philadelphia at the time and *for the purposes afore-said.* [Emphasis added] [26]

In May of 1787, the General Assembly of the State of Connecticut formally commissioned that State's delegates to the Grand Convention in these words:

> Whereas the Congress of the United States by their Act of the twenty first of February 1787 have recommended that on the second Monday of May instant, a Convention of Delegates, who shall have been appointed by the several States, be held at Philadelphia *for the sole and express purpose of revising the Articles of Confederation.*
> Be it enacted by the Governor, Council of Representatives in General Court and by the Authority of the same.
> That [the specified individuals]...be and they hereby are appointed Delegates to attend the said Convention,...and *are hereby authorized and empowered* to Represent this State therein, and to confer with such Delegates appointed by the several States, *for the purposes mentioned in the said Act of Congress* that may be present and duly empowered to act in said Convention, and to discuss upon such Alterations and Provisions *agreeable to the general Principles of Republican Government* as they shall think proper *to render the Federal Constitution adequate to the exigencies of Government and, the preservation of the Union;* And they are further directed, *pursuant to the said Act of Congress* to report *such alterations and provisions* as may be agreed to *by a majority of the United States* represented in Convention to the Congress of the United States, and to the General Assembly of this State. [Emphasis added] [27]

The Assembly of New York, on March 6, 1787, formally commissioned its delegates to the Philadelphia Convention with the following resolution:

> Resolved that [the individuals specified]...are hereby declared *duly nominated and appointed Delegates,* on the part of this State, to meet such Delegates as may be appointed on the part of the other States respectively, on the second Monday in May next, at Philadelphia, *for the sole and express purpose of revising the Articles of Confederation,* and reporting to Congress, and to the several Legislatures, *such alterations and provisions therein,* as shall, when agreed to in Congress, and confirmed by the several States, *render the Federal Constitution adequate to the exigencies of Government, and the*

[26] *Ibid.*, pp. 56-57.
[27] *Ibid.*, pp. 57-58.

preservation of the Union. [Emphasis added] [28]

The State of New Jersey empowered its several deputies to the Federal Convention in three separate commissions, dated November 23, 1786, May 18, 1787, and June 5, 1787. The first commission authorized a portion of its delegates to attend the Philadelphia Convention "*for the purpose of* taking into consideration the state of the Union, as to trade and other important objects, and of devising such other Provisions as shall appear to be *necessary to render the Constitution of the Federal Government adequate to the exigencies thereof.*" [29] The authorizations within the other two commissioning acts were expressed *in precisely the same language.* The only difference was that, in the last commission, the plural form of the word "purpose" was used and the singular form of the word "Provisions" was employed.

The State of Pennsylvania, which hosted the Grand Convention, formally commissioned all of its delegates, except Benjamin Franklin, in an act by the General Assembly that was formally styled, "An Act Appointing Deputies to the Convention Intended to Be Held in the City of Philadelphia for the Purpose of Revising the Federal Constitution." Within this act, adopted on December 13, 1786, the General Assembly stated that it was "fully convinced of the necessity of *revising the Federal Constitution* for the purpose of making *such Alterations and amendments* as the exigencies of our Public Affairs require." That body was also "fully sensible of the important advantages which may be derived to the United States...from co-operating with...the *other States of the Confederation* in the said Design." [Emphasis added] [30]

With these considerations in mind, the General Assembly declared:

> Be it enacted, and it is hereby enacted by the Representatives of the Freemen of the Commonwealth of Pensylvia in General Assembly met, and by the Authority of the same, That [the named individuals]... *are hereby constituted and appointed Deputies from this State*, with Powers to meet such Deputies as may be appointed and authorized by the other States, to assemble in the said Convention at the City aforesaid, and to join with them in devising, deliberating on, and discussing, all such alterations and further Provisions, as may be necessary *to render the Federal Constitution fully adequate to the exigencies of the Union*, and in reporting such Act or Acts for that purpose to the United States in Congress Assembled, as when agreed to by them and duly confirmed by the several States, will *effectually provide for the same.* [Emphasis added] [31]

---

[28] *Ibid.*, p. 60.
[29] *Ibid.*, p. 61.
[30] *Ibid.*, p. 63.
[31] *Ibid.*, p. 64.

In a supplemental act, adopted on March 8, 1787, Benjamin Franklin – who, at the time of the Federal Convention, was the Governor of Pennsylvania – received his commission from his State. By the terms of its provisions, his authority was the same as that given to those delegates who had been previously commissioned. In other words, he was instructed to attend the Convention for the purpose of rendering "the Federal Constitution fully adequate to the exigencies of the Union."

On February 3, 1787, in "the Eleventh Year of the Independence of the Delaware State," the sovereign State of Delaware adopted "An Act Appointing Deputies from This State to the Convention Proposed to Be Held in the City of Philadelphia for the Purpose of Revising the Federal Constitution." Within this official act of the legislature, the credentials of that State's delegates to the Grand Convention were presented in the following language:

> Whereas the General Assembly of this State are fully convinced of the Necessity of *revising the Federal Constitution*, and adding thereto such further Provisions, as may *render the same more adequate to the Exigencies of the Union*;...And this State being willing and desirous of co-operating with...the *other States in the Confederation*, in so useful a design.
>
> Be it therefore enacted by the General Assembly of Delaware, that [the named individuals]...*are hereby appointed Deputies from this State*...with Powers to meet such Deputies as may be appointed and authorized by the other States to assemble in the said Convention at the City aforesaid, and to join with them in devising, deliberating on, and discussing, *such Alterations and further Provisions* as may be necessary *to render the Federal Constitution adequate to the Exigencies of the Union*; and in reporting such Act or Acts for that purpose to the United States in Congress Assembled, as when agreed to by them, and duly confirmed by the several States, *may effectually provide for the same*: So always and Provided, *that such Alterations or further Provisions*, or any of them, *do not extend to that part of the Fifth Article of the Confederation of the said States*,...which declares that "in determining Questions in the United States in Congress Assembled *each State shall have one Vote*." [Emphasis added] [32]

The credentials of the delegates from Maryland were established within "An Act for the Appointment of, and Conferring Powers in Deputies from this State to the Federal Convention," which was adopted by the General Assembly on May 26, 1787. This act declared:

> Be it enacted by the General Assembly of Maryland, That [the specified individuals]...*be appointed and authorised on behalf of this State*, to meet such Deputies as may be appointed and authorised by any other of

---

[32] *Ibid.*, pp. 66-67.

the United States to assemble in Convention at Philadelphia *for the purpose of revising the Federal System*, and to join with them in considering *such Alterations and further Provisions as may be necessary to render the Federal Constitution adequate to the Exigencies of the Union* and in reporting such an Act for that purpose to the United States in Congress Assembled as when agreed to by them, and duly confirmed by the several States will *effectually provide for the same*....[Emphasis added] [33]

The General Assembly of Virginia, on October 16, 1786, provided authorization to its delegates to the Federal Convention in "An Act for Appointing Deputies from This Commonwealth to a Convention to Be Held in the City of Philadelphia in May Next for the Purpose of Revising the Federal Constitution." The act was prefaced by a statement of intent or motive, which began by noting the recommendation of the Annapolis Convention on "the necessity of extending *the revision of the federal System* to all its defects." This preface then noted the concern of the Old Dominion for "the actual *situation of the Confederacy*," reflected on the patriotic sentiments that had induced Virginians "to unite with their Brethren of the other States *in establishing a Federal Government*," and concluded that it was wise to consider provisions "necessary *to secure the great Objects for which that Government was instituted* and to render the United States as happy in peace as they have been glorious in War." [Emphasis added] [34]

Following this introduction, the legislation formally commissioned Virginia's delegation:

> BE IT THEREFORE ENACTED by the General Assembly of the Commonwealth of Virginia *that seven Commissioners be appointed... who or any three of them are hereby authorized as Deputies from this Commonwealth* to meet such Deputies as may be appointed and authorized by other States to assemble in Convention at Philadelphia as above recommended and to join with them in devising and discussing all *such Alterations and farther Provisions as may be necessary to render the Federal Constitution adequate to the Exigencies of the Union* and in reporting such an Act for that purpose to the United States in Congress as when agreed to by them and duly confirmed by the several States will *effectually provide for the same.* [Emphasis added] [35]

On January 6, 1787, the General Assembly of North Carolina officially provided credentials to that State's delegates to the Grand Convention in "An Act for Appointing Deputies from This State to a Convention Proposed to Be

---

[33] *Ibid.*, pp. 67-68.
[34] *Ibid.*, p. 69.
[35] *Ibid.*, pp. 69-70.

Held in the City of Philadelphia in May Next, for the Purpose of Revising the Federal Constitution." The General Assembly enacted:

> That five Commissioners be appointed by joint-ballot of both Houses of Assembly who, or any three of them, *are hereby authorized as Deputies from this State* to meet at Philadelphia on the first day of May next, then and there to meet and confer with such Deputies as may be appointed by the other States *for similar purposes*, and with them to discuss and decide upon *the most effectual means to remove the defects of our Federal Union*, and to procure *the enlarged Purposes which it was intended to effect*, and that they report such an Act to the General Assembly of this State as when agreed to by them, will *effectually provide for the same.* [Emphasis added] [36]

The authorization to commission the deputies appointed by the State of South Carolina was approved by an act adopted by the State legislature on March 8, 1787. Pursuant to this legislation, Governor Thomas Pinckney officially commissioned each of the State's delegates in this language:

> *I do hereby Commission You [the named delegate]...as one of the Deputies appointed from this State* to meet such Deputies or Commissioners as may be appointed and authorized by other of the United States to assemble in Convention at the City of Philadelphia in the Month of May next, or as soon thereafter as may be, and to join with such Deputies or Commissioners (*they being duly authorized and empowered*) in devising and discussing all *such Alterations, Clauses, Articles and Provisions, as may be thought necessary to render the Federal Constitution entirely adequate to the actual Situation and future good Government of the Confederated States,* and that you together with the said Deputies or Commissioners or a Majority of them who shall be present (provided the State be not represented by less than two) do join in reporting such an Act, to the United States in Congress Assembled as when approved and agreed to by them, and duly ratified and confirmed by the several States *will effectually provide for the Exigencies of the Union.* [Emphasis added] [37]

In "An Ordinance for the Appointment of Deputies from This State for the Purpose of Revising the Federal Constitution," which was adopted by the General Assembly on February 10, 1787, the delegates from Georgia were commissioned as follows:

> BE IT ORDAINED by the Representatives of the Freemen of the State of Georgia in General Assembly met and by the Authority of the

---

[36] *Ibid.,* p. 75.
[37] *Ibid.,* p. 78.

same, that [the named individuals]..., Be, and they *are hereby appointed Commissioners,* who, or any two or more of them *are hereby authorized as Deputies from this State* to meet such deputies as may be appointed and authorized by other States to assemble in Convention at Philadelphia and to join with them in devising and discussing *all such Alterations and farther Provisions as may be necessary to render the Federal Constitution adequate to the exigencies of the Union,* and in reporting such an Act for that purpose to the United States in Congress Assembled as when agreed to by them, and duly confirmed by the several States, will *effectually provide for the same.* [Emphasis added] [38]

In pursuance of this act, each of Georgia's delegates to the Federal Convention received the following formal notice of his commission:

WHEREAS you [the named delegate]...are in and by an Ordinance of the General Assembly of our said State *Nominated and Appointed a Deputy* to represent the same in *a Convention of the United States* to be assembled at Philadelphia, *for the Purposes of revising and discussing all such Alterations and farther Provisions as may be necessary to render the Federal Constitution adequate to the Exigencies of the Union.*
　　　　You are therefore hereby Commissioned to proceed on *the duties required of you in virtue of the said Ordinance.* [Emphasis added] [39]

The Purpose of the Federal Convention

From this review of the credentials of the delegates appointed by the several States, the powers and duties of those delegates, as well as the purposes and limitations of the Convention itself, may be readily ascertained. The *purpose* of the Grand Convention was to revise the then existing Federal Constitution to render it adequate to the exigencies of the Federal Government and the preservation of the Federal Union. The objective was purely *federal* in nature, and one State even went so far as to stipulate that the equality of the voting rights enjoyed by the States within the general legislature could not be infringed. Yet another State added the restriction that the Convention must confine its efforts to the principles of *republican* government. Monarchy, like nationalism, would officially be beyond the pale within the Convention.

In his book, *New Views of the Constitution of the United States,* John Taylor of Caroline conducted his own examination of the commissions enacted by the several States. Regarding the authorizations given to the delegates by their respective State governments, Mr. Taylor made these lucid observa-

---

[38] *Ibid.,* p. 84.
[39] *Ibid.,* p. 82.

tions:

> Thus the States unanimously rejected the recommendation of a *National* Government, and by excluding the word national from all their credentials, demonstrated that they well understood the wide difference between a *Federal* and a *National* Union. The distinction was enforced in Massachusetts and Connecticut by the words "sole purpose." The reference of sole, is to the word national, used by Congress, and in all the credentials the word federal is used also in opposition to the word national. There existed no other object but the suggestion of a National Government, for the restrictions in the credentials of the States to operate upon; and their unanimity, without consulting each other, is a complete proof that they all comprehended the difference between a Federal and a National form of government. The word Constitution is also uniformly considered by the States as equivalent to the word Confederation. [40]

Jefferson Davis also reviewed the credentials of the delegates to the Constitutional Convention in his 1881 masterpiece, *The Rise and Fall of the Confederate Government*, and made four conclusions:

> From an examination and comparison of the enactments and instructions above quoted, we may derive certain conclusions, so obvious that they need only to be stated:
>
> 1. In the first place, it is clear that the delegates to the Convention of 1787 represented, *not the people of the United States* in mass, as has been most absurdly contended by some political writers, but *the people* of the several States, *as States* – just as in the Congress of that period – Delaware, with her sixty thousand inhabitants, having entire equality with Pennsylvania, which had more than four hundred thousand, or Virginia, with her seven hundred and fifty thousand.
>
> 2. The object for which they were appointed was not to organize a *new* Government, but "solely and expressly" to amend the "Federal Constitution" already existing; in other words, "to revise the Articles of Confederation," and to suggest such "alterations" or additional "provisions" as should be deemed necessary to render them "adequate to the exigencies of the Union."
>
> 3. It is evident that the term "Federal Constitution," or its equivalent, "Constitution of the Federal Government," was as freely and familiarly applied to the system of government established by the Articles of Confederation – undeniably a league or compact between States expressly retaining their sovereignty and independence – as to that amended system which was substituted for it by the Constitution that superseded those Articles.
>
> 4. The functions of the delegates to the Convention were, of

---

[40] John Taylor, *Op. cit.*, p. 15.

course, only to devise, deliberate, and discuss. No validity could attach to any action taken, unless and until it should be afterward ratified by the several States. It is evident, too, that what was contemplated was the process provided in the Articles of Confederation for their own amendment – first, a recommendation by the Congress; and, afterward, ratification "by the Legislatures of every State," before the amendment should be obligatory upon any. [41]

The general sentiments of the States during the Constitutional Era may be gleaned from the slogan that appeared on the official notices of commission tendered to the delegates from the State of Georgia. At the top of each of these formal notices were the words, "The State of Georgia by the grace of God, free, Sovereign and Independent."[42] Such were the undisguised sentiments of those proud sovereignties that sent delegates to meet in Convention in Philadelphia during the long, hot summer of 1787.

[41] Jefferson Davis, *Ibid.*, Volume 1, pp. 93-94.
[42] Charles Callan Tansill (ed.), *Op. cit.*, p. 82.

Chapter Seven

The Nationalist Conspiracy

Convinced that the exigencies of the Federal Union necessitated amending the existing Federal Constitution, twelve of the thirteen sovereign States sent delegates to the Philadelphia Convention of 1787. Although most States placed, within the credentials of their respective commissioners, no limits on the *range of topics* that might be discussed at the Federal Convention, *all* of the States who sent delegates placed a very *clear and strict limitation* on the *purpose and objective* of the Grand Convention. The States sent their delegates to the Philadelphia Convention *for the sole and express purpose of revising the Articles of Confederation.*

It was universally understood throughout the Union that, by placing this clearly defined limit on the *objective* of the Grand Convention of the States, the delegates would confine their deliberations to the *means* necessary to attain the specified *end*. The delegates were clearly not empowered to propose an entirely new plan of government for the United States, much less to recommend a new Constitution based on principles fundamentally different from the form and system of government established by the Articles of Confederation. What was widely anticipated as a result of the Convention was nothing more than a few proposed amendments to those Articles.

As the American people – and, indeed, the whole world – watched with keen interest, delegates from several of the States assembled at the State House in Philadelphia on May 14, 1787, the scheduled starting date of the Convention, only to discover that the number of States present was insufficient to constitute the quorum needed to officially begin proceedings. It was not until eleven days later, on Friday, May 25th, that a quorum of the States – Massachusetts, New York, New Jersey, Pennsylvania, Delaware, Virginia, North Carolina, South Carolina, and Georgia – was finally present and the Convention could begin.

With the eyes of mankind on them, the delegates quickly went to work organizing themselves. George Washington of Virginia, having been nominated by Robert Morris of Pennsylvania and seconded by John Rutledge of South Carolina, was unanimously elected Chairman of the Convention. William Jackson, who was nominated by Alexander Hamilton of New York, was then elected Secretary. Following the elections of these two officers, the credentials of those delegates present were officially read and, in the words of James Madison of Virginia, "it was noticed that those from Delaware were prohibited from changing the Article in the Confederation establishing an equality of votes among the States." [1] The Convention next appointed Nicholas Weaver as Messenger and Joseph Fry as Door-Keeper. This was followed by the appointment of a Rules Committee consisting of George Wythe of Virginia, Charles Pinckney of South Carolina, and Alexander Hamilton. The Convention then adjourned until Monday morning.

As the American people watched, the delegates resumed business on May 28th by reading the credentials of several newly arrived delegates. George Wythe, reporting from the Rules Committee, then presented a list of rules to guide the Convention. These rules ranged from one requiring that a minimum of seven States must be present for the Convention to do business, to one that required that every delegate, upon adjournment, stand in his place until George Washington had passed him.

Rufus King of Massachusetts objected to one proposed rule that authorized any delegate to require, upon request, the official recording of each delegate's vote on matters before the Convention. George Mason of Virginia seconded the objection, stating that a record of each delegate's votes "in case of its being hereafter promulgated must furnish handles to the adversaries of the Result of the Meeting." [2] In accordance with these sentiments, the proposed rule that would have allowed the official recording of individual votes was rejected by the Convention.

Pierce Butler of South Carolina then moved that the Convention provide against "interruption of business by absence of members, and against licentious publications of their procedings." [3] The meaning of the last proposal was not misunderstood. *This was a proposal that the Convention conduct its business in absolute secrecy!* After referring the matter to the Rules Committee, the delegates adjourned for the day.

The next day – the third day of the Convention – George Wythe reported on additional official rules of the Convention. Among these new rules were the following:

> That no member be absent from the House so as to interrupt the representation of the State without leave.
> That Committees do not sit whilst the House shall be, or ought to be, sitting.
> *That no copy be taken of any entry on the Journal during the sitting of*

[1] Max Farrand (ed.), *The Records of the Federal Convention of 1787*, Volume I, Yale University Press, New Haven, 1966, p. 4.
[2] *Ibid.*, Volume I, p. 10.
[3] *Ibid.*, Volume I, p. 13.

the House without the leave of the House.
  That members only be permitted to inspect the Journal.
  That nothing spoken in the House be printed, or otherwise published,
or communicated without leave. [Emphasis added] [4]

With the adoption of these rules, an impenetrable curtain of secrecy descended around the State House in Philadelphia. To many on the outside, this decision was both surprising and a cause for concern. Writing to John Adams in London, Thomas Jefferson probably expressed the sentiments of most Americans when asserted that, "I am sorry they began their deliberations by so abominable a precedent as that of tying up the tongues of their members." [5]

If the rule of secrecy was cause for concern among the American people, so too was the duration of the Convention. The delegates had officially convened only to deliberate upon and draft a few amendments to the Articles of Confederation. Such a task could be expected to require the labors of only a few days, or perhaps a few weeks at most. Yet, as curious Americans awaited the results of the Convention, May quickly gave way to June, which in turn gave way to July. While the American people celebrated the eleventh anniversary of the Declaration of Independence, it appeared that there was still no end in sight to the Grand Convention of the States.

Although the veil of secrecy surrounding the Philadelphia Convention remained tight, outside observers noticed with concern that two of the three delegates from New York withdrew from the Convention in early July, thereby leaving that State officially unrepresented in that assemblage. Adding to the widespread concern, it appeared that the two delegates – John Lansing and Robert Yates – had withdrawn under the conviction that the Convention posed a threat to American liberty. It was also noticed that the third delegate from New York – Alexander Hamilton – had separately walked out of the Convention only to mysteriously return near its conclusion.

As anxiety and concern mounted throughout the Union, August came and went. Still, the Federal Convention remained in session behind closed doors. It was not until September 18th – 117 days after it had begun – that the Convention finally concluded its business. And it was only then that millions of Americans understood why the Convention had been in continuous session for nearly four months. Rather than deliberate upon and draft several amendments to the Articles of Confederation, the Federal Convention had deliberated upon and drafted an entirely new Constitution for the United

---

[4] *Ibid.*, Volume I, p. 15.
[5] Dumas Malone, *Jefferson and His Time*, Volume 2, Little, Brown and Company, Boston, 1951, quoted on p. 164.

States!

To many Americans, this revelation was not only a surprise, but a keen disappointment. Thomas Jefferson, for one, could not conceal his dismay at the Convention's decision to abandon the Articles of Confederation. "I think all the good of this new Constitution," he wrote, "might have been couched in three or four new articles to be added to the good, old, and venerable fabric, which should have been preserved even as a religious relic." [6]

What had compelled the Convention to exceed its authority and draft an entirely new Constitution? The new plan of government, on its face, certainly appeared to be based on republican and federal principles, just as the Articles of Confederation were. Why, then, did the Convention need to draft a new Constitution? Could not the same results have been more easily effected by a few choice amendments to the Articles, as Mr. Jefferson believed?

The only explanation publicly offered by the Convention for its conduct was a letter to the President of the Congress drafted by the delegates and signed by George Washington. In this letter, dated September 17, 1787, the Convention stated that, in delegating sufficient powers to the Federal Government to fully conduct the foreign affairs of the United States, it was decided that these powers should not be vested in one body or set of hands, but should instead be distributed among three separate branches of government. This *restructuring of the Federal Government* was given as the *reason* for a new Constitution.

Within this letter, the Convention referred to the government it proposed as a "*Federal Government of these States*" and acknowledged that, under the new Constitution, the States would retain their sovereignty. By delegating additional powers to the new government, however, the States would be required to refrain from individually exercising some of the powers and rights *associated* with their sovereign status. When individuals create civil society, it was explained, they are required to yield some of the rights associated with their personal liberty for the good of the whole. Yet, such individuals still remain free, and individual liberty still remains as the *cornerstone* of the society. And so it should be with the sovereign States under the new Constitution. The letter then hinted that a strong clash of interests had been displayed within the Convention, and that the Constitution represented a bundle of compromises. After acknowledging that perhaps not all of the States would approve of the new compact, the Convention concluded with its wish that all of the States would accede to it.

This letter to the Congress was in these words:

---

[6] *Ibid.*, quoted on p. 165.

We have now the honor to submit to the consideration of the United States in Congress assembled, that Constitution which has appeared to us the most adviseable.

The friends of our country have long seen and desired, that the power of making war, peace, and treaties, that of levying money and regulating commerce, and the correspondent executive and judicial authorities should be fully and effectually vested in the general government of the Union: But the impropriety of delegating such extensive trust to one body of men is evident – Hence results the necessity of a different organization.

It is obviously impracticable in the Federal Government of these States, to secure all rights of independent sovereignty to each, and yet provide for the interest and safety of all: Individuals entering into society, must give up a share of liberty to preserve the rest. The magnitude of the sacrifice must depend as well on situation and circumstance, as on the object to be obtained. It is at all times difficult to draw with precision the line between those rights which must be surrendered, and those which may be reserved; and on the present occasion this difficulty was encreased by a difference among the several States as to their situation, extent, habits, and particular interests.

In all our deliberations on this subject we kept steadily in our view, that which appears to us the greatest interest of every true American, the consolidation of our Union, in which is involved our prosperity, felicity, safety, perhaps our national existence. This important consideration, seriously and deeply impressed on our minds, led each State in the Convention to be less rigid on points of inferior magnitude, than might have been otherwise expected; and thus the Constitution, which we now present, is the result of a spirit of amity, and of that mutual deference and concession which the peculiarity of our political situation rendered indispensable.

That it will meet the full and entire approbation of every State is not perhaps to be expected; but each will doubtless consider, that had her interest been alone consulted, the consequences might have been particularly disagreeable or injurious to others; that it is liable to as few exceptions as could reasonably have been expected, we hope and believe; that it may promote the lasting welfare of that country so dear to us all, and secure her freedom and happiness, is our most ardent wish. [7]

This official letter from the Constitutional Convention, which briefly explained the *motives* for drafting a new Federal Constitution for the United States, was the only explanation offered by the delegates. *Conspicuously missing from the documents tendered by the Convention to the Congress was the official Journal of the meeting.* This omission was especially significant considering that one State, in authorizing the Convention, had specifically instructed that the *proceedings*, as well as the *results*, of the Convention should be re-

---

[7] Charles Callan Tansill (ed.), *The Making of the American Republic: The Great Documents, 1774-1789*, Arlington House, New Rochelle, pp. 1003-1004.

ported to the State governments. Even without such an expressed stipulation, however, the magnitude of the Convention's decision to draft a new Constitution seemed to mandate that it publish the official *Journal* of its debates.

Yet the *Journal* seemed to have disappeared. What had happened to it? Had it been destroyed? Was someone hiding it? If the *Journal* no longer existed, perhaps some of the delegates had taken personal notes of the debates. If so, why were these notes not made public along with the new Constitution? Had these personal notes also been destroyed? Many years would pass before the American people discovered the answers to these very pertinent questions.

The Records of the Federal Convention

The *Journal* of the Federal Convention had not been destroyed, at least not completely, although some of the delegates certainly hoped that the official record of their words and deeds behind the closed doors of the Philadelphia State House would never see the light of day. The fate of the *Journal* had been secretly decided on September 17th, the Convention's last day of business. In James Madison's notes for that day, it is revealed that Rufus King – the same delegate who, at the start of the Convention, had persuaded his fellow delegates that their individual votes should not be recorded for posterity – moved that the *Journal* be destroyed, or at least hidden from public view.

As Mr. Madison recorded this incident:

> Mr. King suggested that *the Journals of the Convention should be either destroyed, or deposited in the custody of the President. He thought if suffered to be made public, a bad use would be made of them by those who would wish to prevent the adoption of the Constitution* —
> Mr. [George] Wilson [of Pennsylvania] *prefered the second expedient. He had at one time liked the first best*; but as false suggestions may be propagated it should not be made impossible to contradict them –
> A question was then put on depositing the Journals and other papers of the Convention in the hands of the President, on which,
> N-H – ay. Mtts ay. Ct. ay – N.J. ay. Pena. ay. Del. ay. Md. no. Va. ay. N.C. ay – S.C. ay. Geo. ay. [Ayes 10; noes – 1.] [Emphasis added] [8]

Maryland's lone dissenting vote against hiding the *Journal* from the American people was undoubtedly based on the instructions given to her delegates by the Maryland State government to officially report on the *proceedings* of the Convention after it had concluded its business. In spite of this

---

[8] Max Farrand (ed.), *Op. cit.*, Volume II, p. 648.

specific requirement, however, the Convention voted to hide the *Journal* by placing it in the hands of George Washington for safekeeping. This sudden and strange maneuver seemed to have taken General Washington by surprise, for Mr. Madison added the following to his notes:

> The President having asked what the Convention meant should be done with the Journals &c, whether copies were to be allowed to the members if applied for. It was Resolved mem: con: "that he retain the Journal and other papers, subject to the order of Congress, if ever formed under the Constitution.
>
> The members then proceeded to sign the instrument. [9]

From Mr. Madison's notes, it is apparent that, during the Ratification Period, George Washington was hiding the *Journal* at the request of the Convention. By the instructions given to him, he was to surrender the *Journal* to the new Congress *after* the new Constitution had been adopted. It is not clear from Mr. Madison's notes what would have been the fate of the *Journal* had the Constitution *not* been adopted by the States. It may be presumed from the tenor of the debates on the matter, however, that the *Journal*, in such an event, would have been quietly destroyed.

In pursuance of the resolution of the Convention, William Jackson, the Convention's Secretary and sole superintendent of the minutes, tendered the *Journal* to George Washington, but only after burning "all the loose scraps of paper" [10] associated with it. General Washington, in turn, retained the *Journal* in his possession for nearly a decade, finally depositing the official minutes of the Convention with the State Department in 1796, where it lay dormant for more than twenty years.

The first breach in the veil of secrecy occurred almost immediately after the Federal Convention when Luther Martin, who had been a delegate from Maryland, gave a detailed report on the Convention's proceedings to the legislature of his State. To the shock and amazement of many, Mr. Martin explained in his *Genuine Information* that, behind the closed doors of the Philadelphia State House, a fierce battle had been waged between the forces of liberty and the advocates of totalitarian government. His lengthy address was the first serious indication that something sinister had taken place behind the Convention's veil of secrecy.

The general public received another shocking revelation about the Constitutional Convention in 1808, during the Presidential election campaign in which James Madison was a candidate. This breach in the wall of se-

---

[9] *Ibid.*, Volume II, p. 648.
[10] *Ibid.*, Volume I, quoted on p. xi.

crecy was made, not by a delegate but by Edmond C. Genet, a former minister from France who had taken up residence in New York. In an apparent effort to harm Mr. Madison's candidacy, Mr. Genet published extracts from the Convention's proceedings in *A Letter to the Electors of President and Vice-President of the United States*. Within this letter, Mr. Genet portrayed the man historically dubbed the "Father of the Constitution" as being a leader in the Federal Convention of a ill-fated nationalist conspiracy to destroy the State governments and to establish a centralized despotism in the United States. This startling and disturbing portrayal, moreover, was supported by a large number of direct quotations demonstrating Mr. Madison's role in such a conspiracy against the States.

Aside from Luther Martin's *Genuine Information* and Edmund Genet's 1808 public letter, the tight veil of secrecy surrounding the Convention's proceedings remained intact until 1818, more than thirty years after the Convention, when Congress, by a joint resolution, finally ordered the belated publication of the official *Journal*. The sorry state of the *Journal*, combined with the excessive number of years that had elapsed since the Philadelphia Convention, made the task of publication extremely difficult.

As the noted historian, Max Farrand, observed:

> President Monroe requested the Secretary of State, John Quincy Adams, to take charge of the publication of the Journal. The task proved to be a difficult one. The papers were, according to Adams, "no better than the daily minutes from which the regular Journal ought to have been, but never was, made out." Adams reports that at his request William Jackson, the Secretary of the Convention, called upon him and "looked over the papers, but he had no recollection of them which could remove the difficulties arising from their disorderly state, nor any papers to supply the deficiency of the missing papers." With the expenditure of considerable time and labor, and with the exercise of no little ingenuity, Adams was finally able to collate the whole to his satisfaction. General Bloomfield supplied him with several important documents from the papers of David Brearley; Charles Pinckney sent him a copy of the plan he "believed" to be the one he presented to the Convention; Madison furnished the means of completing the records of the last four days; and Adams felt that "with all these papers suitably arranged, a correct and tolerably clear view of the proceedings of the Convention may be presented."
>
> The results of his labor were printed at Boston in 1819 in an octavo volume of some 500 pages, entitled, *Journal, Acts and Proceedings of the Convention,...which formed the Constitution of the United States*. As Adams had nothing whatever to guide him in his work of compilation and editing, mistakes were inevitable, and not a few of these were important....
>
> ...With notes so carelessly kept, as were evidently those of the Secretary, the Journal cannot be relied upon absolutely. [11]

retary, the Journal cannot be relied upon absolutely. [11]

With the publication of the official *Journal*, the curtain of secrecy surrounding the Federal Convention's proceedings began to be lifted, and the personal notes of some of the individual delegates were eventually made public, beginning in 1821. In that year, the notes of Robert Yates were published under the title of *Secret Proceedings and Debates of the Convention Assembled at Philadelphia, in the Year 1787, for the Purpose of Forming the Constitution of the United States of America*. With the publication of these notes, Mr. Genet's secret source for his 1808 letter was no longer a secret, for it was obvious that the ex-minister from France had drawn his extracts of the proceedings from the notes of the distinguished delegate from New York.

The notes of Mr. Yates proved far superior, in terms of detail, to those of the official *Journal*; and unlike the *Journal*, which merely reported the Convention's resolutions and votes on issues, Mr. Yates's notes contain lengthy excerpts from the debates in support of and in opposition to the various resolutions moved by the delegates. Unfortunately, the Yates notes only covered the Convention's proceedings to July 5th, the date on which Robert Yates and John Lansing walked out the Convention, never to return again.

Following the publication of the *Journal* and the notes of Robert Yates, the notes of other delegates who attended the Philadelphia Convention were either published or discovered. Among these are the notes of James McHenry of Maryland, Rufus King of Massachusetts, William Pierce of Georgia, Alexander Hamilton of New York, William Paterson of New Jersey, and George Mason of Virginia. The most copious and thorough notes, of course, were those taken by James Madison of Virginia.

Although Mr. Madison was often urged by his contemporaries to publish his notes, he steadfastly refused to do so during his lifetime, and it was not until four years after his death in 1836 that his notes were finally made public. The *reason* why this Virginian opted for posthumous publication of his notes is open to speculation. One compelling reason, no doubt, was the fact that his own notes *proved* that the accounts given by Luther Martin, Edmund Genet, and Robert Yates were essentially accurate!

After the publication of James Madison's notes, contemporary scholars and historians quickly seized upon them as being the most accurate recorded account of what had really taken place within the Constitutional Convention of 1787. Over the course of time, however, some scholars became convinced that a reassessment of the accuracy of Mr. Madison's notes was in order. This reassessment was necessitated when it became apparent that Mr. Madison had

---

[11] *Ibid.*, Volume I, pp. xii-xiii.

made a large number of *changes* in his original notes during the years following the Convention.

In his analysis of Mr. Madison's notes, Max Farrand noted:

> It is well known that James Madison had taken full and careful
> notes of the proceedings in the Convention, and he had often been urged
> to publish them. He had, however, decided that a posthumous publication
> was advisable. Madison died in 1836. His manuscripts were purchased by
> Congress, and shortly afterwards, in 1840, under the editorship of H.D.
> Gilpin, *The Papers of James Madison* were published in three volumes.
> More than half of this work was given over to his notes of the debates in
> the Federal Convention, and at once all other records paled into insignifi-
> cance....

> Indeed Madison was evidently regarded by his fellow-delegates to
> the Convention as a semi-official reporter of their proceedings, for several
> of them took pains to see that he was supplied with copies of their speeches
> and motions. *And from the day of their publication until the present, Madi-
> son's notes of the Debates have remained the standard authority for the proceed-
> ings of the Convention.*

> Madison's correspondence and the manuscript itself reveal the fact
> that Madison went over his notes after the publication of the *Journal* in
> 1819. He not only noted differences between his own record and that of
> the *Journal*, but also in many cases corrected his own notes from the *Jour-
> nal*....Nor is it surprising, when we remember that Madison accepted the
> printed *Journal* as authoritative, to find him in not a few cases copying
> from it proceedings of which he had no record....

> But Madison went even one step further and actually *changed his re-
> cords of votes* in the Convention in order to bring them into conformity
> with the *Journal*. This might involve the change of the vote of a single
> State, or of several States, or even reverse his record of the decision of the
> Convention. On what basis or for what reasons Madison felt justified in
> changing his records of votes is not to be ascertained conclusively. Some-
> times it seems to have been done because the records of *Journal* and Yates
> were in accord in their disagreement with him; sometimes he probably saw
> that subsequent action in the Convention proved the record of *Journal* to
> be correct, and his own to be wrong; sometimes it was done because the
> vote of a State as recorded in *Journal* harmonized better with the senti-
> ments of the delegates from that State as expressed in their speeches; and
> sometimes there is no apparent reason.

> The matter might be merely of antiquarian interest, were it not for
> the fact that the printed Journal is itself unreliable, and that there are not a
> few cases in which Madison has made corrections from the *Journal* that are
> undoubtedly mistaken: Votes ascribed in the *Journal* to the wrong ques-
> tions were used, in several cases, to change records that were probably cor-
> rect as first made. Questions and votes were copied into his manuscript
> from the printed *Journal* without observing that these same questions and
> votes were recorded in other places, sometimes even on the same day; an

examination of the original records shows that in most of these cases the questions were not to be found in the body of the Journal, but were incorporated into the text by John Quincy Adams; they are only to be found in the Detail of Ayes and Noes, and their relative position in the proceedings could only be inferred from the order in which the votes happened to be recorded.....

Another extensive set of corrections is to be found in the speeches made in debate. These are generally in the form of additions to Madison's original record. Because of [alleged] misquotations of his own remarks, Madison condemned Yates's notes severely, as being a "very erroneous edition of the matter." *It is more than surprising, then, to discover that these additions were taken from Yates. Such proves to have been the case, however, and in over fifty instances.* There were a number of speeches or remarks, *including several of his own,* that Madison failed to note in any form, but later thought worthy of inclusion. *And there were also new ideas or shades of thought which Yates had noticed but which Madison failed to catch.*

The fact of these changes being made does not rest merely upon the wording of the text and Madison's statement in 1821 that he was intending to prepare his notes for posthumous publication. The manuscript shows that most of the changes thus made are easily recognizable. *The ink which was used at the later date has faded quite differently from that of the original notes, so that most of the later revisions stand out from the page almost as clearly as if they had been written in red ink.* [Emphasis added] [12]

For these reasons, Mr. Farrand made this conclusion regarding the reliably of the notes taken of the Convention's proceedings:

In view of the fact that the *Journal* is so imperfect and not altogether reliable, and that Madison made so many changes in his manuscript, all other records of the Convention take on a new importance. Formerly they have been regarded only in so far as they might supplement our information; now it is seen that they may be of service also in determining what the action really was in doubtful cases. [13]

Proofs of a Conspiracy

As unreliable as the existing *Journal* and sundry personal notes are of the proceedings of the Grand Convention of the States, they constitute the only known records that reveal what happened behind the closed doors of the Philadelphia State House during the summer of 1787. And the amazing story they reveal provides ample proof that a veritable *conspiracy* existed within that

---

[12] *Ibid.*, Volume I, pp. xv-xviii.
[13] *Ibid.*, Volume I, p. xix.

Constitutional Convention to destroy the Federal Republic and replace it with either a National Republic or a National Monarchy.

The startling revelations within the once-secret records of the proceedings of the Philadelphia Convention shocked a number of Americans when they were first published. And upon reading those records, many Americans finally realized, perhaps for the first time, why a number of prominent individuals had been so desirous to keep the records concealed from the public eye for so many years. John Taylor of Caroline, after reading the official *Journal*, the notes of Robert Yates, and the writings of Luther Martin, was so moved by what he discovered that he wrote a book, entitled *New Views of the Constitution of the United States*, to analyze the amazing battle between nationalists and federalists within the Convention.

Regarding the sinister *veil of secrecy* which had surrounded the records of the Federal Convention for so many years, Mr. Taylor wrote in 1823:

> The fact of this jealous secrecy is ascertained by the Journal, and the perseverance in it for years. Even now, the veil is imperfectly removed; the Journal has not come to the general knowledge of the publick, and it appears in a mutilated state. It stops, or is impenetrably obscure, precisely at the period when the projected plan for a national form of government was supplanted by the federal system; and a suppression of the important steps by which this radical change was effected, must have taken place in the Convention, or subsequently. Thus the vindicators of a federal construction of the Constitution are deprived of a great mass of light, and the consolidating school have gotten rid of a great mass of detection. Secrecy is intended for delusion, and delusion is a fraud. If it was dictated by an apprehension, that a knowledge of the propositions and debates, would have alarmed the settled preference of the States and of the publick, for a federal form of government, it amounts to an acknowledgement that these propositions and debates were hostile to that form and to the publick opinion. If, by an apprehension that a publication of the Journal and debates, would produce a construction hostile to the rejected national form of government, it is an acknowledgement that constructions in favour of that form, are hostile to the Constitution adopted. To avoid these consequences, and no others that I can discern, it was necessary to keep the people in the dark, and this stratagem to obtain a victory over their most sacred right in the ambuscade mode, can only be accounted for upon a supposition, that a real hostility of opinion existed between the publick and a party of politicians behind the curtain, which rendered it necessary that the people should be worked as puppets, first by the wire of concealment, and secondly by the wire of construction, into the catastrophe of a consolidated government, either national or monarchical. [14]

---

[14] John Taylor, *New Views of the Constitution of the United States*, Da Capo Press, New York, (orig. pub. in 1823) 1971, pp. 40-41.

The records of the Federal Convention of 1787 indicate that no less than three distinct parties or *factions* existed within the Convention. These three factions, of course, were the same ones that had arisen and taken form during the "Critical Period" prior to the Convention, consisting of the *National Monarchists*, *National Republicans*, and *Federal Republicans*. The various records also indicate that the first two factions formed an alliance or coalition against the third faction, pooling their resources in a vain attempt to force the acceptance of a consolidated or supreme National Government on the Convention.

So apparent was the existence of these factions within the Convention that a delegate from Maryland, the distinguished Luther Martin – a staunch defender of State sovereignty, federalism, and republican government – was able to accurately identify and describe their nature in precise terms:

> One party, whose object and wish it was to abolish and annihilate all State governments, and to bring forward one general government over this extensive continent of a monarchial nature, under certain restrictions and limitations. Those who openly avowed this sentiment were, it is true, but few; yet it is equally true that there was a considerable number, who did not openly avow it, who were, by myself and many others of the Convention, considered as being in reality favorers of that sentiment....
>
> The second party was not for the abolition of the State governments nor for the introduction of a monarchial government under any form; but they wished to establish such a system as could give their own States undue power and influence in the government over the other States.
>
> The third party was what I considered truly federal and republican. This party was nearly equal in number with the other two, and was composed of the delegates from Connecticut, New York [excluding Alexander Hamilton], New Jersey, Delaware, and in part from Maryland; also of some individuals from other representations. This party were for proceeding upon terms of federal equality: they were for taking our present federal system as the basis of their proceedings, and, as far as experience had shown that other powers were necessary to the Federal Government, to give those powers. They considered this the object for which they were sent by their States, and what their States expected from them. [15]

The coalition or alliance formed between the National Monarchists and the National Republicans was also noted by Mr. Martin. "The first party, *conscious that the people of America would reject their system*, if proposed," he wrote, "joined the second, well knowing that by departing from a federal system, they paved the way for their favourite object, the destruction of the State

---

[15] Jefferson Davis, *The Rise and Fall of the Confederate Government*, Volume 1, Thomas Yoseloff, Cranbury, (orig. pub. in 1881) 1958, quoted on p. 95.

governments, and the introduction of monarchy." [Emphasis added] [16]

From the various records now available for inspection, it can be seen that the National Monarchists and the National Republicans were willing to stoop to any level of fraud and deception to give force to their indecent proposals. In James Madison's notes, for example, we find that, *even before the first day of the Convention*, an unscrupulous and secret plot to rob the States of their equal voting rights *within the Convention* was attempted. The schemers who were determined to subvert the federal system realized that the smaller and weaker States, which significantly outnumbered the larger States, would naturally fear and vigorously oppose any attempt to destroy the sovereign equality of the States within the Union.

This plot is related in Mr. Madison's notes in the following words:

> Previous to the arrival of a majority of the States, the rule by which they ought to vote in the Convention had been made a subject of conversation among the members present. It was pressed by Gouverneur Morris and favored by Robert Morris and others from Pennsylvania, that the large States should unite in firmly refusing to the small States an equal vote, as unreasonable, and as enabling the small States to negative every good system of government, which must in the nature of things, be founded on a violation of that equality. The members from Virginia, conceiving that such an attempt might beget fatal altercations between the large & small States, and that it would be easier to prevail on the latter, in the course of the deliberations, to give up their equality for the sake of an effective government, than on taking the field of discussion, to disarm themselves of the right & thereby throw themselves on the mercy of the large States, discountenanced & stifled the project. [17]

The plot to subvert the Federal Convention within its very rules was thus "silenced," not because of its wrongness, but only because it was deemed impractical and doomed to failure. Had the plot not been stifled – had the attempt been made at the very outset of the Convention to deny to the smaller States the equal vote to which they were entitled by the federal principle of the sovereign equality of States – those smaller States would undoubtedly have bolted from the Convention. And in such an event, the American people would have been alerted to the conspiracy to destroy the Federal Republic, and the conspirators would have found themselves confronted by an outraged public.

Although this specific plot was never attempted within the Philadelphia Convention, the very fact that it was *considered* illustrates that the nationalists

---

[16] John Taylor, *Op. cit.*, quoted on p. 42.
[17] Max Farrand (ed.), *Op. cit.*, Volume I, pp. 10-11.

understood that they faced an up-hill battle within the Convention, and that a considerable number of States would be very hostile to what they considered to be a "good system of government." Such an assessment, as it turned out, was highly accurate.

The nationalists did indeed encounter stiff resistance, and from the very sources they had originally identified as the centers of opposition. And as they had feared, the small States were sufficiently strong enough, under the rule of equality of suffrage, to outvote them. The decision to not pursue the disenfranchisement plot within the Convention's rules, therefore, saved not only the Convention, but the Federal Republic as well.

Nationalist Subversion of the Federal Convention

The nationalist conspiracy manifested itself *immediately* after the Convention adopted its rule of secrecy on May 29, 1787. After announcing the cloak of secrecy and determining that only one man – William Jackson, the elected Secretary who had been nominated by Alexander Hamilton – should superintend the minutes, Edmund Randolph arose to open the main business of the Convention.

The Governor of Virginia began by painting a sad and dreary picture of the United States during the "Critical Period," alluding to Shays' Rebellion, among other things, and noting that the existing Federal Government, in general, was wholly inadequate to meet the crisis. The very fact that he could condemn the want of power in the Federal Government to concern itself with such domestic matters as a local police matter within a sovereign State was indicative of his political views and suggestive of what he intended to propose as a "solution" to the alleged crisis.

"Thus we see that the Confederation is incompetent to any *one* object for which it was instituted," Mr. Randolph stated. "The framers of it [were] wise and great men; but human rights were the chief knowledge of the times when it was framed so far as they applied to oppose Great Britain." [18]

From these remarks, it may be deduced that governments founded on human rights, while appealing to the great masses of the American people, were not very appealing to the nationalists within the Federal Convention. This remark proved to be only the first of many contrasts made by the nationalists within the Convention, between *power* and *liberty*, in which they candidly stated their preference for the former.

"Our chief danger arises from the democratic parts of our constitu-

---

[18] *Ibid.*, Volume I, p. 26.

tions," Mr. Randolph informed his fellow delegates. His use of the plural form of the word – *constitutions* – suggested that he was interested in replacing more than just the existing Constitution of the United States. "It is a maxim which I hold incontrovertible," he added, "that the powers of government exercised by the people swallows up the other branches. None of the constitutions have provided sufficient checks against democracy. The feeble Senate of Virginia is a phantom." [19] In spite of these denunciations by Mr. Randolph of the existing *republican* constitutions throughout the Union of the States, Mr. Madison stated in his notes that, "He then proceeded to the *remedy; the basis of which he said, must be the republican principle.*" [Emphasis added] [20]

Robert Yates, in his notes, succinctly described the "remedy" proposed by Edmund Randolph in these words:

> He closed these remarks with a set of resolutions, fifteen in number, which he proposed to the Convention for their adoption, and *as leading principles whereon to form a new government – He candidly confessed that they were not intended for a Federal Government – he meant a strong consolidated Union, in which the idea of States should be nearly annihilated.* [Emphasis added] [21]

Thus, the curtain of secrecy had barely descended over the Federal Convention before the nationalist plot was unfolded before the eyes of the delegates present. Forget the Articles of Confederation, they were informed by the Governor of the largest State in the Union. The Articles are dead, and they should be buried before the rotting carcass fouls the air with its stench. In their place should be installed a government founded upon precisely opposite principles – an energetic, supreme National Government built on the ruins of once sovereign States – a government strong enough to control every aspect of the national economy and powerful enough to crush any semblance of disorder in any quarter of the Union – a government whose very nature would defy all attempts to limit its powers.

Not only was the Convention off to a very bad and disagreeable start, but its very reason for existence was subverted by its very first speaker! The Convention lawfully existed for the *sole and express* purpose of revising the Articles of Confederation, to make it adequate to the exigencies of the Federal Union. Replacing the existing Federal Constitution with a National Constitution, and erecting a consolidated nation on the ruins of a Federal Union be-

---

[19] *Ibid.*, Volume I, p. 27.
[20] *Ibid.*, Volume I, p. 19.
[21] *Ibid.*, Volume I, p. 24.

tween sovereign States, was certainly not calculated to render the Articles more adequate to a Federal Union. Although George Washington, as President of the Convention, maintained his silent neutrality throughout the Convention, he could have – and should have – chastised his fellow Virginian for being out of order in proposing a National Government to the delegates.

After deciding to refer Mr. Randolph's radical proposal to a committee of the whole house for consideration, the Convention heard from Charles Pinckney of South Carolina, who "laid before the house the draught of a *Federal Government* which he had prepared to be agreed upon *between the free and independent States of America*." [Emphasis added] [22]

Although this new plan was referred to as one for a "Federal Government" in Mr. Madison's notes, there was, in fact, little difference between the two plans before the Convention. In Robert Yates' notes, we read that even Mr. Pinckney confessed that his plan "was grounded on the same principle" [23] as the Randolph proposal. Owing to this consideration, little attention was given to Mr. Pinckney's plan by the Convention, and the nationalists, to a man, immediately gravitated to Mr. Randolph's proposition, which was referred to thereafter as the *Virginia Plan*.

Before adjourning for the day, the Convention heard briefly from Alexander Hamilton, who summarized the immediate task facing the delegates by noting that, "it struck him as a necessary and preliminary inquiry to the propositions from Virginia whether the United States were susceptible of one government, or required a separate existence connected only by leagues offensive and defensive and treaties of commerce." [24] The immediate task, in other words, would be to decide whether the United States of America should have a National Government or a Federal Government.

Thus, *on its very first day of serious business*, the Philadelphia Convention had been successfully subverted by a nationalist conspiracy. A *Federal* Convention convened for the sole and express purpose of revising the *Federal* Constitution to render it adequate to the exigencies of a *Federal* Government had been swiftly perverted into a movement to crush the sovereign peoples of the States under a supreme *National* Government founded on principles incompatible with a Federal Republic. If any delegate had previously entertained doubts as to why the cloak of secrecy was so eagerly desired by certain delegates, the events of the Convention's first day of real business should have removed all trace of doubt.

---

[22] *Ibid.*, Volume I, p. 23.
[23] *Ibid.*, Volume I, p. 24.
[24] *Ibid.*, Volume I, p. 27.

The Virginia Plan

The plan of government introduced by Edmund Randolph on May 29th consisted of fifteen comprehensive resolutions, which, in their original form, read as follows:

    1. Resolved that the Articles of Confederation ought to be so corrected & enlarged as to accomplish the objects proposed by their institution; namely. "common defence, security of liberty and general welfare."

    2. Resd. therefore that *the rights of suffrage in the National Legislature ought to be proportioned* to the Quotas of contribution, or to the number of free inhabitants, as the one or the other may seem best in different cases.

    3. Resd. that the *National Legislature* ought to consist of two branches.

    4. Resd. that the members of the first branch of the *National Legislature* ought to be elected by the people of the several States every _____ for the term of _____; to be of the age of _____ years at least, to receive liberal stipends by which they may be compensated for the devotion of their time to public service; to be ineligible to any office established by a particular State, or under the authority of the United States, except those beculiarly [peculiarly] belonging to the functions of the first branch, during the term of service, and for the space of _____ after its expiration; to be incapable of re-election for the space of _____ after the expiration of their term of service, and to be subject to recall.

    5. Resold. that *the members of the second branch of the National Legislature ought to be elected by those of the first*, out of a proper number of persons *nominated by the individual Legislatures*, to be of the age of _____ years at least; to hold their offices for a term sufficient to ensure their independency, to receive liberal stipends, by which they may be compensated for the devotion of their time to public service; and to be ineligible to any office established by a particular State, or under the authority of the United States, except those peculiarly belonging to the functions of the second branch, during the term of service, and for the space of _____ after the expiration thereof.

    6. Resolved that each branch ought to possess the right of originating Acts; that the *National Legislature* ought to be impowered to enjoy the Legislative Rights vested in *Congress* by the Confederation & moreover *to legislate in all cases to which the separate States are incompetent, or in which the harmony of the United States may be interrupted by the exercise of individual Legislation; to negative all laws passed by the several States, contravening in the opinion of the National Legislature the articles of Union*; and *to call forth the force of the Union agst. any member of the Union failing to fulfill its duty under the articles thereof.*

    7. Resd. that a *National* Executive be instituted; *to be chosen by the National Legislature* for the term of _____ years, to receive punctually at

stated times, a fixed compensation for the services rendered, in which no increase or diminution shall be made so as to affect the Magistracy, existing at the time of increase or diminution, and to be ineligible a second time; and that besides a general authority to execute the *National* laws, it ought to enjoy the Executive rights vested in *Congress* by the Confederation.

8. Resd. that the Executive and a convenient number of the *National* Judiciary, ought to compose *a council of revision with authority to examine every act of the National Legislature before it shall operate, & every act of a particular Legislature before a Negative thereon shall be final*; and that the dissent of the said Council shall amount to a rejection, unless the Act of the *National Legislature* be again passed, or that of a particular Legislature be again negatived by _____ of the members of each branch.

9. Resd. that a *National* Judiciary be established to consist of one or more *supreme* tribunals, and of *inferior* tribunals to be chosen by the *National Legislature, to hold their offices during good behaviour*; and to receive punctually at stated times compensation for their services, in which no increase or diminution shall be made so as to affect the persons actually in office at the time of such increase or diminution. That the jurisdiction of the inferior tribunals shall be to hear & determine in the first instance, and of the supreme tribunal to hear and determine in the dernier resort, all piracies & felonies on the high seas, captures from an enemy; cases in which foreigners or citizens of other States applying to such jurisdictions may be interested, or which respect the collection of the *National* revenue; impeachments of any *National* officers, and *questions which may involve the national peace and harmony*.

10. Resolvd. that provision ought to be made for the admission of States lawfully arising within the limits of the United States, whether from a voluntary junction of government & territory or otherwise, with the consent of a number of voices in the *National legislature* less than the whole.

11. Resd. that *a Republican Government & the territory of each State*, except in the instance of a voluntary junction of government & territory, *ought to be guaranteed by the United States to each State*.

12. Resd. that provision ought to be made for the continuance of *Congress* and their authorities and privilege, until a given day after the reform of the articles of Union shall be adopted, and for the completion of all their engagements.

13. Resd. that provision ought to be made for the amendment of the articles of Union whensoever it shall seem necessary, and that the assent of the *National Legislature* ought not to be required thereto.

14. Resd. that the Legislative Executive & Judiciary powers within the several States ought to be bound by oath to support the articles of Union.

15. Resd. that *the amendments which shall be offered to the Confederation, by the Convention* ought at a proper time, or times, after the approbation of *Congress* to be submitted to an assembly or assemblies of representatives, recommended by the several Legislatures to be expressly chosen by the people, to consider & decide thereon. [Emphasis added] [25]

by the people, to consider & decide thereon. [Emphasis added] [25]

Within these fifteen resolutions, the word *national* runs like a refrain, echoing and re-echoing from one resolution to the next. Under the Virginia Plan, there would be a "National Legislature," a "National Executive," and a "National Judiciary," as well as "National laws," "National revenue," "National officers," and "national peace and harmony." Indeed, the word *national* appears in these original fifteen resolutions no less than *nineteen* times, and before long the nationalists would increase the usage of that repugnant term, until it would appear in the Virginia Plan no less than *twenty-six* times!

It is also of significance to note that, throughout the Randolph resolutions, the term "Congress" is used only in reference to the existing legislative authority under the Articles of Confederation. That terminology was dropped by the nationalists, however, for their proposed new National Government, inasmuch as a *Congress* implies an assembly of representatives from sovereign States.

Although the first resolution entertained the notion that the new National Government would be offered as a fulfillment of the "objects proposed by" the Articles of Confederation, the nationalists quickly realized the inherent contradiction within such an idea, and the first resolution was promptly abandoned by them. The second resolution proposed to destroy all semblance of equality of suffrage in the "National Legislature," for the obvious reason that State sovereignty was incompatible with the idea of a National Government.

The sixth resolution provided a glimpse at the magnitude of powers such a proposed National Government should possess. Among other things, it would be empowered to legislate in all cases "to which the separate States are incompetent, or in which the harmony of the United States may be interrupted by the exercise of individual legislation." Such a concept of powers seemed better calculated to produce a government of unlimited powers than one of carefully enumerated powers.

The National Government would also be empowered to veto any law of any State, utterly destroying State sovereignty and independence in the process. Furthermore, the proposed National Government would be authorized to raise an army and wage a war of conquest against any State that refused to submit to it.

It would appear from the seventh and eighth resolutions that the Virginia Plan was not based on the concept of a division of powers within the Federal Government. The eighth resolution specifically called for a highly

---

[25] *Ibid.*, Volume I, pp. 20-22.

disagreeable *unification of the Executive and Judicial Branches* within a "Council of Revision." Within the seventh resolution, we see an unhealthy *merger of the Executive and Legislative Branches* of government, similar to what is routinely practiced in a Parliamentary form of government. The overall effect of these two resolutions unmistakably pointed to a very strong and dominant executive authority within the government, a trait more suited for a monarchical government than for a republican form of government.

Within the ninth resolution, provision was made for a Judicial Branch of government, wherein Judges *chosen by the Legislative Branch* would "*hold their offices during good behaviour.*" It is remarkable, in light of events that have occurred over the course of history since the adoption of the Constitution of 1787, that the Federal Republicans within the Convention made so little effort to expunge the decidedly monarchical nature of the judicial *life tenure* of office from the new compact of government.

The widespread sentiment in the Convention seemed to be that the Judicial Branch was of little consequence and could never pose a threat to the rights of the States and the liberties of the people. Under this consideration, consequently, few objections were raised to the proposition that federal Judges should hold their offices during "good behavior," or for life.

The eleventh resolution contained a seemingly innocent proposal that the National Government should guarantee the territorial integrity and the republican form of government of every State. Under the surface, however, there was nothing innocent about this proposition. It was a blatant proposal to transfer the *Police Powers* of the States to a National Government, as the Federal Republicans within the Convention wisely recognized.

By allowing a National Government to *define* what constitutes a "rebellion" and to crush such a rebellion with force, neither States nor individuals would be secure. Such a National Government, thus empowered, might attempt to declare that an entire State is in a *state of rebellion* and thereby move to crush the whole State with martial force, overthrow its government, and extinguish its local laws.

After these sundry proposals for a radical change in the American system of government had been made, the last of the Randolph resolutions reverted to the pacific tone of the first resolution, by referring to the proposed National Government as nothing more than a collection of "amendments...offered to the Confederation." Would these reassuring words deceive the delegates in the Convention? Would they deceive the American people? The nationalists, bolstered by their early successes in the Convention, had reason to think that their deception might well succeed.

The Nationalists in the Saddle

On May 30th, the day after the Virginia Plan was introduced, the Convention transformed itself into a Committee of the Whole, with Nathaniel Gorham of Massachusetts as Chairman, to consider and debate the merits of that plan of government. Edmund Randolph then proposed three resolutions to the Convention:

> 1. *Resolved*, That a Union of the States, *merely federal*, will not accomplish the objects proposed by the Articles of the Confederation, namely common defence, security of liberty, and general welfare.
> 2. *Resolved*, That no treaty or treaties among any of the States *as sovereign*, will accomplish or secure their common defence, liberty or welfare.
> 3. *Resolved*, That a *National Government* ought to be established, consisting of a *supreme* judicial, legislative and executive. [Emphasis added][26]

Within these three resolutions, which summarized the objectives of the nationalist movement within the Grand Convention of the States, a Federal Republic was openly rejected in favor a consolidated Empire in North America. The Federal Government, by this proposal, would be replaced by a National Government – or, more specifically, a *supreme National Government*. The States, if allowed to exist under this plan, could exist only as local branches or divisions of the supreme centralized authority. The sovereignty of the States would be relegated to the pages of history by this proposal, as if the concept of free and independent States had been only a passing fantasy entertained by those who adopted the Declaration of Independence. If the spirit of *liberty* had produced the sovereign States, then the spirit of centralized *power* was determined to abolish them.

It is evident from the notes taken by James McHenry that the bold swiftness displayed at this early stage by the consolidating nationalists seems to have taken most of the delegates by surprise. After Mr. Randolph proposed his three resolutions, a strangely troubled silence descended upon the whole house. Mr. McHenry wrote in his notes that, upon observing the unusual silence of the delegates, George Wythe of Virginia spoke up to assert that the silence should be interpreted as universal agreement with Mr. Randolph's three resolutions, and he therefore moved that the resolutions be adopted without further debate or consideration.

The silence, however, was hardly due to a widespread approbation of

---

[26] *Ibid.*, Volume I, p. 39.

the radical proposition to destroy the Federal Republic. Many of the delegates, judging from their remarks made soon afterwards, were apparently too stunned and surprised to speak immediately after hearing Mr. Randolph's proposal. According to Mr. McHenry's notes, Pierce Butler was the first shocked delegate to find his voice: "Mr. Butler – does not think the house prepared, that he is not. Wishes Mr. Randolph to shew that the existence of the States cannot be preserved by any other mode than a National Government." [27]

Within this initial objection raised by the delegate from South Carolina may be observed a key factor that explains why the nationalists were able to easily dominate the early stages of the Convention. The scheming nationalists had arrived at the Convention fully prepared and firmly united to press forward their radical agenda. The Federal Republicans, on the other hand, had come to the Federal Convention totally unprepared to face such a challenge to the existence of the Federal Republic.

Pierce Butler's request of Edmund Randolph – that the latter show that *"the existence of the States cannot be preserved by any other mode than a National Government"* – highlighted the dilemma faced by the nationalists. *Sovereign States are incompatible with a National Government, and for that very reason it was impossible for the nationalists to show that the States could be preserved under such a government.* Mr. Butler's inquiry struck at the very heart of the Virginia Plan and exposed the deceit inherent in the claims made by many of the nationalists that the States could somehow continue to exist under their imperial National Government. Try as they may, the nationalists would never be able to convince the other delegates that such a great contradiction could be sustained in the American constitutional system.

After Pierce Butler had voiced his opposition, other delegates spoke up in opposition to the proposed national system. In his notes for this day, James Madison stated that the opposition was directed not so much at the idea of drafting a new Constitution for the United States, as it was at "the force and extent of the particular terms *national & supreme.*" [28] Charles Pinckney "wished to know of Mr. Randolph whether he meant to abolish the State governts. altogether." [29] General Pinckney of South Carolina stated that he thought "agreeing to the resolve is declaring that the Convention does not act under the authority of the recommendation of Congress." [30] The General then read the authorization of the Convention derived from Congress, wherein it was stated that the purpose of the Convention was only to revise

---

[27] *Ibid.*, Volume I, p. 41.
[28] *Ibid.*, Volume I, p. 33.
[29] *Ibid.*, Volume I, pp. 33-34.
[30] *Ibid.*, Volume I, p. 41.

the Articles of Confederation. The Convention, he therefore surmised, had no authority to adopt the Virginia Plan.

In his notes, Robert Yates summarized the opposition made to the three nationalist resolutions of Edmund Randolph:

> In considering the question on the first resolve, various modifications were proposed, when Mr. Pinkney observed, at last, that *if the Convention agreed to it, it appeared to him that their business was at an end*; for as the powers of the house in general were to *revise the present Confederation*, and to alter or amend it as the case might require; to determine its insufficiency or incapability of amendment or improvement, must end in the dissolution of the powers.
>
> *This remark had its weight, and in consequence of it, the 1st and 2nd resolve was dropt, and the question agitated on the third.*
>
> *This last resolve had also its difficulties*; the term *supreme* required explanation – It was asked whether it was intended to annihilate State governments? [Emphasis added] [31]

John Dickinson, the author of the Articles of Confederation and a delegate from the small but proud State of Delaware, urged that the Convention abandon the wild proposal for a supreme National Government and stick to its true business of revising the Articles. His words were recorded as follows in James McHenry's notes:

> Under obligations to the gentlemen who brought forward the systems laid before the house yesterday. Yet differs from the mode of proceeding to which the resolutions or propositions before the Committee lead. Would propose a more simple mode. All agree that the Confederation is defective [and] all agree that it ought to be amended. We are a nation altho' consisting of parts or States – we are also confederated, and he hopes we shall always remain confederated. The enquiry should be –
>
> 1. What are the legislative powers which we should vest in Congress.
> 2. What judiciary powers.
> 3. What executive powers.
>
> We may resolve therefore, in order to let us into the business. That the Confederation is defective; and then proceed to the definition of such powers as may be thought adequate to the objects for which it was instituted. [32]

Elbridge Gerry of Massachusetts, although from a large State, voiced his opposition to a *National* Government and proposed that a *Federal* Gov-

---

[31] *Ibid.*, Volume I, p. 39.
[32] *Ibid.*, Volume I, p. 42.

ernment be adopted:

> A distinction has been made between a *Federal* and *National* Government. We ought not to determine that there is this distinction for if we do, *it is questionable not only whether this Convention can propose an government totally different or whether Congress itself would have a right to pass such a resolution as that before the house.* The commission from Massachusetts empowers the deputies to proceed agreeably to the recommendation of Congress. *This [is] the foundation of the Convention. If we have a right to pass this resolution we have a right to annihilate the Confederation.*
>
> Proposes – In the opinion of this Convention, provision should be made for the establishment of a *federal* legislative, judiciary, and executive. [Emphasis added] [33]

The proposed National Government, as is apparent, quickly came under severe attack by those determined to sustain the Federal Republic, and the nationalists were quickly forced to go on the defensive. Gouverneur Morris of Pennsylvania, an ardent National Monarchist, accordingly addressed the Convention and attempted to confound the issue by expounding false definitions of the key terms "federal," "national," and "supreme." He insinuated that the proposed supreme National Government was, in reality, a genuine Federal Government, and that the existing Federal Government under the Articles was not really a Federal Government at all. The credentials of the delegates, he insisted, authorized the Convention to draft a plan for a *supreme National Government* – such a government was precisely what the States and Congress expected from the Philadelphia Convention. This National Monarchist contended that "in all communities there must be one supreme power, and only one."[34] Mr. Morris concluded by stating that if a supreme National Government were not immediately adopted by the United States, within twenty years the American people would be ruled by a despot.

Despite his efforts, Gouverneur Morris failed to convert a single Federal Republican to the nationalist cause. The federalists readily agreed that, within any political system, there can be only "*one supreme power,* and only one." Either the peoples of the several States must be supreme, they realized, or the Federal Government must be supreme. Since both could not be supreme, the Federal Republicans were determined that supremacy should remain with the people. Nor were they convinced by Mr. Morris's assurance that only a supreme National Government could save America from despotism. As they wisely recognized, a supreme National Government would be, in itself, a principal *source* of despotism.

---

[33] *Ibid.*, Volume I, pp. 42-43.
[34] *Ibid.*, Volume I, p. 34.

The nationalists, however, carried the day, at least on the third resolution proposed by Mr. Randolph. When put to a vote, with each State present having only one vote, six States – Massachusetts, Pennsylvania, Delaware, Virginia, North Carolina, and South Carolina – voted *for* the third resolution. Two States – Connecticut and New Jersey – voted *against* the resolution, while New York was divided (John Lansing against the resolution; Alexander Hamilton for it).

The fact that the vote on this highly significant matter was made *before* all the delegates from the twelve participating States had arrived is in itself highly significant. By this date, May 30th, *only nine States were present.* When the delegates from the other three participating States arrived later, they would discover, much to their astonishment, that by the vote of six States the Convention had decided to annihilate all thirteen States.

Fresh from this decisive, albeit temporary, victory over federalism, the nationalists next broached the delicate subject of representation in the proposed National Government, by proposing that representation in the new national legislature should be based on population and/or property, and not on the sovereign equality of the States. Equal suffrage among the States, they correctly reasoned, was wholly inconsistent with and subversive of the National Government they wished to create. And as they had anticipated, opposition was immediately forthcoming from a small State.

George Read of Delaware quickly spoke up to object to the idea of abandoning equality of suffrage in the legislature. Not only was equality of suffrage guaranteed under the Articles of Confederation, he reminded the Convention, but the credentials given to Delaware's deputies prohibited them from supporting any other principle of suffrage. Should the nationalist proposal be adopted, he concluded, "it might become their duty to retire from the Convention." [35]

Here was the first serious sign that a State might *withdraw* from the Federal Convention in protest to the violence being wrought against State sovereignty by the nationalists, and the nationalists could not conceal their concern. Not only would such an early departure of a State threaten to ultimately wreck the Convention, but the withdrawing delegates might violate the rule of secrecy and spread a wholesale alarm throughout the Union. Gouverneur Morris was probably sincere when he "observed that the valuable assistance of those members could not be lost *without real concern,* and that *so early a proof of discord in the Convention as a secession of a State,* would add much to the regret." The National Monarchist from Pennsylvania insisted, however, "that the change proposed was...*so fundamental an article in a Na-*

---

[35] *Ibid.,* Volume I, p. 37.

tional Govt. that it could not be dispensed with." [Emphasis added] [36]

That uncompromising nationalist from Virginia, James Madison, added his voice to that of Mr. Morris, insisting that, "whatever reason might have existed for the equality of suffrage *when the Union was a federal one among sovereign States*, it must cease when a *National Governt.* should be put into the place." [Emphasis added] [37] According to Mr. Madison's notes, several of the nationalists then attempted to persuade the delegates from Delaware how they could easily extricate themselves from the confining limits imposed by their State's credentials by resorting to clever and artful methods of interpretation.

The line of reasoning put forth to persuade Delaware's delegates to abandon their State's instructions was consistent with the system of government proposed by the nationalists. If they could cleverly interpret a provision limiting them to a revision of the Articles of Confederation as an authorization to annihilate the principles on which the Articles were founded, there was no reason why the delegates from Mr. Read's State could not interpret Delaware's commandment to uphold the equality of suffrage in the legislature as an authorization to annihilate that principle of representation. Although George Read, the leader of the Delaware delegation, was no friend of States' Rights, he could not bring himself to accept the mode of construction urged by the nationalists. At his insistence, it was agreed to *postpone* this critical and explosive issue, and the house adjourned for the day.

If the Federal Republicans were alarmed by these developments, the events of the next day proved even more disturbing, for the Convention turned its attention briefly to the *powers* that should be vested in the proposed supreme National Government. The house considered, among other things, a national power to "negative all laws, passed by the several States, contravening, in the opinion of the national legislature, the articles of union." The delegates were also entertained with the radical idea that the National Government should be empowered "to call forth the force of the Union against any member of the Union, failing to fulfil it's duty under the articles thereof." Also discussed was a very sweeping proposal to authorize "legislative power in all cases to which the State legislatures were individually incompetent." [38]

To the Federal Republicans, these proposals carried the highly disagreeable odor of *totalitarianism*. Two delegates, Mr. Madison recorded in his notes, "objected to the *vagueness* of the term *incompetent*" within the last cited resolution, "and said they could not well decide how to vote until they should see *an exact enumeration of the powers* comprehended by this definition."

---

[36] *Ibid.*, Volume I, p. 37.
[37] *Ibid.*, Volume I, p. 37.
[38] *Ibid.*, Volume I, p. 47 and 53.

Pierce Butler of South Carolina then "*repeated his fears* that we were running into an *extreme* in *taking away the powers of the States*, and called on Mr. Randolph for the extent of his meaning." [Emphasis added] [39]

In response, the Virginia Governor assured the Convention that he did not wish to create a government having "indefinite powers," [40] although he refused to state what limits, if any, should be placed on the powers of his supreme government. "Mr. Randolph was of opinion," William L. Pierce of Georgia wrote in his notes for this day, "that *it would be impossible to define the powers and the length to which the federal [sic] legislature ought to extend just at this time*." James Wilson, a cunning and unscrupulous nationalist from Pennsylvania, gave his "assurances" to the Federal Republicans by observing "that *it would be impossible to enumerate the powers which the federal [sic] legislature ought to have*." [Emphasis added] [41]

James Madison then sought to alleviate the fears of those concerned about liberty by saying "that he had brought with him into the Convention a strong bias in favor of an enumeration and definition of the powers necessary to be exercised by the *national* legislature; *but had also brought doubts concerning its practicability*." He added that, "His wishes remained unaltered; but *his doubts had become stronger. What his opinion might ultimately be he could not yet tell*." [Emphasis added] [42]

Such "reassurances," needless to say, were not very comforting to the Federal Republicans. By the end of May, they had come to realize a crucial distinction between a supreme National Government and a Federal Government. A Federal Government, it appeared from the evasiveness of the nationalists, was one whose authority and powers could be easily defined and limited, whereas a supreme National Government could only be vested with powers that defied definition and limitation.

It may have been a wise strategy on the part of the nationalists to continuously delay and postpone serious discussion on the *powers* to be vested in their proposed National Government. The powers of government, they realized, would invariably flow from the very nature of the government. An imperially *supreme government* would naturally lay claim to imperially *supreme powers* over States and individuals alike. It would appear from the records of the debates that the nationalist strategy was to first eliminate all opposition to a supreme National Government before fully revealing the true extent of its awesome powers. The great difficulty they encountered in fulfilling this objective is indicated within William Pierce's notes for the last day of May.

---

[39] *Ibid.*, Volume I, p. 53.
[40] *Ibid.*, Volume I, p. 53.
[41] *Ibid.*, Volume I, p. 60.
[42] *Ibid.*, Volume I, p. 53.

James Madison, Mr. Pierce noted, "said it was necessary to adopt some general principles on which we should act, — that *we were wandering from one thing to another without seeming to be settled in any one principle.*" George Wythe of Virginia "observed that it would be right to establish general principles before we go into detail, or very shortly Gentlemen would find themselves in confusion, and would be obliged to have recurrence to the point from whence they sat out." The crafty National Monarchist from Massachusetts, Rufus King, "was of opinion that the principles ought first to be established before we proceed to the framing of the Act." [Emphasis added] [43]

The nationalists, it becomes evident, feared nothing more than a deep, penetrating, careful analysis by the other delegates of the *principles* they advocated. For this reason, they urged that their principles be hastily adopted without further debate or consideration, and that the Convention quickly turn its attention to fulfilling the details of those principles. Delays in implementing their principles could only result in allowing sufficient time for the opponents of a supreme National Government to unify their resistance efforts. This sense of great urgency was undoubtedly augmented by the knowledge that delegates from States not yet present would soon be arriving, and these new delegates would only strengthen the champions of the Federal Republic. Time was clearly on the side of the Federal Republicans, as the nationalists understood all too well.

Ideological Warfare

The early stages of the Philadelphia Convention were devoted almost exclusively to a clash of ideology as to what constituted a good form and system of government for the United States of America. When the nationalists insisted that the Convention should, as the first order of business, establish the basic principles of the government that should be created, no one disagreed. *The general nature of the government to be created would, in itself, determine all the other issues.*

Should the Convention draft a plan of government wherein all powers were granted to a supreme central government, and in which the State governments would exist only as local branches of a supreme national authority? Or should a plan be drafted for a limited plan of centralization, wherein the Federal Government would be empowered only to conduct foreign affairs, and the States governments would retain their independent jurisdictions over domestic affairs? Was good government best achieved by centralizing power,

---

[43] *Ibid.*, Volume I, p. 60.

or by distributing power as close to the people as possible? Which, in summary, was more important, liberty or power?

It was on these issues that an ideological war was waged during the early stages of the Convention, and all other issues partook of its nature and sprang directly from these considerations. The debates that occurred during the first half of June, in particular, highlight the ideological battle over political principles that came to dominate the Federal Convention.

On June 2nd, for instance, James Wilson "repeated his arguments in favor of an election without the intervention of the States." [44] Accordingly, he moved that "the States should be divided into districts, consisting of one or more States," [45] for purposes of electing officers to the proposed National Government. By dividing the United States into *national districts*, he was convinced, the States would be virtually annihilated. The States might continue to exist under such a system, but they would be of interest only to mapmakers. In time, perhaps, even this last vestige of Statehood might be done away with.

John Dickinson, on the same day, announced that he, for one, "had no idea of abolishing the State governments as some gentlemen seemed inclined to do." "The happiness of this country...," he added, "required considerable powers to be left in the hands of the States." [46] Later in the same day, the author of the Articles of Confederation spoke at some length on the subject, and his speech was recorded by Mr. Madison as follows:

> *Mr. Dickenson considered the business as so important that no man ought to be silent or reserved.* He went into a discourse of some length, the sum of which was, that *the Legislative, Executive, & Judiciary departments ought to be made as independt. as possible.*...One source of stability is the double branch of the Legislature. *The division of the country into distinct States formed the other principal source of stability. This division ought therefore to be maintained, and considerable powers to be left with the States. This was the ground of his consolation for the future fate of his country.* Without this, and in case of *a consolidation of the States into one great Republic* we might read its fate in the history of smaller ones....One of these remedies he conceived to be the accidental *lucky division of this country into distinct States*; a division which some seemed desirous to abolish altogether. [Emphasis added] [47]

Mr. Dickinson suggested that, although the Virginia Plan pushed by the nationalists appeared on its surface to be a plan for a National Republic, it

---

[44] *Ibid.*, Volume I, p. 80.
[45] *Ibid.*, Volume I, p. 89.
[46] *Ibid.*, Volume I, p. 85.
[47] *Ibid.*, Volume I, pp. 86-87.

bore many disturbing resemblances to scheme calculated to produce a National Monarchy. Two days later, while debating the nature of the "National
Executive," George Mason of Virginia voiced the same concern:

> We are not indeed constituting a British Government, but a more
> dangerous monarchy, an elective one. We are introducing a new principle
> into our system, and not necessary....Do gentlemen mean to pave the way
> to hereditary Monarchy? Do they flatter themselves that the people will
> ever consent to such an innovation? If they do I venture to tell them, they
> are mistaken. The people never will consent. [48]

James Madison attempted to allay such concerns by asserting the in-
credibly ludicrous idea "that no man would be so daring as to place a veto on
a law that had passed with the assent of the legislature." This Virginia nationalist then insisted that there could be nothing improper in merging the Judicial and Executive Branches of government. In response to the ideas put forth
by Mr. Madison and other nationalists, Mr. Dickinson stated that he "could
not agree with gentlemen in blending the national judicial and the executive,
because the one is the expounder, and the other the executor of the laws." [49]

The ideological battle began to wax warm on June 6th. James Wilson
of Pennsylvania asserted that a National Government must have a national,
not a federal, constituency. Not only should such a government possess vigorous "force," but also the "mind or sense of the people at large." A National
Government required a monolithic, single *nation* of Americans to give it
force, not a league of sovereign States. He expected strong opposition from
the State governments, he said, because the "State officers were to be losers of
power." The American people, in sentiment, would be more attached to a
centralized government than to local governments. "There is no danger of
improper elections," he claimed, "if made by *large* districts," referring again to
his pet project for replacing the States with several large *national districts*.
"Bad elections proceed from the smallness of the districts which give an opportunity to bad men to intrigue themselves into office." [50]

In response, Roger Sherman of Connecticut stated that, if the State
governments are to continue to exist, they must play a role in the system of
government to be established. "The objects of the Union, he thought were
few." A Federal Government should be established, vested only with powers
sufficient to conduct the foreign affairs of the United States. "All other matters civil & criminal would be much better in the hands of the States." He

---

[48] *Ibid.*, Volume I, p. 101.
[49] *Ibid.*, Volume I, p. 109-110.
[50] *Ibid.*, Volume I, pp. 132-133.

disagreed with Mr. Wilson, that an election within the latter's proposed large national districts would produce better government than the smaller and more localized elections held by the States. "He was for giving the general govt. power to legislate and excute [only] within a defined province." Such a government, he concluded, would be based on "the independence and confederation of the States." [51]

James Madison arose to challenge the principles espoused by the delegate from Connecticut. He agreed that a Federal Government should possess the powers associated with conducting foreign affairs. But that should be only the starting point, not the limit of its powers. A general government, he claimed, should also concern itself with "the security of private rights" and with "the steady dispensation of justice" throughout the Union. The liberties of the people required that these objects be centralized in the hands of a National Government. It was for this purpose, he claimed, that the Federal Convention had been called. When the Convention "agreed to the first resolve of having a National Government, consisting of a supreme executive, judicial and legislative power, it was then intended to operate to the exclusion of a Federal Government." Thus, he insisted, "the more extensive we made the basis, the greater probability of duration, happiness and good order." [52]

John Dickinson believed it was absolutely necessary, both in terms of necessity and as a matter of practicality, that the State governments should play vital roles in the proposed system of government. He therefore "considered it as essential that one branch of the legislature" should "be drawn immediately from the people; and as expedient that the other" should "be chosen by the legislatures of the States." [53]

George Read then addressed the Convention to express the opinion that, "Too much attachment is betrayed to the State" governments. "We must look beyond their continuance." The State governments must be "swept away," he proclaimed, and the United States must undergo a "consolidation" into a single, monolithic society. As for the States, the proposed National Government "must soon of necessity swallow all of them up. They would soon be reduced to the mere office of electing the National Senate." He was firmly against the idea of merely "patching up the old federal system" and he hoped the idea would be abandoned by the Federal Republicans. "It would be like putting new cloth on an old garment." "The Confederation was founded on temporary principles," he insisted. "It cannot last" and "it cannot be amended." [54]

---

[51] *Ibid.*, Volume I, p. 133 and 143.
[52] *Ibid.*, Volume I, pp. 134 and 141.
[53] *Ibid.*, Volume I, p. 136.
[54] *Ibid.*, Volume I, pp. 136-137 and 143.

"If we are to establish a National Government," James Wilson said the next day, "that government ought to flow from *the people at large*." He "hoped that the National Government would be *independent of the State governments, in order to make it vigorous*." He therefore moved that the sovereign States be replaced by national districts, proposing, "*That the second branch of the national legislature be chosen by districts, to be formed for that purpose*." [Emphasis added] [55]

In a bid to destroy the influence of the State governments in the proposed government, George Read was willing to subvert the concept of an independent legislature by proposing that the President of the United States should appoint the Senate. "He said he thought it his duty, to speak his mind frankly," Mr. Madison noted in his records. "Gentlemen he hoped would not be alarmed at the idea." His proposal, fortunately, "was not seconded nor supported." [56]

The author of the Articles of Confederation attempted to restore the sanity of some delegates by comparing "the proposed National System to the Solar System." The States, he said, were like the planets revolving around the sun. The sun clearly existed to warm the planets, not to burn them to a cinder. Mr. Wilson, he stated, "wished...to extinguish these planets." "If the State governments were excluded from all agency" in the general government, and if "all power" were drawn "from the people at large," the resulting tendency of the National Government to produce "mischiefs" would prove more dangerous than any alleged mischief ever committed by a State government. "The reform would only unite the 13 small streams into one great current pursuing the same course without any opposition whatever." [57]

In response, James Wilson stated that he could see no danger to the States from an all-powerful, supreme National Government. On the contrary, he insisted, the only real threat would be that posed by the States to a supreme National Government. "He was not however for extinguishing these planets as was supposed by Mr. D. – neither did he on the other hand, believe that they would warm or enlighten the sun. Within their proper orbits they must still be suffered to act for subordinate purposes." He therefore repeated his insistence "for an election by the people in large districts," rather than by the peoples of the several States, "subdividing the districts only for the accommodation of voters." "I therefore propose," said he, "that the Senate be elected by the people and that the Territory [*i.e.*, States] be thrown into convenient Districts." [58]

---

[55] *Ibid.*, Volume I, pp. 151 and 157.
[56] *Ibid.*, Volume I, p. 151.
[57] *Ibid.*, Volume I, p. 153.
[58] *Ibid.*, Volume I, pp. 153-154 and 159.

Mr. Dickinson spoke out in opposition to the proposal "because the same is either impracticable or unfair." The proposed national electoral districts, he observed, "must be either parts of States, or entire States, or parts of distinct States united." Not only was there a danger of "fraudulent or corrupt elections" inherent in such a scheme, but if the smaller States were merged into a single national district, "the small States will never have a member" of the Senate. Therefore "it is unfair." [59]

George Mason of Virginia noted that "a certain portion" of power "must necessarily be left in the States." He favored letting the State legislatures elect members to the Senate in order to provide to the States "some means of defending themselves" against "encroachments" of the proposed National Government. The danger to be apprehended, he pointed out, "is that the national, will swallow up the State legislatures." "In every other department we have studiously endeavored to provide for its self-defence. Shall we leave the States alone unprovided with the means for this purpose?" he asked. "There is danger on both sides no doubt; but we have only seen the evils arising on the side of the State" governments. "Those on the other side remain to be displayed." [60]

On June 8th, the Convention turned its attention to the fanatical proposition that a National Government should possess the power to veto the laws of the State governments. This proposal, as it stood, empowered the general government "to negative all laws passed by the several States contravening, in the opinion of the national legislature, the articles of Union; or any treaties subsisting under the authority of the Union." Dangerous as this proposition was to freedom, the nationalists did not think it sufficiently vigorous and moved to strengthen the hand of the proposed National Government against the States. Charles Pinckney, seconded by James Madison, therefore moved to replace the clause with the words, "*to negative all laws which to them shall appear improper.*" [Emphasis added] [61]

In support of his motion, Mr. Pinckney "urged that such a universality of the power was indispensably necessary to render it effectual." Such a broad power was necessary because "the States must be kept in due subordination to the nation" and because "if the States were left to act of themselves in any case, it" would "be impossible to defend the national prerogatives." He grounded his motion "on the necessity of *one supreme controlling power.*" The "universal negative," he emphasized, "was in fact *the corner stone of an efficient National*" Government – "as the *corner-stone* of the present system." He candidly acknowledged that, by this proposal, the National Government would

---

[59] *Ibid.*, Volume I, p. 159.
[60] *Ibid.*, Volume I, pp. 155-156 and 160.
[61] *Ibid.*, Volume I, p. 162.

hold the same status over the States as once held by the British Government over the American colonies. He insisted, however, that under the British Government, "*the negative of the Crown had been found beneficial, and the States are more one nation now, than the Colonies were then.*" [Emphasis added][62]

Mr. Madison seconded the motion, asserting that, "*He could not but regard an indefinite power to negative legislative acts of the States as absolutely necessary to a perfect system.*" "Should no such precaution be engrafted," he added, "the only remedy" would "lie in an appeal to coercion." *Legal* coercion, he claimed, would make *military* coercion of the States unnecessary, inasmuch as the results of both would be the same. "But in order to give the negative this efficacy," he emphasized, "*it must extend to all cases.*" [Emphasis added][63]

Hugh Williamson of North Carolina responded by saying that he was against "giving a power that might restrain the States from regulating their internal police." Elbridge Gerry of Massachusetts also had doubts. A National Government vested with such a power, he said, would be "abused" and "may enslave the States." "Such an idea as this will never be acceded to," he concluded, noting that, "It has never been suggested or conceived among the people."[64]

For his part, James Wilson "would not say what modifications of the proposed power might be practicable or expedient. But however novel it might appear the principal of it when viewed with a close & steady eye, *is right.*" Defining or limiting the powers of the proposed National Government, he insinuated, should not be attempted, for he considered "*the surrender of the rights of a Federal Government to be surrender of sovereignty.*" "True," he said, "we may define some of the rights, but *when we come near the line it cannot be found.* One general excepting clause must therefore apply to the whole." And he again emphasized that, under a National Government, the States would not exist. "*We are now one nation of brethren. We must bury all local interests & distinctions.*" [Emphasis added][65]

To the Federal Republicans, it appeared as though the nationalists wished *to bury the States.* Nor was this nationalist desire to terminate the existence of the States interpreted as over-zealous patriotism. In the eyes of the Federal Republicans, the nationalist conspiracy was fueled by ambition, greed, and lust for power. Gunning Bedford, Jr., of Delaware stated that he saw in the Virginia Plan a plot "to strip the small States of their equal right of suf-

---

[62] *Ibid.*, Volume I, p. 164.
[63] *Ibid.*, Volume I, pp. 164-165.
[64] *Ibid.*, Volume I, pp. 165-166.
[65] *Ibid.*, Volume I, pp. 166 and 170.

frage" to the exclusive benefit of the three large States – Virginia, Massachusetts, and Pennsylvania. It was not the lofty motives of national patriotism that induced those three delegations to support an unlimited National Government. On the contrary, it was the selfish motive of seeking to aggrandize their own States at the expense of the other States. "Will not these large States crush the small ones whenever they stand in the way of their ambitions or interested views," he soberly inquired. [66]

"It seems as if Pa. & Va. by the conduct of their deputies wished to provide a system in which they would have an enormous & monstrous influence," Mr. Bedford added. "Besides, How can it be thought that the proposed negative can be exercised?" Are "the laws of the States to be suspended in the most urgent cases until they can be sent seven or eight hundred miles, and undergo the deliberations of a body who may be incapable of judging of them?" he asked. "Is the national legislature too to sit continually in order to revise the laws of the States?" [67]

James Madison sought to justify the national negative over the States by citing as precedent the British policy toward the colonies: "This was the practice in Royal Colonies before the Revolution and would not have been inconvenient; if the supreme power of negativing had been faithful to the American interest, and had possessed the necessary information." But in the event that the small States still refused to become the colonies of a supreme National Government, Mr. Madison suggested that the larger States might expel the smaller ones from the Union, thereby abandoning them to the mercy of powerful foreign nations. "If the large States possessed the avarice & ambition with which they are charged," said he, "would the small ones in their neighbourhood be more secure when all controul of a" general government "was withdrawn." "It is impossible that the Articles of Confederation can be amended," he stressed, because "they are too tottering to be invigorated." Only "the present system, or something like it, can restore the peace and harmony of the country." [68]

Pierce Butler of South Carolina, for one, remained unconvinced. As Mr. Madison recorded in his notes, Mr. Butler's opposition to the negative over State laws was "vehement," for it cut off "all hope of equal justice to the distant States." The people would never consent to such extreme centralization of power, he warned the Convention. "Will a man throw afloat his property & confide it to a government a thousand miles *distant?*" [69]

Addressing his fellow delegates on June 9th, Judge David Brearly from

---

[66] *Ibid.*, Volume I, p. 167.
[67] *Ibid.*, Volume I, pp. 167-168.
[68] *Ibid.*, Volume I, p. 168 and 171.
[69] *Ibid.*, Volume I, pp. 168 and 173.

New Jersey stated that, "He had come to the Convention with a view of being as useful as he could in giving energy and stability to the Federal Government. When the proposition for destroying the equality of votes came forward, he was astonished, he was alarmed." [70] The learned Judge would undoubtedly have been even more astonished and alarmed had he but known of the aborted nationalist plot to deny the equality of the States *within the Convention itself.*

William Paterson of New Jersey then arose to address the Federal Convention in a very moving speech on behalf of federalism and republican principles. He "considered the proposition for a proportional representation as striking at the existence of the lesser States." The Philadelphia Convention had not been called so that certain ambitious nationalists could draft a government agreeable to their own personal principles. The true purpose was to proceed according to the principles of those States the delegates were supposed to *represent* within the Convention. If there could exist any doubt as to what those legitimate principles might be, the delegates needed to look no further than the credentials given to them by their respective States. "Let us consider with what powers are we sent here?" [71]

At Mr. Paterson's request, the credentials from the State of Massachusetts were read to the Convention. "By this and the other credentials we see, that the basis of our present authority is founded on a revision of the Articles of the present Confederation," he pointed out, "and to alter or amend them in such parts where they may appear defective." "Can we on this ground form a National Government?" he asked. "I fancy not." "Our commissions give a complexion to the business; and can we suppose that when we exceed the bounds of our duty, the people will approve our proceedings?" "We are met here as the deputies of 13 independent, sovereign States, for federal purposes," the New Jersey delegate emphasized. "Can we consolidate their sovereignty and form one nation, and annihilate the sovereignties of our States who have sent us here for other purposes?" [72]

Unless the Convention confined itself to its proper limits, the learned farmer from New Jersey stated, "we should be charged by our constituents with usurpation." "But the commissions under which we acted were not only the measure of our power," he emphasized, for "they denoted also the sentiments of the States on the subject of our deliberation." The American people, he said, were devoted to republican and federal principles. "The democratick spirit beats high" among them, and they would not accept any form of government other than a Federal Government. "The idea of a National" Gov-

---

[70] *Ibid.*, Volume I, p. 177.
[71] *Ibid.*, Volume I, pp. 177 and 182.
[72] *Ibid.*, Volume I, p. 182 .

ernment, he said, "as contradistinguished from a federal one, never entered into the mind of any of them, and to the public mind we must accommodate ourselves." "We must follow the people; the people will not follow us." [73]

The great question before the Convention, Mr. Paterson stated, centered around the "words national and federal." "We have no power to go beyond the federal scheme, and if we had the people are not ripe for any other." Each State, he added, is sovereign, free, and independent, and inherent in the concept of sovereignty is the idea of *equality* among the States. The "sovereign and independent States can never constitute one Nation, and at the same time be States." Sovereign States may, however, "by treaty make one confederated body." "Upon the whole," he solemnly asserted, "every sovereign State according to a confederation must have an equal vote, or there is an end to liberty." [74]

William Paterson wryly observed that the nationalists, in their frenzied zeal to shove their project through the Convention, were basing their arguments on deceptive reasoning. *Their insistence that only a National Government could operate directly on individual citizens was simply not true, for even a Federal Government could be constructed to operate on individual citizens.* The logic of their principles in denying any semblance of equality of suffrage was similarly deceptive, he noted. *To insist that representation within the Federal Union be based solely upon the wealth and population of each State, he observed, was tantamount to stating that, within civil society, a rich man should be entitled to more votes than a poor man.* Such a concept had no basis in a republican form of government, he pointed out. The "individuals" within a Federal Union are the sovereign States. Republican and federal principles thus united, he observed, in mandating that the States should have an equal suffrage in the upper branch of the federal legislature.

The New Jersey delegate then concluded with these words:

> He alluded to the hint thrown out heretofore by Mr. Wilson of the necessity to which the large States might be reduced of *confederating among themselves*, by a refusal of the others to concur. *Let them unite if they please, but let them remember that they have no authority to compel the others to unite.* N. Jersey will never confederate on the plan before the Committee. She would be swallowed up. *He had rather submit to a monarch, to a despot, than to such a fate.* He would not only oppose the plan here but on his return home do everything in his power to defeat it there. [Emphasis added] [75]

---

[73] *Ibid.*, Volume I, pp. 178 and 186.
[74] *Ibid.*, Volume I, pp. 178 and 183-185.
[75] *Ibid.*, Volume I, p. 179.

Rising to respond to Mr. Paterson, James Wilson asserted that "a majority, nay even a minority, of the States have a right to confederate with each other, and the rest may do as they please." The concept of federalism, he insisted, was "unjust" to the larger States, and he vowed to never "confederate" under such a principle. "The gentlemen from New-Jersey is candid in declaring his opinion – I commend him for it – I am equally so. I say again I never will confederate on his principles." If New Jersey "will not part with her sovereignty," he insisted, "it is in vain to talk of" forming a general government for all of the States. "A new partition of the States is desireable," he concluded, perhaps in reference to his idea of replacing sovereign States with national districts, "but evidently & totally impracticable." [76]

This should be a sufficient sampling of the debates during the first few weeks of the Convention to illustrate the great battle of principles which quickly came to dominate the federal meeting whose only *legitimate* purpose was to revise the Articles of Confederation in order to make the Federal Constitution adequate to the exigencies of the Federal Republic. Not since the darkest days of the American Revolution had so many voices been raised in fear of despotism, oppression, injustice, and tyranny. Perhaps the clash of ideology was best and most succinctly epitomized by the comments made in the early days of the Convention by George Read of Delaware, Edmund Randolph of Virginia, and Elbridge Gerry of Massachusetts.

Said Mr. Read: "There can be no cure for this *evil* [*i.e., sovereign States*] but *in doing away States altogether and uniting them all into one great Society.*" Proclaimed Mr. Randolph: "We are erecting a *supreme National Government*; ought it not to be supported, and *can we give it too many sinews?*" Responded Mr. Gerry: "Mr. Gerry rather supposes that the national legislators ought to be sworn to *preserve the State Constitutions, as they will run the greatest risk to be annihilated.*" "Mr. Gerry is afraid *the people will be alarmed, as savoring of despotism.*" [Emphasis added] [77]

The Philadelphia Convention, which had been called for the sole and express purpose of revising the Articles of Confederation, had thus been subverted at its very threshold by a nationalist conspiracy whose goal was to destroy the Federal Republic and to erect a supreme national system in its place. The conspirators had come to the Convention fully prepared and firmly united in purpose, and by using the element of surprise they had succeeded in launching the Federal Convention down the path of the destruction of the States. But the Federal Republicans, although taken by surprise and totally unprepared for such a confrontation, were determined to save the Federal Re-

[76] *Ibid.*, Volume I, pp. 180 and 183.
[77] *Ibid.*, Volume I, pp. 202, 207, and 220.

public from destruction. A bitter and passionate battle royal lay ahead.

Chapter Eight
Three Plans of Government

Nationalist conspirators, as has already been demonstrated, initially succeeded in diverting the Philadelphia Convention of 1787 from its true purpose of revising the Articles of Confederation. Using the element of surprise, the united nationalists had managed to persuade the Federal Convention to adopt, at its very outset, a dangerous plan introduced by Edmund Randolph to erect in the United States of America a *supreme National Government*. By the terms of this *Virginia Plan*, the States would continue to exist in form, but not in substance. The States, by this plan, were to be reduced to the status of colonies, governed by an all-powerful and imperial National Government, which was to possess authority to veto any State laws.

Although the States would continue to exist, it was quickly made evident that some nationalists wanted to abolish them altogether. This had become apparent when desires were expressed to replace the States with *national districts* for electoral purposes. Some nationalists had spoken candidly of their desire to merge the States into a consolidated American nation of people, and to transfer sovereignty from the peoples of the several States to their proposed National Government. Perhaps most alarming of all, the very nature of such a government seemed to defy all attempts to limit its powers.

Appalled and horrified by this blatant attempt to annihilate the sovereignty of the States, a growing resistance movement quickly surfaced in the Grand Convention. Led by the Federal Republicans, these delegates were determined to abide by the instructions of the States and to proceed along lines calculated to *amend* the Federal Constitution and *preserve* the Federal Republic. A strong clash of ideology between the nationalists and federalists was made manifest in the earliest debates, and many delegates raised the cry of tyranny and despotism.

The battle between disparate forces, although comprehensive and general, quickly focused on the question of equality of suffrage in the proposed second branch of the legislature. This question, both sides seemed to agree, would decide the issue of a Federal or a National Government for the United States. So severe was the clash of conflicting principles over this and other questions related to the great issue that serious doubts arose whether the Convention itself would dissolve in discord. Despite the patriotic efforts of the Federal Republicans, however, the nationalists succeeded in controlling the early proceedings of the Convention, for they had the initial double advantage of surprise and unity. For a season it appeared as though the Federal Republic had met its demise.

The Revised Virginia Plan

By June 13, 1787, the initial round of debates on the Virginia Plan had ended, and the Committee of the Whole submitted a report on Mr. Randolph's original fifteen propositions to the Convention. Within this *revised* Virginia Plan, which now consisted of nineteen resolutions, the creation of a *supreme National Government* was frankly and openly proclaimed to be the sole objective of the Convention. The objectionable and divisive word *national* now appeared no less than *twenty-six times* in the Virginia Plan, and the proposed general government – *not the Constitution and laws made in pursuance of it, but the National Government itself* – was openly and boldly declared to be *supreme!*

This revised Virginia Plan was in the following words:

> 1. *Resolved*, That it is the opinion of this committee, that *a National Government ought to be established, consisting of a supreme legislative, executive, and judiciary*.
>
> 2. *Resolved*, That the *national* legislature ought to consist of two branches.
>
> 3. *Resolved*, That the members of the first branch of the *national legislature* ought to be elected by *the people of the several States* for the term of three years; to receive fixed stipends by which they may be compensated for the devotion of their time to the public service, to be paid out of the *national* treasury; to be ineligible to any office established by a particular State, or under the authority of the United States, (except those peculiarly belonging to the functions of the first branch,) during the term of service, and under the *National Government*, for the space of one year after its expiration.
>
> 4. *Resolved*, That the members of the second branch of the *national legislature* ought to be *chosen by the individual legislatures*; to be of the age of thirty years at least; to hold their offices for a term *sufficient to insure their independence*, namely, seven years; to receive fixed stipends by which they may be compensated for the devotion of their time to the public service, to be paid out of the *national* treasury; to be ineligible to any office established by a particular State, or under the authority of the United States, (except those primarily belonging to the functions of the second branch,) during the term of service, and, under the *National Government*, for the space of one year after its expiration.

5. *Resolved*, That each branch ought to possess the right of originating acts.

6. *Resolved*, That the *national legislature* ought to be *empowered* to enjoy the legislative rights vested in *Congress* by the Confederation; and moreover, *to legislate in all cases to which the separate States are incompetent, or in which the harmony of the United States may be interrupted by the exercise of individual legislation; to negate all laws passed by the several States contravening, in the opinion of the national legislature, the Articles of Union or any treaties subsisting under the authority of the Union.*

7. *Resolved*, That the rights of suffrage in the *first branch* of the *national legislature* ought *not* be according to the rule established in the Articles of Confederation, but according to some equitable ratio of representation; namely, in *proportion* to the whole number of white and other free citizens and inhabitants, of every age, sex, and condition, including those bound to servitude for a term of years, and *three fifths of all other persons*, not comprehended in the foregoing description, except Indians not paying taxes in each State.

8. *Resolved*, That the right of suffrage in the *second branch* of the *national legislature* ought to be *according to the rule established for the first.*

9. *Resolved*, That a *national* executive be instituted, to consist of a single person; to be chosen by the *national legislature*, for the term of seven years; with power to carry into execution the *national* laws, to appoint to offices in cases not otherwise provided for, to be ineligible a second time, and to be removed on impeachment and conviction of malpractices of neglect of duty; to receive a fixed stipend by which he may be compensated for the devotion of his time to the public service, to be paid out of the *national* treasury.

10. *Resolved*, That the *national* executive shall have a right to negate any legislative act which shall not be afterwards passed by two thirds of each branch of the national legislature.

11. *Resolved*, That a *national* judiciary be established, to consist of one supreme tribunal, the judges of which shall be appointed by the second branch of the national legislature, *to hold their offices during good behavior*, and to receive punctually, at stated times, a fixed compensation for their services, in which no increase or diminution shall be made so as to effect the persons actually in office at the time of such increase or diminution.

12. *Resolved*, That the *national legislature* be empowered to appoint inferior tribunals.

13. *Resolved*, That the jurisdiction of the *national* judiciary shall extend to all cases which respect the collection of the *national* revenue, impeachments of any *national* officers, and questions which involve the *national* peace and harmony.

14. *Resolved*, That provision ought to be made for *the admission of States* lawfully arising within the limits of the United States, whether from a voluntary junction of government and territory, or otherwise, with the consent of a number of voices in the *national legislature* less than the whole.

15. *Resolved*, That provision ought to be made for the continuance

of *Congress*, and their authorities and privileges, until a given day after the reform of the *Articles of Union* shall be adopted, and for the completion of all their engagements.

16. *Resolved*, That a *Republican Constitution*, and *its existing laws*, ought to be *guaranteed to each State by the United States*.

17. *Resolved*, That provision ought to be made for the amendment of the *Articles of Union*, whensoever it shall seem necessary.

18. *Resolved*, That the legislative, executive, and judiciary powers, within the several States, ought to be bound by oath to support the *Articles of Union*.

19. *Resolved*, That the *amendments which shall be offered to the Confederation by the Convention*, ought, at a proper time or times after the approbation of Congress, to be submitted to an assembly or assemblies recommended by *the several legislatures*, to be expressly chosen by the people to consider and decide thereon. [Emphasis added] [1]

The Virginia Plan illustrated the difficulties and contradictions inherent in the nationalist plan of government for the United States. As much as the nationalists may have abhorred the entire concept of sovereign States, those States did in fact exist. Yet, the National Government they were trying to construct was designed for a single consolidated nation of Americans, a nation that simply did not exist. The *foundation* of their government was thus at discord with the existing reality of the United States.

In a vain attempt to make a National Government compatible with a league of sovereign States, the nationalists were forced to pervert theory, distort principles, and go to absurd lengths to deny plain facts. They could, for instance, state unequivocally that the States, as sovereign political bodies, could freely confederate with whomever they pleased. Yet, they could also assert the incredible fiction that the States were not sovereign and never were sovereign – not by the Declaration of Independence nor under the Articles of Confederation!

Undoubtedly realizing the inconsistency of their principles, some of the bolder nationalists attempted to remove the conflict of contradictions by openly advocating the *annihilation of the States*. Others, such as James Wilson, attempted to partially expunge the contradictions by urging the creation of *national districts* that would exist in parallel with the States. Still others, such as James Madison, attempted to exorcise the demon of inconsistency by repeatedly and vainly referring to the federal election of members to the U.S. House of Representatives by *the peoples of the sovereign States* as a *national election*.

---

[1] Jonathan Elliot (ed.), *Elliot's Debates*, Volume V, Published under the Sanction of Congress, Washington, 1845, pp. 189-190.

The nationalists could piously claim their devotion to liberty, yet frankly admit that their proposed government would dominate the American States more thoroughly than Great Britain had ever dominated them in their colonial status! They claimed that the people supported their principles, yet insisted on concealing their conduct behind a veil of secrecy. The friends of the Virginia Plan insisted that their proposed government was genuinely republican in nature, yet acknowledged that it might be impossible to limit its powers. And they affirmed, with an air of authority, that their proposed government was "partly national" and "partly federal," while accusing any who might challenge such a contradiction of speaking irreverently of a mystery. The nationalist hypocrisy was perhaps nowhere more blatantly displayed than in the last resolution of the revised Virginia Plan, wherein it was resolved that the proposed *supreme National Government* should be offered by the Convention as "amendments" to the "Confederation" established by the Articles of Confederation!

The States, the nationalists understood all too well, could not be literally annihilated. *The proposed Constitution, if adopted, could only be adopted by the sovereign States, and the resulting Union could exist only between those States.* As the nationalists readily admitted, a strong enmity would invariably and naturally exist between their proposed *supreme National Government* and the *federal system* in which such a government must be erected, just as a monarchy and a republican form of government would be natural enemies if both were established within the same jurisdiction. Either the *federal system* would subvert the National Government, or the *National Government* would destroy the States as sovereign political societies. To sufficiently arm and equip their National Government for inevitable warfare with the States, the nationalists were willing to go to any length to vest the former with awesome and dangerous powers. Such a supreme National Government, had the Convention been foolish enough to adopt it and the States so blinded as to ratify it, would have very quickly enslaved the American people.

The nationalists had expected to encounter opposition to their proposed National Government, but not in the form and to the degree which that opposition quickly assumed. During the early stages of the Convention, while the delegates were debating the resolutions introduced by Edmund Randolph, the Federal Republicans were busy organizing themselves into a united front to defend federalism. Writing of these events at a later date, Luther Martin of Maryland noted:

> The resolutions of the members from Virginia were discussed with great coolness in a committee of the whole house, and hopes were formed that the farther we proceeded in their examination, the better the house

might be satisfied of the impropriety of adopting them, and that they would be finally rejected. Whilst they were under discussion, a number of the members who disapproved them, were preparing another system, such as they thought more conducive to the happiness and welfare of the States. The committee, by a *small majority*, agreed to a report [*i.e.*, the revised Virginia Plan], declaring, among other things, that a *National Government* ought to be established, consisting of a *supreme legislative, judiciary, and executive*. That the national legislature ought to be empowered to legislate *in all cases to which the separate States are incompetent*, or *in which the harmony of the United States may be interrupted by the exercise of individual legislation*, and *to negative all laws passed by the several States*, contravening, *in the opinion of the legislature of the United States*, the Articles of the Union. And that the jurisdiction of the national judiciary, shall extend to questions which involve the *national peace and harmony*. [Emphasis added] [2]

Unlike the nationalists, who had united in their conspiracy against the Federal Republic before the start of the Convention, the Federal Republicans required time to unify their actions. By the middle of June, however, they were sufficiently organized to offer their first unified challenge to the nationalists. On June 14th, the day after the revised Virginia Plan was reported to the Convention, William Paterson of New Jersey arose to make an announcement on behalf of the united Federal Republicans. Mr. Madison recorded his address in these words:

> Mr. Paterson, observed to the Convention that it was the wish of several deputations, particularly that of N. Jersey, that further time might be allowed them to contemplate the plan reported from the Committee of the Whole, and to digest one purely federal, and contradistinguished from the reported plan. He said they hoped to have such an one ready by tomorrow to be laid before the Convention: and the Convention adjourned that leisure might be given for the purpose. [3]

William Paterson's announcement signaled the beginning of the end for the proposed supreme National Government. "The eagerness displayed by the members opposed to a Natl. Govt....," James Madison soberly wrote in his notes, "*began now to produce serious anxiety for the result of the Convention. – Mr. Dickenson said to Mr. Madison you see the consequence of pushing things too far.*" [Emphasis added] [4]

---

[2] John Taylor, *New Views of the Constitution of the United States*, Da Capo Press, New York (orig. pub. in 1823) 1971, quoted on pp. 41-42.
[3] Max Farrand (ed.), *The Records of the Federal Convention of 1787*, Revised Edition, Volume I, Yale University Press, New Haven, p. 240.
[4] *Ibid.*, Volume I, p. 242.

The New Jersey Plan

The following day, on June 15th, William Paterson introduced an entirely new plan of government which, he said, several of the States present wished to be subsisted for the Virginia Plan. Although this new plan had actually been prepared by a number of Federal Republican delegates from New Jersey, Connecticut, Delaware, New York, and Maryland, the new proposal was often referred to in debate as the New Jersey Plan, inasmuch as Mr. Paterson, its primary mover, was from that State.

The plan laid before the Philadelphia Convention by Mr. Paterson consisted of the following nine resolutions:

1. *Resolved, That the Articles of Confederation ought to be so revised, corrected and enlarged, as to render the Federal Constitution adequate to the exigencies of government, and the preservation of the Union.*

2. *Resolved,* That, in addition to *the powers vested in the United States in Congress by the present existing Articles of Confederation,* they be authorized to pass acts for raising a revenue, by levying a duty on all goods or merchandise of foreign growth or manufacture, imported into any part of the United States; by stamps on paper, vellum, or parchment; and by a postage on all letters or packages passing through the general post-office; – to be applied to such *federal* purposes as they shall deem proper and expedient: to make rules and regulations for the collection thereof; and the same, from time to time, *to alter and amend in such manner as they shall think proper:* to pass acts for the regulation of trade and commerce, *as well with foreign nations as with each other,* – provided that all punishments, fines, forfeitures, and penalties, to be incurred for contravening such acts, rules, and regulations, shall be adjudged by *the common-law judiciaries of the State* in which any offence contrary to the true intent and meaning of such acts, rules, and regulations, shall have been committed or perpetrated, with liberty of commencing in the first instance all suits and prosecutions for that purpose in *the superior common-law judiciary in such State;* subject, nevertheless, for the correction of all errors, both in law and fact, in rendering judgment, to an appeal to the judiciary of the United States.

3. *Resolved,* That whenever requisitions shall be necessary, instead of the rule for making requisitions mentioned in the Articles of Confederation, *the United States in Congress* be authorized to make such requisitions in proportion to the whole number of White and other free citizens and inhabitants, of every age, sex, and condition, including those bound to servitude for a term of years, and three fifths of all other persons not comprehended in the foregoing description, except Indians not paying taxes; that, if such requisitions be not complied with in the time specified therein, to direct the collection thereof in the non-complying State, and for that purpose to devise and pass acts directing and authorizing the same; – provided, that none of the powers hereby vested in *the United States in Congress* shall

be exercised without the consent of at least _____ States; and in that proportion, if the number of *Confederated States* hereafter be increased or diminished.

4. *Resolved,* That *the United States in Congress* be authorized to elect a *federal* executive, to consist of _____ persons; to continue in office for the term of _____ years; to receive punctually, at stated times, a fixed compensation for their services, in which no increase nor diminution shall be made so as to effect the persons composing the executive at the time of such increase or diminution; to be paid out of the *federal* treasury, to be incapable of holding any other office or appointment during their time of service, and for _____ years thereafter; to be ineligible a second time, and removable by *Congress,* on application by a majority of the executives of the several States: that the executive, besides their general authority to execute the *federal* acts, ought to appoint all *federal* officers not otherwise provided for, and to direct all military operations; — provided, that none of the persons composing the *federal* executive shall, on any occasion, take command of any troops, so as personally to conduct any military enterprise, as general, or in any other capacity.

5. *Resolved,* That a *federal* judiciary be established, to consist of a supreme tribunal, the judges of which to be appointed by the executive, and *to hold their offices during good behavior;* to receive punctually, at stated times, a fixed compensation for their services, in which no increase nor diminution shall be made so as to affect the persons actually in office at the time of such increase or diminution. That the judiciary so established shall have authority to hear and determine, in the first instance, on all impeachments of *federal* officers, and by way of appeal, in the dernier resort, in all cases touching the rights of ambassadors; in all cases of captures from an enemy; in all cases of piracies and felonies on the high seas; in all cases in which foreigners may be interested; in the construction of any treaty or treaties, or which may arise on any of the acts for the regulation of trade, or the collection of the *federal* revenue: that none of the judiciary shall, during the time they remain in office, be capable of receiving or holding any other office or appointment during their term of service, or for _____ thereafter.

6. *Resolved,* That all acts of the United States in Congress, *made by virtue and in pursuance of the powers hereby, and by the Articles of Confederation, vested in them, and all treaties made and ratified under the authority of the United States, shall be the supreme law of the respective States,* so far forth as those acts or treaties shall relate to the said States or their citizens; and that *the judiciary of the several States shall be bound thereby in their decisions,* any thing in the respective laws of the individual States to the contrary notwithstanding; and that if any State, or any body of men in any State, shall oppose or prevent the carrying into execution such acts or treaties, *the federal executive shall be authorized to call forth the power of the Confederated States, or so much thereof as may be necessary, to enforce and compel an obedience to such acts, or an observation of such treaties.*

7. *Resolved,* That provision be made for the admission of new States

into the Union.

8. *Resolved,* That the rules for naturalization ought to be the same in every State.

9. *Resolved,* That a citizen in one State, committing an offence in another State of the Union, shall be guilty of the same offence as if it had been committed by a citizen of the State in which the offence was committed. [Emphasis added] [5]

The word "national," as is readily apparent, appeared nowhere within the New Jersey Plan. That term, *and the concepts associated with it,* were rejected in favor of a federal system of government. Accordingly, the term *federal* and its associated concept of *Confederated States* appeared numerous times. The former word appeared within the plan introduced by Mr. Paterson no less than *eleven times,* and the latter words appeared *twice* in reference to the States that would comprise the Federal Union under the new Constitution.

By the terms of the New Jersey Plan, which was termed a "Federal Constitution," provision was made for a "federal executive," a "federal judiciary," and *a federal legislature appropriately termed a Congress,* as well as other "federal officers." Funded by means of a "federal treasury" acquired from "federal revenue," the proposed Government of the United States would perform "federal acts" for "federal purposes" for the benefit of the "Confederated States."

Special attention should be directed to the sixth resolution in the plan proposed by the Federal Republicans within the Convention. Unlike the Virginia Plan, which provided for a supreme National Government, the New Jersey Plan revived the concept of *supremacy* contained within the Articles of Confederation. Instead of a *supreme government,* the latter plan provided for a *supreme Constitution.* This crucial and highly significant difference between the concepts of supremacy sharply contrasted the two proposed plans. The concept of supremacy contained within the Virginia Plan transferred sovereignty to the National Government, while that of the New Jersey Plan left sovereignty in the peoples of the several States.

One idea contained within the New Jersey Plan was ironically in sharp contrast to its other principles. This peculiar and dangerous provision would have authorized the proposed Federal Government "to call forth the power of the Confederated States, or so much thereof as may be necessary, to enforce and compel an obedience" to its laws and edicts. Such a provision, it is apparent, would have sanctioned the use of military coercion against a sovereign State, and that, in turn, would have laid the foundations for a War Between

---

[5] Jonathan Elliot (ed.), *Op. cit.,* Volume 5, pp. 191-193.

the States. This particular provision was undoubtedly inserted into the New
Jersey Plan in a moment of haste and without sufficient thought, perhaps in
an effort to counter the highly dangerous nationalist proposal for a national
veto over State laws.

Fortunately, the Federal Republicans came to recognize the danger to
liberty inherent in such a coercive power, and the proposition was wisely
dropped altogether. The Convention would ultimately reject not only the
proposed national veto over State laws, but also the proposed military coercion of a sovereign State by the Federal Government. The *Supremacy Clause*,
as eventually adopted by the Convention, would be based largely on the sixth
resolution of the New Jersey Plan, *but only after expunging the portion of the
resolution providing for federal coercion.*

The plan proposed by the Federal Republicans provided for a Congress
consisting of only *one* house or body. This *unicameral legislature* was undoubtedly proposed with a view to a *compromise* in mind. The federalists, in
fact, had hinted at such a compromise prior to introducing the New Jersey
Plan. By the terms of their proposed compromise, representation in the U.S.
House of Representatives would be based on the respective *populations of the
several States*, while representation in the Senate would be based on the *sovereign equality of the several States.*

To the nationalists, the proposed compromise was no compromise at
all, for it spelled total defeat for the system of government they advocated.
*The very existence of equality of suffrage in any department of the general gov-
ernment would stand as a constant reminder of the fact that the States, and not a
consolidated nation of Americans, form the foundation of the Union, and that
those States are sovereign.* Although the dispute between the large and the small
States might be resolved by such a compromise, between federalism and nationalism there could be no compromise. Accordingly, the nationalists appealed to the greed of the large States and fought against equality of suffrage
in the Senate with all their might.

Debate on the New Jersey Plan and on the Virginia Plan, which was
now resubmitted to the Committee of the Whole for re-examination, commenced on June 16, 1787, when John Lansing of New York took the floor.
James Madison recorded his words as follows:

> Mr. Lansing called for *the reading of the 1st resolution of each plan,
> which he considered as involving principles directly in contrast; that of Mr.
> Patterson says he sustains the sovereignty of the respective States, that of Mr.
> Randolph destroys it: the later requires a negative on all the laws of the particu-
> lar States; the former, only certain general powers for the general good. The
> plan of Mr. R. in short absorbs all power except what may be exercised in the*

> *little local matters of the States which are not objects worthy of the supreme cognizance.* He grounded his preference of Mr. P'.s plan, chiefly on two objections agst that of Mr. R. *1. Want of power in the Convention to discuss & propose it. 2 The improbability of its being adopted.* 1. He was decidedly of opinion that *the power of the Convention was restrained to amendments of a federal nature, and having for their basis the Confederacy in being.* The Act of Congress [and] the tenor of the Acts of the States, the commissions produced by the several deputations all proved this. And this *limitation of the power to an amendment of the Confederacy,* marked the opinion of the States, that it was unnecessary & improper to go farther. He was sure this was the case with his State. *N. York would never have concurred in sending delegates to the Convention, if she had supposed the deliberations were to turn on a consolidation of the States, and a National Government.* 2. Was it probable that the States would adopt & ratify a scheme, which they had never authorized us to propose? And which so far exceeded what they regarded as sufficient?...*The States will never feel a sufficient confidence in a general government to give it a negative on their laws.* The scheme is itself totally novel. There is no parallel to it to be found. The authority of [the existing] Congress is familiar to the people, and an augmentation of the powers of Congress will be readily approved by them. [Emphasis added] [6]

"If we form a government, let us do it on principles which are likely to meet the approbation of the States," stated the delegate from New York. The Virginia Plan, he observed, proposed to "absorb the State sovereignties & leave them mere corporations," although the "States will never sacrifice their essential rights to a National Government. New plans, annihilating the rights of the States...can never be approved." [7]

William Paterson then addressed the Convention. "If the Confederacy was radically wrong, let us return to our States, and obtain larger powers, not assume them of ourselves." "I came here not to speak my own sentiments, but the sentiments of those who sent me," he said, adding:

> If we argue the matter on the supposition that no Confederacy at present exists, it can not be denied that all the States stand on the footing of equal sovereignty....*If a proportional representation be right, why do we not vote so here?* If we argue on the fact that a federal compact actually exists, and consult the Articles of it we still find an equal sovereignty to be the basis of it. He reads the 5th. art: of Confederation giving each State a vote – & the 13th. declaring that no alteration shall be made without unanimous consent. *This is the nature of all treaties.* [Emphasis added] [8]

---

[6] Max Farrand (ed.), *Op. cit.*, Volume I, pp. 249-250.
[7] *Ibid.*, Volume I, pp. 258 and 263.
[8] *Ibid.*, Volume I, p. 250.

Judging from Mr. Paterson's comment regarding the mode of voting within the Constitutional Convention, it is apparent that he and the other Federal Republicans were unaware of the plot entertained by the nationalists to rob them of their equality of suffrage *within* the Federal Convention. Had the aborted plot been common knowledge, the hostility of the Federal Republicans to the proposed National Government undoubtedly would have been far more intense than it was.

"When independent societies confederate for mutual defence, they do so in their collective capacity; and then each State for those purposes must be considered as *one* of the contracting parties," Mr. Paterson continued. "Destroy this balance of equality, and you endanger the rights of the *lesser* societies by the danger of usurpation in the greater." "It therefore follows, that a National Government...is unjust, and destructive of the common principles of reciprocity," he concluded. "Much has been said that this" National "Government" – as contradistinguished from a Federal Government – "is to operate on persons, not on States. This, upon examination, will be found equally fallacious." [9]

Responding to these attacks on the proposed national system, James Wilson asserted that, "With regard to the *power of the Convention*, he conceived himself authorized to *conclude nothing*, but to be at liberty to *propose any thing*." Obviously realizing that only a Convention possessing unlimited powers could draft a plan of a National Government with unlimited powers, the delegate from Pennsylvania denied the existence of any limits on the authority of the Philadelphia Convention. "With *regard to the sentiments of the people*, he conceived it difficult to know precisely what they are," although he did not suggest lifting the veil of secrecy to discover what those sentiments might be. Mr. Wilson pressed the idea that, by adopting the proposed National Constitution, the "original authority of *the people at large* is brought forward," as distinguished from the authority of the people of the States. And in demagogic fashion, he proclaimed that, under the proposed National Government, in all cases whatsoever and without limitation "a majority of the" people of the "United States are to control."[Emphasis added] [10]

Governor Randolph brought the day's debates to a close by making a passionate appeal for nationalism. "The true question," said he, "is whether we shall adhere to the federal plan, or introduce the national plan." "We must resort...to *a national legislation over individuals*," which could only be provided by a National Government. The existing Congress, he insisted, was seriously defective because its members were "not elected by the people, but by

---

[9] *Ibid.*, Volume I, p. 259.
[10] *Ibid.*, Volume I, pp. 253 and 270.

the legislatures who retain even a power of recall." The wily politician completely ignored the fact that, under the Articles of Confederation, members of Congress from several of the States actually were *elected by the peoples of their respective States*. Because this fact did not fit his theory as to the necessity of a supreme National Government, however, it was conveniently ignored. Only such a government, he concluded, "will answer the purpose; and he begged it to be considered that the present is the last moment for establishing one." [Emphasis added] [11]

The sands of time were indeed running out for the nationalist conspiracy, although not in the sense in which Mr. Randolph attempted to portray the crisis. The economic and fiscal situation confronting the United States was actually improving, not growing worse. The depression had already bottomed out a year earlier, and prosperity was in sight. With each passing day, the defects of the Articles of Confederation became less glaring in the eyes of the American people. The opportunity to force a National Constitution on the United States, the nationalists consequently realized, would soon be lost.

As soon as the business of the house was resumed on Monday, June 18th, John Dickinson moved that further consideration of the first resolution in the New Jersey Plan be postponed in order to introduce the following resolution: "*Resolved* that the Articles of Confederation ought to be *revised and amended*, so as to render the *Government of the United States* adequate to the exigencies, the preservation, and the prosperity of the Union." [Emphasis added] [12]

The highly significant phraseology of this resolution introduced on behalf of the Federal Republicans merits close scrutiny, for it introduces for our consideration the term "Government of the United States" *as being the equivalent of the term Federal Government*. This, of course, is precisely the phraseology used in the Federal Constitution, as finally adopted by the Convention, to describe the government instituted by it. We see here in this very resolution proof positive that the term in question – *Government of the United States* – was used in contradistinction to a *National Government*, which the term was intended to replace.

The resolution introduced by Mr. Dickinson easily passed in the Convention. Of the eleven States present, *ten* voted for it, *none* voted against it, and *one* State – Pennsylvania – was divided. The situation confronting the nationalists had now become critical, for their proposed National Government was in imminent danger of being pulled down by the determined Federal Republican party.

---

[11] *Ibid.*, Volume I, pp. 255-256.
[12] *Ibid.*, Volume I, p. 281.

It was precisely at this critical juncture that a theretofore largely obscure delegate from New York stepped forward to address the Federal Convention in order to urge the delegates to abandon both the Virginia Plan and the New Jersey Plan in favor of his own plan of government. For the next five hours, the delegates sat spellbound as Alexander Hamilton – the man destined to become the most famous leader of the Society of the Cincinnati and Number "7" in the British cipher – candidly shared with them his concept of what constituted an ideal government for the United States of America.

The Orator of Nationalism

The man who gave the longest speech to the Grand Convention of the States was, beyond doubt, the strangest delegate in attendance. Although Mr. Hamilton had served as an aide to General Washington during the War of Independence, his conduct after the war gave rise to much speculation as to his true loyalties. We have previously cited one illustration, in the case of New York's Trespass Act, wherein the New York nationalist had openly identified with the Tories. That case, however, was only one of many that served to demonstrate his fondness for powerful and wealthy Loyalists.

In his book, *Alexander Hamilton and the Growth of the New Nation*, which was published in 1959, biographer John C. Miller made this observation of Mr. Hamilton's pro-British sentiments:

> Inevitably, therefore, by championing the Loyalists, Hamilton exposed himself to the charge of being a Tory-lover. It was said that he swooned with joy whenever a blue-blooded monarchist gave him a civil word. He was accused of being "the bell-wether of the flock" of the Loyalists and of being in British pay. Newspaper writers speculated as to the number of pieces of silver for which he had sold his country. [13]

According to this author, "Among the members of Congress," under the existing Articles of Confederation "to whom Hamilton was instantly drawn by an affinity of interests and ideas was James Madison of Virginia." [14] While a member of Congress, the brilliant young nationalist from New York also came into contact with the Superintendent of Finance, Robert Morris of Pennsylvania. Mr. Morris, who is often referred to by historians as the "Financier of the Revolutionary War," was firmly convinced that what the United

---

[13] John C. Miller, *Alexander Hamilton and the Growth of the New Nation*, Harper & Row, Publishers, New York, 1959, p. 103.
[14] *Ibid.*, p. 85.

States needed was a vigorous National Government to be erected on the ruins of the sovereign States. Such a supreme National Government, however, was not intended to serve the interests of the common man, but of the financially powerful – of the international bankers.

In an early first attempt to effect the goal of rearing a monied aristocracy in the United States, Robert Morris had established the Bank of North America in 1781. This had been followed by other attempts, under the Articles, to convert the Federal Government into an engine for *socialistic plutocracy*. Alexander Hamilton, for his part, quickly gravitated toward Robert Morris's plans for America and so thoroughly adopted the principles of plutocracy that he eventually came to personify the early drive to socialize the United States on behalf of the financial elite. As John C. Miller noted, "Morris undertook to introduce into American fiscal policy the methods and objectives that later became known as Hamiltonianism." [15]

Under the Articles of Confederation, however, the promoters of a monied aristocracy in the United States encountered a major obstacle in the form of sovereign States and the federal system inherent in the existing Confederacy. By its very nature, a plutocracy requires an all-powerful, highly centralized general government, and as long as sovereign States existed, such a government could never exist. According to his biographer, Alexander Hamilton therefore came to the Philadelphia Convention for the sole and express purpose of abolishing the Articles of Confederation and replacing the existing Congress with a supreme National Government.

As Mr. Miller noted:

> Hamilton came to the Constitutional Convention armed with a philosophy which eminently qualified him to be the spokesman of a new order. *He was a complete and uncompromising nationalist....*
>
> For Hamilton, the pursuit of happiness led straight to a *strong National Government*. But he no longer *pretended* that it could be attained within the Articles of Confederation; a sound and enduring government, he observed, could not be built upon rubble. He considered the Articles to be designed for a *league of nations*, not for a *nation*; *nationalism* could not live within that narrow and oppressive framework.
>
> He was resolved *to change the league into an effective centralized government*, clothed with *high sovereign powers* for *national* objects and operating directly upon the people as individuals – in short, a government capable of *dealing with national problems in a national way. But standing squarely in Hamilton's path were the Articles of Confederation, still the fundamental law of the land.* [Emphasis added] [16]

---

[15] *Ibid.*, p. 86.
[16] *Ibid.*, pp. 153-154.

"The delegates had no more than taken their seats," John C. Miller wrote, "before Hamilton made clear that despite his respect for constitutional authority, he was not averse to doing it violence when his objectives could not otherwise be attained." [17] Thus, from the very outset of the Convention, Mr. Hamilton presented the basic philosophy that would guide his conduct throughout his entire political career – not only as a delegate within the Federal Convention, but even later as the Secretary of the Treasury within the Administration of President George Washington.

Although Alexander Hamilton arrived at the Federal Convention secretly armed with a plan of government previously prepared by extreme nationalists, he remained unusually quiet during the early stages of the proceedings. As long as it appeared that the Virginia Plan could be carried, he kept his own plan under cover and allowed the other key nationalists – James Madison and James Wilson – to parry blows with the Federal Republicans. "On the rare occasions when Hamilton took the floor," wrote Mr. Miller, "it was usually in order to amend the Virginia Plan in the direction of *greater centralization of authority and more power in the Presidency*." [Emphasis added] [18]

When James Wilson moved on June 4th, for example, that the Chief Executive should have an *absolute veto* over legislative acts, Alexander Hamilton heartily seconded the motion, arguing that there would be little danger of abusing such a sweeping power. But when the Convention finally voted on the proposal, only Mr. Hamilton, Mr. Wilson, and Gouverneur Morris were found to favor such broad authority for the President of the United States.

With the introduction of the New Jersey Plan by the Federal Republicans, the fiery nationalist from New York was aghast. The only thing worse than a proposal that the Convention seriously *consider* the retention of the Federal Republic, in his view, was the very real possibility that the Convention might just *decide* to retain the federal system. The time had come, he was convinced, to unveil his own plan of government.

According to Mr. Hamilton's biographer:

> Although Hamilton spoke on June 18 with such magisterial and provocative assurance that some delegates felt that no young man had a right to imagine himself to be as right as Hamilton obviously did, his oratorical effort was generally well received. The longest speech delivered in the Constitutional Convention, it established his reputation as the *Orator of Nationalism*. [Emphasis added] [19]

---

[17] *Ibid.*, p. 154.
[18] *Ibid.*, p. 158.
[19] *Ibid.*, p. 171.

During the course of his incredible five-hour address to the Federal Convention, this *Orator of Nationalism* bluntly stated that the time had come to wipe the States off the map, to merge the peoples of the States into a single body politic, to institute a supreme National Government vested with unlimited powers, to place at the head of such government a monarch, and to attach to this undisguised totalitarian dictatorship a monied aristocracy. Most historians agree that the plan he introduced to the Grand Convention truly represented Alexander Hamilton's concept of the *ideal government for America*. Considering the crucial role Mr. Hamilton was to play in shaping American affairs *after* the adoption of the Constitution of 1787, this fact carries special significance.

Alexander Hamilton's true *motives* for candidly addressing the Philadelphia Convention and introducing his plan for a National Monarchy is open to speculation. Perhaps he regarded the Convention to be in confusion and chaos, and thus susceptible of being persuaded to adopt his radical plan. On the other hand, he may have perceived an opportunity, in the clash of interests between the large and the small States, to persuade the delegates to end the large-small State conflict by literally annihilating the States once and for all. Or, perhaps he hoped that, by introducing his plan, the Virginia Plan would appear less radical to the delegates, and that the Virginia Plan could then serve as a *compromise* between two extremes.

The Longest Speech in the Convention

Whatever may have been his true motives, Alexander Hamilton began the longest speech in the Convention on June 18th by denouncing *both* the Virginia Plan and the New Jersey Plan. "He was particularly opposed to that from N. Jersey," he emphasized, "being fully convinced, that no amendment of the Confederation, *leaving the States in possession of their sovereignty* could possibly answer the purpose." "As to the *powers of the Convention*, he thought the doubts started on that subject had arisen from distinctions & reasonings too subtle." [Emphasis added] [20]

In James Madison's notes of the address of the strange delegate from New York, we read the following:

A *Federal Govt.* he conceived to mean *an association of independent communities into one*. Different *Confederacies* have different powers, and exercise them in different ways. In some instances the powers are exercised

---

[20] Max Farrand (ed.), *Op. cit.*, Volume I, p. 283.

over *collective bodies*; in others over *individuals....Great latitude therefore must be given to the signification of the term.* The [New Jersey] Plan last proposed departs itself from the *federal* idea, as understood by some, since it is to operate eventually on *individuals*. He agreed moreover with the Honble. gentleman from Va. (Mr. R.) that we owed it to our country, to do on this *emergency* whatever we should deem essential to its happiness. *The States sent us here to provide for the exigencies of the Union.* To rely on & propose any plan not adequate to these exigencies, merely because *it was not clearly within our powers, would be to sacrifice the means to the end.* [Emphasis added] [21]

Within this remarkable passage, the student of constitutional government will note that the Orator of Nationalism acknowledged that sovereign States can constitute a *Federal* Government to operate on the people in their capacity as individual citizens as well as in their collective capacities as sovereign States. Even the Federal Government proposed by the New Jersey Plan, he observed, would contain both features of operation. Although the intent of such statements was to strengthen the case for the Virginia Plan, Mr. Hamilton actually undermined one of the chief excuses that had been previously offered in favor of a National Government.

In spite of these favorable words for federalism, however, the delegate from New York had no intention of supporting the federal system of government. The United States, he insisted, was in a state of "emergency" that required the delegates to cast aside the commissions authorizing and limiting their powers and to assume whatever powers they wished. To do otherwise would be "to sacrifice the *means* to the *end*," an *end* which he identified as "the exigencies of the Union."

In Alexander Hamilton's opinion, *the end always justifies the means*; and, if necessary, the desired *end* can always be confounded, obscured, and even transformed into a wholly different end. No one knew better than he that the States, in their commissions to the delegates, had specifically stated the *end* to be attained by the Convention, but had left the *means* necessary to acquire that *specified end* largely unspecified. *The end specified was to render a Federal Constitution adequate to the exigencies of a Federal Government, to the preservation of the Federal Union, and to the strengthening of the Federal Republic.* Replacing that Federal Republic with a National Monarchy was clearly not a *means* calculated to produce the officially mandated *end*. *Mr. Hamilton's goal, like that of the other nationalists in Convention, was to replace the legitimate end of the Philadelphia Convention with an entirely different end.* Such an object could be obtained only by deliberately confusing the *unspecified means*

---

[21] *Ibid.*, Volume I, p. 283.

with the *specified end,* so that the *means* could become an *end* in itself.

In addressing the Convention, the Orator of Nationalism thus concluded that, *since the States had not specifically prohibited the delegates from proposing a National Government, the power must necessary exist.* This peculiar line of reasoning – *that all powers not specifically prohibited may be assumed –* bears a striking resemblance to the preferred mode of construing the Federal Constitution that would be promoted by Alexander Hamilton after its adoption.

As Robert Yates recorded the incredible speech in his notes, Mr. Hamilton audaciously asserted before the Grand Convention:

> Let us now review *the powers with which we are invested.* We are appointed for *the sole and express purpose of revising the Confederation, and to alter or amend it,* so as *to render it* effectual for the purposes of a good government. Those who suppose it must be *federal,* lay great stress on the terms *sole* and *express, as if those words intended a confinement to a Federal Government;* when the manifest import is no more than that the institution of a good government must be the *sole* and *express* object of your deliberations. Nor can we suppose an annihilation of our powers by forming a *National Government,* as many of the States have made in their Constitutions no provision for any alteration....This appears reasonable, and therefore leaves us at liberty to form such a *National Government* as we think best adapted for the good of the whole. I have therefore no difficulty as to the extent of our powers, *nor do I feel myself restrained in the exercise of my judgment under them.* We can only propose and recommend – the power of ratifying or rejecting is still in the States. [Emphasis added] [22]

Having thus done away with all of the restrictions imposed on the delegates by their respective States, and having substituted the specified *end* of a *Federal* Government with a new *end* of a *National* Government, Mr. Hamilton turned his attention to some general observations on what should constitute a "good government" for the United States of America. His observations were recorded in detail by James Madison:

> The great question is what provision shall we make for the happiness of our country? He would first make a comparative examination of the two plans – prove that there were essential defects in both – and point out such changes as might render a *national one,* efficacious. – *The great & essential principles necessary for the support of government. are 1. An active & constant interest in supporting it.* This principle does not exist in the States in favor of the Federal Govt. They have evidently in a high degree, the esprit de corps. They constantly pursue internal interests adverse to those of

---

[22] *Ibid.,* Volume I, pp. 294-295.

the whole. They have their particular debts – their particular plans of finance &c. All these when opposed to, invariably prevail over the requisitions & plans of Congress. *2. The love of power, men love power.* The same remarks are applicable to this principle. The States have constantly shewn a disposition rather to regain the powers delegated by them than to part with more, or to give effect to what they had parted with. The *ambition* of their demagogues is known to hate the controul of the genl. government. It may be remarked too that the citizens have not that anxiety to prevent a dissolution of the genl. govt as of the particular govts. *A dissolution of the latter would be fatal: of the former would still leave the purposes of govt. attainable to a considerable degree.* Consider what such a State as Virga. will be in a few years, a few compared with the life of nations. How strongly will it feel its importance & self-sufficiency? *3. An habitual attachment of the people.* The whole force of this tie is on the side of the State govt. *Its sovereignty is immediately before the eyes of the people: its protection is immediately enjoyed by them.* From its hand distributive justice, and all those acts which familiarize & endear govt. to a people, are dispensed to them. *4. Force by which may be understood a coertion of laws or coertion of arms.* Congs. have not the former except in few cases. In particular States, this coercion is nearly sufficient; tho' he held it in most cases, not entirely so. *A certain portion of military force is absolutely necessary in large communities.* Massts. is now feeling this necessity & making provision for it. *But how can this force be exerted on the States collectively. It is impossible. It amounts to a war between the parties....5. Influence.* He did not mean *corruption,* but a dispensation of those regular honors & emoluments, which produce an attachment to the govt. *Almost all the weight of these is on the side of the States; and must continue so as long as the States continue to exist.* All the *passions* then we see, of *avarice, ambition, interest,* which govern most individuals, and all public bodies, fall into the current of the States, and do not flow in the stream of the genl. govt. The former therefore will generally be an overmatch for the genl. govt. and render any *Confederacy,* in its very nature precarious. [Emphasis added] [23]

To rule mankind, the Orator of Nationalism asserted, required a proper understanding and usage of both *force* and *interest*. And no one was more willing than Mr. Hamilton to use *force* against the States, nor did any man better understand than he how to recruit patrons to his cause by appealing to their greedy *interests*. The political party he would later found would be based squarely on an appeal to the very *passions, avarice, ambition,* and *interest* he spoke of in the Convention. By such means, he asserted, the allegiance of the wealthy and powerful could be transferred from the States to the general government. With the patronage of interest thus acquired, all vestiges of State sovereignty could be crushed. And in the event such patronage and privilege proved insufficient to acquire the desired end, there could always be a resort

---

[23] *Ibid.*, Volume I, pp. 284–285.

to military coercion.

"Men always love power," observed the shrewd nationalist from New York, "and States will prefer their particular concerns to the general welfare." As time progressed, the States would obviously increase in population and strength; and as their strength grew, their mutual dependency on one another for self-defense – the key reason for their interest in the Federal Union – was destined to diminish. Citing as an example the State of Virginia, he could ask, "as the States become large and important, will they not be less attentive to the general government?" "Feeling her own weight and importance, must she not become indifferent to the concerns of the Union?," he inquired. "And where, in such a situation, will be found national attachment to the general government?" [24]

The States, he was convinced, constituted the worst plague to ever blight the American continent. The very existence of the States governments made it next to impossible for a supreme National Government to lay claim to the primary devotion and attachment of the American people. "The State governments, by either plan," he insisted, "will exert the means to counteract it." Although he was fond of the Virginia Plan, he found that it fell short in one key area. While it proposed to erect a supreme National Government over an American nation of people, *it left the States intact*. The Virginia Plan therefore planted the seeds of civil strife and a War Between the States. Either the National Government would crush the States, or the States would undermine it. The State governments "have their State judges and militia all combined to support their State interests; and these will be influenced to oppose a National Government," he noted. "Either plan is therefore precarious. The National Government cannot long exist when opposed by such a weighty rival." [25]

"How then are all these evils to be avoided?" asked the nationalist from New York. Certainly not by any proposal for a Federal Government, such as that contained in the New Jersey Plan, for "all Federal Governments are weak and distracted." There could be only one cure for the evil of sovereign States: "Only by such a compleat sovereignty in the general government as will turn all the strong principles & passions above mentioned on its side." "What does the Jersey Plan propose?" he inquired. "It surely has not this for its object. By this we grant the regulation of trade and a more effectual collection of the revenue, and some partial duties." [26]

As we read in Mr. Yates's notes, Colonel Hamilton's hatred of the federal system knew no bounds:

---

[24] *Ibid.*, Volume I, pp. 295-296.
[25] *Ibid.*, Volume I, p. 296.
[26] *Ibid.*, Volume I, pp. 286 and 297.

Another objection against the Jersey Plan is, the unequal representation. Can the great States consent to this? If they did it would eventually work its own destruction. How are forces to be raised by the Jersey Plan? By quotas? Will the States comply with the requisition? As much as they will with the taxes.

Examine the present Confederation, and it is evident they can raise no troops nor equip vessels before war is actually declared. They cannot therefore take any preparatory measure before an enemy is at your door. *How unwise and inadequate their powers! And this must ever be the case when you attempt to define powers. — Something will always be wanting.* Congress, by being annually elected, and subject to recall, will ever come with the prejudices of their States rather than the good of the Union. Add therefore additional powers to a body thus organized, and you establish a sovereignty of the worst kind, consisting of a single body. Where are the checks? None. They must either prevail over the State governments, or the prevalence of the State governments must end in their dissolution. This is a conclusive objection to the Jersey Plan.

Such are the insuperable objections to both plans.... [Emphasis added] [27]

"The general power whatever be its form if it preserves itself, must swallow up the State powers," Mr. Hamilton insisted. "Otherwise it will be swallowed up by them." "Two sovereignties can not co-exist within the same limits," he correctly observed. By insisting that the general government must be supreme and, hence, sovereign, he acknowledged the inherent contradiction between the sovereignty of the peoples of the States and the sovereignty proposed to be invested in a National Government. The New Jersey Plan proposed to leave sovereignty with the peoples of the States. But he wished it to be vested in the general government. "The plan of N. Jersey therefore," he concluded, "will not do." [28]

The proposed "solution" to the "emergency" confronting the United States, Mr. Hamilton surmised, lay in the political creation of a monied aristocracy. He even cited the example of the British Government in support of his concept. A monied aristocracy had been attached to it, and under its auspices a mercantile system had been created for the socialistic exploitation of the British Empire. By adopting a similar system in the United States, could not a wonderful plutocracy be created for the socialistic exploitation of an American Empire? Colonel Hamilton's statements in favor of a monied aristocracy constituted the most candid expressions ever uttered on American soil on behalf of plutocratic government.

In his notes, Robert Yates recorded Mr. Hamilton's statements as fol-

---

[27] *Ibid.*, Volume I, pp. 297-298.
[28] *Ibid.*, Volume I, p. 287.

lows:

> I am at a loss to know what must be done – *I despair that a republican form of government can remove the difficulties.* Whatever may be my opinion, I would hold it however *unwise to change that form of government. I believe the British Government forms the best model the world ever produced,* and such has been its progress in the minds of the many, that this truth gradually gains ground. This government has for its object *public strength* and *individual security.* It is said with us to be unattainable. *If it was once formed it would maintain itself. All communities divide themselves into the few and the many. The first are the rich and well born, the other the mass of the people.* The voice of the people has been said to be the voice of God; and however generally this maxim has been quoted and believed, it is not true in fact. *The people are turbulent and changing; they seldom judge or determine right. Give therefore to the first class a distinct, permanent share in the government. They will check the unsteadiness of the second, and as they cannot receive any advantage by a change, they therefore will ever maintain good government.* Can a democratic assembly, who annually revolve in the mass of the people, be supposed steadily to pursue the public good? *Nothing but a permanent body can check the imprudence of democracy. Their turbulent and uncontrouling disposition requires checks.* The Senate of New-York, although chosen for four years, we have found to be inefficient. Will, on the Virginia Plan, a continuance of seven years do it? It is admitted that you cannot have a good executive upon a democratic plan. *See the excellency of the British executive – He is placed above temptation –* He can have no distinct interests from the public welfare. *Nothing short of such an executive can be efficient.* The weak side of a republican government is the danger of foreign influence. This is unavoidable, unless it is so constructed as to bring forward its first characters in its support. *I am therefore for a general government, yet wish to go the full length of republican principles.* [Emphasis added] [29]

The republican form of government, said Alexander Hamilton, did not provide for good government. Good government only resulted from totalitarian monarchies, such as that of Great Britain. He deemed it "unwise," however, to openly replace the republican form of government in the United States with a monarchy. But the same desired goal could be effected by going "the full length of republican principles." Let the people have their elections and be deluded into thinking that such elections fulfilled the requirements for republican government. Once elected, the *tenure of office* and *extent of powers* wielded by these elected officials would result in the desired form of government.

As for the balance of power between the State governments and the de-

---

[29] *Ibid.*, Volume I, pp. 299-300.

sired supreme National Government, that, too, could be easily decided in favor of the latter by adopting his plan. All that was required to establish an
elitist, centralized government, he noted, was to trick the American people
into adopting the plan. "If it was once formed," he assured the delegates, "it
would maintain itself." No State or combination of States would dare challenge his National Government, if it could ever be installed in power.

The great bulk of the American people, Mr. Hamilton asserted, were
ignorant, turbulent, changing, and utterly incapable of deciding upon questions of right and wrong. This seemed to be inherent in human nature, he
noted. He made no attempt to explain why, however, the *rich* and the *well-
born* could do a better job of deciding what was right and good. Rather than
prove that human nature dictated a strong, energetic, supreme National Government ruled by an elitist aristocracy, his observations actually pointed to
precisely the opposite solution. The nature of man itself dictated that no set
of politicians should ever be entrusted with such sweeping powers as proposed
by Mr. Hamilton. Yet, Mr. Hamilton flatly rejected the true lessons taught by
a study of human nature and insisted that the only way to check the avarice
and greed of the *masses* was to appease the avarice and greed of the *money
power*.

"Their turbulent and uncontrouling disposition requires checks," the
Orator of Nationalism stated, speaking of the masses of the people. In this he
was correct, although he ignored completely the greatest and most foolproof
checks against unbridled majority rule ever invented by mankind. What better "check" against unbridled majority rule at the federal level could exist than
the watchful eyes of *the State governments*, who would jealously guard the local rights of the States against encroachments from an otherwise uncontrollable federal majority? And what better "check" could be placed against unbridled majority rule within the government itself, than by balancing the interests of *a majority of the people* in the House of Representatives with the interests of *a majority of the States* in the Senate? *Yet, Mr. Hamilton arrogantly insisted that both of these great "checks" on rampant democracy should be abolished!*
To fill the vacuum left by the abolition of these natural checks against unbridled majority rule, he advocated the creation of a monied aristocracy and the
conversion of the U.S. Senate into a *House of Lords!*

It would appear that the real reason why Alexander Hamilton urged a
rejection of all the true and real checks on otherwise uncontrollable power lay
in the fact that he really did not want to suppress the role of avarice and ambition in the councils of government. His objective evidently was not to prevent greedy motives and passions from dominating the general government,
but to encourage such passionate motives. This undeniable fact is borne out by
the personal notes he prepared for his speech, wherein he candidly stated his

desire to foster and promote the worst passions of mankind. As he wrote, "the government must be so constituted as to offer strong motives." "In short," he added, the true objective was "to interest all the *passions* of individuals. And turn them into that channel." [30]

The Hamiltonian Plan of Government

Having laid the foundations for his proposed plan of government, Alexander Hamilton next directed his attention to its details. "Let one body of the legislature be constituted during good behaviour or life," he stated. "Let one executive be appointed who dares execute his powers." "It may be asked is this a republican system?" The answer, of course, was self-evident to all honest delegates in the Convention. A republican form of government is characterized by the *rule of law*. Mr. Hamilton's government, however, would be characterized by the *rule of men*. Nonetheless, the fact that his proposed despots would be *elected* to office was deemed sufficient to pronounce his plan *republican* in principle. "It is strictly so, as long as they remain elective." "And let me observe," he emphasized, "that an executive is less dangerous to the liberties of the people when in office during life, than for seven years." [31]

What Alexander Hamilton said before the Convention in this regard seems to have been a diluted version of his original intention. In his *personal notes* prepared for his great speech, for instance, Mr. Hamilton repeatedly referred to his proposed chief executive as a "monarch," and he stated that the monarchy should be *hereditary*, not elective. "The *monarch* must have proportional strength," he had written in his notes. "*He ought to be hereditary, and to have so much power, that it will not be his interest to risk much to acquire more.*" He also wrote that, "The advantage of a monarch is this – he is above corruption – He must always intend, in respect to foreign nations, the true interest and glory of the people." [Emphasis added] [32]

In his address before the Convention, however, he attempted to dodge the label of monarchy for his plan of totalitarian government:

> It may be said this constitutes an *elective monarchy? Pray what is a monarchy?* May not the governors of the respective States be considered in that light? But by making the executive subject to impeachment, *the term monarchy cannot apply.* These elective monarchs have produced tumults in Rome, and are equally dangerous to peace in Poland; but this cannot apply

---

[30] *Ibid.*, Volume I, p. 311.
[31] *Ibid.*, Volume I, p. 300.
[32] *Ibid.*, Volume I, p. 310.

to the mode in which I would propose the election. Let electors be appointed in each of the States to elect the executive — ...[and the national legislature is] to consist of two branches — and I would give them the *unlimited power of passing all laws without exception.* The Assembly to be elected for three years by the people in districts — the Senate to be elected by electors to be chosen for that purpose by the people, and *to remain in office during life.* The executive to have *the power of negativing all laws — to make war or peace,* with the advice of the Senate — to make treaties with their advice, but to have the sole direction of all military operations, and to send ambassadors and appoint all military officers, and to pardon all offenders, treason excepted, unless by advice of the Senate. On his death or removal, the President of the Senate to officiate, with the same powers, until another is elected. Supreme judicial officers to be appointed by the executive and the Senate. The legislature to appoint courts in each State, *so as to make the State governments unnecessary to it.*

All State laws to be absolutely void which contravene the general laws. An officer to be appointed in each State to have a negative on all State laws. All the militia and the appointment of officers to be under the National Government. [Emphasis added] [33]

In presenting his plan of government to the Convention, the man destined to become the most influential British spy in American history acknowledged that, of the three plans then before the house, the New Jersey Plan was the one that would be preferred by the American people:

I confess that this plan and that from Virginia are very remote from the idea of the people. Perhaps the Jersey Plan is nearest their expectation. But the people are gradually ripening in their opinions of government — they begin to be tired of an excess of democracy — and what even is the Virginia Plan, but *pork still, with a little change of the sauce.* [Emphasis added] [34]

The Hamiltonian Plan of government introduced by the New York nationalist consisted of eleven articles, which were recorded in James Madison's notes as follows:

I. The *Supreme* Legislative power of the United States of America to be vested in two different *bodies of men*; the one to be called the Assembly, the other the Senate who together shall form *the Legislature of the United States* with *power to pass all laws whatsoever* subject to the Negative hereafter mentioned.

II. The Assembly to consist of persons *elected by the people to serve for three years.*

III. The Senate to consist of persons *elected to serve during good be-*

[33] *Ibid.,* Volume I, pp. 300-301.
[34] *Ibid.,* Volume I, p. 301.

haviour; their election to be made by *electors* chosen for that purpose by the *people*: in order to do this *the States to be divided into election districts*. On the death, removal or resignation of any Senator his place to be filled out of the *district* from which he came.

IV. The *supreme* Executive authority of the United States to be vested in a Governour to be *elected to serve during good behaviour* – the election to be made by *Electors* chosen by the people in the *Election Districts aforesaid* – The authorities & functions of the Executive to be as follows: *to have a negative on all laws about to be passed*, and the execution of all laws passed, to have the direction of war when authorized or begun; to have with the advice and approbation of the Senate the power of making all treaties; to have the sole appointment of the heads or chief officers of the departments of Finance, War and Foreign Affairs; to have the nomination of all other officers (Ambassadors to foreign Nations included) subject to the approbation or rejection of the Senate; to have the power of pardoning all offences except Treason; which he shall not pardon without the approbation of the Senate.

V. On the death resignation or removal of the Governour his authorities to be exercised by the President of the Senate till a Successor be appointed.

VI. *The Senate to have the sole power of declaring war*, the power of advising and approving all Treaties, the power of approving or rejecting all appointments of officers except the heads or chiefs of the departments of Finance War and foreign affairs.

VII. The *Supreme* Judicial authority to be vested in _____ Judges *to hold their offices during good behaviour* with adequate and permanent salaries. This Court to have original jurisdiction in all causes of capture, and an appellative jurisdiction in *all causes in which the revenues of the general Government or the citizens of foreign nations are concerned*.

VIII. The *Legislature of the United States* to have power to institute Courts in each State for the determination of *all matters of general concern*.

IX. The Governour Senators and all officers of the United States to be liable to impeachment for mal – and corrupt conduct; and upon conviction to be removed from office, & disqualified for holding any place of trust or profit – all impeachments to be tried by a Court to consist of the Chief _____ or Judge of the Superior Court of Law of each State, *provided such Judge shall hold his place during good behavior*, and have a permanent salary.

X. *All powers of the particular States contrary to the Constitution or laws of the United States to be utterly void; and the better to prevent such laws being passed, the Governour or president of each State shall be appointed by the General Government and shall have a negative upon the laws about to be passed in the State of which he is Governour or President.*

XI. *No State to have any forces land or Naval; and the Militia of all the States to be under the sole and exclusive direction of the United States, the officers of which to be appointed and commissioned by them.* [Emphasis added] [35]

Alexander Hamilton's chief objection to a Federal Republic was the concept of *constitutionally limited government*, and his main criticism of the Articles of Confederation was that it sought to *define* and *enumerate*, and thereby to *limit*, the powers of the Federal Government. In his own plan, he successfully overcame such alleged defects in the political kingdom with the simple remedy of granting *all conceivable powers* to his proposed supreme National Government. By the provisions of this Hamiltonian Plan, the national legislature would be vested "with power to pass all laws whatsoever," the very same sweeping powers that, when claimed by Parliament, had caused the colonies to revolt. Although the articles Mr. Hamilton presented hinted at a sole limitation to this absolute power, in his speech he indicated that this grant of power would have no limitation whatsoever. "I would give them," he stated, "the unlimited power of passing all laws *without exception*." And like the Virginia Plan, the word *Congress* is not used to describe the proposed Legislative Branch, further proof that the term is applicable only to a federal system of government.

The lower house of Mr. Hamilton's bicameral legislature was to be elected directly by the people, and the members of this proposed Assembly would serve for three-year terms. It is of interest to note that the second article of his plan does not specify *which* people would elect the Assembly. The omission of the expression *of the several States* after the word "people" was probably not an oversight, for Mr. Hamilton's stated goal was to abolish those sovereignties. It is not until the third article that Mr. Hamilton gives a clue as to his conception of the "people" under his system. By this provision, the States would be replaced by *national districts*, in a manner similar to that proposed by James Wilson and other nationalists.

The people of the States, in other words, would not exist under Mr. Hamilton's plan. There would only exist the people of a consolidated American Empire to be ruled by an imperial government possessing totalitarian power. The objective to be attained by replacing the States with a consolidated nation of Americans was to *diminish* the influence of the people in the affairs of the general government. "There ought to be a principle in government," Mr. Hamilton was convinced, "capable of resisting the popular current." [36] Herding the peoples of the several States into an amalgamated nation was merely one of the means to effect this goal.

Although the people of the American Empire would directly elect the

---

[35] *Ibid.*, Volume I, pp. 291-293.
[36] *Ibid.*, Volume I, p. 309.

Assembly, the upper branch of Mr. Hamilton's proposed supreme legislature would be elected by *electors*, not directly by the people. "The aristocracy ought to be entirely separated" from the people, he wrote. The aristocratic Senate, in this scheme, would constitute the dominant branch of the legislature, and it would exist to serve the interests of the money power. The Senate would be empowered to declare war by itself, with or without the approval of the popular branch of the legislature. It would also have the exclusive power of approving treaties and of confirming appointments, except those to important executive posts, which would not require any approval at all by the legislature. To protect the Senators from the wrath of an outraged public, the Senators would hold their offices *for life*. Or, as Mr. Hamilton expressed it, "their power should be permanent," and the Senators "should be so circumstanced that they can have no interest in a change." [37]

The Chief Executive was to be also elected by *electors*, not directly elected by the people, and once elected the dictator would not be responsible to the people, but would serve *a life tenure of office*. The election of this "Governor," like that of the elitist Senators, would be a *national election*, with the people organized by the nationally mandated electoral districts. The "monarch" would comprise the dominant branch of the supreme National Government, and he would be vested with so much power that he could not possibly be tempted to usurp additional authority. Among other things, the American King would be empowered to veto all laws passed by the legislature, and his veto would be final. Even if the legislature were unanimously in favor of a law, that branch would be powerless to override His Majesty's imperial veto. So extensive was to be this veto power that the Governor could kill a law even before the legislature had passed it! And he would be empowered to fill the most important executive posts without legislative approval.

Although the articles presented by Mr. Hamilton vested the power to declare war solely in the elitist Senate, it would appear that his real preference was to vest this power in the Executive Branch of government. As recorded by Robert Yates, the Orator of Nationalism stated that, "The executive to have the power of negativing all laws — *to make war or peace*, with the *advice* of the Senate." Under this scheme of government, it is apparent that the Chief Executive of the United States would have at his disposal, at all times, a mighty military force — and he could use this force to wage war whenever he pleased. The Legislative Branch of government, in many respects, would exist primarily for consultation purposes. In this regard, there is a striking resemblance between what Mr. Hamilton proposed to the Convention and the war powers that have been *usurped* by the Presidency in the later half of the Twentieth

---

[37] *Ibid.*, Volume I, p. 309.

Century. This similarity becomes even more remarkable when it is considered that the Philadelphia Convention overwhelmingly *rejected* Mr. Hamilton's plan of government.

The Hamiltonian Plan also provided for a supreme judiciary, with judges to serve life tenures of office. The jurisdiction of this national judiciary, like the authority of the other two branches, would know no limits. Its jurisdiction would extend to "all causes in which the revenues of the general government...are concerned." There would be, of course, no limitations on the sources of revenue and objects of expenditure under the proposed supreme National Government, for it was empowered to tax and spend without restriction. Mr. Hamilton's stated objective was to extend the authority of the national judiciary to such an extent that the State judicial systems would no longer need to exist. To this end, the national judiciary would be empowered determine upon "all matters of general concern," an expression well calculated to effect his goal.

In the tenth article of his plan, this National Monarchist put forth a nationalist conception of a *Supremacy Clause*. According to this definition of *supremacy*, not only would the Constitution be the supreme law of the land, but so too would be *all laws* of the United States – not merely the laws passed in pursuance of the Constitution, but *all laws, without exception*. By this definition, even *unconstitutional laws* would be the supreme law of the land.

It is of interest to observe that, in the Hamiltonian Plan, the National Government would be empowered to enforce an observance of the so-called Supremacy Clause. In this regard, he was of a similar mind with the other nationalists who supported the Virginia Plan. Rather than merely require that the State officials be bound by oath to support the supremacy of the Constitution, the nationalists insisted that the National Government should enforce such observance by possessing a veto power over all State laws. The Orator of Nationalism, however, went one step further. Under his plan, the Governor of each State would be appointed by the National King, and these Governors would then guard the national interest against local popular will. Like the supreme National Monarch, these nationally appointed State Governors could veto a law even before it had passed in the legislature!

There is nothing more feared by a consolidating nationalist than an armed citizenry. We thus observe that, by the provisions of the last article in the Hamiltonian Plan, the States were to be totally disarmed and left defenseless against the imperial National Government. Not only would the States be prohibited from possessing a standing military force for their defense, but their militias – organized bodies of armed citizens – were to "be under the *sole* and *exclusive* direction of the United States, the officers of which to be appointed and commissioned by them." No one knew better than Mr. Hamilton that such militias, or citizen armies, had formed the backbone of the American defense against the British in the Revolutionary War, beginning with the encounter between the Redcoats and the "embattled farmers" at Lexington and Concord. If these independent State militias were converted into a type of *National Guard*, the peoples of the States would be naked and helpless when confronted by the tyranny of a supreme National Government.

With the introduction of the Hamiltonian Plan, the Grand Convention had before it *three different plans* of government. In the Virginia Plan, it had a plan for a *National Republic*. Under the auspices of the New Jersey Plan, the delegates had a plan for a *Federal Republic*. And by means of the Hamiltonian Plan, they had one for a *National Monarchy*. By June 18th, therefore, the three factions within the Federal Convention had each produced its own version of what constituted a "good" government for the United States of America. By Alexander Hamilton's own candid admission, the principles contained in the New Jersey Plan were those that best conformed to the will of the American people, an admission all the more remarkable considering its source. And in making this candid confession, Mr. Hamilton actually proved himself to be more honest than the nationalists promoting the Virginia Plan.

The Reaction of the Convention

If many of the delegates had been alarmed by the Virginia Plan's radical proposition to annihilate the sovereignty of the States and to establish a supreme National Government, then it should not be difficult to image the reaction of those delegates to Alexander Hamilton's proposal for a totalitarian socialist dictatorship for the United States. A few delegates, it is true, were thrilled by the Hamiltonian Plan of government. The National Monarchist from Pennsylvania – Gouverneur Morris – thought Mr. Hamilton's speech was best one delivered before the Convention, and George Read of Delaware did not hesitate to express his preference for the Hamiltonian Plan. The vast majority of the delegates, however, were alarmed by Mr. Hamilton's radical ideas.

As John C. Miller has noted in his book, *Alexander Hamilton and the Growth of the New Nation*:

> Of Hamilton's speech, one of the delegates [William S. Johnson of Connecticut] observed that although the delegate from New York was praised by everyone, he was supported by none. In truth, however, Hamilton was not praised by everyone and he was supported by some.

> By no means all the delegates approved of Hamilton's ideas even as pure theory. Such *staunch supporters of the sovereign rights of the States* as Luther Martin, Elbridge Gerry, John Lansing and William Yates *were horrified* by Hamilton's suggestion that the States be reduced to administrative districts of the general government. [Emphasis added] [38]

Alexander Hamilton's candor and sincerity in regard to his desire to obliterate the States was truly horrifying to the Federal Republicans. But if Mr. Hamilton had hoped that such terror would induce a stampede to the support of the Virginia Plan, he was sorely disappointed. To many of the Federal Republicans, there was very little real difference between the Virginia Plan and the Hamiltonian Plan. Both plans, it appeared to them, would have the same ultimate consequences it terms of the rights of the States and the liberties of the people.

In his book, *New Views of the Constitution of the United States*, John Taylor of Caroline made this comparison of the two proposed plans for a supreme National Government:

> There was no substantial difference between the Virginia Plan and Mr. Hamilton's. One proposed that States should continue to exist as corporations or counties, but as subjects of a government invested with *supreme* legislative, executive, and judicial powers; the other, that the State governments should be directly and not indirectly abolished. One gave them rights on paper, subject to supreme negatives, without any means of defending those rights; the other more candidly denied to them any rights at all. The two plans resemble two plans for defending a country; one, by a mercenary army combined with a militia, but refusing to intrust the militia with arms, lest they should use them against the army; the other, by a mercenary army alone. The Virginia Plan opposed paper to power; Mr. Hamilton's tore the frail sanction to pieces, to save power the trouble of disorganizing conflicts, or of quelling abortive oppositions whilst doing the same thing gradually. Those who approved of but could not carry Mr. Hamilton's plan, saw in the Virginia Plan a kindred alternative; and deriding its federal preachment, adopted its circuitous and strifeful mode of effecting their objective, because they could effect it in no other. Although neither the Virginia Plan nor Mr. Hamilton's succeeded in the Convention, they embraced a mass of talents, too proud and powerful for humility and submission; and they resorted to the engine of construction, to be directed by many an Archimedes. But at this point the two parties began to split. Encroachments upon the paper rights of the States soon appeared, and then Mr. Hamilton and Mr. Madison divided. One acted and the other preached, each in accordance with his own principles as displayed in the Convention....
> The origin of the coalition between the monarchists and consolida-

---

[38] John C. Miller, *Op. cit.*, p. 171.

tors in the Convention, is visible in the Journal.... [39]

The five-hour oration made by Mr. Hamilton on behalf of extreme nationalism marked the high tide of nationalism within the Grand Convention of the States. Although the consolidators would continue to control the proceedings for some period afterwards, they were cognizant of the fact that the tide was turning in favor of federalism. The speech made by the Orator of Nationalism only convinced the Federal Republicans to be even more determined to save the Federal Republic from those forces bent on its destruction.

As Mr. Miller noted in his biography of the National Monarchist, the unfavorable impact of Mr. Hamilton's fantastic speech before the Convention was felt *immediately* by all of the nationalists:

> The first reaction to Hamilton's speech came from the *nationalists*, the men whose support, it might be supposed, he could most confidently rely. In actuality, however, Hamilton had succeeded in putting Madison, Wilson, and other advocates of centralized government in an awkward position. For if the impression were established in the minds of the delegates that *the nationalists intended to abolish the States*, the partisans of the States *could muster sufficient strength in the Convention to defeat any plan of centralized government*. With good reason, therefore, Madison exclaimed that Hamilton was up to his old trick of letting the cat out of the bag; and this time the cat was a particularly ugly specimen that seemed quite capable of breaking up the Convention. To aggravate Madison's exasperation, he felt that Hamilton was gratuitously stirring up opposition to the Virginia Plan: until Hamilton undertook to take the Convention into his confidence, the supporters of that plan had been careful to avoid any imputations of seeking to establish a *monarchy* or a *consolidated government*. The bag Hamilton incautiously opened to the Convention contained nothing to which Madison was willing to admit ownership: the cat was a stray that the New Yorker had picked up somewhere – certainly not in Virginia – and smuggled into the Convention.
>
> *To undo the damage wrought by Hamilton's speech became to the nationalists an urgent necessity.* Both Wilson and Madison took the floor to register their disapproval of the policies recommended by their colleague from New York. Madison declared that he prized *the rights of the States* as highly as he did civil liberties and James Wilson offered assurances that *the States would not be swallowed up by the general government*. The co-existence of the States and the *Federal* Government Wilson declared to be essential to *good government* in the United States: *the country was too extensive to be ruled by a single authority*; and *if the States did not exist, the Convention would have to invent them....*
>
> *From the expositions of his friends, Hamilton realized that he had spo-*

---

[39] John Taylor, *Op. cit.*, pp. 60-61.

ken too candidly of his plans for centralizing power in the United States. He had laid violent hands upon the holy of holies, the sovereignty of the States, and the temple rocked upon its foundations. [Emphasis added] [40]

Realizing the damage he had done to the cause of nationalism, Mr. Hamilton attempted to undo that damage by addressing the Convention on June 19th. "He had not been understood yesterday," he exclaimed. "I did not intend yesterday a total extinguishment of State governments;" he explained, "but my meaning was, that a National Government ought to be able to support itself without the aid or interference of the State governments, and that therefore it was necessary to have full sovereignty." "By an abolition of the States," he clarified, "he meant that no boundary could be drawn between the National & State legislatures; that the former must therefore have indefinite authority." [41]

"Even as Corporations," he insisted, "the extent of some of them as Va. Massts. &c. would be formidable." "Even with corporate rights the States will be dangerous to the National Government, and ought to be extinguished, new modified, or reduced to a smaller scale." The reference here undoubtedly was to the proposed *national districts* favored by Mr. Hamilton, Mr. Wilson, and other nationalists. "*As States,*" the Orator of Nationalism concluded, "he though they ought to be abolished. But he admitted the necessity of leaving in them, subordinate jurisdiction." [42]

As Mr. Miller noted:

> Despite Madison's and Wilson's efforts to portray themselves *as friends of the States*, between them and Hamilton the proponents of State rights found little to choose. No members of the Convention were more eager than Madison and Wilson to give the Federal Government a negative upon State laws in all cases whatsoever; and Madison agreed with Hamilton that it was better to prevent the passage of a State law than to declare it void after it had been passed. True, Madison, Wilson and Morris did not propose to abolish the States, but they would have made them *subordinate jurisdictions* which, in the course of time, would probably have become little more than *adjuncts of an all-embracing centralized government*. With some justice, therefore, a member of the Constitutional Convention compared the nationalists' strategy to "the conduct of a number of jockeys who had thirteen young colts to break; they begin with the appearance of kindness, giving them a lock of hay, or a handful of oats, and stroking them while they eat, until being sufficiently gentle they suffer a halter to be put round their necks." Hamilton's approach, on the other hand, was to break

---

[40] John C. Miller, *Op. cit.*, p. 172.
[41] Max Farrand (ed.), *Op. cit.*, Volume I, pp. 323 and 328.
[42] *Ibid.*, Volume I, pp. 323 and 328.

the spirit of these mettlesome colts with a whip and then lock them up in the stable....

Hamilton's plan of making the States *administrative districts of the central government* had at least the merit of resolving the struggle between the large and small States. As he said, "the more close the Union of the States, and the more compleat the authority of the whole, the less opportunity will be allowed to the stronger States to injure the weaker." The small States would have nothing to fear from their larger neighbors: *they would all be in the same boat struggling for survival against Leviathan.*

Not surprisingly, therefore, Hamilton's ideas found advocates among some of the more *nationally minded* delegates from the small States. In particular, George Read of Delaware...was prepared to make a strategic retreat to an *all-powerful central government in which the sovereignty of the States was utterly dissolved....*

As an ally, Read was anything but a tower of strength to Hamilton....

Except for these brief flare-ups, Hamilton's forensic effort created little stir. Having cleared themselves as well as they could of the charge of being Hamilton's accomplices in *a plot to do away with the States,* the nationalists were happy to drop his plan....[Emphasis added] [43]

Although Colonel Hamilton's radical plan was quickly dropped like a hot potato, the foul odor it had left on nationalism *in general* could not be as easily dismissed by the nationalists. As Mr. Hamilton's biographer noted, the father of the Hamiltonian Plan found it necessary to abandon his own plan and go to the defense of the Virginia Plan in an effort to save it from defeat:

It was plain that Hamilton's ultranationalistic ideas had not made the Virginia Plan appear by comparison more palatable to the champions of the States: Lansing declared that Hamilton's speech had confirmed his suspicions that *the Virginia Plan would establish a centralized despotism in which the States would be as effectually destroyed as even Hamilton could desire.*

Instead of pushing his own plan in the Convention, *Hamilton found himself defending the Virginia Plan....*[Emphasis added] [44]

Alexander Hamilton, to be sure, was quite a curiosity. When the Convention became embroiled in a heated debate on one occasion, Benjamin Franklin recommended that the house should begin each day with a prayer to Almighty God. In response to Mr. Franklin's proposal, the Orator of Nationalism arrogantly retorted that "he did not see the necessity of calling in foreign aid!" Whereupon George Washington is said to have "fixed his eye upon

---

[43] John C. Miller, *Op. cit.,* pp. 172-174.
[44] *Ibid.,* pp. 174-175.

Hamilton with a mixture of surprise and indignation." [45]

Frustrated by the disastrous defeat of his own plan and by the inevitable defeat of the Virginia Plan, Alexander Hamilton eventually walked out of the Federal Convention in despair. Although he returned near the conclusion of the Convention and added his signature to the Constitution, he did so with undisguised reservations. No man's ideas, he confessed, were more remote from the final plan of government adopted by the Convention, than his own were known to be. It was a sentiment that was shared by Gouverneur Morris, Robert Morris, James Wilson, James Madison, Edmund Randolph, and a number of other consolidating nationalists.

The Last Nationalist Victory

On June 19th, the day after Alexander Hamilton's infamous five-hour oration, Rufus King of Massachusetts moved that the Committee of the Whole should resolve in favor of the Virginia Plan, and thereby resolve to reject the New Jersey Plan. On the vote to retain the Virginia Plan and reject the New Jersey Plan, Maryland was divided. Connecticut, Pennsylvania, Virginia, North Carolina, South Carolina, and Georgia voted in favor of the motion. Only New York, New Jersey, and Delaware voted against it. New Hampshire's delegates had not yet arrived at the Convention, so that State was denied the opportunity to vote on the issue.

Thus, by a vote of 7 *ayes*, 3 *noes*, and 1 *divided*, the Federal Convention voted on June 19, 1787, to reject the New Jersey Plan and to retain the Virginia Plan. The vote was clearly a setback for the Federal Republicans and stood as yet another victory for the nationalist coalition. This nationalist victory, however, was only temporary in nature. *In fact, this was destined to be the last significant victory for the nationalists in the Convention!* Even the nationalists seemed to sense their inevitable defeat, and they immediately began to change their strategy.

To allay the concerns of the federalists, the nationalists had repeatedly assured the Convention that no plot existed to abolish the States. James Wilson, for one, claimed emphatically that he was a true friend of the State governments, stating that, by a National Government, "he did not mean one that would swallow up the State Govts. as seemed to be wished by some gentlemen. He was tenacious of the idea of preserving the latter." He conceived that States "were absolutely necessary for certain purposes," and, "He thought, contrary to the opinion of Col. Hamilton that they might not only subsist

---

[45] *Ibid.*, quoted on p. 175.

but subsist on friendly terms with the" proposed National Government. [46]

Even Alexander Hamilton addressed the delegates in an attempt to clarify and soften his position on the subject of annihilating the States. Following these reassuring speeches, however, the nationalists promptly launched their new assault upon the existence of the States by denying that they were or had ever been sovereign! This new strategy was inaugurated by Rufus King, who spoke to the Convention following Mr. Hamilton's address in an effort to obscure and confound the meanings of certain primary terms and concepts. He "wished as everything depended on this proposition," that the Convention should have a better understanding of the "phraseology" used by the nationalists and the federalists. "He conceived that the import of the terms 'States' 'Sovereignty' *national* 'federal,' had been often used & applied in the discussion inaccurately & delusively." [47]

By this new strategy, the nationalist objective was unmistakable. If the States were not sovereign under the Articles of Confederation, then why should they be regarded as sovereign under a new Constitution? If the American people already existed as a consolidated nation under those Articles, should not the Convention draft a new Constitution for that already-existing nation? This incredible attempt to deny the obvious was made despite the fact that, within the Articles, the sovereignty of the States was not only positively acknowledged, but the very purpose of the Federal Union was clearly identified as the preservation of that sovereignty! Nonetheless, the wily nationalist from Massachusetts assured the Convention that, "The States were not 'sovereigns' in the sense contended for by some." "None of the States," he boldly proclaimed, "are now sovereign or independent." [48]

Mr. King's rationale for such an absurd claim was the fact that the States had *delegated* some of their powers to the existing Congress. Having thus delegated powers to the Federal Government, the States no longer possessed "the peculiar features of sovereignty. They could not make war, nor peace, nor allegiances, nor treaties." "Congress, by the Confederation, possesses the rights of the United States," he stated, completely obscuring the very real difference between *rights* and *powers*, an obscurity necessary for the sustenance of the novel theory now put forth on behalf of a *sovereign Federal Government*. "This is a union of the men of those States," and not of the States, *as States*. "The magistracy in Congress possess the sovereignty — To certain points we are now a united people. Consolidation is already established." [49]

---

[46] Max Farrand (ed.), *Op. cit.*, pp. 322-323.
[47] *Ibid.*, Volume I, p. 323.
[48] *Ibid.*, Volume I, pp. 323 and 328.
[49] *Ibid.*, Volume I, pp. 323 and 328.

"A Union of the States is a union of the men composing them, from whence a *national* character results to the whole," Rufus King insisted. By such clever logic, it was thus possible to conjure up a consolidated nation of Americans in the midst of a league of States. "If they formed a Confederacy in some respects — they formed a Nation in others." The Federal Union under the Articles, he asserted, was *partly federal* and *partly national!* The States, he proclaimed, "are now subordinate corporations or societies and not sovereigns," for the existing Federal Government under the Articles possessed a "national sovereignty." [50]

"He made these remarks," he explained, "to obviate some scruples which had been expressed" against a National Government. By asserting such absurdities, he was stating, in essence, that the Convention could adopt a supreme National Government without doing violence to the existing Federal Union between the States. "He doubted much the practicability of annihilating the States; but thought that *much of their power ought to be taken from them.*" [51]

Hearing these outrageous ideas, Luther Martin of Maryland, a staunch champion of the Federal Republic, arose to reply to the nationalists. As James Madison recorded in his notes:

> Mr. Martin, said he considered that the separation from G.B. placed the 13 States in a state of nature towards each other; that they would have remained in that state till this time, but for the Confederation; that they entered into the Confederation on the footing of equality; that they met now to amend it on the same footing, and that he could never acede to a plan that would introduce an inequality and lay 10 States at the mercy of Va. Massts. and Penna. [52]

The purpose of the Declaration of Independence, Mr. Martin stated, was to declare the sovereignty and independence *of the States*, not of a single nation known as the United States. The latter entity was created by the Confederation of those sovereign States for federal, not national, purposes. "Our acession to the Union has been by States," he correctly observed. "If any other principle is adopted by this Convention," he warned, "he will give it every opposition." [53]

In response, James Wilson said that he "could not admit the doctrine that when the colonies became independent of G. Britain they became independent also of each other." This absurdity was stated in spite of the fact that

---

[50] *Ibid.*, Volume I, pp. 323, 328, and 331.
[51] *Ibid.*, Volume I, p. 324.
[52] *Ibid.*, Volume I, p. 324.
[53] *Ibid.*, Volume I, p. 329.

the thirteen States had not even been dependent *on each other* prior to the Declaration of Independence. Although Mr. Wilson had been a signer of that Declaration, he apparently had never understood its basic purpose or principles. He read to the Convention the Declaration of Independence and observed "that the *United Colonies* were declared to be free & independent States," and he inferred from this "that they were confederated as they were independent, States." "The power of war, peace, alliance and trade, are declared to be vested in Congress." [54]

This not-so-subtle attempt to deny the very existence of sovereign States indicates the low esteem placed by the Pennsylvania nationalist on the intelligence of those he addressed. If the Declaration of Independence had the effect he ascribed to them, there would have been no necessity to draft and adopt the Articles of Confederation. According to this twisted nationalist view of American history, the Declaration of Independence not only conveyed sovereignty on the United States as a single nation, but it also created the Federal Union, provided for the Federal Government, and delegated powers to it!

By this strange and novel interpretation of the great charter of American independence, the Declaration was much more than a Declaration of Independence – *it was also a Federal Constitution!* Such a conception, however, does not conform to a true interpretation of the Declaration. Nor does it conform in the slightest degree with the very plain words of the Articles of Confederation. The fact that the nationalists were willing to stoop to such a level of theoretical treachery is indicative of the frantic despair they must have felt.

Following Mr. Wilson's incredible speech trashing the true meaning of the Declaration of Independence, Alexander Hamilton rose to speak, stating that he "assented to the doctrine of Mr. Wilson. He denied the doctrine that the States were thrown into a state of nature." The Orator of Nationalism was, however, slightly more honest than James Wilson by acknowledging the sovereign equality of the States under the Articles of Confederation. "He admitted that the States met now on equal footing but could see no inference from that against concerting a change of the system in this particular." If the sovereign States wished to merge into a single consolidated nation, they were at liberty to do so. And he urged them to do so, stating that, "The three great objects of government, *agriculture, commerce and revenue,* can only be secured by a general government." [55]

By the time the Philadelphia Convention adjourned for the day on June 19, 1787, the nationalist conspiracy against the States stood unchal-

---

[54] *Ibid.*, Volume I, p. 324 and 329.
[55] *Ibid.*, Volume I, pp. 324, 325, and 329.

lenged. The day had witnessed the demise of the New Jersey Plan and the confirmation of the Virginia Plan. It had also witnessed the birth of a new strategy on the part of the nationalists, in which the very existence of the sovereignty of the States was denied altogether, even under the Articles of Confederation. By this new stratagem, it was hoped, a supremely sovereign National Government could be carried under the pretense of conforming to the principles of the existing Federal Union.

But if the nationalists were determined to succeed by a new and deceitful strategy, the Federal Republicans were equally determined to emerge victorious from the Constitutional Convention. Like the nationalist schemers, they also had a new strategy, which they intended to introduce the following day. They were firmly resolved to save the Federal Republic; and this time, they would not be defeated.

Chapter Nine
The Battle Royal

When the sovereign States had agreed to dispatch commissioners to a Federal Convention, to be held in Philadelphia during the summer of 1787, the express purpose of the Grand Convention was solely and exclusively to revise the Articles of Confederation, so that the Federal Constitution could be rendered more adequate to the exigencies of the Federal Government and the preservation of the Federal Union. Yet, as we have already seen, the moment the decision was made to conduct their proceedings in secret, the delegates were propelled down the path toward a *supreme National Government* by a well-organized and well-prepared group of nationalists whose avowed goal was to destroy the existing Federal Republic.

The nationalist conspiracy was inaugurated even before all of the delegates had arrived at the Philadelphia Convention, when Edmund Randolph's fifteen resolutions calling for a supreme National Government were swiftly adopted by a majority of States present. By this sudden and bold maneuver, the nationalists were able to dominate the early stages of the proceedings and to lead the Convention in the direction of a political system designed to effectually destroy the States by subordinating them to a supreme centralized authority. The relationship between the States and the general government, under this system, was candidly described as being similar to the one that had existed between the colonies and the British Government prior to the War of Independence, with one significant difference. Under the proposed *Virginia Plan*, the States would have fewer rights and powers than they had possessed during their prior existence as British *colonies*.

Some nationalists even talked of replacing the States with national districts, and the proposed National Government was to be vested with an absolute veto power over the State governments. Although the nationalists refused to enumerate all the powers their proposed government would possess, they made it clear that attempting to define and limit its powers would be nearly impossible. The proposed Leviathan state would ostensibly be accountable to a non-existent American *nation* of people, and elections of officers to the proposed central regime would be regarded as *national elections*. The States, *as States*, would have nothing whatsoever to do with the National Government, other than to obey its orders, and as distinct political societies they would not be represented in it.

Although this scheme of government was loosely referred to as republican in nature, its inherent concept of *supremacy* made the government, and not the people, sovereign. The government – *not the Constitution and laws made in pursuance of it, but the general government itself* – was frankly and arrogantly declared to be supreme. By preferring the supremacy of the rule of men to the supremacy of the law, such a government scarcely qualified to be termed republican in nature.

Rallying to the defense of the Federal Republic, patriotic delegates succeeded in drafting their own plan of government, which was formally introduced by William Paterson and generally referred to as the *New Jersey Plan*. This plan was calculated to preserve the principles of a Federal Republic and was based on the idea that sovereign States not only existed, but should continue to exist. This plan, unlike the Virginia Plan, was presented in conformity with and in fulfillment of the commissions given to the delegates by their respective States; and, as candidly conceded by the Orator of Nationalism in the Convention, this plan represented the principles shared by a majority of the American people. The New Jersey Plan was based on the concept that the people, not the government, should be sovereign, and that only the Constitution and laws made in pursuance of it should be supreme.

In opposition to both plans, Alexander Hamilton had presented his own plan of government, which brazenly advocated the annihilation of the States and the erection of a supreme and sovereign National Government. By the terms of the *Hamiltonian Plan*, the United States of America should be ruled by a monarch, and His Majesty should reign over the American Empire for his entire life. Attached to this all-powerful central regime would be a monied aristocracy, whose interests would be jealously guarded by a House of Lords, in the form of Senators who would hold office for life. The United States would be divided into national districts for electoral purposes, and the States would be ruled by Royal Governors appointed by the kingly dictator of the United States.

Thus, after nearly four weeks of continuous business, the Constitutional Convention had before it three plans of government. One called for the creation of a National Republic; the other provided for a Federal Republic; and the third constituted a National Monarchy. The Virginia Plan was based on the concept that *that government is best that governs most*. The New Jersey Plan was based on the opposite principle, that *that government is best that governs least*. The Hamiltonian Plan, in turn, was based on the concept that *that government is best that governs worst*.

Mr. Hamilton's proposal, although similar in many respects to the Virginia Plan, was deemed too candid and straightforward in its approach toward the States by the other nationalists. It was therefore dropped very quickly and swept under a rug by the embarrassed nationalists. The real struggle facing the nationalists was with the Federal Republicans, and the enemies of the States managed to defeat the New Jersey Plan.

Thereafter, the nationalists boldly launched a new strategy by insisting that the States had never been sovereign. According to this twisted reasoning, the Declaration of Independence declared the sovereignty and independence, not of thirteen States, but of a single and consolidated American nation. Those provisions in the Articles of Confederation which described the States as sovereign were nothing more than lies. Under the Articles, it was the Federal Government, and not the States, who was sovereign. Simply by delegating powers to the general government, the nationalists insisted, the States surrendered their supremacy or sovereignty to that government. This novel theory, it scarcely needs to be mentioned, subverted the principles on which the Declaration of Independence was founded and undermined the entire American Theory of Government.

The Federal Republicans, although initially defeated, did not give up the fight to save the rights of the States and the liberties of the people. Following the defeat of the New Jersey Plan, the champions of the Federal Republic resolved to pursue a new strategy of their own, a strategy that ultimately proved successful in every respect. Before directing our attention at this new strategy, however, we should first pause to summarize the key issues that separated the Federal Republicans from the nationalist coalition within the Constitutional Convention.

Nationalism Versus Federalism

The differences in principle between the Federal Republicans and the coalition forces of the National Republicans and the National Monarchists were profound and distinctive. The fifteen significant issues that divided these two forces, as evinced from the debates within the Federal Convention, are listed in the table shown below. As indicated within this table, these issues revolved around the concepts of the type of government to be established, the form that government should assume, the source of its authority, the seat of sovereignty in the United States, the level of government that should be primary, the role to be filled by the State governments in the political system, the main source of military strength in the Union, the level of government that should be vested with police powers and responsibility for domestic affairs, the type of elections to be held, the nature of representation in the general government, the predominant influence that should control the general government, and the interests that government should serve.

Key Issue	Nationalism	Federalism
Type of Government	National Government	Federal Government
Form of Government	Republican or Monarchical	Republican
Source of Authority	Consolidated American Nation	Distinct and Independent States
Seat of Sovereignty	Sovereignty Vested in Government	Sovereignty Vested in the People
Primary Government	National Government	State Governments
State Governments	Subordinate Corporate Role	Independent of Federal Government
Military Dominance	All Martial Power Centralized	Most Military Power Left in States
Police Powers	Vested in National Government	Reserved to the States Exclusively
Domestic Affairs	Regulated by National Government	Reserved Exclusively to the States
Type of Elections	National Elections in National Districts	Federal Elections Conducted by States
Minority Rights	Exposed to Unlimited Majority Rule	Protected by Limiting Majority Rule
Equality of the States	Certain States to Dominate the Others	All States to Have Equal Rights
Representation	Based Exclusively on Population	Based Also on Sovereign Equality
Dominant Influence	Elitist Aristocracy of Wealth	Democratic Popular Will
Interests Served	Rich and Well-Born, Money Power	Peoples of the Several States

Let us consider, in more detail, each of these key issues that divided the delegates at the Philadelphia Convention into opposing camps. The **Type of Government** advocated by the National Monarchists and the National Republicans, needless to say, was a *National Government* to be established within a *national system*. The Federal Republicans, of course, advocated precisely the opposite – a *Federal Government* to be established within a *federal system* of government. All other principles effectually flowed from this primary difference between the factions present in the Federal Convention. In fact, the only point on which all the delegates seemed to agree was that the type of government to be established would necessarily determine the other issues.

In regard to the **Form of Government** to be established, the nationalists were divided. The monarchists within the coalition preferred the creation of some type of *monarchy*, and while they openly appeared content with the prospects of an elective monarchy, most secretly dreamed of establishing an hereditary monarchy. Chief among the monarchists were Alexander Hamilton, Gouverneur Morris, and George Read. The other nationalists, such as James Madison and James Wilson, advocated a republican form of government, at least most of the time. On one occasion, Mr. Madison, realizing that the nationalists were losing badly, swung over to the side of the monarchists in desperation. For the most part, however, the National Republicans maintained a high degree of loyalty to republicanism.

The **Source of Authority** for each political system was dictated by the nature of the government proposed. Those advocating the establishment of a Federal Government looked to the already-existing *sovereign States* as the natural sources of authority for their proposed system of government. Since those States already existed, it was not necessary to conjure up new schemes to divide the American people into districts. The people of the United States were already divided into States, and by such a natural division, government could be kept as close as possible to the people. The American people seemed quite satisfied with that natural division, and so were the Federal Republicans.

The nationalists, on the other hand, deemed the division of the people into distinct States as a horrible natural disaster. To overcome this natural calamity, they proposed that a National Government should derive its authority from *a single nation of Americans*. The only difficulty they encountered was the unfortunate fact that such a consolidated nation of Americans did not exist. Adding to their dilemma, they realized that a consolidated nation could never be legitimately created, for if the issue were presented honestly to the American people, the people would overwhelmingly reject it. To overcome this weighty difficulty, the nationalists found it necessary to rewrite American history, misconstrue the Declaration of Independence, and pretend that the Articles of Confederation did not exist. Only by this means were they able to conjure up an imaginary consolidated nation of Americans vested with a national sovereignty. Their proposed National Government would supposedly derive its authority from this non-existent nation of people.

The **Seat of Sovereignty** within each political system was to be quite different. The Articles of Confederation plainly stated that the States were sovereign and that the Federal Union between those States – styled the "United States of America" – existed for the sole and express purpose of preserving and defending that sovereignty. And by the principles of the Declaration of Independence, the sovereignty of the States was vested in the *peoples* of those States, and not in any government, either State or federal. The Federal Republicans were quite content with this arrangement, insisting that the peoples of the States, as the supreme masters of the political kingdom, could *delegate* powers *associated* with their sovereignty to a government, while yet retaining their supremacy over the government thus established.

Not only did the nationalists deny that the States were sovereign, but they also insisted that, in the event the States actually are sovereign, they should not remain so under a new compact of government. Although they professed the idea that sovereignty was vested in a mythical nation of Americans, they proceeded to rob that fictional nation of people of its sovereignty by proclaiming that their National Government, in and of itself, should be supreme in the political kingdom. They candidly confessed that there could be only *one* supreme power in the kingdom, and some of the more honest nationalists clearly stated that it would be their *National Government*, not an imaginary nation of Americans, which would be vested with sovereignty. Indeed, the nationalists insisted that whenever the people – whether the people of the States or the people a phantom consolidated nation – delegate powers to a government, no matter how carefully enumerated and limited those powers might be, they must also surrendered their sovereignty to that government.

Under the federal system of government, each *State government* would remain the **Primary Government** within the United States. All of the ordinary powers of government, including the establishment of a common law, would remain with the States. For the individual citizen, his State government would be the one having the most influence over his life and daily affairs. Inasmuch as the State governments were closer to the people, the Federal Republicans deemed it essential to the preservation of liberty to keep the primary role of government at this level. The Federal Government, meanwhile, would be confined and restricted to the foreign and interstate affairs of the Union of States. In most cases, the Federal Government would have little direct influence over the individual citizen.

The nationalists, on the other hand, wished to fully centralize all concerns – in little as in great things – in the hands of their proposed *National Government*. This government would serve as the primary government for the people of the United States, establishing a uniform common law, and having a direct and profound influence over the daily lives of its subjects. This proposed National Government would be the dominant force regulating and controlling all aspects of the social and economic activities of the American people.

Within the federal system advocated by the Federal Republicans, the **State Governments** would be *independent* of the Federal Government. The Federal Government, however, would not be independent of the State governments. Those governments would send ambassadors to the United States Senate and would establish voting qualifications for federal elections within their own jurisdictions. Although the States would be obliged to acknowledge the supremacy of the Federal Constitution, *enforcement* of such obligations would remain in the respective State governments.

The role played by the State governments under the proposed national system, on the other hand, would be insignificant and negligible. Some nationalists preferred that the very existence of the State governments cease, while others realized that a total abolition was not attainable. If suffered to exist, the States could exist only as subordinate corporations, similar to colonial possessions or like the counties within a State. The national authority would possess an absolute veto over all State laws, and no mutual system of checks-and-balances would be tolerated. Once a State law was vetoed by the national authority, the State could not override the veto under any circumstances. Such an arbitrary veto power over the States was proclaimed to be the *cornerstone* of a national system of government, and many of the nationalists anticipated the day when the States and their respective governments would no longer exist. Until that day arrived, the absolute veto over the States would serve the purpose of nationalism.

In terms of **Military Dominance**, the nationalists would not countenance any suggestion that any vestige of military authority should remain under the control of the State governments. Governments close to the governed and responsive to the will of the people were deemed highly dangerous to imperial goals and objectives. A *supreme National Government*, they agreed, must maintain exclusive control over all armed forces in the United States. Viewed as especially dangerous were the local State militias, those citizen armies that had paved the way for victory in the Revolutionary War. If such State forces could successfully challenge an imperial British Government, they could just as easily pose a challenge to an imperial American Government. Converting the State militias into a type of National Guard, under the absolute and exclusive control of the supreme central authority, was therefore deemed essential to the preservation of totalitarian government in the United States.

The Federal Republicans also understood the age-old concept that *political power grows from the barrel of a gun*. Liberty demanded that the control over the military power in the United States should remain as close to the people as possible. While it was necessary for the combined martial strength of the States to coalesce in time of war against a foreign enemy, in times of peace, the Federal Republicans realized, large standing armies controlled by the Federal Government posed a genuine threat to freedom. And they were adamant that the States should retain their control over the local citizen soldiers known as militias. By this means, in times of peace, most of the military might in the United States would remain in the hands of the States, not in the hands of the Federal Government.

In taking such a stance, the Federal Republicans proved that they well remembered how the British had attempted to secretly march on Lexington and Concord to disarm the Massachusetts militia in 1775. They also demonstrated their felicity to the wise maxim asserted by that sturdy patriot Samuel Webster, who had proclaimed in 1777 that, "Tyrants always support themselves with standing armies! And if possible the people are disarmed." [1] The Federal Republicans were determined that this would never happen in America.

The two camps also disagreed about where to vest **Police Powers** in the United States. This issue was, in many respects, a corollary of the one relating to the primary Military Power. The Federal Republicans were adamant

[1] The Peoples Bicentennial Commission, *Voices of the American Revolution*, Bantam Books, Inc., New York, 1974, quoted on p. 167.

in their insistence that Police Powers should *remain exclusively in the hands of the States*. If Police Powers were centralized, they feared, the result would be a *supreme National Police State*, in which liberty would be suffocated.

What especially concerned the champions of a Federal Republic was that, if vested with Police Powers, the Federal Government would be authorized to crush civil unrest and what it fancied to term a *rebellion*. Such a highly centralized government, vested with this authority, might attempt to use force to crush a genuine grassroots political opposition movement under the claim that it was fighting a "rebellion." Even more alarming, such a government might use force against a State government, claiming that the State government was in a state of "rebellion" against the United States.

The nationalists were equally adamant that their proposed *National Government* must assume the Police Powers of the States. Such authority was needed, they asserted, in order to crush rebellions like the one led by Daniel Shays in Massachusetts. Some of the nationalists candidly acknowledged that the Police Powers would be used against States in their organized capacities *as States*. Gouverneur Morris, for one, claimed that it might be necessary for a National Government to overthrow one or more State governments in the name of crushing a "rebellion" against the supreme central authority.

Regarding the **Type of Elections** to be held under each concept of government, the Federal Republicans maintained that such elections should be *federal elections*, by the peoples of the several States, *as States*. The representatives thus elected to the various federal offices would be properly regarded as the representatives of *the peoples of the States*. The nationalists, on the other hand, insisted that elections to fill the offices of a National Government should be *national elections*. Accordingly, they proposed that, at least for purposes of election, the States should be amalgamated into *national districts*. But even if this were not possible, they insisted, the elections to the House of Representatives could still be viewed, at least with a very dim and fuzzy eye, as a *national election*, inasmuch as representation in that house of Congress was to be based on the respective *populations* of the States. The fact that the representatives elected to the lower branch of the federal legislature would represent the *peoples of the States*, and not a consolidated American nation of people, was conveniently ignored by the national theorists.

Minority Rights under the two contending systems of government would have very different fates. Under the plan pushed by the nationalists, *legitimate minority rights did not exist*. Regarding the rights of the individual citizen, only the avarice and greed of the majority mattered, and there would be no limit to what the majority might do to the interests of the private citizen. The same held true for the rights of the weaker and smaller States, who would be forced in a national system to submit to the unlimited greed and ambitions of the larger and more powerful States. The only minority interest worthy of protection, in the opinion of the nationalists, was the interest of an aristocratic money power.

Although the Federal Republicans did acknowledge the right of the majority to rule, they insisted that the right of the majority to rule must be *properly limited to protect the rights of the legitimate minority interests*. In their opinion, an elitist monied aristocracy was *not* a legitimate minority interest — *only individual citizens and sovereign States could be properly regarded as having legitimate minority interests that deserved special consideration and protection.* Based on these considerations, they insisted that a *majority of the States*, for example, should serve as a counterbalance in the Senate to a *majority of the people* in the House of Representatives.

The Federal Republicans firmly believed in the **Equality of the States**, not merely of the original thirteen States, but also of all new States that might be later admitted into the Federal Union. Such newly admitted States, they insisted, must possess all the *equal rights of sovereignty and independence* enjoyed by the original thirteen. Some of the more die-hard nationalists, however, such as Gouverneur Morris, were strident in their opposition to this concept. New States might be admitted into the Union, they agreed, but *not* at the same level or status as the original thirteen States. The Western Territories, they frankly stated, should forever remain in a *subordinate and colonial status* in relationship to the original States, even after the Territories had been admitted into the Union as *bona fide* States.

Regarding the nature of **Representation** in the general government, the two camps were bitterly divided. This issue, in fact, proved to the one that generated the most passionate and bitter debates, for it was universally acknowledged on both sides that the outcome of this issue would, by its very nature, determine the type of government to be established. And that issue, in turn, would decide all the remaining issues, including the type and extent of powers to be vested in the general government.

The intransigent nationalists insisted that representation in both houses of Congress should be based *solely* on the populations of the several States. Not only would this eliminate any State-majority check in the Senate on the population-majority in the House of Representatives, but it would also significantly eliminate the influence of the State governments in the general government. Even more importantly, by removing all vestiges of equality of suffrage in the general government, the nationalists could claim that the States were not sovereign under the new government. Yet, it would be impossible to make that claim if *one branch of the federal legislature stood as a perpetual monument to the sovereign equality of the States.*

The Federal Republicans were equally intransigent in their insistence that representation in the Senate be based on *equality of suffrage*. They fully understood the importance of this issue to the preservation of the Federal Republic. Not only was equality of suffrage deemed essential as proof that the States retained their sovereignty, but the mode of appointing Senators – by the State legislatures – was deemed essential to maintain the control and influence of the State governments in the Federal Government. Rather than having the Senate serve as an elitist House of Lords, or as a carbon copy of the House of Representatives, the Senate would serve as an *assembly of Ambassadors* from the State governments.

Under the proposed nationalist plan of government, the **Dominant Influence** was to be an *elitist aristocracy of wealth*. Alexander Hamilton was by no means alone in his desire to attach a monied aristocracy to the general government. And the nationalists realized that there were other ways, besides a House of Lords, to achieve that objective. At one point during the Convention, for instance, Gouverneur Morris proposed that this goal be attained by attaching a bloated, socialistic *bureaucracy* to the general government. The Federal Republicans, determined that the dominant influence in the Federal Government should be the *democratic popular will* of the people of the States, opposed all such schemes.

Finally, in regard to the true **Interests Served**, it hardly needs to be mentioned that the nationalists wished to create a general government that would serve the interests of the *money power*, or as Alexander Hamilton put it, *the rich and the well-born*. The Federal Republicans, on the other hand, had only one true interest to serve – *the peoples of the several States*. At one point during the debates, Gouverneur Morris paid the Federal Republicans a supreme compliment, although his remark was not intended as complimentary. *The federalists, he grumbled, acted as though they had come to the Convention to look after the interests of their own States.* Indeed, they had! It is a shame that the nationalists in the Convention could not bring themselves to represent the States which they were commissioned to represent.

The struggle between the nationalists and federalists within the Federal Convention was perhaps best summarized by the repeated nationalist assertion that *power*, and not liberty, was their chief concern. At the time the Declaration of Independence and the Articles of Confederation were drafted, they sadly observed, the chief concern had been *liberty*. Because the Founding Fathers had erred on the side of freedom, insisted the nationalists, the American people had too much liberty. In advocating that the pendulum should be swung back toward the side of power, the nationalists defiantly ignored the precautions urged by the more rationale Federal Republicans and repeatedly insisted that it was impossible to go too far in the direction of concentrated authority. By arrogantly promoting power at the expense of liberty, the nationalists merely highlighted the central fallacy of their whole theory of government and thereby ultimately doomed their own cause.

The Tide Turns

Following the defeat of the New Jersey Plan, the Federal Republicans put into force a new strategy for defeating the nationalist conspiracy against the States. Their failure to carry the New Jersey Plan, they correctly surmised, had resulted from attempting to knock out a supreme National Government in an instant, by proposing that the Convention totally abandon the Virginia Plan in favor of an entirely new set of resolutions. Having learned a lesson from this experience, the new strategy of the Federal Republicans was to attack the Virginia Plan *piecemeal* – one key point at a time – until its nationalist features had been completely replaced by federal features.

One measurement of the extent of success realized by this new approach may be ascertained by the conduct of Edmund Randolph at the conclusion of the Federal Convention. The Virginia Governor, of course, was the nationalist who had first introduced the plan for a supreme National Government to the Convention at its inception in May. Although the final version of the Constitution evolved from the Virginia Plan, it had been so thoroughly revised and altered by the Federal Republicans that Governor Randolph no longer recognized its principles as his own. For that reason, he would refuse the sign the Federal Constitution at the conclusion of the Philadelphia Convention.

The task of transforming the proposed supreme National Government into a Federal Government was not as difficult as it might first appear, at least in regard to the actual alterations required in the plan itself. In terms of structure, for instance, there was really little if any differences between the nationalists and the federalists. Both sought to establish a general government consisting of executive, legislative, and judicial branches. And both camps wished to delegate to the general government the powers necessary to conduct the foreign affairs of the United States.

As historian Richard B. Morris has observed in this regard:

> What stands out in the debates of the Convention are the points of similarity among the various plans rather than their differences. Both the Virginia and New Jersey Plans had granted Congress the power to levy and

collect taxes; and every plan presented at the Convention gave Congress the right to regulate foreign and interstate commerce. The Convention was unanimous in vesting in Congress the power to pay the debts and "provide for the common defense and general welfare of the United States." There was, too, widespread agreement about incorporating into the Constitution a prohibition of the issue by the States of paper money. [2]

Thus, the task of making the necessary changes to convert the evolving Constitution into a federal one was not especially difficulty. The only difficulty encountered was the obstinate resistant of the combined factions of National Monarchy and National Republicanism, who were determined to resist any significant change in their proposal for a supreme National Government. The new strategy was put into effect the day after the defeat of the New Jersey Plan. Significantly, the first target of the Federal Republicans was the objectionable word "nationalist" with which the Virginia Plan was highly adorned. That objectionable word, the defenders of the Federal Republic insisted, had to go. In its place, they wished to substitute terminology applicable to a Federal Government.

This challenge, which was formally moved by Oliver Ellsworth of Connecticut in reference to the first resolution of the Virginia Plan, was recorded as follows by James Madison in his notes:

> Mr. Elseworth 2nd. by Mr. Gorham moves to alter it so as to run "that the *Government of the United States* ought to consist of a supreme legislative, executive and judiciary." This alteration he said would *drop* the word *national,* and *retain the proper title "the United States."*...It would be *highly dangerous* not to consider the Confederation *as still subsisting. He wished also the plan of the Convention to go forth as an amendment to the Articles of Confederation,* since under this idea the authority of the [State] legislatures could ratify it. If they are unwilling, the people will be so too....
>
> Mr. Randolph did not object to the change of expression, but apprised the gentleman who wished for it that he did not admit it for the reasons assigned; *particularly that of getting rid of a reference to the people for ratification. The motion of Mr. Elsewth was acquiesced in.* nem: con:
>
> The 2nd Resoln. "That the *national* legislature ought to consist of two branches." Taken up. *The word "national" struck out as of course.* [Emphasis added] [3]

The significance of these measures – Mr. Ellsworth's proposal, Edmund Randolph's response, and the favorable vote obtained – merits careful

---

[2] Richard B. Morris, *The Framing of the Federal Constitution,* Handbook 103, U.S. Department of the Interior, Washington, 1986, pp. 61 and 64.
[3] Max Farrand (ed.), *The Records of the Federal Convention of 1787,* Revised Edition, Volume I, Yale University Press, New Haven, 1966, pp. 335-336.

consideration. In moving that the expression "National Government" be rejected in favor of the term "Government of the United States," the delegate from Connecticut cited *two specific effects* of his motion. The first stated effect would be to "drop" the repugnant and offensive word "national" from the Constitution. But this word was not dropped so that a different but equivalent expression could be substituted for it.   According to Mr. Ellsworth, the second effect of his motion would be the *retention of the proper title "the United States."* The words "proper title" were here used to differentiate and underscore the opposing concepts inherent in the two titles. The title "Government of the United States" was *proper* for Confederacy, while the title "National Government" was *improper* for a league of States.

But the substitution did more than merely replace an *improper* title with a *proper* title – it also *retained* an existing title. The term "the United States" was not invented by the Convention on this occasion. The term was widely recognized throughout the States, and its precise meaning had been firmly and concisely fixed by the provisions of the Articles of Confederation. As Article I of our first Federal Constitution stated, "The Stile of this *Confederacy* shall be *'The United States of America.'*" [4]

The new terminology for the Federal Government, stated Oliver Ellsworth, would *"retain the proper title 'the United States.'"* The new Constitution, in a word, would thus provide for a Federal Government for an already defined and existing Confederacy styled the United States of America. A *Government of the United States*, a *Government of the States United*, a *Government of a Confederation Styled the United States*, a *Government of a League of Sovereign States*, a *Confederate Government*, and a *Federal Government*, are all *equivalent expressions* referring to the same system of government.

The victory won by the Federal Republicans on June 20th, although it was but the first of many such victories, has long been regarded as one of the most significant in the history of the Convention. It is true, of course, that the change was merely in name only, and that the evolving Constitution, as it stood on this day, contained the essential elements of a supreme National Government. More battles would have to waged, and more victories realized, before the compact would truly be federal in nature. The significance of the June 20th victory, however, cannot be minimized by such considerations, for in accordance with this first major victory of federalism in the Convention, the word "national" – which appeared in the evolving Constitution no less than twenty-six times – was deliberately *stricken out* wherever it occurred. By the vote secured in the Grand Convention, the new Constitution would offi-

---

[4] Charles Callan Tansill (ed.), *The Making of the American Republic: The Great Documents, 1774-1789*, Arlington House, New Rochelle, p. 27.

cially and formally provide for a *Federal Government* that could "*go forth as an amendment to the Articles of Confederation,*" if not literally, then at least in principle.

Commenting on this significant victory of principle in his book, *The Rise and Fall of the Confederate Government*, Jefferson Davis of Mississippi noted:

> The prompt rejection, after introduction, of the word "national," is obviously much more expressive of the intent and purpose of the authors of the Constitution than its mere absence from the Constitution would have been. It is a clear indication that they did not mean to give any countenance to the idea which, "scotched, not killed," has again raised its mischievous crest in these latter days – that the government which they organized was a consolidated *nationality*, instead of a Confederacy of sovereign members. [5]

Bolstered by their significant victory, a galaxy of spokesmen for States' Rights rose in the Convention on June 20th to champion the cause of the Federal Republic. When the second resolution of the Virginia Plan was brought up for consideration, John Lansing of New York took strong issue with its *terminology*, particularly the word "legislature." Such a word might be compatible with a *National Government*, he observed, but only the term "Congress" was proper for a *Federal Government*. Noting that "the true question here was, whether the Convention would adhere to or depart from the *foundation* of the present Confederacy," he accordingly moved that, instead of the second resolution, "that the powers of legislation be vested in the U. States in *Congress*." [Emphasis added] [6]

Mr. Lansing then stated:

> He had already assigned two reasons agst. such an innovation as was proposed. *1. the want of competent powers in the Convention – 2. The state of the public mind.* It had been observed by Mr. Madison in discussing the first point, that in two States the delegates to Congrs. were *chosen by the people*. Notwithstanding the first appearance of this remark, it had in fact no weight, as the delegates however chosen, did not represent the people merely as so many [unorganized] individuals; but *as forming a sovereign State.* Mr. Randolph put it, he said, on its true footing namely that *the public safety superseded the scruple arising from the review of our powers.* But in order to feel the force of this consideration, the same impression must be had of the public danger. *He had not himself the same impression, and could*

---

[5] Jefferson Davis, *The Rise and Fall of the Confederate Government*, Volume 1, Thomas Yoseloff, Cranbury, (orig. pub. in 1881) 1958, p. 97.
[6] Max Farrand (ed.), *Op. cit.*, Volume I, p. 336.

not therefore dismiss his scruple. Mr Wilson contended that as the Convention were only to recommend, they might recommend what they pleased. *He differed much from him.* Any act whatever of so respectable a body must have a great effect, and if it does not succeed, will be a source of great dissentions. [Emphasis added] [7]

"I am clearly of opinion that I am not authorized to accede to a system which will annihilate the State governments," the delegate from New York stated, "and the Virginia Plan is declarative of such extinction." "It could not be expected that those possessing sovereignty could ever voluntarily part with it," he observed, adding that, "It was not to be expected from any one State, much less from thirteen." Even if the States could be tricked into throwing away their sovereignty, it would accomplish nothing worthwhile. "It had been said that Congress [under the Articles] represent the State Prejudices: will not any other body whether chosen by the legislatures or people of the States, also represent their prejudices?" [8]

Mr. Lansing next directed his critical eye on the proposed national legislative veto over State laws:

> It is proposed that the genl. legislature shall have a negative on the laws of the States. Is it conceivable that there will be leisure for such a task? There will on the most moderate calculation, be as many acts sent up from the States as there are days in the year. Will the members of the general legislature be competent judges? Will a gentleman from Georgia be a judge of the expediency of a law which is to operate in N. Hamshire. Such a Negative would be more injurious than that of Great Britain heretofore was. [9]

Then there was the disturbing concept of the proposed vast patronage to be exercised by the Federal Government. "If this influence is to be attained," John Lansing surmised, "the States must be entirely abolished." Then, too, there was the disturbing problem associated with the novelty of the nationalist scheme. "The system was too novel & complex," he noted, pointing out that the American people were accustomed to their States and to federal principles. National principles would certainly be alien on these shores. "No man could foresee what its operation will be either with respect to the genl. govt. or the State govts. One or the other it has been surmised must absorb the whole." [10]

George Mason of Virginia then addressed the Convention to assert strong opposition to any plan that could countenance the use of federal force

---

[7] *Ibid.*, Volume I, p. 336.
[8] *Ibid.*, Volume I, pp. 337 and 345.
[9] *Ibid.*, Volume I, p. 337.
[10] *Ibid.*, Volume I, pp. 337-338.

to coerce a sovereign State. "There will be no Coercion in this government," he stated, adding that, "He will not consent to abolition of State Sovereignties." [11] He also asserted his strong support for the State governments, stating emphatically that, "I never will consent to destroy State governments." [12] Colonel Mason reminded the delegates that it was preferable to err on the side of caution, when empowering the Federal Government, than to err on the other side. In the event that the Government of the United States should require enlarged powers in the future, the remedy could be found in the amendment process. But what remedy could exist to easily remove dangerous powers from the Federal Government, once that government had been vested with such powers?

Luther Martin next addressed the delegates, stating that he "agreed with Col Mason as to the importance of the State Govts.," adding that, "I know that government must be supported; and if the one was incompatible with the other, I would support the State government at the expense of the Union – *for I consider the present system as a system of slavery.*" [Emphasis added] [13]

Maryland's Attorney General then directed his attention to the historical evolution of the United States:

> At the separation from the British Empire, the people of America preferred the establishment of themselves into *thirteen separate sovereignties* instead of incorporating themselves into one: to these they look up for the security of their lives, liberties & properties: to these they must look up – The Federal Govt. they formed, to defend the whole agst. foreign nations, in case of war, and to defend the lesser States agst. the ambition of the larger: They are afraid of granting powers unnecessarily, lest they should defeat *the original end of the Union*; lest the powers should prove *dangerous to the sovereignties of the particular States which the Union was meant to support*; and expose the lesser to being swallowed up by the larger. He conceived also that the people of the States having already vested their powers in their respective legislatures, could not resume them without *a dissolution of their governments*. [Emphasis added] [14]

"I confess when the Confederation was made," Luther Martin stated, "Congress ought to have been invested with more extensive powers." "The time is now come that we can *constitutionally grant* them not only new powers, but to modify their government, *so that the State governments are not en-*

---

[11] James H. Hutson (ed.), *Supplement to Max Farrand's the Records of the Federal Convention of 1787*, Yale University Press, New Haven, 1987, p. 99.
[12] Max Farrand (ed.), *Op. cit.*, Volume I, p. 346.
[13] *Ibid.*, Volume I, pp. 340 and 347.
[14] *Ibid.*, Volume I, pp. 340-341.

dangered." "But whatever we have now in our power to grant, *the grant is a State grant*," he concluded, "and therefore it must be so organized that the State governments are interested in supporting the Union." [Emphasis added][15]

The Convention also heard from Roger Sherman of Connecticut, who rose to second Mr. Lansing's motion. He reminded the nationalists that a federal system was preferable to a national one from the simple consideration that, in the former, the Government of the United States would possess only those powers requisite to effect *the common good of all the States equally.* Oppression of a State, under a federal system, as a consequence, could not occur. The same, however, could not be said of a national system. "In all the great and general points," he emphasized, "the interests of all the States were the same." [16] Common sense dictated, therefore, that the general government should be based on the common interests of all the States, an observation that mandated the retention of the federal system of government.

Mr. Sherman next directed his attention to the existing treaties of the United States. "Foreign states have made treaties with us as Confederated States," he reminded the delegates, "not as a National Government." If the nationalists were to succeed in abolishing the United States of America and replacing the Confederation with a new nation of people, he observed, the results could be disastrous to our foreign affairs. "Suppose we put an end to that government under which those treaties were made, will not these treaties be void?" [17]

After making these statements, the noted statesman from Connecticut proposed the celebrated *Connecticut Compromise* to the Federal Convention, which would serve as a *bona fide* compromise between the *large* and the *small* States, *while yet retaining the federal system of government.* By the terms of this compromise, representation in the House of Representatives would be based on the *populations of the States*, while representation in the Senate would be based on the *sovereign equality of the States.* This compromise, of course, had been proposed much earlier by other Federal Republicans, but the die-hard nationalists had always refused to consider it. *To accept such a compromise, they understood all too well, would have been a total concession of defeat to federalism.* No National Government could possibly be created on the basis of *the sovereign equality of the States* in any of its branches!

Roger Sherman, however, now offered the compromise again, and his words were recorded by James Madison as follows:

If the difficulty on the subject of representation can not be other-

---

[15] *Ibid.*, Volume I, p. 347.
[16] *Ibid.*, Volume I, p. 342.
[17] *Ibid.*, Volume I, p. 348.

wise got over, he would agree to have two branches, and a proportional representation in one of them, provided each State had an equal voice in the other. This was necessary to secure the rights of the lesser States; otherwise three or four of the large States would rule the others as they please. Each State like each individual had its peculiar habits usages and manners, which constituted its happiness. It would not therefore give to others a power over this happiness, any more than an individual would do, when he could avoid it. [Emphasis added] [18]

Before the house adjourned for the day, James Wilson addressed the Convention and attempted to parry some of the principles espoused by the Federal Republicans. But the day clearly belonged to the advocates of States' Rights. It had witnessed the downfall of a National Government, at least in name, an event which had occasioned a number of moving speeches in favor of a Federal Government. It had also witnessed the re-introduction of the highly significant and valuable Connecticut Compromise.

Unfortunately, not all of the speeches on behalf of States' Rights drafted for delivery by the friends of a Federal Government were delivered. One particularly masterful, undelivered address has been discovered by historians, which was originally believed to be Luther Martin's. Scholars later credited it to Roger Sherman, but more recently it has been ascribed to the silent delegate from Pennsylvania, Jared Ingersoll. It is not clear why this well-written speech was not delivered in the Convention. Perhaps Mr. Ingersoll, if he was indeed the author, feared the reaction and repercussions to himself that the speech might have engendered from the others in his State's delegation, many of whom were unyielding in their zeal for a supreme National Government.

As the author of this undelivered speech wrote:

> Suppose for a moment, that the thirteen united States should be extinguished & annihilated, & that we were about to devise the best & most eligible System of Government *unembarrassed by Instructions*, & without any reasonable apprehensions of difficulty from the prejudices or prepossessions of the people of this Country and which would be best a *National Government* or a *Federal Government? Some Members will be surprised when I add, that I am by no means clear that a National Government would deserve the preference!* [19]

This delegate then illustrated the vast differences between the various States of the Union, relative to their customs, habits, economies, industries, and geography. No single set of laws, he asserted, could ever govern such a

---

[18] *Ibid.*, Volume I, p. 343.
[19] James H. Hutson (ed.), *Op. cit.*, p. 103.

vast continent without doing violence and injury to one or more regions. The geography of the United States, he therefore concluded, rendered a National Government unwise and impracticable – so, too, did human nature, which dictated that men are naturally more inclined to disregard interests that do not directly or locally affect them. Only a federal system, which left with each State jurisdiction over its own internal affairs, could result in good government for all Americans.

The events of June 20th clearly demonstrated that federalism was waxing in the Convention, while nationalism was waning. The undelivered address on behalf of States' Rights, assuming that it truly was written by Jared Ingersoll, serves to illustrate that, even within the delegations of the large States, support for federalism was greater than many nationalists realized. Equally clear was the fact that the battle between a Federal Government and a supreme National Government would soon intensify until one side emerged victorious over the other. Between the large States and the small States, compromise was possible; but between federalism and nationalism, there could be no compromise. As to which side would emerge victorious from the battle, by June 20th the handwriting was already on the wall. Just three-and-one-half weeks after this noteworthy day, which witnessed the death of the word "national," the Federal Republicans would deliver the decisive death blow to a supreme National Government.

The Battle Intensifies

The battle between the nationalists and the federalists within the Federal Convention began to intensify as the month of June drew to an end, as indicated by these selections from the notes of James Madison, Robert Yates, and other delegates from June 21st through the 29th day of the month:

> **William S. Johnson**, on June 21st: "It is agreed on all hands that a portion of government is to be left to the States. How can this be done? It can be done by joining the States in their legislative capacity with the right of appointing the second branch of the national legislature, *to represent the States individually*." [Emphasis added] [20]
>
> **James Madison**, on June 21st: "The right of negativing in certain instances the State laws, affords one security to the National Government....*And if it was the case that the National Government usurped the State government, if such usurpation was for the good of the whole, no mischief could arise.* — To draw the line between the two, is a difficult task. *I believe it*

---

[20] Max Farrand (ed.), *Op. cit.*, Volume I, p. 363.

cannot be done, and therefore I am inclined for a general government." [Emphasis added] [21]

Alexander Hamilton, on June 21st: "It is essential to the democratic rights of the community, that this branch [*i.e.*, the U.S. House of Representatives] be directly elected by the people. Let us look forward to probable events — *There may be a time when State legislatures may cease, and such an event ought not to embarrass the National Government.*" [Emphasis added] [22]

James Wilson, on June 21st: "The legislature of the States by the proposed motion will have an uncontrolable sway over the general government. *Election is the exercise of original sovereignty in the people — but if by representatives, it is only relative sovereignty.*" [23]

Alexander Hamilton, on June 21st: "The public mind is perhaps not now ready to receive the best plan of government, but certain circumstances are now progressing which will give a different complexion to it." [24]

Alexander Hamilton, on June 22nd: "It has been asserted, that the interests of the general and of the State legislatures are precisely the same. This cannot be true. *The views of the governed are often materially different from those who govern.* The science of policy is the knowledge of human nature. *A State government will ever be the rival power of the general government.*...All political bodies love power, and it will often be improperly attained." [Emphasis added] [25]

Oliver Ellsworth, on June 22nd: "If we are so exceedingly jealous of State legislatures, will they not have reason to be equally jealous of us. If I return to my State and tell them, we made such and such regulations for a general government, because we dared not trust you with any extensive powers, will they be satisfied? Nay, will they adopt your government? *And let it be remembered, that without their approbation your government is nothing more than a rope of sand.*" [Emphasis added] [26]

Alexander Hamilton, on June 22nd: "Take mankind in general, *they are vicious* — their passions may be operated upon....Take mankind as they are, and what are they governed by? *Their passions....One great error is that we suppose mankind more honest than they are.* Our prevailing passions are *ambition* and *interest*; and it will ever be the duty of a wise government *to avail itself of those passions*, in order to make them subservient to the public good — for these ever induce us to action." [Emphasis added] [27]

Elbridge Gerry, on June 23rd: "At the beginning of the [Revolutionary] War we possessed more than Roman virtue. It appears to me it is now the reverse. We have more land and stock-jobbers than any place on

[21] *Ibid.*, Volume I, pp. 363-364.
[22] *Ibid.*, Volume I, p. 364.
[23] *Ibid.*, Volume I, p. 365.
[24] *Ibid.*, Volume I, p. 366.
[25] *Ibid.*, Volume I, pp. 378-379.
[26] *Ibid.*, Volume I, p. 379.
[27] *Ibid.*, Volume I, p. 381.

earth." [28]

James Wilson, on June 25th: "A citizen of America may be considered in two points of view – as a citizen of the general government, and as a citizen of the particular State, in which he may reside. *We ought to consider in what character he acts in forming a general government.* I am both a citizen of Pennsylvania and of the United States. *I must therefore lay aside my State connections and act for the general good of the whole. We must forget our local habits and attachments.* The general government should not depend on the State governments. This ought to be a leading distinction between the one and the other; nor ought the general government to be composed of an assemblage of different State governments – We have unanimously agreed to establish a general government....If the National Government does not act upon State prejudices, State distinctions will be lost. I therefore move, *that the second branch of the legislature of the National Government be elected by electors, chosen by the people of the United States.*" [Emphasis added] [29]

Oliver Ellsworth, on June 25th: "I cannot see the force of the reasoning in attempting to detach the State governments from the general government. In that case, *without a standing army*, you cannot support the general government, but on the pillars of the State governments....We know that the people of the States are strongly attached to their own Constitutions. If you hold up a system of general government, destructive of their constitutional rights, they will oppose it." [Emphasis added] [30]

William S. Johnson, on June 25th: "The State governments must be preserved: but this motion leaves them at the will and pleasure of the general government." [31]

Hugh Williamson, on June 25th: "[He]...professed himself a friend to such a system as would secure the existence of the State govts. The happiness of the people depended on it." [32]

James Madison, on June 25th: "I find *great differences of opinion in this Convention* on the clause now under consideration. Let us postpone it...." [Emphasis added] [33]

George Mason, on June 25th: "All agree that a more efficient government is necessary. It is equally necessary to preserve the State governments, as *they ought to have the means of self-defence*. On the motion of Mr. Wilson, the only means they ought to have would be destroyed." [Emphasis added] [34]

George Read, on June 25th: "[He]...moved (though not seconded) that they [*i.e.*, U.S. Senators] ought to continue in office *during good behaviour*." [Emphasis added] [35]

James Madison, on June 25th: "*We are proceeding in the same*

---

[28] *Ibid.*, Volume I, p. 393.
[29] *Ibid.*, Volume I, pp. 413-414.
[30] *Ibid.*, Volume I, p. 414.
[31] *Ibid.*, Volume I, p. 415.
[32] *Ibid.*, Volume I, p. 407.
[33] *Ibid.*, Volume I, p. 415.
[34] *Ibid.*, Volume I, p. 415.
[35] *Ibid.*, Volume I, p. 415.

*manner that was done when the Confederation was first formed....*By the vote already taken, will not the temper of the State legislatures transfuse itself into the Senate? Do we create a free government?" [Emphasis added] [36]

Charles Pinckney, on June 26th: "The States he said had different interests. Those of the *Southern*, and of S. Carolina in particular were different from the *Northern*." [Emphasis added] [37]

James Madison, on June 26th: The Senate "ought to be so constituted as *to protect the minority of the opulent against the majority*....[T]hey ought to have *permanency* and *stability*. Various have been the propositions; but my opinion is, *the longer they continue in office, the better will these views be answered*." [Emphasis added] [38]

Roger Sherman, on June 26th: "Govt. is instituted for those who live under it. It ought therefore to be so constituted as not to be dangerous to their liberties. *The more permanency it has the worse if it be a bad govt.* Frequent elections are necessary to preserve the good behavior of rulers. They also tend to give permanency to the government, by preserving that good behavior, because it ensures their *re-election*." [Emphasis added] [39]

George Read, on June 26th: "[He]...wished it to be considered by the small States that it was their interest that we should become *one people* as much as possible, that State attachments shd. be *extinguished* as much as possible, that the Senate shd. be so constituted as to have the feelings of citizens *of the whole*." [Emphasis added] [40]

Alexander Hamilton, on June 26th: "He concurred with Mr. Madison in thinking we were now to decide for ever the fate of republican government....*He acknowledged himself not to think favorably of republican government*; but he addressed his remarks to those who did think favorably of it, in order to prevail on them *to tone their government as high as possible*." "*Those who mean to form a solid republican government, ought to proceed to the confines of another government*." [41]

Elbridge Gerry, on June 26th: "It appears to me that the American people have the greatest aversion to monarchy, and the nearer our government approaches to it, the less chance we have for their approbation." [42]

James Wilson, on June 26th: "Every nation attends to its foreign intercourse – to support its commerce – to prevent foreign contempt and to make war and peace. Our Senate will be possessed of these powers, and therefore ought to be dignified and *permanent*....But give them those powers, and give them the stability proposed by the motion, and they will have *more permanency than a monarchical government*." [Emphasis added] [43]

James Madison, on June 26th: "Congress heretofore depended on

---

[36] *Ibid.*, Volume I, p. 416.
[37] *Ibid.*, Volume I, p. 421.
[38] *Ibid.*, Volume I, p. 431.
[39] *Ibid.*, Volume I, p. 423.
[40] *Ibid.*, Volume I, p. 424.
[41] *Ibid.*, Volume I, pp. 424 and 432.
[42] *Ibid.*, Volume I, p. 432.
[43] *Ibid.*, Volume I, p. 433.

State interests – *we are now going to pursue the same plan.*" [Emphasis added] [44]

James Wilson, on June 26th: "Congress has been ill managed, because particular States controlled the Union. In this Convention, if a proposal is made promising independency to the general government, before we have done with it, *it is so modified and changed as to amount to nothing.*...Is this the way you are to erect an independent government?" [Emphasis added] [45]

Pierce Butler, on June 26th: "The second branch [of the legislature]...must be controlled by the States, or they [*i.e.*, Senators] will be too independent." [46]

Charles Pinckney, on June 26th: "The States and general government must stand together." [47]

Roger Sherman, on June 28th: "In society, the poor are equal to the rich in voting, although one pays more than the other. This arises from *an equal distribution of liberty* amongst all ranks; and it is, on the same grounds, *secured to the States in the Confederation.*...A gentleman from New-York thinks a limited monarchy the best government, and no State distinctions. *The plan now before us gives the power to four States to govern nine States.* As they will have the purse, they may raise troops, and can also *make a King when they please.*" [Emphasis added] [48]

William S. Johnson, on June 29th: "The controversy must be endless whilst gentlemen differ in the grounds of their arguments; those on one side considering the States as *districts* of people composing *one political society*; those on the other considering them as *so many political societies*, and a govt. is to be formed for them *in their political capacity*, as well as for the individuals *composing them*. Does it not seem to follow, that if the States as such are to exist *they must be armed with some power of self-defence.* This is the idea of Col. Mason who appears to have looked to the bottom of this matter." [Emphasis added] [49]

George Read, on June 29th: "I would have no objection, if the government was more national – but the proposed plan is so great a mixture of both, that it is best to drop it altogether. *A State government is incompatible with a general government.*" "These [State] jealousies are inseparable from the scheme of leaving the States in existence. *They must be done away.*...He repeated his approbation of the plan of Mr. Hamilton, & wished it to be substituted in place of that on the table." [50]

James Madison, on June 29th: "Some gentlemen are afraid that the plan is not sufficiently national, while others apprehend that it is too much so....Some contend that States are sovereign, when in fact they are

---

[44] *Ibid.*, Volume I, p. 434.
[45] *Ibid.*, Volume I, p. 434.
[46] *Ibid.*, Volume I, p. 434.
[47] *Ibid.*, Volume I, p. 434.
[48] *Ibid.*, Volume I, p. 457.
[49] *Ibid.*, Volume I, p. 461.
[50] *Ibid.*, Volume I, pp. 463 and 471.

only political societies." "We are vague in our expressions – We speak of *the sovereignty of the States – They are not sovereign –* ...They are corporations with power of bye laws." "*The States never possessed the essential rights of sovereignty.* These were always vested in Congress. Their voting, as States, is no evidence of sovereignty....*The States ought to be placed under the control of the general government – at least as much so as they formerly were under the King and British Parliament.*" [Emphasis added] [51]

   Elbridge Gerry, on June 29th: "[He] urged that we never were independent States, were not such now, & never could be even on the principles of the Confederation. *The States & the advocates for them were intoxicated with the idea of their sovereignty.*...He lamented that instead of coming here like a band of brothers, belonging to the same family, we seemed to have brought with us the spirit of political negociators." [Emphasis added][52]

   Luther Martin, on June 29th: "[He] remarked that the language of the States being *sovereign & independent*, was once familiar & understood; though it seemed now so strange & obscure. *He read those passages in the Articles of Confederation, which described them in that language.*" [Emphasis added] [53]

This should be a sufficient sampling of the debates to obtain an adequate comprehension of the battle of principles in the Philadelphia Convention during the latter portion of June. The statements of Mr. Madison, Mr. Hamilton, and Mr. Wilson, when combined, starkly illustrate the nature of the type of government desired by the nationalist coalition.

   The American people, said Alexander Hamilton, are motivated by passions of ambition and interest, and a "wise government" should have the "duty" to "avail itself of those passions." Rather than seek to minimize the influence of greed and avarice in the Government of the United States by limiting its sphere of influence to the common interests of all the States, the nationalist objective was to create an energetic, *high-toned* government that would cultivate and foster such unhealthy passions.

   Such a government, all three of these leading nationalists agreed, should be wedded to a permanent monied aristocracy that would serve the special interests of rich and the well-born. The elitist branch of the Government of the United States, stated Mr. Madison, "ought to be so constituted as to protect the *minority of the opulent* against the majority." Such a body of plutocrats should be vested with "permanency and stability," preferably having life tenures of office. Empowered with sovereign power and great stability, this aristocracy could enjoy, in the words of James Wilson, "more perma-

---

[51] *Ibid.*, Volume I, pp. 471 and 477.
[52] *Ibid.*, Volume I, p. 467.
[53] *Ibid.*, Volume I, p. 468.

nency than a monarchical government." Thus constituted, a supreme Government of the United States would serve as a perpetual machine for nurturing and fostering ambition, avarice, greed, and interest.

There would be no protection under a national system, however, for the interests of a *minority of the States* in the Federal Union, for, in the words of Mr. Hamilton, "There may be a time when State legislatures may cease, and such an event ought not to embarrass the National Government." "And if it was the case that the National Government usurped the State government...," Mr. Madison pointed out, "no mischief could arise." Limiting the powers of the Government of the United States, therefore, was not only unnecessary, but could not actually be done. A supreme National Government empowered to usurp whatever authority it pleased from the States, "for the good of the whole," could obviously not admit to limitations or restrictions on its authority.

The States are not sovereign, James Madison firmly insisted. By *delegating* powers to a Federal Government, they surrendered their sovereignty to it and became its slaves. The States must therefore continue to remain in their inferior, colonial, servile status within the Federal Union under the new Federal Constitution. "The States ought to be placed under the control of the general government," he opined, as much as, or even more so, than they were formerly under the totalitarian control of a British King and Parliament.

"We ought to consider in what character" an American is to "act in forming a general government," stated James Wilson. Ostensibly having *dual citizenship* in both his *real* Nation-State and in an *imaginary* American nation that was unknown to the Founding Fathers and to the Federal Constitution, such a citizen should not hesitate to abandon loyalty to his State in favor a fictional nation that did not exist. "We must forget our local habits and attachments," he stated. As to why the abandonment of "State connections" should not be considered as treasonous, *even under his concept of dual citizenship*, no explanation was offered.

In compensation for being robbed of their real nations – *their States* – the American citizens *at large* would be allowed to exercise their "original sovereignty" in every popular election, a highly novel concept well-calculated to transform the ordinary republican process whereby citizens periodically select officers to administer a constitutionally defined and limited government into a perpetual Constitutional Convention. By this twisted concept of the nature of federal elections, the fate of liberty and the destiny of America itself would be determined each time an election was held. Had the Convention been so foolish as to adopt this bizarre concept of the electoral process, it would have marked the first time in the history of the world that the security of human rights had been placed on such an unstable foundation.

As the cited selections from the debates of late June indicate, the nationalists realized that all their efforts were being successfully challenged and undermined by the Federal Republicans, who were now able to muster strength equal to, or perhaps greater than, that of the nationalist coalition. "Congress heretofore depended on State interests – we are now going to pursue the same plan," Mr. Madison grumbled, complaining that, "We are proceeding in the same manner that was done when the Confederation was first formed." And James Wilson dismally noted that, "if a proposal is made promising independency to the general government, before we have done with it, it is so modified and changed as to amount to nothing." Even Elbridge Gerry, who was not himself wedded to the nationalist coalition, found occasion to point out the new mood that seemed to be seizing control of the Convention. "The States & the advocates for them," he lamented, "were intoxicated with the idea of their sovereignty." The new strategy of the Federal Republicans was clearly succeeding.

The Orator of Federalism

Symbolic of the strength the nationalist coalition had wielded during the early stages of the Convention was the five-hour speech delivered by Alexander Hamilton that earned him the reputation of being the *Orator of Nationalism*. It was only proper and fitting that, as the Federal Republicans should gain strength in the latter part of June, they should produce a great *Orator of Federalism* who would deliver a lengthy and penetrating speech to the Convention delineating the principles and merits of the federal system of government. That title of honor and distinction was clearly earned by *Luther Martin*, the scholarly and well-read Attorney General of Maryland, who began his great speech on June 27th and ended it the following day. This address, which spanned a total of approximately four hours, was probably the second longest one delivered to the Federal Convention.

The great issue confronting the Convention "is important," stated the Orator of Federalism, one that deserved a careful analysis. "My opinion is, that the general government ought to protect and secure the State governments – others, however, are of a different sentiment, and reverse the principle." "The present reported system," he noted, "is a perfect medley of Confederated and National Government, without example and without precedent." [54]

After making these introductory remarks, Mr. Martin stressed the ne-

---

[54] *Ibid.*, Volume I, p. 439.

cessity of constitutionally *defining* and *limiting* the authority of the Government of the United States. His words were recorded as follows by Robert Yates:

> Many who wish the general government to protect the State governments, are anxious to have t*he line of jurisdiction well drawn and defined,* so that they may not clash. This suggests the necessity of having this line *well detailed* – possibly this may be done. If we do this, the people will be convinced that we meant well to the State governments; and should there be any defects, they will trust *a future convention* with the power of making further *amendments*. [Emphasis added] [55]

Luther Martin was especially concerned by the radical and repugnant theory expressed by some of the nationalists, to the effect that the American people were no longer politically united as sovereign States, but had somehow been magically transformed into a consolidated American Empire. The Articles of Confederation rejected such a fallacious conception, common sense rejected it, and so did he.

The United States of America existed to serve the American people in their organized capacities as sovereign States, Mr. Martin reminded the Convention, not as individual citizens of a great continental Empire. Inasmuch as the true purpose of a Federal Government is to conduct the foreign affairs of the States, he stated, "its powers ought to be kept within narrow limits." [56]

When defining and limiting the powers of the Federal Government, stated the Orator of Federalism, prudence dictated caution, for "if too little power was given to it, more might be added." But "if too much" power were delegated to the Government of the United States, "it could never be resumed." He denied that the State governments posed a threat to a Federal Government. No State government would wish to hamper the operations of a general government as long as that government "pursues proper measures." [57]

The Maryland delegate took strong issue with those nationalists who insisted that only a supreme National Government could operate on individual citizens. Even a Federal Government, although founded on the concept of sovereign States, could be properly constituted to operate on citizens *within its federal sphere* without ceasing to be a Federal Government and without the States ceasing to be sovereign. What truly differentiated a Federal Government from a National Government was the *object* of its power and authority.

As he pointed out:

---

[55] *Ibid.*, Volume I, p. 439.
[56] *Ibid.*, Volume I, p. 437.
[57] *Ibid.*, Volume I, p. 437.

A general government may operate on individuals *in cases of general concern, and still be federal.* This distinction is with the States, *as States,* represented by the people *of those States. States will take care of their internal police and local concerns.* The general government has no interest, but the protection *of the whole.* Every other government must fail. [Emphasis added] [58]

"We are proceeding in forming this government as if there were no State governments at all," Mr. Martin chastised the nationalists, adding that, "The States must approve, or you will have none at all." But if the *supremacy of the general government,* as evinced by a veto power over the States, constituted the *cornerstone* of a National Government, then the *equality of the States* within the Union constituted the *cornerstone* of a federal system. Nowhere could this sovereign equality be more manifestly requisite than in an *equality of suffrage* within the Federal Government. "The corner-stone of a Federal Government is equality of votes. States may surrender this right; but if they do, their liberties are lost." [59]

"The first principle of government is founded on the natural rights of individuals, and in perfect equality," the Orator of Federalism reminded the delegates. "Locke, Vattel, Lord Somers, and Dr. Priestly, all confirm this principle." [60] Luther Martin then read selected passages from the great works of these highly respected authorities. Although neither Mr. Madison nor Mr. Yates recorded any of these quotations in their notes of the speech, it is probable that Mr. Martin cited illustrations from Emerich de Vattel's authoritative *Law of Nations* like those shown below:

"The law of nature...declares every nation free and independent of others." [61]

"Nations, or States, are bodies-politic. Societies of men, united together for the purpose of their mutual safety and advantage by the efforts of their combined strength. Such society has her affairs and her interests; she deliberates and takes resolutions in common, thus becoming a moral person, who possesses an understanding and a will peculiar to herself and is susceptible of obligations and rights." [62]

"Several sovereign and independent States may *unite* themselves together by a perpetual *Confederacy,* without ceasing to be, each individually, *a perfect State. They will together constitute a Federal Republic;* their joint de-

---

[58] *Ibid.,* Volume I, p. 439.
[59] *Ibid.,* Volume I, pp. 439-440.
[60] *Ibid.,* Volume I, p. 440.
[61] Joseph Allan Montgomery (ed.), *Christian History of the Constitution,* Volume II, The American Christian Constitution Press, San Francisco, 1962, p. 218.
[62] Alexander H. Stephens, *A Constitutional View of the Late War Between the States,* Volume I, Kraus Reprint Co., New York, (orig. pub. in 1868) 1970, quoted on p. 204.

liberations will not impair the *sovereignty* of each member, though they may, in certain respects, put some *restraint* on the *exercise* of it in virtue of *voluntary engagements*." [Emphasis added] [63]

After quoting selected excerpts from imminent and respected authorities on the laws of nature with respect to the equality of rights of sovereign States, Luther Martin stated:

> This *principle of equality*, when applied to individuals, is lost in some degree, when he becomes a member of society, to which it is transferred; and this society, by the name of State or kingdom, is, with respect to others, again *on a perfect footing of equality – a right to govern themselves as they please*. Nor can any other State, of right, deprive them of this *equality*. If such a State *confederates*, it is intended for the *good of the whole*; and if it again *confederate*, those rights must be well guarded. Nor can any [other] State demand a surrender of any of those rights; if it can, equality is already destroyed. *We must treat as free States with each other, upon the same terms of equality that men originally formed themselves into societies*. Vattel, Rutherford and Locke, are united in support of the position, that States, as to each other, are in a *State of Nature*.
>
> Thus...have I travelled with the most respectable authorities in support of principles, all tending to prove *the equality of independent States*. This is equally applicable to the smallest as well as the largest States, on the true principles of reciprocity and political freedom. [Emphasis added] [64]

Soberly noting that the proposals of the nationalists constituted "a system of slavery for 10 States," Luther Martin stated:

> *Unequal Confederacies* can never produce good effects. Apply this to the *Virginia Plan*. Out of the number 90 [representatives proposed for the general government], Virginia has 16 votes, Massachusetts 14, Pennsylvania 12 – *in all 42*. Add to this a State having four votes, and it gives a *majority* in the general legislature. Consequently *a combination of these States* will govern the remaining nine or ten States. Where is the safety and independency of those States? Pursue this subject farther. The executive...becomes the executive in consequence of this undue *influence*. And hence flows the appointment of all your offices, civil, military and judicial. The executive is also to have a negative on all laws. Suppose the possibility of a *combination* of ten States – he negatives a law – it is totally lost, because those States cannot form two thirds of the legislature. I am willing to give up private interest for the public good – but I must be satisfied first, that it is the public interest – and who can decide this point? *A majority only of the Union [of States].*

---

[63] *Ibid.*, Volume I, quoted on p. 170.
[64] Max Farrand (ed.), *Op. cit.*, Volume I, p. 440.

The Lacedemonians insisted, in the amphicitonic council to exclude some of the smaller States from a right to vote, in order that they might tyrannize over them. If the plan now on the table be adopted three States in the Union have the controul, and they may make use of their power when they please.

If there exists no *separate interests*, there is no danger of an *equality of votes*; and if there be danger, the smaller States cannot yield. *If the foundation of the existing Confederation is well laid, powers may be added — You may safely add a third story to a house where the foundation is good.*...The partial representation in Congress is not the cause of its weakness, but the want of power. I would not trust a government organized upon the reported plan, for all the slaves of Carolina or the horses and oxen of Massachusetts. Price says, that *laws made by one man or a set of men, and not by common consent, is slavery* — And it is so *when applied to States*, if you give them an unequal representation. What are called human feelings in this instance are only the feelings of *ambition* and the *lust of power*. [Emphasis added] [65]

The next morning, Luther Martin resumed his discourse, stating that the only recognized political *individuals* within a federal system are the sovereign States who are equal members of the Union. The chief objective of a federal system, therefore, must be the preservation and security of the rights and sovereignty of the member States. Security for the rights of individual Americans "cannot be the object of a general government," because those rights "are already secured by their guardians, the State governments. The general government is therefore intended only to protect and guard the rights of the States as States." [66]

Good government, stated the Orator of Federalism, must be based on the wide distribution of powers, not on their concentration in one centralized set of hands. Local government, such as that afforded by the State governments, are closer to the peoples they represent than any Federal Government could ever be. Such governments would therefore better reflect the popular will and would better serve the true interests of the American people. Prudence thus dictated that the Federal Government have only foreign and interstate affairs as its objects, and that the primary concern of the Convention should be to vest that government with powers sufficient only for that purpose and to provide security against usurpation of the other powers reserved to the States.

As Mr. Martin stated:

This general government, I believe, is the first upon earth which

---

[65] *Ibid.*, Volume I, pp. 438, 440, and 441.
[66] *Ibid.*, Volume I, p. 453.

gives checks against democracies or aristocracies. *The only necessary check in a general government ought to be a restraint to prevent its absorbing the powers of the State governments. Representation on federal principles can only flow from State societies. Representation and taxation are ever inseparable* – not according to the quantum of property, but *the quantum of freedom.* [Emphasis added] [67]

The power and effect of Mr. Martin's great speech must have been felt by all the delegates who heard it, for several key nationalists arose in the Convention in an effort to counter that effect. "There has been much fallacy in the arguments advanced by the gentleman from Maryland," James Madison claimed. The gist of Mr. Madison's rebuttal may be ascertained from his concluding remarks, to the effect that the greatest security a minority interest can have is to throw itself on the mercy of a more powerful interest. "And let me remark," he said, "that the weaker you make your Confederation, the greater the danger to the lesser States. They can only be protected by a strong Federal Government."

Only by voluntarily surrendering all their rights and powers to a supreme National Government, and by becoming its colonial possessions, could the States find true security and liberty in the Union. "The true policy of the small States therefore," Mr. Madison concluded, "lies in promoting those principles & that form of govt. which will most approximate the States to the condition of Counties." [68]

James Wilson attempted briefly to parry one or two blows which Mr. Martin had directed against the proposed national system, and on the following day Alexander Hamilton also attempted a rebuttal. What is especially remarkable about the latter's rebuttal is that *he began his address by acknowledging the truthfulness of Mr. Martin's principles.* "The gentleman from Maryland has been at great pains to establish positions *which are not denied,*" said Mr. Hamilton. "Many of them, as drawn from the best writers on government, are become almost *self-evident principles.*" [Emphasis added] [69]

Following this tribute to the *principles* of the Orator of Federalism, the Orator of Nationalism added:

> But I doubt the propriety of his *application* of those principles in the present discussion. He deduces from them the necessity that States *entering into a Confederacy* must retain the equality of votes....*May not the smaller and greater States so modify their respective rights as to establish the general interest of the whole, without adhering to the right of equality?* [Em-

---

[67] *Ibid.*, Volume I, p. 453.
[68] *Ibid.*, Volume I, pp. 449, 455, and 456.
[69] *Ibid.*, Volume I, p. 472.

phasis added] [70]

This admission by Mr. Hamilton is all the more remarkable, considering that he was undoubtedly the most extreme nationalist in the Philadelphia Convention, and considering that his true wish was to utterly annihilate the States. Yet, as he correctly stated, sovereign States are, by the *Law of Nations*, equal moral persons. *When confederating with one another, they may establish whatever contractual relationship they might deem necessary and proper, and yet still retain their sovereignty.* As sovereign States, in other words, they are free to form compacts with each other based on whatever terms they deem necessary and proper. And this observation could be extended to the mode of representation adopted in their common Federal Government, as to any other feature of their common agent.

Alexander Hamilton's acknowledgement of this truth serves to illustrate the forceful effect Luther Martin's address must have had on the Convention. It also serves as an indicator that Mr. Hamilton realized that all hope of establishing a supreme National Government had vanished. Soon after giving his reply to Mr. Martin, the Orator of Nationalism retired in despair from the Grand Convention and returned to New York to deliver the bad news to his nationalist associates in that State. He would not return to the Federal Convention again until near the end of the proceedings.

An Appeal for Divine Intervention

On June 28th, after Luther Martin had concluded his great oration, and after James Madison and Roger Sherman had addressed the Philadelphia Convention, Benjamin Franklin rose to speak. He was, perhaps, the most respected man in America, rivaled only by George Washington in the degree of admiration bestowed upon him by his countrymen. He had vast experience in diplomacy, and had prior experience in constitution-making through his Albany Plan of Union.

Benjamin Franklin's greatness was well known to all the delegates. They knew him as a scholar, an inventor, a publisher of a famous almanac, and the discoverer of lightning-induced electricity. But in spite of his great accomplishments, the Governor of Pennsylvania was a humble and godly man. As such he had become deeply disturbed by the fierce battle taking place in Independence Hall, and he lamented the fact that the delegates had thus far neglected to open any of their sessions with a prayer. The time had come,

---

[70] *Ibid.*, Volume I, p. 472.

Mr. Franklin was convinced, to remedy this omission by urging that the delegates humble themselves before their maker, seek Divine Guidance, and start the practice of beginning each day with a prayer.

As Governor Franklin said to the Convention:

> In this situation of this Assembly, groping as it were in the dark to find political truth, and scarce able to distinguish it when presented to us, how has it happened, Sir, that we have not hitherto once thought of humbly applying to the Father of Lights to illuminate our understandings? In the beginning of the contest with G. Britain, when we were sensible of danger we had *daily prayer in this room* for the Divine Protection. – *Our prayers, Sir, were heard, and they were graciously answered.* All of us who were engaged in the struggle must have observed frequent instances of Superintending Providence in our favor. To that kind Providence we owe this happy opportunity of consulting in peace on the means of establishing our future national felicity. And have we now forgotten that powerful friend? *Or do we imagine that we no longer need his assistance?* I have lived, Sir, a long time, and the longer I live, the more convincing proofs I see of this truth – *that God governs in the affairs of men.* And if a sparrow cannot fall to the ground without his notice, is it probable that an empire can rise without his aid? We have been assured, Sir, in the sacred writings, that "except the Lord build the House they labour in vain that build it." *I firmly believe this; and I also believe that without His concurring aid we shall succeed in this political building no better than the Builders of Babel.*....And what is worse, mankind may hereafter from this unfortunate instance, despair of establishing governments by Human Wisdom and leave it to chance, war and conquest.
>
> I therefore beg leave to move – that henceforth prayers imploring the assistance of Heaven, and its blessings on our deliberations, be held in this Assembly every morning before we proceed to business, and that one or more of the Clergy of this City be requested to officiate in that service. [Emphasis added] [71]

This appeal seemed to touch the heart of a delegate from the State of Connecticut. Like Mr. Franklin, Roger Sherman had a long and distinguished record of service to his country. He had served in nearly every State office in Connecticut except Governor and had served as the Treasurer of Yale. As a member of the Second Continental Congress, Mr. Sherman had been a strong advocate of American independence and had served on the select committee appointed to draft the Declaration of Independence. Like Mr. Franklin, he was an honest statesman and a skilled diplomat. He was also a devout Christian, who was moved to second Benjamin Franklin's proposal for daily prayer.

Most of the other delegates, however, were not moved by the prayer

---

[71] *Ibid.*, Volume I, pp. 451-452.

proposal. As Benjamin Franklin later wrote in his manuscript, "The Convention, except three or four persons, thought Prayers unnecessary." [72] Alexander Hamilton, it appears, objected so vehemently to the prayer proposal that George Washington is said to have stared at him with indignant astonishment. A number of other delegates offered their excuses for not supporting the proposal. No budget existed to pay a clergyman; the American people might become alarmed; it would be a breach in the wall of secrecy; and it was too late in the business of the Convention to start praying now.

Dr. Franklin and Roger Sherman answered these objections by stating that "the past omission of a duty could not justify a further omission," that a rejection of prayer could have bad repercussions on the fate of the Convention, and that "the alarm out of doors that might be excited for the state of things within" would "at least be as likely to do good as ill." [73] The Convention, as it turned out, dodged a vote on the formal motion for prayer, by voting instead for adjournment for the day.

Although many of the delegates may have been under the delusion that the Convention was in no need of God as they planned the fate of the American people, the Almighty may have had another opinion of the matter. Who is to say that it was not by *Divine Intervention* that the two men who had urged the Convention to turn to God – *Benjamin Franklin* and *Roger Sherman* – would soon thereafter unite to deliver the death blow to the nationalist conspiracy within the Federal Convention? By joining forces to urge the adoption of the Connecticut Compromise, these two men assured the triumph of the Federal Republicans.

A Deadlocked Convention

By the last day of June, it had become apparent that the forces of federalism within the Convention were as strong as the coalition forces supporting nationalism, and that any increase in the strength of the former would deliver control of the Convention to the Federal Republicans. As yet, only eleven States were present. Rhode Island, although a small State whose interests would certainly induce her to support the federal system, was not expected to ever send delegates. New Hampshire, however, was expected to dispatch commissioners to the Grand Convention, sooner or later. And the Federal Republicans, knowing that the Granite State would augment their strength in the Convention, desired to ensure the arrival of her delegates as quickly a possible.

---

[72] *Ibid.*, Volume I, p. 452.
[73] *Ibid.*, Volume I, p. 452.

sible.

Thus, on June 30th, David Brearly of New Jersey moved that the President of the Convention — George Washington – write a letter to the Governor of New Hampshire, informing him "that the business depending before the Convention was of such a nature as to require the immediate attendance of the deputies of that State." [74] The motion was heartily seconded by William Paterson.

The nationalists, it hardly needs to be mentioned, strongly objected to the motion. John Rutledge thought such a letter would be improper and expressed the hope that, if such a letter should actually be written, "all the great points" confronting the Convention "would be adjusted before the letter could produce its effect." Rufus King assured the delegates that he had privately written several letters to New Hampshire authorities, and that further correspondence was therefore unnecessary. And James Wilson "wished to know whether it would be consistent with the rule or reason of secrecy" to communicate with New Hampshire's Governor. Such a letter, he informed the house, would "spread a great alarm." [75]

When a vote was taken on the motion, *two* States voted for the proposal, *five* voted against it, *one* was divided, and *three* were absent. Thus, the motion failed to carry – no request would be sent to New Hampshire, urging that State to speedily dispatch its delegates to the Convention. By this vote, the Federal Republicans realized that, if they were to attain a victory, they would have to do it with the forces already present. No help would be forthcoming from either Rhode Island or New Hampshire.

Following this vote, the Convention turned its attention to the proposal of Oliver Ellsworth of Connecticut, that each State should have an equal vote in the United States Senate. "Can we forget for whom we are forming a government?" James Wilson asked, obviously forgetting himself that the government was being formed for the States. "Is it for men, or for the imaginary beings called States?" he queried, conveniently overlooking the fact that the American people *are the States*. "Will our honest constituents be satisfied with metaphysical distinctions?" he posed, apparently confusing the real and meaningful sovereign States with his imaginary consolidated nation of Americans partitioned by his phantom national districts. "It is all a mere illusion of names," stated the master of deceptive rhetoric. "We talk of States, till we forget what they are composed of." [76]

Feigning ignorance of the existence of the States, Mr. Wilson insisted that only people, *in their status as individual citizens*, would be members of

---

[74] *Ibid.*, Volume I, p. 481.
[75] *Ibid.*, Volume I, p. 481.
[76] *Ibid.*, Volume I, p. 483.

the Federal Union. Inasmuch as sovereign political societies were mere meta-physical abstractions, he insisted, to base representation in the Federal Gov-ernment on the existence of States would be unfair to a "majority" of the members of the Union in the three largest States. Mr. Wilson also claimed that the principle of federalism, by serving as a check on the unbridled major-ity-rule democracy he advocated, would allow a minority to rule a majority.

Rising to respond to Mr. Wilson's reasons for opposing the equality of suffrage in the Senate, Oliver Ellsworth stated:

> The capital objection of Mr. Wilson "that the minority will rule the majority" is not true. The power is given to the few to save them from be-ing destroyed by the many. If an equality of votes had been given to them in both branches [of the legislature], the objection might have had weight. Is it a novel thing that the few should have a check on the many?....We are running from one extreme to another. We are razing the foundations of the building. When we need only repair the roof. No salutary measure has been lost for want of *a majority of the States*, to favor it. If security be all that the great States wish for the 1st. branch secures them. The danger of combinations among them is not imaginary....He appealed again to the ob-ligations of the federal pact which was still in force, and which had been entered into with so much solemnity, persuading himself that some regard would still be paid to the plighted faith under which each State small as well as great, held an equal right of suffrage in the general councils. His remarks were not the result of partial or local views. The State he repre-sented (Connecticut) held a middle rank. [77]

The "small States must possess the power of self-defence or be ruined," Mr. Ellsworth concluded. "Will any one say there is no diversity of interests in the States? And if there is, should not those interests be guarded and se-cured? But if there is none, then the large States have nothing to apprehend from an equality of rights." [78]

In rebuttal, James Madison protested against *the federal system of checks-and-balances* urged by the Federal Republicans. He firmly believed in major-ity rule, he claimed, but he adamantly denied the right to govern to a *majority of the States*. Under a federal system, he observed, a *majority of the States* "could *obstruct* the wishes and interests of the majority" of people in the few larger States. The *majority of States* "could *extort* measures, repugnant to the wishes & interest of the majority" of people in the few larger States. Further-more, a *majority of the States* "could *impose* measures adverse thereto." [79]

James Madison conceded that the States had different interests that di-

---

[77] *Ibid.*, Volume I, pp. 484-485.
[78] *Ibid.*, Volume I, p. 496.
[79] *Ibid.*, Volume I, p. 486.

vided them, but the division was not between the large and the small States. The greatest conflict of interest, he stated, was between the *Northern States* and the *Southern States*. And in regard to this difference of interests, he fully acknowledged that each interest had a genuine right to be protected from the other.

Mr. Madison's observance of this undeniable fact, however, only served to confirm the truth and wisdom of the principles espoused by the Federal Republicans. *Only by strictly limiting the authority of the Federal Government and securing the reserved rights of each and every State in the Union – North, South, East, and West – could the separate interests of each State be safeguarded.* Although Mr. Madison apparently could not understand this basic maxim, there were fortunately many champions of States' Rights in the Convention who did.

The failure of many *Southerners* in the Federal Convention to realize this fundamental truth was undoubtedly based on their lack of vision. It is evident from the various remarks made in the Convention by Mr. Madison and many other delegates from the Southern quarter of the Union that these Southerners were suffering from the delusion that the Southern States were destined to be the most populous and dominant influence in the United States. The foolishness of that delusion, however, would not become apparent to James Madison until after the new Federal Constitution had been adopted, when the attacks on Southern rights and interests under the guidance of Alexander Hamilton helped him to understand and appreciate the merits of the federal system of government.

During the course of debate on Saturday, June 30th, Rufus King of Massachusetts ridiculed "the phantom of *State* sovereignty," wistfully spoke of a consolidated nation of American "people," and urged the Convention to detach itself from the "illusion" known as sovereign States. "The Connecticut motion contains all the vices of the old Confederation," he complained to his fellow delegates. "It supposes an imaginary evil – the slavery of State governments. And should this Convention adopt the motion, our business here is at an end." [80]

"Declamation has been substituted for argument," an exasperated Jonathan Dayton of New Jersey replied to the nationalists. "Have gentlemen shewn, or must we believe it, because it is said, that one of the evils of the old Confederation was...[equal] representation?" "We, as distinct societies, entered into the compact," he reminded them. "Will you now undermine the thirteen pillars that support it?" And in response to Rufus King's threat to break up the Convention unless the Federal Republicans surrendered to the

---

[80] *Ibid.*, Volume I, pp. 489, 490, and 499.

nationalists, Luther Martin asserted, "If we cannot confederate on just principles, I will never confederate in any other manner." [81]

"I will not answer for supporting chimerical objects – But has experience evinced any good in the old Confederation?" asked James Madison. "I know it never can answer, and I have therefore made use of bold language against it." In language as bold and irrational as that employed by Alexander Hamilton, Mr. Madison expressed the opinion that, regardless of how the Government of the United States was structured, "the States will usurp the general government." [82]

At this stage of the debates, Gunning Bedford, Jr. of Delaware made one of the most moving speeches delivered in the Convention, in which he clearly stated the principles that divided the house and dared to challenge the *motives* of those who sought to destroy the Federal Republic. His stirring words were recorded by Robert Yates as follows:

> That all the States at present are equally sovereign and independent, has been asserted from every quarter of this house. Our deliberations here are a confirmation of the position; and I may add to it, that each of them act from interested, and many from ambitious motives. Look at the votes which have been given on the floor of this house, and it will be found that their numbers, wealth and local views, have actuated their determinations; and that the larger States proceed as if our eyes were perfectly blinded. Impartiality, with them, is already out of the question – the reported plan is their political creed, and they support it, right or wrong. Even the diminutive State of Georgia has an eye to her future wealth and greatness – South Carolina, puffed up with the possession of her wealth and negroes, and North Carolina, are all, from different views, united with the great States. And these latter, although it is said they can never, from interested views, form a coalition, we find closely united in one scheme of interest and ambition, notwithstanding they endeavor to amuse us with the purity of their principles and the rectitude of their intentions, in asserting that the general government must be drawn from an equal representation of the people [of a consolidated nation]. Pretences to support ambition are never wanting. Their cry is, where is the danger? And they insist that altho' the powers of the general government will be increased, yet it will be for the good of the whole; and although the three great States form nearly a majority of the people of America, they never will hurt or injure the lesser States. *I do not, gentlemen, trust you.* If you possess the power, the abuse of it could not be checked; and what then would prevent you from exercising it to our destruction? You gravely alledge that there is no danger of combination, and triumphantly ask, how could combinations be effected?...This, I repeat, is language calculated only to amuse us. Yes, sir, the larger States

---

[81] *Ibid.*, Volume I, p. 499.
[82] *Ibid.*, Volume I, p. 499.

will be rivals, but not against each other – they will be rivals against the *rest of the States*. But it is urged that such a government would suit the people, and that its principles are equitable and just. How often has this argument been refuted, when applied to a *Federal* Government. The small States never can agree to the Virginia Plan; and why then is it still urged? But it is said that it is not expected that the State governments will approve the proposed system, and that this house must directly carry it to THE PEO-PLE for their approbation! Is it come to this, then, that *the sword* must decide this controversy, and that the horrors of war must be added to the rest of our misfortunes? But what have the people already said? "We find the Confederation defective – Go, and give additional powers to the Confederation – Give to it the imposts, regulation of trade, power to collect the taxes, and the means to discharge our foreign and domestic debts." Can we not then, as their delegates, agree upon these points? As their ambassadors, can we not clearly grant those powers? Why then, when we are met, must entire, distinct, and new grounds be taken, and a government, of which the people had no idea, be instituted? And are we to be told, if we wont agree to it, it is the last moment of our deliberations? I say, it is indeed the last moment, if we do agree to this assumption of power. The States will never again be entrapped into a measure like this. The people will say the *small* States would confederate, and grant further powers to Congress; but you, the *large* States, would not. Then the fault will be yours, and all the nations of the earth will justify us. But what is to become of our public debts if we dissolve the Union? Where is your plighted faith? Will you crush the smaller States, or must they be left unmolested? Sooner than be ruined, there are *foreign powers who will take us by the hand*. I say not this to threaten or intimidate, but that we should reflect seriously before we act. If we once leave this floor, and solemnly renounce your new project, what will be the consequence? You will annihilate your Federal Government, and ruin must stare you in the face. Let us then do what is in our power – *amend and enlarge the Confederation, but not alter the federal system*. The people expect this, and no more. We all agree in the necessity of a more efficient government – and cannot this be done? Although my State is small, I know and respect its rights, as much, at least, as though who have the honor to represent any of the larger States. [83]

On most points raised in this speech, Mr. Madison's notes coincide with those of Robert Yates. There are, however, two significant differences between the two sets of records. In the notes of James Madison, it is recorded that Mr. Bedford acknowledged the possibility that the States might be divided in the future by issues and interests other than those directly related to the sizes of their respective populations. As far as the genuine principles of federalism were concerned, however, this possibility would make no difference. Regardless of how the varied interests of the States might divide them

---

[83] *Ibid.*, Volume I, pp. 500-502.

into opposing camps in the future, the importance of preserving the reserved rights of each and every State remained the same.

The other point of difference between the two sets of notes relates to Mr. Bedford's hint that the smaller States might turn to "foreign powers" if the larger States refused to confederate with them on the principles of sovereign equality. Mr. Madison recorded this portion of the speech in the following words:

> The little States are willing to observe their engagements, but will meet the larger ones on no ground but that of the Confederation. We have been told with a dictatorial air that this is the last moment for a fair trial in favor of a good government. It will be the last indeed if the propositions reported from the Committee go forth to the people. He was under no apprehensions. The large States dare not dissolve the Confederation. If they do the small ones will find some foreign ally of more honor and good faith, who will take them by the hand and do them justice. He did not mean by this to intimidate or alarm. It was a natural consequence; which ought to be avoided by enlarging the federal powers not annihilating the federal system. This is what the people expect. All agree in the necessity of a more efficient govt. and why not make such an one; as they desire. [84]

When the Philadelphia Convention adjourned on June 30th, the marathon debate on the great issue of a supreme National Government versus a Federal Government founded on supreme States had supposedly ended. On Monday, July 2nd, as its first order of business, the house voted on Oliver Ellsworth's motion that the States should have an equal vote in the Senate. It was clearly understood by all the delegates that the *principles* on which the evolving Constitution would be based were to be decided by the outcome of this crucial vote.

One by one the votes were counted. The three large States – Massachusetts, Virginia, and Pennsylvania – all voted against the Connecticut Compromise. They were joined in opposition to the compromise by the States of North Carolina and South Carolina. Connecticut, of course, voted in favor of equal suffrage in the Senate. So, too, did New York, New Jersey, Delaware, and Maryland. The sovereign State of Georgia was officially divided on the issue.

Thus, on the great issue of equal representation in the upper branch of the federal legislature – and on the associated issue involving the great principles of federalism versus nationalism – the vote stood at *five* States for federalism, *five* States for nationalism, and *one* State divided. The battle between the Federal Republicans and the nationalist coalition had thus reached a *stalemate*

---

[84] *Ibid.*, Volume I, p. 492.

– on the great question of federalism versus nationalism, the Convention was now officially *deadlocked.*

Chapter Ten

The Triumph of Federalism

Confronted with a stalemate by the end of June over the great question of representation in the United States Senate, the Philadelphia Convention directed its attention to finding a means for breaking the deadlock. Charles Pinckney of South Carolina moved "to form the States into classes, with an apportionment of Senators among them." [1] In a similar vein, James Wilson of Pennsylvania drafted several resolutions that would have, in essence, abolished the States and replaced them with several *national districts*.

Although neither James Madison's notes nor those of Robert Yates indicate that these Wilson resolutions were ever formally introduced to the Convention, they do serve as concrete evidence that a plot existed to abolish the States and to vest in the Government of the United States the authority to regiment the American people into new political districts. These resolutions, particularly the first and third ones, also serve to possibly indicate what the nationalists within the Convention had in mind when speaking of a consolidated American nation of people.

The first Wilson resolution declared:

> That the second branch of the national legislature shall be elected in the following manner – that the States be divided into _____ Districts; the first to comprehend the States of _____ the second to comprehend the States of _____ the third to comprehend the States of _____ the fourth to comprehend the States of _____ and &c.
> – That the members shall be elected by the said Districts in the proportion following, in the first District [2]

The fact that this resolution abruptly ends in mid-sentence probably reflects the haste with which it was written. In this first resolution, Mr. Wilson had originally written "federal legislature," but had crossed out the word *federal* and replaced it with the word *national*, a clear indication that he realized that such "districts," while compatible with a National Government, would be incompatible with a Federal Government. In front of the word

---

[1] Max Farrand (ed.), *The Records of the Federal Convention of 1787*, Revised Edition, Volume I, Yale University Press, New Haven, 1966, p. 511.
[2] *Ibid.*, Volume I, p. 520.

"Districts" he had originally written the words "four great," thereby indicating that the thirteen sovereign States were to be replaced by four great national districts. But those words had been crossed out by the resolution's author.

The third resolution drafted by James Wilson declared:

> That it shall be in the power of the national legislature, for the convenience and advantage of the good people of the United States, to divide them into such further and other Districts for the purposes aforesaid, as to the said legislature shall appear necessary. [3]

As in the first resolution, Mr. Wilson had originally written the word "federal" before the word "legislature," but had crossed it out and replaced it with the term "national." By the terms of this resolution, which may have been designed to replace the first resolution, a National Government would be empowered to divide and regiment a consolidated nation of Americans in any manner it pleased, and such national districts could be created in utter disregard of any existing State boundaries.

The fact that James Wilson never formally introduced any of his proposals for replacing the States with national districts serves to indicate that he recognized the futility of attempting to abolish the American States. Whatever compromise the Federal Convention devised, it would have to be based on the foundation of the existing sovereign States. The American people would have it no other way, nor would the majority of delegates in the Convention.

Following the suggestion by Mr. Pinckney to regiment the States by rank, and to proportionally base representation in the Senate based on these ranks, General Charles Cotesworth Pinckney rose to address the Constitutional Convention. Although he did not approve of the suggestion to treat the States as anything other than equally sovereign societies, he acknowledged that some compromise between the small and the large States was necessary. He therefore proposed "that a Committee consisting of *a member from each State* should be appointed to devise & report some compromise." [Emphasis added] [4]

Luther Martin, in response, stated that he "had no objection to a commitment, but no modifications whatever could reconcile the smaller States to the least diminution of their equal sovereignty." Roger Sherman also supported the move for a committee of the States, noting that, "It seems we have got to a point, that we cannot move one way or the other. Such a com-

---

[3] *Ibid.*, Volume I, p. 521.
[4] *Ibid.*, Volume I, p. 511.

mittee is necessary to set us right." [5]

Gouverneur Morris, who had now replaced Alexander Hamilton as the Convention's chief *Orator of Nationalism*, then addressed the Convention in a lengthy speech. He, too, was for the appointment of a committee of the States to resolve the deadlock confronting the Federal Convention. But his reasons for supporting the appointment of such a committee was vastly different from those of the Federal Republicans.

Mr. Morris observed that the fears of the advocates of States' Rights were justifiably grounded on a genuine apprehension that a numerical majority in the House of Representatives might run rampant and invade the rights of a minority in the Union. Because such an event was a distinct possibility, he agreed that the Senate should be constituted to serve as a check or brake on unbridled majority rule in the other branch of the legislature. However, he denied that the federal check provided by a majority of States could ever serve as an effective brake on the majority of the people in the federal legislature. Rather than look to the sovereign equality of the States as the guarantor of good government, he urged the Convention to instead rely on an aristocracy of the rich and well-born to serve that purpose. The Senate, therefore, should be converted into a House of Lords appointed by the President, so that plutocracy could serve as a check on a numerical majority of the people.

Referring to the Senate as "the checking branch" of the federal legislature, the new Orator of Nationalism informed the Convention that one vice must be opposed by a different vice, that "one interest must be opposed to another interest." The Senate "must have the aristocratic spirit," and Senators "must love to lord it thro' pride," for "pride is indeed the great principle that actuates both the poor & the rich. It is this principle which in the former resists, in the latter abuses authority." The Senate must also be "independent," stated Mr. Morris, independent of both the individual citizens and of the States. "The aristocratic body, should be as independent & as firm as the democratic." [6]

As Gouverneur Morris informed the delegates:

> The second branch ought to be composed of men of *great and established property – an aristocracy*. Men, who from *pride* will support *consistency* and *permanency*; and to make them *completely independent* they must be chosen *for life*, or they will be a useless body. Such an *aristocratic body* will keep down the turbulency of democracy. But if you elect them for a shorter period, they will be only a name, and we had better be without them. Thus constituted, I hope they will shew us the *weight of aristocracy*.

[5] *Ibid.*, Volume I, pp. 511 and 517.
[6] *Ibid.*, Volume I, p. 512.

[Emphasis added] [7]

The National Monarchist from Pennsylvania acknowledged that such a monied aristocracy would "do wrong" by attempting to invade the rights of the people and to enslave the American people. "He believed so," acknowledging the legitimacy of this concern, and he also "hoped so." "The Rich," he stressed, "will strive to establish their dominion & enslave the rest. They always did. They always will." Turning the Senate over to these forces of evil, he claimed, would constitute the great beauty of the American political system. In fact, only by posing this great evil against the evil of democracy could good government could be attained in the United States. In other words, said Mr. Morris, evil could only be countered by more evil: "There will be a mutual check and mutual security." [8]

Mr. Morris also acknowledged that politicians in the State governments would be horrified by his scheme, but claimed that they could be *bribed* into accepting an official aristocracy in the Government of the United States. "He hoped there was strength of mind eno' in this house to look truth in the face," James Madison wrote in his notes. "He did not hesitate therefore to say that loaves & fishes must bribe the Demagogues. They must be made to expect higher offices under the general than the State govts. A Senate for life will be a noble bait." "Without such captivating prospects," Mr. Morris insisted, "the popular leaders will oppose & defeat the plan." [9]

As Mr. Madison recorded in his notes, the Convention's new Orator of Nationalism was very displeased with the general direction in which the house seemed to be going:

> He perceived that the 1st. branch was to be chosen *by the people of the States*: the 2d. *by those chosen by the people. Is not here a govt. by the States.* A governt. by *Compact* between Virga. in the 1st. & 2d. branch; Massts. in the 1st & 2d. branch &c. *This is going back to mere treaty.* It is no govt. [*i.e.*, no National Government] at all. It is altogether dependent — *on the States*, and will act over again the part which Congs. has acted. [Emphasis added] [10]

"I avow myself the advocate of a strong government," Gouverneur Morris confessed. Accordingly, he urged the Philadelphia Convention to exclude the influence of "local government" in the Government of the United States by reserving the U.S. Senate as the domain, not of the State govern-

---

[7] *Ibid.*, Volume I, p. 517.
[8] *Ibid.*, Volume I, pp. 512-513.
[9] *Ibid.*, Volume I, pp. 513-514.
[10] *Ibid.*, Volume I, p. 514.

ments, but of the money power. "These latter remarks," he concluded, "I throw out only for the consideration of the committee who are to be appointed." [11]

The other leaders of the nationalist conspiracy in the Grand Convention were adamantly *against* the appointment of a committee to resolve the great issue confronting the house. They realized that *any compromise between the small and the large States would forever doom all hope of erecting a National Government.* They also realized that the very composition of the proposed committee – *wherein the States would be equally represented* – violated the improper principles they advocated. Thus, James Wilson "objected to the committee, because it would decide according to that very rule of voting which was opposed on one side." And James Madison complained that "if you appoint one [representative] from each State, we shall have in it the whole force of State prejudices. The great difficulty is to conquer former opinions." [12]

The Grand Committee

When it came time to vote at the conclusion of debates on July 2nd, the great mass of the Convention decided, against the wishes of most nationalist leaders, to accept General Pinckney's proposal. On the question of appointing the committee, *nine* States voted in favor of the motion, and only *two* States voted against it. Then, on the question for committing "to a member from each State," [13] *ten* States voted *aye*, and only *one* State – Pennsylvania – voted *no*. The Convention then *elected*, by ballot, the members of the **Grand Committee**, on which *each State would have one delegate.*

By ballot, the delegates listed below were elected to represent their States on the Grand Committee:

Connecticut	Oliver Ellsworth
Delaware	Gunning Bedford, Jr.
Georgia	Abraham Baldwin
Maryland	Luther Martin
Massachusetts	Elbridge Gerry
New Jersey	William Paterson
New York	Robert Yates
North Carolina	William R. Davie

---

[11] *Ibid.*, Volume I, pp. 518-519.
[12] *Ibid.*, Volume I, pp. 515 and 519.
[13] *Ibid.*, Volume I, p. 516.

Pennsylvania	Benjamin Franklin
South Carolina	John Rutledge
Virginia	George Mason

The composition of the Grand Committee reveals the undeniable fact that the majority of the Philadelphia Convention had resolved to abandon the nationalists, *for there was not a single outspoken nationalist elected to the committee.* As it can be seen, George Mason was elected to represent Virginia, not James Madison. Elbridge Gerry, and not Rufus King, was elected to represent Massachusetts. And rather than elect either Gouverneur Morris or James Wilson to represent the State of Pennsylvania, Dr. Franklin was selected.

But if the die-hard nationalists were deliberately excluded from the Grand Committee, the same could not be said for the most ardent advocates of States' Rights and federalism. The Federal Republicans were well represented by Robert Yates, William Paterson, Luther Martin, Oliver Ellsworth, and Gunning Bedford, Jr. The strength of the Federal Republicans was actually increased when Mr. Ellsworth, due to illness, was unable to sit on the committee. In his place, Connecticut sent Roger Sherman, the delegate who had been responsible for formulating the celebrated *Connecticut Compromise.*

After selecting the committee members, the Federal Convention officially adjourned until July 5th, in order to allow the Grand Committee an entire day to draft a compromise between the large and the small States. The day after the adjournment – on July 3rd – the Grand Committee convened and elected Elbridge Gerry as its Chairman. As the extreme nationalists had feared, the Grand Committee had little difficulty in resolving the *legitimate* differences between the large States and the small States. By the end of the day, a genuine compromise had been reached on the matter of representation in the Federal Government.

The very fact that these select delegates from all the States could reach a compromise so quickly and easily starkly demonstrates that it was the extreme nationalists, and not the Federal Republicans, who had been severely hampering genuine progress in the Convention for more than a month. By excluding the handful of nationalist radicals from the discussion, the large States easily negotiated acceptable terms with the smaller States. And in accomplishing this, the Grand Committee of the States assured the victory of federalism over nationalism within the Federal Convention.

Within the Grand Committee, the man responsible for bringing the large and small States into agreement was *Benjamin Franklin*, a wise and skillful diplomat who urged the committee to adopt the Connecticut Compromise previously proposed by *Roger Sherman*. These two patriotic Americans, as the advocate of constitutional government will recall, had been associated

on a previous issue – an ill-fated attempt to persuade the Convention to turn
to God for guidance. Although they had failed on that earlier question, on the
great issue facing the Grand Committee of the States they succeeded.

After agreeing to adopt the Sherman-Franklin proposal, the Grand
Committee drafted the following report to the Convention:

> That the subsequent propositions be recommended to the Conven-
> tion, *on condition that both shall be generally adopted.*
>
> That in the first branch of the legislature, each of *the States* now in
> the Union, be allowed *one member for every 40,000 inhabitants,* of the de-
> scription reported in the seventh resolution of the Committee of the
> Whole house – That *each State*, not containing that number, shall be al-
> lowed *one member.*
>
> That all bills for *raising or apportioning money*, and for *fixing salaries*
> of the officers of Government of the United States, shall *originate* in the
> first branch of the legislature, and shall not be altered or amended by the
> second branch; and that no money shall be drawn from the public treasury,
> but in pursuance of appropriations to be *originated* in the first branch.
>
> That in the second branch of the legislature, *each State shall have an
> equal vote.* [Emphasis added] [14]

By the terms of this compromise agreement, a supreme National Government was conclusively rejected in favor of a Federal Government. By its
provisions, the new Constitution would be, as the Articles of Confederation
had been, founded on the pillars of sovereign States. There would be no *consolidated nation* of people, no *national districts*, and no *ranking system* based
on the supposed relative importance of the States. There would be, instead,
only the sovereign States. Those States would be represented in the lower
chamber based upon their *respective populations.* In the upper branch, they
would be represented based on their *sovereign equality.* Yet, in *both* branches,
it would be sovereign States – not a consolidated American Empire – that
would be represented. By this compromise, the large-small State issue could
be easily settled *without sacrificing the federal system.*

Nationalism in Despair

When the report of the Grand Committee was presented to the Committee of the Whole on July 5th, the nationalists could not conceal their horror and anguish. The general drift of the dialogue may be ascertained from
the notes recorded by Robert Yates:

---

[14] *Ibid.*, Volume I, p. 523.

Met pursuant to adjournment.

The report of the [Grand] Committee was read.

Mr. Gorham. I call for an explanation of the principles on which it is grounded.

Mr. Gerry, the Chairman, explained the principles.

Mr. Martin. The one representation is proposed as an expedient for the adoption of the other.

Mr. Wilson. The Committee has exceeded their powers.

Mr. Martin proposed to take the question on the whole of the report.

Mr. Wilson. I do not chuse to take a leap in the dark. I have a right to call for a division of the question on each distinct proposal.

Mr. Madison. I restrain myself from animadverting on the report, from the respect I bear to the members of the Committee. But I must confess I see nothing of concession in it. [15]

James Wilson's comical charge that "the Committee had exceeded their powers" [16] undoubtedly resulted in a few smiles from some of the other delegates. Earlier, when urging the Convention to abandon the federal system of government, Mr. Wilson and the other nationalists had casually brushed aside the truthful accusation that, by doing so, the Convention would be exceeding its powers. They had repeatedly stressed that the Federal Union was in "crisis" and was confronted by an "emergency" that required the delegates to ignore all limitations on their powers. Yet, when the Grand Committee recommended a federal solution to the large-small State issue, he dared to complain that it somehow entailed a usurpation of powers! A *national solution* to a *federal crisis* was within the power of the Convention, but a *federal solution* to that same *federal crisis* was not.

After James Madison had denounced the report of the Grand Committee at some length, Pierce Butler spoke briefly, urging that the Senate "ought to represent the States according to their property." [17] He was followed by Gouverneur Morris. No man present was more upset by the recommendation of the Grand Committee than the National Monarchist from Pennsylvania, and the new Orator of Nationalism made no attempt to conceal his disgust.

Mr. Morris's comments were duly recorded by Mr. Madison:

Mr. Govr. Morris. Thought the form as well as the matter of the report objectionable. It seemed in the first place to render amendments impracticable. In the next place, it seemed to involve a pledge to agree to the 2d. part if the 1st. shd. be agreed to. He conceived the whole aspect of it to be wrong. He came here as a Representative of America; he flattered

---

[15] *Ibid.*, Volume I, p. 535.

[16] *Ibid.*, Volume I, p. 527.

[17] *Ibid.*, Volume I, p. 529.

himself as he came here in some degree as a Representative of the whole human race; for the whole human race will be affected by the proceedings of this Convention. He wished gentlemen to extend their views beyond the present moment of time; beyond the narrow limits of place from which they derive their political origin. If he were to believe some things which he had heard, he should suppose that we were assembled to truck and bargain for our particular States....Much has been said of the sentiments of the people. They were unknown. They could not be known. [18]

If Gouverneur Morris ever wished to know what the sentiments of the people were, all he needed to do was to read the *commission* from the *State of Pennsylvania* that authorized his presence in the Federal Convention. He refused to do so, of course, for the reason stated by himself. As he indicated, he did not regard himself as a delegate from Pennsylvania, but as a delegate from "America," or even as a representative of the "whole human race." As far as he was concerned, the *peoples of the States* were not entitled to any representation in the Federal Convention, and he accordingly urged the other delegates to stop representing the States they were commissioned to represent.

There are several highly significant points regarding this portion of Gouverneur Morris's speech which should be noted with great attention. The most obvious consideration, of course, is that, by refusing to represent his State in the Convention, Mr. Morris – like the other nationalist delegates who ascribed to his philosophy – was willfully *neglecting* his official duty to represent the interests of *the people of his State*. The Convention should have expelled him and requested that Pennsylvania send a new delegate who would agree to represent that State in the proceedings. Indeed, had the debates not been conducted in secrecy, and had the good people of Pennsylvania read his speech, it is quite probable that they would have demanded his recall.

Another highly significant point to consider is that the term *nationalists*, as we have used it in reference to those seeking to destroy the Federal Union, is actually inaccurate and inappropriate to describe these conspirators. Within the United States, the only *nations* that exist are the States. The connection between the States – styled the *Federal Union* – is merely a political association between these American Nations or States. The Federal Republicans, by remaining loyal to their own States, were therefore the true *nationalists* within the Grand Convention, when that term is considered in its patriotic and proper sense.

Those who fancied themselves to be the representatives of an American Continent, or of Planet Earth, and who according sought to replace the federal system with a national system, were actually *internationalists*. What they

---

[18] *Ibid.*, Volume I, p. 529.

sought was the destruction of the American Nations or States, the theft of sovereignty from the peoples of those Nation-States, and the creation of a sovereign and supreme "National" Government to dictatorially rule over the American Continent. This represents the principles of *internationalism* in the truest sense of the word, and their objectives certainly should not be confused with *patriotic* nationalism. There is nothing nationalistic or patriotic in the destruction of a sovereign State.

In light of these observations, we would certainly be justified to speak of the federalists in the Convention as the true patriotic nationalists. To avoid confusion and conflict with sundry other accounts of the Constitutional Era, however, we have and will continue to use the term "nationalist" to describe the internationalists within the Federal Convention. The advocate of constitutional government, however, should always bear in mind the true nature of the issues that divided the Philadelphia Convention of 1787 into its opposing *federal* and *national* camps.

Elsewhere in his address to the Convention, Gouverneur Morris issued a *threat* or *warning*, asserting that if the States refused to submit to the demands for a supreme National Government, such a government would be forced on the American people *by the sword.* Any American who remained loyal to his own sovereign State would then be branded a *traitor* and would meet his fate on the *gallows!* And the conquerors of the American people would thereafter place *halters* on the States and make them *slaves of a supreme National Government.*

James Madison recorded this threat or warning in his notes:

> This Country *must* be united. *If persuasion does not unite it, the sword will.* He begged that this consideration might have *its due weight.* The *scenes of horror* attending civil commotion *can not be described,* and *the conclusion of them will be worse than the term of their continuance. The stronger party will then make traytors of the weaker; and the Gallows & Halter will finish the work of the sword.* [Emphasis added] [19]

Taking his own brief notes on Gouverneur Morris's threatening speech, William Paterson summarized the nationalist threat against the American people in words that illustrate how his remarks were interpreted by the Federal Republicans:

> The Sword must decide —
> The strongest Party will make the weaker Traitors and hang them....

---

[19] *Ibid.*, Volume I, p. 530.

– The larger States must prevail – They must decide; they are most powerful. [20]

The student of constitutional government is again reminded that there is nothing *patriotic* about conquering sovereign States, either by persuasion or by the sword. Neither the States, nor an American continent, nor the whole human race could possibly reap any genuine benefits from such a conquest. Only by respecting, preserving, and defending the sovereign rights of all States – in America as well as elsewhere – can mankind secure to themselves the blessings of peace, harmony, and liberty.

Gouverneur Morris's threat did not go unnoticed by the Federal Republicans. For those harsh words, as well as for other unbecoming conduct on the part of the nationalist conspirators, the friends of federalism demanded an apology. "But is there not an apology in what was said by Mr. Govr. Morris that the sword is to unite: by Mr. Ghorum that Delaware must be annexed to Penna. and N. Jersey divided between Pena. and N. York," avowed Gunning Bedford, Jr. "To hear such language without emotion, would be to renounce the feelings of a man and the duty of a citizen." [21]

A nationalist delegate from North Carolina, Hugh Williamson, sought to minimize the damage wrought to the nationalist cause by Mr. Morris's threat. "He hoped...that the meaning of those expressions would not be misconstrued or exaggerated," James Madison wrote in his notes. "He did not conceive that Mr. Govr. Morris meant that the sword ought to be drawn agst. the smaller States." Referring to Mr. Morris, the North Carolina delegate stated that, "He only pointed out the probable consequences of anarchy in the U.S. A similar exposition ought to be given of the expressions of Mr. Ghorum." [22]

William Paterson, however, was unmoved by these reassurances of the innocence and purity of heart of the nationalists. "He acknowledged that the warmth" of Mr. Bedford's remarks against the nationalists "was improper; but he thought the Sword & the Gallows as little calculated to produce conviction." Mr. Paterson also complained, according to Mr. Madison's notes, "of the manner in which Mr. M[adison] – & Mr. Govr. Morris had treated the small States." [23]

Rather than uniting the States, the nationalists had succeeded in nothing more than to divide the States into hostile and quarrelsome groups. Neither nationalist persuasion nor nationalist threats of swordplay, it seemed,

---

[20] *Ibid.*, Volume I, p. 537.
[21] *Ibid.*, Volume I, p. 531.
[22] *Ibid.*, Volume I, p. 532.
[23] *Ibid.*, Volume I, p. 532.

could make a supreme National Government palatable to the Grand Convention. While most Federal Republicans were content to vent their anger and frustration at nationalist treachery through speeches, two of their number decided to abandon the Convention altogether. When *Robert Yates* and *John Lansing*, both representing New York, decided to walk out on July 5th, it signified the official withdrawal or secession of their State from the Constitutional Convention. It was a clear signal that, if the nationalists continued in their efforts to destroy the Federal Republic, the Federal Convention itself would end in dissolution.

The Withdrawal of New York

The exact date and time of the departure of John Lansing and Robert Yates is open to speculation. Although the official *Journal* of the Convention continued to record the votes of New York through July 10th, Robert Yates's notes end on July 5th with a statement indicating that the two New Yorkers "left the Convention" *on that date*. What is especially interesting is the point at which Mr. Yates stopped taking notes. The notes end with the address given by James Madison, wherein the Virginia nationalist indicated his refusal to accept the report of the Grand Committee. Could this have been the final nationalist move that drove them from the Convention?

According to Mr. Madison's notes, his own address to the Federal Convention was immediately followed by a few remarks from Pierce Butler; and he, in turn, was followed by Gouverneur Morris, who stated that the States would be forced to accept a National Government at the point of a sword, and that the federalists would be hanged as traitors. Could these have been the words that convinced Mr. Lansing and Mr. Yates to walk out of the Convention?

With the departure of the two Federal Republicans from New York, that State no longer had a single delegate in the Convention. Although Alexander Hamilton, who had walked out at an earlier date, would eventually return to the Federal Convention, he could neither vote nor officially represent the Empire State in the absence of his colleagues. But unlike Mr. Hamilton, neither Robert Yates nor John Lansing would ever return to the Constitutional Convention.

Based on what they had witnessed, Mr. Yates and Mr. Lansing were firmly convinced that the Convention amounted to nothing more than a conspiracy against the peoples and governments of the States. The significance of their departure was noted by Mr. Hamilton's biographer, John C. Miller, who observed in his book, *Alexander Hamilton and the Growth of the New Nation*, that their departure represented a breach in the tight veil of secrecy in which the Convention was shrouded. "Shortly after Hamilton returned to New York," Mr. Miller noted, "Yates and Lansing walked out of the Convention, *swearing that there was a plot afoot to establish a 'consolidated government'* and that Hamilton was *one* of the chief *conspirators*." [Emphasis added] [24]

Upon their return to New York, these two staunch advocates of federalism and republicanism assumed the task of warning others of the nefarious plot, acting upon the assumption that the final product of the Philadelphia Convention would be based on a supreme National Government. The concern thus generated spread quickly, giving rise to many rumors and preparing many Americans to oppose the Constitution of 1787 even before the Federal Convention had ended.

In a letter addressed to George Clinton, the Governor of New York, Mr. Yates and Mr. Lansing stated:

> Sir: We do ourselves the honor to advise your excellency that, in pursuance to concurrent resolutions of the honorable Senate and Assembly, we have, together with Mr. Hamilton, attended the Convention appointed for revising the Articles of Confederation, and reporting amendments to the same.
>
> It is with the sincerest concern we observe that, in the prosecution of the important objects of our mission, we have been reduced to the disagreeable alternative of either exceeding the powers delegated to us, and giving assent to measures which we conceive destructive to the political happiness of the citizens of the United States, or opposing our opinions to that body of respectable men, to whom those citizens had given the most unequivocal proofs of confidence. Thus circumstanced, under these impressions, to have hesitated would have been culpable. We therefore gave the principles of the Constitution, which has received the sanction of a majority of the Convention, our decided and unreserved dissent; but we must candidly confess that we should have been equally opposed to any system, however modified, which had in object the consolidation of the United States into one government....
>
> Our powers were explicit, and confined to the sole and express purpose of revising the Articles of Confederation, and reporting such alterations and provisions therein as should render the Federal Constitution adequate to the exigencies of government and the preservation of the Union.
>
> From these expressions, we were led to believe that a system of consolidated government could not, in the remotest degree, have been in contemplation of the legislature of this State; for that so important a trust as the adopting measures which tended to deprive the State government of its

---

[24] John C. Miller, *Alexander Hamilton and the Growth of the New Nation*, Harper & Row, Publishers, New York, 1959, p. 176.

most essential rights of sovereignty, and to place it in a dependent situation, could not have confided by implication; and the circumstance, that the acts of the Convention were to receive a State approbation in the last resort, forcibly corroborated the opinion that our powers could not involve the subversion of a Constitution which, being immediately derived from the people, could only be abolished by their express consent, and not by a legislature, possessing authority vested in them for its preservation....

...We were of opinion that the leading feature of every amendment ought to be the preservation of the individual States in their uncontrolled constitutional rights....

These reasons were, in our opinion, conclusive against any system of consolidated government....

We were not present at the completion of the new Constitution; but before we left the Convention, its principles were so well established as to convince us that no alteration was to be expected, to conform it to our ideas of expediency and safety. A persuasion, that our further attendance would be fruitless and unavailing, rendered us less solicitous to return.

We have thus explained our motives for opposing the adoption of the National Constitution, which we conceived it our duty to communicate to your excellency, to be submitted to the consideration of the honourable legislature. [25]

Such views, of course, were the results of leaving the Federal Convention prior to the triumph of the Federal Republicans within that body. Contrary to what Mr. Yates and Mr. Lansing stated in their letter to Governor Clinton, there were very fundamental alterations made in the evolving Constitution after they retired from the Convention. As noted author John C. Miller observed, the new Constitution, during the first half of the Convention, was *radically different* from the final version that was eventually adopted by the delegates:

At this time, the form of government under discussion was radically different from that which was finally adopted: it still incorporated a negative on State laws and gave virtually unlimited powers to the National Government. Undoubtedly the small States were right: the plan as it then stood would have been rejected incontinently by the people and the Convention's work would have gone for naught. [26]

New York's secession from the Federal Convention undoubtedly had a significant impact on the delegates who remained. The first blow to total harmony in the Federal Union had resulted when Rhode Island refused to commission delegates to the Philadelphia Convention. The second blow had

---

[25] Jonathan Elliot (ed.), *Elliot's Debates*, Second Edition, Volume I, Published under the Sanction of Congress, Washington, 1836, pp. 480-482.
[26] John C. Miller, *Op. cit.*, p. 177.

resulted from New Hampshire's severe tardiness in sending her delegates to the Convention. The deputies from the Granite State would not arrive until the latter part of July! But the most serious breach in State unity was occasioned by the secession of New York.

Although not then a populous and wealthy member of the Union, it was clear to all that the Empire State had a bright future and was destined to attain the status of great power and wealth. It would be difficult to form a more perfect Union without New York. Another concern that was undoubtedly shared by the remaining delegates in the Convention was that the departure of New York might be followed by the withdrawal of a number of other States. Unless the nationalist conspiracy was defeated, there might soon be a virtual stampede of frightened delegates heading towards the door!

Nationalist Hypocrisy

During his first speech on July 5, 1787, Gouverneur Morris had proclaimed himself to be the *Representative of America* and a *Representative of the Entire Human Race*, detached from all local interests. He had also ridiculed the other delegates for representing the authorities who commissioned them, accusing them of *trucking* and *bargaining* for their own States. Later in the same day, however, he delivered a second speech, wherein he urged the Convention to adopt a policy that would prevent all the *new* States which would be admitted into the Union in the future from ever having a greater number of votes in the federal legislature than the thirteen original States.

Recording the words of the delegate who styled himself the Representative of America, James Madison noted that, "He looked forward also to that range of New States which wd. soon be formed in the west. He thought the rule of representation ought to be so fixed as to secure the Atlantic States a prevalence in the national councils." After noting that the new States would have different interests than the original States, Mr. Morris stated that, "Provision ought therefore to be made to prevent the maritime States from being hereafter outvoted by them." "He thought this might be easily done," wrote Mr. Madison, "by irrevocably fixing the number of representatives which the Atlantic States should respectively have, and the number which each new State will have." [27]

Although this opinion was shared by a few other extreme nationalists, the Convention's new Orator of Nationalism was quickly discovering that he was becoming a minority of one. Speaking on behalf of the Grand Commit-

---

[27] Max Farrand (ed.), *Op. cit.*, Volume I, pp. 533-534.

tee, George Mason of Virginia stated that "the case of new States was not unnoticed in the committee; but it was thought and he was himself decidedly of
opinion that if they made a part of the Union, they ought to be subject to no
unfavorable discriminations." He finished his remarks by adding that, "Obvious considerations required it." [28]

On July 6th, Nathaniel Gorham of Massachusetts indicated the great
lengths the nationalists were willing to go to destroy the States, when he
stated that he "hoped to see all the States made small by proper divisions."
The more powerful the central government, he noted, the more swiftly the
States could be carved up into nationally regimented "divisions." He was even
willing to destroy his own State in the process, although it then enjoyed the
status of being one of the most populous in the Union. Elbridge Gerry, also
from Massachusetts, was alarmed by such an idea, stating that he "did not
think with his colleague that the large States ought to be cut up." "Ambitious
men," he added, "will be apt to solicit needless divisions, till the States be reduced to the size of counties." [29]

The gist of the debates on the report of the Grand Committee may be
ascertained from the following passages taken from James Madison's notes:

> **Benjamin Franklin**, on July 6th: "[He] observed that this question
> [to consider State equality in the Senate] could not be properly put *by itself,*
> the committee having reported several propositions as *mutual conditions* of
> each other. He could not vote for it if *separately* taken, but should vote for
> *the whole together.*" [Emphasis added] [30]
>
> **Gouverneur Morris**, on July 6th: "As to the alarm sounded, of an
> *aristocracy,* his creed was that *there never was, nor ever will be a civilized so-
> ciety without an Aristocracy.*" [Emphasis added] [31]
>
> **Elbridge Gerry**, on July 7th: "This [proposition for State equality
> in the Senate] is the critical question. He had rather agree to it than have
> no accomodation." [32]
>
> **Roger Sherman**, on July 7th: "Supposed that it was the wish of
> every one that some genl. govt. should be established. An equal vote in the
> 2d. branch would, he thought, be most likely to give it the necessary
> vigor." [33]
>
> **James Wilson**, on July 7th: "[He] was not deficient in a conciliat-
> ing temper, but firmness was sometimes a duty of higher obligation. Con-
> ciliation was also misapplied in this instance." [34]

---

[28] *Ibid.*, Volume I, p. 534.
[29] *Ibid.*, Volume I, p. 540-541.
[30] *Ibid.*, Volume I, p. 543.
[31] *Ibid.*, Volume I, p. 545.
[32] *Ibid.*, Volume I, p. 550.
[33] *Ibid.*, Volume I, p. 550.
[34] *Ibid.*, Volume I, p. 550.

Elbridge Gerry, on July 7th: "[He] thought it would be proper to proceed *to enumerate & define the powers to be vested in the genl. govt.* before a question on the report should be taken as to the rule of representation in the 2d. branch." [Emphasis added] [35]

James Madison, on July 7th: "[He] observed that it wd. be *impossible to say what powers could be safely & properly vested in the govt.* before it was known, in what manner the States were to be represented in it. He was apprehensive that if a just representation were not the basis of the govt. it would happen, as it did when the Articles of Confederation were depending, that every effectual prerogative would be withdrawn or withheld, and the new govt. wd. be rendered as impotent and as short lived as the old." [Emphasis added] [36]

William Paterson, on July 7th: "[T]he small States would never be able to defend themselves without an equality of votes in the 2d. branch. There was no other ground of accommodation. His resolution was fixt. He would meet the large States on that ground and no other." [37]

Gouverneur Morris, on July 7th: "He was agst. the report because it maintained the improper constitution of the 2d. branch. *It made it another Congress, a mere whisp of straw.*....Among the many provisions which had been urged, *he had seen none for supporting the dignity and splendor of the American Empire.* It had been one of the greatest misfortunes that the great objects of the nation had been sacrificed constantly to local views; in like manner as the general interests of States had been sacrificed to those of the counties. What is to be the check in the Senate? None; unless it be to keep the majority of the people from injuring particular States. But *particular States ought to be injured for the sake of a majority of the people*, in case their conduct should deserve it....Ought they to be protected....They were originally nothing more than *colonial corporations*. On the Declaration of Independence, a governnt. was to be formed....We must have an efficient govt. and if there be an efficiency in the local govts. the former is impossible....Do gentlemen wish this to be ye case here. Good God, Sir, is it possible they can so delude themselves. What if all the *Charters & Constitutions* of the States were thrown into the fire, and all their demagogues into the ocean. What would it be to the happiness of America. And will not this be the case here if we pursue the train in wch. the business lies. *We shall establish an Aulic Council without an Emperor to execute its decrees.*" [Emphasis added] [38]

Rufus King, on July 9th: "[He] had always expected that as *the Southern States are the richest*, they would not league themselves with the *Northn.* unless some respect were paid to their superior wealth. If the latter expect those preferential distinctions in Commerce & other advantages which they will derive from the connection they must not expect to receive them without allowing some advantage in return. Eleven out of 13 of the

---

[35] *Ibid.*, Volume I, p. 551.
[36] *Ibid.*, Volume I, p. 551.
[37] *Ibid.*, Volume I, p. 551.
[38] *Ibid.*, Volume I, pp. 551-553.

States had agreed to consider Slaves in the apportionment of taxation; and *taxation and representation ought to go together.*" [Emphasis added] [39]

Rufus King, on July 10th: "The *Eastern* people will...be very desirous of uniting with their *Southern* brethren but did not think it prudent to rely so far on that disposition as to subject them to any gross inequality. *He was fully convinced that the question concerning a difference of interests did not lie where it had hitherto been discussed, between the great & small States; but between the Southern & Eastern.* For this reason he had been ready to yield something in the proportion of representatives *for the security of the Southern.* No principle would justify the giving them a majority. *They were brought as near an equality as was possible. He was not averse to giving them a still greater security, but did not see how it could be done.*" [Emphasis added] [40]

Charles Cotesworth Pinckney, on July 10th: "[He]...dwelt on *the superior wealth of the Southern States*, and insisted on its having its due weight in the government." [Emphasis added] [41]

Gouverneur Morris, on July 10th: "He dwelt much on the danger of throwing such a preponderancy into the *Western* Scale, suggesting that in time the *Western* people wd. outnumber the *Atlantic States. He wished therefore to put it in the power of the latter to keep a majority of votes in their own hands.*" [Emphasis added] [42]

George Mason, on July 11th: "Strong objections had been drawn from the danger to the *Atlantic interests* from new *Western States.* Ought we to sacrifice what we know to be right in itself, lest it should prove favorable to States which are not yet in existence. If the *Western States* are to be admitted into the Union as they arise, they must, he wd. repeat, *be treated as equals*, and subjected to no degrading discriminations. They will have the same pride & other passions which we have, and will either not unite with or *will speedily revolt from the Union*, if they are not in all respects placed on an *equal footing* with their brethren. It has been said they will be poor, and unable to make equal contributions to the general Treasury. *He did not know but that in time they would be both more numerous & more wealthy than their Atlantic brethren.*" [Emphasis added] [43]

Edmund Randolph, on July 11th: "*Congs. have pledged the public faith to New States, that they shall be admitted on equal terms. They never would nor ought to accede on any other.*" [Emphasis added] [44]

Gouverneur Morris, on July 11th: "The remarks of Mr Mason relative to the *Western Country* had not changed his opinion on that head. Among other objections it must be apparent they would not be able to furnish men equally *enlightened*, to share in the administration of our common interests. *The busy haunts of men not the remote wilderness, was the proper School of Political Talents.* If the *Western* people get the power into

---

[39] *Ibid.*, Volume I, p. 562.
[40] *Ibid.*, Volume I, p. 566.
[41] *Ibid.*, Volume I, p. 567.
[42] *Ibid.*, Volume I, p. 571.
[43] *Ibid.*, Volume I, pp. 578-579.
[44] *Ibid.*, Volume I, p. 580.

their hands they will ruin the *Atlantic interests. The back members [i.e., representatives from rural America] are always more averse to the best measures*....Another objection with him agst admitting the *blacks* into the census, was that *the people of Pena. would revolt at the idea of being put on a footing with slaves.* They would reject any plan that was to have such an effect." [45]

James Madison, on July 11th: "[He] was not a little surprised to hear this implicit confidence urged by a member who on all occasions, had inculcated so strongly, the political depravity of men, and *the necessity of checking one vice and interest by opposing to them another vice & interest*....But his reasoning was not only inconsistent with his former reasoning, but with itself....*The truth was that all men having power ought to be distrusted to a certain degree*....With regard to the *Western States*, he was clear & firm in opinion that *no unfavorable distinctions were admissible either in point of justice or policy*." [Emphasis added] [46]

George Mason, on July 11th: "As soon as the *Southern & Western* population should predominate, *which must happen in a few years*, the power wd be in the hands of the minority, and would never be yielded to the majority, unless provided for by the Constitution." [Emphasis added] [47]

Gouverneur Morris, on July 11th: "[He] was compelled to declare himself reduced to the dilemma of doing *injustice* to the *Southern States* or to human nature, and *he must therefore do it to the former*." [Emphasis added] [48]

William R. Davie, on July 12th: "[He] said it was high time to speak out. He saw that it was meant by some gentlemen to deprive the *Southern States* of any share of representation for their blacks. He was sure that N. Carola. would never confederate on any terms that did not rate them at least as 3/5. If the *Eastern States* meant therefore to exclude them altogether the business was at an end." [Emphasis added] [49]

Pierce Butler, on July 13th: "*The security the Southn. States want is that their Negroes may not be taken from them* which some gentlemen within or without doors, have a very good mind to do....*The people & strength of America are evidently bearing Southwardly & S. westwdly.*" [Emphasis added] [50]

Luther Martin, on July 14th: "[He] called for the question on *the whole report*, including the parts relating to the origination of money bills, and the equality of votes in the 2d. branch." [Emphasis added] [51]

Elbridge Gerry, on July 14th: "[He] wished before the question should be put, that the attention of the house might be turned to *the dangers apprehended from Western States*. He was for admitting *them* on liberal

---

[45] *Ibid.*, Volume I, p. 583.
[46] *Ibid.*, Volume I, p. 584.
[47] *Ibid.*, Volume I, p. 586.
[48] *Ibid.*, Volume I, p. 588.
[49] *Ibid.*, Volume I, p. 593.
[50] *Ibid.*, Volume I, p. 605.
[51] *Ibid.*, Volume II, p. 2.

terms, but not for putting *ourselves* into their hands. *They will if they acquire power like all men, abuse it.* They will oppress commerce, and drain our wealth into the *Western Country*. To guard agst. these consequences, he thought it necessary *to limit the number of new States to be admitted into the Union*, in such a manner, that they should *never be able to outnumber the Atlantic States*. He accordingly moved 'that in order to secure the liberties of the States already *confederated*, the number of Representatives in the 1st. branch of the States which shall hereafter be established, shall never *exceed in number*, the Representatives from such of the States as shall *accede* to this *Confederation*.'" [Emphasis added] [52]

Rufus King, on July 14th: "[He] seconded the motion." [53]

Roger Sherman, on July 14th: "[He] thought there was no probability that the number of future States would exceed that of the Existing States. If the event should ever happen, it was too remote to be taken into consideration at this time. Besides *we are providing for our posterity, for our children & our grand children, who would be as likely to be citizens of new Western States, as of the old States. On this consideration alone, we ought to make no such discrimination as was proposed by the motion.*" [Emphasis added] [54]

Luther Martin, on July 14th: "He was for letting a separation take place if they [*i.e.,* the large States] desired it. *He had rather there should be two Confederacies, than one founded on any other principle than an equality of votes in the 2d branch at least.*" [Emphasis added] [55]

Jonathan Dayton, on July 14th: "The smaller States can never give up their equality. For himself he would in no event yield that security for their rights." [56]

Roger Sherman, on July 14th: "[He] urged the equality of votes not so much as a security for the small States; as for the State govts. which could not be preserved unless they were represented & had *a negative in the genl. government.*" [Emphasis added] [57]

Rufus King, on July 14th: "He considered the proposed government as substantially and formally, *a General and National Government over the people of America.* There never will be a case in which it will act as a *Federal Government* on the States and not on the individual Citizens....*He preferred the doing of nothing, to an allowance of an equal vote to all the States.* It would be better he thought to submit to a little more *confusion & convulsion*, than to submit to such an evil." [Emphasis added] [58]

Caleb Strong, on July 14th: "The Convention had been much divided in opinion....He thought the small States had made a *considerable concession* in the article of money bills, and that they might naturally expect

[52] *Ibid.,* Volume II, pp. 2-3.
[53] *Ibid.,* Volume II, p. 3.
[54] *Ibid.,* Volume II, p. 3.
[55] *Ibid.,* Volume II, p. 4.
[56] *Ibid.,* Volume II, p. 5.
[57] *Ibid.,* Volume II, p. 5.
[58] *Ibid.,* Volume II, pp. 6-7.

some *concessions on the other side*. From this view of the matter he was compelled to give his vote for the report taken all together." [Emphasis added][59]

James Madison, on July 14th: "[He] expressed his apprehensions that if the proper foundation of governmt was destroyed, by substituting an equality in place of a proportional representation, *no proper superstructure would be raised*....He reminded them of the consequences of laying the existing Confederation on improper principles....He called for a single instance in which the genl. govt. was not to operate on the people individually." [Emphasis added][60]

James Wilson, on July 14th: "That the States ought to be preserved he admitted. But does it follow that an equality of votes is necessary for the purpose?...He was anxious for uniting all the States under one governt. He knew there were some respectable men who preferred three Confederacies, united by offensive & defensive alliances."[61]

Oliver Ellsworth, on July 14th: "[He] asked two questions one of Mr. Wilson, whether he had ever seen a good measure fail in Congs. for want of a majority of States in its favor? He had himself never known such an instance: the other of Mr. Madison whether a negative lodged with *a majority of the States* even the smallest, could be *more dangerous* than the qualified negative proposed to be lodged in *a single Executive Magistrate*, who must be taken from *some one State?*" [Emphasis added][62]

It is evident from these passages that the Convention unanimously agreed that there was a wide range of *different* – even *conflicting* – interests among the various States of the Federal Union. Even the most outspoken nationalists did not hesitate to vociferously defend the interests of their own States when those interests were at stake. And as is apparent, Gouverneur Morris himself, the self-styled Representative of the Entire American Continent, did not hesitate to *truck* and *bargain* when the interests of the monied aristocracy he represented were at stake. Nor were the debates confined to the divergent interests of the existing thirteen States. A number of delegates went so far as to contrast the special interests of their own States with those of States that did not yet exist!

The debates on the report of the Grand Committee serve to amply highlight the true nature of the Federal Constitution of 1787 – from the question of proportional versus equal representation in the Congress to the matter of counting Negro slaves for purposes of taxation and representation. The Constitution, it is plain to discern, embodies nothing more than a *bundle of compromises* or *set of agreements* among sovereign States having unique and often conflicting interests. In other words, *the result of the Convention was a*

---

[59] *Ibid.*, Volume II, p. 8.
[60] *Ibid.*, Volume II, pp. 8-9.
[61] *Ibid.*, Volume II, p. 10-11.
[62] *Ibid.*, Volume II, p. 11.

compact between the States – a Federal Constitution providing for a Federal Government.

During the heated debates between the Northern and Southern States, even Gouverneur Morris acknowledged this truth. Although he had previously ridiculed the concept of a government founded on a *compact between sovereign States*, claiming that a government founded on *compact* was no government at all, he changed his tune dramatically on July 12th and repeatedly stressed that he was desirous of forming a *compact* with the *Southern States.*

As James Madison recorded in his notes:

> Mr. Govr. Morris. It has been said that it is high time to speak out. As one member, he would *candidly* do so. He came here to form a *compact* for the good of America. He was ready to do so with all the States: He hoped & believed that all would enter into such a *Compact.* If they would not he was ready to join with any States that would. But as the *Compact* was to be *voluntary*, it is vain for the Eastern States to insist on what the Southn States will never agree to. It is equally vain for the latter to require what the other States can never admit. [Emphasis added] [63]

Considering the *source* of these words – a man who was undeniably the most extreme nationalist to attend the Convention, with the possible exception of Alexander Hamilton – this candid admission that the Federal Constitution of 1787 would constitute *a voluntary compact among the sovereign States* is all the more remarkable. It was a shame that such honest candor was more the exception than the rule with the leading nationalists in the Philadelphia Convention.

The Decisive Federalist Victory

By Monday, July 16, 1787, the marathon debate on the great question of representation in the Federal Government had come to an end. It was now time to *vote* on the crucial issue that had for so long divided the Convention. On this issue, both the nationalists and the Federal Republicans had staked the fate of their opposing systems of government. The small States and the large States, like the Northern States and the Southern States, could resolve their differences within a federal system by compromise and concession. But between the nationalists and the federalists, as all the delegates realized, no compromise was possible. Either a *Federal Government* founded on supreme and sovereign States must be erected, or a supreme and sovereign *National*

---

[63] *Ibid.*, Volume I, p. 593.

Government would be erected on the ruins of those States. The outcome of this great battle of principle would, it was widely understood, determine the future course of the Convention regarding *all other questions* related to the nature of the Government of the United States, *including its scope of authority and the powers delegated to it.*

Although the Federal Republicans had *gained* additional support from some hesitant delegates in the Convention – most notably Caleb Strong and Elbridge Gerry of Massachusetts – they had also *lost* the valuable vote of New York, following the withdrawal of Robert Yates and John Lansing. Also, the delegates from the small State of New Hampshire had not yet arrived, thus depriving the Federal Republicans of the vote of that State. The vote would thus be guaranteed to be a close one, and the nationalists, as it would appear from their stunned reaction to the vote, apparently were confident that they would once again defeat the defenders of the Federal Republic.

As soon as the house convened on July 16th, the question of agreeing to the *whole* report of the Grand Committee – *including the provision for an equality of suffrage in the Senate* – was brought forward. Connecticut, New Jersey, Delaware, Maryland, and South Carolina all voted *for* the adopting the report. Two of the large States – Virginia and Pennsylvania – voted *against* the Connecticut Compromise. Also voting *against* the compromise measure were the States of North Carolina and Georgia. The four delegates from Massachusetts were evenly divided on the question. While Nathaniel Gorham and Rufus King voted according to their nationalist prejudices, Elbridge Gerry and Caleb Strong sided with the Federal Republicans.

The vote on the great issue of principles that had for so long divided the Grand Convention thus stood at *five* States for the Connecticut Compromise, *four* States against it, and *one* State divided. *The compromise measure had passed!* Despite the fact that they had been denied the assistance of New York and New Hampshire, the Federal Republicans had managed to deliver the decisive death blow to the nationalist conspiracy.

As John Dickinson could thereafter say with a smile of satisfaction, "Let it be remembered that the Senate is to be created by the sovereignties of the several States." [64] Clearly no supreme National Government could ever be built on that kind of foundation – only a Federal Government could be founded on the sovereignties of the several States. *Federalism had triumphed over nationalism!*

As soon as the vote had been taken, the Federal Convention began the process of considering the *powers* to be delegated to the Federal Government.

---

[64] Warren L. McFerran, "States' Rights: Foundation of the Federal Republic," *The New American*, June 6, 1988, quoted on p. 27.

First came the resolution, "That the natl. legislature ought to possess the leg-islative rights vested in Congs. by the Confederation." [65] No objections were raised against this proposal to vest in the new Federal Government the same powers that had been vested in the old Federal Government under the Arti-cles of Confederation, and it therefore passed easily.

Attention was then directed at the next proposed resolution, which de-clared that, "And moreover to legislate in all cases to which the separate States are incompetent; or in which the harmony of the U.S. may be interrupted by the exercise of individual legislation." This proposed sweeping power was immediately challenged by the Federal Republicans. Pierce Butler called "for some explanation of the extent of this power; particularly of the word *incom-petent*. The vagueness of the terms rendered it impossible for any precise judgment to be formed." [66]

Nathaniel Gorham responded that, "The vagueness of the terms consti-tutes the propriety of them. We are now establishing general principles, to be extended hereafter into details which will be precise & explicit." But the Fed-eral Republicans did not find the "vagueness" of the delegated powers in this resolution to be at all proper. John Rutledge "urged the objection started by Mr. Butler and moved that the clause should be committed to the end that a specification of the powers comprised in the general terms, might be re-ported." [67]

The motion for commitment was then put for a vote, and on this issue the States were evenly divided. *Five* voted for the commitment, and *five* voted against it. After this vote was made, Governor Randolph of Virginia arose to address the Convention, and his words undoubtedly shocked many of the delegates. Within this remarkable speech, Edmund Randolph made what amounted to a *concession* or *acknowledgement of defeat* to the victorious Fed-eral Republicans. He acknowledged that the *powers* proposed to be delegated to the Government of the United States within the Virginia Plan had been based on the *assumption* that a *supreme National Government* would be consti-tuted. With the rejection of such a government, he stated, the nationalists now found themselves *extremely embarrassed*. He implored the Convention to *suspend* the proceedings to allow the nationalists time to regroup and devise a new strategy.

Mr. Randolph's concession speech was recorded in James Madison's notes, and we here quote it in its entirety:

The vote of this morning (involving an equality of suffrage in 2d.

---

[65] *Ibid.*, Volume II, pp. 16-17.
[66] *Ibid.*, Volume II, p. 17.
[67] *Ibid.*, Volume II, p. 17.

branch) had *embarrassed* the business *extremely*. *All the powers given in the report* from the Come. of the Whole [*i.e.*, the revised Virginia Plan], were *founded on the supposition* that a proportional representation was to prevail in *both* branches of the legislature – When he came here this morning his purpose was to have offered some propositions that might if possible have united a great majority of votes, and particularly might provide agst. the danger suspected on the part of the smaller States, by *enumerating* the cases in which it might lie, and allowing an equality of votes in such cases. But finding from the preceding vote that they persist in demanding an equal vote in all cases, that *they have succeeded in obtaining it*, and that *N. York if present would probably be on the same side*, he could not but think we were *unprepared* to discuss this subject further. It will probably be *in vain* to come to any final decision with a bare majority on either side. For these reasons he wished the Convention might *adjourn*, that the larger States might consider the steps proper to be taken in the present *solemn crisis of the business*, and that the small States might also deliberate on the means of conciliation. [Emphasis added] [68]

The nationalists did indeed face a "solemn crisis," for they now found themselves "unprepared" to pursue their conspiracy against the States any farther. Would the Federal Republicans take sympathy on them and consent to the bizarre request for a recess? William Paterson immediately arose to give a brilliant response to Mr. Randolph's plea for an emergency adjournment. His words were recorded as follows by Mr. Madison:

> Mr. Patterson, thought with Mr. R. that *it was high time for the Convention to adjourn* that *the rule of secrecy ought to be rescinded*, and that *our constituents should be consulted*. No conciliation could be admissible on the part of the smaller States on any other ground than that of an equality of votes in the 2d. branch. If Mr Randolph would reduce to form his motion for *an adjournment sine die, he would second it with all his heart*. [Emphasis added] [69]

William Paterson's words were undoubtedly intended to terrify, or at least further embarrass, the die-hard nationalists in the Federal Convention. Lifting the obnoxious veil of secrecy and consulting with the peoples they were supposed to represent, the delegate from New Jersey knew, were not proposals that would be welcomed by those who preferred concealment and special interests.

The reaction produced by Mr. Paterson's remarks were recorded as follows by James Madison:

---

[68] *Ibid.*, Volume II, pp. 17-18.
[69] *Ibid.*, Volume II, p. 18.

Genl. Pinckney wished to know of Mr. R. whether he meant an adjournment sine die, or only an adjournment for the day. If the former was meant, it differed much from his idea. He could not think of going to S. Carolina, and returning again to this place. Besides it was chimerical to suppose that the States if consulted would ever accord separately, and beforehand.

Mr. Randolph, had never entertained an idea of an adjournment sine die; & was sorry that his meaning had been so readily & strangely misinterpreted. He had in view merely an adjournment till tomorrow in order that some conciliatory experiment might if possible be devised, and that in case the smaller States should continue to hold back, the larger might then take such measures, he would not say what, as might be necessary.

Mr. Patterson seconded the adjournment till tomorrow, as an opportunity seemed to be wished by the larger States to deliberate further on conciliatory expedients.

On the question for adjourning till tomorrow, the States were equally divided.

Mas. no. Cont. no. N.J. ay. Pa. ay. Del. no. Md. ay. Va. ay. N.C. ay. S.C. no. Geo. no. So it was lost. [Ayes – 5; noes – 5.] [70]

If the nationalists had been embarrassed by their defeat at the start of the day, their embarrassment was compounded by this vote on the adjournment motion. The Convention had refused to grant their request for an adjournment! From Mr. Madison's notes on the proceedings that followed this embarrassing vote, it is readily apparent that William Paterson's words had a remarkable effect on the delegates:

Mr. Broome thought it his duty to declare his opinion agst. an adjournment sine die, as had been urged by Mr. Patterson. Such a measure he thought would be fatal. Something must be done by the Convention tho' it should be by a bare majority.

Mr. Gerry observed that Masts. was opposed to an adjournment, because they saw no new ground of compromise. But as it seemed to be the opinion of so many States that a trial shd be made, the State would now concur in the adjournmt.

Mr. Rutlidge could see no need of an adjournt. because he could see no chance of a compromise. The little States were fixt. All that the large States then had to do, was to decide whether they would yield or not. For his part he conceived that altho' we could not do what we thought best, in itself, we ought to do something. Had we not better keep the govt. up a little longer, hoping that another Convention will supply our omissions, than abandon every thing to hazard. Our constituents will be very little satisfied with us if we take the latter course.

Mr. Randolph & Mr. King renewed the motion to adjourn till to-

---

[70] *Ibid.*, Volume II, pp. 18-19.

morrow.

On the question Mas. ay. Cont. no. N.J. ay. Pa. ay. Del. no. Md. ay. Va. ay. N.C. ay. S.C. ay. Geo. divd. [Ayes – 7; noes – 2; divided – 1.] Adjourned. [71]

The crisis now confronting the nationalists resulted in an unusual meeting the next day — on July 17th — *prior* to the start of regular business by the house. The great issue confronting them was how to resurrect their defeated supreme National Government. The atmosphere was understandably gloomy, and many of the war-weary nationalists seemed despondent and resigned to defeat.

James Madison attended the emergency meeting and took these notes:

> On the morning following before the hour of the Convention a number of the members from the larger States, by common agreement met for the purpose of consulting on the proper steps to be taken in consequence of the vote in favor of an equal representation in the 2d. branch, and the apparent inflexibility of the smaller States on that point – Several members from the latter States also attended. *The time was wasted in vague conversation on the subject, without any specific proposition or agreement. It appeared indeed that the opinions of the members who disliked the equality of votes differed so much as to the importance of that point, and as to the policy of risking a failure of any general act of the Convention by inflexibly opposing it.* Several of them supposing that no good governnt could or would be built on that foundation, and that as a division of the Convention into two opinions was unavoidable it would be better that the side comprising the principal States, and a majority of the people of America, should propose a [separate] scheme of govt. to the States, than that a scheme should be proposed on the other side, would have concurred in a firm opposition to the smaller States, and in a separate recommendation, if eventually necessary. *Others seemed inclined to yield to the smaller States,* and to concur in such an Act however imperfect & exceptionable, as might be agreed on by the Convention as a body, tho' decided by a bare majority of States and by a minority of the people of the U. States. It is probable that the result of this consultation satisfied the smaller States that they had nothing to apprehend from a Union of the larger, in any plan whatever agst. the equality of votes in the 2d. branch. [Emphasis added] [72]

Thus, the nationalist coalition had been completely shattered. The former unity which had characterized the coalition had now given way to confusion, chaos, and bickering. Following the successful conclusion of the small-large State controversy, those desiring the creation of a supreme Na-

---

[71] *Ibid.*, Volume II, p. 19.
[72] *Ibid.*, Volume II, pp. 19-20.

tional Government could no longer take refuge behind the greed of the larger States for an unequal share of power in the Federal Union. But this did not stop the most extreme nationalist radical then present in the Convention from making one last attempt to rally partisans to the lost cause. As soon as the Convention resumed business following the nationalist emergency meeting, Gouverneur Morris made a desperate plea on behalf of nationalism.

As Mr. Madison noted:

> Mr. Governr. Morris *moved to reconsider the whole resolution agreed to yesterday* concerning the constitution of the 2 branches of the legislature. *His object was to bring the house to a consideration in the abstract of the powers necessary to be vested in the general government.* It had been said, *Let us know how the govt. is to be modelled, and then we can determine what powers can be properly given to it.* He thought the most eligible course was, *first to determine on the necessary powers, and then so to modify the governt. as that it might be justly & properly enabled to administer them.* He *feared* if we proceded to a consideration of the *powers*, whilst *the vote of yesterday* including an equality of the States in the 2d. branch, remained in force, *a reference to it, either mental or expressed, would mix itself with the merits of every question concerning the powers. – This motion was not seconded.* (It was probably approved by *several* members, who either *despaired of success*, or were *apprehensive* that the attempt would *inflame the jealousies of the smaller States*.)[Emphasis added] [73]

As a very unhappy Gouverneur Morris realized, the *type of government* adopted by the Convention would naturally determine the nature and extent of its *powers*. The rejection of a National Government, he correctly foresaw, would inevitably result in a rejection of national powers. Or, stated differently, the reaffirmation of a Federal Government would only result in a government vested with limited, enumerated, and clearly defined *federal powers*!

Mr. Morris's candid acknowledgement of this basic truth indicates that the delegates fully comprehended the consequences of their decision to reject a National Government. And the fact that he could not find another nationalist in the Convention willing to second his motion indicates that the nationalists fully realized that they had been decisively beaten. Gouverneur Morris was certainly correct in observing that a *new mentality* had now taken hold of the house. The Federal Republicans were now in control of the Constitutional Convention, and they would maintain that control to the very end.

On July 17, 1787, in a personal letter to Euphemia Paterson, William Paterson expressed his general satisfaction with the new turn of events in the Convention:

---

[73] *Ibid.*, Volume II, p. 25.

The business is difficult and unavoidably takes up much time, but I think we shall eventually agree upon and adopt a system that will give strength and harmony to the Union and render us a great and happy people. This is the wish of every good, and the interest of every wise man. [74]

Five days later, on July 22nd, Hugh Williamson wrote a private letter to James Iredell, wherein he referred to the evolving Constitution as a plan for amending the Articles of Confederation, an admission all the more remarkable considering his pro-nationalist sentiments:

After much labor, the Convention have nearly *agreed on the principles and outlines of a system* which we hope *may fairly be called an amendment of the Federal Government.* This system we expect will in three or four days be referred to small committee to be properly dressed; and if we like it when clothed and equipped, we shall submit it to Congress; and advise them to recommend it to *the hospitable reception of the States.* [Emphasis added] [75]

And by August 1, 1787, Pierce Butler could write to Weedon Butler in London on the purpose of the Grand Convention, stating that, "No doubt you have heard of the purpose of the meeting — to form a stronger Constitution on strictly Federal Principles." [76] And that is indeed precisely what the Convention, under the control of the champions of States' Rights, proceeded to do — *to form a stronger Constitution on strictly Federal Principles!*

Demolishing the Twin Pillars of Nationalism

The day after their great victory within the Constitutional Convention, the Federal Republicans quickly attacked and destroyed the two great pillars on which the proposed National Government was to have been built — the obnoxious *national veto* over State laws and the equally obnoxious *supremacy* of the Government of the United States. And with the destruction of these twin pillars of nationalism, the supreme National Government was well on its way to becoming a tame Federal Government.

During the course of the earlier debates within the Philadelphia Convention, James Madison had spoken fondly of the proposed national veto on State laws, referring to it as the *cornerstone* of a National Government. This

---

[74] James H. Hutson (ed.), *Supplement to Max Farrand's The Records of the Federal Convention of 1787,* Yale University Press, New Haven, 1987, p. 172.
[75] *1787: The Day-to-Day Story of the Constitutional Convention,* Exeter Books, New York, 1987, quoted on pp. 93-94.
[76] *Ibid.,* quoted on p. 108.

frightening power, as it stood on July 17th, was proposed in the following words: "To negative all laws passed by the several States contravening in the opinion of the nat: legislature the articles of Union, or any treaties subsisting under the authority of ye Union." [77]

In his notes for this date, Mr. Madison relates how this key pillar of nationalism was rejected by the Convention:

> Mr. Govr. Morris *opposed* this power *as likely to be terrible to the States, and not necessary, if sufficient legislative authority should be given to the genl. government.*
>
> Mr. Sherman thought it *unnecessary,* as the *Courts of the States* would not consider as valid any law contravening the Authority of the Union, and which the legislature would wish to be negatived.
>
> Mr. L. Martin considered the power as *improper & inadmissable.* Shall all the laws of the States be sent up to the genl. legislature before they shall be permitted to operate?
>
> Mr. Madison, considered the negative on the laws of the States as *essential to the efficacy & security of the genl. govt.* The necessity of a general govt. proceeds from the propensity of the States to pursue their particular interests in opposition to the general interest. This propensity will continue to disturb the system, unless effectually controuled. *Nothing short of a negative on their laws will controul it....Confidence can not be put in the State Tribunals as guardians of the National authority and interests....*A power of negativing the improper laws of the States is at once the most mild & certain means of preserving the harmony of the system. *Its utility is sufficiently displayed in the British System.* Nothing could maintain the harmony & subordination of the various parts of *the Empire,* but the prerogative by which the Crown, stifles in the birth every Act of every part tending to discord or encroachment. It is true the prerogative is sometimes misapplied thro's ignorance or a partiality to one particular part of ye. Empire: but we have not the same reason to fear such misapplication in our system. As to the sending all laws up to the natl. legisl: that might be rendered unnecessary by some emanation of the power into the States, so far at least, as to give *a temporary effect to laws of immediate necessity.*
>
> Mr. Govr. Morris was *more & more opposed to the negative. The proposal of it would disgust all the States. A law that ought to be negatived will be set aside in the Judiciary department. And if that security should fail; may be repealed by a nationl. law.*
>
> Mr. Sherman. *Such a power involves a wrong principle,* to wit, that a law of a State contrary to the articles of the Union, would if not negatived, be valid & operative.
>
> Mr. Pinkney urged the *necessity* of the Negative.
>
> On the question for agreeing to the power of negativing laws of States &c....*it passed in the negative.*

---

[77] *Ibid.*, Volume II, p. 27.

Mas. ay. Ct. no. N.J. no. Pa. no. Del. no. Md. no. Va. ay. N.C. ay.
S.C. no. Geo. no. [Ayes – 3; noes – 7.]

Mr. *Luther Martin* moved the following resolution "that the legislative acts of the U.S. made *by virtue & in pursuance of the Articles of Union*,
and all treaties made & ratified *under the authority of the U.S.* shall be the
*supreme law of the respective States, as far as those acts or treaties shall relate to
the said States, or their citizens and inhabitants* – & that *the Judiciaries of the
several States shall be bound thereby in their decisions, any thing in the respective laws of the individual States to the contrary notwithstanding*" which was
agreed to nem: con:. [Emphasis added] [78]

Several highly significant concepts raised in these debates merit our
careful attention. It is evident from the speech given by James Madison that
he was still thinking in terms of *Empire*. "Its utility is sufficiently displayed in
the British System," he pleaded. But if he was still thinking in terms of an
imperial government, the majority of the other delegates were thinking more
in terms of a *Republic* for the United States.

It is also of great significance to note that *two different reasons* were expounded for *opposing* the vesting of a negative power over State laws in the
hands of the Federal Government. One of these reasons was expressed by
Gouverneur Morris. Although he had once strongly favored such a dangerous
power, he was now "more & more opposed to the negative." Such a power,
openly delegated to the Federal Government, was "likely to be terrible to the
States." "The proposal of it would disgust all the States," he correctly observed.

Mr. Morris therefore urged, in essence, that the power be *secretly* vested
in the Federal Government. If the mention of such a power appeared in the
new Constitution, *all* of the States would be *disgusted* and would reject the
compact. The politically correct approach, he therefore concluded, was to
conceal the power behind the concept of the supremacy of the Government of
the United States. "A law that ought to be negatived will be set aside in the
Judiciary department," he stated. "And if that security should fail; may be repealed by a *nationl. law*." He could thus conclude that a clear delegation of
the negative was "not necessary, if sufficient *legislative authority* should be
given to the genl. government." The States would not be *disgusted* by this
form of the negative, it would appear from his reasoning, because they would
not know that this *secret power* had been delegated by them to their common
agent until it was too late. But would a *deception* be binding on the States?
Would a *fraud* be enforceable on the American people?

The Federal Republicans also opposed the negative over State laws, but

---

[78] *Ibid.*, Volume II, pp. 27-29.

for a very different reason. Such a dangerous power was, as Luther Martin stated, simply "improper & inadmissable" in a federal system of government, for it would transfer sovereignty from the States to the Federal Government, thereby converting it into a supreme National Government. "Such a power involves a wrong principle," Roger Sherman observed. The *wrong principle* was derived from the rejected national system. The *correct principle* on which a federal system is based is that the States are supreme and that the Federal Constitution is whatever they say it is. Not only would the States create the Constitution, but they alone would be empowered to alter its provisions by the amendment process. Therefore, he concluded, the correct principle of federalism required that the final or ultimate responsibility for maintaining and upholding the supreme law of the land lay with the State governments, or more specifically, said he, "the Courts of the States."

To an ardent nationalist like James Madison, such a concept was anathema. "Nothing short of a negative on their laws will" suffice, he insisted. "Confidence can not be put in the *State Tribunals* as guardians of the national authority and interests." The *overwhelming majority* of the delegates, it would appear, did not agree with Mr. Madison. When the vote was taken on the question of the proposed negative over State laws, only three States were found to still favor it. This victory over the *cornerstone of nationalism* was immediately followed by a victory over the *supremacy* claimed for the Federal Government, thereby destroying Mr. Morris's scheme of relying on that alleged supremacy as a concealed vehicle for resurrecting the defeated negative over States laws.

When Luther Martin, the champion of States' Rights and the great Orator of Federalism, introduced what has since been termed the *Supremacy Clause* to the Convention, all the delegates understood its true meaning and import. This clause was not introduced to support the concept of supremacy in the Federal Government, *but to defeat it*. The origin of the Supremacy Clause adopted by the Convention can, in fact, be traced back directly to the New Jersey Plan introduced earlier by the Federal Republicans, and still further back to Supremacy Clause of the Articles of Confederation.

Article XIII of the first Federal Constitution of the United States begins with these words: "Every State shall abide by the determinations of the United States in Congress assembled, on all questions which by this Confederation are submitted to them." It then adds: "And the Articles of this Confederation shall be inviolably observed by every State...." Under the Articles of Confederation, this was the *Supremacy Clause*, and the *enforcement of its observance* was left with the respective States.

The objective of the national veto over the States proposed by the nationalists had been to reverse this concept by vesting supremacy in the general government itself and thereby empowering the central regime with authority to enforce an observance of its supremacy. Such a concept was not only subversive of federalism, but also tended to undermine republican principles by making the *government* itself, and not the Constitution, supreme. In other words, it would have resulted in the *rule of men*, not in the *rule of law*.

Luther Martin's objective, in reintroducing the federal concept of supremacy, was to preserve the supremacy of the law and the sovereignty of the States. By the principles of his resolution – *which the Convention adopted without opposition* – the Constitution itself, all federal laws *made in pursuance of the Constitution*, and all treaties *made and ratified under the constitutional authority of the United States*, would be the "supreme law of the respective States," or the *supreme law of the land*. Unconstitutional laws and treaties involving matters not within the authority vested in the Federal Government would, of course, not be part of this "supreme law of the respective States." They would simply be unconstitutional, illegal, non-binding, null, and void.

By adopting Mr. Martin's resolution, the Convention agreed to retain the form of *enforcement* that existed under the Articles of Confederation. In opposition to that mode of enforcement, James Madison had railed that the State governments could not be trusted to enforce an observance of the federal compact in their respective jurisdictions. The Convention, however, thought otherwise. With the adoption of the Supremacy Clause, the delegates directly killed the idea that any branch of the Federal Government could enforce the supremacy of the Constitution. That important power was reserved exclusively to the State governments.

Preserving the Federal Republic

Following the great victory of federalism in mid-July, the Federal Convention proceeded to draft a Federal Constitution designed to remodel the Federal Government, to improve the Federal Union, and to preserve the Federal Republic. The once-formidable nationalist coalition no longer existed in the Grand Convention, and on many issues the nationalists found themselves quarreling with and opposing one another. Their lack of unity helped to ensure that the course set by the Federal Republicans was not altered. Although some of the more extreme nationalists continued to introduce measures compatible only with a supreme National Government, their efforts were easily defeated.

The desperation the nationalists must have felt is evident from their ill-fated attempt on July 17th to convert the President of the United States into a King serving a life-tenure of office. Even James Madison, obviously frantic at the loss of his pet project – the national veto over State laws – was willing to consider abandoning his republican principles to join the monarchists. The debates over this ill-fated but interesting maneuver were as follows:

> **James McClurg:** "[He] moved to strike out 7 years, and insert *'during good behavior.'* By striking out the words declaring him [*i.e.*, the President of the United States] not re-eligible, he was put into a situation that would keep him dependent for ever on the legislature; and he conceived the independence of the executive to be equally essential with that of the Judiciary Department." [Emphasis added] [79]
>
> **Gouverneur Morris:** "[He] 2ded. the motion. *He expressed great pleasure in hearing it. This was the way to get a good government.* His fear that so valuable an ingredient would not be attained had led him to take the part he had done. *He was indifferent how the executive should be chosen, provided he held his place by this tenure.*" [Emphasis added] [80]
>
> **Jacob Broom:** "[He] highly approved the motion. It obviated all his difficulties." [81]
>
> **Roger Sherman:** "*[He] considered such a tenure as by no means safe or admissible.* As the executive magistrate is now re-eligible, he will be on good behavior as far as will be necessary. If he behaves well he will be continued; if otherwise, *displaced on a succeeding election.*" [Emphasis added] [82]
>
> **James Madison:** "He conceived it to be absolutely necessary to a well constituted Republic that the [Executive and Legislative Branches]...shd. be kept distinct & independent of each other. Whether the plan proposed by the motion was a proper one was another question....*On the other hand, respect for the mover entitled his proposition to a fair hearing & discussion*, until a less objectionable expedient should be applied...." [Emphasis added] [83]
>
> **George Mason:** "This motion was made some time ago, & *negatived by a very large majority.* He trusted that it wd. be again negatived....*He considered an executive during good behavior as a softer name only for an executive for life. And that the next would be an easy step to hereditary Monarchy.* If the motion should finally succeed, he might himself live to see such a *Revolution.* If he did not it was probable his children or grandchildren would. *He trusted there were few men in that house who wished for it.* No State he was sure had so far revolted from republican principles as to have the least bias in its favor." [Emphasis added] [84]
>
> **James Madison:** "[He] was not apprehensive of being thought to favor any step towards *monarchy.* The real object with him was to prevent

---

[79] *Ibid.*, Volume II, p. 33.
[80] *Ibid.*, Volume II, p. 33.
[81] *Ibid.*, Volume II, p. 33.
[82] *Ibid.*, Volume II, pp. 33-34.
[83] *Ibid.*, Volume I, p. 35.
[84] *Ibid.*, Volume II, p. 35.

its introduction." [Emphasis added] [85]

Gouverneur Morris: "*[He] was as little a friend to monarchy as any gentleman.* He concurred in the opinion that the way to keep out monarchial govt. was to establish such a repub. govt. as wd. make the people happy and *prevent a desire [means?] of change.*" [Emphasis added] [86]

James McClurg: "[He] was not so much afraid of *the shadow of monarchy* as to be unwilling to approach it; nor so wedded to republican govt. as not to be sensible of the tyrannies that had been & may be exercised under that form. It was an essential object with him to make the executive independent of the legislature; and the only mode left for effecting it, after the vote destroying his ineligibility a second time, was to appoint him during good behavior." [Emphasis added] [87]

The Convention, of course, was too wise to be misled by this maneuver, and Dr. McClurg's motion was rejected by a vote of six to four. On July 19th, Gouverneur Morris again attempted to persuade the Convention to convert the President into a King; and on the following day he urged that the President should not be subject to impeachment. But he found little support from the other delegates for either of his radical recommendations. The President of the United States, the Convention finally resolved, should serve a term of *four years*, not a term for life like a monarch. Furthermore, resolved the Convention, the President should be subject to impeachment.

In accordance with the principles of republican government, the Philadelphia Convention determined that all three branches of the Federal Government should be constituted as separate divisions of that government. And in accordance with a federal system of government, the delegates resolved that the proper title of the federal legislature should be *Congress*. That term, of course, was borrowed from the Articles of Confederation and from the New Jersey Plan, and its inclusion into the Constitution of 1787 served to illustrate the intentions of the Federal Convention.

The Convention also decided that the House of Representatives, rather than represent the *people of America*, as desired by the nationalists, would instead represent the *peoples of the States*. There would be no national districts and no national elections. Instead, there would be only States and federal elections to select the officers of the Federal Government. Members of the House of Representatives would thus be regarded in the Constitution as the *representations from the several States*. Inasmuch as all elections of federal officers were to be *federal elections* – not national elections – the Federal Convention wisely decided that the right of establishing *voting qualifications* should

---

[85] *Ibid.*, Volume II, p. 35.
[86] *Ibid.*, Volume II, pp. 35-36.
[87] *Ibid.*, Volume II, p. 36.

be reserved exclusively to the States.

Although representation and voting in the lower branch of the federal legislature would be based on the respective population sizes of the several States, a notable exception to this rule was made by the Grand Convention. In the event that the election of the President of the United States should result in tie, the House of Representatives would settled the matter, *wherein each State would be allowed only one vote!*

While the House of Representatives would represent the *peoples of the States*, the Senate would represent the *governments of the States*. This federal feature, the Convention decided, was necessary to make the State governments a part of the common or general government. Furthermore, federalist arguments in favor of this type of representation stressed the need for the State governments to have a *State veto* or *negative* within the Federal Government! And not only would each State have an equal representation and vote in the United States Senate, but the Federal Republicans added a proviso to the Constitution that specifically prohibited any future amendment from ever altering the nature of this permanent monument to the sovereign equality of the States.

The method of selecting the President was widely debated by the delegates. Some were of the opinion that the Chief Executive should be selected by a direct popular vote by the peoples of the States, while others thought that the President should be appointed by the federal legislature. Still others supported the idea that the President should be appointed by the State governments. The Convention finally decided that the election should be *indirectly* by the peoples of the States by means of an *Electoral College* system. Under this *federal voting system*, the States were each awarded a number of votes that equaled the sum of their representatives in the two branches of Congress. The election of the President, in other words, would clearly be a *federal election*, not a national act.

There were two primary considerations that induced the Convention to provide for an indirect election of the Chief Executive of the United States. The most widely known and recognized reason for this provision was the fear of rampant democracy entertained by some of the delegates. The other reason is less well understood, although it was urged by at least two of the delegates. These delegates supported an indirect election of the President because they feared the harmful influences of rampant aristocracy. It is evident from their expressed concerns that they believed that an elitist or aristocratic organization might deceive the people and thereby subvert the electoral process. Nor did those delegates harboring such fears attempt to conceal the specific organization that gave rise to such concerns.

On July 25, 1787, Elbridge Gerry of Massachusetts said before the

Convention:

> A popular election in this case is radically vicious. The ignorance of the people would put it in the power of some one set of men dispersed through the Union & acting in concert to delude them into any appointment. He observed that such a Society of men existed in the Order of the Cincinnati. They were respectable, united, and influencial. They will in fact elect the Chief Magistrate in every instance, if the election be referred to the people. – His respect for the characters composing this Society could not blind him to the danger & impropriety of throwing such a power into their hands. [88]

Inasmuch as nearly half of the delegates listening to his speech were members of the aristocratic Society of the Cincinnati, the significance and importance of Mr. Gerry's speech should not be minimized. And in the event that the message was not made clear enough by Mr. Gerry, on the next day George Mason of Virginia again raised the same concern:

> A popular election in any form, as Mr. Gerry has observed, would throw the appointment into the hands of the Cincinnati, a Society for the members of which he had a great respect; but which he never wished to have a preponderating influence in the govt. [89]

Rejection of a National Police State

The more extreme radicals in the nationalist camp urged the Convention to vest Police Powers in the Federal Government, and to vest total military control within that government. But the great mass of the Convention, now under the leadership of the Federal Republicans, were too wise to be misled by their councils, and both provisions were rejected. There would be no constitutionally established National Police State in America. Nor would the compact authorize the Government of the United States to govern an American Empire as a Military Dictatorship.

The debates on these topics merit the careful attention of the student of constitutional government, and the following selected passages from James Madison's notes on July 17th serve to illustrate the nature of the arguments raised by both schools of thought:

Roger Sherman: "[He] observed that it would be difficult to draw

---

[88] *Ibid.*, Volume II, p. 114.
[89] *Ibid.*, Volume II, p. 119.

the line between the powers of the genl. legislatures, and those to be left with the States; that *he did not like the definition contained in the resolution*, and proposed in place of the words 'of individual legislation' line 4 inclusive, to insert 'to make laws binding on the people of the United States in all cases which may concern the common interests of the Union; *but not to interfere with the government of the individual States in any matters of internal police which respect the govt. of such States only, and wherein the general welfare of the U. States is not concerned.'*" [Emphasis added] [90]

James Wilson: "[He] seconded the amendment as better expressing the general principle." [91]

Gouverneur Morris: "[He] opposed it. The *internal police*, as it would be called & understood by the States *ought to be infringed in many cases*, as in the case of paper money & *other tricks* by which citizens of other States may be affected." [Emphasis added] [92]

Gunning Bedford, Jr.: "[He] moved that the 2d. member of Resolution 6. be so altered as to read 'and moreover to legislate *in all cases for the general interests of the Union*, and *also in those to which the States are separately incompetent,*...or in which the harmony of the U. States may be interrupted by the exercise of individual legislation." [Emphasis added] [93]

Gouverneur Morris: "[He] 2ds. the motion." [94]

Edmund Randolph: "*This is a formidable idea indeed. It involves the power of violating all the laws and Constitutions of the States, and of intermeddling with their police.*" [Emphasis added] [95]

The same general subject was again brought up for discussion on July 18th, when the Convention considered the Sixteenth Resolution, "That a Republican Constitution & its existing laws ought to be guaranteid to each State by the U. States." [96]

Mr. Madison recorded the following notes during the debates:

Gouverneur Morris: "[He] thought the resol: very objectionable. *He should be very unwilling that such laws as exist in R. Island should be guaranteid.*" [Emphasis added] [97]

James Wilson: "The object is merely to secure the States agst. *dangerous commotions, insurrections and rebellions.*" [Emphasis added] [98]

George Mason: "If the genl govt. should have no right to suppress *rebellions* agst. particular States, it will be in a bad situation indeed. As Re-

---

[90] *Ibid.*, Volume II, p. 25.
[91] *Ibid.*, Volume II, p. 26.
[92] *Ibid.*, Volume II, p. 26.
[93] *Ibid.*, Volume II, p. 26.
[94] *Ibid.*, Volume II, p. 26.
[95] *Ibid.*, Volume II, p. 26.
[96] *Ibid.*, Volume II, p. 47.
[97] *Ibid.*, Volume II, p. 47.
[98] *Ibid.*, Volume II, p. 47.

bellions agst. itself originate in & agst. individual States, *it must remain a passive spectator of its own subversion.*" [Emphasis added] [99]

Edmund Randolph: "*The resoln. has 2. objects. 1. To secure Republican Government. 2. To suppress domestic commotions.* He urged the necessity of both these provisions." [Emphasis added] [100]

James Madison: "[He] moved to substitute 'that the constitutional authority of the States shall be guaranteed to them respectively agst. domestic as well as foreign violence.'" [101]

James McClurg: "[He] seconded the motion." [102]

William Houstoun: "*[He] was afraid of perpetuating the existing Constitutions of the States.* That of Georgia was a very bad one, and he hoped would be revised & amended. *It may also be difficult for the genl. govt. to decide between contending parties each of which claim the sanction of the Constitution.*" [Emphasis added] [103]

Luther Martin: "*[He] was for leaving the States to suppress Rebellions themselves.*" [Emphasis added] [104]

Nathaniel Gorham: "[He] thought it strange that a Rebellion should be known to exist in the *Empire*, and the genl. govt. shd. be restrained from interposing to subdue it....With regard to different parties in a State; as long as they confine their disputes to words they will be harmless to the genl. govt. & to each other. If they appeal to the sword it will then be necessary for the genl. govt., however difficult it may be to decide on the merits of their contest, to interpose & put an end to it." [Emphasis added] [105]

Daniel Carroll: "Some such provision is essential. *Every State ought to wish for it.* It has been doubted whether it is a *casus federis* at present. And *no room ought to be left for such a doubt hereafter.*" [Emphasis added] [106]

Edmund Randolph: "[He] moved to add as amendt. to the motion; 'and that no State be at liberty to form any other than a republican govt.'" [107]

James Madison: "[He] seconded the motion." [108]

John Rutledge: "[He] thought it unnecessary to insert any guarantee. No doubt could be entertained but that Congs. had the authority if they had the means to co-operate with any State in subduing a rebellion. It was & would be involved in the nature of the thing." [109]

James Wilson: "[He] moved as a better expression of the idea, 'that a republican form of governmt. shall be guaranteed to each State & that

---

[99] *Ibid.*, Volume II, p. 47.
[100] *Ibid.*, Volume II, p. 47.
[101] *Ibid.*, Volume II, pp. 47-48.
[102] *Ibid.*, Volume II, p. 48.
[103] *Ibid.*, Volume II, p. 48.
[104] *Ibid.*, Volume II, p. 48.
[105] *Ibid.*, Volume II, p. 48.
[106] *Ibid.*, Volume II, p. 48.
[107] *Ibid.*, Volume II, p. 48.
[108] *Ibid.*, Volume II, p. 48.
[109] *Ibid.*, Volume II, p. 48.

each State shall be protected agst. foreign & domestic violence." [110]

On August 17, 1787, the Convention again turned its attention to this general subject, focusing on the resolution, "To subdue a rebellion in any State, on the application of its legislature." [111]

In Mr. Madison's notes, we find the following debate on this topic:

Charles Pinckney: "*[He] moved to strike out 'on the application of its legislature.'*" [Emphasis added] [112]

Gouverneur Morris: "[He] 2ds." [113]

Luther Martin: "*[He] opposed it as giving a dangerous & unnecessary power. The consent of the State ought to precede the introduction of any extraneous force whatever.*" [Emphasis added] [114]

John F. Mercer: "[He] supported the opposition of Mr. Martin."[115]

Oliver Ellsworth: "[He] proposed to add after 'legislature' *'or executive.'*" [Emphasis added] [116]

Gouverneur Morris: "*The Executive may possibly be at the head of the Rebellion. The genl govt. should enforce obedience in all cases where it may be necessary.*" [Emphasis added] [117]

Oliver Ellsworth: "In many cases *the genl. govt. ought not to be able to interpose unless called upon.* He was willing to vary his motion so as to read, 'or without it when the legislature cannot meet.'" [Emphasis added][118]

Elbridge Gerry: "*[He] was agst. letting loose the myrmidons of the U. States on a State without its own consent. The States will be the best Judges in such cases. More blood would have been split in Massts in the late insurrection [i.e., Shays' Rebellion], if the genl. authority had intermeddled.*" [Emphasis added] [119]

John Langdon: "[He] was for striking out as moved by Mr. Pinkney. The *apprehension of the national force,* will have a salutary effect in *preventing insurrections.*" [Emphasis added] [120]

Edmund Randolph: "If the natl. legislature is to judge whether the State legislature can or cannot meet, that amendment would make the clause *as objectionable as the motion of Mr Pinkney.*" [Emphasis added] [121]

Gouverneur Morris: "*We are acting a very strange part. We first*

---

[110] *Ibid.*, Volume II, pp. 48-49.
[111] *Ibid.*, Volume II, p. 316.
[112] *Ibid.*, Volume II, p. 317.
[113] *Ibid.*, Volume II, p. 317.
[114] *Ibid.*, Volume II, p. 317.
[115] *Ibid.*, Volume II, p. 317.
[116] *Ibid.*, Volume II, p. 317.
[117] *Ibid.*, Volume II, p. 317.
[118] *Ibid.*, Volume II, p. 317.
[119] *Ibid.*, Volume II, p. 317.
[120] *Ibid.*, Volume II, p. 317.
[121] *Ibid.*, Volume II, p. 317.

form a strong man to protect us, and at the same time wish *to tie his hands behind him.* The legislature may surely be *trusted* with such a power to preserve the public tranquillity." [Emphasis added] [122]

On this crucial issue, the nationalists once again were defeated. The Federal Republicans succeeded in convincing the Convention that there was more to fear from a National Police State than there was from occasional civil unrest. As Elbridge Gerry wisely noted, if the Federal Government were to dispatch jack-booted soldiers and federal marshals to police America, *the bloodshed would be incredible.* Also, there existed the very real possibility that, if vested with such draconian powers, the Federal Government might, under the guise of crushing a "rebellion," *overthrow a State government.* In a word, the Federal Government *itself* might well become the *chief threat* to, rather than the guarantor of, republican government in the several States. One of the delegates – Gouverneur Morris – had even indicated that the power, had it been granted, would be used in this sinister fashion!

Under these considerations, the Federal Convention wisely adopted the principles espoused by the Orator of Federalism. As Luther Martin had indicated, the sovereign States should be left "to suppress rebellions themselves." If this duty were transferred to the Federal Government, he warned, it would be "dangerous" to the liberties of the citizens and destructive of the States. "The consent of the State," he therefore concluded, "ought to precede the introduction of any extraneous force whatever." Thus, the Convention included in the Constitution a provision to guarantee to each State a republican form of government and to provide military assistance to that end. *But a specific proviso was affixed to this clause, stipulating that the Federal Government could not act unless and until so invited to intervene by the State government!*

Without such an invitation, the Government of the United States would be powerless to act. And even with the invitation, it could only intervene *to assist the State government* in the enforcement of the laws of that State. By this means, and only by this means, the Convention finally resolved, could a republican form of government be truly guaranteed to each State in the Federal Union.

The effect of this measure and of the other resolutions of a similar nature adopted by the Constitutional Convention all reinforced the concept that the new Constitution was to be founded on strictly federal principles. The *Police Powers* in the United States were be reserved exclusively to the sovereign States by the new Constitution. And while a limited *Military Power* would be vested in the Government of the United States, the vast *majority* of

---

[122] *Ibid.*, Volume II, p. 317.

all *peacetime* Military Power was to remain in the respective States. Of particular significance in this regard were the State militias. The delegates wisely rejected the proposals to transfer all control over these citizen-soldiers to the Federal Government, thereby converting them into a National Guard. Although the State militias could be called into *federal* service in time of war to help defend the United States, at all other times they were to remain under the control of the State governments.

The delegates even inserted a clause into the new Constitution that recognized the *reserved war powers* left to each sovereign State. By this provision, each State could, by itself, wage a war against a hostile foreign enemy whenever that enemy attacked it and the Government of the United States refused to adequately defend the invaded State. The Convention's reasons for leaving most Military Power with the States, therefore, were two-fold: 1. To provide the States with a means of defending themselves, if and when necessary, against the Federal Government; and 2. To provide the States with a means of defending themselves, in the last resort, against a hostile foreign power.

A clue as to the great success realized by the Federal Republicans in reserving the majority of the Military Power to the sovereign States may be found in this passage from the book, *1787: The Day-to-Day Story of the Constitutional Convention*, which was published on the two-hundredth anniversary of the Federal Convention:

> One result was that in every peace time year between 1789 and 1946, the forty-eight [State] Governors collectively had command of a larger army than did the President of the United States. Thus, even had the President or a commanding general thought about seizing power, he couldn't because he didn't control even half of the nation's armed services. [123]

This fact is even more noteworthy when it is recalled that the United States *decisively won* every war it fought prior to 1946. The same cannot be said for the wars waged after that date. Reserving the majority of Military Power to the sovereign States was clearly a wise decision on the part of the Constitutional Convention, in more ways than one.

A Strictly Federal Constitution

With the defeat of nationalism in the Federal Convention, as we have

---

[123] *1787: The Day-to-Day Story of the Constitutional Convention*, *Op. cit.*, p. 140.

already observed, the Federal Republicans were able to expunge all vestiges of nationalism from the evolving compact and to thereby transform it into a strictly Federal Constitution. All powers to be delegated to the Federal Government were placed under the stern and critical eye of those interested in preserving States' Rights, and only those powers deemed absolutely necessary were approved by them. Even the concept of the *regulation of commerce* did not escape their close scrutiny.

When delegating this power to the Federal Government, the intent was to merely ensure that a system of *free enterprise* would prevail in the United States. By "regulation," the Convention did not intend for the Government of the United States to assume the power of *interferring with* or *controlling* commerce. The goal of the framers of the Constitution was to prevent the several States from erecting any trade barriers between one another. But even this limited power was sliced in half by the Federal Republicans when they insisted that the Federal Government's powers to regulate commerce should apply only to *imports*, not to exports.

Roger Sherman, for instance, informed the Convention on August 21st that, "The States will never give up all power over trade." And Elbridge Gerry stated that, unless regulation of exports were prohibited to the Federal Government, "It will enable the genl govt to oppress the States." He warned that, "It might be made use of to compel the States to comply with the will of the genl government, and to grant it any new powers which might be demanded." [124] Both Gouverneur Morris and James Wilson were bitterly opposed to this severe restriction on the power of regulating commerce. "To deny this power," said the latter, "is to take from the common govt. half the regulation of trade." [125] Despite the protests of the nationalists, however, the Convention decided to cut the power in half and to prohibit the Federal Government from regulating exports from the States.

On August 20th, the nationalists made several bold efforts to resurrect the deceased supreme National Government. On that date, Charles Pinckney introduced a number of resolutions, one of which declared that, "The U.S. shall be for ever considered as one Body corporate and politic in law, and entitled to all the rights privileges, and immunities, which to Bodies corporate do or ought to appertain." [126] In vain do we search the Constitution of the United States for any such clause as this, and there is a very good reason why such a provision cannot be found. This proposal to create a single American nation was not adopted by the Constitutional Convention.

Gouverneur Morris, together with Mr. Pinckney, then introduced a

---

[124] *Ibid.*, Volume II, p. 361-362.
[125] *Ibid.*, Volume II, p. 362.
[126] *Ibid.*, Volume II, p. 342.

comprehensive plan for the creation of an elaborate and extensive socialist bureaucracy. In addition to a *Department of Foreign Affairs*, a *Department of War*, a *Department of the Marine*, and a *Department of State*, this plan also provided for a *Council of State*, wherein the wise check provided by the separation of the three branches of government could be easily and conveniently evaded. Such a Council would serve to recommend laws to Congress and to promote education and look after the morality of the American people.

In addition, the plan introduced by Mr. Morris provided for a *Department of Domestic Affairs*, which would rule and meddle in such internal or domestic affairs as that involved with manufacturing, navigation, construction, communications, and agriculture, and which would also serve as the headquarters of the *General Police*. Furthermore, under this plan, there would be a *Department of Commerce and Finance* that would rule and meddle in the affairs of domestic trade. If a King and a House of Lords were unacceptable to the Convention, the movers of this plan apparently were convinced that a bloated socialistic bureaucracy could ultimately produce the same desired end.

The plan urged by the two nationalists was in these words:

[1.] To assist the President in conducting the public affairs there shall be a Council of State composed of the following officers – 1. The Chief Justice of the Supreme Court, who shall from time to time recommend such alterations of and additions to the laws of the U.S. as may in his opinion be necessary to the due administration of Justice, and such as may promote useful learning and inculcate sound morality throughout the Union; He shall be President of the Council in the absence of the President.

2. The Secretary of Domestic Affairs who shall be appointed by the President and hold his office during pleasure. It shall be his duty to attend to matter of general police, the State of Agriculture and manufactures, the opening of roads and navigations, and the facilitating communications thro' the U. States; and he shall from time to time recommend such measures as may tend to promote those objects.

3. The Secretary of Commerce and Finance who shall also be appointed by the President during pleasure. It shall be his duty to superintend all matters relating to the public finances, to prepare & report plans of revenue and for the regulation of expenditures, and also to recommend such things as may in his judgment promote the commercial interests of the U.S.

4. The Secretary of Foreign Affairs who shall also be appointed by the President during pleasure. It shall be his duty to correspond with all foreign ministers, prepare plans of treaties, & consider such as may be transmitted from abroad; and generally to attend to the interests of the U-S- in their connections with foreign powers.

5. The Secretary of War who shall also be appointed by the Presi-

dent during pleasure. It shall be his duty to superintend every thing relating to the War-Department, such as the raising and equipping of troops,
the care of military stores – public fortifications, arsenals & the like – also
in time of war to prepare & recommend plans of offence and defence.

6. The Secretary of the Marine who shall also be appointed during
pleasure – It shall be his duty to superintend every thing relating to the
Marine-Department, the public ships, Dock-Yards, Naval-Stores & arsenals
– also in the time of war to prepare and recommend plans of offence and
defence.

The President shall also appoint a Secretary of State to hold his office during pleasure; who shall be Secretary to the Council of State, and
also public Secretary to the President. It shall be his duty to prepare all
public despatches from the President which he shall countersign.

The President may from time to time submit any matter to the discussion of the Council of State, and he may require the written opinions of
any one or more of the members: But he shall in all cases exercise his own
judgment, and either conform to such opinions or not as he may think
proper; and every officer abovementioned shall be responsible for his opinion on the affairs relating to his particular Department.

Each of the officers abovementioned shall be liable to impeachment
& removal from office for neglect of duty malversation, or corruption. [127]

The Pennsylvania National Monarchist, it would appear, was a man
well ahead of his own time. Such a draconian, bureaucratic nightmare would
have been most welcomed by the New Dealers of the Roosevelt Era, or even
by Lyndon Johnson's Great Society policy makers. But his proposed bureaucratic government was not welcomed in the Constitutional Convention of
1787, and it very appropriately ended up in the discard pile.

On at least one occasion during the Federal Convention, some nationalists attempted to vest in the federal judiciary the power of *judicial review*, or
the authority to veto or negative a law of Congress. James Madison, on August 15, 1787, for example, proposed a type of judicial review that would
have required a newly passed federal law to be submitted to both the Chief
Executive and to the Supreme Court for their *mutual* approbation. In the
event that *one* of these branches – either the executive or the judicial – should
veto the law, Congress would be empowered to override the veto by a two-
thirds majority vote in each house. But if *both* the executive and the judiciary
should veto the law, it would require a three-fourths majority vote in each
house of Congress to override the double veto. James Wilson seconded Mr.
Madison's formal proposal for judicial review.

Opposition was immediately voiced to this new and bizarre role for the
Judicial Branch of the Federal Government. As Mr. Pinckney observed, it

---

[127] *Ibid.*, Volume II, pp. 342-344.

would entail "the interference of the Judges in the legislative business" and would "involve them in parties, and give a previous tincture to the opinions." John F. Mercer of Maryland stated that he, too, "disapproved of the Doctrine that the Judges as expositors of the Constitution should have authority to declare a law void." [128]

When Mr. Madison's proposal for judicial review was put to the vote, only three States were found to support it. *The other eight States voted it down.* After the vote, Gouverneur Morris spoke up to say that he "regretted that something like the proposed check could not be agreed to," lamenting that, "The legislature will contrive to soften down the President." In rebuttal, John Dickinson asserted that he "was strongly impressed with the remark of Mr. Mercer as to the power of the Judges to set aside the law," concluding that, "He thought no such power ought to exist." [129]

Although Gouverneur Morris continued to insist that judicial review was essential to good government, he found himself confronted by overwhelming opposition. He therefore proposed that, in lieu of judicial review, the Convention should adopt "the expedient of an absolute negative in the Executive." [130] The Federal Republicans, however, were not convinced by his arguments. "Can one man be trusted better than all the others if they all agree?" asked Roger Sherman. "This was neither wise nor safe." Stating that he "disapproved of Judges meddling in politics and parties," the Connecticut delegate concluded that, "We have gone far enough in forming the negative as it now stands." [131] The mass of the Convention agreed with Mr. Sherman, *and no power of judicial review was delegated to the federal judiciary.* The fact that such a power had been formally proposed, fully debated, and deliberately rejected by the Convention is far more conclusive that such a power does not constitutionally exist than its mere absence from the compact would have otherwise suggested.

In light of these considerations, we may state that, perhaps excepting a handful of extreme nationalist radicals, there was not a single delegate who attended the Constitutional Convention who would have been anything but stunned to know that a future Chief Justice of the Supreme Court – John Marshall – could ever haughtily proclaim that, "It is emphatically the province and duty of the Judicial Department, to say what the law is." [132] Furthermore, nearly all of the delegates would have been horrified had they but

---

[128] *Ibid.*, Volume II, p. 298.
[129] *Ibid.*, Volume II, p. 299.
[130] *Ibid.*, Volume II, p. 299.
[131] *Ibid.*, Volume II, p. 300.
[132] Otis H. Stephens, Jr. and John M. Scheb, II, *American Constitutional Law: Essays and Cases*, Harcourt Brace Jovanovich, Publishers, San Diego, 1988, quoted on insert facing p. 432.

known that another Chief Justice – Charles Evan Hughes – could royally proclaim that, "We are under a Constitution, but the Constitution is what the Judges say it is." [133] The delegates who attended the Constitutional Convention, as is evident from the numerous recorded debates, clearly thought they had constituted a Republic, not a monarchy, wherein a few Judges could arrogantly and imperially decree – in the spirit of Louis XIV – *"I am the state!"*

Nationalism's Dying Gasp

During the latter half of the Constitutional Convention, and especially toward its conclusion, many of the nationalists were unable to conceal their keen disappointment in the system of government on which the new Constitution was being built. Long after the defeat of his pet project, for instance, James Madison was openly lamenting the rejection of the veto power over State laws. And on July 20th, after the decisive victory of the federalists, Rufus King "expressed his apprehensions that an extreme caution in favor of liberty might enervate the government we were forming." [134] *And he was quite correct.* Whereas the first half of the Convention had been dominated by those who preferred power to liberty, the situation was reversed in the latter half of the Convention.

The other nationalists, also sensing that the pendulum had swung away from power to the side of liberty, shared Mr. King's gloomy attitude. Gouverneur Morris, for one, stated on August 31st that he "was ready for a postponement. He long wished for another Convention, that will have the firmness to provide a vigorous government, which we are afraid to do." [135] Although he consented to sign the new Constitution on the last day of the Convention, he did so with strong mental reservations, stating that he "had objections, but considering the present plan as the best that was to be attained, he should take it with all its faults." [136]

Alexander Hamilton was also bitterly disappointed in the new Constitution, a feeling that he expressed on a number of occasions, especially toward the end of the Convention. In Mr. Madison's notes for September 6th, for example, we find this passage:

> Mr. Hamilton said that he had been restrained from entering into

---

[133] *Ibid.*, quoted on insert facing p. 432.
[134] *Ibid.*, Volume II, p. 66.
[135] *Ibid.*, Volume II, p. 479.
[136] *Ibid.*, Volume II, p. 645.

the discussions by his dislike of the Scheme of Govt in General; but as he meant to support the plan to be recommended, as better than nothing, he wished in this place to offer a few remarks. [137]

Although Mr. Hamilton did sign the Constitution on September 17th, he expressed the strongest mental reservations heard in the Convention. "No man's ideas were more remote from the plan than his own were known to be," he informed his fellow delegates, "but is it possible to deliberate between anarchy and convulsion on one side, and the chance of good to be expected from the plan on the other." [138]

Then there was Governor Edmund Randolph of Virginia, the man who had first proposed to the Grand Convention that a *supreme National Government* should be established in the United States. It had been this delegate who had introduced the Virginia Plan to the Convention. By the end of the Convention, however, he candidly confessed that his plan had been so drastically altered that he no longer wished to claim ownership of it. Although he would later consent to lend his support to the ratification of the new Constitution, so strong was his opposition to the compact that he dramatically declined to add his signature to it at the end of the Convention!

From the records of the Convention's proceedings, it is apparent that the nationalists made one last attempt to breathe life into the deceased corpse of their supreme National Government on September 14, 1787. This maneuver entailed an attempt to incorporate into the Federal Constitution a wide range of powers that would be improper for a Federal Government to exercise. The range of proposed nationalist powers included a power to incorporate, a power over education, and a power over internal improvements such as canals. The Federal Republicans, however, objected to all of these additional powers, and *every one of the objectionable powers was summarily rejected.*

It began when Benjamin Franklin suggested that, among the powers delegated to Congress in Section 8 of Article I of the Constitution, there should be added "a power to provide for cutting canals where deemed necessary." Although James Wilson seconded the motion, Roger Sherman objected, stating that, "The expence in such cases will fall on the U-- States, and the benefit accrue to the places where the canals may be cut." [139]

James Madison proposed enlarging the grant of power so that the Federal Government would be authorized "to grant charters of incorporation where the interest of the U.S. might require & the legislative provisions of individual States may be incompetent." His motion was seconded by Edmund

---

[137] *Ibid.*, Volume II, p. 524.
[138] *Ibid.*, Volume II, pp. 645-646.
[139] *Ibid.*, Volume II, p. 615.

Randolph. When Rufus King indicated that he "thought the power unnecessary," James Wilson countered by claiming, "It is necessary to prevent *a State* from obstructing the *general* welfare." [140]

A very interesting exchange of words then took place between Rufus King, James Wilson, and George Mason, an exchange that was recorded by Mr. Madison as follows:

> Mr. King – The States will be *prejudiced* and *divided into parties* by it – In Philada. & New York, it will be referred to *the establishment of a Bank*, which has been *a subject of contention* in those cities. *In other places it will be referred to mercantile monopolies.*
>
> Mr. Wilson mentioned the importance of facilitating by canals, the communication with the Western Settlements – As to *Banks* he did not think with Mr. King that the power in that point of view would excite the prejudices & parties apprehended. *As to mercantile monopolies they are included in the power to regulate trade.*
>
> Col: Mason was for limiting the power to the single case of canals. *He was afraid of monopolies of every sort, which he did not think were by any means already implied by the Constitution as supposed by Mr. Wilson.* [Emphasis added] [141]

Faced with stiff opposition, the general power to incorporate was dropped from Mr. Madison's motion, and the Convention voted on the question of granting the power to cut canals. By a vote of eight to three, the measure failed. Yet, as the above-cited passage indicates, a sinister new development had arisen within the Convention. It is apparent from Mr. Madison's notes that some of the more dishonest nationalists had resolved to adopt a *new strategy*, to the effect that, *if the Convention refused to grant the powers desired by the nationalists, the nationalists would simply conjure them up by false interpretations of the Constitution.* This existence of this new and ominous strategy is starkly revealed in the exchange of words between James Wilson and George Mason on the nature of *regulating commerce*. This power, which was intended to ensure free enterprise in the United States, was perverted by Mr. Wilson into a power to establish, by government sanction, commercial monopolies!

Following the failure of the motion to grant the power of incorporation and to cut canals, James Madison and Charles Pinckney moved to grant to Congress a power "to establish an University, in which no preferences or distinctions should be allowed on account of religion." James Wilson seconded the motion. Gouverneur Morris, perhaps to the astonishment of many of the

---

[140] *Ibid.*, Volume II, p. 615.
[141] *Ibid.*, Volume II, p. 616.

delegates, then spoke up to state that, "It is not necessary," adding that, "The exclusive power at the Seat of Government, will reach the object." [142]

Here again, we see an expression of this new strategy of the *dishonest* wing of the nationalist camp: *delegating powers to the Federal Government would not be necessary, since all powers could be assumed by that government at pleasure!* It is of interest to note, however, that the great majority of the Convention seemed to disagree with Gouverneur Morris's diabolical mode of constitutional construction, deciding that such a power, if it were to be exercised by the Government of the United States, must be *specifically delegated* to it in the Constitution. Accordingly, the motion was put to vote. The majority of States voted *against* the idea of granting a power over education in the United States to the Federal Government, and the motion failed. And by voting on this motion, the Convention established the precedent that the Government of the United States could only exercise those powers expressly delegated to it by the Constitution.

The Plot to Subvert the Constitution

The appearance of the new nationalist strategy near the conclusion of the Convention is of great consequence, especially in light of the artfully contrived constructions that were placed on the Constitution *after* its adoption by the States. Although the *vast majority* of the delegates sincerely labored to draft a plan of government that would be based on carefully enumerated and defined powers, the notes of James Madison and those of other delegates clearly reveal that there did exist within the Convention a concerted plot among a handful of extreme nationalists to undermine and ultimately subvert the labors of the other delegates.

Those who resorted to such a tactic realized that all hope of drafting a Constitution based on a supreme National Government had been lost. If such a government were to be obtained, they realized, it could be derived only by *false interpretations* of the Federal Constitution, particularly its general phrases, such as "regulating commerce," "general welfare," and "necessary and proper." Although these clauses were all completely innocent and harmless in themselves and, in one case – the General Welfare Clause – had been copied literally from the Articles of Confederation, in the hands of these shrewd construers, the words of the evolving Constitution took on a new and sinister meaning.

We have already observed two instances of this new and sinister strat-

---

[142] *Ibid.*, Volume II, p. 616.

egy, in the form of James Wilson's ominous misinterpretation of the Commerce Clause and in the manner in which Gouverneur Morris was able to see a federal power over education in the evolving compact which no other delegate could see. In the book, *1787: The Day-to-Day Story of the Constitutional Convention*, its authors relate a most interesting encounter between James McHenry, Gouverneur Morris, Nathaniel Gorham, and Thomas Fitzsimmons on September 6th that sheds some light on the existence of this new plot:

> Either before the session began or shortly after, McHenry (MD) spoke to Morris (PA), Fitzsimmons (PA) and Gorham (MA) about *adding a power* to build piers to protect shipping in the winter. One of them, either Morris or Gorham, thought it could be done under the words "provide for the common defence and general welfare," *a thought that shocked McHenry.* [Emphasis added] [143]

It would appear from the records of the Federal Convention that James Madison, to his credit, played *no part* in the development of this new nationalist strategy, an observation that is confirmed by the far more *honest mode* of constitutional construction he advocated after the adoption of the new Constitution. Following the ratification of the instrument, when he discovered that certain scheming nationalists sought to subvert the Constitution through false constructions, he made no attempt to conceal his outrage and disgust at such treachery. It would be his honest revulsion of this new nationalist strategy, in fact, that would ultimately cause him to part company with the nationalist forces of Alexander Hamilton and to align himself with Thomas Jefferson in defense of the true principles of the Constitution.

This letter written by James Madison to Edmund Pendleton on January 21, 1792, is a typical illustration of Mr. Madison's sentiments towards the new nationalist strategy:

> If Congress can do whatever in their *discretion* can be *done by money*, and will promote the *general welfare*, the Government is no longer a limited one possessing enumerated powers, but an indefinite one subject to particular exceptions. It is to be remarked that the phrase out of which this doctrine is elaborated, is copied from the old Articles of Confederation, where it was always understood as nothing more than a general caption to the specified powers, and it is a fact that it was preferred in the new instrument for that very reason as less liable than any other to misconstruction. [144]

---

[143] *1787: The Day-to-Day Story of the Constitutional Convention, Op. cit.*, p. 172.
[144] James H. Hutson (ed.), *Op. cit.*, p. 299.

The Federal Convention itself, as is plainly evident from the many labors and votes of the delegates, emphatically and overwhelmingly rejected the idea that anything other than a *strict interpretation* of their product would constitute a fraudulent construction. The vote given by the States to the motion made by Elbridge Gerry and Charles Pinckney on September 14th serves as conclusive proof of this fact. On that date, Mr. Gerry and Mr. Pinckney moved that "the liberty of the Press should be inviolably observed." Roger Sherman objected to the motion, not because he wished to see the liberty of the press violated, but because such a clause would imply that the Federal Government could exercise assumed powers, or powers that had not been specifically delegated to it. The provision, he observed, would thus be "unnecessary," inasmuch as, "The power of Congress does not extend to the Press." [145]

After Roger Sherman had voiced his objection to the motion, the Convention, by a vote of seven to four, decided to *reject* the Gerry-Pinckney motion. The significance of this vote, as well as the argument used by Mr. Sherman to urge the measure's defeat, merit careful attention. In urging that the measure be *adopted*, both Mr. Gerry and Mr. Pinckney were acting under the assumption that, in cases of doubt, the Federal Government might be authorized to exercise powers not specifically prohibited to it by the Constitution. In urging that the measure be *rejected*, on the other hand, Roger Sherman advocated precisely the opposite mode of constitutional construction – that the Federal Government would be authorized to exercise only those powers delegated to it, and that no implied or undefined power could be assumed by that government.

The Constitutional Convention, as already indicated, adopted Mr. Sherman's recommendation and voted against the provision to guarantee the freedom of the press. *But why?* There can be only two possible explanations for the decision of the delegates to not adopt the Gerry-Pinckney resolution. Either the majority of the delegates agreed with Roger Sherman's mode of constitutional construction and thought the Federal Government could only exercise the powers specifically delegated to it, or they wished to see the freedom of the press violated. Which reason seems to be the more probable one?

If there could possibly be any doubt in this regard, then it might be noted that George Mason thought that the Convention should include in the Constitution an *entire* Bill of Rights, covering a sweeping range of rights which no government should invade. The majority of the Convention, however, disagreed with him, and *no Bill of Rights was added to the compact by the Convention*. Once again, we must ask *why?* Either the great mass of the Fed-

---

[145] *Ibid.*, Volume II, p. 617-618.

eral Convention wished to see human rights perish in America, or the majority of delegates were convinced that the rights of the people were secured by the fact that the authority of the Federal Government was restricted to only the delegated powers. Again, which reason seems more probable?

We may safely conclude, therefore, that the Constitutional Convention had firmly resolved that the proper mode of construing the compact should be one based on the concept that *all powers not delegated to the Federal Government by the Constitution are reserved exclusively to the several States*. Indeed, such a mode of interpretation represented the only one compatible with the concept of a Federal Government, which the Convention had resolutely determined to establish. To have affirmed any other mode of construction would have been inconsistent with the system of government adopted.

It may also be stated that the majority of the delegates understood that such an honest mode of constitutional interpretation was the only one consistent with *common sense*. Had the Convention intended to grant vague and undefined – and hence, unlimited – powers to the Federal Government within the general phrases of the Constitution, then nothing would have been more frivolous than an enumeration of powers. Why else would they have labored to define the powers of the new government and to debate with such exacting precision the wording of specific phrases? It was clearly their intention to create a government of carefully defined and enumerated powers. To suggest otherwise would be to insult the intelligence of those who wrote the Federal Constitution.

The development of the new nationalist plot to misconstrue the Constitution of the United States undoubtedly helps to explain why so many concerned Americans, during the Ratification Period, insisted upon the addition of the *Bill of Rights* to the new Federal Constitution – *to serve as a constitutional check or barrier against cunning and dishonest misinterpretations of the compact*. The *Tenth Amendment*, in particular, was designed to effect this purpose with its bold and unmistakable language: "The powers not delegated to the United States by the Constitution, nor prohibited by it to the States, are reserved to the States respectively, or to the people." [146]

Although such an amendment did not alter a single delegated power or make any alteration in the foundation of the system of government adopted by the Convention, it did serve notice to anyone who might be inclined to think otherwise, that the Federal Government could not lawfully take a single step beyond the boundaries established by the Constitution. In the event that it did, its acts would be null, void, and of no force.

---

[146] Alexander H. Stephens, *A Constitutional View of the Late War Between the States*, Volume I, Kraus Reprint Co., New York, (orig. pub. in 1868) 1970, p. 569.

The Committee of Style

During the course of the Grand Convention of the States, the Federal Constitution underwent several revisions to keep its phraseology, provisions, and format sufficiently updated to reflect the decisions of the delegates. On July 26th, for instance, the Constitution was sent to a Committee of Detail, chaired by John Rutledge, where Edmund Randolph wrote a revised draft of the evolving plan of government. James Wilson then put the Randolph draft into smoother phraseology. Following lengthy debates by the delegates, the instrument was eventually sent to a Committee of Style so that the Federal Constitution could be written in its completed, polished phraseology, a task that was completed by September 12th, five days before the end of the Convention.

The five members of the Committee of Style entrusted with the task of changing the *style*, but not the *meaning*, of the finished product were Judge William S. Johnson of Connecticut, James Madison of Virginia, Alexander Hamilton of New York, Rufus King of Massachusetts, and Gouverneur Morris of Pennsylvania. Although the committee was chaired by Judge Johnson, the job of actually stylizing the new compact was assumed by the delegate from Pennsylvania. Unfortunately, it is not known how so many extreme nationalists managed to obtain positions on this committee, nor is it known how Gouverneur Morris ended up being the one to actually perform the assignment delegated to the committee by the Convention.

Inasmuch as it was the National Monarchist from Pennsylvania who actually stylized the Constitution into its final verse and format, the question naturally arises, did Gouverneur Morris take advantage of the trust delegated to him by attempting to alter the meaning of parts of the Federal Constitution? His authorization, as noted previously, extended only to changing the *style*, not the *meaning*, of the various constitutional provisions approved by the Convention. But did he confine himself to that duty?

As noted by the authors of *1787: The Day-to-Day Story of the Constitutional Convention*, this is a question that historians have long asked:

> While historians have suspected that Gouverneur Morris, through careful selection and arrangement of words and punctuation marks, artfully bent the meaning of some provisions closer to his personal views (*and he later claimed as much*), this was not a Convention which could be easily tricked. [Emphasis added] [147]

It is a matter of record that Gouverneur Morris *did* make very *funda-*

---

[147] *1787: The Day-to-Day Story of the Constitutional Convention, Op. cit.*, p. 181.

mental alterations that resulted in significant changes in the *meanings* of at least two clauses in the Constitution. Fortunately, these profound changes were detected by the alert Federal Republicans, who insisted that the clauses in question be reworded to restore their original meaning and intent. One highly significant change made by Mr. Morris related to the amendment process. By the final determination of the Convention, either the Congress *or the States* would be authorized to *propose* future amendments to the compact. After this constitutional provision had been written by Gouverneur Morris, however, *the States had been mysteriously robbed of their right to propose future amendments!* Fortunately, George Mason noticed the dangerous omission and confronted Mr. Morris on the matter.

After the Convention had ended, George Mason gave an account of this interesting attempt by Gouverneur Morris to rob from the States much of their control over the supreme law of the land:

> Anecdote. The Constn as agreed at first was that amendments might be proposed either by Congr. or the legislatures a Commee was appointed to digest & redraw. Gov. Morris & King were of the Commee. One morng. Gov. M. moved an instrn for certain atlerns (not 1/2 the members yet come in) in a hurry & without understanding it was agreed to. The Commee reported so that Congr. shd have the exclusve power of proposg. amendmts. G. Mason observd it on the report & opposed it. King denied the constrn. Mason demonstrated it, & asked the Commee by what authority they had varied what had been agreed. G. Morris then impudently got up & said by authority of the Convention & produced the blind instruction beforementd. Which was unknown by 1/2 of the house & not till then understood by the other. They then restored it as it stood originally. [148]

Gouverneur Morris apparently attempted to also pervert the meaning of the *General Welfare Clause* of the Constitution, an attempt that was referred to by Albert Gallatin in a speech delivered in the House of Representatives on June 19, 1798. Note the use of the word "trick" in Mr. Gallatin's speech:

> Mr. G[allatin] said he was well informed that those words had originally been inserted in the Constitution as a limitation to the power of laying taxes. After the limitation had been agreed to, and the Constitution was completed, a member of the Convention, (he was one of the members who represented the State of Pennsylvania) being one of a Committee of revisal and arrangement, attempted to throw these words into a distinct paragraph, so as to create not a limitation, but a distinct power. The trick,

---

[148] Max Farrand (ed.), *Op. cit.*, Volume III, pp. 367-368.

however, was discovered by a member from Connecticut, now deceased,
and the words restored as they now stand. [149]

Luther Martin, who had become disgusted at the conduct of certain
nationalists and had accordingly walked out of the Convention before its conclusion, was convinced that numerous small alterations in the meaning of the
Constitution's various provisions had been made by Gouverneur Morris; and
this fact helped persuade him to oppose the adoption of the new compact
during the Ratification Period. While it may be doubted if all of Mr. Martin's
criticisms were justified, it is of interest to note that Mr. Morris himself admitted that he not only had attempted to deceive the Convention, but had
actually *succeeded* in the trickery in that portion of the Constitution providing
for the *federal judiciary*. In a letter written to Timothy Pickering on December 22, 1814, Gouverneur Morris stated that he had deliberately worded that
portion of the compact in sufficiently vague phraseology as to leave a handle
for cunning interpreters to later seize and exploit it in an effort to subvert the
remainder of the instrument.

As Mr. Morris stated in this letter:

> But, my dear Sir, what can a history of the Constitution avail to-
> wards interpreting its provisions. This must be done by comparing the
> plain import of the words, with the general tenor and object of the instru-
> ment. That instrument was written by the fingers, which write this letter.
> Having rejected redundant and equivocal terms, I believed it to be as clear
> as our language would permit; *excepting, nevertheless, a part of what relates to
> the judiciary*. On that subject, conflicting opinions had been maintained
> with so much professional astuteness, that it became necessary to select
> phrases, *which expressing my own notions would not alarm others*, nor shock
> their selflove, and to the best of my recollection, this was the only part
> which passed without cavil. [150]

It is apparent that Gouverneur Morris, by his own confession, did attempt to instill a little more *vigor* into the Federal Government than was authorized by the Federal Convention, an attempt that carries special significance in regard to the federal judiciary. This fact merely reinforces the view
that the true interpretation of the Federal Constitution is founded on *strict
constructionism* — a mode of interpretation designed to ascertain meanings of
various clauses and phrases of the compact that make each part of the Constitution conform to the general spirit and tenor of the whole document, as well
as to derive meanings that conform with the intent of those who wrote and

---

[149] *Ibid.*, Volume III, p. 379.
[150] *Ibid.*, Volume III, p. 420.

adopted the compact.

Considering the known attempts made by Mr. Morris to alter the meaning of portions of the Constitution, we might inquire as to whether this attempt was extended as well to the *Preamble*, particularly to the key words, "We, the People of the United States." Prior to submitting the Constitution to the Committee of Style, the Preamble had begun with the words, "We the People of the States of..." [151] – words which were followed by the name of each one of the thirteen then-existing States of the Union.

Some change in phraseology in the Preamble, it should be acknowledged, was clearly warranted by two primary considerations. The Convention had already resolved that the Constitution could be adopted by as few as nine States, and the possibility existed that not all of the States would consent to join the new and amended Union. Since no one could say with certainty which States would adopt the new compact, and which ones would not, it would have been improper to have listed all thirteen States in the Preamble. The second consideration mandating some type of change in the Preamble was the knowledge that new States would eventually join the Federal Union, although no one could say with certainty what the names of these new States would be.

These two considerations combined to dictate that a change should be made in the *wording* of the Preamble. But why were the words, *We, the People of the United States*, selected to replace the words, *We the People of the States*? If the intention was to provide another ambiguous expression on which the nationalists could later hang an inference allegedly "proving" the existence of a non-existent consolidated American nation, then the words so chosen served their purpose, for that is precisely the interpretation later claimed by the nationalists for the Preamble. Yet, as Mr. Morris was not authorized or empowered to change the *meaning* of a single syllable in the Constitution, we may conclude that the true intent and meaning of the Preamble remained unaltered by the change in phraseology. *We, the People of the United States* can mean nothing more than *We, the Peoples of the States in the Federal Union*.

Providing for the Constitution's Ratification

Although the Federal Convention had resolved to present the new Constitution as an "amendment" to the Articles of Confederation, it was clearly understood that the new compact would in fact *replace* the Articles with an *amended federal system* of government. But to have followed the

---

[151] *1787: The Day-to-Day Story of the Constitutional Convention, Op. cit.*, quoted on p. 181.

amendment procedure specified in the Articles, it was widely feared, would doom all hope of adoption of the new instrument. The amendment process stipulated by those Articles required the unanimous approval of all the States before such an amendment could be declared ratified, and experience had already demonstrated the impracticality of that procedure for constitutional reformation. The Convention therefore made two bold moves to remedy the situation.

The first significant alteration made by the Convention was in the amendment process itself. To amend the new Federal Constitution, after it had been adopted, would require the approval of only three-fourths of the States. Although this new amendment process would still require more than a simple majority of the States to approve an amendment, the process was clearly less stringent than that which had existed under the old Articles of Union. The second significant alteration made by the Convention, although temporary in nature, was deemed more urgent and more requisite to the very adoption of the compact. By this alteration, only nine of the thirteen States would be required to duly ratify the new Constitution and give it force. Furthermore, the Federal Convention stipulated that the approval should come directly from the *peoples of the States*, by means of special State Ratification Conventions called for the purpose of considering the proposed Constitution, and not from the State governments.

Regarding this novel method of ratifying the Constitution of 1787, Jefferson Davis made these comments:

> In this emergency the Convention took the responsibility of transcending the limits of their instructions, and recommending a procedure which was in direct contravention of the letter of the Articles of Confederation. This was the introduction of a provision into the new Constitution, that the ratification of nine States should be sufficient for its establishment among themselves. In order to validate this provision, it was necessary to render it to authority higher than that of Congress and the State legislatures – that is, to the people of the States, assembled, by their representatives, in convention. Hence, it was provided, by the seventh and last article of the new Constitution, that "the ratification of the *Conventions* of nine States" should suffice for its establishment "between the States so ratifying the same."
>
> There was another reason, of a more general and perhaps more controlling character, for this reference to conventions for ratification, even if entire unanimity of the State legislatures could have been expected. Under the American theory of republican government, conventions of the people, duly elected and accredited as such, are invested with the plenary power inherent in the people of an organized and independent community, assembled in mass. In other words, they represent and exercise what is properly the *sovereignty* of the people. State legislatures, with restricted powers,

do not possess or represent sovereignty. Still less does the Congress of a Union or Confederacy of States, which is by two degrees removed from the seat of sovereignty. We sometimes read or hear of "delegated sovereignty," "divided sovereignty," with other loose expressions of the same sort; but no such thing as a division or delegation of sovereignty is possible.

In order, therefore, to supersede the restraining article above cited and to give the highest validity of the compact for the delegation of important powers and functions of government to a common agent, an authority above that of the State legislatures was necessary. Mr. Madison, in the "Federalist," says: "It has been heretofore noted among the defects of the Confederation, that in many of the States it had received no higher sanction than a mere legislative ratification." This objection would of course have applied with greater force to the proposed Constitution, which provided for additional grants of power from the States, and the conferring of larger and more varied powers upon a general government, which was to act upon individuals instead of States, if the question of its confirmation had been submitted merely to the several State legislatures. Hence the obvious propriety of referring it to the respective *people* of the States in their sovereign capacity, as provided in the final article of the Constitution. [152]

The mode of ratification adopted by the Convention, although novel, was consistent with the system of government adopted – both were decidedly *federal* in nature. Two facts regarding the mode of ratification clearly prove that the act of ratification would be a federal, and not a national, act. The first indisputable fact is that the new Constitution was submitted to the peoples of the thirteen States, and not to any single American nation of people. The minimum requirement for ratification – 9 out of 13, or approximately 70% – applied to the States, not to the whole people of America. The possibility thus existed that the Constitution could be duly ratified even though opposed by a substantial majority of Americans!

Let us pursue this consideration further. In 1790, the combined population of the original thirteen States was approximately 3.5 million people, with each State having the population indicated in the table shown above. Assuming that these figures were also valid for the period from 1787 to 1789, the validity of our previously stated supposition can be easily demonstrated. For sake of argument, let us assume that the peoples of the four most populous States – Virginia, Massachusetts, Pennsylvania, and North Carolina – were unanimous in their opposition to the proposed Constitution. Let us also assume that the Constitution was supported by a majority of only one or two persons in the other nine States, while opposed by the remainder of the peoples in those States. Under this scenario, 2,893,164 – or more than 77% of

---

[152] Jefferson Davis, *The Rise and Fall of the Confederate Government*, Volume 1, Thomas Yoseloff, Cranbury, (orig. pub. in 1881) 1958, pp. 98-100.

the 3,734,916 Americans – would be opposed to the Constitution, and only 841,752 people – or less than 23% of Americans – would be in favor of it. Yet, under this scenario, *the Constitution would still be ratified by the requisite number of States*, because the ratification process was based on federal, not national, principles.

State	Population	State	Population
Virginia	747,610	South Carolina	249,073
Massachusetts	475,199	New Jersey	184,139
Pennsylvania	433,611	New Hampshire	141,899
North Carolina	395,005	Georgia	82,548
New York	340,241	Rhode Island	69,112
Maryland	319,728	Delaware	59,096
Connecticut	237,655		

The second highly significant factor proving that the ratification process was designed to be a federal and not a national act, was that the new Constitution, if adopted, would go into effect *between only those States who ratified it*. Because each State was recognized by the Federal Constitution as a sovereign body politic, *no State could be bound without its own consent*. Such a concept of ratification, it hardly needs to be mentioned, would have been wholly illogical and irrational had the Constitution recognized the American people as a single, consolidated nation.

The Final Adjournment

The Constitutional Convention, which had been in continuous session since May 25th, ended on September 17th with a final meeting of the delegates. The summer of 1787 had indeed been long and hot. From the introduction of a proposal for a supreme National Government in its earliest days, through the great battle between the federalists and the nationalists, to the ultimate triumph of the defenders of the Federal Republic, the Convention had witnessed a battle royal between men of opposing principles, all conducted under a tight veil of secrecy.

Although the Federal Republicans had emerged victorious from the struggle, the great battle of principle had not been without casualties. Several delegates and one sovereign State had been frightened away by the heat of battle. Of the 55 delegates who had attended the Philadelphia Convention, only 42 remained to attend the last session, and three of them – Edmund

Randolph, George Mason, and Elbridge Gerry – *refused* to add their names to the finished product. But the battle had been won – the Federal Republic had been saved.

After Benjamin Franklin read an appeal, written by Gouverneur Morris, urging all the delegates to sign the new compact, several short speeches on the subject of signing the Constitution were made by a few delegates. Then Rufus King raised the subject of the Convention's records, suggesting that the official *Journal* should be either destroyed or given to George Washington so that it could be safely hidden from public scrutiny. James Wilson spoke up to say that he, at one time, had favored the first fate for the official minutes, but had since decided in preference of the second mode of concealment.

In accordance with the wishes of these two nationalists, the Convention voted *ten* to *one* – with Maryland being the lone dissenter – to instruct George Washington to hide the *Journal* until after the government under the new Constitution should be formed. The *Journal*, as turned out, would remain hidden from the general public for more than three decades, and it was not until its publication in 1819 that the curtain of secrecy surrounding the Convention was finally lifted. The generation of Americans who adopted the Constitution of 1787, as a consequence, never knew the true story of the Constitutional Convention that wrote it.

Once the matter of the *Journal* had been decided, the delegates proceeded to sign the Constitution, and the Convention then adjourned *sine die*. According to legend, when Benjamin Franklin walked out the door, a woman asked him what kind of government the Convention had finally adopted. "*A Republic*," he is said to have responded, "*if you can keep it.*" And thus the Federal Convention ended on this paradoxical note hinting of future promise and of future danger.

Chapter Eleven
The Ratification Period

Having successfully completed its business of drafting a new Federal Constitution for the United States of America, the Constitutional Convention unanimously adopted two resolutions during its last session that specified how the new compact should be ratified by the States and how the new government under that instrument should be implemented upon the successful adoption of the Constitution. These two published resolutions, which were signed by George Washington and William Jackson, were in the following words:

In Convention Monday September 17th 1787.
Present
The States of
New Hampshire, Massachusetts, Connecticut, Mr. Hamilton from New York, New Jersey, Pennsylvania, Delaware, Maryland, Virginia, North Carolina, South Carolina and Georgia. Resolved,

That the preceeding Constitution be laid before the United States in Congress assembled, and that it is the Opinion of this Convention, that it should afterwards be submitted to a Convention of Delegates, chosen in each State by the People thereof, under the Recommendation of its Legislature, for their Assent and Ratification; and that each Convention assenting to, and ratifying the Same, should give Notice thereof to the United States in Congress assembled.

Resolved, That it is the Opinion of this Convention, that as soon as the Conventions of nine States shall have ratified this Constitution, the United States in Congress assembled should fix a Day on which Electors should be appointed by the States which shall have ratified the same, and a Day on which the Electors should assemble to vote for the President, and the Time and Place for commencing Proceedings under this Constitution. That after such Publication the Electors should be appointed, and the Senators and Representatives elected: That the Electors should meet on the Day fixed for the Election of the President, and should transmit their Votes certified, signed, sealed and directed, as the Constitution requires, to the Secretary of the United States in Congress assembled, that the Senators and Representatives should convene at the Time and Place assigned; that the Senators should appoint a President of the Senate, for the sole Purpose of receiving, opening and counting the Votes for President; and, that after he shall be chosen, the Congress, together with the President, should, without Delay, proceed to execute this Constitution.

By the Unanimous Order of the Convention. [1]

Also on September 17th, the Philadelphia Convention approved a letter to the President of the existing Congress under the Articles of Confederation to *explain* the new plan of government. Inasmuch as the Convention had resolved to hide from the public the record of its proceedings, this letter signed by George Washington represented the only official explanation for the reason and purpose of a new Federal Constitution. Within this letter, the Convention began by observing that it was desire of all Americans to fully vest in a general government sufficient powers to adequately conduct the foreign affairs of the United States. But such powers, the Convention stated, should not be entrusted to a single body of men. "Hence results the necessity of a different organization." [2]

Referring to the agency to be established by the new compact as "the Federal Government of these States," the letter indicated that it would be necessary for the States to yield some of the powers associated with their sovereignty to a new general government. "Individuals entering into society," the Convention said, resorting to an analogy, "must give up a share of liberty to preserve the rest." [3] The import of this analogy was intended to dispel any apprehensions among the States. Like individuals forming a society, the States, upon entering the new Confederation, would be required yield some of their powers to a common agent in order to better safeguard their sovereignty.

The letter then alluded to the vast differences among the States "as to their situation, extent, habits, and particular interests" and noted that the Constitution "is the result of a spirit of amity, and of that mutual deference and concession which the peculiarity of our political situation rendered indispensable." [4] The Constitution of 1787, in other words, was acknowledged as being an agreement, compact, or bundle of compromises between sovereign States. The letter then concluded with the observation that, although the new Constitution might not be approved and ratified by every State, the Convention sincerely hoped that the compact would promote the interests of the United States.

On September 28, 1787, the Congress initiated the Ratification Period by enacting the following resolution:

Resolved Unanimously that the said Report with the resolutions
and letter accompanying the same be transmitted to the several legislatures

---

[1] Charles Callan Tansill (ed.), *The Making of the American Republic: The Great Documents, 1774-1789*, Arlington House, New Rochelle, pp. 1005-1006.
[2] *Ibid.*, p. 1003.
[3] *Ibid.*, p. 1003.
[4] *Ibid.*, pp. 1003-1004.

in Order to be submitted to a Convention of Delegates chosen in each State by the people thereof in conformity to the resolves of the Convention made and provided in that case. [5]

On the same date, a copy of the new Constitution, together with an official letter from the Secretary of Congress, was sent to the head of state of each of the thirteen American States. The accompanying letter stated:

> In obedience to an unanimous resolution of the United States in Congress Assembled, a copy of which is annexed, I have the honor to transmit to Your Excellency, the Report of the Convention lately Assembled in Philadelphia, together with the resolutions and letter accompanying the same; And have to request that Your Excellency will be pleased to lay the same before the Legislature, in order that it may be submitted to a Convention of Delegates chosen in Your State by the people of the State in conformity to the resolves of the Convention, made & provided in that case. [6]

The Constitutional Convention had completed its work by the middle of September, and Congress had obligingly and dutifully referred the Convention's work to each of the State governments. By the end of September, the fate of the recommended plan of government was in the hands of the sovereign States, who alone would pass final judgment on the work of the Federal Convention. The Ratification Period had begun.

Federalist and Antifederalist

Even before the Philadelphia Convention had completed its task of drafting a new Constitution for the United States, a substantial portion of the opposition to the new plan of government had already developed. Some Americans, such as Patrick Henry, were suspicious of the Convention before it convened for its first session, and the suspicions of other Americans were aroused the moment the Convention resolved to conduct its proceedings in secrecy. The fact that the records of the Convention, at its conclusion, were not surrendered to the proper authorities for inspection only augmented such suspicions.

During its sessions, the Federal Convention had attempted to enforce the rule of secrecy to the maximum extent possible, so much so, in fact, that with certain delegates the pursuit of concealment bordered on paranoia. A

---

[5] *Ibid.*, p. 1007.
[6] *Ibid.*, p. 1008.

case in point may be found in the notes of William Pierce, regarding the printed copies of the various proposed plans of government which all delegates had been given in the early stages of the Convention. Shortly after these had been given to the delegates, a copy of the plans was found laying on the floor, apparently having been accidentally dropped by one of the delegates. At the end of the day, George Washington solemnly rose from his chair to severely reprimand the unknown owner of the papers in front of the whole house and, according to Mr. Pierce, thoroughly alarmed every delegate present. The papers were then laid on a table so that the owner could come forward to claim his lost copy of the various proposals. No delegate ever came forward.

Despite this tight rein of secrecy, total concealment was an impossibility. Alexander Hamilton, for one, left the Convention on several occasions to report on the progress of the Convention to his political cronies in New York. And when Robert Yates and John Lansing walked out of the Convention in early July, they regarded it as their duty to their State to report on the efforts within the Convention to enslave the sovereign States and to establish a despotic rule in America.

Even among those delegates who remained in the Federal Convention throughout most of its proceedings, an evolving opposition to the new Constitution was developing. After doing battle with the extreme nationalists in the Convention for nearly four months, Elbridge Gerry and George Mason, for example, became fearful for the fate of liberty under the new compact. Upon leaving the Convention, these delegates were determined to oppose the ratification of the new instrument.

Perhaps the most damning indictment of the Federal Convention came from Luther Martin, who had served as the Orator of Federalism within the Convention. Although he had personally witnessed many victories over nationalism within the Convention – including the rejection of the repugnant word *National*, the establishment of a Senate based on the sovereign equality of the States, the rejection of a federal veto power over the States, the replacement of a supreme government with a supreme Constitution, and the rejection of a Police State – he had nonetheless become frightened by the existence of nationalist conspiracy against the Federal Republic.

Upon leaving the Convention, Mr. Martin regarded it as his duty to the State of Maryland to report on the proceedings of the Convention and to state why he could not endorse the new plan of government. His report was delivered to the Maryland legislature on November 29, 1787, and was subsequently published from December 28, 1787, to February 8, 1788, in the *Maryland Gazette and Baltimore Advertiser*. Although the full title of this formal address was "The Genuine Information, Delivered to the Legislature of the State of Maryland, Relative to the Proceedings of the General Convention, Held at Philadelphia, in 1787, by LUTHER MARTIN, Esquire, Attorney-General of Maryland, and One of the Delegates in the Said Convention," it was widely and popularly referred to as simply the *Genuine Information*.

Within the *Genuine Information*, Luther Martin directed his attention to some 110 points of significance concerning the proposed Constitution, which he believed should be known by the American people. One of these points of criticism, for example, was the following:

> The part of the system which provides, that *no religious test* shall ever be required as a qualification to any office or public trust under the United States, was adopted by a great majority of the Convention, and without much debate; however, there were some members *so unfashionable* as to think, that a *belief of the existence of a Deity*, and of a *state of future rewards and punishments* would be some security for the good conduct of our rulers, and that, in a Christian country, it would be *at least decent* to hold out some distinction between the professors of Christianity and downright infidelity or paganism. [7]

Although Mr. Martin did criticize the final product of the Convention – as is evident from the selection just cited – his chief complaint was against the nationalist conspiracy that had made itself manifest within the Federal Convention. So important was this, in his mind, that the first one-third of his *Genuine Information* consisted of an historical account of the maneuverings of this conspiracy within the Grand Convention of the States. And so revealing and horrifying was his historical account of the Convention's proceedings that many of the nationalists, including James Madison, would continue to rail against him and his candid exposé for the rest of their lives.

In a letter written to Thomas Jefferson on July 11, 1788, J.B. Cutting gave an indication of the extensiveness of the indictment against the nationalist conspiracy given by Mr. Martin:

> So far did Mr Martin proceed in his avowed hostility, as even to detail in the face of decency – before the assembled legislature of Maryland – the petty dialogues and paltry anecdotes of every description – that came to his knowledge in conventional committees and private conversations with the respective members of the Convention – when at Philadelphia. I blush'd in my own bed-chamber when I read his speech on this side of the Atlantic. [8]

---

[7] Max Farrand (ed.), *The Records of the Federal Convention of 1787*, Volume III, Yale University Press, New Haven, 1966, p. 227.
[8] *Ibid.*, Volume III, p. 339.

Luther Martin's critics evidently believed that he should have kept his mouth shut and said nothing about the conspiracy against the Federal Republic he had witnessed within the Federal Convention. But if the tale he told was sufficiently shocking to make grown men blush, then the blame should have been placed on those who acted the part, not on the one who brought the matter to the attention of the public. Indeed, if Mr. Martin's knowledge of this conspiracy caused him to display an undue bias against the proposed Constitution, then his bias can be excused by his concern for the liberties of the American people. And if the indictment he presented was highly critical of the secretive and sinister conduct of the nationalists within the Grand Convention, then he may again be excused by his willingness to publicly report on the *proceedings* of that Convention.

Those nationalists, such as James Madison, who so vehemently condemned Luther Martin and his *Genuine Information*, should have been honorable and decent enough to follow his example by promptly tendering their own hidden records of the proceedings to the proper authorities, rather than to wait decades to perform that solemn public duty. Instead, they preferred to keep their own records of the Convention's proceedings hidden from the public eye for as long as possible, while bitterly condemning those Federal Republicans who dared to publish their own notes in a more timely manner. It was manifestly evident from this embittered battle over the publication of the proceedings of the Convention which side had the most to hide.

As a consequence of these fears and suspicions, a great and formidable opposition to the proposed Constitution was quickly organized in many States. Those most concerned with preserving the rights of the States and most fearful of federal tyranny – men like Samuel Adams, George Clinton, John Hancock, John Lansing, Elbridge Gerry, George Mason, Patrick Henry, James Monroe, Luther Martin, John Taylor of Caroline, and Thomas Jefferson – aligned themselves with the opposition movement. In general, the opposition consisted almost exclusively of individuals who may be described as *Federal Republicans*.

Proponents of ratification, on the other hand, were much less well-defined, and to this movement were drawn some *Federal Republicans* who recognized that the compact posed no threat to State sovereignty, as well as a host of *National Republicans* and *National Monarchists* who supported the Constitution *only* because they preferred it to the Articles of Confederation. To the ranks of the proponents of ratification flocked such die-hard *nationalists* as James Madison, Gouverneur Morris, James Wilson, John Jay, Alexander Hamilton, Edmund Randolph, Rufus King, and John Marshall. Also supporting ratification were some of those who had helped to *defeat* the nationalist conspiracy within the Philadelphia Convention, such as Roger

Sherman, Oliver Ellsworth, John Dickinson, Pierce Butler, and Gunning Bedford, Jr.

Considering the fierce battles that erupted over the ratification issue in many of the States, an observation must be made. Had no Convention ever occurred, and had the new Constitution been suddenly recommended to the States out of the clear blue sky by a patriotic and widely respected American, it is highly doubtful if serious opposition to it would have been created. On its own merits, the Constitution of 1787 contained few objectionable provisions. Indeed, many of those who opposed ratification, such as Thomas Jefferson, actually liked the compact itself and would have raised little objection under normal circumstances. But these were not normal circumstances.

Despite the curtain of secrecy drawn around the Convention, knowledge of the nationalist conspiracy was widespread. In opposing the new Constitution, therefore, much – *if not all* – of the opposition was battling, not the compact itself, but the nationalist conspiracy. These opponents of ratification were convinced that every clause and syllable in the proposed compact, particularly those that appeared even slightly questionable, required very close scrutiny. Such scrutiny, they believed, was required in order to clarify and fix the true meaning of the compact's various provisions, thereby stifling any plot that might exist to subvert the Constitution by misconstruing it. To facilitate this strategy, the opponents of ratification often deliberately misconstrued the various provisions of the Constitution, giving the proponents of ratification, in the process, ample opportunity to prove the ridiculousness and absurdity of such false interpretations. By such means, the true interpretation of the compact could be determined and forevermore fixed with certainty.

Especially significant in this strategy of the opponents of ratification was a great effort to determine, once and for all, whether the proposed plan was for a *Federal* Government or a *National* Government. This question, it was quickly perceived, would conclusively decide all the other issues associated with the proposed compact. The proponents of ratification quickly recognized that the fate of the Constitution hinged on this issue, and they acted accordingly. Not only did they repeatedly insist that the new Constitution would provide for a *Federal Government*, but they insisted on styling themselves *Federalists*. Inasmuch as the opposition was opposing a Federal Constitution, they therefore insisted that the opposition should be styled the *Antifederalists*. And when several proponents of ratification wrote a series of essays promoting the new Constitution in the State of New York, these papers were collected and published under the name of *The Federalist Papers*.

Writing in his work, *The Framing of the Federal Constitution*, noted historian Richard B. Morris observed:

Lines were quickly drawn. The country was far less united over the merits of the Constitution than were the delegates who adopted it. Its supporters drew their strength from the commercial and manufacturing interests, from the people resident in or accessible to main arteries of commerce, both along the seaboard and in the interior, from creditors, Revolutionary War officers, and professional men. Its opponents – States'-Righters, agrarians, paper money men, various categories of debtors, and other particularists and special interests not represented at the Convention – displayed anything but enthusiasm for the Constitution.

The Federalists, as the supporters of the Constitution quickly were called, had one solid advantage: they came with a concrete proposal. Their opponents, the Antifederalists, were opposing something with nothing; their objections, though often sincerely grounded, were basically negative, not constructive. The Antifederalists stood for a policy of drift while the Federalists were providing clear signposts. The former claimed to be the democratic party, but the touchstone of their democracy in the State was their insistence on more explicit guarantees of personal liberties and their advocacy of a unicameral legislature, a popularly-elected judiciary, and a weak executive.

...Many of the Antifederalists were as distrustful of the masses as their opponents. In New York, for example, Gov. George Clinton, the leader of the State's Antifederalists, criticized the people for their fickleness and their tendency to "vibrate from one extreme to another." Elbridge Gerry, who refused to sign the Constitution, asserted in the Convention that "the evils we experience flow from the excess of democracy," and expressed great concern at "the danger of the levelling spirit." John F. Mercer of Maryland professed little faith in his neighbors as voters, for "the people cannot know and judge the character of candidates. The worst possible choice will be made."...It is true, however, that these men were more concerned than the Federalists about the threat posed to individual liberties by a powerful central authority. The Federalists, while sharing the opponents' fear of tyranny, had directed their full attention to the problems of investing the central government with power, energy, and efficiency adequate to its needs. The Antifederalists, by concentrating their heaviest fire on the absence in the proposed Constitution of safeguards for civil liberties, contributed significantly to the final product, the Constitution with the initial Ten Amendments. [9]

The name selected for themselves by the proponents of ratification is most revealing in itself. Although many of them preferred a supreme National Government, they did not style themselves *Nationalists*. Nor did they style themselves *National-Federalists* or *Federal-Nationalists*, to imply that the new government would be some type of *mixture* between the opposing systems. Instead, they called themselves *Federalists*, pure and simple, to convey the

---

[9] Richard B. Morris, *The Framing of the Federal Constitution*, Handbook 103, U.S. Department of the Interior, Washington, 1986, pp. 69-70.

unmistakable message that, *despite the personal sentiments of some of their rank*, what they advocated now was a *Federal Constitution*, pure and simple.

Some nationalists, it is true, found it difficult to conceal their own personal desires during the Ratification Period, and many of the arguments they put forward in defense of the new compact were tinctured by occasional statements reflecting their personal preference for a supreme National Government. The conduct of Alexander Hamilton in New York is illustrative in this regard. In opposition to Governor Clinton, who opposed the Constitution under the pseudonym "Cato," Mr. Hamilton initially sought to promote the new plan of government under the ominous pseudonym of "Caesar." While the pseudonym may have aptly fit the character of Mr. Hamilton, it did not fit the character of the new Constitution.

Writing as "Caesar," Alexander Hamilton arrogantly asserted that he was "not much attached to the majesty of the multitude" and that he refused to gain "influence by cajoling the unthinking mass...and ringing in their ears the gracious sound of their absolute Sovereignty. I despise the trick of such dirty policy." [10] The vast majority of Americans, "Caesar" insisted, were too ignorant to capably judge the merits of the proposed Constitution. "The mass of the people of America (any more than the mass of other countries) cannot judge with any degree of precision concerning the fitness of this New Constitution to the peculiar situation of America." [11] Only an elite and aristocratic group of *experts*, he insisted, like those who had been delegates to the late Grand Convention, were capable of making such a determination.

The great bulk of the American people, wrote this American "Caesar," should "just take it as it is and be thankful," without further debate and consideration. The alternative, Mr. Hamilton warned, would be a despotic government forced upon America at gun point. If the new compact were not adopted and George Washington not induced to become the first President of the United States, the General "should be solicited again to accept of the command of *an army*." [12]

Commenting on the early methods of persuasion employed by Alexander Hamilton, John C. Miller wrote in his book, *Alexander Hamilton and the Growth of the New Nation*:

> By raising the subject of military despotism as an alternative to the adoption of the Constitution, Hamilton gave Clinton an opportunity to portray him as something far more sinister than a brash and intolerant man. "Caesar," Clinton exclaimed, was living up to his reputation as an advocate of forceful methods of persuasion. "If perchance you should happen

---

[10] John C. Miller, *Alexander Hamilton and the Growth of the New Nation*, Harper & Row, Publishers, New York, 1959, quoted on p. 185.
[11] *Ibid.*, quoted on p. 185.
[12] *Ibid.*, quoted on p. 186.

to differ from Caesar," asked the Governor, "are you to have Caesar's principles crammed down your throats with an army?" [13]

Alexander Hamilton quickly realized that the new Constitution could never be forced upon the American people at the point of a bayonet. Thus, the man who fancied himself to be a modern-day Caesar was forced to drastically alter his style and his pseudonym. Ten days after Mr. Hamilton had written his last essay as "Caesar," the first number of *The Federalist Papers* was published in the New York *Independent Journal* of October 27, 1787. Not only was the tone of these essays drastically different from that used by "Caesar," but so too was the pseudonym adopted by the three authors of those essays.

The National Monarchist from New York now wrote under the pseudonym of "Publius," a name derived from the legendary hero, *Publius Valerius*, who established a just and durable republican government following the fall of Tarquin, Rome's last King. Of this Roman champion of free, limited, republican government, Plutarch observed that, "He resolved to render the government, as well as himself, instead of terrible, familiar and pleasant to the people" by dispelling their fears of oppression and tyranny. [14] By this remarkable change of strategy, Alexander Hamilton had gone from *Caesar*, the conqueror of nations, to *Publius*, the champion of the common man.

Even the most extreme National Monarchists, as is evident, were forced to set aside their personal sentiments and desires during the Ratification Period. If the new Constitution were to be adopted, the Federalists universally understood, the compact would have to be promoted on its own merits and the sovereign rights of the States would have to be recognized and openly acknowledged. Accordingly, it was in this manner that the Constitution was urged upon the American people, and it was in this sense and general understanding that the peoples of the several States finally assented to and ratified the new Constitution.

That the States who assented to the Constitution understood it to be a Federal Constitution, as opposed to a national one, is clearly evident from the debates that took place within the State Ratification Conventions, convened for the sole purpose of considering the proposed compact, and from the official acts of ratification promulgated by the several States. As better understanding of the true merits of the Constitution of 1787 became known and recognized over the course of the next three years, all thirteen States were ultimately convinced to ratify the new compact, with the dates of their respective ratifications, Convention votes, as well as 1790 population and popula-

---

[13] *Ibid.*, p. 186.
[14] *Ibid.*, quoted on p. 188.

tion rank indicated in the table shown below.

State	Date	Vote	Pop. Rank	Population
1. Delaware	Dec. 7, 1787	Unanimous	13	59,096
2. Pennsylvania	Dec. 12, 1787	46 to 23	3	433,611
3. New Jersey	Dec. 18, 1787	Unanimous	9	184,139
4. Georgia	Jan. 2, 1788	Unanimous	11	82,548
5. Connecticut	Jan. 9, 1788	128 to 40	8	237,655
6. Massachusetts	Feb. 6, 1788	187 to 168	2	475,199
7. Maryland	Apr. 28, 1788	63 to 11	6	319,728
8. South Carolina	May 23, 1788	149 to 73	7	249,073
9. New Hampshire	June 21, 1788	57 to 46	10	141,899
10. Virginia	June 26, 1788	89 to 79	1	747,610
11. New York	July 26, 1788	30 to 27	5	340,241
12. North Carolina	Nov. 21, 1789	195 to 77	4	395,005
13. Rhode Island	May 29, 1790	34 to 32	12	69,112

To facilitate our understanding of how the States received the new Constitution and in what light they regarded it, we should examine the ratification process in each of them and observe the spirit manifested in the their respective debates and the precise terms in which they formally adopted the compact. As we shall discover, in ratifying the instrument, each State was acting under the impression, and with the repeated assurances of the Federalists, that what they were adopting was a Federal Constitution providing for a Federal Government within a Federal Union between sovereign States.

The State of Delaware

The first State to assent to the Federal Constitution was Delaware, which formally ratified the compact on December 7, 1787. Delaware's prompt ratification becomes all the more remarkable when it is considered that she was, at the time, the least populous of all the States, and that she had been the only State to insist, within the credentials given to her delegates to the Constitutional Convention, that the States should not be robbed of their equality of suffrage within Congress. The Connecticut Compromise adopted by the Grand Convention evidently satisfied Delaware that the sovereign equality of the States would be preserved in the new Federal Union. And by adopting the new compact by a *unanimous* vote, this State clearly signaled her understanding that, under the new Constitution, the rights of even the smallest State in the Union would be safe and secure.

Delaware's assention to the Constitution was expressed in this manner:

We the Deputies of *the People of the Delaware State*, in Convention met, having taken into our serious consideration the *Federal Constitution* proposed and agreed upon by the Deputies of the United States in a General Convention held at the City of Philadelphia on the seventeenth day of September in the year of our Lord one thousand seven hundred and eighty seven, Have *approved, assented to, ratified,* and *confirmed,* and by these Presents, Do, in virtue of the Power and Authority to us given for that purpose, for and in behalf of ourselves and our Constituents, fully, freely, and entirely *approve of, assent to, ratify,* and *confirm* the said Constitution. [Emphasis added] [15]

This statement was then followed by the signatures of the delegates who represented the people of Delaware in the State Ratification Convention. The official act of ratification was then concluded by these words of Thomas Collins, the Governor of this sovereign State:

> To all whom these Presents shall come Greeting, I Thomas Collins President of the Delaware State do hereby certify, that the above instrument of writing is a true copy of the original *ratification of the Federal Constitution* by the *Convention of the Delaware State,* which original ratification is now in my possession. In Testimony whereof I have caused the seal of the Delaware State to be hereunto an'exed. [Emphasis added] [16]

It is clear from Delaware's official ratification that the Delaware State understood the new compact to be a *Federal Constitution*. It is thus referred to in her official assention act, and in the certification of authenticity of that ratification written by Governor Collins. Not once is the term *national* used in either the act of ratification or in the statement of certification. Delaware had specifically and unequivocally "approved, assented to, ratified, and confirmed" a Federal Constitution for a league of sovereign States, not a National Constitution for a consolidated nation.

The State of Pennsylvania

The sovereign State of Pennsylvania became the second to ratify the new plan of government, on December 12, 1787, but not without a serious struggle between that State's Federalists and Antifederalists. The struggle, unfortunately, was not confined to debates, but was marked by fraud and occasional violence and strong-armed action on the part of the Federalists. Regarding the ratification battle in this State, historian Richard B. Morris has

---

[15] Charles Callan Tansill, *Op. cit.,* p. 1009.
[16] *Ibid.,* p. 1009.

written:

> The first real battle occurred in Pennsylvania. There the Antifeder-
> alists sought frantically to delay action; they wanted to get more informa-
> tion. By refusing to attend a session of the legislature, they killed a quorum
> and kept it from acting. A band of Constitutionalists broke into their lodg-
> ings, dragged them through the streets to the State House, and forcibly
> kept them in the Assembly until a vote was taken to call a Ratification
> Convention. The feverish haste with which the Convention was sum-
> moned and the fact that only a fraction of the voters of Pennsylvania bal-
> loted for delegates provided the Antifederalists with plenty of ammunition.
> [17]

The struggle for ratification within Pennsylvania is especially interesting, inasmuch as that State's delegates within the Federal Convention had
been among those foremost in the conspiracy to subvert State sovereignty and
to destroy the federal system. It is of special significance, furthermore, to note
that the *leader* of the Federalist faction in the Keystone State was none other
than James Wilson, who had been one of the key leaders of the nationalist
conspiracy within the Constitutional Convention.

In an "Address to a Meeting of the Citizens of Philadelphia on October
6, 1787," James Wilson spoke of the "extent of the *Confederated States*" and
said: "Let it be remembered, then, that the business of the *Federal Constitution* was not local, but general – not limited to the views and establishments
of a single State, but... comprehending the views and establishments of *thirteen independent sovereignties.*" [18] This same theme was also conveyed by Mr.
Wilson within the State Ratification Convention.

Addressing the Ratification Convention on November 28, 1787, James
Wilson stated:

> The truth is, Sir, that the framers of this system were particularly
> anxious, and their work demonstrates their anxiety, to *preserve the State
> governments unimpaired – it was their favorite object*; and, perhaps, however
> proper it might be in itself, it is more difficult to defend the plan on ac-
> count of the *excessive caution* used in that respect than from any other ob-
> jection that has been offered here or elsewhere....I trust it is unnecessary to
> dwell longer upon this subject; for, when gentlemen assert that it was the
> *intention of the Federal Convention to destroy the sovereignty of the States*,
> they must conceive themselves better qualified to judge of the intention of
> that body than its own members, of whom *not one*, I believe, entertained so
> *improper an idea.* [Emphasis added] [19]

---

[17] Richard B. Morris, *Op. cit.*, p. 70.
[18] Max Farrand (ed.), *Op. cit.*, Volume III, pp. 101-102.
[19] *Ibid.*, Volume III, p. 144.

Politics, as is evident from this passage, certainly brings out the best features in men. And in politics, perhaps more than in any other pursuit of man, truth is a commodity to be used and abused for profit. As to the final results of the Federal Convention, Mr. Wilson clearly spoke the truth. But as to the *unanimity* of the delegates within the Grand Convention, his assertions were most false, for no one knew better than he that a concerted effort had been made in the Convention to subvert the sovereignties of the several States. The picture portrayed by Mr. Wilson to the State of Pennsylvania, however, was that no such nationalist conspiracy had ever existed. The final product of the Philadelphia Convention was even offered as proof that all the delegates assembled in that Convention had been of one mind in the preservation of the Federal Republic.

The extreme nationalist who had, behind the closed doors of the Grand Convention, denied that the States were sovereign, even under the Articles of Confederation, was forced to acknowledge within the State Ratification Convention that they indeed were sovereign. Speaking on November 24th, Mr. Wilson spoke of the American States as "13 distinct and independent States" and as "thirteen independent and sovereign States." He also explained that the Philadelphia Convention, after taking into consideration the vast expanse of the United States, had determined that no single or consolidated government could ever govern such an extensive continent without being tyrannical in nature. "In this dilemma," he informed the Ratification Convention, "a Federal Republic naturally presented itself to our observation, as a species of government which secured all the internal advantages of a Republic, at the same time that it maintained the external dignity and force of a monarchy." [20]

Later, in the same speech, James Wilson presented the alternatives before the American States and indicated which of these options had been recommended by the proposed Constitution:

> At this period, America has it in her power to adopt either of the following modes of government: She may dissolve the *individual sovereignty of the States*, and become *one consolidated Empire*; she may be divided into thirteen separate, independent and unconnected commonwealths; she may be erected into *two or more Confederacies*; or, lastly, she may become *one comprehensive Federal Republic*....
>
> Of these [first] three species of government, however, I must observe, that *they obtained no advocates in the Federal Convention*, nor can I presume that they will find advocates here, or in any of our sister States. The general sentiment in that body, and, I believe, the general sentiment of the citizens of America, is expressed in the motto which some of them have

---

[20] *Ibid.*, Volume III, pp. 138-139.

chosen, UNITE OR DIE; and while we consider the extent of the country, so intersected and almost surrounded with navigable rivers, so separated and detached from the rest of the world, it is natural to presume that Providence has designed us for an united people, under *one great political compact.* If this is a just and reasonable conclusion, supported by the wishes of the people, *the Convention did right in proposing a single Confederated Republic.* [Emphasis added] [21]

Aside from lying about the existence of a nationalist conspiracy within the Federal Convention, James Wilson told the truth regarding the *final product* of that Convention. The Philadelphia Convention, said he, contained not a single advocate for any political system for the United States other than a Federal Republic, and no threat could possibility exist to State sovereignty under the new Constitution, which he termed "one great political *compact.*" Furthermore, Mr. Wilson indicated, all Americans could rejoice in the preservation of States' Rights, for "the Convention did *right* in proposing a single *Confederated Republic.*"

James Wilson, it would appear from the records of the debates in the State Ratification Convention, did an admirable job of concealing his own personal preferences and in advocating the legitimate merits of the new Federal Constitution. But on December 11, 1787, in an apparent fit of rage, he momentarily blew his cover and launched into a nationalist tirade against those who conceived the instrument to be a *compact* among sovereign States, although he himself had previously admitted that it was indeed *a compact between sovereign States.*

On this occasion, Mr. Wilson ranted:

> We were told some days ago, by the honorable gentleman from Westmoreland (Mr. Findley), when speaking of this system and its objects, that the Convention, no doubt, thought they were forming a *compact* or *contract* of the greatest importance. Sir, I confess I was much surprised at so late a stage of the debate to hear such principles maintained. It was matter of surprise to see the great leading principle of this system still so very much misunderstood. "The Convention, no doubt, though they were forming 'a contract!'" *I cannot answer for what every member thought*; but I believe it cannot be said that they thought they were making a *contract*, because *I cannot discover the least trace of a compact in that system. There can be no compact unless there are more parties than one.* It is a new doctrine that one can make a compact with himself. "The Convention were forming compacts!" *With whom? I know no bargains that were made there. I am unable to conceive who the parties could be.* The State governments make a bargain with one another; that is the doctrine that is endeavored to be estab-

---

lished by gentlemen in opposition; *their State sovereignties wish to be represented!* But far other were the ideas of this Convention, and far other are those conveyed in the system itself. [Emphasis added] [22]

It would be difficult to cram more falsehoods and lies in the same amount of space, and it is apparent that Mr. Wilson had a very low regard for the intelligence of those he addressed. The Federal Constitution, he thundered, could not possibly be a contract or compact among sovereign States! Yet, in his earlier speech, on November 24th, as we have already observed, he had emphatically asserted that the new Constitution was *"one great political compact."* But he now insisted that such terminology could not possibly be applied to the proposed compact.

"I cannot discover the least trace of a compact in that system," the extremely dishonest nationalist insisted. "I know no bargains that were made there." Either James Wilson slept through the entire Federal Convention or was suffering from a severe and acute case of amnesia. The whole Philadelphia Convention of 1787, from beginning to end, was little more than a series of compromises and concessions among the various States, from the celebrated *Connecticut Compromise* between the large and small States to the famous *Three-Fifths Compromise* between the Northern and Southern States. Even Mr. Wilson's colleague in the Grand Convention, Gouverneur Morris, had repeatedly grumbled and complained in the Federal Convention that the other delegates had come to Philadelphia to "truck and bargain" for their respective States. As a consequence, the Constitution itself represents little more than a *bundle of bargains* between the States, and its very text reveals the nature and extent of all those compromises!

"I am unable to conceive who the parties could be," Mr. Wilson claimed, affecting total ignorance of the existence of the State Ratification Conventions, one of which he was addressing at the time. The fact that the Constitution had been drafted by the *representatives of sovereign States* and could only be ratified by *representatives of those same States*, each State acting for itself and bound only by its own consent, apparently was insufficient to give him a clue as to who the parties to the federal compact might be. All he knew was that the Constitution would not be a compact between the State *governments*. The possibility that the Constitution might be a compact between the *peoples* of the States, *in their sovereign capacities*, apparently never occurred to him.

It should be noted that Max Farrand, the distinguished editor of *The Records of the Federal Convention of 1787*, affixed a telling footnote to this

---

[22] *Ibid.*, Volume III, p. 166.

outrageous speech made by James Wilson. As Mr. Farrand noted, "Yet Wilson had said on November 24...,'Providence has designed us for an united people, under one great political compact.'" [23] If Mr. Farrand detected the heretical contradiction, it is safe to assume that the majority of delegates in the Pennsylvania Ratification Convention observed it as well and regarded Mr. Wilson's speech as little more than the ravings of a defeated nationalist.

Convinced that, in Mr. Wilson's more truthful and rationale words, "the Convention did *right* in proposing a single *Confederated Republic*" — a federal system based on the concept of sovereign States – Pennsylvania assented to the "great political compact" in these words:

> *In the Name of the People of Pennsylvania*
> Be it Known unto all Men that We the Delegates of the People of the Commonwealth of Pennsylvania in general Convention assembled Have assented to, and ratified, and by these presents Do in the Name and by the authority of the same People, and for ourselves, assent to, and ratify the foregoing Constitution for the United States of America. Done in Convention at Philadelphia the twelfth day of December in the year of our Lord one thousand seven hundred and eight seven and of the Independence of the United States of America the twelfth. In witness whereof we have hereunto subscribed our names. [Emphasis added] [24]

The State of New Jersey

Within the Constitutional Convention of 1787, the State of New Jersey had distinguished herself by being the leading advocate of federalism, and one of her delegates — William Paterson — had been given the honor of introducing the New Jersey Plan. On December 18, 1787, she became the third State to ratify the Federal Constitution. The fact that New Jersey's ratification was made with the *unanimous* vote of the delegates in the Ratification Convention may be regarded as concrete proof that this State saw no threat to her sovereignty in the new plan of government.

During the Philadelphia Convention, William Paterson – who later became Governor of New Jersey – had addressed the Grand Convention in the following manner:

> Can we, on this ground, form a National Government? I fancy not. Our commissions give a complexion to the business; and can we suppose that, when we exceed the bounds of our duty, the people will approve our

---

[23] *Ibid.*, Volume III, p. 166.
[24] Charles Callan Tansill (ed.), *Op. cit.*, p. 1010.

proceedings?

We are met here as the deputies of *thirteen independent, sovereign States, for federal purposes. Can we consolidate their sovereignty and form one nation*, and annihilate the sovereignties of our States, who have sent us here for other purposes? [25]

On another occasion, Mr. Paterson had asked the Constitutional Convention: "Can we, *as representatives of independent States*, annihilate the essential powers of independency? Are not the votes of this Convention taken on every question under the idea of independency?" [26]

Even with such unyielding devotion to the principles of federalism, the Garden State ratified the Constitution *without any opposition*! The sentiment of this small State was that the new compact secured the sovereignty and reserved rights of New Jersey as much as the plan introduced in the Federal Convention by Mr. Paterson would have. One week before Christmas, this State assented to the federal compact in these words:

> Now be it known that we the Delegates of the State of New-Jersey *chosen by the People thereof* for the purposes aforesaid having maturely deliberated on, and considered the aforesaid proposed Constitution, do hereby *for and on the behalf of the People of the State of New-Jersey agree to, ratify* and *confirm* the same and every part thereof. [Emphasis added] [27]

The State of Georgia

On January 2, 1788, Georgia became the fourth State in the Federal Union to ratify the new Federal Constitution. And like New Jersey, the Peach State assented to the compact *without opposition*, a fact in which the native Georgian, Alexander H. Stephens, writing in 1868, could take special pride: "In the Georgia Convention, there was no opposing voice. The Constitution was unanimously assented to, ratified, and adopted as 'a Constitution for the Government of the United States of America.' A Government of States. A Federal Republic." [28]

The Georgia Ratification Convention adopted the federal compact in the following language:

[25] Jefferson Davis, *The Rise and Fall of the Confederate Government*, Volume 1, Thomas Yoseloff, Cranbury, (orig. pub. in 1881) 1958, quoted on p. 106.
[26] *Ibid.*, Volume 1, quoted on p. 106.
[27] Charles Callan Tansill, *Op. cit.*, p. 1012.
[28] Alexander H. Stephens, *Op. cit.*, Volume 1, p. 227.

Now Know Ye, That We, the Delegates of *the People of the State of Georgia* in Convention met, pursuant to the Resolutions of the Legislature aforesaid, having taken into our serious consideration the said Constitution, Have *assented to, ratified* and *adopted,* and by these presents DO, in virtue of the powers and authority to Us given by *the People of the said State* for that purpose, for, and in behalf of ourselves and our Constituents, fully and entirely *assent to, ratify* and *adopt* the said Constitution. [Emphasis added] [29]

By her act of ratification, the sovereign State of Georgia became the first *Southern State* to adopt the new Constitution. And Georgia's unanimous vote in favor of the compact indicated that this State of the Deep South was satisfied that the peculiar rights of the Southern States would be preserved and safeguarded in the new Federal Union.

The State of Connecticut

Within the Constitutional Convention of 1787, delegates from Connecticut had been firmly aligned with the other Federal Republicans in the effort to defeat nationalism. Oliver Ellsworth, and especially Roger Sherman, had been responsible for formulating and promoting the successful *Connecticut Compromise* that doomed the nationalist conspiracy within the Convention and ensured that the U.S. Senate would forever stand as a monument to the *sovereign equality of the States.*

On September 26, 1787, shortly after the conclusion of the Federal Convention, Mr. Sherman and Mr. Ellsworth sent a joint dispatch to the Governor of Connecticut to explain the new Constitution and to certify that the proposed instrument posed no threat to sovereignty of the States:

Sir,

We have the honour to transmit to your excellency a printed copy of the Constitution formed by the Federal Convention, to be laid before the legislature of the State.

The general principles, which governed the Convention in their deliberations on the subject, are stated in their address to Congress.

We think it may be of use to make some further observations on particular parts of the Constitution.

The Congress is differently organized: yet the whole number of members, and this State's proportion of suffrage, remain the same as before.

The equal representation of the States in the Senate, and the voice

---

[29] Charles Callan Tansill (ed.), *Op. cit.,* p. 1015.

of that branch in the appointment to offices, *will secure the rights of the lesser, as well as of the greater States.*

Some additional powers are vested in Congress, which was a principal object that the States had in view in appointing the Convention. Those powers extend *only* to matters respecting *the common interests of the Union,* and are *specially defined,* so that *the particular States retain their sovereignty in all other matters.*

The objects, for which Congress may apply monies, are the same mentioned in the Eighth Article of the Confederation, viz. for the common defence and general welfare, and for payment of the debts incurred for those purposes. It is probable that the principal branch of revenue will be duties on imports; what may be necessary to be raised by direct taxation is to be *apportioned on the several States,* according to the numbers of their inhabitants, and although Congress may raise the money by their own authority, if necessary, yet *that authority need not be exercised, if each State will furnish its quota.*

The restraint on the legislatures of the several States respecting emitting bills of credit, making any thing but money a tender in payment of debts, or impairing the obligation of contracts by *ex post facto* laws, was thought necessary as a security to commerce, in which the interest of foreigners, as well as of the citizens of different States, may be affected.

The Convention endeavoured to provide for the energy of government on the one hand, and *suitable checks* on the other hand, *to secure the rights of the particular States, and the liberties and properties of the citizens.* We wish it may meet the approbation of the several States, and be *a mean of securing their rights,* and lengthening out their tranquility. [Emphasis added] [30]

Within the Nutmeg State, Roger Sherman and Oliver Ellsworth became leading figures in the Federalist movement. The latter, who was destined to become the third Chief Justice of the United States, was elected as a delegate to his State's Ratification Convention. Addressing that Convention, Mr. Ellsworth's opening words were:

Mr. President: – It is observable that there is no preface to the proposed Constitution, but it evidently presupposes two things; one is the necessity of a *Federal Government;* the other is the inefficiency of the *old* Articles of Confederation. [31]

Oliver Ellsworth concluded his speech with this observation:

The Constitution before us is a complete system of Legislative, Judicial, and Executive power. It was designed to supply the *defects* of the former system; and I believe, upon a full discussion, it will be found to an-

---

[30] Max Farrand (ed.), *Op. cit.,* Volume III, pp. 99-100.
[31] Alexander H. Stephens, *Op. cit.,* Volume 1, quoted on p. 228.

swer the *purposes* for which it was designed. [32]

Addressing the Ratification Convention on January 7, 1788, Oliver Ellsworth directed his attention to the "coercive principle" on which the Federal Government would operate. Such a principle, he emphasized, allowed the Government of the United States to apply coercion only to an *individual citizen* guilty of violating the law. Under no circumstances could coercion be applied to a *sovereign State*.

As Mr. Ellsworth stated:

> No man pretends the contrary: we all see and feel this necessity. *The only question is, Shall it be a coercion of law, or a coercion of arms?* There is no other possible alternative. Where will those who oppose a coercion of law come out? Where will they end? A necessary consequence of their principles is *a war of the States one against the other. I am for coercion by law — that coercion which acts only upon delinquent individuals. This Constitution does not attempt to coerce sovereign bodies, States, in their political capacity. No coercion is applicable to such bodies, but that of an armed force.* If we should attempt to execute the laws of the Union by sending an armed force against a delinquent State, it would involve the good and bad, the innocent and guilty, in the same calamity.
> But this legal coercion singles out *the guilty individual,* and punishes him for breaking the laws of the Union. [Emphasis added] [33]

Other Connecticut Federalists — including Governor Huntingdon and Richard Law — added their voices to that of Oliver Ellsworth. "Consider that this general government rests upon the State governments for its support," Mr. Law informed the Ratification Convention. "It is like a vast and magnificent bridge, built upon thirteen strong and stately pillars." "Now, the rulers, who occupy the bridge," he added, "cannot be so *beside themselves* as to knock away the pillars which support the whole fabric." [34]

Even Oliver Wolcott, a nationalist by sentiment and an intimate political friend of Alexander Hamilton, promoted the cause of ratification in the Connecticut Convention by stressing the *federal* nature of the Constitution. "*The Constitution effectually secures the States in their several rights,*" said this future Secretary of the Treasury. "It must secure them, for its own sake; for *they are the pillars which uphold the general system.*" He then alluded to the Senate, "a constituent branch of the general legislature, without whose assent no public act can be made, are appointed by the States, and *will secure the*

---

[32] *Ibid.*, Volume 1, quoted on p. 229.
[33] Max Farrand (ed.), *Op. cit.*, Volume III, p. 241.
[34] Alexander H. Stephens, *Op. cit.*, Volume 1, quoted on p. 232.

rights of the several States." "So well guarded is this Constitution throughout," Mr. Wolcott emphasized, "that *it seems impossible that the rights either of the States or of the people should be destroyed.*" [Emphasis added] [35]

The spirit manifested in the State of Connecticut, it is clearly evident, was that the proposed Constitution provided for a Federal Government, that the reserved rights of the sovereign States would remain secure in the new Union, and that no federal coercion of a State could possibly occur. Acting under these considerations and with this understanding, on January 9, 1788, Connecticut became the fifth State to ratify the Federal Constitution.

Her formal act of assention was in these words:

> *In the Name of the People of the State of Connecticut.*
> We the Delegates of *the People of said State* in general Convention assembled, pursuant to an Act of the Legislature in October last, Have *assented to* and *ratified,* and by these presents do *assent to, ratify* and *adopt* the Constitution, reported by the Convention of Delegates in Philadelphia, on the 17th day of September AD. 1787. for the United States of America. [Emphasis added] [36]

The State of Massachusetts

The State of Massachusetts, the second most populous member of the Federal Union, became the sixth to give its formal assention to the proposed Constitution. This ratification, however, was secured only after a long and bitter struggle in the State Ratification Convention, wherein many of the delegates expressed concern for the preservation of the sovereignty of the Bay State. Demonstrating that Massachusetts was still a *Cradle of Liberty*, the Antifederalists remained unrelenting in their opposition until the Federalists finally agreed that certain amendments should be incorporated into the Constitution to safeguard human rights and the sovereignty of the members of the Federal Union. But even with this assurance, the Constitution was approved in the Ratification Convention by a very close vote of 187 to 168. Without the promise of the *Bill of Rights*, it is probable that the Constitution would have been *rejected* by this proud State!

Within the Massachusetts Ratification Convention, a number of prominent and distinguished individuals – including Samuel Adams, Fisher Ames, Rufus King, Theophilis Parsons, James Bowdoin, and John Hancock – aligned themselves into opposing camps. Leading the Antifederalist cause

---

[35] *Ibid.*, Volume 1, quoted on p. 232.
[36] Charles Callan Tansill (ed.), *Op. cit.*, p. 1016.

were the two sturdy patriots of the American Revolution, John Hancock and Samuel Adams. The general sentiments of these Antifederalists is perhaps best revealed by the statement made by Mr. Adams when he first read the new Constitution. Upon seeing in the Preamble the words, "We, the People," rather than the words, "We, the States," the Bostonian exclaimed that he had *stumbled at the threshold!* The challenge confronting the Federalists in Massachusetts, thus, was clearly discernible. Unless they could convincingly demonstrate that the new compact posed no threat to State sovereignty, the Bay State would not ratify the Constitution.

Determined to allay the fears of the Antifederalists, Fisher Ames declared:

> The State governments are *essential parts* of the system, and the defence of this article [providing for six-year terms for Senators] is drawn from *its tendency to their preservation. The Senators represent the Sovereignty of the States....They are in the quality of Ambassadors of the States....The State governments* represent the wishes, and feelings, and local interests, *of the people. They are the safeguard and ornament of the Constitution; they will protract the period of our liberties; they will afford a shelter against the abuse of power, and will be the natural avengers of our violated rights.*
>
> ...This article seems to be an excellence of the Constitution, and affords just ground to believe that it will be, *in practice as in theory, a Federal Republic.* [Emphasis added] [37]

Another Federalist also assured the Ratification Convention that the States would form the pillars of the proposed federal system:

> But some gentlemen object further and say the delegation of these great powers will destroy the State legislatures; but, I trust, *this never can take place,* for *the general government depends on the State legislatures for its very existence....*If gentlemen consider this, they will, I presume, alter their opinion; for nothing is clearer than that the existence of the legislatures in the different States, is *essential to the very being of the general government.* I hope, Sir, we shall all see the necessity of a *Federal Government,* and not make objections unless they appear to us to be of some weight. [Emphasis added] [38]

Even Rufus King, who had acted as an extreme nationalist in the Constitutional Convention, informed the State Ratification Convention that the proposed compact was genuinely federal in nature: "To conclude, Sir, if we mean to support an efficient *Federal Government,* which under the *old* Con-

---

[37] Alexander H. Stephens, *Op. cit.,* Volume 1, quoted on pp. 239-240.
[38] *Ibid.,* Volume 1, quoted on p. 241.

federation, can never be the case, the proposed Constitution is, in my opinion, the only one that can be *substituted*." [Emphasis added] [39]

Despite such strong assurances, however, it had become apparent by January 30, 1788, that the opposition forces outnumbered the proponents of ratification. At that point, the President of the Ratification Convention – John Hancock – offered a number of amendments to the Constitution that would serve as the basis for a compromise between the Federalists and the Antifederalists. By this compromise, the Federalists could be satisfied by the adoption of the compact, and the Antifederalists could be satisfied by written guarantees in the Constitution to protect individual liberty and States' Rights. This compromise measure sufficed to induce Samuel Adams, who by then had assumed leadership of the Antifederalist cause, to agree to yield his opposition to the new Federal Constitution.

Addressing the Ratification Convention, Mr. Adams paid particular attention to the first of the proposed amendments, which he considered to be the crux of the whole issue:

> Your Excellency's first proposition is, *"that it be explicitly declared, that all powers not expressly delegated to Congress are reserved to the several States, to be by them exercised."* This appears to my mind, to be *a summary of a Bill of Rights*, which gentlemen are anxious to obtain. *It removes a doubt which many have entertained respecting the matter*, and gives assurance that, if any law made by the *Federal Government* shall be extended beyond the power granted by the proposed Constitution and *inconsistent with the Constitution of this State, it will be an error*, and adjudged by the courts of law to be *void. It is consonant with the Second Article in the present Confederation,* that *each State retains its sovereignty, freedom, and independence, and every power, jurisdiction, and right, which is not, by this Confederation, expressly delegated to the United States in Congress assembled.* I have long considered the watchfulness of the people over the conduct of their rulers the strongest guard against the encroachments of power; and *I hope the people of this country will always be thus watchful.* [Emphasis added] [40]

By thus deciding to propose the list of amendments to the compact, the majority of representatives in the Ratification Convention were finally able to agree with Fisher Ames when he stated:

> Very few among us now deny that a *Federal Government* is necessary to save us from ruin; that the Confederation is not that government; and that the proposed Constitution, *connected with the amendments*, is wor-

---

[39] *Ibid.*, Volume 1, quoted on p. 242.
[40] *Ibid.*, Volume 1, quoted on pp. 243-244.

thy of being adopted. [Emphasis added] [41]

On February 6, 1788, the proud and sovereign State of Massachusetts formally assented to the Constitution in these words:

> *In Convention of the Delegates of the People of the Commonwealth of Massachusetts February 6th 1788*
>
> The Convention have impartially discussed, & fully considered the Constitution for the United States of America, reported to Congress by the Convention of Delegates from the United States of America, & submitted to us by a resolution of the General Court of the said Commonwealth, passed the twenty fifth day of October last past, & acknowledging with grateful hearts, the goodness of the *Supreme Ruler of the Universe* in affording the People of the United States in the course of his Providence an opportunity deliberately & peaceably without fraud or surprize of entering into an explicit & solemn *Compact* with each other by *assenting to & ratifying* a New Constitution in order to form a more perfect Union, establish Justice, insure Domestic tranquillity, provide for the common defence, promote the general welfare & secure the blessings of Liberty to themselves & their posterity; Do in the name & in behalf of *the People of the Commonwealth of Massachusetts assent to & ratify* the said Constitution for the United States of America. [Emphasis added] [42]

These words were then followed by a formal declaration that a Bill of Rights should be added to the new Constitution:

> And as it is the opinion of this Convention that certain amendments & alterations in the said Constitution would *remove the fears & quiet the apprehensions of many of the good people of this Commonwealth & more effectually guard against an undue administration of the Federal Government,* The Convention do therefore recommend that the following alterations & provisions be introduced into the said Constitution. [Emphasis added] [43]

A total of nine amendments were recommended by the Ratification Convention, many of which would serve as the basis for the Bill of Rights that was later incorporated into the Federal Constitution. First and foremost in the list was the proposal which Samuel Adams had correctly identified as *the summary of the whole Bill of Rights*. This Massachusetts proposal provided, "That it be explicitly declared that all Powers not expressly delegated by the aforesaid Constitution are reserved to the several States to be by them exer-

---

[41] *Ibid.*, Volume 1, quoted on pp. 244-245.
[42] Charles Callan Tansill (ed.), *Op. cit.*, p. 1018.
[43] *Ibid.*, p. 1018.

cised." [44] This proposition, together with similar ones subsequently made by other States, would serve as the basis for the *Tenth Amendment* to the Federal Constitution.

The State of Maryland

On April 28, 1788, Maryland became the seventh State to ratify the amended Articles of Union. Although Luther Martin had dutifully warned the Maryland legislature about the existence of the nationalist conspiracy within the Federal Convention, that State could find little fault with the Constitution *itself* and deemed it to be a federal compact that posed no threat to her sovereignty. There was, as a consequence, very little debate in the State Ratification Convention, and the Constitution was readily approved by a vote of 63 to 11.

The Free State ratified the Constitution of the United States in these words:

> *In Convention of the Delegates of the People of the State of Maryland*
> *28 April 1788.*
> We the Delegates of *the people of the State of Maryland* having fully considered the Constitution of the United States of America reported to Congress by the Convention of Deputies from the United States of America held in Philadelphia on the seventeenth Day of September in the Year Seventeen hundred and eighty seven of which the annexed is a Copy and submitted to us by a Resolution of the General Assembly of Maryland in November Session Seventeen hundred and eighty seven do for ourselves and in the Name and on behalf of *the People of this State assent to* and *ratify* the said Constitution. [Emphasis added] [45]

The State of South Carolina

Within the Federal Convention of 1787, Pierce Butler of South Carolina had distinguished himself by demonstrating his fealty to the Federal Republic on a number of occasions. And his devotion to the cause of ratification of the new compact was enthusiastic and without reservation, for he recognized the instrument for what it was — *a strictly Federal Constitution founded on the sovereignty of the States.* An indication of his satisfaction of this fact may

---

[44] *Ibid.*, p. 1018.
[45] *Ibid.*, p. 1021.

be ascertained from the letter he wrote to Weedon Butler on October 8, 1787.

In this letter, Mr. Butler stated:

> View the system then as resulting from *a spirit of Accomodation to different Interests,* and not the most perfect one that the Deputies cou'd devise for a Country better adapted for the reception of it than America is at this day, or perhaps ever will be. *It is a great Extent of Territory to be under One free Government; the manners and modes of thinking of the Inhabitants, differing nearly as much as in different Nations of Europe.* If we can secure tranquillity at Home, and respect from abroad, they will be great points gain'd. We have, as you will see, taken *a portion of power* from the Individual States, to form a General Government for the whole to preserve the Union.... *The powers of the General Government are so defined as not to destroy the Sovereignty of the Individual States.* These are the outlines, if I was to be more minute I shou'd tire your patience. [Emphasis added] [46]

During the debates over ratification, some Antifederalists accused the Federal Convention of usurping authority and exceeding the limits imposed on the delegates by the States they had represented. In response, General Charles Cotesworth Pinckney denied this charge in a speech delivered on January 17, 1788, in the South Carolina House of Representatives:

> [I]t had been alleged that, when there, they exceeded their powers. He thought not....
>
> Every member who attended the Convention, was, from the beginning, sensible of the necessity of giving greater powers to the *Federal Government.* This was the very purpose for which they were convened. [Emphasis added] [47]

The following day, in another speech to the South Carolina House of Representatives, General Pinckney explained why the Federal Convention had not affixed a Bill of Rights to the proposed Constitution:

> With regard to the liberty of the press, the discussion of that matter was not forgotten by the members of the Convention. *It was fully debated,* and the impropriety of saying any thing about it in the Constitution clearly evinced. *The general government has no powers but what are expressly granted to it; it therefore has no power to take away the liberty of the press.* That invaluable blessing, which deserves all the encomiums the gentleman has justly bestowed upon it, is *secured by all our State Constitutions*; and to have mentioned it in our general Constitution would perhaps *furnish an argu-*

---

[46] Max Farrand (ed.), *Op. cit.,* Volume III, p. 103.
[47] *Ibid.,* Volume III, pp. 252-253.

ment, hereafter, that the general government had a right to exercise powers not expressly delegated to it. For the same reason, we had no Bill of Rights inserted in our Constitution; for, as we might perhaps have omitted the enumeration of some of our rights, it might hereafter be said we had delegated to the general government a power to take away such of our rights as we had not enumerated; but *by delegating express powers, we certainly reserve to ourselves every power and right not mentioned in the Constitution.* [Emphasis added] [48]

Although impressed by the lucid logic and truthfulness of General Pinckney's reasoning, the Antifederalists were determined that certain amendments should be incorporated into the proposed Constitution, especially one that would clearly acknowledge the rights reserved to the sovereign States. The Federalists agreed to this request, and on May 23, 1788, South Carolina became the eighth State to assent to the federal compact.

South Carolina's act of ratification was expressed in the following language:

> The Convention having maturely considered *the Constitution or Form of Government* reported to Congress by the Convention of Delegates from the United States of America and submitted to them by a Resolution of the Legislature of this State passed the seventeenth and eighteenth days of February last in order to form a more perfect Union, establish Justice, ensure Domestic tranquillity, provide for the common defence, promote the general Welfare and secure the blessings of Liberty to the people of the said United States and their posterity DO *in the name and behalf of the people of this State* hereby *assent to* and *ratify* the said Constitution. [Emphasis added] [49]

Similar to the example set by Massachusetts, the Palmetto State affixed to her act of assention a set of principles or understandings that would serve as the basis for certain amendments to the compact. Unlike Massachusetts, however, South Carolina presented these proposals in the form of a basic *Declaration of Understanding*, which was accepted by the other States, consisting of a *set of conditions* upon which she entered the new Federal Union.

This Declaration of Understanding was expressed by the sovereign State of South Carolina in this language:

> And Whereas *it is essential to the preservation of the rights reserved to the several States, and the freedom of the people under the operations of a general government that the right of prescribing the manner time and places of holding the elections to the Federal Legislature, should be for ever inseparably*

---

[48] *Ibid.*, Volume III, p. 256.
[49] Charles Callan Tansill (ed.), *Op. cit.*, p. 1022.

annexed to the sovereignty of the several States. This Convention doth *declare* that the same ought to remain to all posterity *a perpetual and fundamental right in the local,* exclusive of the *interference* of the general government except in cases where the legislatures of the States, shall refuse or neglect to perform and fulfil the same according to the tenor of the said Constitution.

This Convention doth also *declare* that no Section or paragraph of the said Constitution warrants a *Construction* that the States do not *retain every power not expressly relinquished by them and vested in the General Government of the Union.* [Emphasis added] [50]

This Declaration of Understanding was then followed by two resolutions wherein the South Carolina Ratification Convention proposed several specific amendments to the new Constitution. Commenting on the exceptional act of ratification by this Southern State, Alexander H. Stephens made the following observations in his great work, *A Constitutional View of the Late War Between the States*:

In these proceedings we see, clearly, that the understanding was that the Constitution was Federal in its character. The Congress is styled "The Federal Legislature," and, in the accompanying paper, proposing amendments, the reserved Sovereignty of the several States is mentioned as a matter understood, and an express declaration that the Constitution had been assented to and ratified, with the understanding that no section or paragraph of the Constitution warranted a construction that the States did not retain every power not expressly relinquished by them. This was in the nature of a Protocol, which went with the paper, forever fixing the understanding of the State, with which she had entered into the Compact, and the understanding with which her ratification was accepted by the other States. [51]

The Federal Constitution was adopted by the State of South Carolina by a vote of 149 to 73 in her Ratification Convention. Although the proposed amendments and the Declaration of Understanding had managed to assure some of the Antifederalists that there was no need to fear the new Federal Government, not all the opponents of ratification were convinced by such assurances. Rawlins Lowndes, for instance, concluded his speech before the Ratification Convention with these impassioned sentiments: "He wished for no other epitaph, than to have inscribed on his tomb, *'Here lies the man that opposed the Constitution, because it was ruinous to the liberty of America.'* [Emphasis added]" [52] Such were the heart-felt concerns shared by many Antifederalists throughout the States.

---

[50] *Ibid.,* p. 1023.
[51] Alexander H. Stephens, *Op. cit.,* Volume 1, p. 249.
[52] *Ibid.,* Volume 1, quoted on p. 250.

With the assention of South Carolina, a total of eight States had rati-fied the new compact. All that was thereafter required to duly ratify the Con-stitution and officially put it into effect *between the ratifying States* was the approval of only one more State. And the honor of being the key State to as-sure the adoption of the Federal Constitution was bestowed upon the small but proudly sovereign State of New Hampshire.

The State of New Hampshire

On June 21, 1788, the Granite State assured the successful adoption of the Federal Constitution by being the ninth member of the league of States to assent to it. As was the case in Massachusetts and South Carolina, many of the delegates to the New Hampshire Ratification Convention were concerned that insufficient safeguards existed to adequately secure the sovereignty and reserved rights of the several States. The vote in the Ratification Convention was thus very close, with 57 delegates voting for the compact and 46 delegates voting against it.

New Hampshire's act of ratification declared:

> The Convention haveing Impartially discussed and fully considered the Constitution for the United States of America, reported to Congress by the Convention of Delegates from the United States of America & submit-ted to us by a Resolution of the General Court of said State passed the fourteenth Day of December last past and acknowledgeing with grateful Hearts the goodness of the Supreme ruler of the Universe in affording the People of the United States in the Course of His Providence an Opportu-nity, deliberately & peaceably without fraud or surprize of entering into an *Explicit and solemn compact* with each other by *assenting to & ratifying* a new Constitution, in Order to form a more perfect Union, establish Jus-tice, Insure domestick Tranquility, provide for the common defence, pro-mote the general welfare and secure the Blessings of Liberty to themselves & their Posterity – Do In the Name & behalf of *the People of the State of New-Hampshire assent to & ratify* the said Constitution for the United States of America. [Emphasis added] [53]

This formal act of ratification was then followed by a declaration that certain amendments, consisting of a Bill of Rights, should be incorporated into the federal compact:

> And as it is the Opinion of this Convention that certain amend-

---

[53] Charles Callan Tansill (ed.), *Op. cit.*, p. 1024.

ments & alterations in the said Constitution would remove the *fears* &
quiet the *apprehensions* of many of the good People of this State & *more Effectually guard against an undue Administration of the Federal Government* –
The Convention do therefore recommend that the following alterations &
provisions be introduced into the said Constitution. [Emphasis added] [54]

A total of twelve amendments were proposed by New Hampshire,
many of which would help form the foundation for the Bill of Rights. The
last of these proposed amendments, for example, declared that "Congress
shall never disarm any Citizen unless such as are or have been in Actual
Rebellion." Another proposed amendment provided that "Congress shall
make no Laws touching Religion, or to infringe the rights of Conscience."
Still another proposed amendment asserted, "That no standing Army shall be
Kept up in time of Peace unless with the consent of three fourths of the
Members of each branch of Congress, nor shall Soldiers in Time of Peace be
quartered upon private Houses without the consent of the Owners." And
another interesting recommendation provided, "That Congress shall erect no
Company of Merchants with exclusive advantages of Commerce." [55]

First and foremost among the amendments proposed by New Hampshire was one that would help to form the foundation of the Tenth Amendment to the Constitution: "That it be Explicitly declared that all Powers not
expressly & particularly Delegated by the aforesaid Constitution are reserved
to the several States to be, by them Exercised." [56] It is abundantly clear from
this proposed amendment, as well as from the official language used in the act
of ratification, that New Hampshire – like all the other States who had earlier
adopted the new plan of government – understood the Constitution of 1787
to be a *compact* between sovereign States, providing for a *Federal Government*
with expressly *defined* and *limited* powers.

With the assention of the Granite State, the new Federal Constitution
had been officially adopted by the minimum number of States required to
give it validity and authority between the States who had ratified it. A new
Federal Union was thus formally inaugurated between the nine ratifying
States, to wit: Delaware, Pennsylvania, New Jersey, Georgia, Connecticut,
Massachusetts, Maryland, South Carolina, and New Hampshire. Regardless
of whether or not the other four States ever ratified the new Constitution,
these nine sovereign bodies would be united with one another in a Confederacy styled the United States of America.

All that officially remained to inaugurate the new Federal Union was to

---

[54] *Ibid.*, p. 1024.
[55] *Ibid.*, pp. 1025-1025.
[56] *Ibid.*, p. 1025.

hold elections for federal offices and to launch the new Federal Government. Before this could be accomplished, however, two more States – Virginia and New York – voluntarily joined the new Union by ratifying the Federal Constitution. By the time the new compact went into effect, the new Union would thus consist of a total of eleven States. The two final holdouts – North Carolina and Rhode Island – refused to join the new Union until after it had been inaugurated, and for a period of time these two States maintained an existence independent of the United States.

The State of Virginia

Within the Constitutional Convention, Virginia's delegation – particularly Edmund Randolph and James Madison – had taken the initiative in the drive to destroy the Federal Republic and to build on the ruins of sovereign States a supreme National Government. So thoroughly defeated were they that Mr. Randolph, who had introduced the Virginia Plan to the Convention, later refused to sign the Federal Constitution. He did, however, lend his support to its ratification, as did Mr. Madison. These Federalists were supported in their efforts by John Marshall and Edmund Pendleton.

If the Federalists could boast of great talent and ability, so too could the Antifederalists of the Old Dominion. A stellar cast of statesmen and orators stepped forward to oppose the ratification of the new Constitution, including Patrick Henry, James Monroe, George Mason, Richard Henry Lee, and John Taylor of Caroline. The ratification contest in Virginia was truly a *battle of titans*, which witnessed two future Presidents pitted against one another and which witnessed the man destined to become the most historically famous Chief Justice of the United States pitted against America's foremost Orator of Liberty.

In a very thorough examination of virtually every phrase in the new Constitution, the Virginia Ratification Convention painstakingly ascertained the principles of the compact in explicit detail. The Antifederalists candidly expressed fear that the Federal Government had been delegated too much power, that certain general clauses in the Constitution were too ambiguous and liable to misconstruction, and that the sovereignty of the States was threatened by the compact. The general drift of their arguments may be ascertained by the tenor often expressed in debate by Patrick Henry.

As the great Orator of Liberty fearfully exclaimed before the Convention on one occasion:

This proposal of altering our Federal Government is of a most alarming nature! Make the best of this new government – say it is composed of anything but inspiration – you ought to be extremely cautious, watchful, jealous of your liberty; for, instead of securing your rights, you may lose them forever. [57]

Speaking further of the items which made him fearful of the new Constitution, Mr. Henry focused his attention on the Preamble of the proposed compact:

> I have the highest veneration for those gentlemen; but, Sir, give me leave to demand, What right did they have to say, "*We, the People?*" My political curiosity, exclusive of my anxious solicitude for the public welfare, leads me to ask, who authorized them to speak the language of, "*We, the People*," instead of, "We, the States?" States are the characteristics and the soul of a Confederation! If the States be not the agents of this Compact, it must be one great, consolidated, National Government, of all the States! [58]

Like that sturdy patriot, Samuel Adams of Massachusetts, Patrick Henry had *stumbled at the threshold* of the new Constitution, and his inquiry posed an excellent question that demanded a satisfactory answer. The records of the proceedings of the Federal Convention, of course, were still being hidden at this time, which meant that the reason for the wording of the Preamble remained a mystery. Had those records been available, all would have known that the Preamble had begun with the words, "We, the People of the States," until the Committee of Style changed the *style*, but not the *meaning*, of the Preamble. In the absence of any records of the Federal Convention, James Madison was obliged to explain to the Ratification Convention that the term "We, the People" meant nothing more than *We, the Peoples of the Several States*.

One of the chief fears of the Antifederalists was that the new compact, although appearing to provide for a Federal Government, might be construed as an instrument providing for a supreme National Government. This topic, no doubt, caused Mr. Madison to squirm uncomfortably in his chair, for there was one Antifederalist within the Ratification Convention who had witnessed his ardent efforts within the Federal Convention to secure the adoption of precisely such a despotic government. And at one point during the debates, on June 19, 1788, that Antifederalist came very close to exposing the awful truth about Mr. Madison's conduct in the Constitutional Convention, which resulted in a verbal altercation between the two gentlemen.

This altercation between George Mason and James Madison was re-

---

[57] Alexander H. Stephens, *Op. cit.*, Volume 1, quoted on p. 257.
[58] *Ibid.*, Volume 1, quoted on p. 257.

corded as follows:

> Mr. *George Mason*....There are many gentlemen in the United States who think it right, that we should have one great National Consolidated Government, and that it was better to bring it about slowly and imperceptibly, rather than all at once. This is no reflection on any man, for I mean none. To those who think that one National Consolidated Government would be best for America, this extensive judicial authority will be agreeable; but I hope there are many in this Convention of a different opinion, and who see their political happiness resting on their State governments. I know, from my own knowledge, many worthy gentlemen of the former opinion. – (Here Mr. *Madison* interrupted Mr. *Mason*, and demanded an unequivocal explanation. As those insinuations might create a belief, that every member of the late Federal Convention was of that opinion, he wished him to tell who the gentlemen were to whom he alluded.) – Mr. *Mason* then replied – I shall never refuse to explain myself. It is notorious that this is a prevailing principle. – It was at least the opinion of many gentlemen in Convention, and many in the United States. I do not know what explanation the honorable gentleman asks. I can say with great truth, that the honorable gentleman, in private conversation with, expressed himself against it: Neither did I ever hear any of the delegates from this State advocate it.
>
> Mr. *Madison* declared himself satisfied with this, unless the committee thought themselves entitled to ask a further explanation.
>
> After some desultory remarks, Mr. *Mason* continued. – I have heard that opinion advocated by gentlemen, for whose abilities, judgment, and knowledge, I have the highest reverence and respect. [59]

Although George Mason refused to name *Edmund Randolph* and *James Madison* as among the nationalist conspirators, it is probable that the Ratification Convention realized the truth. The real issue to be determined by the Ratification Convention, however, was not whether such a conspiracy had *existed* within the Federal Convention, but whether such a conspiracy had *succeeded* in Philadelphia. The great question, thus, became: Does the Constitution provide for a Federal Government or for a National Government?

To Patrick Henry, this question was of paramount importance. Whenever he attempted to solicit an explanation from the Federalists, however, all James Madison would say was that the new government would be partly federal and partly national. For his part, Mr. Henry did not find this attempt to dodge the question amusing. "We are told that this government, collectively taken, is without an example; that it is National in this part, and Federal in that part, etc.," he observed. "We may be amused, if we please, by a treatise of political anatomy." Then he relentlessly pressed forward with his question

---

[59] Max Farrand (ed.), *Op. cit.*, Volume III, pp. 330-331.

again, urging Mr. Madison to forget his own nationalistic bias long enough to provide a truthful answer. "I beg gentlemen to consider: lay aside your prejudices. *Is this a Federal Government?*" [60]

With great reluctance, James Madison finally consented to provide a truthful answer to the question posed by Mr. Henry. Yes, he admitted, it is a Federal Government, as that term was understood by the Antifederalists. He reminded the Antifederalists that nine States had already adopted the Constitution, but the new compact would not be binding on Virginia without her own consent. This proved, Mr. Madison said, that the Constitution was a compact among the States, not between the governments of the States, but between the peoples of the States. Were it a National Government, as suggested by Mr. Henry, the Constitution would be binding upon Virginia due to the fact that nine States had already duly ratified it. This was the key confirmation that the Antifederalists wanted to hear from Mr. Madison.

To quiet the fears of the opponents of ratification, James Madison also asserted that the States, under the proposed Federal Constitution, would retain most of the rights and powers they had formally enjoyed under the old Articles of Confederation. And he offered an illustration to prove that sovereignty would remain with the States under the new compact:

> Let us suppose, for a moment, that the acts of Congress, requiring money from the States, had been as effectual as the paper on the table; suppose all the laws of Congress had complete compliance; will any gentleman say that, as far as we can judge from past experience, the State governments would have been debased, and all consolidated and incorporated into one system? My imagination cannot reach it. I conceive that had those acts that effect, which all laws ought to have, the States would have retained their Sovereignty. [61]

Considering that Mr. Madison had, within the Federal Convention, denied that the States were ever sovereign – even under the Articles of Confederation – and that the States ought to be reduced to the status of colonies, as they were prior to July 4, 1776, this admission becomes all the more remarkable. It illustrates that no one knew better than he that the project for a supreme National Government had been totally defeated in the Federal Convention.

John Marshall, another leading Federalist, also verified the federative principles of the proposed system within the Virginia Ratification Convention by asserting that a State could rightfully secede from the new Federal Union:

---

[60] Alexander H. Stephens, *Op. cit.*, Volume 1, quoted on pp. 258-259.
[61] *Ibid.*, Volume 1, quoted on p. 263.

> We are threatened with the loss of our liberties by the possible abuse of power, notwithstanding the maxim, that those who give may take away. It is the people that give power, and can take it back. What shall restrain them? They are the masters who give it, and of whom their servants hold it. [62]

Another serious concern expressed by the Virginia Antifederalists related to the nature of the federal judiciary under the proposed Federal Constitution. William Grayson, for example, speaking in reference to the U.S. Supreme Court, declared that, "This Court has more power than any court under heaven....What has it in view, unless to subvert the State governments?" And George Mason asserted fear that, "When we consider the nature of these courts, we must conclude that their effect and operation will be utterly to destroy the State governments; for they will be the judges how far their laws will operate." "The principle itself goes to the destruction of the legislation of the States, whether or not it was intended," he added. "I think it will destroy the State governments." [63]

The Virginia Federalists repeatedly sought to allay such concerns by assuring the Ratification Convention that such a construction of the judicial powers was improper. Even John Marshall, who was destined to become the fourth Chief Justice of the United States, assured the Virginia delegates that the federal judiciary posed no threat to the sovereign States. "I hope that no gentleman will think that a State will be called at the bar of the federal court...," he informed the Ratification Convention. "It is not rational to suppose that the sovereign power should be dragged before a court." [64]

The only other key issue that divided the Virginia State Ratification Convention was the question of a Bill of Rights. The Federalists insisted that, inasmuch as the new government would be federal, vested only with enumerated and limited powers, such a Bill of Rights was wholly unnecessary. "Is the disputed right enumerated?" asked George Nicholas. "If not, Congress cannot meddle with it." [65]

George Mason, however, was not convinced that such an understanding constituted a sufficient safeguard for human rights and the reserved rights of the States. What *practical* safeguard, he wished to know, existed to oppose federal encroachments on the rights of the States? In reply, John Marshall assured the Ratification Convention that such attempted usurpations of power could be, and would be, successfully resisted by the State governments. A Bill

---

[62] *Ibid.*, Volume 1, quoted on p. 261.
[63] James Ronald Kennedy and Walter Donald Kennedy, *The South Was Right!*, Pelican Publishing Company, Gretna, 1994, quoted on p. 230.
[64] *Ibid.*, quoted on p. 229.
[65] Alexander H. Stephens, *Op. cit.*, Volume 1, quoted on p. 262.

of Rights, he thus concluded, would not be necessary.

Patrick Henry, however, remained unconvinced. "A Bill of Rights may be summed up in a few words," he pointed out. "What do they tell us? That our rights are reserved. Why not say so? Is it because it will consume too much paper?" "Gentlemen's reasoning against a Bill of Rights," Mr. Henry continued, "does not satisfy me – without saying which has the right side, it remains doubtful." [66]

The great Orator of Liberty then waxed eloquent and delivered the most moving speech heard by the Ratification Convention:

> The Honorable gentleman (Gov. Randolph), who was up some time ago, exhorts us not to fall into a repetition of the defects of the Confederation. He said, we ought not to declare that each State retains every power, jurisdiction, and right, which is not expressly delegated, because experience has proved the insertion of such a restriction to be destructive, and mentioned an instance to prove it. That case, Mr. Chairman, appears to me to militate against himself....They can exercise power, by implication, in one instance as well as in another. Thus, by the gentleman's own argument, they can exercise the power, though it be not delegated....We have nothing local to ask. We ask rights which concern the general happiness. Must not justice bring them into the concession of these? The honorable gentleman was pleased to say that the new government, in this policy, will be equal to what the present is. If so, that amendment will not injure that part....
>
> He speaks of war and bloodshed. Whence do this war and bloodshed come? I fear it, from not from the source he speaks of. I fear it, Sir, from the operation and friends of the Federal Government. He speaks with contempt of this amendment. But whoever will advert to the use made, repeatedly, in England, of the prerogative of the King, and the frequent attacks on the privileges of the people, notwithstanding many legislative acts to secure them, will see the necessity of *excluding implications*. Nations who have trusted to logical deductions have lost their liberty!...
>
> The worthy member who proposed to ratify has also proposed that what amendments may be deemed necessary should be recommended to Congress, and that a committee should be appointed to consider what amendments were necessary. But what does it all come to at last? That it is a vain project, and that it is indecent and improper! I will not argue unfairly, but I will ask him if amendments are not unattainable? Will gentlemen, then, lay their hands on their hearts, and say that they can adopt it in this shape? When we demand this security of our privileges, the language of Virginia is not that of respect! Give me leave to deny! She only asks amendments previous to her adoption of the Constitution....
>
> He tells you of the important blessings which, he imagines, will result to us and mankind in general from the adoption of this system. I see

---

[66] *Ibid.*, Volume 1, quoted on p. 264.

the awful immensity of the dangers with which it is pregnant! I see it! I feel it! I see beings of a higher order anxious concerning our decision! When I see beyond the horizon that bounds human eyes, and look at the final consummation of all human things, and see those intelligent beings which inhabit the ethereal mansions, reviewing the political decisions and revolutions which, in the progress of time, will happen in America, and the consequent happiness or misery of mankind, I am led to believe that much of the account, on one side or the other, will depend on what we now decide! Our own happiness alone is not affected by the event! All nations are interested in the determination! We have it in our power to secure the happiness of one half of the human race! Its adoption may involve the misery of the other hemisphere! [67]

Alexander H. Stephens, writing in 1868, made these remarks on this extraordinary oration by Patrick Henry:

> Just at this point in Mr. Henry's speech, the heavens blackened with a gathering tempest, which burst with so terrible a fury as to put the whole House in such disorder that he could proceed no farther! It was the last speech that Patrick Henry made in that Convention!
>
> Did he possess a superhuman vision, or had he caught something of the spirit of the ancient prophets, which enabled him to see farther into the future, and understand better the workings of political systems controlled by human passion, than any of his many great and equally patriotic colleagues, in that renowned body of sages and statesmen? Did he see farther in the future than Pendleton, Madison, or Marshall, when he said, "I see it! I feel it!" Did he get glimpses of the terrible scenes of the last seven years [*i.e.*, the War Between the States and Radical Reconstruction]? or, of the still more horrible ones yet ahead of us – ? [68]

As the historical record attests, the Old Dominion ratified the Federal Constitution on June 26, 1788, by the very close vote of 89 to 79. Her act of ratification, which followed that of New Hampshire by only one week, was the first one made with the explicit assertion that each sovereign State had the right to *secede* from the new Union whensoever such a course should be deemed necessary to preserve the rights and liberties of her people. The official ratification was also made with the understanding that the States respectively reserved all powers not expressly delegated by the Constitution to the Government of the United States. It was with this *Declaration of Understanding* that the most populous American State adopted the compact, and it was with this understanding that the other States accepted her act of ratification.

As the Virginia act of ratification stated:

---

[67] *Ibid.*, Volume 1, quoted on pp. 266-268.
[68] *Ibid.*, Volume 1, p. 268.

We the Delegates of *the People of Virginia* duly elected in pursuance of a recommendation from the General Assembly and now met in Convention having fully and freely investigated and discussed the proceedings of the Federal Convention and being prepared as well as the most mature deliberation hath enabled us to decide thereon Do *in the name and in behalf of the People of Virginia* declare and make known that *the powers granted under the Constitution being derived from the People of the United States may be resumed by them whensoever the same shall be perverted to their injury or oppression and that every power not granted thereby remains with them and at their will*: That therefore no right of any denomination can be cancelled abridged restrained or modified by the Congress by the Senate or House of Representatives acting in any Capacity by the President or any Department or Officer of the United States except in those instances in which power is given by the Constitution for those purposes: & That among other essential rights the liberty of Conscience and of the Press cannot be cancelled abridged restrained or modified by any authority of the United States. *With these impressions* with a solemn appeal to the Searcher of hearts for the purity of our intentions and under the conviction that whatsoever imperfections may exist in the Constitution ought rather to be examined in the mode prescribed therein than to bring the Union into danger by a delay with a hope of obtaining Amendments *previous* to the Ratification, We the said Delegates *in the name and in behalf of the People of Virginia* do by these presents *assent to* and *ratify* the Constitution recommended on the seventeenth day of September one thousand seven hundred and eighty seven by the Federal Convention for the Government of the United States hereby announcing to all those whom it may concern that the said Constitution is binding upon the said People according to an authentic Copy hereto annexed in the Words following. [Emphasis added] [69]

Attached to the Virginia act of ratification was a recommendation for a Bill of Rights that began by stating, "That there be a Declaration or Bill of Rights asserting and securing from encroachment the essential and unalienable Rights of the People in some such manner as the following." [70] In all, some twenty propositions were offered by the Virginia Ratification Convention.

One of the more interesting provisions in this section was aimed at stifling all claims for *judicial review,* by asserting, "That all power of suspending laws or the execution of laws by any authority, without the consent of the representatives of the people in the legislature is injurious to their rights, and ought not to be exercised." [71] It is evident that the Virginia Ratification Convention was firmly convinced that the law should be what the *legislature* says

---

[69] Charles Callan Tansill (ed.), *Op. cit.,* pp. 1027-1028.
[70] *Ibid.,* p. 1028.
[71] *Ibid.,* p. 1029.

it is, not what the *judiciary* says it should be. It is also evident that the wisdom of that Convention conceived that any other mode of legislation would be subversive of the rights of the people.

Other recommendations for a Declaration or Bill of Rights included the following provisions:

> **Seventeenth Provision:** "That the people have a right to keep and bear arms; that a well regulated Militia composed of the body of the people trained to arms is the proper, natural and safe defence of a free State. That standing armies in time of peace are dangerous to liberty, and therefore ought to be avoided, as far as the circumstances and protection of the Community will admit; and that in all cases the military should be under strict subordination to and governed by the Civil power." [72]
>
> **Nineteenth Provision:** "That any person religiously scrupulous of bearing arms ought to be exempted upon payment of an equivalent to employ another to bear arms in his stead." [73]
>
> **Twentieth Provision:** "That religion or the duty which we owe to our Creator, and the manner of discharging it can be directed only by reason and conviction, not by force or violence, and therefore all men have an equal, natural and unalienable right to the free exercise of religion according to the dictates of conscience, and that no particular religious sect or society ought to be favored or established by Law in preference to others." [74]

This list of twenty *propositions* asserting the inalienable rights of man was then followed by a list of twenty proposed *amendments* to be incorporated into the body of the Federal Constitution. First and foremost among the list was a declaration, "That each State in the Union shall respectively retain every power, jurisdiction and right which is not by this Constitution delegated to the Congress of the United States or to the departments of the Federal Government." [75]

Other proposed amendments recommended by this State included the following:

> **Ninth Proposal:** "That no standing army or regular troops shall be raised or kept up in time of peace, without the consent of two thirds of the members present in both houses." [76]
>
> **Eleventh Proposal:** "That each State respectively shall have the power to provide for organizing, arming and disciplining it's own Militia, whensoever Congress shall omit or neglect to provide for the same. That

---

[72] *Ibid.*, p. 1030.
[73] *Ibid.*, p. 1030.
[74] *Ibid.*, pp. 1030-1031.
[75] *Ibid.*, p. 1031.
[76] *Ibid.*, p. 1032.

the Militia shall not be subject to Martial law, except when in actual service in time of war, invasion, or rebellion; and when not in the actual service of the United States, shall be subject only to such fines, penalties and punishments as shall be directed or inflicted by the laws of its own State." [77]

Seventeenth Proposal: "That those clauses which declare that Congress shall not exercise certain powers be not interpreted in any manner whatsoever to extend the powers of Congress. But that they may be construed either as making exceptions to the specified powers where this shall be the case, or otherwise as inserted merely for greater caution." [78]

Summarizing the proceedings and conclusions of the Virginia Ratification Convention, Alexander H. Stephens noted the following in his book, *A Constitutional View of the Late War Between the States*:

> These proceedings conclusively show how the Convention of Virginia understood the Constitution. That is, that it was Federal in its character, and that the Government under it was to be a Federal Government, one founded upon Compact between Sovereign States. Not a member of the Convention advocated the Constitution upon any other principles. The opposition of Patrick Henry, George Mason, and others, was altogether argumentative, and sprung mainly from apprehensions that the Constitution would not be construed as its friends maintained that it would be, and that powers not delegated would be assumed, by construction and implication. These proceedings also show clearly, that Virginia understood by the declaration, in her ratification, that her people had the right to resume the powers that they had delegated, in case these powers, in their judgment, should be perverted to their injury. [79]

As the student of constitutional government undoubtedly detected during our analysis of the proceedings of the Virginia Ratification Convention, there was one very prominent Virginian – other than George Washington – whose name was not mentioned in connection with it. Inasmuch as Mr. Jefferson was, at the time, stationed in Paris, serving as the American Ambassador to France, he did not *directly* participate in the proceedings of the Ratification Period. Nonetheless, he did participate *indirectly* in those proceedings, and his name was raised a number of times in the Virginia Ratification Convention, especially by the Antifederalists, who claimed to have knowledge that Mr. Jefferson did not approve of the new Constitution. Such an assertion significantly bolstered the Antifederalist cause and embarrassed James Madison, for the author of the Declaration of Independence was the most revered man in Virginia, rivaled only by George Washington.

---

[77] *Ibid.*, p. 1032.
[78] *Ibid.*, p. 1033.
[79] Alexander H. Stephens, *Op. cit.*, Volume 1, p. 270.

Although Thomas Jefferson never *publicized* his opinion of the proposed compact or his stand on the ratification issue, what the Antifederalists had said in the Virginia Ratification Convention was basically the truth. When the Philosopher of the Revolution first read the Constitution shortly after the Federal Convention ended, he found himself evenly divided in sentiment, liking half of it and disliking the other half. He was especially disturbed by the Presidency, an office which he thought resembled a bad edition of a Polish King. Not only did the President have too much power, he felt, but it was dangerous for the President to be eligible for re-election. His initial impression, candidly expressed in *private* communications, was that all of the good in the new compact could have been added as a few amendments to the Articles of Confederation, which he thought should have been preserved.

The more he studied the Constitution, however, the more his position on it softened. To secure the good that it contained, he therefore urged his friends, in *private* correspondence, to *support* the ratification of the compact until it had been approved by the requisite minimum number of States. After that point had been reached, he was convinced, the Constitution should be *opposed* until the Federalists agreed to the addition of a Bill of Rights. *The action taken by the Virginia Ratification Convention was in complete harmony with his wishes.* Once it became obvious that a Bill of Rights would indeed be added to the compact, Mr. Jefferson *privately* urged universal ratification of the new Constitution.

In his book, *The Constitutional Principles of Thomas Jefferson*, Caleb Perry Patterson made this assessment of the position taken on the question of ratification by the author of the Declaration of Independence:

> After receiving a copy of the Constitution from Madison with almost twenty pages of explanations,...Jefferson expressed himself in favor of ratification by nine States – the necessary number for adoption. "My first wish," he told Hopkinson, "was that the 9. first Conventions might accept the Constitution, as the means of securing to us the great mass of good it contained, and that the 4. last might reject it, as the means of obtaining amendments." He wrote another one of his friends that if he were in America, he "would advocate it warmly til nine should have adopted & then as warmly take, the other side to convince the remaining four that they ought not to come into it till the declaration of rights is annexed to it."
>
> When he learned that the State Ratifying Conventions were proposing amendments in the nature of a Bill of Rights (126 were proposed) and that few shared his attitude toward the re-eligibility of the President Jefferson changed his mind and became an advocate of unanimous ratification. "With respect to the declaration of rights I suppose the majority of the United States are of my opinion: for I apprehend all the Antifederalists, and a very respectable proportion of the Federalists think that

such a declaration should now be annexed." The ninth State ratified, and Jefferson wrote: "I sincerely rejoice at the acceptance of our new Constitution by nine States. It is a good canvas, on which some strokes only want retouching. What these are, I think are sufficiently manifested by the general voice from North to South, which calls for a Bill of Rights."...

Jefferson's expectation that a Bill of Rights would be forthcoming was soon realized. He persuaded Madison to reverse himself and to become a champion of such a bill, though Madison acted more from the motive of placating the critics of the Constitution and of facilitating its ratification than from a feeling that a Bill of Rights was necessary. Madison really agreed with Hamilton and Wilson that such a bill was illogical in a Constitution containing only granted powers and that its annexation would create an implication of powers which had not been granted. Jefferson asked of such critics why the Constitution had denied certain powers to Congress, contending that the document itself furnished a precedent for the denying of powers which had not been granted. He admitted that a Constitution could be so meticulous in its wording that a Bill of Rights would be unnecessary and that he had proposed that type of Constitution for Virginia. But he contended, and rightly so, that the Constitution under consideration was so general in character as to provide a basis for broad implications which, under the general tendency of governments to assume powers, would doubtless be taken advantage of....

Here then is the picture of this great advocate of constitutional government, willing to accept the fiat accompli, but unwilling to be labelled and placed in a straight jacket. As a champion of liberty and self-government he would continue to maintain his vigilance. [80]

After the adoption of the Constitution and the formation of the new Federal Government, Alexander Hamilton and Thomas Jefferson became leaders of opposing political parties, despite the fact that both men were members of President Washington's Cabinet. In an attempt to discredit his archenemy in the eyes of the President, Mr. Hamilton accused Mr. Jefferson of being an unyielding Antifederalist enemy of the Constitution during the Ratification Period. To counter this untruthful charge, the latter wrote a letter to President Washington on September 9, 1782, in which he explained his conduct during the time in question.

As Thomas Jefferson informed George Washington:

Spelling my name and character at full length to the public, while he [Mr. Hamilton] conceals his own under the signature of "An American," he charges me, first, with having written letters from Europe to my friends to oppose the present Constitution, while depending....The first charge is most false. No man in the United States, I suppose, approved of

---

[80] Caleb Perry Patterson, *The Constitutional Principles of Thomas Jefferson*, Peter Smith, Gloucester, 1953, pp. 38-40.

every title in the Constitution; no one, I believe, approved more of it than I did, and more of it was certainly disapproved by my accuser than by me, and of its parts most vitally Republican. Of this the few letters I wrote on the subject (not half a dozen I believe) will be a proof: and for my own satisfaction and justification, I must tax you with the reading of them when I return to where they are. You will see that my objection to the Constitution was, that it wanted a Bill of Rights securing freedom of religion, freedom of the press, freedom from standing armies, trial by jury, and a constant habeas corpus act. Col. Hamilton's was, that it wanted a King and House of Lords. The sense of America has approved my objection and added the Bill of Rights, not the King and Lords. I also thought a longer term of service, insusceptible of renewal, would have made a President more independent. My country has thought otherwise, I have acquiesced implicitly. He wishes the general government should have power to make laws binding the States in all cases whatsoever. Our country has thought otherwise; has he acquiesced? Notwithstanding my wish for a Bill of Rights, my letters strongly urged the adoption of the Constitution, by nine States at least, to secure the good it contained. I at first thought that the best method of securing the Bill of rights would be for four States to hold off till such a bill should be agreed to. But the moment I saw Mr. Hancock's proposition to pass the Constitution as it stood, and give perpetual instructions to the representatives of every State to insist on a Bill of Rights, I acknowledged the superiority of his plan and advocated universal adoption. [81]

Here, then, is the position taken during the Ratification Period by Thomas Jefferson, as honestly related in his own words. Because of the agreement to incorporate a Bill of Rights into the Federal Constitution, many of the Antifederalists could be persuaded to withdraw their chief objections and allow the compact to pass in the State Ratification Conventions. *Without such assurances for a Bill of Rights, it is highly doubtful if States like Massachusetts and Virginia would have acceded to the instrument.* Having received such an assurance from the Federalists, the Old Dominion adopted the compact, and her ratification marked a decisive turning point for the new Constitution and helped to persuade the deeply divided New York Ratification Convention to assent to the new plan of government.

The State of New York

The New York delegation to the Federal Convention of 1787, as we have already noted, had been deeply divided. Robert Yates and John Lansing

---

[81] Richard S. Poppen (ed.), *Thomas Jefferson*, St. Louis, 1904, pp. 56-57.

had consistently sided with the cause of the Federal Republicans in the Philadelphia Convention, while Alexander Hamilton had, with equal persistence, taken a stand on the side of extreme nationalism. All three delegates had walked out of the Grand Convention, and only Mr. Hamilton had been willing to return near its conclusion. Inasmuch as New York had been the only State to officially secede from the Federal Convention, it was clear to all that the battle for ratification in the Empire State would be intense.

The chief Federalists in New York were Robert Livingston, John Jay, and Alexander Hamilton. Although Mr. Hamilton was the leader of this State's Federalist faction, his initial methods of "persuasion" and his unethical conduct probably did more to help the Antifederalists than his own cause. Writing under the pseudonym of "Caesar," for example, he threatened that, if New York refused to ratify the Constitution by peaceful means, the State might be forced to do so at the point of a sword. He also threatened to agitate a treasonous rebellion in New York City against the rest of the State, for the avowed purpose of dismembering the State and joining New York City – *by itself* – to the new Federal Union!

Such "persuasive" methods, needless to say, did little to advance the cause of the Constitution in New York, as noted by historian Richard B. Morris:

> Hamilton was the main Federalist orator, but he was considered an arrogant extremist by his opponents and his pleas failed to turn the tide. He and Robert R. Livingston then let it be known that New York City would secede and ratify on its own if the State withheld approval. John Jay proved the more tactful and understanding in efforts to reassure the Antifederalists. [82]

John Jay managed to persuade Alexander Hamilton that his bullying tactics and menacing approach would only doom the cause of the Constitution in New York. Accordingly, Mr. Hamilton agreed to drop the style of the arrogant "Caesar" and to adopt the pleasant and reassuring style of "Publius." Under that pseudonym, Mr. Hamilton and Mr. Jay – in collaboration with James Madison of Virginia – produced a remarkable series of essays on the Constitution that were subsequently published under the title, *The Federalist Papers*. The sole purpose of these essays was to help secure ratification of the compact in the Empire State, and Mr. Madison was invited to participate in the effort only after Gouverneur Morris had declined Mr. Hamilton's request to help him author the essays.

But Alexander Hamilton's change of tactics did not eliminate all of his

---

[82] Richard B. Morris, *Op. cit.*, p. 77.

problems. There still remained the matter of his personal conduct within the Constitutional Convention, and especially his notorious five-hour oration, wherein he had candidly stated his preference for a totalitarian dictatorship, a highly centralized government ruled by a monied aristocracy, and the total destruction of the States. Although his words had been spoken in total concealment from the public eye, two eye witnesses from New York had heard every word he spoke, and one of them – John Lansing – was *an Antifederalist delegate in the State Ratification Convention!* Would Mr. Lansing "spill the beans" and inform the Ratification Convention of Mr. Hamilton's conduct in the late Federal Convention? The answer was provided on June 28, 1788, when Mr. Lansing rose to speak.

Here is the official record of the verbal encounter between Mr. Hamilton and Mr. Lansing in the Ratification Convention:

> Hon. Mr. Lansing....It has been admitted by an honorable gentleman from New York, (Mr. Hamilton,) that the State governments are necessary to secure the liberties of the people. He has urged several forcible reasons why they ought to be preserved under the new system; and he has treated the idea of the general and State governments being hostile to each other as chimerical. I am, however, firmly persuaded that an hostility between them will exist. *This was a received opinion in the late Convention at Philadelphia. That honorable gentleman was then fully convinced that it would exist, and argued, with much decision and great plausibility, that the State governments ought to be subverted, at least so far as to leave them only corporate rights, and that, even in that situation, they would endanger the existence of the general government.* But the honorable gentleman's reflections have probably induced him to correct that sentiment.
>
> (Mr. Hamilton here interrupted Mr. Lansing, and *contradicted, in the most positive terms,* the charge of inconsistency included in the preceding observations. This produced a *warm personal altercation* between those gentlemen, which engrossed *the remainder of the day*.) [Emphasis added] [83]

It is unfortunate that the official record does not provide more details on that "warm personal altercation" that "engrossed the remainder of the day." It may be presumed, however, that many details were brought to light before the Ratification Convention that Mr. Hamilton wished could have remained concealed in darkness. It may also be presumed that this altercation, coupled with the failure of Mr. Hamilton's other crass attempts at persuasion, convinced the New York Federalist that the Constitution could and should be defended only on its true merits, *as a strictly Federal Constitution.* As a consequence of this conviction, Alexander Hamilton – although a confirmed Na-

---

[83] Max Farrand (ed.), *Op. cit.*, Volume III, p. 338.

tional Monarchist – became, *at least for the duration of the Ratification Period,* the most ardent advocate of the *federal principles* inherent in the proposed American Constitution in the State of New York!

The concerns expressed by the Antifederalists in the Ratification Convention may be ascertained from this speech delivered by an opponent of ratification, whose alarm was aroused by the so-called *General Welfare Clause* in the Constitution:

> Sir, I yesterday expressed my fears that this clause would tend to annihilate the State governments. I also observed, that the powers granted by it were indefinite, since the Congress are authorized to provide for the common defence and general welfare, and to pass all laws necessary for the attainment of these important objects. The legislature is the highest power in a government....Now, if the Congress should judge it a proper provision, for the common defence and general welfare, that the State governments should be essentially destroyed, what, in the name of common sense, will prevent them? Are they not constitutionally authorized to pass such laws? Are not the terms, *common defence and general welfare,* indefinite, undefinable terms? *What checks have the State governments against such encroachments?* [Emphasis added] [84]

The construction applied to the clause in question was, of course, highly absurd, as perhaps even the Antifederalists fully realized, for the phrase under consideration had actually been copied directly from the old Articles of Confederation, and it was widely known and understood that no powers could be derived from such generalized terminology. The New York Antifederalists, however, evidently preferred to leave nothing to implication, and were determined to fix for all time the true meaning of the general phrases of the compact. They also wished to draw from the Federalists an understanding of how the State governments could maintain themselves when confronted by federal encroachments.

In response to the fears raised by the Antifederalists, Alexander Hamilton gave these unequivocal assurances:

> [The State legislatures will be] *standing bodies of observation, possessing the confidence of the people, jealous of federal encroachments, and armed with every power to check the first essays of treachery.* They will institute regular modes of inquiry. The complicated domestic attachments, which subsist between the State legislators and their electors, will ever make them *vigilant guardians of the people's rights. Possessed of the means and the disposition of resistance,* the spirit of opposition will be easily communicated to the people, and, under the conduct of *an organized body of leaders,* will act with *weight*

---

[84] Alexander H. Stephens, *Op. cit.,* Volume 1, quoted on p. 279.

and system. Thus, it appears that *the very structure of the Confederacy* affords the surest preventions from error, and *the most powerful checks to misconduct.* [Emphasis added] [85]

It is abundantly evident from Mr. Hamilton's words that he did not entertain the slightest idea that either he, Gouverneur Morris, James Wilson, or James Madison had been victorious in the Federal Convention. The Constitution, said he, would rest upon the pillars of sovereign States, whose governments would serve as the guardians of the liberties of the people. Such governments would constitute vigilant watch dogs, always ready to defend the people against encroachments from the Federal Government. Not only would the State governments hold the confidence and loyalty of the people, but they would also possess the means to hold the Government of the United States in check. And this means of resistance would stem directly from "the very structure of the Confederacy." Considering the source of these words, this was a most remarkable admission.

Continuing in the same vein, Alexander Hamilton told the New York Ratification Convention:

> The gentlemen are afraid that the State governments will be abolished. But, Sir, their existence does not depend upon the laws of the United States. *Congress can no more abolish the State governments, than they can dissolve the Union.* The whole Constitution is repugnant to it, and yet the gentleman would introduce an additional useless provision against it. [86]

Mr. Hamilton also informed the Ratification Convention:

> It has been observed, *to coerce the States is one of the maddest projects that was ever devised.* A failure of compliance will never be confined to a single State. This being the case, can we suppose it wise to hazard a *civil war?* Suppose Massachusetts, or any large State, should refuse, and Congress should attempt to compel them, would they not have influence to procure assistance, especially from those States which are in the same situation as themselves? *What picture does this idea present to our view? A complying State at war with a non-complying State;* Congress marching the troops of one State into the bosom of another; this State collecting auxiliaries, and forming, perhaps, a majority against its federal head. *Here is a nation at war with itself. Can any reasonable man be well disposed towards a government which makes war and carnage the only means of supporting itself — a government that can exist only by the sword?* Every such war must involve the innocent with the guilty. *This single consideration should be sufficient to dispose every peaceable citizen against such a government.* But can we believe that

---

[85] *Ibid.*, Volume 1, quoted on p. 280.
[86] *Ibid.*, Volume 1, quoted on p. 280.

one State will ever suffer itself to be used as an instrument of coercion? *The thing is a dream; it is impossible.* [Emphasis added] [87]

As history attests, the *impossible* dream – *the maddest project ever imagined* – which Mr. Hamilton presented to the State Ratification Convention in 1788, became *a tragic nightmare* some 73 years later under the leadership of Abraham Lincoln and the Radical Republicans. Yet, despite the deplorable fact that Mr. Lincoln's policy of war and conquest against sovereign States has been glorified ever since the War Between the States by those who worship all-powerful government, the undeniable truth – as so honestly and candidly stated by Alexander Hamilton – is that such coercion of a State is totally subversive of the foundations of our Federal Republic. What honest, peaceable, reasonable man, he declared, could be "well disposed towards a government which makes war and carnage the only means of supporting itself – a government that can exist only by the sword?"

To the representatives of the people of New York assembled in Convention, Mr. Hamilton said:

> The State governments possess inherent advantages, which will ever give them an influence and ascendancy over the National Government, and will forever preclude the possibility of federal encroachments. That their liberties, indeed, can be subverted by the federal head, is repugnant to every rule of political calculation. Is not this arrangement, then, Sir, a most wise and prudent one? Is not the present representation fully adequate to our present exigencies, and sufficient to answer all the purposes of the Union? I am persuaded that an examination of the objects of the Federal Government will afford a conclusive answer. [88]

We may excuse Alexander Hamilton's inappropriate usage of the term "National Government" in this portion of his address, for it is apparent that he is herein clearly describing a *Federal Government*, not a National Government. Nor was Mr. Hamilton alone in affirming that the new Constitution would truly be federal in nature. John Jay referred to the government to be established by the compact as a "strong, energetic, Federal Government." [89] And Robert Morris, another proponent of ratification, confirmed these sentiments when he asserted that, "I am happy, Mr. Chairman, to perceive that it is a principle *on all sides conceded*, and adopted by this committee, that an energetic Federal Government is essential to the preservation of our Union." [90]

---

[87] *Ibid.*, Volume 1, quoted on pp. 281-282.
[88] *Ibid.*, Volume 1, quoted on p. 282.
[89] *Ibid.*, Volume 1, quoted on p. 283.
[90] *Ibid.*, Volume 1, quoted on p. 283.

Robert Livingston, speaking on behalf of ratification, referred to the Government of the United States as a "Federal Government" and indicated that it was possible for such a government to operate directly on individual citizens without mitigating against the concept of a league of States:

> The gentleman from Duchess appears to have misapprehended some of the ideas which dropped from me. My argument was, that a Republic might very properly be formed by a *league of States*, but that the laws of the general legislature must act, and be enforced upon individuals. The gentlemen who have spoken in opposition to me have either misunderstood or perverted my meaning; but, Sir, I flatter myself, it has not been misunderstood by the Convention at large. [91]

Perhaps it was Alexander Hamilton who best summarized the arguments of the Federalists when he made these remarkably candid and truthful statements to the Ratification Convention:

> The States can never lose their powers till the whole people of America are robbed of their liberties. These must go together; they must support each other, or meet one common fate....
> I imagine, I have stated to the committee abundant reasons to prove the entire *safety of the State governments* and of the people. [92]

On July 26, 1788, New York became the eleventh State to ratify the Federal Constitution by the extremely narrow margin of 30 to 27 within her Ratification Convention. However, the Empire State at first desired to make her assention to the compact *conditional* on the addition of a Bill of Rights to it. An urgent exchange of correspondence then took place between Alexander Hamilton and James Madison, and the latter solemnly assured the New York Ratification Convention that such a Bill of Rights would indeed be incorporated into the Constitution as soon as possible. With this assurance, New York's conditional ratification was changed to complete ratification, although the Empire State still insisted on incorporating a *Declaration of Understanding* within her act of assention. Like Virginia, New York wanted it to be clearly understood that the States reserved to themselves all powers not delegated to the Federal Government and that a sovereign State had the inalienable right to *secede* from the new Union whensoever such action was deemed necessary by the State.

New York's act of ratification began with these words:

---

[91] *Ibid.*, Volume 1, quoted on p. 277.
[92] *Ibid.*, Volume 1, quoted on pp. 283 and 285.

We the Delegates of *the People of the State of New York*, duly elected and Met in Convention, having maturely considered the Constitution for the United States of America, agreed to on the seventeenth day of September, in the year One thousand Seven hundred and Eighty seven, by the Convention then assembled at Philadelphia in the Common-wealth of Pennsylvania (a Copy whereof precedes these presents) and having also seriously and deliberately considered the present situation of the United States, *Do declare and make known*. [Emphasis added] [93]

These introductory words were then followed by a lengthy Declaration of Understanding that contained no less than twenty-three propositions. Some of the more interesting statements of understanding were the following:

"That all Power is originally vested in and consequently derived from the People, and that government is instituted by them for their common Interest Protection and Security." [94]

"That the enjoyment of Life, Liberty and the pursuit of Happiness are essential rights which every Government ought to respect and preserve." [95]

"That the Powers of Government may be reassumed by the People, whensoever it shall become necessary to their Happiness; that every Power, Jurisdiction and right, which is not by the said Constitution clearly delegated to the Congress of the United States, or the departments of the Government thereof, remains to the People of the several States, or to their respective State Governments to whom they may have granted the same; And that those Clauses in the said Constitution, which declare, that Congress shall not have or exercise certain Powers, do not imply that Congress is entitled to any Powers not given by the said Constitution; but that such Clauses are to be construed either as exceptions to certain specified Powers, or as inserted merely for greater Caution." [96]

"That the People have an equal, natural and unalienable right, freely and peaceably to Exercise their Religion according to the dictates of Conscience, and that no Religious Sect or Society ought to be favoured or established by Law in preference of others." [97]

"That the People have a right to keep and bear Arms; that a well regulated Militia, including the body of the People capable of bearing Arms, is the proper, natural and safe defence of a free State." [98]

"That the Militia should not be subject to Martial Law except in time of war, Rebellion or Insurrection." [99]

"That standing Armies in time of Peace are dangerous to Liberty,

---

[93] Charles Callan Tansill (ed.), *Op. cit.*, p. 1034.
[94] *Ibid.*, p. 1034.
[95] *Ibid.*, p. 1034.
[96] *Ibid.*, pp. 1034-1035.
[97] *Ibid.*, p. 1035.
[98] *Ibid.*, p. 1035.
[99] *Ibid.*, p. 1035.

and ought not to be kept up, except in Cases of necessity; and that at all times, the Military should be under strict Subordination to the civil Power." [100]

"That no Person ought to be taken imprisoned or disseised of his freehold, or be exiled or deprived of his Privileges, Franchises, Life, Liberty or Property but by due process of Law." [101]

"That nothing contained in the said Constitution is to be construed to prevent the Legislature of any State from passing Laws at its discretion from time to time to divide such State into convenient Districts, and to apportion its Representatives to and amongst such Districts." [102]

"That the Jurisdiction of the Supreme Court of the United States, or of any other Court to be instituted by the Congress, is not in any case to be encreased enlarged or extended by any Fiction Collusion or mere suggestion; – And That no Treaty is to be construed so to operate as to alter the Constitution of any State." [103]

After the presentation of the Declaration of Understanding came the actual act of ratification, which was expressed in this language:

> *Under these impressions and declaring that the rights aforesaid cannot be abridged or violated, and that the Explanations aforesaid are consistent with the said Constitution,* And in confidence that the Amendments which shall have been proposed to the said Constitution will receive an early and mature Consideration: We the said Delegates, *in the Name and in the behalf of the People of the State of New York* Do by these presents *Assent to* and *Ratify* the said Constitution. In full Confidence nevertheless that until a Convention shall be called and convened for proposing Amendments to the said Constitution, the Militia of this State will not be continued in Service out of this State for a longer term than six weeks without the Consent of the Legislature thereof; – that the Congress will not make or alter any Regulation in this State respecting the times places and manner of holding Elections for Senators or Representatives unless the Legislature of this State shall neglect or refuse to make Laws or regulations for the purpose, or from any circumstance be incapable of making the same, and that in those cases such power will only be exercised until the Legislature of this State shall make provision in the Premises; – that no Excise will be imposed on any Article of the Growth production or Manufacture of the United States, or any of them within this State, Ardent Spirits excepted; And that the Congress will not lay direct Taxes within this State, but when the Monies arising from the Impost and Excise shall be insufficient for the public Exigencies, nor then, until Congress shall first have made a Requisition upon this State to assess levy and pay the Amount of such Requisition made agreeably to the Census fixed in the said Constitution in such way and manner as the

---

[100] *Ibid.*, p. 1035.
[101] *Ibid.*, p. 1035.
[102] *Ibid.*, p. 1037.
[103] *Ibid.*, p. 1037.

Legislature of this State shall judge best, but that in such case, if the State shall neglect or refuse to pay its proportion pursuant to such Requisition, then the Congress may assess and levy this States proportion together with Interest at the Rate of six per Centum per Annum from the time at which the same was required to be paid. [Emphasis added] [104]

Affixed to the formal act of ratification was a list of some thirty-two proposed amendments to the Federal Constitution, of which the following three are representative examples:

> "That the Congress do not grant Monopolies or erect any Company with Exclusive Advantages of Commerce." [105]
> "That the Congress shall not declare War without the concurrence of two-thirds of the Senators and Representatives present in each House." [106]
> "That the Senators and Representatives and all Executive and Judicial Officers of the United States shall be bound by Oath or Affirmation not to infringe or violate the Constitution or Rights of the respective States." [107]

The Empire State was the last of the States to ratify the new Constitution before it went into effect between those States that had adopted it. On July 2, 1788, after receiving notification of the ratification by New Hampshire – the ninth State to adopt the Constitution – the Congress under the Articles of Confederation initiated proceedings to put the new compact into operation. By September 13th, the Congress resolved:

> That the first Wednesday in Jany next be the day for appointing Electors in the several States, which before the said day shall have ratified the said Constitution; that the first Wednesday in Feby next be the day for the electors to assemble in the respective States and to vote for a President; And that the first Wednesday in March next be the time and the present seat of Congress the place for commencing proceedings under the said Constitution. [108]

On March 4, 1789, the new Federal Government was launched. George Washington, who had been unanimously elected President of the United States, was sworn into office, as was the Vice President, John Adams of Massachusetts. Twenty-two Senators, having been appointed by the legisla-

---

[104] *Ibid.*, pp. 1037-1038.
[105] *Ibid.*, p. 1040.
[106] *Ibid.*, p. 1040.
[107] *Ibid.*, pp. 1043-1044.
[108] *Ibid.*, p. 1062.

tures of the eleven States in the new Union, took their seats in the upper
branch of the new Congress; and Representatives elected by the peoples of
those same eleven States took their seats in the House of Representatives.

All this took place, it must be strongly emphasized, with only *eleven*
States participating in the launching of the new Federal Government. Neither
North Carolina nor Rhode Island took part in any of the federal elections,
because *those two States were not members of the new Federal Union.* Nor
would they become members of the new Union unless and until they ratified
the Constitution of 1787. Membership in the Federal Union, it will be remembered, was to be based on *voluntary consent,* and no State could be *forced*
or *coerced* to maintain membership in the United States of America. Until
these two States saw fit to adopt the new Constitution, they would remain in
their status as completely independent Nations in the North American Continent and as *foreign powers* to the United States.

The State of North Carolina

Nine months after the new Federal Government was launched, North
Carolina formally resolved to take her place alongside her sister States in the
new Union. Her reason for holding out so long was an earnest and strong desire for a Bill of Rights. The decision to delay ratification had been made on
August 2, 1788, when the State formally resolved that mere verbal *assurances*
of a Bill of Rights would be insufficient to induce her to adopt the Federal
Constitution.

At that time, the State Ratification Convention passed the following
declaration:

> *Resolved,* That a declaration of rights, asserting and securing from
> encroachment the great principles of civil and religious liberty, and the un-
> alienable rights of the people, together with amendments to the most am-
> biguous and exceptionable parts of the said Constitution of government,
> ought to be laid before Congress and the Convention of the States that
> shall or may be called for the purpose of amending the said Constitution,
> for their consideration, previous to the ratification of the Constitution
> aforesaid on the part of the State of North Carolina. [109]

This temporary *rejection* of the Federal Constitution was followed by a
Declaration of Rights, which consisted of some nineteen propositions. Some of
the more noteworthy of these declarations were the following:

---

[109] Jefferson Davis, *Op. cit.,* quoted on pp. 110-111.

Third Declaration: "That Government ought to be instituted for the common benefit, protection and security of the people; and that the doctrine of non-resistance against arbitrary power and oppression is absurd, slavish, and destructive to the good and happiness of mankind." [110]

Seventh Declaration: "That all power of suspending laws, or the execution of laws by any authority without the consent of the representatives, of the people in the legislature, is injurious to their rights, and ought not to be exercised." [111]

Eleventh Declaration: "That in controversies respecting property, and in suits between man and man, the ancient trial by jury is one of the greatest securities to the rights of the people, and ought to remain sacred and inviolable." [112]

Seventeenth Declaration: "That the people have a right to keep and bear arms; that a well regulated militia composed of the body of the people, trained to arms, is the proper, natural and safe defence of a free State. That standing armies in time of peace are dangerous to Liberty, and therefore ought to be avoided, as far as the circumstances and protection of the community will admit; and that in all cases, the military should be under strict subordination to, and governed by the civil power." [113]

Nineteenth Declaration: "That religion, or the duty which we owe to our Creator, and the manner of discharging it, can be directed only by reason and conviction, not by force or violence, and therefore all men have an equal, natural and unalienable right to the free exercise of religion according to the dictates of conscience, and that no particular religious sect or society ought to be favoured or established by law in preference to others." [114]

The Declaration of Rights was followed by a list of twenty-six proposed amendments to the federal compact, which included the following selections:

First Proposal: "That each State in the Union shall, respectively, retain every power, jurisdiction and right, which is not by this Constitution delegated to the Congress of the United States, or to the departments of the Federal Government." [115]

Eighteenth Proposal: "That those clauses which declare that Congress shall not exercise certain powers, be not interpreted in any manner whatsoever to extend the powers of Congress; but that they be construed either as making exceptions to the specified powers where this shall be the case, or otherwise, as inserted merely for greater caution." [116]

Twenty-Second Proposal: "That Congress erect no company of

---

[110] Charles Callan Tansill (ed.), *Op. cit.*, p. 1045.

[111] *Ibid.*, p. 1045.

[112] *Ibid.*, p. 1046.

[113] *Ibid.*, p. 1047.

[114] *Ibid.*, p. 1047.

[115] *Ibid.*, p. 1047.

[116] *Ibid.*, p. 1050.

merchants with exclusive advantages of commerce." [117]

Twenty-Sixth Proposal: "That Congress shall not introduce foreign troops into the United States without the consent of two-thirds of the members present of both houses." [118]

North Carolina's patience was rewarded. When the first Congress under the new Constitution convened in New York City in 1789, one of its first tasks was to draft a Bill of Rights. Guided by James Madison, Congress took the sundry proposals of the States and condensed them into twelve amendments, which were then submitted to the States for ratification. Such a course of action was convincing proof to North Carolina that her conditions had been met, and her Convention ratified the Constitution on November 21, 1789.

The Tar Heel State assented to the Constitution in these words:

> Whereas The General Convention which met in Philadelphia in pursuance of a recommendation of Congress, did recommend to the Citizens of the United States a Constitution or form of Government in the following words Viz....
>
> Resolved, that this Convention in behalf of *the freemen, citizens and inhabitants of the State of North Carolina*, do *adopt* and *ratify* the said Constitution and form of Government. [Emphasis added] [119]

When the Antifederalists in North Carolina had pressed the charge that the Constitutional Convention of 1787 had exceeded its power, the Federalists denied it, claiming that the Grand Convention had only recommended a new "Federal Government" to replace the old one. William R. Davie, who had attended the Federal Convention as part of the North Carolina delegation, assured the Ratification Convention that the States would retain their sovereignty under the new Constitution, pointing to the equality of suffrage in the Senate as proof.

During the course of debates in the Ratification Convention, Mr. Davie gave this explanation of the purpose of the new Federal Constitution:

> The business of the Convention was to amend the Confederation, by giving it additional powers....The weakness and inefficiency of the old Confederation produced the necessity of calling the Federal Convention. Their plan is now before you; and, I hope, on a deliberate consideration, every man will see the necessity of such a system....A consolidation of the States is said by some gentlemen to have been intended....If there were any

---

[117] *Ibid.*, p. 1051.

[118] *Ibid.*, p. 1051.

[119] *Ibid.*, p. 1051.

seeds in this Constitution which might, one day, produce a consolidation, it would, Sir, with me, be an insuperable objection, I am so perfectly convinced that so extensive a country as this, can never be managed by one consolidated government. The Federal Convention were as well convinced as the members of this House, that the State governments were absolutely necessary to the existence of the Federal Government. [120]

Following the adoption of the compact by the State of North Carolina, only one State of the former Confederation remained outside the new Federal Union. Inasmuch as Rhode Island had not sent any commissioners to the Federal Convention of 1787 and seemed anything but enthusiastic toward the new Constitution, it was widely believed that this small but proud New England State would never consent to join the new Union. And for it time, it appeared as though those who held such views were correct in their judgment.

The State of Rhode Island

In Rhode Island, the question of ratification was submitted directly to the people of that State, rather than to a special Ratification Convention elected by them. The result was an overwhelming *rejection* of the Constitution by Rhode Islanders. Acting under the assumption that this State would never ratify the compact, the first Congress of the United States actually initiated the process of formulating trade legislation that would have officially recognized Rhode Island as a foreign nation.

Governor John Collins of Rhode Island quickly dispatched a letter to the President of the United States, praying that the United States would remain patient until such time as Rhode Islanders could see their way clear to adopting the new compact. But until such an event occurred, the Governor asserted, Rhode Island intended to pursue friendly foreign relations with the United States of America.

President George Washington promptly forwarded this letter to the Senate on September 26, 1789, with the following remarks:

> Having yesterday received a letter written in this month by the Governor of Rhode Island, at the request and in behalf of the General Assembly of that State, addressed to the President, the Senate, and the House of Representatives of the eleven United States of America in Congress assembled, I take the earliest opportunity of laying a copy of it before you. [121]

---

[120] Alexander H. Stephens, *Op. cit.*, Volume 1, quoted on pp. 287-288.
[121] Jefferson Davis, *Op. cit.*, Volume 1, quoted on p. 112.

In his letter to the Government of the United States, Governor Collins had said:

> The critical situation in which the people of this State are placed engages us to make these assurances, on their behalf, of their attachment and friendship to their sister States, and of their disposition to cultivate mutual harmony and friendly intercourse. They know themselves to be a handful, comparatively viewed, and, although they now stand as it were alone, they have not separated themselves or departed from the principles of that Confederation, which was formed by the sister States in their struggle for freedom and in the hour of danger....
>
> Our not having acceded to or adopted the new system of government formed and adopted by most of our sister States, we doubt not, has given uneasiness to them. That we have not seen our way clear to it, consistently with our idea of the principles upon which we all embarked together, has also given pain to us. We have not doubted that we might thereby avoid present difficulties, but we have apprehended future mischief....
>
> Can it be thought strange that, with these impressions, they (the people of this State) should wait to see the proposed system organized and in operation? – to see what further checks and securities would be agreed to and established by way of amendment before they could adopt it as a Constitution of government for themselves and their posterity?...
>
> We are induced to hope that we shall not be altogether considered as foreigners having no particular affinity or connection with the United States; but that trade and commerce, upon which the prosperity of this State much depends, will be preserved as free and open between this State and the United States, as our different situations at present can possibly admit....
>
> We feel ourselves attached by the strongest ties of friendship, kindred, and interest, to our sister States; and we can not, without the greatest reluctance, look to any other quarter for those advantages of commercial intercourse which we conceive to be more natural and reciprocal between them and us. [122]

The question of ratification was again raised in Rhode Island. This time, however, a Ratification Convention was called to consider the question. By the extremely close vote of 34 to 32, this Convention resolved on May 29, 1790, to accede to the new Federal Constitution. Had just a single delegate changed his mind and voted against the compact, tiny Rhode Island would not have ratified the Constitution.

The Ocean State's act of ratification began with these words:

We the Delegates of *the People of the State of Rhode-Island, and*

---

[122] *Ibid.*, Volume 1, quoted on pp. 112-113.

Providence Plantations, duly elected and met in Convention, having maturely considered the Constitution for the United States of America, agreed to on the seventeenth day of September, in the year one thousand seven hundred and eighty seven, by the Convention then assembled at Philadelphia, in the Commonwealth of Pennsylvania (a Copy whereof precedes these presents) and having also seriously and deliberately considered the present situation of this State, *do declare and make known.* [Emphasis added] [123]

These words were followed by a *Declaration of Understanding*, consisting of eighteen propositions or basic assertions. It is especially interesting to note that Rhode Island, following the example set by Virginia and New York, became the third State to enter the new Union with the expressed understanding that a State has the right to *secede* from the Union whensoever such action is deemed necessary to the preservation of the welfare and safety of the people of the State.

Among the declarations mentioned by Rhode Island were these basic assertions:

Second Declaration: "That all power is naturally vested in, and consequently derived from the People; that magistrates therefore are their trustees and agents, and at all times amenable to them." [124]

Third Declaration: "That the powers of government may be reassumed by the people, whensoever it shall become necessary to their happiness: – That the rights of the States respectively, to nominate and appoint all State Officers, and every other power, jurisdiction and right, which is not by the said Constitution clearly delegated to the Congress of the United States or to the departments of government thereof, remain to the people of the several States, or their respective State governments to whom they may have granted the same; and that those clauses in the said Constitution which declare that Congress shall not have or exercise certain powers, do not imply, that Congress is entitled to any powers not given by the said Constitution, but such clauses are to be construed as exceptions to certain specified powers, or as inserted merely for greater caution." [125]

Fourth Declaration: "That religion, or the duty which we owe to our Creator, and the manner of discharging it, can be directed only by reason and conviction, and not by force or violence, and therefore all men, have an equal, natural and unalienable right to the free exercise of religion, according to the dictates of conscience, and that no particular religious sect or society ought to be favoured, or established by law in preference to others." [126]

---

[123] Charles Callan Tansill (ed.), *Op. cit.*, p. 1052.
[124] *Ibid.*, p. 1052.
[125] *Ibid.*, p. 1052.
[126] *Ibid.*, p. 1053.

Seventh Declaration: "That all power of suspending laws or the execution of laws, by any authority without the consent of the representatives of the people in the legislature, is injurious to their rights, and ought not to be exercised." [127]

Seventeenth Declaration: "That the people have a right to keep and bear arms, that a well regulated militia, including the body of the people capable of bearing arms, is the proper, natural and safe defence of a free State; that the militia shall not be subject to martial law except in time of war, rebellion or insurrection; that standing armies in time of peace, are dangerous to liberty, and ought not to be kept up, except in cases of necessity; and that at all times the military should be under strict subordination to the civil power; that in time of peace no soldier ought to be quartered in any house, without the consent of the owner, and in time of war, only by the civil magistrate, in such manner as the law directs." [128]

Following the Declaration of Understanding came the official act of ratification, which was in this language:

> *Under these impressions, and declaring, that the rights aforesaid cannot be abridged or violated, and that the explanations aforesaid, are consistent with the said Constitution,* and in confidence that the amendments hereafter mentioned, will receive an early and mature consideration, and conformably to the Fifth Article of the said Constitution, speedily become a part thereof; We the said delegates, in the name, and in the behalf of *the People, of the State of Rhode-Island and Providence-Plantations,* do by these Presents, *assent to,* and *ratify* the said Constitution. [Emphasis added] [129]

Affixed to the official act of ratification was a list of twenty-one proposed amendments to the Federal Constitution. Among these proposals were the following amendments:

First Proposed Amendment: "The United States shall guarantee to each State its sovereignty, freedom and independence, and every power, jurisdiction and right, which is not by this Constitution expressly delegated to the United States." [130]

Sixth Proposed Amendment: "That no person shall be compelled to do military duty, otherwise than by voluntary enlistment, except in cases of general invasion; any thing in the second paragraph of the Sixth Article of the Constitution, or any law made under the Constitution to the contrary notwithstanding." [131]

Ninth Proposed Amendment: "That Congress shall lay no direct

---

[127] *Ibid.,* p. 1053.
[128] *Ibid.,* p. 1055.
[129] *Ibid.,* p. 1055.
[130] *Ibid.,* p. 1056.
[131] *Ibid.,* p. 1057.

taxes, without the consent of the legislatures of three fourths of the States in the Union." [132]

Twelfth Proposed Amendment: "As standing armies in time of peace are dangerous to liberty and ought not to be kept up, except in cases of necessity; and as at all times the military should be under strict subordination to the civil power, that therefore no standing army, or regular troops shall be raised, or kept up in time of peace." [133]

Thirteenth Proposed Amendment: "That no monies be borrowed on the credit of the United States without the assent of two thirds of the Senators and Representatives present in each house." [134]

Fourteenth Proposed Amendment: "That the Congress shall not declare war, without the concurrence of two thirds of the Senators and Representatives present in each house." [135]

Eighteenth Proposed Amendment: "That the State Legislatures have power to recall, when they think it expedient, their federal Senators, and to send others in their stead." [136]

Twentieth Proposed Amendment: "That Congress erect no company with exclusive advantages of commerce." [137]

It is abundantly evident that Rhode Island, like all the other States, understood the compact to be a Federal Constitution founded on the sovereignty of the States, that the Federal Government would be limited to those powers expressly delegated to it, and that all powers not delegated would remain exclusively with the respective States. With the assention of Rhode Island, the Union of States was once again complete. All that remained to complete the adoption of the new plan of government was to incorporate into it a Bill of Rights.

The Bill of Rights

As we have already observed, the Federalists were initially opposed to incorporating a Bill of Rights into the Federal Constitution. James Madison, for one, had repeatedly stressed that, inasmuch as the Federal Government could exercise only the powers delegated to it, a declaration of rights was unnecessary. Alexander Hamilton also took that position, both within the New York Ratification Convention and within the pages of *The Federalist Papers*.

Writing in the *Federalist*, No. 84, Mr. Hamilton stated:

---

[132] *Ibid.*, p. 1058.
[133] *Ibid.*, p. 1058.
[134] *Ibid.*, p. 1058.
[135] *Ibid.*, p. 1058.
[136] *Ibid.*, p. 1059.
[137] *Ibid.*, p. 1059.

> But a minute detail of particular rights is certainly far less applicable to a Constitution like that under consideration, which is merely intended to regulate the general interests of the nation, than to a constitution which has the regulation of every species of personal and private concerns. [Emphasis added] [138]

This Federalist went on to assert that, not only was a Bill of Rights unnecessary, but would actually be dangerous:

> I go further and affirm that bills of rights, in the sense and to the extent in which they are contended for, are not only *unnecessary* in the proposed Constitution *but would even be dangerous*. They would contain various exceptions to powers which are granted; and, on this very account, would afford a colorable *pretext* to claim more than were granted. *For why declare that things shall not be done which there is no power to do?* Why, for instance, should it be said that the liberty of the press shall not be restrained, when no power is given by which restrictions may be imposed? I will not contend that such a provision would confer a regulating power; but it is evident that it would furnish, *to men disposed to usurp*, a plausible pretense for claiming that power. [Emphasis added] [139]

While the Antifederalists could appreciate the logic raised against a Bill of Rights by Mr. Hamilton, in regard to the limited authority of the Federal Government, they did not agree with the effect that such a Bill of Rights would have. In their view, "men disposed to usurp" preferred nothing more than ambiguity and uncertainty, and for that very reason they deemed it essential to liberty that nothing should be left to inference and assumption. By insisting on a Bill of Rights, the Antifederalists intended to write into the Constitution living barriers and obstacles to thwart those "men disposed to usurp" to which Mr. Hamilton referred.

Confronted by unyielding insistence for a Bill of Rights from the Antifederalists during the Ratification Period, the Federalists had no choice but to concede to their demands for such a declaration. In fulfillment of the bargain made with the Antifederalists, James Madison accordingly introduced in the U.S. House of Representatives a series of resolutions proposing constitutional amendments, "To quiet the apprehensions of many, that without some such declaration of rights the government would assume, and might be held to possess the power to trespass upon those rights of persons and property which by the Declaration of Independence were affirmed to be unalienable." [140]

---

[138] Alexander Hamilton, James Madison, and John Jay, *The Federalist Papers*, New American Library, New York, 1961, p. 513.

[139] *Ibid.*, pp. 513-514.

[140] Lawrence P. McDonald, *We Hold These Truths*, '76 Press, Seal Beach, 1976, quoted on o. 37.

In all, James Madison consolidated the sundry recommendations of the States into seventeen amendments, which he introduced in Congress. Upon deliberation, Congress rejected five of Mr. Madison's proposals, and the remaining twelve proposed amendments were then submitted to the sovereign States for their consideration and action. The resolution of the first Congress, made on March 4, 1789, presented these twelve proposed amendments with this introduction:

> The Conventions of a number of the States, having at the time of their adopting the Constitution, expressed a desire, *in order to prevent misconstruction or abuse of its powers*, that further *declaratory* and *restrictive* clauses should be added: And as extending the ground of public confidence in the Government, will best ensure the beneficent ends of its institution:
>
> RESOLVED by the Senate and House of Representatives of the United States of America, *in Congress assembled*, two thirds of both Houses concurring, that the following Articles be proposed to the *Legislatures of the several States*, as Amendments to the Constitution of the United States, all or any of which Articles, when ratified by three fourths of the said Legislatures, to be valid to all intents and purposes, as part of the said Constitution; viz
>
> ARTICLES in addition to, and Amendment of the Constitution of the United States of America, proposed by Congress, and ratified by the Legislatures of the several States, pursuant to the Fifth Article of the original Constitution. [Emphasis added] [141]

The twelve amendments submitted to the several States made the following provisions:

> **First Proposed Amendment** (*Not Ratified*): "After the first enumeration required by the First Article of the Constitution, there shall be one Representative for every thirty thousand, until the number shall amount to one hundred, after which, the proportion shall be so regulated by Congress, that there shall be not less than one hundred Representatives, nor less than one Representative for every forty thousand persons, until the number of Representatives shall amount to two hundred, after which the proportion shall be so regulated by Congress, that there shall not be less than two hundred Representatives, nor more than one Representative for every fifty thousand persons." [142]
>
> **Second Proposed Amendment** (*Not Ratified*): "No law, varying the compensation for the services of the Senators and Representatives, shall take effect, until an election of Representatives shall have intervened." [143]
>
> **Third Proposed Amendment** (*Adopted as First Amendment*):

---

[141] Charles Callan Tansill (ed.), *Op. cit.*, p. 1063.
[142] *Ibid.*, pp. 1063-1064.
[143] *Ibid.*, p. 1064.

"Congress shall make no law respecting an establishment of religion, or prohibiting the free exercise thereof; or abridging the freedom of speech, or of the press; or the right of the people peaceably to assemble, and to petition the Government for a redress of grievances." [144]

Fourth Proposed Amendment (*Adopted as Second Amendment*): "A well regulated Militia, being necessary to the security of a free State, the right of the people to keep and bear Arms, shall not be infringed." [145]

Fifth Proposed Amendment (*Adopted as Third Amendment*): "No soldier shall, in time of peace be quartered in any house, without the consent of the Owner, nor in time of war, but in a manner to be prescribed by law." [146]

Sixth Proposed Amendment (*Adopted as Fourth Amendment*): "The right of the people to be secure in their persons, houses, papers, and effects, against unreasonable searches and seizures, shall not be violated, and no Warrants shall issue, but upon probable cause, supported by Oath or affirmation, and particularly describing the place to be searched, and the persons or things to be seized." [147]

Seventh Proposed Amendment (*Adopted as Fifth Amendment*): "No person shall be held to answer for a capital, or otherwise infamous crime, unless on a presentment or indictment of a Grand Jury, except in cases arising in the land or naval forces, or in the Militia, when in actual service in time of War or public danger; nor shall any person be subject for the same offence to be twice put in jeopardy of life or limb; nor shall be compelled in any criminal case to be a witness against himself, nor be deprived of life, liberty, or property, without due process of law; nor shall private property be taken for public use, without just compensation." [148]

Eighth Proposed Amendment (*Adopted as Sixth Amendment*): "In all criminal prosecutions, the accused shall enjoy the right to a speedy and public trial, by an impartial jury of the State and district wherein the crime shall have been committed, which district shall have been previously ascertained by law, and to be informed of the nature and cause of the accusation; to be confronted with the witnesses against him; to have compulsory process for obtaining witnesses in his favor, and to have the Assistance of Counsel for his defence." [149]

Ninth Proposed Amendment (*Adopted as Seventh Amendment*): "In Suits at common law, where the value in controversy shall exceed twenty dollars, the right of trial by jury shall be preserved, and no fact tried by a jury, shall be otherwise re-examined in any Court of the United States, than according to the rules of the common law." [150]

Tenth Proposed Amendment (*Adopted as Eighth Amendment*): "Excessive bail shall not be required, nor excessive fines imposed, nor cruel

---

[144] *Ibid.*, p. 1064.
[145] *Ibid.*, p. 1064.
[146] *Ibid.*, p. 1064.
[147] *Ibid.*, p. 1064.
[148] *Ibid.*, p. 1064.
[149] *Ibid.*, pp. 1064-1065.
[150] *Ibid.*, p. 1065.

and unusual punishments inflicted." [151]

     Eleventh Proposed Amendment (*Adopted as Ninth Amendment*): "The enumeration in the Constitution, of certain rights, shall not be construed to deny or disparage others retained by the people." [152]

     Twelfth Proposed Amendment (*Adopted as Tenth Amendment*): "The powers not delegated to the United States by the Constitution, nor prohibited by it to the States, are reserved to the States respectively, or to the people." [153]

Upon receiving these twelve proposed amendments, the States acted on them without hesitation. New Hampshire, New York, Pennsylvania, and New Jersey approved of all the amendments, except for the second one. Delaware acceded to all of the proposals, except for the first amendment in the list. Maryland approved of all twelve recommendations, as did South Carolina, North Carolina, Rhode Island, and Virginia. No action on the proposed amendments was taken by Massachusetts, Connecticut, Georgia, and the first State to be formed from the Western Territories, Kentucky. Thus, the first two proposed amendments were declared defeated, while the last ten were adjudged duly ratified and adopted by the requisite number of States.

     The remarkable feature about the American Bill of Rights is the manner in which it differs from the sundry imitations that have since been adopted by many other countries around the world. While the many imitators are based on the fraudulent assumption that all rights originate from government and that all power is inherent in government, the American Bill of Rights is based upon the opposite maxim, that rights originate from God and that all power is inherent in the peoples of the several States. That is why the concept that *the Federal Government shall not* runs like a refrain throughout the Bill of Rights – because the people *do* have certain inalienable rights, the powers of government *must* be limited. The Bill of Rights is thus predicated on the notion that the greatest potential threat or danger to life, liberty, and property is the Government of the United States. *The purpose of the American Bill of Rights is to protect the American people from a potentially abusive Federal Government.*

     Special attention should be directed to the Ninth and Tenth Amendments to the Federal Constitution. These are the only true *sweeping clauses* in the whole Constitution, and they clearly demonstrate that, while the powers delegated to the Government of the United States are *few* and *defined*, the rights reserved to individual citizens and to sovereign States and *numerous* and

---

[151] *Ibid.*, p. 1065.

[152] *Ibid.*, p. 1065.

[153] *Ibid.*, p. 1065.

indefinite. The most important provision of the American Bill of Rights is, of course, the last amendment in the group. The entire theory on which the Federal Constitution is founded is contained in the famous and widely cherished Tenth Amendment, which serves to define both the *republican* form of limited majority rule as well as the *federal* nature of our system of sovereign States.

In his monograph, *The Sabotage of the Tenth Amendment*, Edward Albertson made these observations on the sweeping implications of Amendment Ten:

> In these twenty-eight words, the people of the United States find assurance that they are secure from the threat of tyranny so long as the Constitution shall live....
>
> Among the amendments constituting the "Bill of Rights," the Tenth outweighs all the rest. At once, the objection may be raised: what of the freedoms protected by the First Amendment, religion, speech, press and assembly? But such an objection is not well-taken. The Tenth Amendment, when strictly construed, prohibits the denial of these rights. Only those powers delegated by the Constitution may be exercised by Congress, and no power has been so delegated which would permit Congress to establish a religion, or prohibit the free exercise thereof; or to abridge the freedom of speech, or of the press; or the right of the people peaceably to assemble, and to petition the government for a redress of grievances. [154]

The adoption of the Bill of Rights successfully concluded the Constitutional Era of American history, and both sides in the ratification struggle deserve the eternal gratitude of succeeding generations of Americans. The Federalists gave us the Constitution of the United States, and the Antifederalists gave us the Bill of Rights. And with the successful adoption of the Constitution and the Bill of Rights, *power* had at long last been reconciled with *liberty*. The Federal Constitution would forevermore serve as the touchstone and inspiration for all who champion the sovereignty of the States and the natural rights of man.

---

[154] Edward Albertson, *The Sabotage of the Tenth Amendment*, Citizens Legal Defense Alliance, Los Angeles, 1975, pp. 3-4.

Chapter Twelve
The Enduring Legacies

With the adoption of the Federal Constitution of 1787 and the Bill of Rights, the Constitutional Era came to an end. It had been a period of great constitutional reformation, involving a significant restructuring of the Federal Government while simultaneously preserving intact the fraternal league of friendship between the North American States styled the United States of America. That the new compact of government adopted by the States proved highly satisfactory to the young Republic may be ascertained by its longevity and by the high esteem in which all Americans have long held it. So enduring, in fact, was the amended work of the Constitutional Convention that the Federal Constitution today holds the distinction of being the oldest surviving written constitution in the world.

The Federal Constitution and the Bill of Rights, however, did not emerge from the Constitutional Era in a vacuum. A number of *enduring legacies* also emerged from that great Era which are, in many respects, of significance nearly equal to the compact itself. These legacies include a variety of concepts that range from the profoundly wise, to the inherently dangerous, to the deceptively mythological. Although quite a number of legacies emerged from the Constitutional Era, the attention of the student of constitutional government should be directed to only a few of the more important ones. These include the concepts vaguely referred to as the "Founding Fathers" and the "Father of the Constitution," as well as the manner in which Americans have, over the years, viewed the actions of the Constitutional Convention. Closely associated with this latter legacy are the early efforts to conceal the secret records of the Federal Convention from public view.

Other legacies that have endured include the concept of divergent interests, the notion of federal coercion of sovereign States, the enduring battle between the federalists and the nationalists that gave rise to political parties, and the immoral doctrine of "implied powers." And of course, we would certainly be remiss not to give special attention to the most significant enduring legacy of all, *The Federalist Papers*, that collection of essays written by Alexander Hamilton, James Madison, and John Jay. In conjunction with this last consideration, we should also devote consideration to the views and careers of the two principal authors of those famous essays. Although defeated in the

Federal Convention, both Alexander Hamilton and James Madison have, it would appear, emerged victorious in the enduring myths built around the Constitutional Convention. One myth holds that the former contributed significantly to the drafting of the federal compact, and another bestows upon the latter the laudatory title of *Father of the Constitution*.

The Founding Fathers of the United States

In the aftermath of the Constitutional Convention, a new term was added to the political vocabulary of the American people – the *Founding Fathers*. Just exactly *who* this term was designed to refer to has always been unclear, although it has often been used in speeches, debates, and literary works as a vague reference to those who played important roles in the American Revolution, the War of Independence, the drafting of the Declaration of Independence and the Articles of Confederation, the Constitutional Convention, and the State Ratification Conventions. The term, thus, could be stretched to include all individuals from Thomas Jefferson, Samuel Adams, Luther Martin, and Patrick Henry, to George Washington, James Madison, Gouverneur Morris, and Alexander Hamilton.

In and of itself, there is nothing improper in the term, an observation that seems to be reinforced by the fact that no one has ever seriously challenged its usage. The same cannot be said, however, for some of the concepts and implications associated with the usage of that term. The phrase is often used to imply or to signify that the Founding Fathers were all of *one mind* and *one heart* in their principles. While this may have been essentially true of the Founders of the Republic during the American Revolution, the War of Independence, and the adoption of the Articles of Confederation, it most certainly was not true in regard to the Constitutional Convention. As we have already observed, the delegates to that Convention were deeply divided by questions that involved the most fundamental and basic of principles, both as to the form and as to the system of government that should be established.

Mythology, however, has often been preferred to historical truths in regard to the Constitutional Era. According to one fable, George Washington played a leading role in the framing of the new government, when in fact, as the records indicate, he rarely spoke in the Convention, preferring to keep his own sentiments and preferences to himself. Another myth holds that James Madison of Virginia is the Father of the Constitution. As to why Mr. Madison has been crowned with such an honorary title is not exactly known, although the defeated nationalists may have hoped to bolster their lost cause by insisting that one of their own had fathered the instrument cherished by all Americans.

It is true, of course, that the noted Virginian played a leading role in securing the call for the Philadelphia Convention and that he played a key role in securing the adoption of the new compact. But the same could also be said of Alexander Hamilton. Unlike Mr. Hamilton, however, Mr. Madison faithfully attended every meeting at the Federal Convention and took the most comprehensive set of notes on the debates. If the honorary title conferred upon him is in reference to these services he performed, then the title bestowed upon him may have some justification. But if the title is meant to imply that Mr. Madison contributed the most to the debates, or that the Constitution represents his concept of a general government, then it is unjustly given, for neither of these implications is true.

If participation in the debates is to be the criterion for determining who is the Father of the Constitution, then the award should go to Gouverneur Morris, who spoke more often than any other delegate in the Convention, including Mr. Madison. The fact that the Constitution is the exact opposite of the one Mr. Morris desired merely indicates the error of attempting to use this standard for selecting the recipient of the coveted title. And if the honor is to be conferred upon an individual whose ideas are best represented in the compact, then other candidates seem more qualified for it than Mr. Madison, whose three leading principles – a National Government, a national veto over State laws, and proportional representation in the Senate – were all *rejected* by the Convention. In this regard, William Paterson, in recognition of his role in defeating the proposed National Government, deserves the title more than Mr. Madison. Or perhaps Roger Sherman, for his invaluable service in proposing the Connecticut Compromise, deserves the title more than any other delegate. A case might even be made that Luther Martin, in recognition of his contribution of the Supremacy Clause, deserved the honor more than the Virginia nationalist.

The truth, of course, is that the Constitution of the United States has no *Father*, at least not in the form of one man. And in this regard, the Constitution of 1787 stands apart from the Declaration of Independence and the Articles of Confederation, both of which were largely the work of individual authors. Thomas Jefferson may thus be properly regarded as the *Father of the Declaration of Independence*, and John Dickinson may be justly termed the *Father of the Articles of Confederation*. The Constitution of 1787, however, was written by *all* of the delegates in the Convention, not just one man. It represents the results of many *compromises* between the States, and not the ideas of one Virginia nationalist.

As we have already observed, the delegates who drafted the Federal

Constitution certainly were not of one mind or even remotely in agreement as to the *form* and *system* of government that should exist in the United States. Some of them preferred a monarchical form of government, while others favored the republican form. And some favored nationalism and the destruction of the States, while others advocated the preservation of the federal system and of the States. So divided were the delegates on *fundamental principles* that the hostility among the opposing interests threatened to break up the Convention on several occasions.

Hostility among factions within the Convention, as we have documented previously, gave rise to undisguised distrust and open discussion of the possibility of war and coercion between the States. Not only did the delegates focus on the inherent differences between the large States and the small States, but they also acknowledged the strong and enduring differences between the Northern States and the Southern States. During the heat of debate, one delegate could actually say to the nationalists that *he did not trust them*. And a prominent nationalist dared to suggest that the conflicting interests might be resolved by a *War Between the States*, with the stronger side forcing a supreme National Government on the American people and making traitors and rebels out of all who opposed it.

Although the prevailing opinion of the Constitutional Convention held by the American people has largely been highly favorable throughout the years – owing chiefly to the great respect Americans have for the Constitution – many of the delegates understood that this view might change dramatically if the people knew the full story of what took place behind the veil of secrecy that surrounded the Philadelphia Convention. For this reason, the decision was made by the delegates to perpetuate the rule of secrecy *beyond the end of Convention*. The degree of importance placed on secrecy *after* the Convention ended can be ascertained by the incident involving the list of names written out by John F. Mercer of Maryland.

During the Federal Convention, while listening to the various debates and observing the votes given by the other delegates, Mr. Mercer happened to write down the names of the delegates on the back of a printed copy of an early report of the Committee of Detail. Next to each name was written the word "for" or "against." Upon seeing the list and noting that the word *for* had been written next to the names of some twenty delegates, James McHenry asked what it meant. In response, Mr. Mercer stated that the list indicated which delegates were *for* or *against* the destruction of the Republic and the establishment of a monarchical government. Realizing the importance of the list, Mr. McHenry copied it and later allowed Luther Martin to copy his copy. When Mr. Martin eventually went public with the list, the reaction was profound and extreme.

Not only had Luther Martin broken the seal of secrecy – a very serious infraction in itself, according to some – but, according to his critics, he had seriously misinterpreted the meaning of the list. *For* and *against*, they insisted, could only mean for or against a National Government, not a monarchical government. Then the story was changed again by Mr. Martin's critics. *For* and *against* meant nothing at all, claimed the critics, a reference to neither a monarchy nor a supreme National Government. Such was the extent of the desire to maintain secrecy *even after the Convention had ended*. Not one man who had ever advocated in the Grand Convention either a monarchical form or a national system of government wished to ever have his conduct known by the American people.

The secrecy surrounding the Federal Convention remained in effect until its official *Journal* was published some three decades after the end of the Convention. Shortly after the publication of the official record came the publication of the notes of Robert Yates. Although Mr. Yates' notes ended on July 5, 1787, when he and his colleague from New York, John Lansing, walked out of the Convention, the details they provided of the debates gave to the general public its first true picture of what really occurred in the Philadelphia State House during the summer of 1787. The effect of these notes, coupled with Mr. Martin's *Genuine Information*, had a shocking effect, even among those individuals who had been previously prone to view the Constitutional Convention with a suspicious eye.

John Taylor of Caroline, after reading the *Journal* and Robert Yates' notes of the secret debates, was so moved by the new revelations that he authored a book on the subject, entitled *New Views of the Constitution of the United States*. He introduced readers to his work, which was published in 1823, with this short and sober introduction:

> That many eminent and respectable men have ever preferred, and ever will prefer, a consolidated National Government to our federal system; that the Constitution, under the influence of this predilection, has been erroneously construed; that these constructions are rapidly advancing towards their end, whether it shall be consolidation or disunion; that they will become a source of excessive geographical discord; and that the happiness and prosperity of the United States will be greater under a Federal than under a National Government, in any form, are the opinions which have suggested the following treatise. If the survey taken of these subjects is not proportioned to their importance, it yet may not be devoid of novelty, nor wholly ineffectual towards attracting more publick attention towards a question involving a mass of consequences either very good or very bad. [1]

---

[1] John Taylor, *New Views of the Constitution of the United States*, Da Capo Press, New York, (orig. pub. in 1823) 1971, Introductory Page.

More than the image of a few delegates who had acted as "Founding Fathers" by attending the Federal Convention was tarnished by the publication of the records of their debates. Although Americans have always preferred to think highly of *all* of the Founding Fathers – from Thomas Jefferson to Alexander Hamilton – knowledge of the proceedings of the Constitutional Convention significantly changed the way Americans perceived the role of Conventions *in general*. This transformation of opinion is even more noteworthy when we consider the high degree of confidence placed in such Conventions of the States *prior* to the Philadelphia Convention of 1787.

Prior to the Constitutional Convention, the American people took it for granted that such Conventions could be safely *trusted* to adequately represent the respective States and to properly *limit* their conduct to the officially sanctioned and authorized duties. From the *Stamp Act Congress* to the *Continental Congresses* to the *Annapolis Convention*, all such gatherings of representatives from the States had demonstrated faithful allegiance to the instructions and intentions of those who had authorized the meetings. *The Constitutional Convention, however, marked a dramatic and significant break from this tradition of trust.*

Never again would the States favor a call for another Federal Convention, despite the fact that our present Federal Constitution allows for the convening of such Conventions as a means of proposing amendments. Even in modern times, whenever the question is raised of convening a Convention of the States to propose, say, a Balanced Budget Amendment, fears are inevitably expressed. *"How can such a Convention be controlled?"* "What will prevent it from becoming a *runaway* Convention?" It is actually assumed by many that, if a Convention were called today to propose amendments to the Federal Constitution, the result would be, not amendments, but an entirely new Constitution! This fear may be ascribed to yet another enduring legacy of the last Federal Convention held in Philadelphia during the summer of 1787, which had been convened for the *sole and express purpose* of revising the Articles of Confederation. If that Convention had not been truly faithful to the States it represented, why should any future Conventions be trusted?

The Heresy of Implied Powers

Yet another enduring legacy of the Constitutional Era is the highly dangerous and heretical doctrine of *implied powers*. This concept, as we have previously observed, originated as a plot within the Constitutional Convention among those favoring a supreme National Government, especially among those within the National Monarchy faction. Realizing that the Convention was fixed in its resolution to adopt a Federal Constitution with strictly defined and limited powers, these extreme nationalists indicated their desire to *misconstrue* the new compact in a hope to resurrect the defeated plan for an imperial National Government. Both Gouverneur Morris and James Wilson, as we have documented previously, gave voice to this new conspiracy in the final days of the Constitutional Convention.

In his book, *Inquiry into the Origin and Course of Political Parties in the United States*, which was posthumously published in 1867, Martin Van Buren of New York – who had served as the eighth President of the United States – provided some additional proof of this *early design* to subvert the Constitution:

> The subject of internal improvements by the Federal Government, in regard as well to the power of the latter over the subject as to the expediency of the exercise, was repeatedly and very fully discussed in Congress, whilst Mr. Rufus King and myself represented the State of New York in the Senate of the United States. Upon the question of power we concurred in opinion, he adhering to that of Hamilton – the construction of such works being one of the very few powers which the latter did not claim for the Federal Government. Notwithstanding this agreement the subject was often canvassed between us in respect to the arguments advanced, from time to time, in Congress, by others. On one of those occasions, he told me that on Gouverneur Morris's visit to the city of New York, soon after his return from the Federal Convention, he was congratulated by his friends on the circumstance that the Convention had succeeded upon a Constitution which would realize the great object for which it had been convened, and that Morris promptly and, as Mr. King seemed to have understood it, significantly replied – *"That will depend upon the construction that is given to it!"* Mr. King did not state any inference he had drawn from the remark and seemed to me indisposed to prolong the conversation upon that point, and, knowing his habitual reserve in speaking of his old associates, I yielded to what I believed to be his wish not to be questioned, although I was at the moment strongly impressed by the observation. I referred to it afterwards in a speech I made in the Senate upon the powers of the government, which was extensively published. At a subsequent period this ready answer of Morris would not have attracted notice; but spoken before even a single officer had been elected to carry the Constitution into effect, and of course before any question as to its construction had arisen, it was to my mind, and, as I believe, to the mind of Mr. King, evidence of a foregone conclusion to claim under that instrument powers not anticipated by the great body of those who framed it, or by those who had given it vitality by their approval. The facts that this reply had been so long remembered by Mr. King, a prominent and sagacious member of the Convention, and repeated under the circumstances I have detailed, were calculated to create

such an impression. It gave, at least to my view, a decided direction in respect to the source from whence the doctrine of *implied powers* originated. [2]

Thus, the battle royal between the Federal Republicans, the National Republicans, and the National Monarchists was destined to continue even beyond the Convention which had witnessed the decisive victory of the champions of the Federal Republic. Although defeated in that Convention, the forces of nationalism neither repented nor evaporated into smoke. After the adoption of the new Constitution and the Bill of Rights, a new attempt was made to once again unite the forces of nationalism under the banner of implied powers, an attempt that resulted in the rise of *political parties* in the United States. As a consequence, the same friction that had previously divided the Federal Convention quickly divided all Americans.

The National Monarchists and many of the National Republicans again joined forces, under the leadership of Alexander Hamilton, to form the *Federalist Party*. The name chosen for itself by this party was *doubly* deceitful. In adopting this name, the uncompromising nationalists pretended to be the very same pro-ratification coalition that had advocated the adoption of the new Constitution. The new party also adopted the name in a fraudulent attempt to delude the public into thinking that they were friends and supporters of the Federal Republic. Both the leader they elected to follow and the measures they advocated, however, revealed the hypocrisy of these claims.

The new Federalist Party, while pretending to be the true friends of the Federal Constitution, advocated the subversion of that very instrument by *false constructions* of the compact. Gouverneur Morris perhaps best illustrated the party's mode of interpreting the Constitution in a speech delivered before the Senate on January 8, 1802, when he declared that, "The people of America bound the States down by this compact." [3] The objective of this mode of interpretation, thus, was to so pervert and distort the meaning of the Constitution as to transform it into the chains by which the peoples of the States could be conquered and enslaved. By this means, State sovereignty could be destroyed, all powers could be assumed by the Federal Government, and a supreme National Government could rise like a phoenix from its grave.

Under the leadership of Thomas Jefferson, an opposition party, styled the *Democratic-Republican Party* or simply the *Republican Party*, arose to oppose the misnamed Federalists. To the ranks of this party flocked a considerable number of Federal Republicans and a few National Republicans. This

---

[2] Martin Van Buren, *Inquiry into the Origin and Course of Political Parties in the United States*, Augustus M. Kelley, Publishers, New York, (orig. pub. in 1867) 1967, pp. 129-131.
[3] Max Farrand (ed.), *The Records of the Federal Convention of 1787*, Revised Edition, Volume III, Yale University Press, New Haven, 1966, p. 391.

party advocated the preservation of the true principles of the Federal Constitution, both in regard to its republican features as well as in regard to the federal system established by it.

Writing in 1823, Thomas Jefferson summarized the views of his party in these words:

> I ask for no straining of words against the general government, nor yet against the States. I believe the States can best govern over home concerns and the general government over foreign ones. I wish, therefore, to see maintained that wholesome distribution of powers established by the Constitution for the limitation of both, and never to see all offices transferred to Washington. [4]

This was the essence of the views held by the Jeffersonians, as expressed by the founder of the party. The formidable opposition that confronted the efforts of this party in its quest to preserve constitutional government in the early days of the Republic amply attests to the fact that *eternal vigilance* was indeed requisite to safeguarding the Federal Republic despite the victory obtained by the Federal Republicans in the Constitutional Convention.

The Federalist Papers

One of the most significant legacies that have endured from the Constitutional Era, as previously noted, is the series of essays advocating ratification of the Constitution in the State of New York that have since been published under the style of *The Federalist Papers*. Nearly all Americans since the founding of the Republic — even school children — are familiar with these famous essays, although only a few have actually read them. Their significance stems largely from the importance placed upon the papers by historians, constitutional scholars, and Supreme Court Justices. The advocate of constitutional government, therefore, must take note of these important essays on the Constitution.

These celebrated essays, eighty-five in number, were published in New York City newspapers over a period stretching from October 27, 1787, to August 16, 1788. The idea of writing the essays may be attributed to John Jay, who persuaded Alexander Hamilton to change his threatening "Caesar" method of persuasion in favor of the "Publius" approach. For assistance in writing the essays, Mr. Hamilton first approached Gouverneur Morris, who

---

[4] Thomas James Norton, *The Constitution of the United States: Its Sources and Application*, America's Future, Inc., New York, 1943, quoted on p. 226.

declined the request. Afterwards, Mr. Hamilton approached James Madison, who was then in New York City to represent Virginia in the Congress under the Articles of Confederation. Mr. Madison agreed to collaborate in the effort, and all three writers – Alexander Hamilton, James Madison, and John Jay – used the same pseudonym to conceal their true identities.

Although the identities of the three authors eventually became public knowledge, a dispute arose as to exactly who had written which particular essay. The source of the dispute stemmed from Mr. Hamilton's false claims of authorship of a number of essays that were clearly written by his Southern collaborator, as historian Clinton Rossiter has noted:

> Throughout the long months during which *The Federalist* was running in the New York newspapers, and indeed until several years after publication of the collected essays, the identity of Publius was a well-guarded secret. This mask of anonymity...made it possible for Hamilton, in a note written just before his death and discovered just after, to lay claim to a full sixty-three numbers of *The Federalist*, some of which very plainly belonged to Madison. Just why this man of honor and sound memory should have engaged in this extraordinary action is impossible to explain. In any case, he touched off a tortuous dispute that went on for generations between his political heirs and those of Madison over the authorship of the various papers, especially number 49-58, 62 and 63. Thanks chiefly to the scholarly labors of Professor Douglas Adair, we can say with some confidence that Hamilton wrote fifty-one numbers (1, 6-9, 11-13, 15-17, 21-36, 59-61, 65-85), Madison twenty-six (10, 14, 37-58, and probably 62, 63), and Jay five (2-5, 64), while three (18-20) were the product of a joint effort by Madison and Hamilton. [5]

In his introduction to the 1961 New American Library edition of *The Federalist Papers*, Clinton Rossiter began by stating that, "*The Federalist* is the most important work in political science that has ever been written, or is likely ever to be written, in the United States. It is, indeed, the one product of the American mind that is rightly counted among the classics of political theory." [6]

Thus it is that *The Federalist Papers* take precedence, as "the most important work in political science that has ever been written," over such great masterpieces as *New Views of the Constitution of the United States, Tyranny Unmasked,* and *Construction Construed and Constitutions Vindicated* by John Taylor of Caroline; *A Disquisition on Government* and *A Discourse on the Constitution and Government of the United States* by John C. Calhoun; *A Constitu-*

---

[5] Alexander Hamilton, James Madison, and John Jay, *The Federalist Papers*, New American Library, New York, 1961, pp. x-xi.
[6] *Ibid.*, p. vii.

tional View of the Late War Between the States by Alexander H. Stephens; and *The Rise and Fall of the Confederate Government* by Jefferson Davis.

The Federalist Papers, it would appear from the manner in which they are so highly esteemed by certain individuals, even take precedence over the debates in the State Ratification Conventions and the records of the Federal Convention itself, in terms of importance in contributing to our understanding of the federal compact. Why is this so? Why should the writings of a *National Monarchist* and a *National Republican – both of whose main ideas were rejected in the Constitutional Convention* – take precedence over the records of the very Convention which wrote the Constitution, or the records of those Ratification Conventions which adopted the compact? A clue may be gleaned from the words of Mr. Rossiter.

Continuing with his introduction, Clinton Rossiter wrote:

> This work has always commanded widespread respect as the first and still most authoritative commentary on the Constitution of the United States. It has been searched minutely by lawyers for its *analysis of the powers of Congress*, quoted confidently by historians for its *revelations of the hopes and fears of the framers of the Constitution*, and cited magisterially by the Supreme Court for its *arguments in behalf of judicial review, executive independence*, and *national supremacy*. It would not be stretching the truth more than a few inches to say that *The Federalist* stands third only to the Declaration of Independence and the Constitution itself among all the *sacred writings* of American political history. [Emphasis added] [7]

At the risk of being branded as heretics and infidels for daring to question the accuracy of the sacred writings of nationalism, our great inquiry into the true principles of constitutional government in the United States requires that we examine *The Federalist Papers* with a critical eye, to determine for ourselves if those essays are truly compatible with the plan of government adopted by the Constitutional Convention. If indeed they are compatible, then the religious adulation may have some merit; but, if not, then the temple has been desecrated and the Constitution supplanted by the false idol of nationalism.

Before directing our attention to an examination of *The Federalist Papers*, however, we should first inquire into the political ideology of its authors, particularly the two distinguished writers who contributed most significantly to the essays. Both Alexander Hamilton and James Madison attended the Constitutional Convention of 1787, both were active in their respective State Ratification Conventions, and both had distinguished political careers follow-

---

[7] *Ibid.*, p. vii.

ing the adoption of the Constitution. An analysis of their conduct and political careers, therefore, will tell us much about the famous essays they wrote. We may begin with the man from New York.

The Strange Career of Alexander Hamilton

Alexander Hamilton, a foreign immigrant from the West Indies, began his political career by joining the Continental Army and serving as an aide to General George Washington. On at least one occasion, Mr. Hamilton engaged in heated words with his superior and returned home to New York in disgust. Those who had envisioned a promising political career for the young man, however, realized the importance of being in the good graces of General Washington and, at their urging, Mr. Hamilton resumed his duties as aide to the General.

Although a veteran of the War of Independence and a key leader of the Society of the Cincinnati, Alexander Hamilton quickly became known after the war as a Tory lover, consistently championing the cause of those who had opposed the Declaration of Independence. Mr. Hamilton's hostility to the Articles of Confederation began *before* those Articles had been ratified by all thirteen States, and he accordingly began agitating for a Constitutional Convention to modify the compact at an early date. And from the very start of this political agitation, he was firmly aligned with the monied interests favoring a very strong central government and a National Bank.

At the Annapolis Convention, it was this delegate from New York who wrote the famous appeal letter on behalf of the Convention, which called for a more general Convention with fewer restrictions on its authority. When the States responded favorably to the call for a Grand Convention, the New York nationalists used all the political clout they could muster to ensure that Mr. Hamilton was commissioned as a delegate. Although it was obvious from the start that his nationalist vote in the Philadelphia Convention would always be overruled by his two federalist colleagues – Robert Yates and John Lansing – the New York nationalists deem it essential that he represent their interests in that assemblage. To assist him in the part he was to play, the nationalists helped Mr. Hamilton draft a plan of government which he could introduce to the Federal Convention if and when conditions were ripe for such a plan.

In his book, *Jefferson and Hamilton*, the distinguished historian Claude G. Bowers gave this highly descriptive and accurate summary of Mr. Hamilton's conduct in the Constitutional Convention:

Unless we divest ourselves of the Hamiltonian myths in reference to the Constitution, an intelligent comprehension of his political character will be impossible. We must rid ourselves of the fallacious notion that he was satisfied with the Constitution or believed it adequate. No one contributed more mightily to making the Constitutional Convention possible. In the preliminary Convention at Annapolis, no one did more to crystallize sentiment for it, and it was his persuasive pen that wrote the history-making address there determined upon. About his dining-table in New York he did yeoman service in coaxing skeptical and reluctant members of Congress to call a Convention. There, under a simulation of gayety, his eloquence and wit and banter made converts of the most stubborn....

But in the Convention itself he played no such part as is popularly ascribed to him. After the presentation of his own plan in the early stages, he played an inconspicuous part, and much of the time he was not only absent from the Convention, but out of the State. This was not because of indifference to the event, but to a realization that he could accomplish nothing for his plan.

This plan was a direct contradiction of that which was adopted. There is nothing conjectural about that fact – the records are indisputable. We have the plan, the brilliant five-hour oration in its behalf, the brief from which he spoke. These have come down to us, not from his enemies, but from his partial biographers, his son the editor of his "Works," and the report of Madison on the authenticity of which he himself passed. This plan provided for the election of a President for life; for Senators for life or during good behavior, and by electors with a property qualification; and for the crushing of the sovereignty of States through the appointment by the President of Governors with a life tenure and the power to veto any act of the State legislatures, though passed unanimously. Not only was the President enabled under this plan to negative any law enacted, but he had the discretionary power to enforce or ignore any law existing. Though his President, serving for life, was not called a King, he was to be armed with more arbitrary power than was possessed by the King of England. His English eulogist does not overstate when he says that "what he had in mind was the British Constitution as George III had tried hard to make it," and failed because the English people would not tolerate it. This interpretation of Hamilton's purpose is reenforced by another of his most brilliant disciples who asserts that "Hamilton's Governor [President] would have been not dissimilar to Louis XIV and could have said with him, 'L'état c'est moi.'...Thinly veiled, his plan contemplated an elective King with greater powers than those of George III, an imitation House of Lords, and a popular House of Commons with a limited tenure." Even so this plan confessedly fell far short of his conception of an ideal government. In the brief for his speech we are left in no doubt as to his partiality for a Monarchy, in which the aristocracy should have a special power. "The monarch...ought to be hereditary, and to have so much power that it would not be his interest to risk much to acquire more." As for the aristocracy, "they should be so circumscribed that they can have no interest in a change." We should be "rescued from the democracy." As to the republican form of government – "Republics are liable to corruption and intrigue," and, since "a republican government does not admit of a vigorous execution, it is therefore bad."

Later, in one of his few discussions, he said that "those who mean to form a solid republican government ought to proceed to the confines of another government." His Republic, and in his great speech he had conceded that no other form would be accepted by the people, "was to be an aristocratic as distinguished from a democratic Republic, and the power of the separate States was to be effectually crippled." Even after the Constitution had been adopted, he believed that one of the objects of administration should be "to acquire for the Federal Government more consistency than the Constitution seems to promise for so great a country," to the end that it "may triumph altogether over the State governments and reduce them to an utter subordination, dividing the large States into simpler districts." Such were the ideas urged by Hamilton in the forceful five-hour speech which Gouverneur Morris thought the most brilliant intellectual exhibition he had ever witnessed. After this exhaustive exposition, he took but little part. Toward the close he explained his comparative silence: "He had been restrained from entering into the discussions by his dislike of the scheme of government in general." This distaste did not diminish as the Convention closed its labors, and he accepted the Constitution in the end "as better than nothing." His motive for joining in recommending it to the people is conclusively shown in his last Convention utterance: "No man's ideas are more remote from the plan than my own are known to be; but is it possible to deliberate between anarchy and convulsion on one side, and the chance of good to be expected from the plan on the other?"

Nor did he ever lose faith in his own plan, or gain confidence in the Constitution which was adopted. Just before retiring from the Cabinet he avowed himself a monarchist who had "no objections to a trial being made of this thing of a Republic." Two years before his death he wrote bitterly to [Gouverneur] Morris of his support of a Constitution in which he had never had faith "from the beginning," in which he described it as "a frail and worthless fabric." And the night of his death, when his bosom friend and confident [Mr. Morris] was meditating the funeral oration he was to deliver on the steps of Trinity Church, he wrote in his diary, "He was in principle opposed to republican and attached to monarchical government, but then his opinions were generally known and have been long and loudly proclaimed. His share in the forming of our Constitution must be mentioned, and his unfavorable opinion cannot therefore be concealed." [8]

Following the adoption of the Federal Constitution, Alexander Hamilton secured a strategic position in the Cabinet of President George Washington. As the Secretary of the Treasury, the National Monarchist was in an ideal position to advance his personal political views, including the rearing of a monied aristocracy. And in conjunction with his avowed maxim that *a national debt is a national blessing*, he urged measures calculated to plunge the

---

[8] Claude G. Bowers, *Jefferson and Hamilton: The Struggle for Democracy in America*, Houghton Mifflin Company, Boston, 1925, pp. 30-32.

United States deeply into debt.

Although the Constitutional Convention had considered vesting in the Federal Government the power to charter a National Bank and to incorporate in general, upon deliberation and discussion these two powers had been deliberately withheld from that government. Yet, as the basis for his monied aristocracy, Mr. Hamilton insisted that such a National Bank was necessary and proper. When the *constitutionality* of the bank bill was challenged in Congress by James Madison, who had by then parted company with the extreme nationalists, President Washington sought the advice of his Cabinet.

On February 15, 1791, Secretary of State Thomas Jefferson gave his written opinion that the bank bill was indeed unconstitutional, citing among other things that very fact that the Constitutional Convention had rejected such a power to incorporate a bank. "It is an established rule of construction where a phrase will bear either of two meanings," he wrote, "to give it that which will allow some meaning to the other parts of the instrument, and not that which would render all the others useless." "Certainly no such universal power was meant to be given them." [9]

Mr. Jefferson then directed his attention to the proceedings of the Convention itself:

> It is known that the very power now proposed *as a means* was rejected as *an end* by the Convention which formed the Constitution. A proposition was made to them to authorize Congress to open canals, and an amendatory one to empower them to incorporate. But the whole was rejected, and one of the reasons for rejection urged in debate was, that then they would have a power to erect a bank, which would render the great cities, where there were prejudices and jealousies on the subject, adverse to the reception of the Constitution. [10]

On February 23, 1791, the Secretary of the Treasury gave his opinion of the bill's constitutionality, basing his argument on the concept of *implied powers* and formally establishing the doctrine known as a *loose* or *liberal* interpretation of the Constitution. Regarding the issue raised by Mr. Jefferson, that the Convention had deliberately rejected the power in question, the leader of the Federalist Party artfully took advantage of the fact that the records of the Convention were still locked up in the strong box of secrecy. "What was the precise nature or extent of this proposition, or what the reasons for refusing it," he wrote, "is not ascertained by any authentic document, or even by accurate recollection." No recommendation was made by him,

[9] Max Farrand (ed.), *Op. cit.*, Volume III, p. 363.
[10] *Ibid.*, Volume III, p. 363.

however, that President Washington should resolve the dispute by consulting the Convention's *Journal*, which the President was still hiding from the public. Instead, President Washington was counseled by Mr. Hamilton to completely ignore the question of the intent of the Convention: "In this state of the matter, no inference whatever can be drawn from it." [11]

Alexander Hamilton's fascination with military dictatorship knew no limits. When Thomas Jefferson expressed the sentiment that Sir Francis Bacon and John Locke were among the greatest men the world had ever produced, Mr. Hamilton responded by stating that the greatest man who ever lived was *Julius Caesar*! And when Napoleon Bonaparte established a military despotism in France, Mr. Hamilton referred to him as "that unequalled conqueror, from whom it is painful to detract." [12] As history has recorded, Napoleon's chief claim to fame was his willingness to spread war and carnage over the face of Europe.

Mr. Hamilton, it appears, had secret ambitions of becoming an American Caesar or New World Napoleon. During the Whiskey Rebellion, for example, he marched at the head of the armed forces of the United States to crush the rebellious farmers of Pennsylvania. And when Virginia dared to resist the Hamiltonian plan of government being forced on America, Mr. Hamilton could scarcely conceal his eagerness to lead a federal army against that sovereign State, to conquer and divide it into smaller jurisdictions.

And all the while, Alexander Hamilton was selling out the interests of the United States by secretly working as "Number 7" in the British cipher. Among other things, he deliberately sabotaged the American position in the negotiations conducted with the British Government, resulting in the disaster known as Jay's Treaty. Indirectly, therefore, he helped to create the conditions that ultimately led to the War of 1812.

When the Presidential election of 1800 resulted in a tie between Thomas Jefferson and Aaron Burr, Mr. Hamilton surprised everyone by supporting his arch political enemy from Virginia, thereby ensuring a victory for Mr. Jefferson. As much as he disliked the author of the Declaration of Independence, his hatred for Mr. Burr was even greater, a hatred that ultimately resulted in a fatal duel between the two men. It was said and widely believed that, as a result of Mr. Hamilton's death in the 1804 duel, Mr. Burr had figuratively *blown the brains out of the Federalist Party*.

Despite his faults — and they were legion — Alexander Hamilton was undeniably a brilliant man with a keen intellect, a fluent pen, and ceaseless energy. Thomas Jefferson once described him as a *colossus* to the Democratic-

---

[11] *Ibid.*, Volume III, pp. 363-364.
[12] Claude G. Bowers, *Op. cit.*, quoted on p. 27.

Republican Party, stating that, even without numbers, he was *a host within himself.* The great tragedy is that such energy and genius were not directed toward preserving the Federal Constitution in the true spirit in which it had been adopted by the States.

The Inconsistent Career of James Madison

When James Madison was a young man, his education was placed in the hands of the slightly older Thomas Jefferson, who ensured that the man from Montpellier received the best possible education in law and government. As a result of this early relationship, the two men became life-long close friends, and Mr. Madison always displayed a special deference to the genius of his mentor, even when disagreeing with him on fundamental principles. Despite his friendship with the man from Monticello, however, Mr. Madison, upon assuming his seat in the Congress under the Articles of Confederation, quickly gravitated toward Alexander Hamilton, Robert Morris, and other advocates of extreme nationalism and truly strong government. By the time of the Constitutional Convention, it was nearly impossible to determine who – Alexander Hamilton or James Madison – was more determined to humble the State governments at the feet of a supreme National Government.

When James Madison studied the lessons of history, he drew conclusions which were precisely opposite those of Mr. Jefferson. Thomas Jefferson, of course, was convinced that the great lesson of history taught that the primary threat to liberty was the trend toward centralization of power. The misery of mankind, he was convinced, had long resulted from *too much government.* James Madison, on the other hand, believed that anarchy or *an insufficient quantity of government* was the chief evil that had bedeviled the human race. The greatest threat facing the United States, he was therefore convinced, was the sovereignty of the States and the independent spirits of the State governments.

The fact that Mr. Madison's views were strikingly similar to those held by Alexander Hamilton was not lost upon those who attended the Constitutional Convention and heard both men present their ideas to the house. An indication of this general understanding is revealed in a letter written to Mr. Hamilton by his political comrade, Timothy Pickering, on October 18, 1803. Within this letter, Mr. Pickering stated:

> Dining in company with General Pinckney, as he passed thro' Salem, in September, I was asked, by one of the guests, some question concerning the nature of the propositions you made in the General Convention. I referred the enquirer to the General, who was a member. – He an-

swered, That you proposed, that the Governors of the several States should
be appointed by the President of the U States: But that Mr. Madison
moved, and was seconded by his cousin Charles Pinckney, That all the laws
of the individual States should be subject to the negative of the Chief Executive of the U. States. The General added, That he did not know which
would be deemed the strongest measure. [13]

Unlike Alexander Hamilton, however, James Madison had no real basis
of nationalist support within his home State. He therefore had to use extreme
caution when corresponding with his fellow Virginians throughout the Constitutional Era. Once he made the mistake of taking his friend, Thomas Jefferson, into his confidence, by informing him of his desire to place a national
veto over State laws in the hands of the general government. When Mr. Jefferson responded by stating that he was opposed to such a dangerous power,
Mr. Madison realized that his friend did not share his nationalist fervor. He
therefore distanced himself from his mentor for the remainder of the Constitutional Era, preferring instead to collaborate his efforts with Alexander Hamilton and James Wilson, whose views seemed more synchronized with his
own.

When the time of the Philadelphia Convention arrived, no one was
more prepared to abandon the Articles of Confederation than James Madison.
The Virginia Plan, although introduced in the Constitutional Convention by
Edmund Randolph, was essentially the work of Mr. Madison. This plan, as
we have already observed, called for the erection of a supreme National Government, the vesting in that government of an absolute negative over all State
laws, and representation to be based solely on population. The general government, under this plan, was to be vested with virtually unlimited powers,
and its control over the States was to be greater than that wielded over the
colonies by King George III prior to the issuance of the Declaration of Independence. During the course of the debates, Mr. Madison even went so far as
to deny that the States were ever sovereign, thereby contradicting the very letter of the Articles of Confederation.

Although James Madison always insisted that his political views were
purely republican in nature, on at least one occasion during the Grand Convention he signaled a willingness to swing over to the side of the monarchists
in his ardent opposition to States' Rights. And his strong hostility to the
equality of suffrage in the Senate clearly indicated his desire to ensure that no
fetter or check should be erected to safeguard the public from the uncontrolled tyranny of the numerical majority.

This last observation is especially intriguing, considering the opinions

---

[13] Max Farrand (ed.), *Op. cit.*, Volume III, p. 399.

Mr. Madison had stated to James Monroe in a letter dated October 5, 1786, some seven months *prior* to the Constitutional Convention:

> There is no maxim, in my opinion, which is more liable to be misapplied, and which, therefore, more needs elucidation, than the current one, that the interest of the majority is the political standard of right and wrong. Taking the word "interest" as synonymous with "ultimate happiness," in which sense it is qualified with every necessary moral ingredient, the proposition is no doubt true. But taking it in the popular sense, as referring to immediate augmentation of property and wealth, nothing can be more false. In the latter sense, it would be the interest of the majority in every community to despoil and enslave the minority of individuals; and *in a federal community, to make a similar sacrifice of the minority of the component States*. In fact, it is only re-establishing, under another name and a more specious form, force as the measure of right. [Emphasis added] [14]

In spite of such expressed views, however, James Madison advocated within the Federal Convention that the small States should be divested of all power to check or hamper the will of the numerical majority. Even when it appeared that the small States might abandon the Convention in despair and thus destroy all hope of ever uniting all the States in one Confederacy, Mr. Madison refused to compromise. He remained, to the end of the Convention, an uncompromising nationalist.

The fact that Alexander Hamilton turned to him for help in writing *The Federalist Papers* is indicative of the unshakable confidence placed in Mr. Madison's nationalism by the National Monarchist from New York. In Mr. Hamilton's estimation, it would appear, Mr. Madison's nationalist fervor was second only to that of Gouverneur Morris. The close political camaraderie between the Virginian and the New Yorker remained consistent throughout the Constitutional Era, an association that was shattered only after the organization of the new government under the Federal Constitution.

Had it not been for the fact that Virginia, and the Southern States in general, regarded the measures of Alexander Hamilton, under the new government, with such extreme hostility, it is realistic to assume that James Madison would have remained a loyal Hamiltonian for the duration of his political career. But *political expediency*, aside from all other considerations, was sufficient to induce Mr. Madison to part company with Mr. Hamilton and the other extreme nationalists. *Virginia demanded that its statesmen vigorously oppose the Hamiltonian system and to champion the cause of States' Rights.* The nationalist from Montpellier thus had little choice but to follow the

---

[14] Saul K. Padover (ed.), *The Complete Madison: His Basic Writings*, Harper & Brothers, Publishers, New York, 1971, p. 45.

wishes of his State and join with the Jeffersonians. To have taken any other course would have been political suicide.

Many years later, in a conversation with Nicholas P. Trist on September 27, 1834, James Madison explained the reason for his break with the National Monarchist from New York. Mr. Trist recorded this reason as follows in his notes:

> Mr. M., "As to the other branch of the subject, I deserted Colonel Hamilton, or rather Colonel H. deserted me; in a word, the divergence between us took place – from his wishing to *administration*, or rather to administer the government (these were Mr. M.'s very words), into what he thought it ought to be; while, on my part, I endeavored to make it conform to the Constitution as understood by the Convention that produced and recommended it, and particularly by the State Conventions that *adopted* it. [15]

As a consequence of his change of allegiance from the Hamiltonian Federalists to the champions of the Federal Republic, Mr. Madison found it necessary to drastically alter his publicly stated views. Nowhere was this change of sentiment more apparent than in his concept that one level of government should provide an ultimate check over the conduct of the other level within the federal system. During his career as an unyielding nationalist, Mr. Madison was emphatic in his insistence that the Federal Government should possess such a power over the States. Indeed, such a power was, in his opinion, the *cornerstone* of a supreme National Government.

Writing to Thomas Jefferson on October 24, 1787, shortly after the Convention had ended, the as-of-yet unconverted Virginia nationalist explained his views to his mentor:

> You will herewith receive the result of the Convention, which continued its session till the 17th of September. I take the liberty of making some observations on the subject, which will help to make up a letter, if they should answer no other purpose.
>
> It appeared to be the sincere and unanimous wish of the Convention *to cherish and preserve the Union of the States*. No proposition was made, no suggestion was thrown out, in favor of a partition of the Empire into *two or more Confederacies*.
>
> ...The whole of them together formed a task more difficult than can be well conceived by those who were not concerned in the execution of it. Adding to these considerations the natural diversity of human opinions on all new and complicated subjects, it is impossible to consider the degree of concord which ultimately prevailed as less than a *miracle*.

---

[15] Max Farrand (ed.), *Op. cit.*, Volume III, p. 534.

The first of these objects, as respects the Executive, was peculiarly embarrassing....

The second object, the due *partition of power between the general & local governments*, was perhaps of all, the most nice and difficult. A few contended for an entire abolition of the States; some for indefinite power of legislation in the Congress, with a negative on the laws of the States; some for such a power without a negative; some for a limited power of legislation, with such a negative; *the majority finally for a limited power without the negative*. The question with regard to the negative underwent repeated discussions, and was finally *rejected* by a bare majority. As I formerly intimated to you my opinion *in favor* of this ingredient, I will take this occasion of explaining myself on the subject. *Such a check on the States appears to me necessary*. 1. To prevent encroachments on the general authority. 2. To prevent instability and injustice in the legislation of the States.

...*The Senate will represent the States in their political capacity; the other House will represent the people of the States in their individual capacity*....*The President also derives his appointment from the States*, and is periodically accountable to them. This *dependence of the general [government] on the local authorities*, seems effectually to guard the latter against any dangerous encroachments of the former....It may be said that *the Judicial authority, under our new system will keep the States within their proper limits, and supply the place of a negative on their laws*. The answer is, that it is more *convenient* to prevent the passage of a law than *to declare it void after it is passed*; that this will be particularly the case, where the law aggrieves individuals, who may be unable to support an appeal agst. a State to the supreme Judiciary; that a State which would violate the legislative rights of the Union, would not be very ready to obey a Judicial decree in support of them, and that *a recurrence to force, which, in the event of disobedience would be necessary*, is an evil which the new Constitution meant to exclude as far as possible.

2. *A constitutional negative on the laws of the States seems equally necessary to secure individuals agst. encroachments on their rights*.... [Emphasis added] [16]

Such views were tantamount to rank heresy in the Jeffersonian camp, and this letter illustrates that James Madison still did not understand the great lesson of history. The idea that a central regime within an American "Empire" would constitute *the natural guardian of human rights* against violations committed by local governments was so radical and bizarre in nature that not even Alexander Hamilton would have dared to utter such a strange idea in public. But if Mr. Madison truly expected that the Federal Government would need to interpose its authority and nullify a State act to save liberty in America, then he was destined to be rudely awakened by political reality. A decade after he had bitterly and passionately fought for such a negative within

---

[16] *Ibid.*, Volume III, pp. 131-135.

the Federal Convention, he would be working side-by-side with Thomas Jefferson and John Taylor of Caroline to advance the theory of *State interposition and nullification* against a dangerous *federal* law which threatened American liberty.

Within the Virginia Resolutions of 1798, James Madison wrote:

> That this Assembly doth explicitly and peremptorily declare, that it views the powers of the Federal Government, as resulting from the compact, to which the States are parties, as limited by the plain sense and intention of the instrument constituting that compact — as no further valid than they are authorized by the grants enumerated in that compact; and that in case of a deliberate, palpable and dangerous exercise of other powers, not granted by the said compact, the States who are parties thereto, have the right, and are in duty bound, to interpose, for arresting the progress of the evil, and for maintaining within their respective limits, the authorities, rights and liberties appertaining to them. [17]

After the Virginia Resolutions were published, James Madison penned a lengthy and ardent defense of the principles on which State Interposition and Nullification were based. Writing on behalf of the Virginia House of Delegates during its 1799-1800 session, Mr. Madison stated that he and a committee had scanned the Virginia Resolutions "not merely with a strict, but with a severe eye." Yet, even under this *severe* scrutiny, he could find no fault with the concept of a State negative on dangerous federal acts, noting that "they feel confidence in pronouncing, that, in its just and fair construction, it is unexceptionably true in its several positions, as well as constitutional and conclusive in its inferences." [18]

James Madison went on to write that the powers of the Federal Government are strictly limited to those enumerated in the Constitution, quoting Amendment Ten as proof of this fact, and that the peoples of the several States, *as sovereign States*, are indeed the true *parties* to the federal compact. He then justified the *State negative on federal acts* in this language:

> It appears, to your committee to be a *plain principle, founded in common sense, illustrated by common practice*, and *essential to the nature of compacts* — that, where resort can be had to *no tribunal superior to the authority of the parties*, the parties themselves must be *the rightful judges in the last resort*, whether the bargain made has been pursued or violated. *The Constitution of the United States, was framed by the sanction of the States, given by each in its sovereign capacity. It adds to the stability and dignity, as*

---

[17] Alexander H. Stephens, *A Constitutional View of the Late War Between the States*, Volume 1, Kraus Reprint Co., New York, (orig. pub. in 1868) 1970, quoted on p. 579.
[18] *Ibid.*, Volume 1, quoted on p. 579.

well as to the authority of the Constitution, that it rests on this legitimate and solid foundation. The States, then, being parties to the constitutional compact, and *in their sovereign capacity*, it follows *of necessity*, that *there can be no tribunal above their authority*, to decide *in the last resort*, whether the compact made by them be violated; and, consequently, that, *as the parties to it*, they must themselves decide *in the last resort*, such questions as may be of sufficient magnitude to require their interposition. [Emphasis added] [19]

Furthermore, stated Mr. Madison:

From this view of the resolution, it would seem *inconceivable* that it can incur any just disapprobation from those who, laying aside all momentary impressions, and recollecting the *genuine source and object of the Federal Constitution*, shall candidly and accurately interpret the meaning of the General Assembly. If the deliberate exercise of dangerous powers, palpably withheld by the Constitution, could not justify the parties to it, in *interposing even so far as to arrest the progress of the evil*, and *thereby to preserve the Constitution itself*, as well as to *provide for the safety of the parties to it*, there would be an end to all relief from usurped power, and a direct subversion of the rights specified or recognized under all the State Constitutions, as well as a plain denial of the fundamental principle on which our independence itself was declared. [Emphasis added] [20]

James Madison then directed his attention to the powers of the federal judiciary. Although he still insisted that the U.S. Supreme Court possessed the power of *judicial review* over *federal* laws, he most emphatically denied that the Supreme Court of the United States was superior to those who made the Constitution:

But it is objected, that *the Judicial authority is to be regarded as the sole expositor of the Constitution in the last resort*; and it may be asked for what reason, the declaration by the General Assembly, *supposing it to be theoretically true*, could be required at the present day, and in so solemn a manner.

On this objection it might be observed: *first, that there may be instances of usurped power, which the forms of the Constitution would never draw within the control of the Judicial Department; secondly, that if the decision of the Judiciary be raised above the authority of the sovereign parties to the Constitution, the decisions of the other departments, not carried by the forms of the Constitution before the Judiciary, must be equally authoritative and final with the decisions of that department.* But the proper answer to the objection is, that the resolution of the General Assembly relates to those great and extraordinary cases, *in which all the forms of the Constitution may prove ineffec-*

---

[19] *Ibid.*, Volume 1, quoted on p. 581.
[20] *Ibid.*, Volume 1, quoted on p. 582.

tual against infractions dangerous to the essential rights of the parties to it. The resolution supposes that dangerous powers not delegated, may not only be usurped and executed by the other departments, but that *the Judicial Department, also, may exercise or sanction dangerous powers beyond the grant of the Constitution*; and, consequently, that the ultimate right of the parties to the Constitution, to judge whether the compact has been dangerously violated, must extend to violations by one delegated authority, as well as by another; *by the Judiciary, as well as by the Executive, or the Legislative.*

However true, therefore, it may be that the Judicial Department is, *in all questions submitted to it by the forms of the Constitution,* to decide in the last resort, *this resort must necessarily be deemed the last in relation to the authorities of the other departments of the government; not in relation to the rights of the parties to the constitutional compact, from which the Judicial as well as the other departments hold their delegated trusts. On any other hypothesis, the delegation of Judicial power would annul the authority delegating it;* and the concurrence of this department with the others in usurped powers, *might subvert forever,* and beyond the possible reach of any rightful remedy, the very Constitution, which all were instituted to preserve.

...The authority of Constitutions over Governments, and of the sovereignty of the people over Constitutions, are truths which are at all times necessary to be kept in mind; and at no time, perhaps, more necessary than at present. [Emphasis added] [21]

It was the great principle of States' Rights espoused in the Kentucky and Virginia Resolutions of 1798 that paved the way for the "Revolution of 1800," which witnessed the election of Thomas Jefferson to the Presidency and which doomed the Federalist Party to extinction. Within the Administration of President Jefferson, James Madison held the strategic position of Secretary of State, the most important post in the Cabinet. When President Jefferson declined to serve a third term, the Democratic-Republicans turned to Mr. Madison to be their standard bearer in the 1808 elections. Following the example set by his illustrious and distinguished predecessor, President Madison declined to serve a third term and was succeeded in office by James Monroe, the last the famous *Virginia Dynasty.*

Although James Madison's very successful political career after the adoption of the Federal Constitution was made possible only by his conversion from nationalism to federalism, he was always haunted by the fear that the embarrassing role he had played behind the closed doors of the Constitutional Convention of 1787 would become widely known. When Thomas Jefferson, prior to 1800, urged him to publish his notes of the Grand Convention for public consumption, for example, Mr. Madison was forced to delicately explain to his friend, in a letter written on February 8, 1799, that the

---

[21] *Ibid.,* Volume 1, quoted on pp. 582-583.

publication of his notes would not have the positive effect that Mr. Jefferson believed it would. The man whose political career would be most damaged by a publication of the notes, Mr. Jefferson then understood, would be Mr. Madison himself.

But if James Madison desired to perpetuate the Philadelphia Convention's rule of secrecy indefinitely, then he was to be bitterly dismayed by those who did not share his wishes. Luther Martin, who was the first to cast aside the extended rule of secrecy, would forever remain an object of enmity in Mr. Madison's eyes. President George Washington, who belatedly produced the official *Journal* of the Convention in 1796, also drew criticism from James Madison. Then there was the letter published in 1808 by Edmund Genet that very much embarrassed the Virginian, for it candidly identified him as one of the key nationalist leaders in the Constitutional Convention who had attempted to subvert the State governments.

When Congress finally resolved to publish the Convention's *Journal* nearly thirty years after the conclusion of the Philadelphia Convention, the notes of Robert Yates were soon afterwards made public. Mr. Yates' notes represented another major and significant embarrassment to ex-President Madison, who bitterly condemned them as being grossly inaccurate and unfair to him. The blow to his honor was made worse when John Taylor of Caroline cited the notes of Mr. Yates in his 1823 book, *New Views of the Constitution of the United States*. Thereafter, John Taylor of Caroline – like Robert Yates and Luther Martin – became an object of enmity in the ex-President's eyes.

Then there was John Tyler, an articulate and distinguished rising star in the Old Dominion who ably represented the next generation of statesmen in Virginia. As Mr. Tyler asserted in a speech delivered on February 6, 1833:

> He [Edmund Randolph] proposed [in the Federal Convention of 1787] a Supreme National Government, with a Supreme Executive, a Supreme Legislative, and a Supreme Judiciary, and a power in Congress to veto State laws. Mr. Madison I believe, Sir, was also an advocate of this plan of govt. If I run into error on this point, I can easily be put right. The design of this plan, it is obvious, was to render the States nothing more than the provinces of a great government to rear upon the ruins of the old Confederacy a consolidated Government, one and indivisible. [22]

Against all of these commentators – from Luther Martin and Robert Yates to John Taylor of Caroline and John Tyler – James Madison complained of unjust interpretations of his conduct and grumbled about unfair treatment of his nationalistic views. Despite the grumbling, however, he

---

[22] Max Farrand (ed.), *Op. cit.*, Volume III, p. 524.

steadfastly refused to publish his own notes in an effort to remove the stain from his public image. Instead, he chose to copy a number of passages from Mr. Yates' notes to fill in the missing details in his own notes and insisted that his own notes should not be published until four years after his death. And when his own notes were finally published in 1840, *they merely confirmed that all the charges against him were indeed true.*

While assailing those who dared to tell the truth about what had really taken place within the Constitutional Convention, James Madison began reverting back to his old concepts of nationalism. Particularly after the deaths of John Taylor of Caroline in 1824 and Thomas Jefferson in 1826, Mr. Madison began devoting more and more of his energies toward justifying and excusing his conduct within the Philadelphia Convention. In doing so, he found himself once again defending all of the extremist principles which that Convention had rejected, while denying that such principles were extremist in nature.

On March 25, 1826, for example, Mr. Madison wrote a letter to Andrew Stevenson stating, "Will you pardon me for pointing out an error of fact into which you have fallen, as others have done, by supposing that the term, *National* applied to the contemplated government, in the early stage of the Convention, particularly in the propositions of Mr. Randolph, was equivalent to *unlimited* or consolidated." "This was not the case," he added, although it was in fact the case. "The term was used, not in contradistinction to a limited, but to a *Federal* Government." [23]

Countless other such letters were written by the gentlemen from Montpellier during the closing days of his life, all with the same purpose and objective. Every commentator on the Constitutional Convention, Mr. Madison insisted, who deduced from the records that he favored the creation of a supreme National Government on the ruins of State sovereignty were grossly mistaken. The ongoing project of correcting "errors" in interpretation of the Convention's records became to him a monumental task, inasmuch as nearly everyone who read the published records seemed to arrive at the very conclusion which Mr. Madison vigorously sought to deny.

In his efforts to defend his own conduct in the Constitutional Convention, James Madison insisted that his extremist nationalist views had been correct and proper. The Federal Government, he insisted, should indeed rule over the States with greater authority than the King of England had ruled over the colonies. That government should indeed possess a veto power over State laws, *exercised by the Supreme Court of the United States.* And, as he insisted shortly before his death, State interposition and nullification was all

---

[23] *Ibid.*, Volume III, p. 473.

wrong, both in theory and in practice. The ultimate authority on the powers to be exercised by the Federal Government, he exclaimed in a fit of nationalist fervor, should be the *U.S. Supreme Court*, and not the peoples of the sovereign States!

Thus, the Virginia nationalist had come full circle. The man who had begun his political career as an uncompromising nationalist, and who had later moved to the opposite end of the political spectrum under the guiding influence of the author of the Declaration of Independence, had returned once more to his nationalist roots. Were it not for the great friendship he had had with Mr. Madison, Thomas Jefferson would undoubtedly have turned over in his grave.

A Mixed Blessing

It is apparent from our examination of the political careers of the two primary authors of *The Federalist Papers* that those essays could only be, at best, a *mixed blessing* to the American people. While the celebrated essays do indeed contain many sound and praiseworthy observations on the nature of the form and system of government drafted by the Philadelphia Convention, it was only natural that, try as they may, neither James Madison nor Alexander Hamilton could completely shed his own biases to faithfully explain the principles of a genuinely Federal Constitution.

Should we really expect a man who viewed the compact as a "frail and worthless fabric" – *a man who was an avowed National Monarchist* – to faithfully and accurately explain the merits of a *Federal Republic*, in which he had no confidence? And should we expect that Mr. Madison, who feared that the greatest threat to the political system stemmed from State sovereignty, to adequately do justice to a compact founded on that sovereignty? What is truly remarkable about *The Federalist Papers* is not the nationalist bias profusely expressed by its authors, but the fact that they could ever bring themselves to acknowledge that the Constitution was indeed based on federal principles.

Regarding the efforts of these two nationalists in collaborating in the writing of *The Federalist Papers*, historian Richard B. Morris has noted:

> *The Federalist* papers reflect a certain divergence of opinion between Hamilton and Madison on the role of the States in the new Federal Government. Hamilton saw the proposed Constitution as designed to establish a "consolidated system," one in which the States would be subordinated to the authority of the Union. In *Federalist* No. 22 he asserts: "The fabric of American Empire ought to rest on the solid basis of the consent of the

people." Madison, on the other hand, felt that the people's assent to the Constitution was to be given not as individuals but through their respective States, and that the act establishing the Constitution would be "federal" rather than "national." Hamilton believed that the powerful States and State machines menaced popular liberty and that the Federal Government was the bulwark of the people's rights. However, he could not afford to be too blunt in expressing his views during the contest over ratification, and he constantly sought to reassure the States' Rights politicians that State sovereignty would not be jeopardized and that the first loyalty of the citizens would be to their own States. [24]

Commenting on *The Federalist Papers*, John Taylor of Caroline made these interesting observations:

> The turbulence of a free government is perpetually contrasted with the repose of tyranny, by those who pleade for power, and dread the untractableness of checks devised for its control. Men are apt to see very clearly, whatever they wish or fear; and often surrender the soundest principles to their imaginary apparitions. Tinctures of such impressions are discernible in the Federalist, in suggestions of the disorderly and discordant proceedings of the State governments, and in captivating pictures of the safety and splendour to be expected from a supreme National Government. Its authors had a difficult task to perform, and they performed it with an ability, which must excite our admiration, though it may fail to reconcile contradictions. They laboured to gratify both their own prepossessions and those of the States; and if their success in effecting the ratification of the Constitution, shall be followed by the reinstatement of a rejected National Government, their ingenuity in proving that a federal system is both right and wrong, good and bad, must excite our amazement. [25]

In laboring to gratify the desires of the Federal Republicans and to reassure the Antifederalists, the authors of *The Federalist Papers* made certain to include a number of expositions of the Constitution which were quite sound and wholesome. Indeed, anyone wishing to discover authoritative and conclusive proof that, in adopting the federal compact, the States retained their sovereignty and that the powers of the Federal Government are strictly limited to those enumerated in the Constitution, will be very pleased at the evidence provided to that effect by the authors of those essays.

Writing in the *Federalist*, No. 41, for example, Mr. Madison very ably proved that the General Welfare Clause in the Constitution is perfectly harmless. So far from enlarging the powers of the Federal Government, he pointed

---

[24] Richard B. Morris (ed.), *The Basic Ideas of Alexander Hamilton*, Washington Square Press, Inc., New York, 1956, p. 223.
[25] John Taylor, *Op. cit.*, pp. 63-64.

out, it actually restricted those powers by *limiting* the federal taxing and spending authority to the enumerated purposes. And as he correctly noted, the expression itself was copied verbatim from the Articles of Confederation.

And in the *Federalist*, No. 40, Mr. Madison asserted that the new Constitution rests upon the same *fundamental principles* as the old Articles:

> Will it be said that the *fundamental principles* of the Confederation were not within the purview of the Convention, and ought not to have been varied? I ask, *What are these principles?* Do they require that in the establishment of the Constitution the States should be regarded as *distinct and independent sovereigns? They are so regarded by the Constitution proposed*....Do these principles, in fine, require that the *powers* of the general government should be *limited*, and that, beyond this limit, the States should be left in possession of their *sovereignty and independence?* We have seen that in the new government, *as in the old*, the general powers are *limited*; and that *the States, in all unenumerated cases, are left in the enjoyment of their sovereign and independent jurisdiction.*
>
> The truth is that the great principles of the Constitution proposed by the Convention may be considered *less as absolutely new than as the expansion of principles which are found in the Articles of Confederation.* [Emphasis added] [26]

Even Alexander Hamilton, in his contributions to *The Federalist Papers*, found occasion to expound the limited nature of the Federal Government. In the *Federalist*, No. 33, for instance, Mr. Hamilton focused his attention on two clauses within the federal compact — the *Necessary and Proper Clause* and the *Supremacy Clause* — and he insisted that neither clause posed a threat to State sovereignty or to the concept of constitutionally limited government. Regarding the clause in the Constitution authorizing the Government of the United States to make all laws "necessary and proper" for carrying into effect the *delegated* powers, Mr. Hamilton correctly pointed out that, "it may be affirmed with perfect confidence that the constitutional operation of the intended government would be precisely the same if these clauses were entirely obliterated as if they were repeated in every article." [27]

Furthermore, stated Mr. Hamilton:

> And it is *expressly* to execute these [enumerated] powers that the Sweeping Clause, as it has been affectedly called, authorizes the national legislature to pass all *necessary* and *proper* laws. If there be anything exceptionable, it must be sought for in the specific powers upon which this general declaration is predicated. The declaration itself, though it may be

---

[26] Alexander Hamilton, James Madison, and John Jay, *Op. cit.*, pp. 249-251.
[27] *Ibid.*, p. 202.

chargeable with tautology or redundancy, is at least perfectly harmless. [28]

Regarding the Supremacy Clause, Alexander Hamilton wrote:

> A LAW, by the very meaning of the term, includes suprem-
> acy....But it will not follow from this doctrine that acts of the larger society
> which are *not pursuant* to its constitutional powers, but which are invasions
> of the residuary authorities of the smaller societies, will become the su-
> preme law of the land. These will be merely acts of usurpation, and will de-
> serve to be treated as such. Hence we perceive that the clause which de-
> clares the supremacy of the laws of the Union, like the one we have just be-
> fore considered, only declares a truth which flows immediately and neces-
> sarily from the institution of a Federal Government. It will not, I presume,
> have escaped observation that it expressly confines this supremacy to laws
> made *pursuant to the Constitution*; which I mention merely as an instance of
> caution in the Convention; since that limitation would have been to be
> understood, though it had not been expressed. [29]

Such explanations of the new Constitution as those just cited truly
merit the praise and admiration of all who champion the cause of constitutionally limited government. In terms of deductive reasoning, they stand as
brilliant masterpieces of lucid logic; and these passages serve well to illustrate
that at least some portions of *The Federalist Papers* merit the praise and adulation that has been bestowed upon the essays. Indeed, had the authors of those
papers confined themselves exclusively to this proper mode of exposition, no
man could justifiably raise a voice of criticism against *The Federalist Papers*.

Unfortunately, the brilliance expressed within the passages quoted previously was not consistently maintained throughout *The Federal Papers*. Instead of consistency and complete harmony with the Federal Constitution,
those papers are filled with a number of glaring errors and contradictions.
This fact can be easily demonstrated in the manner in which the authors of
those essays flippantly and casually used the terms *national* and *federal* as
though they were interchangeable and equivalent in meaning. Mr. Hamilton
and Mr. Madison repeatedly referred to the Government of the United States
as a "Confederate Government," a "Federal Government," and a "National
Government." It was even asserted that a *National* Constitution would provide for a *federal* legislature, and that a *Federal* Constitution would provide
for a *national* legislature.

In the *Federalist*, No. 9, for instance, Alexander Hamilton devoted his
whole energy to proving that the United States, under the new compact,

---

[28] *Ibid.*, p. 203.
[29] *Ibid.*, pp. 204-205.

would be a "Confederacy" of sovereign States. As to the form and system of government to be established by the Constitution, he spelled this out in capital letters as being a "CONFEDERATE REPUBLIC." [30] He even quoted the noted philosopher Montesquieu in favor of this type of political system, and then observed:

> The definition of a *Confederate Republic* seems simply to be "an assemblage of societies," or an association of two or more States into one State. The extent, modifications, and objects of the federal authority are mere matters of discretion. So long as the separate organization of the members be not abolished; so long as it exists, by a constitutional necessity, for local purposes; though it should be in perfect subordination [sic] to the general authority of the Union, it would still be, in fact and in theory, an association of States, or a Confederacy. The proposed Constitution, so far from implying an abolition of the State governments, makes them constituent parts of the national [sic] sovereignty, by allowing them a direct representation in the Senate, and leaves in their possession certain exclusive and very important portions of sovereign power. This fully corresponds, in every rational import of the terms, with the idea of a Federal Government.
> [31]

Despite the apparent distortion and subversion of the definition of a Confederacy, it is plain that Mr. Hamilton was here contending for a *Federal Government*, which he correctly identified as the type of government established by the Constitution. Yet, this stands in sharp contradiction to what he said elsewhere within *The Federalist Papers*. In the *Federalist*, No. 85, for example, he contended for a supreme NATIONAL GOVERNMENT – spelled out in all capital letters – based on a single, consolidated NATION – also spelled in all capital letters – of Americans:

> A NATION, without a NATIONAL GOVERNMENT, is, in my view, an awful spectacle. The establishment of a Constitution, in time of profound peace, by the voluntary consent of a whole people, is a PRODIGY, to the completion of which I look forward with trembling anxiety. [32]

Adding to the confusion caused by the abuse of the terms *national* and *federal* was the mutilation of the concept of political *sovereignty*. Alexander Hamilton, in particular, was guilty of excessive mutilation of a term which should not have been difficult to understand. In the *Federalist*, No. 81, for example, he wrote:

---

[30] *Ibid.*, p. 74.
[31] *Ibid.*, p. 76.
[32] *Ibid.*, p. 527.

It is inherent in the nature of *sovereignty* not to be amenable to the suit of an individual *without its consent.* This is the general sense and the general practice of mankind; and the exemption, as one of the attributes of sovereignty, is now enjoyed by *the government of every State in the Union.* [Emphasis added] [33]

In the *Federalist*, No. 82, Mr. Hamilton termed the States "distinct sovereignties." [34] And within the *Federalist*, No. 33, he declared that, "The necessity of a concurrent jurisdiction in certain cases results from *the division of the sovereign power.*" [Emphasis added] [35]

Writing in the *Federalist*, No. 32, Mr. Hamilton asserted:

But as the plan of the Convention aims only at a partial Union or consolidation, *the State governments would clearly retain all the rights of sovereignty which they before had, and which were not, by that act, exclusively delegated to the United States.* This exclusive *delegation*, or rather this *alienation*, of *State sovereignty* would only exist in three cases: where the Constitution in express terms granted an exclusive authority to the Union; where it granted in one instance an authority to the Union, and in another prohibited the States from exercising the like authority; and where it granted an authority to the Union to which a similar authority in the States would be absolutely and totally *contradictory* and *repugnant.* [Emphasis added] [36]

As one final selection, Mr. Hamilton wrote in the *Federalist*, No. 31:

I repeat here what I have observed in substance in another place, that all observations founded upon the danger of usurpation ought to be referred to the composition and structure of the government, not to the nature or extent of its powers. *The State governments by their original Constitutions are invested with complete sovereignty.* [Emphasis added] [37]

Within these selections cited from Alexander Hamilton's contributions to *The Federalist Papers*, we find gross inconsistencies with respect to the question of sovereignty and the new Federal Constitution. Within the *Federalist*, No. 81, as we have seen, he called the *State governments* sovereign. In the *Federalist*, No. 82, the *States, as political societies*, were deemed sovereign. In the *Federalist*, No. 33, Mr. Hamilton advocated a so-called *divided sovereignty* under the new Constitution between the *States* and an American *nation*. In

---

[33] *Ibid.*, p. 487.
[34] *Ibid.*, p. 491.
[35] *Ibid.*, p. 201.
[36] *Ibid.*, p. 198.
[37] *Ibid.*, p. 196.

the *Federalist*, No. 32, this author again advanced the theory of *divided sovereignty* and *delegated sovereignty*, claiming that sovereignty was divided between the two levels of *government*. In the *Federalist*, No. 9, Mr. Hamilton referred to a *national sovereignty*, and in the *Federalist*, No. 31, he insisted that the *State governments* are invested with *complete sovereignty*.

The reader of *The Federalist Papers* is thus presented with the truly novel idea of a Confederate Republic wherein sovereignty is vested in the people of the States, in the people of an American nation, in the State governments, and in the Federal Government. Under this highly creative approach to federalism, not only do the States possess a *complete sovereignty*, but they also possess a portion of a *divided sovereignty*, while simultaneously the Federal Government is vested with a *delegated sovereignty*.

Such recklessness regarding terminology might be excusable had not these key terms – *federal*, *national*, and *sovereignty* – been so thoroughly and extensively discussed and analyzed by the delegates within the Constitutional Convention. For nearly four months, that Convention had wrangled over such terms and their inherent meanings, a fact which could not have been lost on the celebrated writers of *The Federalist Papers*.

No one knew better than Mr. Hamilton and Mr. Madison that a National Government and a Federal Government were not the same, and that the Convention had rejected the former in preference for the latter. Yet, even after the Convention had deliberately rejected the term *national* and its accomplice, a *supreme* general government, those two concepts managed to worm their way into the pages of *The Federalist Papers*, just as though the Convention had expressly bestowed its blessing of approval on them. The fact that improper terminology and concepts were so cleverly mixed with wholesome concepts and proper terms within the essays indicates the diabolically brilliant genius of the nationalist authors to resurrect a system of government that had been positively rejected in the Federal Convention.

If there could ever be any doubt that the reckless terminology and confusing concepts presented in *The Federalist Papers* have not served to mislead succeeding generations of Americans, then we may offer as proof the book, *The Framing of the Federal Constitution*, which was published in 1986 by the U.S. Department of the Interior. In the Foreword to this handbook, the following summary is given of our Constitutional Era:

> The American system of government springs from the work of 55 delegates meeting in Convention in Philadelphia during the summer of 1787. The document they wrote and presented to their countrymen for approval was the *Federal Constitution*. This work gave the *nation* a *National Government* based on the principle of *popular sovereignty* and the *paradoxi-*

cal idea of a "*sovereign Union of sovereign States.*" That a people could, by purposeful deliberation, *make themselves into a nation* was an event heretofore without parallel. [Emphasis added] [38]

This book then begins with these words:

> In the summer of 1787, some 55 delegates met in Convention in the State House in Philadelphia and devised a new *National Government*, then loosely allied in a "league of friendship" under the Articles of Confederation....In mid-September they gave to their countrymen the final document, four pages of parchment setting forth a plan of Union....
>
> This document was the *Federal Constitution*. It provided for a *sovereign government* with clearly *defined powers and responsibilities*. In spare, eloquent language, the delegates created a central government with authority in *national affairs* while reserving *local affairs* to the States. They steered between the equal dangers of tyranny and ineffectualness with...*strict limitations on powers granted*...and the *vesting of sovereignty in the people themselves* and not in offices and institutions. [Emphasis added] [39]

The propositions contained within these passages must excite our curiosity and amazement. Here we see incredible propositions that a *Federal Constitution* provides for a *National Government*, and that by adopting a *Federal Constitution*, the peoples of the States somehow managed to *make themselves into a nation*, an event admittedly without precedent. The Constitution, according to this account, provides for a *sovereign government* while yet *vesting sovereignty in the people themselves* and not in offices and institutions. This supremely *sovereign government* is somehow possessed only of *clearly defined powers and responsibilities* and strangely admits of *strict limitations on powers granted*. According to this account, the States are sovereign, the Union is sovereign, the people are sovereign, and so is their government. To what else may we attribute these blatant contradictions except to the enduring legacy of *The Federalist Papers*, wherein we see precisely the same confused concepts and contradictory terminology?

John Taylor's Views of The Federalist Papers

To no one was this subtle subversion of the Federal Constitution more apparent than to John Taylor of Caroline, who cast his keenly critical eye on

---

[38] Richard B. Morris, *The Framing of the Federal Constitution*, Handbook 103, U.S. Department of the Interior, Washington, 1986, p. 2.
[39] Richard B. Morris, *The Framing of the Federal Constitution*, Handbook 103, U.S. Department of the Interior, Washington, 1986, p. 6.

The Federalist Papers when writing *New Views on the Constitution of the United States*. Commenting on the disagreeable habit of the authors of those essays to mix improper with proper terminology when referring to the American constitutional system, he wrote:

> The stray words and constructive supremacies, interwoven with the Constitution by the Federalist, look rather like the casual over-flowings of an accumulated fund, than the effect of a critical examination into their consistency with the form of government adopted. A National and a Federal form were the rivals for preference; and if the same terms and the same construction were applicable to both, the contest in the Convention was frivolous, and the preference of the latter form unsubstantial. Hence, although many of the interpretations of the Constitution comprised in the Federalist, are profound and correct, it does not follow, that interpolations of words used and of provisions proposed for establishing a National Government, ought to countermine the constructions which are federal. [40]

Elsewhere in his book, this clairvoyant political theorist noted:

> But the two formidable words "national and general" still tingle in our ears....I protest against them, because they are not in the Constitution, although they have been drawn from the recess of the Convention, borrowed from a rejected plan of government, introduced by the high authority of the Federalist, and accepted with avidity by the consolidating school. In contending that we have neither a national nor a general government, nor a national nor a federal sovereignty, nor a judicial supremacy, it is necessary to point out the inconsistency between allowing great political powers to the States, and rescinding them by these illegitimate expressions. [41]

As the premier example of the evil consequences that would flow from the usage of improper terminology, John Taylor of Caroline cited Alexander Hamilton's statement in the *Federalist*, No. 9, that, "The proposed Constitution, so far from implying an abolition of the State governments, makes them constituent parts of the *national* sovereignty, by allowing them a direct representation in the Senate, and leaves in their possession certain exclusive and very important portions of sovereign power."

Commenting on the evils that could be logically deduced from this single sentence in *The Federalist Papers*, the Philosopher of Federalism wrote:

> The ambiguity of this sentence arises from the interpolation of the words national sovereignty, which are not in the Constitution; from admitting that the powers not delegated were sovereign powers belonging to the

---

[40] John Taylor, *Op. cit.*, p. 64.
[41] *Ibid.*, pp. 71-72.

governments of the States; and from making these governments constituent parts of a national sovereignty, in virtue of their representation in the Senate; by which representation they become the subjects of the assumed national sovereignty. State sovereignty is lodged in the people of each State, but by supposing it to be lodged in their governments, and considering these governments as constituents of a national sovereignty in consequence of their representation in the Senate, State Rights are made to derive their security, not from the limitations and reservations of the federal compact, but from this representation of their governments, just as Englishmen derive theirs from their representation in Parliament. Whatever may be the rights of Englishmen, representation invests the Parliament with a supreme power over them; and whatever may be the rights of the political individuals called State governments, representation creates a *national sovereignty* over these also, according to this ingenious sentence.

By taking it for granted that the Constitution has established a national sovereignty, the difficulty of proving it is avoided. The phrase "national sovereignty," is assumed in correspondence with that of the British Parliament; and the State governments are turned into its constituents by the structure of the Senate. Mr. Hamilton thus concedes to himself the essential principle of his plan for a government; knowing that if the concession should succeed, its consequences would certainly follow. A national sovereignty would remove most obstacles to his system, and to use his own sound language, "if it was once formed, it would maintain itself."

...The rights of the States were not reserved to the Senate of the United States, but to the States themselves; and are not conveyed to an imaginary National Government, upon the ground that their governments are represented in the Senate....

...The consolidating school contends that we have two sovereignties; but that one is sovereign over the other; Mr. Hamilton, that we have co-ordinate sovereignties, each invested with exclusive powers, but that one is made superlative by the representation in the Senate. That a *federal* Senate should beget a *national* sovereignty, if we have one, is a political curiosity. [42]

John Taylor of Caroline also analyzed Mr. Hamilton's attempts to vest sovereignty in the *government*, as opposed to the peoples of the several States, and illustrated that the inevitable consequence would be destructive of liberty:

Mr. Hamilton invests the State *governments* with complete sovereignty. Why does he abandon our principle, that complete sovereignty resides only in the people of each State? The reasons are obvious. His prepossession in favour of the English form of government, induced him to deposit a complete sovereignty in governments. Therefore he proposed a National Government in the Convention, empowered, like the British Parliament, to pass all *laws whatsoever*. And the same object would be effected,

[42] *Ibid.*, pp. 65-67.

if a National Government assumed as established by the Constitution, can pass *all laws which it may deem necessary and proper.* [43]

Federal Versus National

In the *Federalist*, No. 39, James Madison devoted his talents to examining the nature of the *form* and *system* of government established by the Constitution of the United States. Although the Philadelphia Convention had conclusively settled this great controversy by resolving on the retention of a Federal Republic, it became apparent from this essay that Mr. Madison was not content with the Convention's final verdict.

Regarding the *form of government*, Mr. Madison wholly agreed with the Convention's decision in favor of the republican form. Yet, his *definition* of a republican form of government is at best dubious and could be easily stretched, with a minimal effort, to cover an elective monarchy as well. In regard to the *system of government*, Mr. Madison was half in agreement and half in disagreement with the Constitution, contending for a political curiosity known as a government half national and half federal. Considering the importance of these topics to our understanding of the basic principles of constitutional government, we should examine the 39th essay of *The Federalist Papers* with a critical and discerning eye.

Commenting on the form of government established by the federal compact, James Madison wrote:

> The first question that offers itself is whether the general form and aspect of the government be strictly republican. It is evident that no other form would be reconcilable with the genius of the people of America; with the fundamental principles of the Revolution; or with that honorable determination which animates every votary of freedom to rest all our political experiments on the capacity of mankind for self-government. If the plan of the Convention, therefore, be found to depart from the republican character, its advocates must abandon it as no longer defensible. [44]

The Federal Constitution, as he correctly noted, is *essentially* or mostly republican in nature, *with one significant exception* which Mr. Madison failed to note – *the federal judiciary*. Neither the Justices of the Supreme Court of the United States, nor any Justices of inferior federal courts, are *elected* by the peoples of the States. They are *appointed* to office by the *President*, and their

---

[43] *Ibid.*, p. 79.
[44] Alexander Hamilton, James Madison, and John Jay, *Op. cit.*, p. 240.

appointments are confirmed by the *Senate*. Nor are federal Judges accountable to the people of the States after they have assumed office. Federal Judges hold their offices for *life tenures*, and the people have no way to remove from office bad Judges. Although *Congress* may impeach and thereby remove a Judge from office, the *people* themselves have no control over the federal judiciary.

In no conceivable manner, therefore, could it be said that the federal judiciary is based on republican principles, for it is neither representative of nor accountable to the people of the States. On the contrary, *that department of the Federal Government constitutes the monarchical branch of Government of the United States*. As Thomas Jefferson correctly observed, the very composition of the Judicial Branch of the Government of the United States constitutes a *solecism* within our Federal Republic.

The *reason* why James Madison failed to note this significant exception to the republican nature of the Constitution may be found in the improper *definition* of republican government he presented:

> If we resort for a criterion to the different principles on which different forms of government are established, we may *define a Republic* to be, or at least may bestow that name on, a government which *derives all its powers directly or indirectly from the great body of the people*, and is *administered by persons holding their offices during pleasure for a limited period, or during good behavior*. It is *essential* to such a government that it *be derived from the great body of the society*, not from an inconsiderable proportion or a favored class of it; otherwise a handful of tyrannical nobles, exercising their oppressions by a delegation of their powers, might aspire to the rank of republicans and claim for their government the honorable title of Republic. It is *sufficient* for such a government that the persons administering it *be appointed, either directly or indirectly, by the people*; and that they hold their appointments by *either of the tenures just specified*; otherwise every government in the United States, as well as every other popular government that has been or can be well organized or well executed, would be degraded from the republican character. [Emphasis added] [45]

Although Mr. Madison has raised a number of good points within this passage, we must beg to disagree with his definition of a republican form of government on at least two counts. The first point is one of omission. One of the key factors that sets a genuine republican form of government apart from other forms is a *limitation of powers* placed on the rule of a majority. Why Mr. Madison failed to note this key aspect of republican government is difficult to explain, especially in light of the fact that the Constitutional Convention deliberately rejected proposals for vague and undefined powers precisely

---

[45] *Ibid.*, p. 241.

because such sweeping powers were un-republican in nature.

The other point of disagreement centers around the matter of *accountability to the people*. As we have before indicated, federal Judges are in no way accountable to the peoples of the several States. Yet, by the definition given by Mr. Madison, even the federal judiciary could be falsely deemed the epitome of republican purity. In fact, by Mr. Madison's definition, even the plan of government proposed in the Philadelphia Convention by Alexander Hamilton would pass the test of republicanism, which no doubt would have surprised no one more than Mr. Hamilton himself. Was this dubious definition of republican government offered as an attempt to soften criticism of the nationalist plot to vest supremacy in the monarchical branch of the Federal Government?

After reviewing the republican nature of the federal system, James Madison focused his attention on the *system of government* established by the Federal Constitution:

> "But it was not sufficient," say the adversaries of the proposed Constitution, "for the Convention to adhere to the republican form. They ought with equal care to have preserved the *federal* form, which regards the Union as a *Confederacy* of sovereign States; instead of which they have framed a National Government, which regards the Union as a *consolidation* of the States." And it is asked by what authority this bold and radical innovation was undertaken? The handle which has been made of this objection requires that it should be examined with some precision.
>
> ...In order to ascertain the real character of the government, it may be considered in relation to the foundation on which it is to be established; to the sources from which its ordinary powers are to be drawn; to the operation of those powers; to the extent of them; and to the authority by which future changes in the government are to be introduced. [46]

Here was the golden opportunity for Mr. Madison to refer to his own notes of the Federal Convention and to cite authoritatively the successful motion made by Oliver Ellsworth to *reject* the concept of a "National Government" in favor of a "Government of the United States" so that the new Constitution could go forward as an amendment to the Articles of Confederation. Such information would undoubtedly have reassured the public and eliminated much of the hostility toward the ratification of the new Constitution. Instead of seeing an opportunity to advance the truth about the compact, however, Mr. Madison saw only an opportunity to mix fiction with fact – to acknowledge that the Constitution was indeed federal in nature while, at the same time, to throw out handles for those determined to pervert it into a Na-

---

[46] *Ibid.*, pp. 242-243.

tional Constitution.

As Mr. Madison wrote in the *Federalist*, No. 39:

> On examining the first relation, it appears, on one hand, that the Constitution is to be founded on the assent and ratification of the *people of America*, given by deputies elected for the special purpose; but, on the other, that this assent and ratification is to be given by the people, *not as individuals composing one entire nation, but as composing the distinct and independent States to which they respectively belong*. It is to be the *assent and ratification of the several States*, derived from the supreme authority in each State – the authority of the people themselves. The act, therefore, establishing the Constitution will not be a *national* but a *federal* act. [Emphasis added] [47]

Herein Mr. Madison has correctly identified the parties to the federal compact – the sovereign States. His reluctance in acknowledging this truth is apparent in the manner in which he at first stated that the parties are the "people of America." After making that absurd remark, however, he proceeded to prove that initial comment incorrect. It was not, he finally concluded, the *people of America*, but the *people of the States*, who ratified and gave validity to the Constitution. The compact is thus the result of the "assent and ratification of the several States," who are the parties to it. So far, the Constitution is wholly federal in nature.

Mr. Madison added further proof of the obvious fact that the States are the parties to the compact:

> That it will be a federal and not a national act, as these terms are understood by the objectors – the act of the people, as forming so many independent States, not as forming one aggregate nation – is obvious from this single consideration; that it is to result neither from the decision of a *majority* of the people of the Union, nor from that of a *majority* of the States. It must result from the *unanimous* assent of the several States that are parties to it, differing no otherwise from their ordinary assent than in its being expressed, not by the legislative authority, but by that of the people themselves. Were the people regarded in this transaction as forming one nation, the will of the majority of the whole people of the United States would bind the minority, in the same manner as the majority in each State must bind the minority; and the will of the majority must be determined either by a comparison of the individual votes, or by considering the will of the majority of the States as evidence of the will of a majority of the people of the United States. Neither of these rules has been adopted. *Each State, in ratifying the Constitution, is considered as a sovereign body independent of all others, and only to be bound by its own voluntary act.* In this relation, then,

---

[47] *Ibid.*, p. 243.

the new Constitution will, if established, be a *Federal* and not a *National* Constitution. [Emphasis added] [48]

After dutifully noting the true nature of the Federal Constitution, Mr. Madison then resorted to some myth making:

> The next relation is to the sources from which the ordinary powers of government are to be derived. The House of Representatives will derive its powers from the people of America; and the people will be represented in the same proportion and on the same principle as they are in the legislature of a particular State. So far the government is *national,* not *federal.* The Senate, on the other hand, will derive its powers from the States as political and coequal societies; and these will be represented on the principle of equality in the Senate, as they now are in the existing Congress. So far the government is *federal,* not *national.* The executive power will be derived from a very compound source. The votes allotted to them are in a compound ratio, which considers them partly as distinct and coequal societies, partly as unequal members of the same society. The eventual election, again, is to be made by that branch of the legislature which consists of the national representatives; but in this particular act they are to be thrown into the form of individual delegations from so many distinct and coequal bodies politic. From this aspect of the government it appears to be of a mixed character, presenting at least as many *federal* as *national* features. [49]

According to Mr. Madison, the "House of Representatives will derive its *powers* from the people of America." Inasmuch as his entire case herein relies upon this assumption, we must look deeper into the matter. Is it true that the House of Representatives derives its powers from the *people of America,* or are those powers derived from the *Constitution?*

Mr. Madison clearly was of the opinion that such powers are derived directly from a consolidated American nation, not from the *compact* to which the peoples of the several States are parties *as sovereign States.* According to this novel concept, the powers of that branch of Congress are apparently determined every two years when a mythical and non-existent American nation elects members to the House of Representatives, a process which constitutes, in essence, a perpetual Constitutional Convention. Perhaps this strange idea explains why Mr. Madison failed to include in his definition of a republican form of government any notion of *constitutionally limited powers.*

According to this bizarre theory of the source of legislative powers, when the Philadelphia Convention labored arduously to detail the enumerated powers to be delegated to the Federal Government, the delegates were

---

[48] *Ibid.,* pp. 243-244.
[49] *Ibid.,* p. 244.

wasting their time. And when the States insisted upon the addition of the Bill of Rights as a condition for adopting the Constitution, they were also acting in vain. The powers of government, said Mr. Madison, are derived directly from the people of America, not from the Constitution. The addition of precautionary statements to the compact like Amendment Ten, therefore, can have no effect, inasmuch as the Constitution has nothing whatsoever to do with the powers of the Federal Government. Can anyone believe that the Constitution would have been ratified by a single State if the peoples of those States had understood the compact in the manner herein described by James Madison?

The Constitution itself contradicts Mr. Madison. Article I, Section 2 of the compact states that, "The House of Representatives shall be composed of Members chosen every second Year by *the People of the several States*, and the Electors in each State shall have the Qualifications requisite for Electors of the most numerous Branch of the state Legislature." [Emphasis added] [50] The House of Representatives is thus elected, not by "the people of America," as Mr. Madison claimed, but expressly by "the People of the several States."

Article I, Section 2, Clause 1 of the Federal Constitution reinforces this concept by stipulating that each Representative elected to the lower branch of Congress must be "an Inhabitant of that State in which he shall be chosen." [51] The Fourth Clause of Article I, Section 2 refers to the Members of the House of Representatives as *Representations from the States*, by declaring, "When vacancies happen in the *Representation from any State*, the Executive Authority thereof shall issue Writs of Election to fill such Vacancies." [Emphasis added][52]

Article II, Section 1, Clause 2 of the compact provides details for the election of the President of the United States, wherein it is described how the House of Representatives shall elect the President in the case of a tie vote in the Electoral College, an event which occurred only once in American history, involving the election of 1800. "But in chusing the President," this clause asserts, "the Votes shall be taken by States, the *Representation from each State* having one Vote." [Emphasis added] [53] How and why would the vote in the lower house of Congress be made *by States, with each State having one vote*, if that branch represented a consolidated, *single nation* of Americans?

We also note that Article I, Section 2, Clause 3 of the federal compact ends with this declaration:

---

[50] Alexander H. Stephens, *Op. cit.*, Volume 1, p. 557.
[51] *Ibid.*, Volume 1, p. 557.
[52] *Ibid.*, Volume 1, p. 557.
[53] *Ibid.*, Volume 1, p. 562.

> The Number of Representatives shall not exceed one for every thirty Thousand, but each State shall have at Least one Representative; and until such enumeration shall be made, the State of New Hampshire shall be entitled to chuse three, Massachusetts eight, Rhode-Island and Providence Plantations one, Connecticut five, New-York six, New-Jersey four, Pennsylvania eight, Delaware one, Maryland six, Virginia ten, North Carolina five, South Carolina five, and Georgia three. [54]

How many Representatives is the *State of America* allowed to have in the House in Representatives? Such a glaring omission to assign within the Constitution even one Representative is highly suggestive. So far from representing the "people of America," it is obvious that the lower branch of Congress represents *the peoples of the several States*. Although the authors of *The Federalist Papers* recognized the existence of a non-existent consolidated nation of Americans, the Constitution of the United States does not.

Speaking before the House of Representatives on January 24, 1792, Congressman Hugh Williamson – who had been a delegate to the Constitutional Convention from North Carolina – verified that the mass of that Convention did not agree with Mr. Madison's thesis espoused in *The Federalist Papers*. This assertion carries more weight when it is considered that, within the Federal Convention, Mr. Williamson had been a supporter of nationalist principles.

Mr. Williamson's remarks were recorded in the *Annals of Congress* in these words:

> Mr. Williamson observed, that although some complaints were made of the fractional parts not being represented, he never could conceive that the framers of the Constitution entertained an idea of a representation of the people distinct from the States, but contemplated the representation of the people of each State, according to some given ratio. [55]

With the explosion of James Madison's fallacious concept of the House of Representatives, his distorted view of the nature of Presidential elections must also collapse, inasmuch as it was based on the former incorrect theory. For proof that the election of the President of the United States is a *federal* – and not a *national* – act, we may cite an informative letter written by Rufus King on March 23, 1824. Considering that he had been an ardent champion of a supreme National Government within the Federal Convention, his views become all the more impressive.

As Mr. King stated:

---

[54] *Ibid.*, Volume 1, p. 557.
[55] Max Farrand (ed.), *Op. cit.*, Volume III, p. 365.

The election of the Pr., as it is one of the most important, so it is one of the most *intricate provisions* of the Constitution, and in its object, except in the first stage of the process, *is assigned to the States acting in their federal equal capacity.* For this reason, measures which may be employed in the several States, under regulations and provisions of simple, and *single sovereignties,* could not be adopted in the balanced system of the Constitution of the U.S. — *a compact between the States,* wh. contains special provisions whereby the executive, legislative and judicial officers must be appointed. [Emphasis added] [56]

As our final and conclusive evidence to disprove the contention put forth by Mr. Madison, we offer none other than the distinguished authority of James Madison himself. Writing to Thomas Jefferson on September 6, 1787, Mr. Madison described the nature of representation in the Federal Government in this manner:

A Governmt. will probably be submitted to the *people of* the *States,* consisting of a *President, cloathed* with *Executive power;* a *Senate chosen* by the *Legislatures,* and another *House chosen* by the *people of* the States, jointly *possessing* the *legislative* power; and a regular *judiciary* establishment. The mode of constituting the *Executive* is among the few points not yet finally settled. The *Senate* will consist of two *members* from each State, and *appointed sexennially.* The other, of *members appointed biennially* by the *people of the States,* in proportion to their number. [57]

On October 24, 1787, in another letter to Thomas Jefferson, James Madison reaffirmed this understanding of the *purely federal nature of representation* inherent in the Federal Government:

The Senate will represent the States in their political capacity; the other House will represent the people of the States in their individual capac[it]y. The former will be accountable to their constituents at moderate, the latter at short periods. The President also derives his appointment from the States, and is periodically accountable to them. This dependence of the general [government] on the local authorities, seems effectually to guard the latter against any dangerous encroachments of the former.... [58]

We may therefore conclude that Mr. Madison's contention for a National Constitution within *The Federalist Papers,* based upon the nature of representation, is totally incorrect, and that the Constitution and the Federal Government both stand, thus far into the consideration of their features,

---

[56] *Ibid.,* Volume III, p. 462-463.
[57] *Ibid.,* Volume III, p. 77.
[58] *Ibid.,* Volume III, p. 134.

wholly *federal* in nature. With this understanding, we may therefore resume our analysis of Mr. Madison's views expressed in the *Federalist*, No. 39.

James Madison next directed his attention to the *operations* of the Federal Government:

> The difference between a Federal and National Government, as it relates to the *operation of the government,* is by the adversaries of the plan of the Convention supposed to consist in this, that in the former the powers operate on the political bodies composing the Confederacy in their political capacities; in the latter, on the individual citizens composing the nation in their individual capacities. On trying the Constitution by this criterion, it falls under the *national* not the *federal* character; though perhaps not so completely as has been understood. In several cases, and particularly in the trial of controversies to which States may be parties, they must be viewed and proceeded against in their collective and political capacities only. But the operation of the government on the people in their individual capacities, in its ordinary and most essential proceedings, will, in the sense of its opponents, on the whole, designate it, in this relation, a *National* Government. [59]

It was a wise strategy on Mr. Madison's part to take refuge under the ill-defined and therefore meaningless cover of *the understanding of the Antifederalists,* whatever that may have been. The operation of the Federal Government, said Mr. Madison, makes that government a national one, but evidently only "in the sense of its opponents." Since we do not know which opponents he had in mind, we must therefore ignore this diversionary tactic and assume that the *sense* of the term Mr. Madison really had in mind was his own and perhaps that of his fellow nationalists.

Within the Constitutional Convention of 1787, the nationalists had repeatedly insisted that *only* a supreme National Government could operate directly on the individual citizens of the several States. Indeed, this had been one of the arguments put forward on behalf of that type of government for the United States. In response, the Federal Republicans within the Convention had repeatedly challenged such an erroneous contention, stating that a Federal Government could also be constituted to operate directly on the citizens of the States, as in the collection of federal taxes.

Here, for example, is what Luther Martin said to the Convention on June 27, 1787:

> A general government may operate on individuals in cases of general concern, and still be federal. This distinction is with the States, as

---

[59] Alexander Hamilton, James Madison, and John Jay, *Op. cit.*, pp. 244-245.

States, represented by the people of those States. States will take care of their internal police and local concerns. The general government has no interest, but the protection of the whole. Every other government must fail.[60]

What differentiates a Federal Government from a National Government is not that one operates exclusively on States in their organized capacities while the other operates on individual citizens. As Mr. Martin correctly indicated, the difference between the two political systems was the nature of the government's *sphere of influence* and the *extent of its powers*. A Federal Government may operate on States and individual citizens in its capacity of governing federal or foreign concerns, while a National Government operates exclusively on individuals within a single society in all domestic as well as all foreign concerns. Can there be any doubt as to which type of government was adopted by the Convention?

If further proof is required to show that James Madison was in error in his assertions, then we may offer an authority that would impress even Mr. Madison – *himself.* Within the Federal Convention on June 19, 1787, while critically analyzing the New Jersey Plan, Mr. Madison strongly emphasized the fact that even a Federal Government could operate directly on individual citizens. As proof of his claim, he cited an example of such a mode of operation that existed under the Articles of Confederation in the case piracies and captures by the then existing Confederate Government.

James Madison recorded his own remarks on this topic as follows:

> Much stress had been laid by some gentlemen on the want of power in the Convention to propose any other than a *federal* plan. To what had been answered by others, he would only add, that neither of the characteristics attached to a *federal* plan would support this objection. One characteristic, was that in a *Federal* Government, the power was exercised not on the people individually; but on the people *collectively*, on the *States.* Yet in some instances as in piracies, captures &c. the existing Confederacy, and in many instances, the amendments proposed to it (proposed by Mr. Patterson) must operate immediately on individuals. [61]

If James Madison was correct in his statements to the Philadelphia Convention – and he *was* correct – then his analysis within *The Federalist Papers* must be incorrect. We may therefore conclude that the Government of the United States remains, thus far in the analysis, wholly *federal* in nature. Although that government may operate directly on the individual citizens of the several States, it remains a Federal Government due to the *federal limita-*

---

[60] Max Farrand (ed.), *Op. cit.*, Volume I, p. 439.
[61] *Ibid.*, Volume I, p. 314.

tions imposed on its range of actions and on the extent of its constitutional powers.

Continuing with his analysis of the system of government established by the Federal Constitution, James Madison wrote in the *Federalist*, No. 39:

> But if the government be national [sic] with regard to the *operation* of its powers, it changes its aspect again when we contemplate it in relation to the extent of its powers. The idea of a National Government involves in it not only an authority over the individual citizens, but an indefinite supremacy over all persons and things, so far as they are objects of lawful government. Among a people consolidated into one nation, this supremacy is completely vested in the national legislature. Among communities united for particular purposes, it is vested partly in the general and partly in the municipal legislatures. In the former case, all local authorities are subordinate to the supreme; and may be controlled, directed, or abolished by it at pleasure. In the latter, the local or municipal authorities form distinct and independent portions of the supremacy, no more subject, within their respective spheres, to the general authority than the general authority is subject to them, within its own sphere. In this relation, then, the proposed government cannot be deemed a *national* one; since its jurisdiction extends to certain enumerated objects only, and leaves to the several States a residuary and inviolable sovereignty over all other objects. It is true that in controversies relating to the boundary between the two jurisdictions, the tribunal which is ultimately to decide is to be established under the general government. But this does not change the principle of the case. The decision is to be impartially made, according to the rules of the Constitution; and all the usual and most effectual precautions are taken to secure this impartiality. Some such tribunal is clearly essential to prevent an appeal to the sword and a dissolution of the compact; and that it ought to be established under the general rather than under the local governments, or, to speak more properly, that it could be safely established under the first alone, is a position not likely to be combated. [62]

While we may be pleased to note that Mr. Madison correctly concluded that the *powers* of the Government of the United States clearly and unmistakably define it as a Federal Government, we must beg to disagree with the tortuous manner in which he arrived a such a conclusion. The highly disagreeable usage of the concept of *government supremacy*, as stressed by Mr. Madison, carries with it a repugnant and un-American tincture. According to the *American Theory of Government*, as established by the acclaimed Declaration of Independence, the Federal Government possesses neither complete nor partial "supremacy" – *supremacy, or sovereignty, is exclusively vested in the peoples of the several States!*

---

[62] Alexander Hamilton, James Madison, and John Jay, *Op. cit.*, pp. 245-246.

The whole idea behind the establishment of written Constitutions to place limits and restrictions on governments is that the people thereby exercise and demonstrate their *supremacy over government*, both State and federal. But even if we may disagree with Mr. Madison's concept of a supreme government, we note that he at least acknowledged the federal nature of the Government of the United States in regard to its powers. Thus far, the purity of the Federal Government remains unblemished.

James Madison next directed his attention to the *amendment process* specified in the federal compact:

> If we try the Constitution by its last relation to the authority by which amendments are to be made, we find it neither wholly *national* nor wholly *federal.* Were it wholly national, the supreme and ultimate authority would reside in the *majority* of the people of the Union; and this authority would be competent at all times, like that of a majority of every national society to alter or abolish its established government. Were it wholly federal, on the other hand, the concurrence of each State in the Union would be essential to every alteration that would be binding on all. The mode provided by the plan of the Convention is not founded on either of these principles. In requiring more than a majority, and particularly in computing the proportion by *States*, not by *citizens*, it departs from the national and advances towards the *federal* character; in rendering the concurrence of less than the whole number of States sufficient, it loses again the *federal* and partakes of the *national* character. [63]

The desperate frustration felt by those whose pet project had been defeated in the Constitutional Convention is readily apparent in this passage from the *Federalist*, No. 39. Attempting to deduce a National Government based on the fact that amendments need not have the unanimous approval of all the States in order to be ratified, is most assuredly a stark illustration of straining at a gnat. The fact that it is the *States*, and *not a consolidated American nation*, that may amend the compact, should be sufficient proof to settle the matter in favor of a Federal Government.

Had a consolidated American nation been given half control over the amendment process, to be shared with the States, then Mr. Madison's conclusions would have been justified. Then, indeed, we could say with him that, in terms of amending the compact, the Constitution is truly half federal and half national. But, alas, the amendment process is not shared at all with any consolidated American nation, because *the Constitution does not recognize the existence of such a nation.* The Constitution recognizes only the existence of the peoples of the several States, who alone are the parties to it, who alone made

---

[63] *Ibid.*, p. 246.

it and ratified it, who alone possess all the powers not delegated by it to the Federal Government, and who alone may amend it. In this regard, then, the chastity of the federal system remains unmolested by nationalism.

Concluding his essay, Mr. Madison wrote:

> The proposed Constitution, therefore, even when tested by the rules laid down by its antagonists, is, in strictness, neither a National nor a Federal Constitution, but a composition of both. In its foundation it is federal, not national; in the sources from which the ordinary powers of government are drawn, it is partly federal and partly national; in the operation of these powers, it is national, not federal; in the extent of them, again, it is federal, not national; and, finally in the authoritative mode of introducing amendments, it is neither wholly federal nor wholly national. [64]

The esteem placed upon the intelligence of the general public by the authors of *The Federalist Papers* must indeed have been very low. The idea that a government whose *foundation* is federal and whose *powers* are federal could ever exercise those *federal* powers in a *national* mode of operation, staggers the imagination. To those who prefer mystery to understanding, Mr. Madison's logic may well offer the means of conjuring up a rejected supreme National Government. But to those who prefer the Constitution of the United States as it was drafted by the Federal Convention and adopted by the States – and not as it has been distorted by the cunning and sophistry of artful constructions – it will forever remain a truly *Federal Constitution*.

Judicial Supremacy

Writing in the *Federalist*, No. 37, James Madison stated:

> The genius of republican liberty seems to demand on one side not only that all power should be derived from the people, but that those intrusted with it should be kept in dependence on the people by a short duration of their appointments; and that even during this short period the trust should be placed not in a few, but in a number of hands. [65]

And in his remarks in October of 1788 on Thomas Jefferson's draft of a Constitution, Mr. Madison wrote:

---

[64] *Ibid.*, p. 246.
[65] *Ibid.*, p. 227.

It sd not be allowed the Judges or the Executive to pronounce a law thus enacted unconstitul & invalid.

In the State Constitutions & indeed *in the fedl. one also, no provision is made for the case of a disagreement in expounding them*; and as the Courts are generally the last in making their decision, *it results to them*, by refusing or not refusing to execute a law, to stamp it with its final character. *This makes the Judiciary Dept. paramount in fact to the Legislature, which was never intended, and can never be proper.* [Emphasis added] [66]

Judicial review – the practice of a federal court declaring a law of Congress unconstitutional and void – said James Madison, is repugnant to the theory on which the Federal Constitution is founded. Such a practice, said he, would make the monarchical branch of government "paramount" to the most republican branch. Furthermore, it would be contrary to the "genius of republican liberty," which requires that all power be vested in those accountable to the people of the States, meaning that the tenure of office of those entrusted with power should be of short duration. Furthermore, that "genius of republican liberty" demands that significant power be vested in numerous hands, as in the case of a Congress, and not in a few hands, as in the case of the Supreme Court. On all counts, therefore, judicial review would be subversive of the Constitution and destructive of republican liberty – such a fearsome power *"was never intended, and can never be proper."*

In spite of this knowledge, however, James Madison was – from the moment his pet project was defeated in the Constitutional Convention to the time of his death – an enthusiastic and persistent advocate of the obnoxious practice of judicial review. And in spite of his honest and correct observation in 1788 that "no provision is made for the case of a disagreement in expounding" the Federal Constitution, he later *changed his mind* and claimed that judicial review could be logically deduced from the glittering general phraseology of the compact.

Typical of his erroneous construction in this regard, Mr. Madison made this claim in a letter written to Thomas Jefferson on June 27, 1823, a claim which, it might be mentioned, failed to persuade the Sage of Monticello that such a power existed:

Believing as I do that the General Convention regarded a provision within the Constitution for deciding in a peaceable & regular mode all cases arising in the course of its operation, as essential to an adequate System of Govt. that it intended the Authority vested in the Judicial Department as a final resort in relation to the States, for cases resulting to it in the

---

[66] James H. Hutson (ed.), *Supplement to Max Farrand's The Records of the Federal Convention of 1787*, Yale University Press, New Haven, 1987, p. 297.

> exercise of its functions, (the concurrence of the Senate chosen by the State Legislatures, in appointing the Judges, and the oaths & official tenures of these, with the surveillance of public Opinion, being relied on as guarantying their impartiality); and that this intention is expressed by the articles declaring that the Federal Constitution & laws shall be the supreme law of the land, and that the Judicial power of the U.S. shall extend to all cases arising under them:...thus believing I have never yielded my original opinion in the "Federalist" No. 39 to the ingenious reasonings of Col: [John] Taylor [of Caroline] agst. this construction of the Constitution. [67]

By this clever and cunning reasoning, the power of judicial review is conjured up from the depths of the imaginations of those longing for a supreme National Government. After first citing the Supremacy Clause, which was written by Luther Martin and adopted by the Philadelphia Convention to emphatically deny the supremacy of the Federal Government, Mr. Madison cites the dubious phraseology of Gouverneur Morris to the effect that the "judicial power" is to extend to all cases arising *under* the Constitution.

But even this construction cannot sustain the deduction made by the Virginia nationalist. *The phrase stating that the "judicial power" extends to all cases arising under the compact does not grant a single power to the federal judiciary.* It merely establishes the *proper limits* of the Supreme Court's *jurisdiction*. If the power of judicial review has been delegated to the federal judiciary, then it must be found among the enumerated powers, inasmuch as ours is a *government of delegated powers*, not a *government of implied powers*.

The power of nullifying an act of Congress is, by all accounts, a very significant and sweeping authority. If the Constitutional Convention had intended to vest such authority in the federal judiciary, common sense dictates that some mention of it would have been included in the Constitution. The fact that the Constitution does not even hint at such power may be regarded as conclusive evidence that such a power does not exist. This conclusion is strengthened by the fact that the Convention had considered adding a form of judicial review to the compact, but when a vote was taken on the subject, the power was expressly *rejected* by the delegates. The rejection of this power could not have failed to escape the notice of James Madison, inasmuch as he had been one of the main proponents of the motion in the Federal Convention.

The task of resurrecting this rejected power within *The Federalist Papers* primarily fell to Alexander Hamilton. Beginning with the *Federalist*, No. 78, Mr. Hamilton turned his attention to the federal judiciary, and he began the discussion by assuring his readers that there could be no reason to fear the

---

[67] *Ibid.*, p. 312.

Supreme Court of the United States. "Whoever attentively considers the different departments of power," he wrote, "must perceive that, in a government in which they are separated from each other, the judiciary, *from the nature of its functions*, will always be the *least dangerous* to the political rights of the Constitution; because it will be *least in a capacity to annoy or injure them.*" [Emphasis added] [68]

After lulling the Antifederalists to sleep with such sweet assurances, Mr. Hamilton then departed from a description of the Constitution of the United States and began describing a supreme federal judiciary that would accommodate his own constitution:

> Limitations [of power] of this kind can be preserved in practice no other way than through the medium of courts of justice, whose duty it must be to declare all acts contrary to the manifest tenor of the Constitution void. Without this, all the reservations of particular rights or privileges would amount to nothing.
>
> Some perplexity respecting the rights of the courts to pronounce legislative acts void, because contrary to the Constitution, has arisen from an imagination that the doctrine would imply a superiority of the judiciary to the legislative power. It is urged that the authority which can declare the acts of another void must necessarily be superior to the one whose acts may be declared void. As this doctrine is of great importance in all the American Constitutions, a brief discussion of the grounds on which it rests cannot be unacceptable.
>
> There is no position which depends on clearer principles than that every act of a delegated authority, contrary to the tenor of the commission under which it is exercised, is void. No legislative act, therefore, contrary to the Constitution, can be valid. To deny this would be to affirm that the deputy is greater than his principal; that the servant is above his master; that the representatives of the people are superior to the people themselves; that men acting by virtue of powers may do not only what their powers do not authorize, but what they forbid.
>
> ...It is far more rational to suppose that the courts were designed to be an intermediate body between the people and the legislative in order, among other things, to keep the latter within the limits assigned to their authority. The interpretation of the laws is the proper and peculiar province of the courts. A Constitution is, in fact, and must be regarded by the judges as, a fundamental law. It therefore belongs to them to ascertain its meaning as well as the meaning of any particular act proceeding from the legislative body....
>
> Nor does this conclusion by any means suppose a superiority of the judicial to the legislative power. It only supposes that the power of the people is superior to both, and that where the will of the legislature, declared in its statutes, stands in opposition to that of the people, declared in

---

[68] Alexander Hamilton, James Madison, and John Jay, *Op. cit.*, p. 465.

the Constitution, the judges ought to be governed by the latter rather than the former. They ought to regulate their decisions by the fundamental laws rather than by those which are not fundamental. [69]

Elsewhere in this essay, Mr. Hamilton wrote that the important role to be played by the federal judiciary necessitated its monarchical nature:

> If, then, the courts of justice are to be considered as the bulwarks of a limited Constitution against legislative encroachments, this consideration will afford a strong argument for the permanent tenure of judicial offices, since nothing will contribute so much as this to that independent spirit in the judges which must be essential to the faithful performance of so arduous a duty. [70]

Mr. Hamilton concluded this essay by reminding his readers of the beauty of the *monarchical* Constitution of Great Britain:

> Upon the whole, there can be no room to doubt that the Convention acted wisely in copying from the models of those Constitutions which have established *good behavior* as the tenure of their judicial offices, in point of duration; and that so far from being blamable on this account, their plan would have been inexcusably defective if it had wanted this important feature of good government. The experience of Great Britain affords an illustrious comment on the excellence of the institution. [71]

This constitutes the rationale for claiming the power of judicial review for the federal judiciary; and we must admit that Mr. Hamilton could be especially persuasive with a pen. The constant references to an all-wise and ever-faithful monarchical branch of government dutifully guarding the Constitution from the abuses of the ignorant and turbulent republican branch of government was presented to the American people in a most impressive style. The arguments used to sustain his deductive conclusions, however, are filled with fallacies

"No legislative act...," said Mr. Hamilton, "contrary to the Constitution, can be valid." This is quite true – yet, it equally true that *no judicial act, contrary to the Constitution, can be valid*. Let us, therefore, put Mr. Hamilton's theory to a practical test to determine if it is calculated to preserve the Constitution, or to subvert it. Let us suppose that Congress enacts a law. According to the Constitution, the President may, within ten days, *veto* the law if he deems it to be unconstitutional. This negative power is not left to as-

---

[69] *Ibid.*, pp. 466-468.
[70] *Ibid.*, p. 469.
[71] *Ibid.*, p. 472.

sumption, but is spelled out in very plain language in the compact *as a check on the power of Congress*. If the President does veto the law, acting under the impression that it is unconstitutional, then Congress may override the veto and pass the law anyway, acting under the assumption that the opinion of the Chief Executive is wrong. The Constitution provides this authority *as a counter-check on the power of the Executive Branch*, and this check is not left to assumption, but is prescribed in very plain words. By providing a check in each of these two branches over the other, neither Congress nor the President may possess a supremacy over the other.

Assuming the law is passed by Congress, with or without the President's approval, Mr. Hamilton contends that the federal judiciary may exercise a negative power and void the law, *as a check on the power of Congress*. Such a power is not described at all in the compact, but is derived only by assumption, as Mr. Hamilton admits. "It is far more rational to *suppose*," he said, in attempting to deduce this very significant power. If a federal court does indeed void a law, what recourse may be had by Congress to prevent the superiority of the monarchical over the republican branch of government? Can Congress override the decision of the Supreme Court, as it can override a Presidential veto – *as a counter-check on the power of the federal judiciary*? To admit the *check* without the *counter-check* would be to destroy the delicate *balance* of the constitutional system and raise the Judicial Branch over the Legislative Branch.

If the Supreme Court can *assume* the power of *judicial review* over acts of Congress, may the Congress *assume* a similar power of *legislative review* over the acts of the federal judiciary? Can the President assume an equivalent power of *executive review* over acts of Congress and refuse to enforce an existing law? Can the Chief Executive assume such a power over judicial decisions that are, in his opinion, unconstitutional? All officers of the Federal Government are bound by oath to support and maintain the Constitution of the United States. If that oath grants *judicial review* to the federal judiciary, then it must also grant *legislative review* to Congress and *executive review* to the President. Also, may not the State governments lay claim to a power of *State review*, based on the oaths that the officers of the State governments are required to take to support and maintain that same Constitution?

Let us carry this deductive reasoning process even farther. Does an officer of the government, upon taking the required oath to support and maintain the Federal Constitution, thereby acquire the broad power to nullify the actions of another department or level of government? Stated differently, does his oath bind the *other* departments or level of government to his views of the Constitution, and make *them* responsible to him? Or does that oath bind *him* to fidelity to the compact and make *him* responsible to the peoples of the several States, whose Constitution he has sworn to uphold? And finally, does it not excite our amazement that a simple oath intended to serve as a *restriction* upon the officers of government can be ingeniously misconstrued as an *expansion* of their power and authority?

The real answer to the claims made by Mr. Hamilton, Mr. Madison, and others who prefer the monarchical branch of government over the republican branch, is that ours is a government founded on powers derived from *enumerations*, not on powers deduced from *suppositions*. If there could ever have been any doubts on this matter, then the matter should have been conclusively settled by the adoption of the Tenth Amendment to the Constitution.

As Thomas Jefferson wisely stated to President Washington on February 15, 1791, when giving his opinion of Mr. Hamilton's proposed National Bank:

> I consider the foundation of the Constitution as laid on this ground: That all powers not delegated to the United States, by the Constitution, nor prohibited by it to the States, are reserved to the States, or to the people....To take a single step beyond the boundaries thus specially drawn..., is to take possession of a boundless field of power, no longer susceptible of any definition. [72]

History itself has condemned the theories espoused by the authors of *The Federalist Papers*, who assured America that judicial review would not instill a supremacy in the U.S. Supreme Court. It was but a small step, after usurping this power, for that Supreme Court to go from haughtily asserting that the law is whatever the federal judiciary says it is – "It is emphatically the province and duty of the Judicial Department," said Chief Justice John Marshall, "to say what the law is." – to arrogantly proclaiming that the Constitution itself is whatever that branch of the Federal Government says it is – "We are under a Constitution," said Chief Justice Charles Evans Hughes, "but the Constitution is what the Judges say it is."[73] The *genius of republican liberty*, however, rejects all such claims of *judicial supremacy* and insists that federal law is whatever the representatives of the people, in Congress assembled, say it is and that the Constitution is whatever the sovereign peoples of the several States say it is. This is the only proper interpretation of the compact that is consistent with both the letter and spirit of the Constitution.

---

[72] Harold C. Syrett (ed.), *American Historical Documents*, Barnes & Noble, Inc., New York, 1960, p. 131.
[73] Otis H. Stephens, Jr. and John M. Scheb, II, *American Constitutional Law: Essays and Cases*, Harcourt Brace Jovanovich, Publishers, San Diego, 1988, quoted on illustration page facing p. 432.

But the authors of *The Federalist Papers* were not content with establishing judicial supremacy within the federal sphere. They also insisted that the Supreme Court of the United States possessed a veto power *over State laws*, despite the fact that such a veto power had been deliberately rejected by the Constitutional Convention of 1787. This awesome and dreadful power over the States was casually explained by Mr. Hamilton within a single paragraph in the *Federalist*, No. 80:

> The first point depends upon this obvious consideration, that there ought always to be a constitutional method of giving efficacy to constitutional provisions. What, for instance, would avail restrictions on the authority of the State legislatures, without some constitutional mode of enforcing the observance of them? The States, by the plan of the Convention, are prohibited from doing a variety of things, some of which are incompatible with the interests of the Union and others with the principles of good government. The imposition of duties on imported articles and the emission of paper money are specimens of each kind. No man of sense will believe that such prohibitions would be scrupulously regarded without some effectual power in the government to restrain or correct the infractions of them. This power must either be a direct negative on the State laws, or an authority in the federal courts to overrule such as might be in manifest contravention of the Articles of Union. There is no third course that I can imagine. The latter appears to have been thought by the Convention preferable to the former, and I presume will be most agreeable to the States. [74]

Here we see the logic used to conjure up a dangerous power that was deliberately withheld by the Convention. Considering that such a power does not exist, it is no surprise to observe that not once did Mr. Hamilton, in an effort to support his contention, make reference to any provision within the Federal Constitution. Instead, reference was repeatedly made to obscure *assumptions* – "obvious consideration," "No man of sense will believe," "This power must either be," "There is no third course that I can imagine," "appears to have been thought by the Convention," and "I presume." This represents a considerable amount of inference and supposition *within a single paragraph*!

Are these *conjectures* a sufficient basis to allow the Supreme Court to conquer the sovereign States? Are Mr. Hamilton's presumptions, suppositions, considerations, and assumptions to be considered part of the supreme law of the land? Was this the understanding of the States when they ratified the compact? Did any State Ratification Convention, when adopting the Constitution, entertain the idea, even for a moment, that the States would be

---

[74] Alexander Hamilton, James Madison, and John Jay, *Op. cit.*, pp. 475-476.

bound by any sophistries that appeared in the anonymously written essays of *The Federalist Papers?* Or did those States believe that they would be bound only by the plain words of the Constitution itself?

If there could be any doubt on this matter, then we may reflect on the reason *why* the States added the Bill of Rights to the Constitution. While a construing Supreme Court may always find inspiration and comfort in the pages of *The Federalist Papers*, the champions of constitutionally limited government will always find solace in the records of the Constitutional Convention, in the debates of the State Ratification Conventions, and in the Federal Constitution itself. Whenever a conflict exists between the sacred writings of nationalism and the Constitution, constitutional liberty demands that the former must be made to yield to the latter. Otherwise, it is chimerical to speak of constitutional government in the United States of America.

We may conclude our analysis of *The Federalist Papers* with these observations made by John Taylor of Caroline in his brilliant masterpiece, *New Views of the Constitution of the United States*:

> Suppose the proceedings of the Convention had been publick, and that all the panoply for the establishment of a National Government, had been displayed in the newspapers. Suppose the States to have been alarmed by the exhibition, and to have remonstrated against the project. That this would have been the case, is demonstrated by the credentials to their deputies, and the opinions annexed to their ratifications. Suppose the States, after the publication of the Constitution, to have retained fears inspired by the attempts to establish a National Government, and that a great number of eminent men had assured them that these fears were groundless. And suppose that the States, still unsatisfied, had, for conclusive security, insisted upon the amendments which they added to the Constitution; particularly that reserving all their rights not delegated. Had the proposals for a National Government, and for negatives over State laws and judgments, been published when they were made, there is no doubt but that they would have provoked the irresistible remonstrances of every State. Now imagine, that in consequence of State oppositions, these projects had been abandoned exactly as they were, in consequence of the opposition by State deputies; that the Federal Constitution had been substituted for them; and that the States had, under the impression which the projects had made, subjoined to it the amendments. Could the States have been honestly told, after all this process, that the apparent rejection of a National Government and its supreme negatives, was only a delusion to appease their fears, and a bait to allure them within the trap, hypocritically abandoned?
>
> Now this very case is that under consideration. The proposals for a National Government and its negative over the State acts, were really made. They were opposed by the State deputies, who had a knowledge of them. They were rejected. A different form of government was promulgated. It contained no such negative. The States expounded its meaning to

be federal, by a positive reservation of rights not delegated. And now they are told that the devil, thus repeatedly exorcised, still remains in the church.

The notoriety of this deception is fully illustrated by recollecting, that the States, by their deputies, (and they could only do it by deputies,) had made themselves sovereign and independent; that they had already united in virtue of that character; that in virtue of that character, they had appointed deputies to frame a more perfect Union; that by these deputies they voted as States; that they ratified the Constitution as States; that they immediately amended it as States; that they vote in the Senate as States; and that they are represented as States in the other federal legislative branch. Further, the Declaration of Independence was never repealed. Its annual commemorations demonstrated, and continue to demonstrate, a publick opinion, that it still lives; and the Constitution did not confer sovereignty and independence upon the Federal Government, as the Declaration of Independence had done upon the States. On the contrary, by the Constitution, the States may take away all the powers of the Federal Government, whilst that government is prohibited from taking away a single power reserved to the States. Under all these circumstances, is it possible that any one State of the Union, in ratifying the Constitution, which literally conformed to previous solemn acts, to previous words and phrases, and to the settled rights of the States, entertained the most distant idea, that it was destroying itself; betraying its people; establishing a National Government; and creating a supreme negative over all its acts, political and civil, or political only, with which the Federal Government, or one of its departments, was invested by implication.

Sovereignty is the highest degree of political power, and the establishment of a form of government, the highest proof which can be given of its existence. The States could not have reserved any rights by the Articles of their Union, if they had not been sovereign, because they could have no rights, unless they flowed from that source. In the creation of the Federal Government, the States exercised the highest act of sovereignty, and they may, if they please, repeat the proof of their sovereignty, by its annihilation. But the Union possesses no innate sovereignty, like the States; it was not self-constituted; it is conventional, and of course subordinate to the sovereignties by which it was formed. Could the States have imagined, when they entered into a Union, and retained the power of diminishing, extending, or destroying the powers of the Federal Government, that they who "created and could destroy," might have this maxim turned upon themselves, by their own creature; and that this misapplication of words was able both to deprive them of sovereignty, and bestow it upon a Union subordinate to their will, even for existence. I have no idea of a sovereignty constituted upon better ground than that of each State, nor of one which can be pretended to on worse, than that claimed for the Federal Government, or some portion of it. Conquest or force would give a much better title to sovereignty, than a limited deputation or delegation of authority. The deputations by sovereignties, far from being considered as killing the sovereignties from which they have derived limited powers, are evidences of their existence; and leagues between States demonstrate their vitality. The sovereignties which imposed the limitations upon the Federal Government, far from supposing that they perished by the exercise of a part of their faculties, were vindicated, by reserving powers in which their deputy, the Federal Government, could not participate; and the usual right of sovereigns to alter or revoke its commissions.

If under all these circumstances, the States could never have conceived that they had, by their Union, relinquished their sovereignties; created by a supreme negative power over their laws; or established a National Government; their opinion ought to be the rule for the construction of the Constitution. And if the Constitution has, by implication, effected all these ends without their knowledge and consent, it is certainly the most recondite speculation that was ever formed, and the States of all cullies, the most excusable. [75]

Of Conquest and Excuses

During the Constitutional Convention of 1787, Gouverneur Morris had intimated that, should the States refuse to submit to a supreme National Government, the matter would ultimately be decided by the sword, with the stronger party making traitors and rebels out of the weaker. And during the ratification contest in New York, Alexander Hamilton – while masquerading as "Caesar" – had threatened to force a government upon what he perceived to be an unwilling people by an army. These two ominous ideas, unfortunately, were among the legacies that endured beyond the American Constitutional Era.

Some three score and eleven years after the new government under the Constitution was inaugurated, the Southern States, doubting their continued safety within the Union, sought to escape from impending danger by resorting to secession and the creation of a separate Southern Confederacy. During the ensuing carnage of the War Between the States, the stronger side conquered the weaker side and did indeed brand them as rebels and traitors. The victors in the War of Conquest haughtily asserted that State sovereignty – both North and South – had been crushed at Appomattox with the surrender of General Robert E. Lee. It was also asserted that, by the point of a sword, a consolidated Nation had been erected on the ruins of the old Federal Republic and that the Federal Government had been violently and savagely replaced by a supreme National Government.

In the words of one of the leading enemies of the Federal Republic – Thaddeus Stevens – these crimes against the Constitution were committed,

---

[75] John Taylor, *Op. cit.*, pp. 35-37.

not because the Radical Republicans had a *right* to perform such acts, but only because they wielded unchallenged *power!* Constitutionally limited government was thus proclaimed to have been supplanted by the rule that *might makes right*, and the delicate balance between power and liberty destroyed. Power, the Radical Republicans resolved with delight, had finally conquered liberty.

Commenting on the results of the War Between the States, William Bennett Bizzell, the President of the College of Industrial Arts, wrote in his 1914 book, *Judicial Interpretation of Political Theory*:

> The history of the transformation of the terms "Federal Government" or "Confederacy" (as the general government was usually referred to up to the time of the Civil War *by both North and South*) into the "Nation" is of interest and consequence in the development of our political ideas. Lincoln, in his debate with Douglas in 1858, used the term "Confederacy," in speaking of the Union, but when Confederacy was applied to the seceding States in the South, the term was generally abandoned by the North, and *with its abandonment the old idea of the word was surrendered also*. Lincoln, in his Gettysburg Address, speaks of "a new Nation conceived in liberty and dedicated to the proposition that all men are created equal." From this time on it was often asserted that we had become *a Nation with a big N*. This is interesting when we *contrast* this sentiment with that of the Constitutional Convention; for in the first draft of the Constitution the word "national" was *struck out twenty-six times* and the words "Government of the United States" substituted. But the new word had taken a deep hold upon the people, and its frequent use by public speakers and the current literature of the period gave it *permanence in our political vocabulary. With the appropriation of this term came the tendency of the party in power to extend the powers of our governmental agencies, especially that of the executive power*....It was but a step for the Republican Party to go from the Reconstruction Acts to *a policy of increased centralization*.... [Emphasis added] [76]

In utter disregard of the Federal Constitution, a Leviathan State has been erected in the United States since the tragic days of the War Between the States. Over the course of time since that war, constitutionally limited government has been replaced by a supreme National Government which haughtily proclaims that it can legislate in all cases whatsoever – a claim very similar to the one made by the British Parliament which induced the American colonies to rebel. The ensuing years have also witnessed the alarming growth of the Presidency, who today closely resembles the dictatorial King of Alexander Hamilton's rejected plan of government, supremely reigning over the States

[76] William Bennett Bizzell, *Judicial Interpretation of Political Theory: A Study in the Relation of the Courts to the American Party System*, G.P. Putnam's Sons, New York, 1914, pp. 67-68.

and vying with the Supreme Court in the arrogant boast, *"I am the law!"*

But in spite of the horrendous growth of Big Government in Washington, D.C. during the Twentieth Century, *the Constitution of the United States still exists!* All that remains to revive constitutional liberty in America and to bring the Federal Government once again within its proper limits is for an outraged people – North, South, East, and West – to rise up and demand that constitutionally limited government be restored to the United States.

When we consider the triumphs and tragedies that have occurred during the more than two hundred years of American history since the founding of the Federal Republic, we are reminded of the words spoken by Rufus King to Thomas Hart Benton of Missouri. As Mr. Benton related in his work, *Thirty Years' View*:

> In one of our conversations, and upon the formation of the Constitution in the Federal Convention of 1787, he [*i.e.*, Rufus King] said some things to me which, I think ought to be remembered by future generations, to enable them to appreciate justly those Founders of our government who were in favor of a stronger organization than was adopted. He said: "You young men who have been born since the Revolution, look with horror upon the name of a King, and upon all propositions for a strong government. It was not so with us. We were born the subjects of a King, and were accustomed to subscribe ourselves 'His Majesty's most faithful subjects;' and we began the quarrel which ended in the Revolution, not against the King, but against his Parliament; and in making the new government many propositions were submitted which would not bear discussion; and ought not to be quoted against their authors, being offered for consideration, and to bring out opinions, and which, though behind the opinions of this day, were in advance of those of that day." – These things were said chiefly in relation to General Hamilton.... [77]

It was thus Rufus King's wish, made in old age, that future generations of Americans, when considering the debates within the Constitutional Convention of 1787, should forgive those delegates who had advocated a supreme National Government for the United States. The men who advocated such a government within the Convention, said he, had been brainwashed by the tyranny that had existed prior to the War of Independence. Having lived under totalitarian government prior to the American Revolution, that was the only type of government they had ever known. Clinging to old habits, they had accordingly carried their prejudices and biases with them into the Federal Convention of 1787.

If we wish to be strict, we would reject this excuse or apology at once,

---

[77] Max Farrand (ed.), *Op. cit.*, Volume III, p. 466.

without further consideration, for it fails to explain why only *certain* delegates were affected by the brainwashing of British tyranny. Thomas Jefferson, Samuel Adams, Patrick Henry, and John Taylor of Caroline – to name but a few American patriots of that age – had all lived under the King prior to the American Revolution. Yet, all of these men were wise enough to realize that the evils which induced the colonies to revolt were *inherent* in totalitarian government. For this reason, they wisely rejected all forms of totalitarianism and staunchly advocated strictly limited, free government. Why is it that these American patriots were immune to the intoxicating influences of strong, centralized government, while others of their generation were not?

It is the expressed wish of one of the nationalist-minded delegates who attended the Constitutional Convention of 1787, however, that future generations find it in their hearts to forgive those political leaders of the Constitutional Era who did not properly learn the lessons of the American Revolution. And in the spirit of a noble and great people, such forgiveness can be extended. But forgiveness can only be extended to those of the generation of the Founding Fathers who lived under King George III and whose minds were poisoned by his tyranny. It will be much harder to excuse the conduct of those who were born *after* the American Revolution and who were accordingly raised in an environment conducive of liberty, yet who strove – and who continue to strive to this very day – to conquer the sovereign States and to centralize all powers in the hands of the Federal Government. What excuse could possibly be offered in their defense?

Chapter Thirteen
The Federal Constitution

Although the actual parchment on which the Constitution was written by the Constitutional Convention is – like the Declaration of Independence – considered a U.S. treasure, more than a century and a half passed before it found a permanent home. In the early years of the Federal Republic, the document migrated with the seat of Federal Government. For two years it remained in New York City, then resided for a decade in Philadelphia, and finally was shipped to Washington, D.C. in 1800. Like many other state papers, the Constitution traveled from office to office as did its custodians.

When the British invaded Washington, D.C. in August of 1814, the Constitution was hastily taken out of the federal city in a wagon. After the War of 1812, it was packed away for safekeeping, and only on rare occasions did anyone refer to actual document itself. Secretary of State John Quincy Adams referred to the original copy of the Federal Constitution in 1823 and checked its punctuation to settle a political dispute, and a publisher referred to it in 1846. Because the original copy of the document was so rarely disturbed or put on display, it survived much better than did the original copy of the Declaration of Independence.

The first adequate treatment of both the Declaration of Independence and the Federal Constitution came in 1921, when the Library of Congress assumed responsibility for them, displaying both under protective conditions for the first time three years later. Aside from several years during World War II, when the two documents were housed in Fort Knox for safekeeping, the Library of Congress maintained custody of the Declaration and the Constitution until 1952. In that year, the Declaration and the Constitution were put on display in the Exhibition Hall of the National Archives Building in Washington, D.C., where they currently reside, housed in air-tight bronze and glass encasements that are filled with a preservative gas. During the day, the two great state papers remain at floor level for viewing by visitors to the National Archives Building. At night, the cases are lowered into a massive vault beneath the floor.

In our great inquiry into the birth of the Federal Republic, we have traced the evolution of the United States of America through the American

Revolution, the Declaration of Independence, the Articles of Confederation, the Philadelphia Convention of 1787, and the State Ratification Conventions. To facilitate a more thorough understanding of constitutional government in the United States, we should now direct our attention to the actual provisions of the Federal Constitution. And in examining the meaning and import of the compact's various provisions, our emphasis will be on presenting the intentions of the Constitutional Convention and the general understanding of the State Ratification Conventions, and not on the perverted interpretations rendered for more than two centuries by a construing Supreme Court.

The Logical Organization of the Constitution

The Federal Constitution of 1787 is, of course, the second compact between the sovereign American States, the first being the Articles of Confederation. Like the first Federal Constitution, the Constitution of 1787 is divided into main sections styled *Articles*, and it is not inappropriate to refer to the newer compact in the same manner in which the older compact was often referred to – as the *Articles of Union*. Specifically, the original Constitution of 1787 consists of a *Preamble* and seven articles, most of which are divided into *Sections*, which in turn are further divided into *Clauses*. When referring to a particular constitutional provision, therefore, we will cite the provision by utilizing the traditional reference style of *Article X, Section Y, Clause Z*, which indicates the exact clause within the specified section of the enumerated article. This style, of course, will be modified when necessary to accommodate sections that are not divided into clauses, and articles that are not divided into sections.

The seven original Articles of Union are followed by the various *Amendments* which have been incorporated into the Constitution over the years following its adoption by the original thirteen States. The first ten amendments are often referred to as the federal *Bill of Rights*, and these were added to the compact immediately after the ratification of the compact at the insistence of the Antifederalists. Two other amendments were subsequently incorporated into the Federal Constitution during the ante-bellum period of American history, and three more amendments were added during the Radical Reconstruction Period. During the so-called Progressive Era, four more amendments were added to the compact, and three additional amendments were incorporated into the instrument during and immediately after the New Deal Period. The final four amendments to the compact were added to the supreme law from 1961 to 1971, during the Second Radical Reconstruction Era of U.S. History.

Although a few of the amendments added to the compact since the War Between the States represented deviations from the original concept of a Federal Republic, by and large the effect and purpose of the Federal Constitution has not been significantly affected by any amendments. Even today, that supreme law clearly provides for a Federal Government within a Federal Union founded upon the pillars of separate and sovereign States. Thus, it is of particular significance to note that all of the profound changes and alterations made in the Government of the United States since its inception – alterations that have worked to transform a strictly limited and defined Federal Government into an undefined and virtually unlimited supreme National Government – have been done in utter violation of the letter and spirit of the Constitution of the United States.

The importance of understanding that the provisions of the original Federal Constitution are logically divided by topic into separate articles must not be minimized. At the start of the War Between the States, when President Abraham Lincoln desired to suspend the right to a writ of *habeas corpus*, for example, he found such a provision authorizing the suspension *in the First Article* of the Constitution. As Article I, Section 9, Clause 2 asserts: "The Privilege of the Writ of Habeas Corpus shall not be suspended, unless when in Cases of Rebellion or Invasion the public safety may require it." [1]

Observing that the clause does not mention which branch of government may determine when a situation exists that warrants a suspension of the right to the writ, President Lincoln felt no qualms about assuming that the Constitution delegated the prerogative to the Presidency. He therefore acted to suspend the right to the writ of *habeas corpus* by his own authority. Such an assumption is all the more remarkable when it is considered that Mr. Lincoln was, by profession, a lawyer who should have known that the entire First Article of the Constitution deals with the Legislative Branch of the Government of the United States. In suspending the right to the writ, he was therefore plainly usurping a power of Congress.

Lest there should remain any doubts as to the layout and structure of the various articles of the second Constitution of the United States, we should briefly describe the organization of the compact. The most important branch of the Federal Government was clearly intended to be the Legislative Branch. That is why this branch is constituted in the very first article, and why nearly half of the text of the original Constitution is contained in Article I of the

---

[1] Richard B. Morris, *The Framing of the Federal Constitution*, Handbook 103, U.S. Department of the Interior, Washington, 1986, quoted on p. 93.

compact.

Article I, which establishes the Legislative Branch of the Federal Government, consists of a total of ten sections. The *First Section* is very brief and declares that *all* legislative powers of the Federal Government shall be vested in a bicameral Congress. *Section Two* defines the organization of the House of Representatives, while *Section Three* defines the organization of the Senate. The *Fourth Section* provides for elections of Representatives and Senators, and the *Fifth Section* provides basic rules for each house of Congress to do business. *Section Six* authorizes compensation to federal legislators and prohibits Congressmen from holding other federal offices. *Section Seven* stipulates that all revenue bills must originate in the more populous branch of the legislature, and also details the nature and extent of Presidential vetoes of acts of Congress. The *Eighth Section* is especially significant, inasmuch as it is this portion of Article I which actually delegates certain enumerated powers to the federal legislative. *Section Nine* provides for several exceptions, prohibitions, and restrictions on the powers of Congress that were inserted for greater caution. And *Section Ten* contains several prohibitions or restrictions on the several States.

The second most important branch of the Federal Government was intended to be the Executive Branch. Article II, which is the second longest major division in the original body of the compact, deals exclusively with this branch and consists of four sections. *Section One* vests the executive power of government in the President of the United States and provides lengthy instructions and requirements for filling the offices of President and Vice President of the United States. *Section Two* of this article delegates specific powers to the President, and *Section Three* stipulates that the President may give to Congress information regarding the *State of the Union*, may convene both houses of Congress in emergencies, may receive foreign ambassadors, should faithfully execute the laws, and may commission all U.S. officers. *Section Four* provides for the removal from office – by impeachment and conviction – of the President, Vice President, and all other civil officers of the Government of the United States.

The least important branch of the Federal Government was intended to be the Judicial Branch. This truth is reflected by the fact that this branch is provided for in the Third Article of the Constitution, which follows those providing for the other two branches and which is significantly shorter in length than either Article I or Article II. This truth is also supported by the fact that, when the federal city in the District of Columbia was constructed for the headquarters of the Government of the United States, separate buildings were provided only for the President and the Congress. The U.S. Supreme Court, due to its relative insignificance, was housed in a small portion of the Capitol Building. More than a century would pass before a separate building was constructed for the Judicial Branch of the Federal Government.

Article III, which establishes the federal judiciary, consists of three sections. *Section One* vests the judicial power of the United States in one Supreme Court and in other inferior federal courts that Congress may deem necessary to establish. This section also provides for life tenures of office for federal Judges. The *Second Section* defines the powers of the Judicial Branch, establishing both original and appellate jurisdiction. *Section Three* details the definition of treason against the United States and vests in Congress the power to declare, with stated restrictions, the punishment for such disloyalty.

Article IV of the Constitution of the United States consists of four sections and deals, in general, with the interstate relations of the members of the Federal Union. *Section One* stipulates that each State shall accord full faith and credit to the lawful acts of the other States in the Union, thereby officially recognizing the sovereign equality of the States. *Section Two* provides for equal recognition of the privileges and immunities of the citizens of the several States, for the extradition of criminals who flee from one State to another, and for the return for fugitive slaves. The *Third Section* guarantees the territorial integrity of the sovereign States, delegates to Congress the power to regulate the U.S. territorial possessions, and authorizes the admission of new States to the Union. *Section Four* guarantees to each State a republican form of government, promises federal protection to each State against foreign invasion, and provides for federal assistance in combating domestic or internal insurrection *when requested by the State government having jurisdiction in the matter.*

In Article V of the Federal Constitution, there are no separate sections, only detailed stipulations for the process of amending the compact. Article VI is also relatively short and is not, therefore, divided into separate sections, although it is divided into three distinct clauses. In addition to the Supremacy Clause, this article assures the assumption of the federal debt under the old Articles of Confederation and requires that all officers, both State and federal, take an oath *to support the Constitution of the United States.* And Article VII provides for the ratification of the compact. This last article of the original Constitution is followed by the signatures of 39 of the delegates who attended the Federal Convention.

The Preamble

The Federal Constitution begins with an introductory sentence styled the *Preamble*. The title of this introductory sentence is derived from the Latin word *praeambulus*, which literally means "walking in front." [2] The word "preamble" is accordingly defined in *Webster's II: New Riverside University Dictionary* as follows: "1. A preliminary statement, esp. the introduction to a formal document that explains its purpose. 2. An introductory fact or occurrence: PRELIMINARY." [3]

The Preamble is thus an introductory or explanatory statement which does not confer any powers on the Government of the United States. It does, however, provide an explanation of the purpose of the Constitution, indicate by whose authority the compact was established, and identify who is the beneficiary of the Constitution. Unfortunately, because of the precise style and brevity of the Preamble, its true meaning has often been confused and misunderstood, and not infrequently *deliberately* distorted by those seeking to deny the existence of sovereign States.

This Preamble consists of a total of 52 words and reads as follows:

> We the People of the United States, in Order to form a more perfect Union, establish Justice, insure domestic Tranquility, provide for the common defence, promote the general Welfare, and secure the Blessings of Liberty to ourselves and our Posterity, do ordain and establish this Constitution for the United States of America. [4]

By breaking this long sentence down into its component parts, the meaning of the Preamble will become more obvious. This Preamble tells who the agents were who established the Constitution, what action they took, why they took such action, and who was the beneficiary of their action. It tells us everything, in fact, *except in what capacity the agents acted and who the parties to the compact would be*. For these missing ingredients, we must turn to Article VII of the Constitution, which declares that, "The Ratification of the Conventions of nine States, shall be sufficient for the Establishment of this Constitution between the States so ratifying the Same." [5] If we combine the Seventh Article with the Preamble, our general picture of the Constitution becomes complete.

Specifically, the Preamble and Article VII combine to clarify the following key concepts about the Federal Constitution:

The Agents Who Acted: "We the People of the United States."
In What Capacity the Agents Acted: "The Ratification of the

---

[2] *Webster's II: New Riverside University Dictionary*, The Riverside Publishing Company, Boston, 1984, p. 925.
[3] *Ibid.*, p. 925.
[4] Richard B. Morris, *Op. cit.*, quoted on p. 88.
[5] *Ibid.*, quoted on p. 100.

Conventions of nine States, shall be sufficient for the Establishment of this Constitution."

The Action Taken: "Do ordain and establish this Constitution."

Why the Action Was Taken: "In Order to form a more perfect Union, establish Justice, insure domestic Tranquility, provide for the common defence, promote the general Welfare, and secure the Blessings of Liberty to ourselves and our Posterity."

The Beneficiary of the Action: "For the United States of America."

The Members of the Union Thus Created: "Between the States so ratifying the same."

It should be noted that the term "United States of America" is nowhere defined in the Constitution of 1787. The reason for the omission of such a definition lies in the fact that the political term had already been precisely defined and its meaning firmly and widely understood by all Americans. This term had first appeared in the *Declaration of Independence* in reference to a loose military alliance between the thirteen newly sovereign and independent American States. The term also appeared in the *Articles of Confederation*, where its meaning was fixed forevermore. As Article I of the first Federal Constitution asserted, "The Stile of this Confederacy shall be 'The United States of America.'" [6] By this provision in the Articles, the *United States of America* was well-defined as a *league of sovereign States*, and the Constitution of 1787 was specifically intended for that very same Confederation – "for the United States of America." And the Federal Union thus established would be, as under the old Articles of Union, "between the States" of the Union.

The agents who adopted the compact on behalf of the United States of America were styled "the People of the United States." In the original Preamble, of course, this had been expressed as "the People of the States of," words which were followed by the names of all thirteen of the original States. The change in phraseology was necessitated only by two pressing considerations, the first of which was the fact that it was not known if all thirteen States would ratify the compact. Furthermore, change was dictated by the fact that new States would later be admitted to the Union, and no one could predict with certainty what the names of these new States would be. For these two reasons – *and only for these two reasons* – the Committee of Style changed the words *We the People of the States* to *We the People of the United States*. The two expressions were regarded by the Constitutional Convention as equivalent.

The use of the word *people*, of course, was intended to signify that the compact's authority would be derived directly from the source of sovereignty

---

[6] Charles Callan Tansill (ed.), *The Making of the American Republic: The Great Documents, 1774-1789*, Arlington House, New Rochelle, p. 27.

– the peoples of the several States – and not from the State governments. The usage of that term in the Preamble also serves to contradict the arrogant claim made by the federal Supreme Court, to the effect that the Constitution is whatever the federal judiciary says it is. In bold and unmistakable language, the Preamble informs us that the Constitution is what the States say it is; and by the terms of Article V, only the States can lawfully amend the compact, because only the American people, *as States*, are sovereign. And should the people of the States choose to once again demonstrate their sovereignty over the Federal Government, they may abolish the federal judiciary by amending the Constitution. The Supreme Court, however, has no constitutional authority to either amend the Constitution or to abolish the States.

With this understanding of the Preamble, it is evident that the introductory section of the Constitution could be reworded as follows without changing its meaning in the slightest degree: *We the Peoples of the several States, in order to unite our respective States in a political league for federal purposes, do ordain and establish this Constitution for the Confederation of sovereign States heretofore styled in the previous Articles of Union, the United States of America.*

Article I, Sections 1 Through 7

Article I of the Federal Constitution is by far the most lengthy one in the instrument, comprising nearly half of the original text of the compact. This Article has a total of ten sections and deals exclusively with the Legislative Branch of the Government of the United States. Article I, Section 1 consists of a single sentence, which makes the following provision: "All legislative Powers herein granted shall be vested in a Congress of the United States, which shall consist of a Senate and House of Representatives." [7]

Three points merit our careful attention in Section One. The first is the usage of the term "Congress." This term was copied from the Articles of Confederation and signifies an assemblage of representatives or deputies from sovereign States. In the three main plans of government introduced in the Constitutional Convention, only one – the *New Jersey Plan* – had proposed retaining the usage of this term in the new government, which was one of the key features that set it apart from the plans providing for a supreme National Government. The usage of the term Congress in the Constitution of 1787 is further proof that the compact establishes a Federal Government, and not a National Government, supreme or otherwise.

---

[7] Richard B. Morris, *Op. cit.*, quoted on p. 88.

It is also of significance to note that Article I, Section 1 specifically states that *all* legislative power of the Federal Government is vested in the Congress. Since all law-making power is delegated to Congress, this means that neither the President nor the Judicial Department can enact legislation, nor can legislative power be "delegated" by Congress to other bodies, such as bureaucracies created by the federal legislature. Although we often hear such loose expressions as that the U.S. Supreme Court can and does *make laws*, or that its rulings are *the law of the land*, it is clear that such concepts are in direct violation of Article I of the supreme law of the land, which emphatically declares that only Congress can make federal laws.

The final point of significance regarding Article I, Section 1, is that it delegates no powers, in itself, to the Congress. It merely states that the legislative powers "herein granted" – in other words, enumerated elsewhere in Article I – shall be vested in the Legislative Branch. The specific federal legislative powers, as previously noted, are enumerated in Section Eight of the First Article.

Article I, Section 2 provides for the House of Representatives and consists of five clauses, which are expressed in the language shown below. Note that the square brackets indicate that portion of Clause 3, known historically as the *Three-Fifths Compromise* between the Northern and Southern States, which has been superseded by the Fourteenth Amendment:

[1] The House of Representatives shall be composed of Members chosen every second Year by the People of the several States, and the Electors in each State shall have the Qualifications requisite for Electors of the most numerous Branch of the State Legislature.

[2] No Person shall be a Representative who shall not have attained to the Age of twenty five Years, and been seven Years a Citizen of the United States, and who shall not, when elected, be an inhabitant of that State in which he shall be chosen.

[3] Representatives and direct Taxes shall be apportioned among the several States which may be included within this Union, according to their respective Numbers, [which shall be determined by adding to the whole Number of free Persons, including those bound to Service for a Term of Years, and excluding Indians not taxed, three fifths of all other Persons.] The actual Enumeration shall be made within three Years after the first Meeting of the Congress of the United States, and within every subsequent Term of ten Years, in such Manner as they shall by Law direct. The Number of Representatives shall not exceed one for every thirty Thousand, but each State shall have at Least one Representative; and until such enumeration shall be made, the State of New Hampshire shall be entitled to chuse three, Massachusetts eight, Rhode-Island and Providence Plantations one, Connecticut five, New-York six, New Jersey four, Pennsylvania eight, Delaware one, Maryland six, Virginia ten, North Carolina five,

South Carolina five, and Georgia three.

[4] When vacancies happen in the Representation from any State, the Executive Authority thereof shall issue Writs of Election to fill such Vacancies.

[5] The House of Representatives shall chuse their Speaker and other Officers; and shall have the sole power of Impeachment. [8]

It is readily apparent from Article I, Section 2 that the election of Members of the House of Representatives is a *federal* election, and not a *national* election, and that members of the lower branch of the federal legislature represent the peoples of the several States, not the people of a consolidated American nation. Representatives are elected "by the People of the several States," must be inhabitants of the States represented at the time of their election, must be "apportioned among the several States," and are constitutionally referred to as the *Representations from the States.* The Third Clause assigns the number of Representatives each of the original States would have prior to the 1790 census, and it must be observed that an American nation is not even mentioned nor is it assigned any Representatives, because the Constitution recognizes the American people only as sovereign States.

Article I, Section 2, Clause 1, as indicated, provides that the right of establishing the qualifications for the franchise shall be reserved exclusively to the separate States. The only stipulation placed on this States' Right is that the qualifications established within a State for federal elections must be the same as those established for electing members of the most numerous branch of the State legislature. Aside from this limitation, however, each State is left free to establish its own qualifications for the franchise in federal elections.

The Third Section of Article I establishes the Senate and consists of seven clauses, which are quoted below. Those portions of the first two clauses within the square brackets have been superseded by the Seventeenth Amendment:

[1] The Senate of the United States shall be composed of two Senators from each State, [chosen by the Legislature thereof,] for six Years; and each Senator shall have one Vote.

[2] Immediately after they shall be assembled in Consequence of the first Election, they shall be divided as equally as may be into three Classes. The Seats of the Senators of the first Class shall be vacated at the Expiration of the second Year, of the second Class at the Expiration of the fourth Year, and of the third Class at the Expiration of the sixth Year, so that one third may be chosen every second Year; [and if Vacancies happen by Resignation, or otherwise, during the Recess of the Legislature of any State, the Executive thereof may make temporary Appointments until the

---

[8] *Ibid.*, quoted on pp. 88-89.

next Meeting of the Legislature, which shall then fill such Vacancies.]

[3] No Person shall be a Senator who shall not have attained to the Age of thirty Years, and been nine Years a Citizen of the United States, and who shall not, when elected, be an Inhabitant of that State for which he shall be chosen.

[4] The Vice President of the United States shall be President of the Senate, but shall have no Vote, unless they be equally divided.

[5] The Senate shall chuse their other Officers, and also a President pro tempore, in the Absence of the Vice President, or when he shall exercise the Office of President of the United States.

[6] The Senate shall have the sole Power to try all Impeachments. When sitting for that Purpose, they shall be on Oath or Affirmation. When the President of the United States is tried, the Chief Justice shall preside: and no Person shall be convicted without the Concurrence of two thirds of the Members present.

[7] Judgment in Cases of Impeachment shall not extend further than to removal from Office, and disqualification to hold and enjoy any Office of honor, Trust or Profit under the United States: but the Party convicted shall nevertheless be liable and subject to Indictment, Trial, Judgment and Punishment, according to Law. [9]

The composition of the U.S. Senate, as John Dickinson once observed, reflects the sovereign equality of the States. For this very reason, the question of representation in the Senate had been one of the most bitter controversies that divided the Philadelphia Convention of 1787. Not only did the issue sharply divide the large and the small States, but it also served as the rallying point for the respective advocates of nationalism and federalism. With the adoption of the *Connecticut Compromise* – providing for representation in the House of Representatives according to State populations and for representation in the Senate according to State sovereign equality – the nationalists were defeated in the Federal Convention and harmony was restored between the large and the small States. The extent of the federalist victory in the Grand Convention can be measured by the provision in Article V which prohibits any amendment to the compact that would deprive any State, without its consent, of its equal suffrage in the Senate.

It is of interest to note that the original intent of the Constitution was that the Senate would directly represent the various State *governments*. And for nearly one and a quarter centuries the upper house of Congress did fulfill this original intention of the Founding Fathers. With the adoption of the Seventeenth Amendment in 1913, however, Senators were thereafter elected by the *peoples* of the several States. Although Amendment XVII was undoubtedly intended to strike a blow at the federal system, it could not alter the fact

---

[9] *Ibid.*, quoted on pp. 89-90.

that *equality of suffrage* among the States remained as before in the Senate. Thus, to this very day, John Dickinson's words remain true, and the Senate continues to stand as a living monument to the sovereignty of the States.

The only powers thus far delegated to Congress are those associated with the impeachment of federal officers. Article I, Section 2, Clause 5 delegates to the House of Representatives "the sole Power of Impeachment" or the power to formally *accuse* a federal official of misconduct. Article I, Section 3, Clause 6 delegates to the Senate "the sole Power to *try* all Impeachments." Upon conviction, the offending official is removed from office for misconduct, and the case may – or may not – go before a court of law for criminal proceedings. Although many of our modern Presidents have deserved impeachment, only once has a President of the United States ever been impeached, when the Radical Republicans in the House of Representatives arrogantly charged Andrew Johnson with misconduct. When tried in the Senate, however, President Johnson was acquitted by an extremely close vote and thus remained in office until the end of his term.

The Fourth Section of Article I deals with the elections of Congressmen and the assembling of Congress. The first of the two clauses in this section stipulates that the States are to conduct, control, and supervise the elections for Representatives and Senators to the Federal Government. Only in the rare and highly unusual circumstance where a State government is unable to coordinate such elections is the Congress to step forward and conduct said elections on behalf of the State in question.

This section is worded in the language shown below. Note that the last clause has been entirely superseded by the Twentieth Amendment and is accordingly placed within square brackets :

[1] The Times, Places and Manner of holding Elections for Senators and Representatives shall be prescribed in each State by the Legislature thereof; but the Congress may at any time by Law make or alter such Regulations, except as to the Places of chusing Senators.

[2] [The Congress shall assemble at least once in every Year, and such Meeting shall be on the first Monday in December, unless they shall by Law appoint a different Day.] [10]

Section Five of Article I prescribes the manner of conducting business in each house of Congress and consists of these four clauses:

[1] Each House shall be the Judge of the Elections, Returns and Qualifications of its own Members, and a Majority of each shall constitute a Quorum to do Business; but a smaller Number may adjourn from day to

---

[10] *Ibid.*, quoted on p. 90.

day, and may be authorized to compel the Attendance of absent Members, in such Manner, and under such Penalties as each House may provide.

[2] Each House may determine the Rules of its Proceedings, punish its Members for disorderly Behaviour, and, with the Concurrence of two thirds, expel a Member.

[3] Each House shall keep a Journal of its Proceedings, and from time to time publish the same, excepting such Parts as may in their Judgment require Secrecy; and the Yeas and Nays of the Members of either House on any question shall, at the Desire of one fifth of those Present, be entered on the Journal.

[4] Neither House, during the Session of Congress, shall, without the Consent of the other, adjourn for more than three days, nor to any other Place than that in which the two Houses shall be sitting. [11]

Attention should be directed to the provision relating to the issue of secrecy. *Government by secrecy* is, by all honest views, not conducive to liberty; and it might be asked, does the Third Clause of this section allow Congress to enact *secret laws* to bind the citizenry? Inasmuch as *ignorance of the law* is not considered a defense in any court of law, this question becomes even more significant. Fortunately for the rights of man, the answer to the question is *no* – secrecy is applicable only to certain *information* presented in Congress which is deemed sensitive to the security of the United States, such as the positioning and movement of troops in time of war. While such information may be kept secret, secrecy cannot be applied to the *laws* debated and passed by Congress.

Another provision that merits attention regards the official Journal of Congress, which is styled the *Congressional Record*. During the Administration of President George Washington, the Chief Executive of the United States set the precedent of placing certain "Executive Orders" within the *Congressional Record* as a means of publishing certain internal housekeeping rules pertinent to the government and within the scope of the Constitution's delegated powers. Over a period of time, however, the Executive Branch of the Federal Government has developed the habit of placing into the *Congressional Record* what amounts to executive-enacted legislation disguised as Executive Orders. This odious practice, it scarcely needs to be mentioned, represents a clear usurpation of the legislative power of Congress and is therefore unconstitutional.

Article I, Section 6 consists of two clauses and is expressed in the following language:

[1] The Senators and Representatives shall receive a Compensation

---

[11] *Ibid.*, quoted on p. 90.

for their Services, to be ascertained by Law, and paid out of the Treasury of the United States. They shall in all Cases, except Treason, Felony and Breach of the Peace, be privileged from Arrest during their Attendance at the Session of their respective Houses, and in going to and returning from the same; and for any Speech or Debate in either House, they shall not be questioned in any other Place.

[2] No Senator or Representative shall, during the Time for which he was elected, be appointed to any civil Office under the Authority of the United states, which shall have been created, or the Emoluments whereof shall have been encreased during such time; and no Person holding any Office under the United States, shall be a Member of either House during his Continuance in Office. [12]

By the terms of the First Clause of Section 6, Congressmen may utter remarks on the floor of Congress that might be deemed slanderous, if such comments were said anywhere else. Although this sweeping immunity can be and is abused, such unrestricted freedom of speech was deemed essential to good government by the Founding Fathers. And while the Second Clause prohibits Congressmen from *holding* other offices, it does not prohibit them from *seeking* other offices. It is not unusual, for instance, for a Senator to enter the Presidential election campaign without losing his seat in the Senate. Only if actually elected or appointed to another position in the government is a member of Congress required to resign from the federal legislature.

Article I, Section 7 consists of three clauses, the first of which stipulates that all revenue or taxation bills must originate in the House of Representatives. Inasmuch as State population was deemed by the Federal Convention to be the best indicator of the respective wealth of each member of the Federal Union, the intention of this constitutional provision was clearly to enshrine in the compact the concept of no taxation without adequately proportional representation. This concept, in fact, had been an integral part of the great compromise between the large and the small States in the Philadelphia Convention of 1787.

The other two clauses of Section 7 deal with the Presidential approval or veto of acts of the legislature. Attention should be given to the exacting detail in which this veto power is provided for, in regard to both the Presidential prerogative itself and the mode in which the Congress can override a Presidential veto. Although a vastly more comprehensive veto power has been claimed for the federal judiciary by the consolidating school, the Constitution nowhere makes mention of such an important power, let alone provides any detail similar to what we find here for the more tame Presidential veto.

As Section 7 of Article I declares:

---

[12] *Ibid.*, quoted on pp. 90-91.

[1] All bills for raising Revenue shall originate in the House of Representatives; but the Senate may propose or concur with Amendments as on other Bills.

[2] Every Bill which shall have passed the House of Representatives and the Senate, shall, before it become a Law, be presented to the President of the United States. If he approve he shall sign it, but if not he shall return it, with his Objections to that House in which it shall have originated, who shall enter the Objections at large on their Journal, and proceed to reconsider it. If after such Reconsideration two thirds of that House shall agree to pass the Bill, it shall be sent, together with the Objections, to the other House, by which it shall likewise be reconsidered, and if approved by two thirds of that House, it shall become a Law. But in all such Cases the Votes of both Houses shall be determined by yeas and Nays, and the Names of the Persons voting for and against the Bill shall be entered on the Journal of each House respectively. If any Bill shall not be returned by the President within ten Days (Sundays excepted) after it shall have been presented to him, the same shall be a Law, in like Manner as if he had signed it, unless the Congress by their Adjournment prevent its Return, in which Case it shall not be a Law.

[3] Every Order, Resolution, or Vote to which the Concurrence of the Senate and House of Representatives may be necessary (except on a question of Adjournment) shall be presented to the President of the United States; and before the Same shall take Effect, shall be approved by him, or being disapproved by him, shall be repassed by two thirds of the Senate and House of Representatives, according to the Rules and Limitations prescribed in the Case of a Bill. [13]

The American constitutional system, it is plain to discern, is very unlike the *parliamentary system* that exist in other countries, such as Great Britain. The primary objective of the parliamentary system is to maintain consistent unity and harmony between the legislative and executive departments of government, and for this reason the majority in the legislature typically appoints the Executive Branch. Although such a system clearly results in a very efficient government, it also endangers liberty by avoiding all semblance of checks and balances.

The constitutional system established by the Federal Constitution is precisely the opposite, in principle and in operation, from the parliamentary system. Under the American constitutional system, the three branches of government are distinct, separate, and independent of one another, and each is designed to supply a check on the other. This fundamental concept rests upon the notion that the division of power and the preservation of liberty are more important than the so-called efficiency of the government. A highly efficient government is the natural breeding ground of tyranny and oppression.

---

[13] *Ibid.*, quoted on p. 91.

Article I, Section 8

Perhaps the most important section in the entire Constitution is Article I, Section 8, which enumerates the *powers* of Congress. In making this broad assessment, we are merely stressing a fundamental truth underlying the compact. *The extent of powers of the Legislative Branch determines the extent of powers for the whole Federal Government.* This fact may be easily ascertained by the single observation that only Congress may *make federal laws*, and these laws provide the basis of operations for the other two branches of the government. The Executive Branch exists solely to *execute the federal laws* passed by Congress, and the Judicial Branch exists solely to *apply the federal laws* to cases arising under its constitutionally limited jurisdiction. It is, in fact, precisely because the limits of authority placed on Congress dictate the limits of the other two branches, that we find the Bill of Rights beginning with the words, "Congress shall make no law...." This restriction on Congress effectually places an equal restriction on *all three branches* of the Government of the United States.

The Eighth Section of Article I contains the longest sentence in the Constitution, a sentence which encompasses a total of eighteen clauses connected together by semi-colons:

[1] The Congress shall have Power To lay and collect Taxes, Duties, Imposts and Excises, to pay the Debts and provide for the common defence and general Welfare of the United States; but all Duties, Imposts and excises shall be uniform throughout the United States;

[2] To borrow Money on the credit of the United States;

[3] To regulate Commerce with foreign Nations, and among the several States, and with the Indian Tribes;

[4] To establish an uniform Rule of Naturalization, and uniform Laws on the subject of Bankruptcies throughout the United States;

[5] To coin Money, regulate the Value thereof, and of foreign Coin, and fix the Standard of Weights and Measures;

[6] To provide for the Punishment of counterfeiting the Securities and current Coin of the United States;

[7] To establish Post Offices and post Roads;

[8] To promote the Progress of Science and useful Arts, by securing for limited Times to Authors and Inventors the exclusive Right to their respective Writings and Discoveries;

[9] To constitute Tribunals inferior to the supreme Court;

[10] To define and punish Piracies and Felonies committed on the high Seas, and Offences against the Law of Nations;

[11] To declare War, grant Letters of Marquee and Reprisal, and make Rules concerning Captures on Land and Water;

[12] To raise and support Armies, but no Appropriation of money

to that Use shall be for a longer Term than two Years;

[13] To provide and maintain a Navy;

[14] To make Rules for the Government and Regulation of the land and naval Forces;

[15] To provide for calling forth the Militia to execute the Laws of the Union, suppress Insurrections and repel Invasions;

[16] To provide for organizing, arming, and disciplining, the Militia, and for governing such Part of them as may be employed in the Service of the United States, reserving to the States respectively, the Appointment of the Officers, and the Authority of training the Militia according to the discipline prescribed by Congress;

[17] To exercise exclusive Legislation in all Cases whatsoever, over such District (not exceeding ten Miles square) as may, by Cession of particular States, and the Acceptance of Congress, become the Seat of the Government of the United States, and to exercise like Authority over all Places purchased by the Consent of the Legislature of the State in which the Same shall be, for the Erection of Forts, Magazines, Arsenals, dock-Yards, and other needful Buildings; – And

[18] To make all Laws which shall be necessary and proper for carrying into Execution the foregoing Powers, and all other Powers vested by this Constitution in the Government of the United States, or in any Department or Officer thereof. [14]

Although the powers delegated to Congress within Article I, Section 8 are clearly enumerated and can admit of no ambiguity, a number of attempts have been made over the years to distort the provisions of this part of the compact in an effort to vest in the Federal Government more powers than are authorized. We should, therefore, examine this particular section of Article I with great care and attention.

Clause One of this Section is often termed the *General Welfare Clause* and has been cleverly perverted and misconstrued into an authorization for Congress to pass all laws which might be proclaimed to be for the common defense or general welfare of the United States. Such a construction, if admitted, would result directly in a government of unlimited powers. But the clause in question will not admit of such a construction, for it merely states that Congress may lay and collect taxes, duties, imposts, and excises *for the purpose of* paying the debts and providing for the common defense and general welfare of the United States. The only power within the clause is that of laying and collecting taxation. The stated *ends* for the enumerated power cannot be converted into a *means* or separate delegation of broad powers to acquire other ends, without completely subverting the Constitution.

The phraseology of the General Welfare Clause which has been most

---

[14] *Ibid.*, quoted on pp. 91-93.

often distorted for dishonest purposes was ironically copied verbatim from the old Articles of Confederation, where no such pretense of broad and sweeping powers could possibly have been admitted. The idea of a *common* defense and of a *general* welfare is, by the very nature of such concepts, *restrictive* in meaning and intent. The Congress may thus tax and spend only to promote the common interests of all the States in the Union, and not to promote the interests of particular citizens, States, or regions of the Confederacy. This is what is meant by the expression "common defence and general welfare." And, if any doubt could possibly exist as to exactly what constitutes the common defense and general welfare of the United States, then the remaining clauses of Article I, Section 8 should remove all ambiguity by precisely defining the concept.

The Third Clause of Section 8 is often referred to as the *Commerce Clause*, and this provision has been cited more than any other in the Constitution by the Supreme Court of the United States in its continuous quest to unlawfully enlarge the powers of the Federal Government and to promote socialism within the United States. Especially subject to cunning misconstructions has been that portion of the Commerce Clause respecting the regulation of commerce "among the several States," often referred to as the *Interstate Commerce Clause*. The original intent of this particular provision, as the historical evidence plainly shows, was essentially *negative* in nature – to merely prohibit the States from erecting barriers to free trade within the Confederation. The true purpose of the Commerce Clause, therefore, is to ensure that a *free enterprise* economic system prevails in the United States.

In the hands of a construing Supreme Court, however, the Interstate Commerce Clause has been often and repeatedly cited as supposed justification for the establishment and enlargement of a socialistic and bureaucratic Regulatory State in the United States. And each time the provision is interpreted by that high court, the distortion of its meaning becomes even greater and more tragically comical. Beginning with a misconstruction of the clause into a *positive* delegation of power to regulate *inter*state commerce, the interpretation was stretched in ensuing years to cover *intra*state commerce as well, and, ultimately, all human activity that might conceivably affect – even indirectly – inter- or intra-state commerce.

By modern interpretation, even a local pizza delivery boy is *engaging in interstate commerce*, and hence subject to federal regulation, simply by delivering his goods to a company that is engaged in interstate commerce. And the deluge of rules and regulations that have resulted from misconstructions of the Interstate Commerce Clause threatens to bury the American people under a mountain of paperwork and to strangle American enterprise in a noose of red tape. The Interstate Commerce Commission alone has issued more than *one trillion* rates to regulate the transportation of goods – more than 20,000 for each family in America!

Those provisions in Section 8 authorizing Congress to "coin Money" and to punish counterfeiting of "the Securities and current Coin of the United States" also require attention. In no conceivable manner could these provisions be interpreted as authorizing the creation of the Federal Reserve System to coin money out of *paper*, or as authorizing anything but gold and silver to be recognized as *money* or *legal tender*. By vesting the power to coin money in Congress, the intention of the Founding Fathers was *to ban paper money from the United States*, an intention that is made even more manifest by Article I, Section 10, Clause 1, which prohibits the States from making anything but gold and silver a legal tender. Although current Federal Reserve Notes bear the statement on their face that, "This note is legal tender for all debts, public and private," the fact remains that such a statement is – like the Federal Reserve System itself – palpably unconstitutional.

Attention should also be given to Article I, Section 8, Clause 8, which delegates to Congress the power to grant *Patents* and *Copyrights*. These two powers constitute the sum total of the extent of the Federal Government's authority to "promote the Progress of Science and useful Arts." Although other *promotional powers* were recommended by some delegates within the Constitutional Convention – including a power over *education* and the encouragement of *agriculture*, *manufactures*, and *commerce* – they were all summarily and deliberately *rejected* by the Convention. Thus, no authority exists for the Federal Government to dictate educational standards, to grant monies to such plays as the Leaping Lesbians in San Francisco, or to promote such art exhibits as the one featuring Christian artifacts floating in jars of human urine. The majority of the Founding Fathers wisely realized that one man's ideas of useful art and science may be another man's definition of objectionable obscenities. For this reason, all promotion of science and art – other than the granting of copyrights and patents – was left to the States and the individual citizens.

The usage of the term "supreme" in Clause Nine of this section requires explanation. That term is used within the Constitution only in reference to two objects. One is the *Supreme Court*, and the other is the Constitution and all laws and treaties made in pursuance of it, which are styled the *supreme law of the land*. It is evident from Article I, Section 8, Clause 9, that the word *supreme*, as used in reference to the Supreme Court of the United States, signifies only that that court is supreme or *superior* to the *inferior* federal courts that Congress may, from time to time, think proper to institute. *It does not signify that the U.S. Supreme Court is superior to the State judiciaries.* Each

State, of course, has its own Supreme Court, which is undeniably the superior court *in all areas of jurisdiction reserved by the Constitution to the States.* Within the *federal sphere*, therefore, the U.S. Supreme Court is truly supreme; yet, within the *State sphere*, the State Supreme Courts are supreme.

Although the primary intention of the States, in forming the Federal Union, was to institute a common agent to conduct their foreign affairs and provide for the common defense, they also wisely feared a large standing federal army in times of peace. For this reason, they retained primary control over their militias, and they stipulated in Clause Twelve that appropriations for the federal military could not span a period of more than two years. It is a fact that, from the inception of the Federal Government until the year 1946, the combined armed forces under the control of the State governments always surpassed the peacetime armed forces controlled by the Federal Government, thus ensuring that a centralized Military Dictatorship could not be sustained. It might also be added, as a point of historical significance, that the United States achieved *victory* in every war fought prior to 1946. The same cannot be said for those wars waged by the United States after that date.

Finally, attention should be given to the last clause in Section 8, which is often referred to as the *Sweeping Clause*, or the *Necessary and Proper Clause*. This provision has been ingeniously misconstrued into an authorization for an unlimited field of implied powers that supposedly permit Congress to pass all laws which the legislators might pretend to be necessary and proper. Yet, the only powers referred to by this clause are "the foregoing powers" and "all other Powers vested by this Constitution" in Congress. There are no implied powers contained in the clause, only references to powers *expressly enumerated* elsewhere in the compact. The Necessary and Proper Clause, in summary, merely authorizes Congress to pass those laws necessary and proper to carry into effect the enumerated powers. Even Alexander Hamilton, writing in *The Federalist Papers*, candidly and expressly acknowledged that this provision was *perfectly harmless*.

Article I, Section 9 and 10

Section Nine of Article I contains eight clauses that deal with certain enumerated *exceptions* to the powers delegated. It was universally understood by all the States which adopted the Constitution that the exceptions contained within Section Nine could not be construed to imply that Congress could claim powers not expressly delegated to it. A number of States, in fact, actually affixed statements to their acts ratifying the Constitution which expressly declared their understanding that the exceptions were inserted into the compact only for greater caution and emphasis.

As this section declares:

[1] The Migration or Importation of such Persons as any of the States now existing shall think proper to admit, shall not be prohibited by the Congress prior to the Year one thousand eight hundred and eight, but a Tax or duty may be imposed on such Importation, not exceeding ten dollars for each Person.

[2] The Privilege of the Writ of Habeas Corpus shall not be suspended, unless when in Cases of Rebellion or Invasion the public safety may require it.

[3] No Bill of Attainder or ex post facto Law shall be passed.

[4] No Capitation, or other direct, Tax shall be laid, unless in Proportion to the Census or Enumeration herein before directed to be taken.

[5] No Tax or Duty shall be laid on Articles exported from any State.

[6] No preference shall be given by any Regulation of Commerce or Revenue to the Ports of one State over those of another; nor shall Vessels bound to, or from, one State, be obliged to enter, clear, or pay Duties in another.

[7] No money shall be drawn from the Treasury, but in Consequence of Appropriations made by Law; and a regular Statement and Account of the Receipts and Expenditures of all public Money shall be published from time to time.

[8] No Title of Nobility shall be granted by the United States: And no Person holding any Office of Profit or Trust under them, shall, without the Consent of the Congress, accept of any present, Emolument, Office, or Title, of any kind whatever, from any King, Prince, or foreign State. [15]

The First Clause, it should be noted, did not *require* that Congress ban the importation of Negro slaves in 1808, or in any year thereafter. On the contrary, it only prohibited a ban on importation *until the year 1808*, while allowing the Congress to tax what was regarded by the Constitution as a species of property. In 1808, the first year in which Congress was allowed to prohibit the further importation of chattel slaves, the Southern States joined with the Northern States to end all further imports of Negro slaves.

Although Clause Four stipulates that all direct federal taxes must be apportioned among the States, this requirement was circumvented in regard to the *income tax* by the Sixteenth Amendment. And as we have previously observed, the prerogative of suspending the right to a writ of *habeas corpus* is vested in the Congress, not in the Executive Branch of the Government of the United States. It is difficult to imagine how anyone could ever honestly enter-

---

[15] *Ibid.*, quoted on pp. 93-94.

tain any other conception of Article I of the compact.

The phraseology utilized in the Eighth Clause of Article I, Section 9 merits close scrutiny: "No Title of Nobility shall be granted by the *United States*: And no Person holding any Office of Profit or Trust under *them*...." The word "them" is a *plural* pronoun that refers back to the words "United States," and it is apparent from the style employed that the constitutional usage of the term *United States* is as a *plural* entity or concept. The treatment of the term "United States" illustrated within Article I, Section 9, Clause 8 is not an isolated case, for, as we shall discover, the main text of the Constitution *consistently* refers to the United States as a plural entity.

A statement such as, "The United States *is* a great country," is therefore constitutionally inaccurate, in terms of proper grammar. In accordance with the grammatical style of the Constitution, this sentence should be written as, "The United States *are* a great country," a proper style that reconciles the verb with the subject. Constitutionally – as well as grammatically – the *subject* of this sample sentence is the word "States," which is used in reference to *all* the States of the Union. The word "United" is, according to the grammatical style of the Constitution, considered to be an *adjective* that describes those States. The two terms – *United States* and *States United* – are thus constitutionally synonymous and could be used interchangeably, inasmuch as both properly refer to the *States of the Union*.

The Tenth Section of Article I consists of three clauses that contain several specific agreements between the members of the Federal Union to refrain from exercising certain portions of their inherent sovereignty:

> [1] No State shall enter into any Treaty, Alliance, or Confederation; grant Letters of Marquee and Reprisal; coin Money; emit Bills of Credit; make any Thing but gold and silver Coin a Tender in Payment of debts; pass any Bill of Attainder, ex post facto Law, or Law impairing the Obligation of Contracts, or grant any Title of Nobility.
>
> [2] No State shall, without the Consent of the Congress, lay any Imposts or Duties on Imports or Exports, except what may be absolutely necessary for executing it's inspection laws; and the net Produce of all Duties and Imposts, laid by any State on Imports or Exports, shall be for the Use of the Treasury of the United States; and all such Laws shall be subject to the Revision and Controul of the Congress.
>
> [3] No State shall, without the Consent of Congress, lay any Duty of Tonnage, keep Troops, or Ships of War in time of Peace, enter into any Agreement or Compact with another State, or with a foreign Power, or engage in War, unless actually invaded, or in such imminent Danger as will not admit of delay. [16]

---

[16] *Ibid.*, quoted on p. 94.

The fact that the States could, by adopting the compact, voluntarily agree to refrain from exercising these powers proves that they are sovereign. And it is of interest to observe that the Constitution specifically recognizes the right of a sovereign State to defend itself by exercising the war power – *the inherent right of every sovereign body to sustain and preserve itself!* By creating the Federal Union, the States sought to establish a common agent that would conduct their foreign affairs – and wage their wars – in a unified manner. Thus, whenever a State is threatened by a hostile foreign power, it is the duty of the other States, through their common Federal Government, to adequately defend the sovereignty and rights of the threatened State. This is the primary reason why the United States of America exists. Yet, whensoever the Union fails to properly defend a State, the threatened State may exercise its war powers to preserve itself. This right is inherent in sovereignty and would exist even if not specifically recognized in the Constitution.

Article II

The Second Article deals with the Executive Branch of the Government of the United States and consists of four sections. The First Section of Article II, which is quoted below, contains eight clauses that define the structure of the Executive Branch and provide for the elections of the President and the Vice President of the United States. The Third Clause was superseded by the Twelfth Amendment and is accordingly placed within square brackets. And the Sixth Clause has been modified, but not superseded, by the Twenty-Fifth Amendment.

As Article II, Section 1 declares:

[1] The executive Power shall be vested in a President of the United States of America. He shall hold his Office during the Term of four Years, and, together with the Vice President, chosen for the same Term, be elected, as follows

[2] Each State shall appoint, in such Manner as the Legislature thereof may direct, a Number of Electors, equal to the whole Number of Senators and Representatives to which the State may be entitled in the Congress: but no Senator or Representative, or Person holding an Office of Trust or Profit under the United States, shall be appointed an Elector.

[3] [The Electors shall meet in their respective States, and vote by Ballot for two Persons, of whom one at least shall not be an Inhabitant of the same State with themselves. And they shall make a List of all the Persons voted for, and of the Number of Votes for each; which list they shall sign and certify, and transmit sealed to the Seat of the Government of the United States, directed to the President of the Senate. The President of the

Senate shall, in the Presence of the Senate and House of Representatives, open all the Certificates, and the Votes shall then be counted. The person having the greatest Number of Votes shall be the President, if such Number be a Majority of the whole Number of Electors appointed; and if there be more than one who have such Majority, and have an equal Number of Votes, then the House of Representatives shall immediately chuse by Ballot one of them for President; and if no Person have a Majority, then from the five highest on the List the said House shall in like Manner chuse the President. But in chusing the President, the Votes shall be taken by States, the Representation from each State having one Vote; A quorum for this purpose shall consist of a Member or Members from two thirds of the States, and a Majority of all the States shall be necessary to a Choice. In every Case, after the Choice of the President, the Person having the greatest Number of Votes of the Electors shall be the Vice President. But if there should remain two or more who have equal Votes, the Senate shall chuse from them by Ballot the Vice President.]

[4] The Congress may determine the Time of chusing the Electors, and the Day on which they shall give their Votes; which Day shall be the same throughout the United States.

[5] No Person except a natural born Citizen, or a Citizen of the United States, at the time of the Adoption of this Constitution, shall be eligible to the Office of President; neither shall any Person be eligible to that Office who shall not have attained to the Age of thirty five Years, and been fourteen Years a Resident within the United States.

[6] In Case of the Removal of the President from Office, or of his Death, Resignation, or Inability to discharge the Powers and Duties of the said Office, the Same shall devolve on the Vice President, and the Congress may by Law provide for the Case of Removal, Death, Resignation or Inability, both of the President and Vice President, declaring what Officer shall then act as President, and such Officer shall act accordingly, until the Disability be removed, or a President shall be elected.

[7] The President shall, at stated Times, receive for his Services, a Compensation, which shall neither be encreased nor diminished during the Period for which he shall have been elected, and he shall not receive within that Period any other Emolument from the United States, or any of them.

[8] Before he enter on the Execution of his Office, he shall take the following Oath or Affirmation: – "I do solemnly swear (or affirm) that I will faithfully execute the Office of President of the United States, and will to the best of my Ability, preserve, protect and defend the Constitution of the United States." [17]

It is plainly evident from the Second and Third Clauses of Article II, Section 1 that the elections of the two constitutionally established offices of the Executive Branch of the Federal Government are decisively *federal* in nature. The States, not a mythical consolidated nation of Americans, elect the

---

[17] *Ibid.*, quoted on pp. 94-96.

President and Vice President of the United States. *"Each State shall appoint...a Number of Electors,"* states the Second Clause, referring to the *Electoral College System* of the several States. In voting for the President and Vice President, each State has a number of votes equal to its total number of Representatives and Senators in the Congress.

Although the number of electoral votes derived from the number of a State's Representatives is directly proportional to the size of her population, the same cannot be said for the electoral votes derived from her two Senators. As a consequence of this method of distribution of electoral votes among the several States, it is quite possible for a candidate for the Presidency to receive a majority of the *electoral vote* without receiving a majority of the *popular vote.* The *federal* nature of Presidential elections made it possible for Abraham Lincoln to win the election in 1860, for example, despite the fact that *he received less than 40% of the popular vote.*

The elaborate constitutional mode of resolving a tied Presidential electoral vote prescribed in the Third Clause of Article II, Section 1 was only utilized once in American history, when a tied vote in the 1800 election between Thomas Jefferson and Aaron Burr was settled by the House of Representatives. Four years later, the Twelfth Amendment was incorporated into the Constitution to supersede the mode of Presidential election detailed in Clause Three of Article II, Section 1. By the terms of Amendment Twelve, *separate electoral ballots* must be cast for President and Vice President.

Although the Third Clause of Article II, Section 1 has been superseded by the Twelfth Amendment, we find within it more evidence showing that the House of Representatives is an assembly of delegates representing the sovereign States, and not a body representing a single American nation. In the event that the House must elect the President, the Constitution states, "the Votes shall be taken *by States,* the *Representation from each State* having *one Vote."* This phraseology, it might be added, was repeated *verbatim* in the Twelfth Amendment.

In the Seventh Clause of Article II, Section 1, we see again the plural usage of the term United States: "The President...shall not receive within that Period any other Emolument from the *United States,* or any of *them."* And in the last clause of this section is the official *Oath of Office* which is required of every President upon entering that office: "I do solemnly swear (or affirm) that I will faithfully execute the Office of President of the United States, and will to the best of my Ability, *preserve, protect and defend the Constitution of the United States."* In no part of this oath does the incoming President pledge to support his campaign promises or to fulfill some peculiar "popular mandate" that allegedly resulted in his successful election. The only mandate the

President is sworn to fulfill is that prescribed by the Constitution. By this oath, he must "preserve, protect and defend the Constitution of the United States," all campaign promises made to the contrary notwithstanding.

There are three clauses in the Second Section of Article II which are devoted to enumerating the *powers* of the President of the United States. There is a startling contrast between the very few powers actually delegated to the Chief Executive by the Constitution and the awesome and breath-taking latitude of authority wielded by modern Presidents. Nowhere in the Constitution, for instance, is the President of the United States authorized to use federal troops to police the planet, to wage undeclared wars around the globe, to rule over the States like a monarch, or to legislate by Executive Order. On the contrary, the Constitution merely delegates a few plain and simple powers to the Presidency that are to be exercised by a humble public servant.

As Article II, Section 2 declares:

> [1] The President shall be Commander in Chief of the Army and Navy of the United States, and of the Militia of the several States, when called into the actual Service of the United States; he may require the Opinion, in writing, of the principal Officer in each of the executive Departments, upon any Subject relating to the Duties of their respective Offices, and he shall have Power to grant Reprieves and Pardons for Offences against the United States, except in Cases of Impeachment.
>
> [2] He shall have Power, by and with the Advice and Consent of the Senate, to make Treaties, provided two thirds of the Senators present concur; and he shall nominate, and by and with the Advice and Consent of the Senate, shall appoint Ambassadors, other public Ministers and Consuls, Judges of the supreme Court, and all other Officers of the United States, whose Appointments are not herein otherwise provided for, and which shall be established by Law: but the Congress may by Law vest the Appointment of such inferior Officers, as they think proper, in the President alone, in the Courts of Law, or in the Heads of Departments.
>
> [3] The President shall have Power to fill up all Vacancies that may happen during the Recess of the Senate, by granting Commissions which shall expire at the End of their next Session. [18]

Within the First Clause of Article II, Section 2, the President is empowered to act as the *Commander in Chief* of the armed forces of the United States, including the State militias, "when called into the actual Service of the United States." In such a capacity, the President of the United States is charged with the responsibility of *conducting* a war after it has been lawfully declared. There are, however, significant restrictions on his authority over the armed forces of the Confederation.

---

[18] *Ibid.*, quoted on p. 96.

While the President may conduct a war after it has been declared, for example, *only Congress* – in accordance with Article I, Section 8, Clause 11 – can lawfully proclaim a *Declaration of War*. Although the President of the United States serves as Commander in Chief of the armed forces, he can neither raise nor support the military forces by his own authority. *Only Congress* – in pursuance of Article I, Section 8, Clauses 12, 13, and 14 – is empowered to raise, support, and maintain the armed forces of the United States. And while the President may act as Commander in Chief of the State militias, *when called into federal service*, he cannot, by his own authority, call them into such service. Once again, *only Congress* – as stipulated by Article I, Section 8, Clause 15 – may "provide for calling forth the Militia" of the several States. Although modern Presidents have routinely violated the letter and spirit of the federal compact in many of these areas, the mandates prescribed by the Constitution are specified in very plain and unmistakable language. Any President that wages war without an official declaration from Congress, or attempts to "federalize" a sovereign State's "National Guard" by his own prerogative, must be considered a very dangerous usurper and deserves to be treated accordingly.

It is evident from the references in Article II, Section 2, Clauses 1 and 2 to "the principal Officer in each of the executive Departments" and to "the Heads of Departments," that the Constitution anticipated – but made no specific provision for – a *Presidential Cabinet* to be associated with the Executive Branch of government. Although such Cabinet Offices or Departments may constitutionally exist, such divisions of the Executive Branch of the government must be *limited* in their scope and authority by the constitutional *limitations* imposed on the President. Inasmuch as the President is constitutionally authorized to act as the American *Head of State* in dealing with foreign powers, for instance, a Department of State would be considered constitutionally proper. On the other hand, since no power is delegated to the President over education, labor, and agriculture, for example, a Department of Education, a Department of Labor, and a Department of Agriculture would all be unconstitutional.

The Third Section of Article II declares:

> He shall from time to time give to the Congress Information on the State of the Union, and recommend to their Consideration such Measures as he shall judge necessary and expedient; he may, on extraordinary Occasions, convene both Houses, or either of them, and in Case of Disagreement between them, with Respect to the Time of Adjournment, he may adjourn them to such Time as he shall think proper; he shall receive Ambassadors and other public Ministers; he shall take Care that the Laws be faithfully executed, and shall Commission all Officers of the United

States.[19]

Although the Constitution authorizes the President, "from time to time," to give to the Congress certain information regarding the *State of the Union*, and to "recommend to their Consideration such Measures as he shall judge necessary and expedient," in modern times this prerogative has been grossly abused. So dominant are modern-day Presidents in the legislative process that, according to reliable studies, more than three-fourths of all laws emanating from Congress originate as proposed legislation in the Executive Branch of the Federal Government. The scope of such recommended legislation ranges from the President's proposed federal budget to a vast array of laws drafted by the President's policy makers. Such abuse of power has resulted, to a large extent, in converting the Legislative Branch into little more than an appendage of a domineering Executive Branch.

Article II, Section 4 consists of a single sentence, which declares that, "The President, Vice President and all civil Officers of the United States, shall be removed from Office on Impeachment for, and Conviction of, Treason, Bribery, or other high Crimes and Misdemeanors." [20] Although it has become quite popular in modern times to speak of being *loyal to the President* – especially whenever American soldiers are facing danger in some remote corner of the globe – this section of Article II reveals that such loyalty is grossly misplaced.

Under a republican form of government, it must be remembered, loyalty is never owed to government officials, not even to the acting Head of State. The President, like all other federal officers, is supposed to be loyal to the peoples of the several States, inasmuch as true loyalty is owed to those who are sovereign. The American people are the *masters* of the political system – the President is a mere public *servant*. That is why the Constitution requires all federal officers, from the President on down, to take a solemn oath to support and maintain the supreme law of the people. As Article II, Section 4 reminds us, even the President of the United States, like all other public servants, can be guilty of bribery, treason, and other high crimes.

Article III

Article III consists of three sections that provide for the Judicial Branch of the Government of the United States. The fact that the federal judiciary is

---

[19] *Ibid.*, quoted on pp. 96-97.
[20] *Ibid.*, quoted on p. 97.

the last of the three branches of the Federal Government to be provided for in the Constitution, combined with the fact that Article III is significantly shorter in length than either Article I or II, illustrates that this branch was considered by the majority of the Founding Fathers to be the least significant division of that government. This observation is further supported by the noteworthy fact that none of the broad and sweeping powers that have been claimed for the U.S. Supreme Court are even hinted at, let alone positively enumerated, in Article III.

The First Section of Article III provides for the establishment of the federal judiciary in these words:

> The judicial Power of the United States, shall be vested in one supreme Court, and in such inferior Courts as the Congress may from time to time ordain and establish. The Judges, both of the supreme and inferior Courts, shall hold their Offices during good Behaviour, and shall, at stated Times, receive for their Services, a Compensation, which shall not be diminished during their Continuance in Office. [21]

As is apparent from this section of Article III, the word *supreme* is used in reference to the U.S. Supreme Court only to distinguish it from *inferior* federal courts. Just as the Supreme Court of the United States is the highest tribunal in the land *within the federal sphere of jurisdiction*, each State has its own Supreme Court that is likewise the highest tribunal in the land within *the sphere of jurisdiction reserved to that State*. It is also apparent from this section that most of the structural organization of the federal judiciary depends for its very existence on the Congress. Aside from the one U.S. Supreme Court, all other federal courts exist only by federal statutory laws, and all such inferior courts may be abolished by a simple act of Congress.

Section Two of Article II enumerates the powers delegated to the Judicial Branch of the Federal Government:

> [1] The judicial Power shall extend to all Cases, in Law and Equity, arising under this Constitution, the Laws of the United States, and Treaties made, or which shall be made, under their authority; – to all Cases affecting Ambassadors, other public Ministers and Consuls; – to all Cases of admiralty and maritime Jurisdiction; – to Controversies to which the United States shall be a party; – to Controversies between two or more States; – between a State and Citizens of another State; – between Citizens of different States, – between Citizens of the same State claiming Lands under Grants of different States, and between a State, or the Citizens thereof, and foreign States, Citizens or Subjects.

---

[21] *Ibid.*, quoted on p. 97.

[2] In all cases affecting Ambassadors, other public Ministers and Consuls, and those in which a State shall be Party, the supreme Court shall have original Jurisdiction. In all the other Cases before mentioned, the supreme Court shall have appellate Jurisdiction, both as to Law and Fact, with such Exceptions, and under such Regulations as the Congress shall make.

[3] The Trial of all Crimes, except in Cases of Impeachment, shall be by Jury; and such Trial shall be held in the State where the said Crimes shall have been committed; but when not committed within any State, the Trial shall be at such Place or Places as the Congress may by law have directed. [22]

Years after the Constitutional Convention, Gouverneur Morris, whose talented pen styled the Constitution in its final phraseology, claimed that he had deliberately stretched or distorted the phraseology of the compact in regard to the Judicial Branch of the Federal Government, in order to secretly delegate more power to that department than was intended by the Convention. Yet, a careful examination of Article III, Section 2 fails to reveal any *significant* alterations or deviations from the intention of the Philadelphia Convention of 1787. We do see, however, another reference to the United States as a plural entity, in that portion of Clause 1 that declares: "The judicial Power shall extend to all Cases, in Law and Equity, arising under this Constitution, the Laws of the *United States*, and Treaties made, or which shall be made, under *their* authority."

What stands out in regard to the Judicial Branch of the Government of the United States is the wide authority over that branch wielded by the Congress. Not only do all inferior federal courts depend on Congress for their existence, but the Legislative Branch of government, as stipulated in Article III, Section 2, Clause 2, has the authority to *restrict* — or to establish *exceptions to* — the "appellate Jurisdiction, both as to Law and Fact," of the U.S. Supreme Court. And according to the terms of the next clause, Congress has the authority to establish the sites for trials for crimes not committed within any State.

Regarding the *powers* of the Judicial Branch of the Federal Government, the enumerations expressly listed in Article III, Section 2 are very straightforward and unambiguous. The federal judicial power extends "to all cases, in law and equity, arising *under this Constitution, the Laws of the United States*, and *Treaties made*, or which shall be made, *under their authority*." All federal laws and treaties, of course, must be made *in pursuance of the Constitution* in order to be legitimate, so that this delegation of power may be interpreted as *limiting* the judicial power to the *federal sphere of power* established

---

[22] *Ibid.*, quoted on pp. 97-98.

by the Constitution.

Inasmuch as the intent of the Constitution is to delegate to the Federal Government control over the *foreign affairs* of the United States, it is appropriate that the Judicial Power also extends "to all Cases affecting Ambassadors, other public Ministers and Consuls" and "to all Cases of admiralty and maritime Jurisdiction." Furthermore, the Judicial Power extends to litigation that crosses State boundaries – "to Controversies to which the United States shall be a Party," "to Controversies between two or more States," "between a State and Citizens of another State" as modified by the Eleventh Amendment, "between Citizens of different States," and "between Citizens of the same State claiming Lands under Grants of different States, and between a State, or the Citizens thereof, and foreign States, Citizens or Subjects." The jurisdiction of the federal judiciary is thus strictly limited and strictly federal in nature, extending only to foreign and interstate cases in law and equity. Outside of this very limited sphere of jurisdiction, the *State Supreme Courts* have final and ultimate jurisdiction.

Article III, Section 3 consists of the following two clauses that define the nature of *treason* against the United States of America:

> [1] Treason against the United States, shall consist only in levying War against them, or in adhering to their Enemies, giving them Aid and Comfort. No Person shall be convicted of Treason unless on the Testimony of two Witnesses to the same overt Act, or on Confession in open Court.
>
> [2] The Congress shall have Power to declare the Punishment of Treason, but no Attainder of Treason shall work Corruption of Blood, or Forfeiture except during the Life of the Person attained. [23]

Several highly significant observations regarding the subject of loyalty and treason merit our consideration. Although Americans routinely recite a *Pledge of Allegiance* to the flag and to the Republic for which it stands, loyalty or allegiance is actually owed to the *sovereign*, who is the *supreme power* or *ultimate authority* within the political system. Under the American Theory of Government, sovereignty is not vested in either a flag or in a government, but only in the *American people* themselves, in their organized capacities as *sovereign States*. Treason may thus be committed against a single State or against all of the States combined.

Perhaps the most historically famous case of treason *against a single State* occurred as a result of an armed invasion of Virginia in October of 1859 by a band of terrorists led by the fanatical abolitionist, John Brown. The pur-

---

[23] *Ibid.*, quoted on p. 98.

pose of this invasion, in addition to "freeing the slaves," was to overthrow the State of Virginia. After the invading army of radical abolitionists had been defeated and their leader captured, John Brown was tried in a Virginia court of law and convicted of the crimes of murder and *treason against the State of Virginia*. He accordingly met his much-deserved fate on the gallows.

In defining treason and in authorizing the Congress to prescribe the punishment for such crime, the scope of Article III, Section 3 of the Federal Constitution is confined only to treason against the United States, or, in other words, against all of the sovereign States jointly. Defining and punishing treason against an individual State is reserved by the Constitution to each State, respectively.

One final observation should be made in regard to treason against the United States. As Article III, Section 3, Clause 1 stipulates, treason against the United States includes "levying War against them," wherein the word *them* refers back to the term *United States*. And as Article II, Section 4 states, all officers of the Federal Government – including the President of the United States – may be guilty of committing the heinous crime of treason, either by adhering to the enemies of the States or by waging war against them.

What shall we therefore conclude regarding the conduct of Abraham Lincoln, who waged a war of conquest against a number of sovereign States? What conclusion can be made regarding Dwight D. Eisenhower, who dispatched the U.S. Army to invade the State of Arkansas in 1957 to overthrow that State's domestic laws by forcing racial integration at Central High School in Little Rock? And what conclusion can be made regarding John F. Kennedy, who invaded the State of Mississippi to force integration of the University of Mississippi at the point of a bayonet?

We have now fully examined that portion of the Constitution which provides for the Judicial Branch of the Federal Government, and the question must raised: Which provision in Article III provides for the highly significant power of *judicial review*? The answer, of course, is that *no provision* in Article III – or in any other part of the Constitution, for that matter – even hints at such a broad and sweeping power to overthrow federal laws. The lack of such a constitutional authorization, however, has not deterred those who wish to vest such an awesome power in the federal judiciary.

In their textbook, *American Constitutional Law: Essays and Cases*, Professors Otis H. Stephens, Jr. and John M. Scheb, II of the University of Tennessee state that the source or origin of judicial review is not the Constitution itself, but rather Chief Justice John Marshall, who arrogantly *assumed* the right to nullify an act of Congress in the case of *Marbury vs. Madison*. As these authors note:

Prior to adoption of the Federal Constitution *several* State courts had invoked this power to invalidate State legislation. This practice continued after establishment of the new National [sic] Government in 1789. The Supreme Court in effect *recognized* the power as early as 1798 when, in *Hylton* v. *United States....*, it upheld a federal tax on carriages as a constitutional exercise of Congressional power. Nevertheless, *Marbury* v. *Madison* was the first case in which the Supreme Court in a published opinion *invalidated an act of Congress* on the ground that it violated the Constitution. Marshall reasoned that in light of the Court's "duty" to interpret the law and the proposition that the Constitution is superior to ordinary statutes in the hierarchy of laws, *judicial review was inevitable.* In other words, the Court could not recognize the supremacy of the Constitution as provided by Article VI and exercise its judicial duty as prescribed in Article III without sooner or later ruling on the constitutionality of acts of government and striking them down if they conflicted with the basic law. Given his premises, Marshall's conclusions followed logically. But some of his contemporaries, Thomas Jefferson among them, did not accept those premises at all. Early critics of judicial rule pointed out that the principle was not explicitly stated in the Constitution....The critics also noted that the President and Congress, no less than the Supreme Court, were required in their oaths of office to uphold the Constitution of the United States.

In one of the most effective refutations of Marshall's position, Justice John B. Gibson of the Pennsylvania Supreme Court contended in 1825 that *each branch of government is ultimately responsible to the people for the constitutionality of its own acts....*Justice Gibson maintained that the Supreme Court has no more authority to invalidate an act of Congress on constitutional grounds than Congress has to declare a Supreme Court decision unconstitutional. In the realm of logic and language, *no final resolution of this conflict over the legitimacy of judicial review has ever been achieved.* [Emphasis added] [24]

The power of judicial review, as is evident, is *assumed* from the oath taken by the federal Judges to support and maintain the Federal Constitution. However, that very same oath of office is also taken by all the officers of the various State governments as well as by all of the officers of the Federal Government. To what limits may the ingenious assumption of powers be carried? If that oath can authorize the U.S. Supreme Court to declare acts of Congress unconstitutional, then the President can also assume the power to ignore existing laws at his pleasure, and Congress may then assume the power to ignore all acts of the other two branches that are, in its opinion, unconstitutional.

The assumption herein made can also be carried over to the federal system as well. If the U.S. Supreme Court may assume, based on the oath taken by its Justices, a power to nullify a State law, then both the President and the

---

[24] Otis H. Stephens, Jr. and John M. Scheb, II, *American Constitutional Law: Essays and Cases*, Harcourt Brace Jovanovich, Publishers, San Diego, 1988, p. 21.

Congress may likewise assume the power to void State laws, based on their oaths of office. Yet, in accordance with Article VI, Clause 3, all State officials are also bound by oath to support and maintain that same Federal Constitution. Thus, by the same logic used to vest judicial review in the U.S. Supreme Court, every court in each State may rightfully declare an act of Congress null and void. So, too, may each State legislature and the Governor of each State. If the oath confers the power on one department in our political system, then it must equally confer it on all the others.

In asserting the power of judicial review in the 1803 case of *Marbury vs. Madison*, Chief Justice John Marshall stated that, "It is emphatically the province and duty of the Judicial Department, to say what the law is." [25] Yet, as we have already observed, the Constitution of the United States – in Article I, Section 1, Clause 1 – emphatically states that it is the province and duty of *the Congress* to say what the law is, within the federal sphere. One hundred years after the Supreme Court had theoretically usurped the power of legislation from Congress, another Chief Justice of the United States attempted to usurp the sovereignty of the States – in utter violation of Article V of the compact – by haughtily proclaiming that the Supreme Court had the authority to amend the Constitution. "We are under a Constitution," opined Chief Justice Charles Evans Hughes in 1907, "but the Constitution is what the Judges say it is." [26]

Although the concept of judicial review has long been advocated by consolidationists as an extra-constitutional check on the abuses of power by the Congress, the question must be raised: Can we realistically expect that an *assumed* and *unconstitutional* power will be used by those who usurped the authority to maintain and support the Constitution? Stated differently, is it to be expected that an action performed in violation and contradiction of the Constitution will maintain that Constitution?

In this regard, the observations made by Professors Stephens and Scheb in their textbook are especially significant:

> The Supreme Court has been chiefly responsible for *defining the scope of powers* exercised by Congress, the President, and the federal bureaucracy under the Constitution. Although it has curbed those powers on a number of occasions, *it has far more often articulated constitutional rationales supporting the enlargement of governmental authority.* Under the briefly enumerated power of Congress to "regulate commerce...among the several States," for example, the Court has upheld the exercise of vast legislative power encompassing labor-management relations, conditions of employment, antitrust policy, highway construction, air safety, environmental pro-

---

[25] *Ibid.*, quoted on illustration page facing p. 432.
[26] *Ibid.*, quoted on illustration page facing p. 432.

tection, and civil rights, among only a few of the most familiar categories. [Emphasis added] [27]

Despite the pretended claims to the contrary, it is thus apparent that judicial review is *not* a part of the checks and balances within the Federal Government. It is, on the contrary, a key part of the conspiracy to usurp all the powers of the States and to centralize all authority in Washington in utter violation of the letter and spirit of the supreme law of the land. For this reason, it comes as no surprise that Professors Stephens and Scheb could write the following in their textbook:

> For the most part the immense growth of government, chiefly characterized by the proliferation of bureaucracy, has taken place gradually and with little fanfare. Over the past two centuries the center of political gravity has shifted from State to national primacy; from legislative supremacy to Presidential leadership; and from limited government to pervasive government engaged in problem-solving on a grand scale. *These changes, however, have not been accompanied by a corresponding change in the basic principles of American constitutional government.* [Emphasis added] [28]

Judicial review has undoubtedly done more damage to the Federal Constitution than has any other catastrophe in American history. And in modern times, this unconstitutional practice has assumed an even more alarming nature in the hands of those "Judges" who make no pretense whatsoever of fidelity to the *original intention* of the Founding Fathers. The original meaning of the various provisions of our Constitution, such Supreme Court Justices as William J. Brennan have candidly and crassly informed us, is totally irrelevant. These construing enemies of the supreme law of the land thus openly and boldly interpret the compact according to their own constitutions, delegating new powers to the Federal Government as they deem proper, awarding new rights and privileges to criminal elements within society, and robbing the States of their last vestiges of constitutionally reserved powers.

When we consider the nature of the federal judiciary, together with the outlandish claims made on behalf of its supremacy, a sobering question invariably arises. Has the nature of our political system been unconstitutionally transformed, *in effect*, from a Federal Republic to a National Monarchy? Is the United States governed, *in effect*, by precisely that type of government which was emphatically rejected by the Constitutional Convention? The reader is left to provide his own answers to these questions.

---

[27] *Ibid.*, p. 19.
[28] *Ibid.*, p. 18.

Article IV

Article IV of the Federal Constitution contains several specific agreements among the States and is divided into four sections. The First Section is intended to ensure harmony and accord within the Union, and its provisions establish beyond cavil the fact that the sovereign equality of the States forms the cornerstone of the Federal Union. As this section declares:

> Full Faith and Credit shall be given in each State to the public Acts, records, and judicial Proceedings of every other State. And the Congress may by general Laws prescribe the Manner in which such Acts, Records and Proceedings shall be proved, and the Effect thereof. [29]

The Second Section of Article IV contains three clauses. The First Clause establishes the concept of *American citizenship*, by stipulating that the citizens of one State have a right to all the "Privileges and Immunities" enjoyed by the citizens of other States in the Federal Union. Inasmuch as the Constitution does not recognize any single, consolidated nation of citizens, the concept of *citizens of the United States* is sustained only by assuring the equality of privileges and immunities among the *citizens of the several States*.

The Second Clause of Article IV, Section 2 provides for the *extradition* of criminals who flee from one State to another in an effort to evade justice in the State wherein the crime was committed. It should be noted that among the crimes mentioned in this clause is *treason* against a single State. Inasmuch as the Third Clause referred only to the restoration of runaway slaves to their rightful owners, it was superseded by the Thirteenth Amendment and is accordingly placed within square brackets in the quotation shown below.

As this section of Article IV states:

> [1] The Citizens of each State shall be entitled to all Privileges and Immunities of Citizens in the several States.
>
> [2] A Person charged in any State with Treason, Felony, or other Crime, who shall flee from justice, and be found in another State, shall on Demand of the executive Authority of the State from which he fled, be delivered up, to be removed to the State having Jurisdiction of the Crime.
>
> [3] [No Person held to Service or Labour in one State, under the Laws thereof, escaping into another, shall, in consequence of any Law or Regulation therein, be discharged from such Service or Labour, but shall be delivered up on Claim of the Party to whom such Service or Labour may be due.] [30]

---

[29] Richard B. Morris, *Op. cit.*, quoted on p. 98.
[30] *Ibid.*, quoted on p. 98.

The Third Section of Article IV contains two clauses that provide for the admission of new States into the Confederation, guarantee the territorial integrity of the existing States, and establish authority for the administration of the territorial possessions of the United States:

> [1] New States may be admitted by the Congress into this Union; but no new State shall be formed or erected within the Jurisdiction of any other State; nor any State be formed by the junction of two or more States, or Parts of States, without the Consent of the Legislatures of the States concerned as well as of the Congress.
>
> [2] The Congress shall have Power to dispose of and make all needful Rules and Regulations respecting the Territory or other Property belonging to the United States; and nothing in this Constitution shall be so construed as to Prejudice any Claims of the United States, or of any particular State. [31]

Only once has the territorial integrity of the States guaranteed by Article IV, Section 3, Clause 1 been violated, and that occurred during the War Between the States, when the Government of the United States unconstitutionally split the State of Virginia into two parts, without the consent of that State, thereby creating the State of West Virginia from a fragment of the Old Dominion. And while the Second Clause delegates to Congress the power to regulate the territorial possessions of the United States, it must be remembered that the republican and federal nature of the Union is incompatible with the concept of *colonies*. The true constitutional course in regard to Territories is to either admit them into the Union as new States or to grant them independence, and not to hold them perpetually in the form of colonial possessions, as in the case of Puerto Rico.

The Fourth Section of Article IV states:

> The United States shall guarantee to every State in this Union a Republican Form of Government, and shall protect each of them against Invasion; and on Application of the Legislature, or of the Executive (when the Legislature cannot be convened) against domestic Violence. [32]

This section of the Constitution provides three closely related guarantees to the sovereign members of the Federal Union. The first is a promise or guarantee to every State to secure to it a republican form of government. And here we might pose a question. When the monarchical U.S. Supreme Court usurps a power of judicial review of State laws and strikes down a law passed

---

[31] *Ibid.*, quoted on pp. 98-99.
[32] *Ibid.*, quoted on p. 99.

by the lawful representatives of the people of a State, is this guaranteeing republican government to that State, or is this a direct violation of the constitutional guarantee?

The second guarantee is that each State shall be protected against invasion. Again, we must pose a query. Is this promise confined only to invasions of a State by foreign powers, or does it also encompass invasions by other States in the Federal Union and even by the Federal Government itself? That portion of the Constitution which defines treason against the United States seems to provide a satisfactory answer to this question.

Finally, the third guarantee entails a solemn pledge to protect the States against "domestic Violence." There are, however, two conditions associated with this particular guarantee that must be met in order to fulfill the constitutional mandate. The first stipulation is that the Federal Government cannot offer any assistance to suppress domestic violence *unless* and *until* it has been formally requested to do so by the State government in whose jurisdiction the violence is perpetrated. The other requirement mandated by the guarantee of protection against "domestic violence" is that federal assistance *must* be provided to any State that requests it, and even then such assistance *must* be directed toward helping that State to enforce its laws. Should the Federal Government fail to fulfill any of these requirements, the constitutional guarantee of a republican form of government to each State would be subverted.

Under no circumstances, it must be stressed, does Article IV, Section 4 – or any other part of the Constitution, for that matter – authorize the Federal Government to coerce a State in its sovereign capacity. Although a few radical extremists in the Constitutional Convention of 1787 desired to vest in the Federal Government the authority to overthrow a State government under the pretense of guaranteeing a republican form of government to all the States, they were decisively defeated in the Convention by those who insisted on inserting into this section of the Constitution the proviso that federal intervention can not be undertaken without an invitation from the State government involved.

Article V

The Fifth Article of the federal compact is devoted exclusively to defining in precise terms the only lawful manner for amending the Constitution of the United States. By its provisions, an amendment may be formally *proposed* either by two-thirds of both houses of Congress or by application of two-thirds of the State legislatures. A proposed amendment may be *ratified* either by the legislatures of three-fourths of the States or by Ratification Conventions in three-fourths of the States.

Although the Federal Government – specifically Congress – is authorized to propose or recommend amendments, only the States can ratify amendments. In fact, the *State governments* can both propose and ratify amendments to the Federal Constitution, proving that those governments are constitutionally much closer to the true seat of sovereignty than is the Federal Government. The U.S. Supreme Court, it will be noted, plays no role at all in the amendment process, proving that the claim made, to the effect that the Constitution is whatever the Supreme Court says it is, is palpably absurd. *The Constitution, proclaims Article V of the compact, is whatever the sovereign States say it is!*

Although Article V allows for the calling of a Federal Convention to propose amendments to the Constitution, it would appear that the States learned a valuable lesson from the Constitutional Convention of 1787, which had been called for the sole and express purpose of amending the Articles of Confederation. Never again would such a Convention be entrusted to amend an existing Federal Constitution. Attention should also be directed to this article's ironclad stipulation that no State can be denied, without its consent, of its equal suffrage in the Senate. The existence of this proviso illustrates the extent of the victory realized by the Federal Republicans within the Philadelphia Convention of 1787.

As Article V declares:

> The Congress, whenever two thirds of both Houses shall deem it necessary, shall propose Amendments to this Constitution, or, on the Application of the Legislatures of two thirds of the several States, shall call a Convention for proposing Amendments, which, in either Case, shall be valid to all Intents and Purposes, as Part of this Constitution, when ratified by the Legislatures of three fourths of the several States, or by Conventions in three fourths thereof, as the one or the other Mode of Ratification may be proposed by the Congress; Provided that no Amendment which may be made prior to the Year One thousand eight hundred and eight shall in any Manner affect the first and fourth Clauses in the Ninth section of the first Article; and that no State, without its Consent, shall be deprived of its equal Suffrage in the Senate. [33]

One final observation should be made regarding the amendment process. By its very nature, an **amendment** is merely an *addition to* or *alteration of* specific provisions within the Federal Constitution. Due to its nature, an inherent limitation must exist over the amendment process. No amendment,

---

[33] *Ibid.*, quoted on p. 99.

for example, should be added to the Constitution that would destroy the sovereignty of the States or transform the American form and system of government. Any amendment of such a nature would not be an amendment at all, but would in fact be *an entirely new Constitution*. And if the purpose actually is to replace the Federal Constitution with a different type of supreme law, then such a change should be openly presented to the States as a new constitutional dispensation, thereby ensuring that no State is bound by a new system of government without its own consent.

Article VI

The Sixth Article contains the following three clauses:

> [1] All Debts contracted and Engagements entered into, before the Adoption of this Constitution, shall be as valid against the United States under this Constitution, as under the Confederation.
>
> [2] This Constitution, and the Laws of the United States which shall be made in Pursuance thereof; and all Treaties made, or which shall be made, under the Authority of the United States, shall be the supreme Law of the Land; and the Judges in every State shall be bound thereby, any Thing in the Constitution or Laws of any State to the Contrary notwithstanding.
>
> [3] The Senators and Representatives before mentioned, and the Members of the several State Legislatures, and all executive and judicial Officers, both of the United States and of the several States, shall be bound by Oath or Affirmation, to support this Constitution; but no religious Test shall ever be required as a Qualification to any Office or public Trust under the United States. [34]

Of particular significance in Article VI is the Second Clause, often referred to as the *Supremacy Clause*. The origin of this provision may be traced back to a motion made on July 17, 1787, in the Federal Convention by Luther Martin of Maryland. Just prior to the introduction of Mr. Martin's motion, the Convention *rejected*, by a vote of 7 to 3, a proposal that the Federal Government should be empowered to negative State laws. After rejecting that power as wholly inappropriate in a federal system of government, the Convention was left with the question of how to assure that the compact between the States could be maintained. At that point, Luther Martin – a staunch champion of States' Rights and the Convention's Orator of Federalism – drew upon the Supremacy Clause of the old Articles of Confederation and

---

[34] *Ibid.*, quoted on pp. 99-100.

moved:

> [T]hat the Legislative acts of the U.S. made by virtue & in pursu-
> ance of the Articles of Union, and all treaties made & ratified under the au-
> thority of the U.S. shall be the *supreme law of the respective States*, as far as
> those acts or treaties shall relate to the said States, or their Citizens and in-
> habitants – & that the Judiciaries of the several States shall be bound
> thereby in their decisions, any thing in the respective laws of the individual
> States to the contrary notwithstanding. [Emphasis added] [35]

The Convention adopted Mr. Martin's motion without objection, and
although the phraseology was changed by the Committee of Style, the meaning of the provision was not. According to the Supremacy Clause, the foundation of the *supreme law of the land* – that is, of the *supreme law of the respective
States* – is the Constitution of the United States. All federal laws and treaties
made in pursuance of the Constitution may become a part of this supreme
law; yet, federal laws and treaties not made in pursuance of the compact are
simply null and void. In similar fashion, all constitutional State laws are also
part of this supreme law of the land, or supreme law of the respective States.

By the terms of Article VI, Clause 2, any State law that violates the
Federal Constitution is unconstitutional. In similar fashion, any federal law
that violates the compact is unconstitutional. The only question is, who is to
decide such cases? Although a false claim has been made that such authority
resides in the U.S. Supreme Court, the precise language of Article VI, Clause
2 points to the State judiciaries. In very plain language, the Supremacy Clause
declares that those State authorities are to decide such cases, charging "the
Judges in every State" to uphold the supremacy of the Federal Constitution.
The federal judiciary is not even mentioned in connection with the Supremacy Clause!

Article VII

Article VII consists of a single sentence which provides for the ratification of the Constitution by the original thirteen American States: "The Ratification of the Conventions of nine States, shall be sufficient for the Establishment of this Constitution between the States so ratifying the Same." [36] As
this provision plainly indicates, the Constitution is a *compact* that exists "be-

---

[35] Max Farrand (ed.), *The Records of the Federal Convention of 1787*, Revised Edition, Volume II, Yale
University Press, New Haven, 1966, pp. 28-29.
[36] Richard B. Morris, *Op. cit.*, quoted on p. 100.

tween the States" who are the parties to it. Such a concept, of course, was copied directly from the Articles of Confederation, which referred to the league of friendship established by it as a Confederation or Union *between the States*.

Article VII is followed by a concluding section that was attached to the compact by the Constitutional Convention:

> Done in Convention by the Unanimous Consent of the States present the Seventeenth Day of September in the Year of our Lord one thousand seven hundred and Eighty seven and of the Independence of the United States of America the Twelfth.
> In witness whereof We have hereunto subscribed our Names. [37]

These words are followed by the signatures of 39 of the delegates to the Convention who had participated in the drafting of the Constitution. Specifically, 38 of those delegates officially signed for the eleven States of Delaware, Maryland, Virginia, North Carolina, South Carolina, Georgia, New Hampshire, Massachusetts, Connecticut, New Jersey, and Pennsylvania. The remaining signer – Alexander Hamilton – officially signed on behalf of no State, since his own State, New York, had previously withdrawn from the Grand Convention.

The Bill of Rights

On December 15, 1791, the first ten amendments to the Federal Constitution – popularly termed the Bill of Rights – were officially incorporated into the compact in fulfillment of a bargain made by the Federalists with the Antifederalists. The various restrictions and guarantees contained within the federal Bill of Rights, it should be noted, apply only to the Government of the United States. The States have long had their own Bills of Rights.

The first eight Amendments to the Federal Constitution deal with specific rights and are expressed in the following terms:

> **Amendment One:** "Congress shall make no law respecting an establishment of religion, or prohibiting the free exercise thereof; or abridging the freedom of speech, or of the press; or the right of the people peaceably to assemble, and to petition the Government for a redress of grievances." [38]
> **Amendment Two:** "A well regulated Militia, being necessary to the

---

[37] *Ibid.*, quoted on p. 100.
[38] *Ibid.*, quoted on p. 100-101.

security of a free State, the right of the people to keep and bear Arms, shall not be infringed." [39]

Amendment Three: "No soldier shall, in time of peace be quartered in any house, without the consent of the Owner, nor in time of war, but in a manner to be prescribed by law." [40]

Amendment Four: "The right of the people to be secure in their persons, houses, papers, and effects, against unreasonable searches and seizures, shall not be violated, and no Warrants shall issue, but upon probable cause, supported by Oath or affirmation, and particularly describing the place to be searched, and the persons or things to be seized." [41]

Amendment Five: "No person shall be held to answer for a capital, or otherwise infamous crime, unless on a presentment or indictment of a Grand Jury, except in cases arising in the land or naval forces, or in the Militia, when in actual service in time of war or public danger; nor shall any person be subject for the same offense to be twice put in jeopardy of life or limb; nor shall be compelled in any criminal case to be a witness against himself, nor be deprived of life, liberty, or property, without due process of law; nor shall private property be taken for public use, without just compensation." [42]

Amendment Six: "In all criminal prosecutions, the accused shall enjoy the right to a speedy and public trial, by an impartial jury of the State and district wherein the crime shall have been committed, which district shall have been previously ascertained by law, and to be informed of the nature and cause of the accusation; to be confronted with the witnesses against him; to have compulsory process for obtaining witnesses in his favour, and to have the Assistance of Counsel for his defense." [43]

Amendment Seven: ""In Suits at common law, where the value in controversy shall exceed twenty dollars, the right of trial by jury shall be preserved, and no fact tried by a jury, shall be otherwise re-examined in any Court of the United States, than according to the rules of the common law." [44]

Amendment Eight: "Excessive bail shall not be required, nor excessive fines imposed, nor cruel and unusual punishments inflicted." [45]

The general tenor of the federal Bill of Rights is established within the first five words of Amendment One: "Congress shall make no law." The general tone thus established is consistent with the American Theory of Government that was established by the Declaration of Independence. According to this theory, *power* and *liberty* are opposing concepts. The more power a gov-

---

[39] *Ibid.*, quoted on p. 101.
[40] *Ibid.*, quoted on p. 101.
[41] *Ibid.*, quoted on p. 101.
[42] *Ibid.*, quoted on p. 101.
[43] *Ibid.*, quoted on pp. 101-102.
[44] *Ibid.*, quoted on p. 102.
[45] *Ibid.*, quoted on p. 102.

ernment is allowed to exercise, the less freedom the people are allowed to enjoy. Under an all-powerful, totalitarian government, for instance, the people have no rights and can exist only as slaves. The idea behind the American Theory of Government, then, is to delegate to the government only powers sufficient to perform its assigned tasks, and not one power more than is absolutely necessary. This maxim applies regardless of the form of government, and is applicable to representative as well as to non-representative governments.

Although the first eight Amendments to the Federal Constitution are unambiguous and require little in the way of explanation, we should clarify a few misconceptions regarding certain portions of the Bill of Rights that have arisen in modern times. The object of the first portion of Amendment One is to guarantee freedom of religion in the United States by prohibiting the Federal Government from favoring one denomination or Church over another. It was not intended, as falsely contended by some, to ban Christianity from all public sectors in the United States, or to promote a separation between God and state.

The long-established practices of the Federal Government reveal the true nature of this portion of the First Amendment. The President of the United States, for instance, has traditionally placed Christmas displays on the White House lawn; the Congress has always started its sessions with a prayer; and the Judicial Branch of government had a long tradition of swearing in witnesses by use of the Holy Bible. The purpose of religious freedom, in a word, is to ensure the survival of Christianity, not to destroy it.

Advocates of "gun control" have long demonstrated a preference for either ignoring or misconstruing the Second Amendment, which guarantees the right to keep and bear arms. It has been falsely claimed that this amendment only guarantees the right to the State militias, which are now often referred to as the misnamed National Guard. When ratifying the Constitution, a number of States proposed that such guarantees as those contained in this amendment be added to the compact, and the phraseology they employed in their proposals left no doubt as to the true meaning of the Second Amendment.

The State of Virginia, for example, in ratifying the federal compact, formally asserted, "That the people have a right to keep and bear arms; that a well regulated Militia composed of the body of the people trained to arms is the proper, natural and safe defence of a free State." [46] Some other States – including New York, North Carolina, and Rhode Island –attached identically worded statements to their official acts of ratification. Those who favored the

---

[46] Charles Callan Tansill (ed.), *Op. cit.*, p. 1030.

adoption of this amendment clearly understood that practical political power grows out of the barrel of a gun, and they were determined that such power should be widely disbursed throughout the Union, and not concentrated in the hands of the Federal Government.

The primary source of this amendment reveals that Amendment Two was intended to secure both the inalienable right of the citizenry to keep and bear arms, and the separate but related right of a sovereign State to rely on its own militia as the most natural and safe means of defending its freedom. Both of these natural rights, tragically, have come under sharp attack by the Government of the United States in recent years.

Although the Fourth Amendment was intended to protect the rights of the American people against an aggressive and obtrusive Federal Government, in recent years the rights secured by this amendment have been seriously undermined. All too often in modern times, agents of the Federal Government have displayed an alarming tendency to serve their *search warrants* with battering rams, attack helicopters, machine guns, and Army tanks. The Bureau of Alcohol, Tobacco, and Firearms (BATF), for instance, once assaulted a domestic residence and murdered its occupant before realizing that it was attempting to "serve" a search warrant at the wrong address. The most glaring abuse of Amendment Four, however, undoubtedly occurred when federal agents attempted to serve a search warrant at the Branch Davidian Church near Waco, Texas. Before the incident was over, nearly one hundred people – including women and children – had been either shot or burned to death.

The Fifth Amendment contains a number of provisions designed to safeguard the rights of the innocent, including a guarantee against *double jeopardy*. In recent times, however, the Government of the United States has discovered a clever mode of evading this constitutional stipulation so that accused persons can be put in double jeopardy whenever that government wishes to rob such persons of their constitutional rights. This clever mode of evasion is effected, ironically, by usage of "civil rights" rhetoric and terminology. The widely publicized case of the four Los Angeles police officers accused of improperly handling the arrest of a brawling, drunken Negro criminal named Rodney King offers an excellent illustration.

The four police officers involved in the arrest were duly tried in a California court on criminal charges, but not one was found guilty of committing a crime. The Federal Government, however, insisted that they be tried again, this time in a federal court. While the charges against the accused assumed a *new name* in the federal case, the change of name could not conceal the fact that it was a clear case of double jeopardy. Some of the officers were nonetheless convicted and sentenced to prison terms in violation of *their* civil rights guaranteed by the Fourth Amendment.

During the Ratification Period, the Federalists had argued against the Bill of Rights on the grounds that such provisions were unnecessary, that the enumeration of specific rights might afford a pretext to deny other rights to the people, and that a Bill of Rights might be falsely construed as implying that the Federal Government could exercise all powers except those specifically prohibited to it. To guard against such a pretext, Amendment Nine and Amendment Ten were incorporated in the compact.

Amendment Nine declares in unmistakable terms that, "The enumeration in the Constitution, of certain rights, shall not be construed to deny or disparage others retained by the people." [47] And the entire Bill of Rights was succinctly summarized by **Amendment Ten**, which boldly proclaims that, "The powers not delegated to the United States by the Constitution, nor prohibited by it to the States, are reserved to the States respectively, or to the people." [48]

The Tenth Amendment represents the foundation of the Federal Constitution and the cornerstone of the Federal Republic, and it is based on the concept of sovereign States forming the pillars on which the Federal Union rests. The *sources* of Amendment Ten reveal the true nature of this crucial constitutional provision. In ratifying the Constitution, the State of Virginia, for example, proposed to amend the compact to the effect, "That each State in the Union shall respectively retain every power, jurisdiction and right which is not by this Constitution delegated to the Congress of the United States or to the departments of the Federal Government." [49]

Other States attached similarly worded proposals to their formal acts of ratification. Rhode Island, for instance, proposed to amend the compact as follows: "The United States shall guarantee to each State its sovereignty, freedom and independence, and every power, jurisdiction and right, which is not by the Constitution expressly delegated to the United States." [50] It was from these various proposals that Amendment Ten was drafted and submitted to the States for their approval.

The Ante-Bellum Amendments

For nearly three-quarters of a century, from 1792 to 1865, the United States of America witnessed a period of remarkable stability, in terms of constitutional alterations. During the Ante-Bellum Period, only two amendments

---

[47] Richard B. Morris, *Op. cit.*, quoted on p. 102.
[48] *Ibid.*, quoted on p. 102.
[49] Charles Callan Tansill (ed.), *Op. cit.*, p. 1031.
[50] *Ibid.*, p. 1056.

were added to the Federal Constitution, and those were added at relatively early dates. **Amendment Eleven**, which was incorporated into the compact on January 8, 1798, in an effort to curb the abuse of power by the federal judiciary, declares that, "The judicial power of the United States shall not be construed to extend to any suit in law or equity, commenced or prosecuted against one of the United States by Citizens of another State, or by Citizens or Subjects of any Foreign State." [51]

When the Presidential election of 1800 resulted in a tie between Thomas Jefferson and Aaron Burr, it was widely realized that the original mode of selecting the President and Vice President of the United States required reformation. Accordingly, on September 25, 1804, **Amendment Twelve**, which is cited below, was added to the Federal Constitution. That portion of this amendment which was later superseded by the Twentieth Amendment is shown in square brackets:

> The Electors shall meet in their respective States, and vote by ballot for President and Vice-President, one of whom, at least, shall not be an inhabitant of the same State with themselves; they shall name in their ballots the person voted for as President, and in distinct ballots the person voted for as Vice-President, and they shall make distinct lists of all persons voted for as President, and of all persons voted for as Vice-President, and of the number of votes for each, which lists they shall sign and certify, and transmit sealed to the seat of the Government of the United States, directed to the President of the Senate; – The President of the Senate shall, in the presence of the Senate and House of Representatives, open all the certificates and the votes shall then be counted; – The person having the greatest number of votes for President, shall be the President, if such number be a majority of the whole number of Electors appointed; and if no person have such majority, that from the persons having the highest numbers not exceeding three on the list of those voted for as President, the House of Representatives shall choose immediately, by ballot, the President. But in choosing the President, the votes shall be taken by States, the representation from each State having one vote; a quorum for this purpose shall consist of a member or members from two-thirds of the States, and a majority of all the States shall be necessary to a choice. [And if the House of Representatives shall not choose a President whenever the right of choice shall devolve upon them, before the fourth day of March next following, then the Vice-President shall act as President, as in the case of the death or other constitutional disability of the President.] The person having the greatest number of votes as Vice-President, shall be the Vice-President, if such number be a majority of the whole number of Electors appointed, and if no person have a majority, then from the two highest numbers on the list, the Senate shall choose the Vice-President; a quorum for the purpose shall

---

[51] Richard B. Morris, *Op. cit.*, quoted on p. 102.

consist of two-thirds of the whole number of Senators, and a majority of the whole number shall be necessary to a choice. But no person constitutionally ineligible to the office of President shall be eligible to that of Vice-President of the United States. [52]

The Radical Reconstruction Amendments

As a result of the conquest of the Southern States by the Federal Government in the War Between the States, the United States underwent a period of Radical Reconstruction that lasted from 1865 to 1876. This tragic and disgraceful period in American history was characterized by Military Dictatorship, the subversion of constitutionally limited government, and a conspiratorially fraudulent 1876 Presidential election that allowed Rutherford B. Hayes to defeat Samuel Tilden. The period was also characterized by an attempt to radically alter the Constitution of the United States with three Radical Reconstruction amendments.

Commenting on this dark time in U.S. history, noted historian Clarence B. Carson made these observations in his five-volume work, *A Basic History of the United States*:

> The Radicals made a shambles of the Constitution during their period of rule. Of that, there should be no doubt. The Civil War had fitted as readily into the Constitution as a round peg of the same size would fit into a square hole. There simply is no provision in the Constitution for the United States Government to use force, i.e., make war, upon States. There are no provisions for the treatment of people within States when war is undertaken against them. And certainly there were no provisions in the Constitution for reconstructing States.
>
> In any case, the Radicals ran roughshod over the Constitution for several years. Lincoln had maintained that the Union was indissoluble, that States could not secede from it. (The Supreme Court later ruled, in *Texas vs. White*, that this was the law.) Yet the Radicals denied to former Confederate States their place in the Union and, though they had no representation, proceeded to levy taxes upon the South. The slaves were freed well before a constitutional amendment was adopted; property was thus taken from the owners without compensation. (Lincoln had several times proposed that provision be made for compensation, but Congress did not concur.) Constitutional amendments were passed after, instead of before, the President or Congress had acted: to free the slaves, to disqualify leading Confederates, to induce the States to grant the vote to Blacks. In effect, martial law was imposed at various times without following the forms for doing so. Time and time again Congress overrode the most serious and

---

[52] *Ibid.*, quoted on pp. 102-103.

weighty constitutional objections raised by President [Andrew] Johnson. [53]

It was under these circumstances – with the Southern States ruled by Military Dictatorship after the War Between the States – that the Radical Republicans sought to add three new amendments to the federal compact. Two of them dealt directly with the Negro race, serving the dual purposes of freeing the slaves without compensation in utter violation of the Bill of Rights and of enfranchising those freed slaves. By enfranchising freed Blacks and by disenfranchising and impoverishing as many Southern Whites as possible, the objective of the Radicals was to destroy free government in the Southern States, ruin the economic vitality of the South, and undermine the social fabric of American civilization. Radical Reconstruction proved to be no more humanitarian in its treatment of Negroes than it was in its treatment of Southern Whites. Many freed Negroes in the Southern States, as a direct consequence of the deliberate destruction of the Southern economy, were left without any means of support by their Northern "liberators," who seemed not to care one whit if they all died of starvation and disease.

Amendment Thirteen, which was declared ratified on December 18, 1865, declares:

> *Section 1.* Neither slavery nor involuntary servitude, except as a punishment for crime whereof the party shall have been duly convicted, shall exist within the United States, or any place subject to their jurisdiction.
> *Section 2.* Congress shall have power to enforce this article by appropriate legislation. [54]

Amendment Fifteen, which was declared ratified on March 30, 1870, asserts:

> *Section 1.* The right of citizens of the United States to vote shall not be denied or abridged by the United States or by any State on account of race, color, or previous condition of servitude.
> *Section 2.* The Congress shall have power to enforce this article by appropriate legislation. [55]

The truly strange and bizarre Radical Reconstruction Amendment was **Amendment Fourteen**, whose puzzling and ambiguously vague phraseology was sufficient to arouse widespread opposition throughout the Federal Union,

---

[53] Clarence B. Carson, *A Basic History of the United States*, Volume III, American Textbook Committee, Wadley, 1985, pp. 192-193.
[54] Richard B. Morris, *Op. cit.*, quoted on pp. 103-104.
[55] *Ibid.*, quoted on p. 105.

even among the Northern States. In his book, *We Hold These Truths*, Lawrence P. McDonald noted that this particular amendment never received the necessary votes in Congress to lawfully propose it to the States. "Two-thirds of both chambers did not vote for the resolution proposing the Fourteenth Amendment, as must be done under the Constitution for legal passage of such a resolution," he wrote. Nonetheless, he added, "The Radical Republican majority resolved that the resolution did pass, and submitted it to the States for ratification." [56]

If the manner in which the Fourteenth Amendment was proposed to the States was illegal, so too was the manner in which it was declared officially ratified by those States, a point which was stressed by Felix Morley in his book, *Freedom and Federalism*:

> In promoting the Fourteenth Amendment,...the Congress usurped power in a manner explicable only by the Radical exploitation of post-war emotionalism and excusable from no viewpoint. What happened was that the Southern States, with the single exception of Tennessee, within eight months flatly rejected the Amendment as certified to them in June, 1866. In several cases these rejections were by unanimous vote of both Houses; in all, by heavy majorities. Faced with this seeming impasse, and the collapse of all their plotting, the [Thaddeus] Stevens junta quickly prepared the infamous Reconstruction Act, adopted March 2, 1867. Although it was then almost two years since the complete collapse of the Confederacy, this Act defined its States as "rebel," declared that "no legal State government" existed in the area, placed these States under military rule, and added the blackmailing provision that this tyranny would continue until new and compliant legislatures "shall have adopted the Fourteenth Amendment." Only thereafter would any recalcitrant Southern State "be declared entitled to representation in Congress."
>
> President Johnson promptly vetoed this "Reconstruction Act" as completely and obviously unconstitutional and many suits against it were brought in the courts. But the Radicals overrode the veto, brought impeachment proceedings against the President "for high crimes and misdemeanors" and further threatened impeachment of the Supreme Court Justices, who thereupon supinely bowed themselves out of the picture on the curious reasoning (*Georgia v. Stanton*) that the issues aroused by the Act were political and not justiciable....
>
> Under military occupation the South perforce caved in. Compliant legislatures, composed for the most part of Negroes and Northern carpetbaggers, were installed and promptly adopted the previously rejected Fourteenth Amendment, though even then with opposition which under the circumstances was remarkable. The procedure was almost too preposterous for Secretary of State Seward, who on July 20, 1868, issued a very tentative proclamation of ratification. This pointed out that the legislatures of Ohio

---

[56] Lawrence Patton McDonald, *We Hold These Truths*, '76 Press, Seal Beach, 1976, p. 55.

and New Jersey had, on sober second thought, repudiated their earlier ratifications, and that in Arkansas, Florida, North Carolina, Louisiana, South Carolina and Alabama, in that order, alleged ratifications had been given "by newly constituted and newly established bodies avowing themselves to be, and acting as legislatures...."

Such back talk was not acceptable to the free-wheeling Radicals. The following day they jammed through a concurrent resolution asserting that the Amendment had been ratified by twenty-nine States, including those questioned by Seward, and ordering him to promulgate it as a part of the Constitution. On July 28, the Secretary of State did so, in a statement which made clear he was acting by command of Congress. And as a highly dubious part of the Constitution the Fourteenth Amendment has remained there ever since. [57]

Regarding the peculiar resolution passed by Congress to proclaim that the Fourteenth Amendment had been duly ratified by the requisite number of States, historian Clarence B. Carson has noted:

> This resolution had no precedent and has no antecedent. Moreover, only 27 States were listed by Congress as having ratified, and counting the Southern States there were 37 States; thus, three-fourths had not ratified by the count of Congress. [58]

In a two-page editorial in the September 27, 1957 issue of *U.S. News & World Report*, David Lawrence assessed the fraudulent methods employed to secure alleged ratification of Amendment Fourteen and candidly concluded that, "No such amendment was ever legally ratified." The very existence of such an amendment in our Federal Constitution, he pointed out, "is a disgrace to free government," and he reminded the American people that, "It is never too late to correct injustice." [59]

On July 28, 1868, the Fourteenth Amendment to the Constitution of the United States was illegally declared to have been duly ratified by the sovereign States. This unconstitutional, and therefore non-binding, amendment consists of five sections and is expressed in the following language:

> *Section 1*. All persons born or naturalized in the United States, and subject to the jurisdiction thereof, are citizens of the United States and of the State wherein they reside. No State shall make or enforce any law which shall abridge the privileges or immunities of citizens of the United States; nor shall any State deprive any person of life, liberty, or property,

---

[57] Felix Morley, *Freedom and Federalism*, Liberty Press, Indianapolis, 1981, pp. 89-91.
[58] Clarence B. Carson, *Op. cit.*, Volume III, p. 195.
[59] James Ronald Kennedy and Walter Donald Kennedy, *The South Was Right!*, Pelican Publishing Company, Gretna, 1994, quoted on pp. 375-376.

without due process of law; nor deny to any person within its jurisdiction the equal protection of the laws.

Section 2. Representatives shall be apportioned among the several States according to their respective numbers, counting the whole number of persons in each State, excluding Indians not taxed. But when the right to vote at any election for the choice of electors for President and Vice President of the United States, Representatives in Congress, the Executive and Judicial officers of a State, or the members of the Legislature thereof, is denied to any of the male inhabitants of such State, being twenty-one years of age, and citizens of the United States, or in any way abridged, except for participation in rebellion, or other crime, the basis of representation therein shall be reduced in the proportion which the number of such male citizens shall bear to the whole number of male citizens twenty-one years of age in such State.

Section 3. No person shall be a Senator or Representative in Congress, or elector of President and Vice President, or hold any office, civil or military, under the United States, or under any State, who, having previously taken an oath, as a member of Congress, or as an officer of the United States, or as a member of any State legislature, or as an executive or judicial officer of any State, to support the Constitution of the United States, shall have engaged in insurrection or rebellion against the same, or given aid and comfort to the enemies thereof. But Congress may by a vote of two-thirds of each House, remove such disability.

Section 4. The validity of the public debt of the United States, authorized by law, including debts incurred for payment of pensions and bounties for services in suppressing insurrection or rebellion, shall not be questioned. But neither the United States nor any State shall assume or pay any debt or obligation, incurred in aid of insurrection or rebellion against the United States, or any claim for the loss of emancipation of any slave; but all such debts, obligations, and claims shall be held illegal and void.

Section 5. The Congress shall have power to enforce, by appropriate legislation, the provisions of this article. [60]

Within the Constitutional Convention of 1787, the State of New Jersey had distinguished herself by displaying fidelity to the Federal Republic and by sponsoring a new plan of government based on strictly federal principles that bore her proud name. It was, therefore, only proper that New Jersey should have been one of the two *Northern* States to resist the illegal ratification process of the Fourteenth Amendment by *withdrawing* her previous ratification of the amendment. In two Joint Resolutions approved by her legislature on September 11, 1866, New Jersey formally rescinded her ratification, claiming, among other things, that the Fourteenth Amendment "is couched in ambiguous, vague and obscure language, the uniform resort of those who

---

[60] Richard B. Morris, *Op. cit.*, quoted on pp. 104-105.

seek to encroach upon public liberty." [61]

This assessment of vagueness and ambiguity has been confirmed repeatedly by succeeding interpreters who strive to find some coherent and consistent meaning in the general phraseology of the Fourteenth Amendment. Felix Morley, for instance, has commented that, "The full effect of this revolutionary change was not contemporaneously advertised. Indeed it was consistently played down by Thaddeus Stevens and his associates." [62] And Dr. Alfred H. Kelly, in the June 1956 issue of the *Michigan Law Review*, has noted that, "Political strategy called for ambiguity, not clarity."[63]

If ambiguity is the political strategy of the enemies of the Constitution, then clarity must be the proper strategy for the friends of liberty. In interpreting the Fourteenth Amendment, therefore, we must construe it in a manner that is consistent with the rest of the Federal Constitution, including the Tenth Amendment, which plainly asserts in language that is anything but ambiguous that the Government of the United States may exercise only powers that are *plainly* and *expressly* delegated to it. If we are to acknowledge the existence and validity of the Fourteenth Amendment, which, in truth, can not and should not be admitted, then we must interpret it as only an *amendment* or *minor addendum* to a Constitution for a league of sovereign States.

The Second, Third, and Fourth Sections of the Fourteenth Amendment, as is apparent from their phraseology, seem to bristle with the harsh invectiveness and punitive fury of the Radical Republicans. However, the precise phraseology employed actually nullifies the whole effect of these three sections. The wrath and fury of these sections, as expressly stated by their terms, are directed solely against those guilty of "insurrection" and "rebellion." Yet, exactly who were these nefarious traitors and rebels?

The Constitution emphatically states, in Article III, Section 3, Clause 1, that *treason* against the United States includes *waging war against the sovereign States*. But nowhere in the Constitution does it state that *secession* from the Union constitutes disloyalty, insurrection, or treason. Therefore, *the punitive portions of Sections Two, Three, and Four of the Fourteenth Amendment seem to have been applicable only to the Radical Republicans and their supporters in the Northern States*. But regardless of to which side – North or South – the punishment may have been applicable, considerations of *due process of law* certainly must have dictated that the punishments stipulated could only apply to those *individuals* who had been found guilty *in a court of law* of violating the stated provisions. To have inflicted the specified punishments without re-

---

[61] James Ronald Kennedy and Walter Donald Kennedy, *Op. cit.*, quoted on p. 373.
[62] Felix Morley, *Op. cit.*, pp. 87-88.
[63] *Ibid.*, quoted on p. 88.

gard to "due process of law" would have been a clear violation of the stipulation mandated in the First Section of this amendment, as well as a violation of the federal Bill of Rights.

It has been universally acknowledged that, of all the sections in Amendment Fourteen, only the First Section contains provisions whose meaningfulness has survived the perfidy of the dark age that gave birth to this obnoxious amendment. Yet, in spite of the fondness displayed by the U.S. Supreme Court for this particular part of the Constitution, it will be observed that Section One contains provisions that, *when properly and strictly construed,* are utterly devoid of significant meaning. For proof of this, let us analyze each and every provision in the First Section of Amendment Fourteen.

"All persons born or naturalized in the United States, and subject to the jurisdiction thereof, are citizens of the United States and of the State wherein they reside." Prior to the adoption of this amendment, U.S. citizenship was derived by virtue of being a citizen of one of the States or Territories of the United States – there was no such thing as a *citizen at large,* or a citizen of the United States who was not also a citizen of some State or Territory. This provision of the Fourteenth Amendment does not alter, in the slightest degree, this original concept of citizenship. It is, therefore, an utterly meaningless provision – it altered nothing.

"No State shall make or enforce any law which shall abridge the privileges or immunities of citizens of the United States." This provision of the Fourteenth Amendment is also totally meaningless, inasmuch as it is redundant, merely repeating the provision found in Article IV, Section 2, Clause 1 of the compact, which states that, "The Citizens of each State shall be entitled to all Privileges and Immunities of Citizens in the several States." The new provision, thus, changed nothing in the federal system, but only repeated what had already been provided for by the original text of the supreme law of the several States.

"Nor shall any State deprive any person of life, liberty, or property, without due process of law." The key issue here is the last four words in this provision. What is meant by *due process of law?* This terminology can only mean that the States, as well as the Federal Government, must confine their actions to *constitutional* means. Would any reasonable person assert that "due process of law" could have any other meaning than *constitutionally authorized proceedings?* Yet, this has always been true, from the moment the Constitution was ratified by the original thirteen States! Within the federal sphere, the Federal Constitution has always been supreme; and within the sphere of authority reserved to the States, the State Constitutions have always been supreme. The portion of Section One of the Fourteenth Amendment under consideration seems to merely reassert this basic truth, and it is, therefore, completely re-

dundant and meaningless.

"Nor deny to any person within its jurisdiction the equal protection of the laws." This last provision of Section One of the Fourteenth Amendment is totally redundant and merely repeats that portion of the Declaration of Independence which asserts that the American Theory of Government is founded on the concept that all men are created equal. Inasmuch as the American constitutional system has always been founded on this concept, the last provision in the First Section of the Fourteenth Amendment is utterly devoid of meaningful change – it effected no change whatsoever to our federal system.

As has been shown, the illegal Fourteenth Amendment, when properly and strictly construed, is utterly devoid of meaning. That Amendment made no change to our constitutional system of sovereign States and limited government. It is especially significant to note that the First Section is completely redundant of other provisions and concepts and cannot be interpreted as delegating a single new power to the Government of the United States.

It is possible, of course, that the Radical Republicans, in forcing this amendment on the States, harbored deceitful and fraudulent motives – motives that are not readily discernible from a plain reading of the Fourteenth Amendment. Even if this were true, however, it would change nothing. It is a long established principle of jurisprudence that a deception is non-enforceable and that a fraud is non-binding. If a fraud was intended, then the deception should be considered as dead as those Radicals who sought to perpetrate their ugly crime on the American people.

The Progressive Era Amendments

During the so-called Progressive Era of American history, four new amendments were incorporated into the Constitution of the United States. The first of these misnamed "progressive" Amendments was based on the confiscatory principles espoused in *The Communist Manifesto*, which advocated that a progressive income tax be utilized to confiscate the property of the more productive members of society and to facilitate the socialization of the means of production.

Amendment Sixteen, often referred to as the *Income Tax Amendment*, was declared ratified on February 25, 1913, and is in these words: "The Congress shall have power to lay and collect taxes on incomes, from whatever source derived, without apportionment among the several States, and without regard to any census or enumeration." [64] By means of this amendment, the

---

[64] Richard B. Morris, *Op. cit.*, quoted on p. 105.

property of all Americans – except for certain key interests associated with the monied aristocracy, whose property is allowed to be shielded from confiscation by *Tax Exempt Foundations* – became subject to seizure on a grand scale, and the financial power of the Federal Government was allowed by grow geometrically.

On May 31, 1913, **Amendment Seventeen**, which contains the three clauses cited below, was added to the federal compact:

> [1] The Senate of the United States shall be composed of two Senators from each State, elected by the people thereof, for six years; and each Senator shall have one vote. The electors in each State shall have the qualifications requisite for electors of the most numerous branch of the State legislatures.
>
> [2] When vacancies happen in the representation of any State in the Senate, the executive authority of such State shall issue writs of election to fill such vacancies: Provided, That the legislature of any State may empower the executive thereof to make temporary appointments until the people fill the vacancies by election as the legislature may direct.
>
> [3] This amendment shall not be so construed as to affect the election or term of any Senator chosen before it becomes valid as part of the Constitution. [65]

The effect of this Amendment was to rob the State *governments* of representation in the Government of the United States, a representation which the majority of the Founding Fathers had considered essential to the preservation of good government in the United States. The amendment, however, did not deny – and, indeed, could not have lawfully denied – to the States their equality of suffrage in the U.S. Senate. Nor did the amendment alter the fact that the Senate is founded on the sovereign equality of the States. The use of the expression, "the representation of any State in the Senate," within the Second Clause should be noted.

Amendment Eighteen, which was declared ratified on January 29, 1919, was based on a grand social experiment historically termed *Prohibition*. Only two major results were realized by the adoption of this ill-advised amendment. The first result was the alarming growth in our large cities of organized crime; and the second result was the equally alarming growth of the Internal Revenue Service. When the impropriety of legislating morality at the federal level became undeniable, this amendment was superseded or voided by the Twenty-First Amendment. Neither organized crime nor the Internal Revenue Service, unfortunately, could be as easily repealed as the Prohibition Era that gave rise to their great powers. Due to the fact that this amendment,

---

[65] *Ibid.*, quoted on p. 105.

which is quoted below, has been repealed, it is placed entirely in square brackets:

> [*Section 1*. After one year from the ratification of this article the manufacture, sale, or transportation of intoxicating liquors within, the importation thereof into, or the exportation thereof from the United States and all territory subject to the jurisdiction thereof for beverage purposes is hereby prohibited.
> *Section 2*. The Congress and the several States shall have concurrent power to enforce this article by appropriate legislation.
> *Section 3*. This article shall be inoperative unless it shall have been ratified as an amendment to the Constitution by the legislatures of the several States, as provided in the Constitution, within seven years from the date of the submission thereof to the States by the Congress.] [66]

Finally, on August 26, 1920, the last of the so-called Progressive Era Amendments was added to the Federal Constitution. Like the Fifteenth Amendment, **Amendment Nineteen** was a small but significant blow against the reserved rights of the States to establish *voting qualifications*. The leftists who had urged the adoption of the latter amendment undoubtedly hoped that, by enfranchising American women, the newly empowered voters would prove as easily gullible and misled as those who had been enfranchised by Amendment Fifteen. The First Clause of Amendment Nineteen declares: "The right of citizens of the United States to vote shall not be denied or abridged by the United States or by any State on account of sex." The remaining clause states: "Congress shall have power to enforce this article by appropriate legislation." [67]

The New Deal Amendments

Two amendments were added to the federal compact at the start of President Franklin D. Roosevelt's long reign over America, and one was added a few years after his death. **Amendment Twenty**, which was incorporated into the Constitution on February 6, 1933, revised some of the rules for electing the President and Vice President of the United States. This amendment reads as follows:

> *Section 1*. The terms of the President and Vice President shall end at noon on the 20th day of January, and the terms of Senators and Repre-

---

[66] *Ibid.*, quoted on pp. 105-106.
[67] *Ibid.*, quoted on p. 106.

sentatives at noon on the 3rd day of January, of the years in which such terms would have ended if this article had not been ratified; and the terms of their successors shall then begin.

Section 2. The Congress shall assemble at least once in every year, and such meeting shall begin at noon on the 3rd day of January, unless they shall by law appoint a different day.

Section 3. If, at the time fixed for the beginning of the term of the President, the President elect shall have died, the Vice President elect shall become President. If a President shall not have been chosen before the time fixed for the beginning of his term, or if the President elect shall have failed to qualify, then the Vice President elect shall act as President until a President shall have qualified; and the Congress may by law provide for the case wherein neither a President elect nor a Vice President elect shall have qualified, declaring who shall then act as President, or the manner in which one who is to act shall be selected, and such person shall act accordingly until a President or Vice President shall have qualified.

Section 4. The Congress may by law provide for the case of the death of any of the persons from whom the House of Representatives may choose a President whenever the right of choice shall have devolved upon them, and for the case of the death of any of the persons from whom the Senate may choose a Vice President whenever the right of choice shall have devolved upon them.

Section 5. Sections 1 and 2 shall take effect on the 15th day of October following the ratification of this article.

Section 6. This article shall be inoperative unless it shall have been ratified as an amendment to the Constitution by the legislatures of three-fourths of the several States within seven years from the date of its submission. [68]

On December 5, 1933, Prohibition *at the federal level* was officially repealed by the adoption of **Amendment Twenty-One**, the only amendment ever ratified by State Ratification Conventions. By the adoption of this amendment, the moral issue of alcohol consumption was returned exclusively to the jurisdiction of the sovereign States. This amendment, as a consequence, did not guarantee that the United States would be universally "wet." It merely affirmed that the decision would remain solely with the States, where it properly belonged. The State of Mississippi, for one, decided to remain "dry" for a number of years after the repeal of federal Prohibition.

As this amendment declares:

Section 1. The eighteenth article of amendment to the Constitution of the United States is hereby repealed.

Section 2. The transportation or importation into any State, Territory, or possession of the United States for delivery to use therein of in-

---

[68] *Ibid.*, quoted on pp. 106-107.

toxicating liquors, in violation of the laws thereof, is hereby prohibited.

    Section 3. This article shall be inoperative unless it shall have been ratified as an amendment to the Constitution by conventions in the several States, as provided in the Constitution, within seven years from the date of the submission hereof to the States by the Congress. [69]

When Thomas Jefferson established a precedent by declining to serve as President for more than two terms, all his successors to that office followed his example, *except for Franklin D. Roosevelt*, whose four successive terms in the Presidency transformed him, in effect, into our first King or Monarch. In response to the bad example set by President Roosevelt, **Amendment Twenty-Two** was added to the Constitution on February 26, 1951. In adopting this amendment, the sovereign States belatedly acknowledged that the Federal Republicans within the Constitutional Convention of 1787, and that such Antifederalists as Mr. Jefferson, had been correct in their opinion that the constitutional structure of the Presidency required the addition of a term limitation provision.

    As this amendment states:

    Section 1. No person shall be elected to the office of the President more than twice, and no person who has held the office of President, or acted as President, for more than two years of a term to which some other person was elected President shall be elected to the office of President more than once. But this Article shall not apply to any person holding the office of President when this Article was proposed by the Congress, and shall not prevent any person who may be holding the office of President, or acting as President, during the term within which this Article becomes operative from holding the office of President or acting as President during the remainder of such term.

    Section 2. This article shall be inoperative unless it shall have been ratified as an amendment to the Constitution by the legislatures of three-fourths of the several States within seven years from the date of its submission to the States by the Congress. [70]

The Second Radical Reconstruction Amendments

    Beginning with the infamous and unconstitutional 1954 Supreme Court school integration decision and the treasonous 1957 invasion of Little Rock, Arkansas by federal troops, the United States entered into a *Second Radical Reconstruction Period*, which lasted for nearly two decades. It was dur-

---

[69] *Ibid.*, quoted on p. 107.
[70] *Ibid.*, quoted on pp. 107-108.

ing this disturbing and distressing period in American history that the last four amendments were incorporated into the Federal Constitution. Three of the four new amendments were designed to further transfer jurisdiction over *voting qualifications* from the States to the Federal Government and to extend, as widely as possible, the franchise to every conceivable voter. The objective, undoubtedly, was to enfranchise those who directly benefit from the Welfare State, by allowing them to vote for those politicians who are willing to support the socialistic redistribution of wealth.

By the provisions of **Amendment Twenty-Three**, which was adopted on March 29, 1961, the *District of Columbia* was officially recognized as the equivalent of a *sovereign State*, at least in regard to electing the President and Vice President of the United States. If the goal had been only to enfranchise the residents of Washington, D.C., such an objective could easily have been accomplished by recognizing those inhabitants as citizens of a neighboring State, either Maryland or Virginia. Or, the same result could have been realized by granting to the residents of the federal capital a number of electoral votes equivalent to the number of Representatives it would have if it were a State. Yet, by granting to the people of Washington, D.C., an electoral vote equivalent to a proportional number of Representatives *plus two Senators*, this repugnant Amendment made a mockery of the concept of Statehood.

As this amendment reads:

> *Section 1.* The district constituting the seat of the United States shall appoint in such manner as the Congress may direct:
> A number of electors of President and Vice President equal to the whole number of Senators and Representatives in Congress to which the District would be entitled if it were a State, but in no event more than the least populous State; they shall be in addition to those appointed by the States, but they shall be considered, for purposes of the election of President and Vice President, to be electors appointed by a State; and they shall meet in the District and perform such duties as provided by the twelfth article of amendment.
> *Section 2.* The Congress shall have power to enforce this article by appropriate legislation. [71]

On January 23, 1964, **Amendment Twenty-Four** was added to the compact, enabling federal politicians to inaugurate the widespread practice of purchasing their offices with funds obtained from the public treasury:

> *Section 1.* The right of citizens of the United States to vote in any primary or other election for President or Vice President, for electors for

---

[71] *Ibid.*, quoted on p. 108.

President or Vice President, or for Senator or Representative in Congress, shall not be denied or abridged by the United States or any State by reason of failure to pay any poll tax or other tax.

    Section 2. The Congress shall have power to enforce this article by appropriate legislation. [72]

Amendment Twenty-Five was incorporated into the Constitution of the United States on February 10, 1967, and provides a detailed process for filling the office of the Presidency in the event a vacancy should occur:

    Section 1. In case of the removal of the President from office or of his death or resignation, the Vice President shall become President.

    Section 2. Whenever there is a vacancy in the office of the Vice President, the President shall nominate a Vice President who shall take office upon confirmation by a majority vote of both Houses of Congress.

    Section 3. Whenever the President transmits to the President pro tempore of the Senate and the Speaker of the House of Representatives his written declaration that he is unable to discharge the powers and duties of his office, and until he transmits to them a written declaration to the contrary, such powers and duties shall be discharged by the Vice President as Acting President.

    Section 4. Whenever the Vice President and a majority of either the principal officers of the executive departments or of such other body as Congress may by law provide, transmit to the President pro tempore of the Senate and the Speaker of the House of Representatives their written declaration that the President is unable to discharge the powers and duties of his office, the Vice President shall immediately assume the powers and duties of the office as Acting President.

    Thereafter, when the President transmits to the President pro tempore of the Senate and the Speaker of the House of Representatives his written declaration that no inability exists, he shall resume the powers and duties of his office unless the Vice President and a majority of either the principal officers of the executive department or of such other body as Congress may by law provide, transmit within four days to the President pro tempore of the Senate and the Speaker of the House of Representatives their written declaration that the President is unable to discharge the powers and duties of his office. Thereupon Congress shall decide the issue, assembling within forty-eight hours for that purpose if not in session. If the Congress, within twenty-one days after receipt of the latter written declaration, or, if Congress is not in session, within twenty-one days after Congress is required to assemble, determines by two-thirds vote of both Houses that the President is unable to discharge the powers and duties of his office, the Vice President shall continue to discharge the same as Acting President; otherwise, the President shall resume the powers and duties of his office. [73]

---

[72] *Ibid.*, quoted on p. 108.
[73] *Ibid.*, quoted on pp. 108-109.

It is an historical curiosity that, shortly after this amendment was added to the Constitution, a bizarre series of events occurred in the Administration of President Richard M. Nixon. It began with the resignation, in disgrace, of Vice President Spiro T. Agnew, and the *appointment* of Gerald R. Ford as a replacement Vice President. This was followed by the coerced resignation, in disgrace over the Watergate Scandal, of President Nixon himself. After assuming the office of the Presidency, Mr. Ford *appointed* Nelson A. Rockefeller to be the new Vice President. As a consequence, the United States had, for the first time in its history, a President and a Vice President, neither of whom had ever been approved for high office by the peoples of the several States. It is left to the student of constitutional government to speculate on the connection, if any, between the Twenty-Fifth Amendment and this strange series of events.

On July 1, 1971, **Amendment Twenty-Six** was incorporated into the Federal Constitution, which further reduced the authority of the States to establish *voting qualifications*. The First Section of this amendment states that, "The right of citizens of the United States, who are eighteen years of age or older, to vote shall not be denied or abridged by the United States or by any State on account of age." Section Two provides that, "The Congress shall have power to enforce this article by appropriate legislation." [74]

It is of interest to note the views of young Americans who, at the time this amendment was before the States for consideration, would be considered its immediate beneficiaries. At Meridian High School in Meridian, Mississippi, for example, a poll was conducted early in January of 1971 to ascertain the opinion of seniors towards this amendment. When asked what changes such an amendment would have on future elections, the answers of the students ranged from no change at all to a "communist landslide." [75] Although many of those polled believed that the younger voters would naturally be inclined to vote as their parents do, others were of the opinion that, as a consequence of lowering the voting age, American politics would become more radicalized and socialist oriented. And that, undoubtedly, was the hope entertained by the forces behind the amendment.

The Revised Articles of Confederation

It is evident from this survey of the various provisions of the Constitu-

---

[74] *Ibid.*, quoted on p. 110.
[75] Allen Brooks and Lisa Bourdeaux, "Eighteen Year Old Vote: Change and Challenge," *The Wildcat*, January 22, 1971, quoted on p. 2.

tion of the United States that, under the new compact, as under the old Articles of Confederation, the Federal Union was designed to rest upon the foundation of sovereign States. So similar was the new Confederation under the Constitution of 1787 to the old one under the Articles of Confederation, that the style of the old Union – the *United States of America* – was retained and perpetuated in the new Union of States.

The Government of the United States, as is evident from the very specific and limited powers delegated to it, was intended only to conduct the foreign affairs of the league of States. All domestic or internal affairs, on the other hand, were reserved to the exclusive control and jurisdiction of the several States, whose governments were intended to serve as the principal or primary level of authority within the American constitutional system. The Constitution of 1787, in a word, was nothing more than *revised Articles of Confederation*!

This is an undeniable fact that even the authors of *The Federalist Papers* willingly acknowledged. In the *Federalist*, No. 45, for instance, James Madison detailed the constitutional or organic nature of our federal system at considerable length. This is how he explained the *system of government* established in the United States of America by the Federal Constitution:

> The State governments will have the advantage of the Federal Government, whether we compare them in respect to the immediate dependence of the one on the other; to the weight of personal influence which each side will possess; to the powers respectively vested in them to the predilection and probable support of the people; to the disposition and faculty of resisting and frustrating the measures of each other.
>
> The State governments may be regarded as constituent and essential parts of the Federal Government; whilst the latter is nowise essential to the organization of the former. Without the intervention of the State legislatures, the President of the United States cannot be elected at all. They must in all cases have a great share in his appointment, and will, perhaps, in most cases, of themselves determine it. The Senate will be elected absolutely and exclusively by the State legislatures. Even the House of Representatives, though drawn immediately from the people, will be chosen very much under the influence of that class of men, whose influence over the people obtains for themselves an election into the State legislatures. Thus, each of the principal branches of the Federal Government will owe its existence more or less to the favor of the State governments, and must consequently feel a dependence, which is more likely to beget a disposition too obsequious than too overbearing towards them. On the other side, the component parts of the State governments will in no instance be indebted for their appointment to the direct agency of the Federal Government, and very little, if at all, to the local influence of its members.
>
> The number of individuals employed under the Constitution of the

United States will be much smaller than the number employed under the particular States. There will consequently be less of personal influence on the side of the former than of the latter. The members of the legislative, executive, and judiciary departments of thirteen or more States, the justices of peace, officers of militia, ministerial officers of justice, with all the county, corporation, and town officers, for three millions and more of people, intermixed, must exceed, beyond all proportion, both in number and influence, those of every description who will be employed in the administration of the federal system. Compare the members of the three great departments of the thirteen States, excluding from the judiciary department the justices of peace, with the members of the corresponding departments of the single government of the Union; compare the militia officers of three millions of people with the military and marine officers of any establishment which is within the compass of probability, or, I may add, of possibility, and in this view alone, we may pronounce the advantage of the States to be decisive. If the Federal Government is to have collectors of revenue, the State governments will have theirs also. And as those of the former will be principally on the seacoast, and not very numerous, whilst those of the latter will be spread over the face of the country, and will be very numerous, the advantage in this view also lies on the same side. It is true, that the Confederacy is to possess, and may exercise, the power of collecting internal as well as external taxes throughout the States; but it is probable that this power will not be resorted to, except for supplemental purposes of revenue; that an option will then be given to the States to supply their quotas by previous collections of their own; and that the eventual collection, under the immediate authority of the Union, will generally be made by the officers, and, according to the rules, appointed by the several States....

The powers delegated by the proposed Constitution to the Federal Government are few and defined. Those which are to remain in the State governments are numerous and indefinite. The former will be exercised principally on external objects, as war, peace, negotiation, and foreign commerce; with which last the power of taxation will, for the most part, be connected. The powers reserved to the several States will extend to all the objects which, in the ordinary course of affairs, concern the lives, liberties, and properties of the people, and the internal order, improvement, and prosperity of the State.

The operations of the Federal Government will be most extensive and important in times of war and danger; those of the State governments in times of peace and security. As the former periods will probably bear a small proportion to the latter, the State governments will here enjoy another advantage over the Federal Government. The more adequate, indeed, the federal powers may be rendered to the national defence, the less frequent will be those scenes of danger which might favor their ascendancy over the governments of the particular States.

If the new Constitution be examined with accuracy and candor, it will be found that the change which it proposes consists much less in the addition of new powers to the Union, than in the invigoration of its original powers. The regulation of commerce, it is true, is a new power; but that seems to be an addition which few oppose, and from which no apprehensions are entertained. The powers regulating to war and peace, armies and fleets, treaties and finance, with the other more considerable powers, are all vested in the existing Congress by the Articles of Confederation. The proposed change does not enlarge these powers; it only substitutes a more effectual mode of administering them. [76]

So far from effecting a great revolution in the American system of government, the Constitution of 1787 merely invigorated the basic principles that had been enshrined in the old Articles of Confederation. Even those Founding Fathers such as James Madison and Alexander Hamilton, who had diligently worked to supplant the federal system with a national system in the Federal Convention, conceded that the Federal Republicans had been victorious in the Philadelphia Convention.

As Mr. Madison candidly observed in the *Federalist*, No. 40, regarding the basic principles on which our current Federal Constitution is founded:

> I ask, What are these principles? Do they require that, in the establishment of the Constitution, the States should be regarded as *distinct and independent sovereigns*? They *are* so regarded by the Constitution proposed....Do these principles, in fine, require that the powers of the general government should be limited, and that, beyond this limit, the States should be left in possession of their *sovereignty and independence*? We have seen that, in the new government *as in the old*, the general powers are limited; and that the States, in all unenumerated cases, are left in the enjoyment of their *sovereign and independent jurisdiction*.
>
> The truth is that the great principles of the Constitution proposed by the Convention may be considered *less as absolutely new, than as the expansion of principles which are found in the Articles of Confederation*. [Emphasis added] [77]

Although the Government of the United States has admittedly grown to gargantuan proportions since the days of its first establishment, this tremendous growth in power, dominance, and influence has been achieved in utter violation of the letter and spirit of the supreme law of the land. While all Americans may today groan under the miseries of a Leviathan State, it will be perceived that our Federal Constitution, although ignored and neglected, still survives. And as long as it continues to live, there is still hope that the American people may someday rise up and, in a thunderous voice, demand

---

[76] Alexander Hamilton, James Madison, and John Jay, *The Federalist Papers*, New American Library, New York, 1961, pp. 290-293.

[77] *Ibid.*, pp. 249-251.

the restoration of constitutionally limited government.

Chapter Fourteen

Conclusions

During the course of our great inquiry into the origin of the United States of America, we have covered considerable ground, discovering a number of significant principles relative to constitutional government in the process. Our inquiry began with the inception of American civilization at the colonies of Jamestown and Plymouth Plantation, and we have traced the evolution of that civilization through the formation of thirteen separate British colonies and through the conversion of those colonies into sovereign States by virtue of the American Revolution and the Declaration of Independence. We have also traced the evolution of the Federal Union between those sovereign States from the Articles of Confederation through the Philadelphia Convention of 1787 and the adoption of our present Federal Constitution.

To conclude our investigation into the development of the American constitutional system, we should summarize the significant principles that have been brought to light as a result of our great inquiry. At this point, the following concepts pertinent to the origin of the United States should be readily apparent to the student of constitutional government:

1. American civilization was conceived during the years 1608 to 1620, with the founding of settlements at Jamestown and Plymouth Plantation. When the early settlers in the New World rejected *socialism* and embraced the concept of *government-by-the-consent-of-the-governed*, the future greatness of American civilization was assured. Over the course of time, other settlements arose in North America, and these various settlements eventually all became the colonial possessions of Great Britain. Although these thirteen colonies – Georgia, South Carolina, North Carolina, Virginia, Maryland, Pennsylvania, Delaware, New Jersey, New York, Connecticut, Rhode Island, Massachusetts, and New Hampshire – belonged to the same Empire and were physically juxtaposed along the Atlantic seaboard of North America, each was *politically independent* from the others. And within each of these colonies, local autonomy through democratic legislatures flourished.

2. By means of the socialistic *mercantile system*, the British Government sought to economically exploit its colonies for the benefit of a monied aristocracy in England. Initially, this oppressive system was enforced with a lack of

vigor. But with the coming to power of King George III, the new Tory regime in Great Britain sought to invigorate the enforcement of the system of socialist exploitation. When the American colonies offered resistance, the British Government moved to rob the American people of their *rights as Englishmen* in violation of the British Constitution. Colonial protests were ignored by the government of England, and when the British Government attempted to inaugurate a campaign to *disarm* the colonial militias, the results were the famous 1775 shot heard 'round the world and the start of the Revolutionary War. Initially, the objective of the colonists in that war was to secure recognition of their basic rights as Englishmen under the British Constitution.

3. After more than a year of warfare, all thirteen colonies resolved to transform the *Revolutionary War* into a *War of Independence*. This transformation was signaled by the publication, on July 4, 1776, of the unanimous Declaration of Independence, written by Thomas Jefferson, the *Philosopher of the Revolution*. Within this Declaration, the colonies – now free, sovereign, and independent States – established the Lockean-Jeffersonian Theory of Government as the foundation of the American constitutional system, enumerated the many crimes of the British Government, and announced the birth of thirteen sovereign American States. *The sole purpose of the War of Independence was to secure the sovereignty of each of the former North American colonies*, an objective that was realized within the Treaty of Paris of 1783, wherein the British Government formally acknowledged the sovereignty of the States, mentioning each State by name.

4. By asserting, within the Declaration of Independence, *that all men are created equal*, the objective of the American Founding Fathers was not to deny the established *laws of nature*, but to conform to them. They were well aware of the fact that certain inequalities existed *naturally* among people – including differences based on race, sex, age, and natural abilities – and that it would be both impossible to remove those inequalities and improper for society to ignore them. For this reason, the American Revolution was waged exclusively as a *political* revolution, and not as a *social* revolution. Its objective was to secure the political rights of the American people, not to subvert the foundations of American civilization.

5. The *American Theory of Government*, as established within the first section of the Declaration of Independence, is based on the concept that all men are created equal, which, as we have determined, means only a rejection of the unnatural Divine Rights Theory of Government. According to the American Theory of Government, God granted certain inalienable rights as well as political powers to all citizens within society. To safeguard their rights,

the people form a *civil society* or *body politic* termed a *State*, institute a representative government for themselves, and delegate some of their political powers to that government. By this means, they establish a *Republic* for themselves, governed by a *republican form of government*. *Sovereignty*, or *political supremacy*, remains vested in the people of the State, who are thereby the *masters* of their political system, while their State government holds its powers only as a *trust*, and is thereby the *servant* of the people.

6. Under the American Theory of Government, two or more sovereign States may unite with one another in a *Federal Union* for purposes of common defense without ceasing to be perfect States. Together, they will form a *Federal Republic*, with a *Federal Government* empowered only to conduct their foreign affairs. By means of this *federal system of government*, the States – who are the *parties* to the *compact* or *Federal Constitution* – may enjoy the advantages of a united front in dealing with foreign powers, while simultaneously enjoying the advantages of local *home rule* over their own internal or domestic affairs. The Union thus formed between the States exists to serve the interests of those States and may be modified or abolished by them at will, and *each member of the Union retains all powers not expressly delegated to the Federal Government by the interstate compact or agreement.* Inasmuch as the *reason* why States form a Federal Union is to better preserve and maintain their separate sovereignties, *each State in the Union obviously retains its sovereignty while yet a member of the political association.*

7. After declaring their independence of the government of Great Britain, the thirteen American States proceeded to act upon the American Theory of Government by forming a Federal Union between themselves under the *Articles of Confederation*, a Union that was formally inaugurated in 1781, five years after the States had been born. The official name or style of the Confederacy was the *United States of America*, and the Articles expressly declared that each State in the Union retained its sovereignty and freedom. Furthermore, those Articles indicated that the reason why the United States of America existed was *to protect, defend, and preserve the sovereignty of the States!*

8. Following the successful conclusion of the War of Independence and the adoption of the Articles of Confederation, the United States entered into a "Critical Period," which was characterized by economic depression and the alarming appearance of *factions* among the American political and military leaders. Specifically, three separate and distinct factions appeared – the *Federal Republicans*, the *National Republicans*, and the *National Monarchists*. Although the Federal Republicans acknowledged that additional powers should be vested in the Federal Government, they were devoted to the republican form and federal system of government established under the Articles of Con-

federation. The National Republicans, while professing loyalty to the republican form of government, were determined that the federal system, including the sovereignty of the States on which that system was founded, should be replaced by a consolidated national system. The National Monarchists shared this desire to annihilate the federal system, and they also wished to replace the republican form of government established in the United States with an elitist monarchical form of government. The desire of some individuals to abolish the existing Federal Government resulted in at least one attempt to use the Continental Army to force a new political system on the United States at the point of a bayonet. Fortunately, this plot to erect a military despotism was thwarted by George Washington.

9. Recognizing the need for constitutional reformation, some of the States sent deputies to a 1786 Convention in Annapolis, Maryland, the result of which was an appeal for a more general Convention of the States. The existing Congress responded favorably to this request of the Annapolis Convention by urging the States to support the call for a Grand Convention. In this appeal from the Congress, the word "national" was employed for the first time, marking this appeal as the first official sign that some individuals had in mind constitutional changes that would be incompatible with a federal system. Twelve of the States responded favorably to this congressional appeal, although each and every one of them rejected the concept of *nationalism*. In the credentials given to their commissioners, all of these States deliberately avoided usage of the word "national" and instead restricted their delegates to the *sole and express purpose* of revising the Articles of Confederation to render the Federal Constitution adequate the exigencies of the Federal Republic. With these instructions and stipulations, the American people expected little more from the Philadelphia Convention of 1787 than a few proposed amendments to the Articles.

10. Shortly after convening in May of 1787, the Federal Convention resolved to conduct its business behind a *curtain of secrecy*, thus preventing the American people from witnessing the conduct of the assembled delegates. Even after the conclusion of the Grand Convention of the States, a deliberate attempt was made to prevent or delay the publication of the *records of the proceedings* of that Convention. Indeed, it was not until some three decades later that the official *Journal* of the Convention was made available to the public. And James Madison, who took the most copious notes in the Convention, refused to allow the publication of his notes during his lifetime. It was evident, by this concerted desire for *prolonged secrecy*, that some of the delegates had a lot to hide from the American people.

11. Within the Philadelphia Convention, all three political factions were represented, and a *coalition* or *alliance* was formed between the National

Republicans and the National Monarchists in an effort to defeat the Federal Republicans. The nationalist coalition sought to attain an early victory by utilizing the *element of surprise* and their initial advantage of *close unity*. Thus, as soon as the rule of secrecy had been adopted by the Convention, the *nationalist conspiracy* against the Federal Republic was earnestly pressed forward, and *before all twelve of the States had even arrived in Philadelphia*, the nationalists managed to secure an *early victory* for their proposition to replace the federal system with a national system. Owing to this early victory, procured by the surprising tactics of the nationalists, the champions of the Federal Republic quickly found themselves on the defensive.

12. After a few weeks of debate, the Federal Convention had before it *three plans of government*, each one representing the desires of a particular political faction. The *Virginia Plan*, urged by the National Republicans, proposed the creation of a *supreme National Government*. Although the States would ostensibly continue to exist under this plan, they would exist only as subordinate branches of the supreme national authority, which would possess the power to negative or veto any State law. The *Hamiltonian Plan* took this concept even farther, by proposing to essentially abolish the States altogether and to transform the proposed National Government into a monarchical government, headed by a President or King serving a life tenure of office and vested with more power than was exercised by either the despotic Louis XIV of France or George III of England. The *New Jersey Plan*, on the other hand, sought to preserve both the republican form and the federal system of government established by the Articles of Confederation. The Hamiltonian Plan was considered as *too extreme* by nearly all the delegates, and the National Monarchists accordingly rallied around the Virginia Plan. The New Jersey Plan, when put to a vote, *was defeated*. The Federal Republicans, however, were determined to secure victory by a *new strategy* – a strategy that entailed *transforming* the Virginia Plan into a plan for a Federal Republic.

13. The first indication that the Federal Republicans would succeed in their new strategy occurred when they successfully *expunged* the objectionable word "national" from the evolving new Constitution. As a consequence of this great victory, that repugnant word was *deliberately stricken out* of the new compact no less than *twenty-six times*! Furthermore, the Convention agreed to the motion of the Federal Republicans that the new Constitution should go forth to the States *as an amendment to the Articles of Confederation*. The truly decisive victory for the Federal Republicans, however, occurred when the Philadelphia Convention agreed to adopt the *Connecticut Compromise*, which provided for representation and suffrage in the U.S. Senate to be based on *the sovereign equality of the States*. Such a basis of representation and suffrage was,

of course, *totally incompatible with a national system*, and this great victory was accordingly regarded by the Federal Convention as *a conclusive defeat for the nationalist conspiracy*. With this decisive victory, the *nationalist coalition* fell apart, and from that point onward, the Federal Republicans were able to *dominate* the Grand Convention and thereby ensure that the Convention's final product would be compatible with a Federal Union between sovereign States.

14. When the proposed compact was presented to the sovereign States for their consideration, the *proponents of ratification* styled themselves *Federalists* and referred to their opponents as *Antifederalists*, all in an attempt to assure the American people that the new government, like the old one, would be federal in nature, and not a National Government. And in each State, the new Constitution was ratified with the understanding that it was a *Federal Constitution*. A number of States, in fact, affixed official *Declarations of Understanding* to this effect to their formal ratification acts. Furthermore, to prevent any possible future misunderstanding in this regard, a host of proposed amendments for a *Bill of Rights* were recommended for adoption by the ratifying States. Chief among these proposals was the one eventually added to the compact as *Amendment Ten*, which expressly defined the system of government established by the Constitution as a *federal system*, wherein all powers not delegated to the Federal Government are reserved to the several States. The Tenth Amendment thus succinctly summarized the foundation of the Federal Union.

15. Several legacies from the Constitutional Era have endured to this very day. Chief among them is the collection of essays written by Alexander Hamilton, James Madison, and John Jay, collectively referred to as *The Federalist Papers*. Although these essays contain a wealth of accurate and valuable explanations of the various principles on which the Federal Constitution is founded, they also contain a number of erroneous concepts and fallacious assumptions. The authors of those papers were especially reckless in their inconsistent usage of terminology, vesting *sovereignty* in everything from the *people* to the *government*, using the terms *federal* and *national* as though they were equivalent, and referring to the United States as everything from a *Confederate Republic* to a consolidated *Nation*. Of particular significance is the dangerous description of the federal judiciary presented by Alexander Hamilton and the confused analysis of our federal system presented by James Madison. None of the fallacious theories espoused by the writers on these subjects is supported by the records of the Grand Convention or by the plain words of the Constitution of 1787.

16. An examination of the provisions of the Constitution of the United

States reveals that it truly is a *Federal Constitution*. The *powers* vested in the Federal Government by it are only those powers necessary to conduct the *foreign affairs* of the American States. All other powers relative to the *internal or domestic affairs* of the American people are expressly *reserved* to the sovereign States of the Federal Union. The *structure* of the Federal Government also reveals it to be genuinely federal in nature. Representation in the *Senate*, of course, is based on *the sovereign equality of the States*. Yet, even representation in the *House of Representatives* is based on Statehood, and the Constitution plainly refers to those Representatives as the *Representation from each State*. The *Executive Branch* of government is likewise based on the principle of federal representation, with *each State* having a number of *electoral votes* equal to the sum of the number of its Senators and Representatives. The *Judicial Branch* of the general government, of course, is appointed by the *federal head* of the Executive Branch, an appointment that must be confirmed by the *federal representatives* in the Senate. Although the Judicial Branch of the Federal Government is *monarchical* in nature, the other two branches are *republican* in form and substance.

17. By the terms of the *Supremacy Clause*, the *supreme law of the land* is declared to be the *Constitution*, all federal laws *made in pursuance of it*, and all treaties *made under the authority of the compact*. Federal laws and treaties *not* made in pursuance of the Constitution are non-binding, but are *null, void, and of no force*. By the terms of this Supremacy Clause, it is the *State governments* who are charged with maintaining and preserving the *supreme law of the several States*. This concept of *supremacy* was copied from the Articles of Confederation and from the New Jersey Plan, and was introduced to the Federal Convention by *Luther Martin*, the great Orator of Federalism and a staunch champion of States' Rights. The *objective* of the Federal Republicans, in introducing the Supremacy Clause in the Convention, was *to defeat nationalism* and to ensure compatibility with the concept of sovereign States.

18. Finally, it must be noted that the States, and only the States, may lawfully *amend* the Federal Constitution. Neither the President of the United States, the Congress, nor the U.S. Supreme Court is lawfully empowered either to change the meaning of a single provision in the compact or to add a new provision to the Constitution. Because the States, and only the States, are the *parties to the compact*, they, and they alone, may alter the Constitution. Consequently, *the Constitution is what the States say it is*, and not what the Federal Government says it is. The States may, for example, constitutionally abolish the federal judiciary, as well as any other branch of the general government. But neither the U.S. Supreme Court nor any other branch of the Federal Government can constitutionally abolish the States, no matter how

much that government may desire to do so. *This fact alone proves that the States are sovereign, and that they comprise the supreme power within the American political system.* The Constitution – the supreme law of the land – represents the sovereign will of the peoples of the several States and serves to limit and confine the Government of the United States to the expressly delegated powers. Should that government escape from the confining chains of the Constitution, it would then have possession of a boundless field of power, and liberty would invariably cease to exist in America.

The Organic Structure of the United States

With a proper understanding of the origin of the United States of America, the true organic nature of the Federal Union becomes readily apparent. The *United States of America* came into existence as a military alliance between sovereign States by virtue of the Declaration of Independence. The *United States of America*, by virtue of the Articles of Confederation, then acquired a political nature as a Confederation of those same sovereign States. And our present Federal Constitution, as expressed within its Preamble, was intended for that same Confederacy, styled the *United States of America*. According to the terms of the Articles, the Confederation from 1781 to 1789 existed *between the States*. And according to Article VII our present federal compact, the Confederation continues to exist *between the States*.

The organic structure of the United States that had existed under the Articles of Confederation remained unaltered by the adoption of the new Articles of Union. Under the old Articles, terminology such as *Federal Government*, *Federal Union*, *Federal Constitution*, and *Federal Republic* were all applicable to the then-existing constitutional system. After the ratification of the Constitution of 1787, those very same terms continued to have validity, proof that the constitutional system remained unaltered. Inasmuch as the Constitutional Convention had deliberately rejected the word "national," it may be said that all terminology based on that word is incompatible with the Constitution of the United States. Thus, words such as *National Constitution*, *National Government*, *National Union*, *National Republic*, and even *Nation* itself, are all inappropriate within our political system, unless, of course, such terms are used in reference to our *States, which comprise the only true nations in our constitutional system.*

Although we often hear such loose expressions as, "The United States is a great nation," or "The United States is the greatest nation the world has ever produced," such sentiments should not be confused with a treatise on the

Constitution. If such statements are expressed in time of war or in order to assert patriotic pride in our *general welfare* and *common defense*, then the sentiments are indeed appropriate, inasmuch as *it was the intention of the Founding Fathers to unite the States into one Republic in all matters relating to foreign nations.* However, inasmuch as *it was the intention of those same Founding Fathers to reserve to each State separately control over all domestic affairs,* such expressed sentiments are hardly patriotic when intended to deny the sovereignty of the States or to deny the existence of States' Rights. It is a point which can never be repeated too often, that *there is nothing patriotic about the subversion of a sovereign State!*

The American constitutional system is founded on the pillars of sovereign States that retain all powers not specifically delegated to the Federal Government. True *patriotism* requires that we support and defend the system of government established by our Constitution. In all matters relating to our foreign affairs, we should patriotically support the common defense of the United States. And in all matters relating to our internal or domestic affairs, we should support with equal patriotic fervor the rights constitutionally reserved to the several States. True *patriotism* demands nothing less from each and every citizen, as well as from each and every officer of the government, both State and federal.

Constitutionally speaking, the United States of America is not a nation in the political sense of the word. *The United States is a federation or league of sovereign Nations, styled States.* The very style of our Confederation – *the United States of America* – reveals its true nature. The words "of America," of course, refer to that portion of the globe in which the United States is located, and it must be noted that the United States is not the only political association situated in the New World. Guatemala, Peru, and Chile, for example, are also *American States*, and their citizens are therefore as much *Americans* as are the citizens of the United States.

The words "United States" also require attention. The first word is merely an *adjective* which describes the *noun* that follows, and the words are used in the Federal Constitution in a *plural sense* – in reference to a number of *States* that have *united* in a Confederation. It is of interest to note that, in Spanish, the title of our Confederacy is *los Estados Unidos*, and in French it is *les Etats Unis*. In each case, the literal translation is *the States United!* Even Americans have long grown accustomed to referring to the United States of America as a league or combination of States. During World War II, for instance, it was popular among U.S. servicemen stationed overseas to refer to their own country as "the States," and to refer to returning home as "going Stateside." Even the official slogan of our Confederation – *E Pluribus Unum* –

reveals the true nature of the organic structure of the United States. It literally means *one out of many*, and it signifies that one Federal Republic has been created from many sovereign Republics.

The official *flag* of the United States, popularly referred to as the *Stars and Stripes*, stands as a monument to American Statehood. What do those *stars* and those *stripes* represent, if not the sovereign States? The thirteen stripes signify the thirteen original States, and the stars represent each and every State that is currently a member of the federation. The blue background of the stars symbolizes the freedom and sovereignty of those States. The white and red colors of the stripes symbolize the purity of the American cause in the War of Independence and the blood that was spilled to secure State sovereignty and independence. *No design for a flag could have been better calculated to glorify the sovereignty of the States than the Stars and Stripes!*

Let us assume, for a moment, that a consolidated nation of Americans actually does exist, which we may refer to as simply the *State of America*. What political rights could this fictional consolidated nation enjoy under our constitutional system of government? By the terms of the Federal Constitution, representation in the House of Representatives is based on the respective populations of the several States, with *each State being guaranteed at least one Representative*. Yet, how many representatives does the *State of America* have in the lower branch of Congress? In the Senate, each State is entitled to equal suffrage and *each State is specifically entitled to two Senators*. How many Senators does the *State of America* have in the upper branch of Congress? In *Presidential elections*, each State is entitled to a number of electoral votes equal to its total number of Senators and Representatives. Inasmuch as the *State of America* has no Senators or Representatives, *it has no electoral votes*. If indeed such a consolidated nation exists, the failure of the Constitution to recognize its existence seems to have been a glaring oversight on the part of the Founding Fathers.

Then, too, there is the matter of exactly who are the *parties* to the federal compact. By the terms of Article VII of the Federal Constitution, the Constitution exists as a compact *between the States* who ratified it. And by the terms of Amendment Ten, those ratifying States reserved all powers not expressly yielded to the Federal Government. By agreement among the States, these same conditions would apply to all new States admitted into the Union after the adoption of the new compact. Furthermore, only the States may amend the Constitution of the United States. Where does all this leave our consolidated *State of America*? The *State of America* never ratified the Constitution, nor was it ever admitted into the Union as a legitimate State. Consequently, the *State of America* is not a party to the compact, is not a member of the Union, is not entitled to any constitutionally guaranteed rights, cannot participate in the amendment process, and has no constitutionally reserved powers!

It may be concluded from this brief analysis that a consolidated nation of Americans, if such a nation actually exists, has neither reserved rights nor any political powers in the federal system. *Such a nation, in short, could only exist as a nation of slaves!* All these observations, of course, are based on the false assumption that a consolidated or single nation of Americans actually exists. But as we have already demonstrated, no such consolidated nation exists. The *American people*, to be certain, do exist, just as *all the people of the world* actually exist. But all the people of the world do not exist as a single, consolidated nation – they exist only as separate and independent nations. In similar fashion, *the American people constitutionally exist only as sovereign States*.

It is only in their politically associated capacities as *sovereign States* that the Constitution recognizes an *American people*, and it is only in this capacity that the American people are represented in the Federal Government and reserve all powers not delegated to that government by the Federal Constitution. Only a desire to commit political suicide could induce the American people to wish to abandon their States in favor of an imaginary consolidated nation devoid of constitutionally recognized rights and reserved powers!

The word *State* is equivalent to the word *Nation*, which signifies that our *States* are actually our *Nations*, that the *State governments* actually constitute our true *National Governments*. As a consequence of this observation, the *United States* could be renamed the *United Nations* without altering the true meaning of the title of the American Confederacy. The word *federal* literally means *of a league – a league of States* – and such terms as Federal Government, Federal Republic, and Federal Constitution, thus literally mean *Government of the League*, *Republic of the League*, and *Constitution of the League*. The term *federal powers* is actually equivalent to the expression *powers over foreign affairs*, and the two expressions have been used interchangeably in such great masterpieces as John Locke's *Second Treatise of Government*.

Word associations are also helpful in ascertaining the true import and meaning of certain primary words. In this regard, the third edition of *Roget's International Thesaurus* is especially useful in further defining such significant terms as *federal, federation, federalize,* and *union*. Regarding the word *federal*, this thesaurus associates the term with the words "associative," "leagued," "associated," "federated," "confederated," "federate," "in league," "uniting," "partners with," "in partnership," and "confederate." [1] In addition, this the-

---

[1] *Roget's International Thesaurus*, Third Edition, Thomas Y. Crowell Company, New York, p. 25.

saurus associates the word *federation* with such words as "combination," "union," "junction," "alliance," "affiliation," "association," "confederation," "federalization," "fusion," and "coalition." [2] The term *federalize* is associated with the words "league," "ally," "join forces," "affiliate," "confederate," "unionize," "associate," "federate," "pool one's interests," "join fortunes with," "make common cause with," "band together," "team up with," and "go in partnership." [3] Finally, the words *federation* and *union* are associated with such terminology as "association," "alliance," "coalition," "league," "combine," "combination," "confederacy," and "confederation." [4] Not once does this thesaurus associate any of these key terms with the word *national*.

Without the existence of sovereign States, the United States would not exist. As we have observed in the course of our great inquiry into the origin of the United States, the States – meaning *representatives of those States* – were the only actors in the entire drama! As Jefferson Davis once noted, remove all reference to the States from the story of the creation of the United States of America, and what would remain would be of less account than the Shakespearean play of *Hamlet* with the role of the Prince of Denmark omitted. The United States, as we have observed, was created *by the States, for the States,* and *of the States*. Indeed, if all reference to the sovereign States were removed from our constitutional system – and we mean here more than a mere grammatical quibble – what, then, would we call our Confederation – the *United Nothing?*

The Lesson of Germany

During the course of the debates in the Constitutional Convention of 1787, some of the delegates — particularly James Madison of Virginia – displayed a strong tendency to cite examples from other federations of sovereign States in history as instructive in guiding the conduct and policy of the American States. If we may follow the example of the Founding Fathers in this regard, perhaps it might be enlightening to survey the sad fates of Federal Republics in other parts of the world during the Twentieth Century. And there are quite a number of fine illustrations that could be cited, all demonstrating the folly and tragedy of allowing centralization to subvert the sovereignty of the member States of a Federal Union.

We could, for instance, cite as a tragic example the disastrous and

---

[2] *Ibid.*, p. 25.
[3] *Ibid.*, p. 25.
[4] *Ibid.*, p. 518.

wicked federation styled the *Union of Soviet Socialist Republics* (USSR), where consolidation of authority and centralization of power in the hands of a Federal Government in Moscow formed the cornerstone of Communist oppression in the Soviet Union. The tyranny spawned by the Soviet Union's supreme National Government spread far beyond the boundaries of the Soviet Confederation and was felt in every quarter of the globe. Both in terms of human misery and in terms military defense expenditures, the consequences of centralizing all power in the Soviet Union cost the American people – and many other peoples around the globe – a vast sum in the latter half of the Twentieth Century. Could any other illustration be cited which would better demonstrate the evils that may arise when centralization converts a Federal Government into a totalitarian National Government?

We could also cite, as another example, the sad case of the *Federal Republic of Mexico*, where the destruction of the reserved rights of the Mexican States and the centralization of all power in the hands of its Federal Government in Mexico City has resulted in Marxist tyranny, characterized by massive poverty, extensive corruption, and fraudulent elections. In an effort to escape from this land of misery, untold numbers of starving Mexican peasants annually strive to slip unobserved across the border into the United States. What lesson may be learned by the American people from the tragic case of the Mexican Federal Republic?

Perhaps the most instructive case in the Twentieth Century, however, is the stark lesson provided by the Germanic federation of sovereign States. During the days of the old Weimer Republic, as history plainly indicates, Germany was a Federal Republic founded upon the sovereignty of its member States, which included Prussia and Bavaria. Following the defeat of Germany in the First World War, a socialist movement arose which sought to establish a Military Dictatorship in Germany. But standing squarely in the way of these conspirators was the federation of sovereign German States! A National Police State, the leader of this socialist movement realized, could never be erected on such a foundation. If an all-powerful, centralized Third Reich was to be established, he therefore concluded, States' Rights in Germany must be destroyed and the Federal Government must be transformed into a supreme National Government.

The name of this scheming politician, of course, was *Adolph Hitler*, and the movement he led was styled *National Socialism*. Years before his *nationalist conspiracy* succeeded in Germany, the future dictator of the Third Reich published the *blueprint* for his enslavement of the sovereign German States in his book, *Mein Kampf*, which, in English, means *My Camp*. Within this work, first published in 1924, Adolph Hitler devoted an entire chapter to "Federalism as a Mask." In the hope that this blueprint for Nazi tyranny may awaken the American people to the inherent dangers of subverting States' Rights, we shall quote some significant extracts from this chapter of *Mein Kampf.*

As Adolph Hitler wrote:

> The struggle between federalism and centralization so shrewdly propagated by the Jews in 1919-20-21 and afterward, forced the National Socialist movement, though absolutely rejecting it, to take a position on its essential problems.
>
> Should Germany be a *federated or a unified state*, and what for practical purposes must be understood by the two? To me the second seems the more important question, because it is not only fundamental to the understanding of the whole problem, but also because it is clarifying and possesses a conciliatory character.
>
> What is a federated state?
>
> By a federated state we understand a league of sovereign States which band together of their own free will, on the strength of their sovereignty; ceding to the totality that share of their particular sovereign rights which makes possible and guarantees the existence of the common federation.
>
> In practice this theoretical foundation does not apply entirely to any of the federated states existing on earth today. Least of all to the American Union, where, as far as the overwhelming part of the individual States are concerned, there can be no question of any original sovereignty, but, on the contrary, many of them were sketched into the total area of the Union in the course of time, so to speak. Hence in the individual States of the American Union we have mostly to do with smaller and larger territories, formed for technical, administrative reasons, and, often marked out with a ruler, States which previously had not and could not have possessed any State sovereignty of their own. For it was not these States that had formed the Union, on the contrary it was the Union which formed a great part of such so-called States. The very extensive special rights granted, or rather assigned, to the individual territories are not only in keeping with the whole character of this federation of States, but above all with the size of its area, its spatial dimensions which approach the scope of a continent. And so, as far as the States of the American Union are concerned, we cannot speak of their State sovereignty, but only of their constitutionally established and guaranteed rights, or better, perhaps, privileges. [5]

It would appear from this extract from *Mein Kampf* that either Adolph Hitler was deeply influenced by the arguments of American nationalists, or that American nationalists were deeply influence by Adolph Hitler. The arguments used by Mr. Hitler bear a disturbing resemblance to those used by the socialists – national as well as international – of both major political par-

---

[5] Adolph Hitler, *Mein Kampf,* Houghton Mifflin Company, Boston, (orig. pub. in 1924) 1971, pp. 565-566.

ties in the United States in their efforts to rob the American States of their reserved rights. If, indeed, our own tribe of modern nationalists has been inspired by *Mein Kampf*, then the exposure of this Nazi blueprint for tyranny truly is a public service to the American people.

The fallacies inherent in Adolph Hitler's analysis of the American Union are so obvious that they need only to be stated. In his entire analysis, not once did he refer to the fact that the original thirteen States existed prior to the Union, that the sovereignty of those original States was explicitly recognized by the Articles of Confederation, and that the Constitution of 1787 was founded on that same State sovereignty. Nor did he acknowledge that the State of Texas existed as the sovereign and independent Lone Star Republic for nearly a decade before being admitted to the American Union. Furthermore, Mr. Hitler failed to mention that, by agreement among the original States, all new States originating from the territorial possessions of the United States would be admitted into the Union *on the same footing*, as regards their sovereignty, as the original thirteen States.

These facts were omitted from his analysis, no doubt, because they did not conform to his predetermined conclusion that the American States exist merely "for technical, administrative reasons" of a supreme National Government. He therefore referred to the sovereign American States as "the individual territories," and spoke of their reserved rights guaranteed by the Tenth Amendment as "special rights granted, or rather assigned" by some supreme National Government in Washington, D.C. States' Rights in the United States, he therefore concluded, are no more than "privileges" that exist only by sufferance of a centralized authority.

After dispensing with State sovereignty in the United States, Adolph Hitler next directed his attention to State sovereignty in Germany:

> The above formulation is not fully and entirely applicable to Germany either. Although in Germany without doubt the individual States did exist first and in the form of States, and the Reich was formed out of them. But the very formation of the Reich did not take place on the basis of the free will or equal participation of the single States, but through the workings of the hegemony of one State among them, Prussia. The great difference between the German States, from the purely territorial standpoint, permits no comparison with the formation of the American Union, for instance. The difference in size between the smallest of the former federated States and the larger ones, let alone the largest, shows the non-similarity of their achievements, and also the inequality of their share in the founding of the Reich, the forming of the federated state. Actually, in most of these States there could be no question of a real sovereignty, except if State sovereignty was taken only as an official phrase. In reality, not only the past, but the present as well, had put an end to any number of these so-called

"sovereign States" and thus clearly demonstrated the weakness of these "sovereign" formations. [6]

The German States, it is apparent, did not survive Mr. Hitler's analysis any better than did the American States. According to Adolph Hitler, it is possible to speak of sovereign States only when such States are equivalent, or nearly equivalent, in *size* and *achievement*. This, of course, is like saying that individual citizens of unequal size and unequal achievement in the same society cannot possess the same rights. Smaller and weaker States, like smaller and weaker individuals in society, have no rights, other than the right to obey the dictates of the larger and more powerful members of the global community. There is a disturbing and uncanny resemblance between the arguments herein used by Mr. Hitler and those used by the larger States within the Constitutional Convention of 1787 to deny equality of suffrage in the Senate. There is also a striking resemblance between Mr. Hitler's arguments, that might makes right, and those which have been employed throughout history to defend the indefensible conduct of bullies, whether individuals or governments.

Looking at the other political factions then existent in Germany, Adolph Hitler ridiculed their pretended loyalty to States' Rights:

> It is an unequaled hypocrisy to bemoan to the masses of voters (for only toward them is the agitation of our present-day parties directed) the loss of the sovereign rights of the individual provinces, while all these parties without exception outbid one another in a policy of fulfillment which in its ultimate consequences could not but lead to deep-seated changes inside Germany. [7]

Elsewhere, he wrote:

> *Solely to blame for this [want of centralized power] are again the parties which incessantly harangue the patient mass of the voters about the necessary independence of the provinces, but at the same time promote and support a Reich policy which must lead inevitably to the elimination of the very last of these so-called "sovereign rights."* [8]

And again, Mr. Hitler wrote:

> Every so-called "theft of sovereign rights" from the Bavarian State by the Reich was accepted practically without resistance except for a repul-

---

[6] *Ibid.*, pp. 566-567.
[7] *Ibid.*, p. 569.
[8] *Ibid.*, p. 571.

sive yelping....The federative state idea, like religion in part, is only an instrument for...often unclean party interests. [9]

With such an unclean "federative state idea," the future ruler of the Third Reich would have no part. He therefore derived a "rule, basic for us National Socialists," which was expressed as follows and placed entirely in italics within his master blueprint:

> *A powerful National Reich, which takes into account and protects the outward interests of its citizens to the highest extent, can offer freedom within, without having to fear for the stability of the state. On the other hand, a powerful National Government can undertake and accept responsibility for great limitations on the freedom of the individual as well as the provinces, without damage to the Reich idea if in such measures the individual citizen recognizes a means toward the greatness of his Nation.* [10]

To justify this destruction of the rights of sovereign States and citizens alike within Germany, Adolph Hitler offered this explanation:

> Certainly all the states of the world are moving toward a certain unification in their inner organization. And in this Germany will be no exception. Today it is an absurdity to speak of a "State sovereignty" of individual provinces, which in reality the absurd size of these formations in itself fails to provide. The techniques of communication as well as administration steadily diminish the importance of the individual States. Modern communications, modern technology, make distance and space shrink more and more. A State of former days today represents only a province, and the states of the present formerly seemed like continents.[11]

Were these arguments sufficient to justify the destruction of inalienable rights and of sovereign States in Germany? Are they sufficient to justify destruction of those rights in the United States? The current state of *technology*, said Mr. Hitler, should ultimately be the determining factor that dictates the seat of political supremacy, and not historical and constitutional requirements. If the horse-and-buggy dictated that Bavaria and Prussia were sovereign States, then the airplane dictated that such sovereignty should be centralized in the German Reich, and the modern jet must now dictate that German sovereignty be surrendered to a New World Order! Had cellular telephones and personal computers been available to the Founding Fathers of the United States, Adolph Hitler would have us believe, they would have been induced,

---

[9] *Ibid.*, p. 573.
[10] *Ibid.*, p. 572.
[11] *Ibid.*, p. 572.

and even justified, to have centralized all power in a supreme National Government.

Against such a weighty argument as that presented on behalf of National Socialism, we can offer only the humble opinion that divisions of power, limited Constitutions, States' Rights, and local sovereignty, are all dictated, not by the nature of technology, but by *the nature of man*. The reason why the Bill of Rights was added to the American Constitution, for instance, had nothing whatsoever to do with the fact that the American people of that day had neither cars, planes, telephones, nor computers. The Tenth Amendment was added to the Federal Constitution only because the American people did not trust the politicians who might be chosen to administer the Government of the United States!

Technology has certainly changed drastically since 1787. *Can the same be said for the nature of man?* Has modern humanity found angels to govern mankind in the form of a Hitler, a Stalin, a Roosevelt, a Mao Tse-tung, or a Kennedy? Or does *human nature* yet dictate that politicians still can not and should not be entrusted with highly centralized and possibly unlimited powers? We leave these questions to verdict of mankind.

After stating his reasons for annihilating States' Rights in Germany, Adolph Hitler concluded his chapter on "Federalism as a Mask" with these words:

> *Moreover, a young victorious idea will have to reject any fetter which might paralyze its activity in pushing forward its conceptions. National Socialism as a matter of principle, must lay claim to the right to force its principles on the whole German Nation without consideration of previous federated State boundaries, and to educate it in its ideas and conceptions. Just as the churches do not feel bound and limited by political boundaries, no more does the National Socialist idea feel limited by the individual State territories of our fatherland.*
>
> *The National Socialist doctrine is not the servant of individual federated States, but shall some day become the master of the German Nation. It must determine and reorder the life of a people, and must, therefore, imperiously claim the right to pass over boundaries drawn by a development we have rejected.*
>
> *The more complete the victory of its ideas will be, the greater may be the particular liberties it offers internally.* [12]

So necessary was the destruction of federalism in Germany to the cause of National Socialism, that the Nazi leader, in his book, italicized every single word in these three paragraphs! The result of the destruction of States' Rights

---

[12] *Ibid.*, pp. 577-578.

in Germany, it scarcely needs to be mentioned, was precisely the opposite of the wonderful end promised by Adolph Hitler. In Germany, the death of State sovereignty signaled the death of freedom for the German people and the dawning of the dictatorship of the Nazi Party.

From the lessons taught by the fates of other federations in the Twentieth Century, the American people may learn much. Wherever centralization of power and the destruction of sovereign States has occurred, the results have invariably been oppression, misery, and tyranny. In Germany, as we have observed, the result of the destruction of States' Rights was *Nazi tyranny*. In Mexico, the subversion of federalism resulted in *Marxist tyranny*. And in the Soviet Union, centralization of power was the cornerstone of *Communist tyranny*. Today, in the United States, as we rush toward complete centralization and the total destruction of State sovereignty, what form of *tyranny* may we expect?

The Challenge We Face

As the student of constitutional government has undoubtedly perceived, the great *bulwark of freedom* within any political federation – whether in Germany, Mexico, the Soviet Union, or the United States – is the *sovereignty of the States*. Indeed, it may be truthfully stated that tyranny over the whole Confederation is completely impossible so long as States' Rights remain intact. When a Federal Government is properly confined to its proper and legitimate sphere of authority, and the States retain exclusive jurisdiction over their own domestic affairs, neither a Military Dictatorship nor a Police State is possible. Of necessity, tyranny requires highly centralized powers – without such centralized powers, tyranny cannot exist.

It is of interest and consequence to note the candid comments, or rather confessions, made to Ambassador Richard Washburn Child midway through the Twentieth Century by a prominent Italian Fascist and by a Soviet Communist. As the Fascist informed Mr. Child:

> The more concentrated are the powers and the wider the activities of government, the better are our final opportunities. Give us one spot where we can find the seed of power in the form of the army, the bureaucracy, also railroads, telegraphs and basic industries; that gives us our ideal target....When government has drawn into its hands power over production, distribution, and communication, it always builds a bureaucracy which taxes, irritates and meddles with labor. The first result is to put into a single basket all that we wish to seize; the second is to irritate the over-

taxed and impoverished mob which we will use to seize it. [13]

And the Communist said:

> The difficulty confronting our propaganda and plans in America is that the political system has in it so much of political self-government....Real power in America politically is that of the community, the real power economically is that of your financial and economic system. That is what constitutes the obstacle to communistic advance in America.[14]

Such candid confessions serve only to remind us of the warnings bequeathed to posterity by two of our Founding Fathers. "What has destroyed liberty and the rights of man in every government which has existed under the sun?" queried Thomas Jefferson, who supplied the answer without hesitation – "the generalizing and concentrating all cares and powers into one body." [15] Yet, perhaps it was, ironically, Alexander Hamilton who most succinctly expressed this warning during an address before the New York Ratification Convention. "The States can never lose their powers till the whole people of America are robbed of their liberties," he stated. "These must go together; they must support each other, or meet one common fate." [16]

As a result of the great efforts made by the friends of liberty during the Constitutional Era, the present Constitution of the United States represents the greatest model of a federal system that has ever been devised by man. It is only natural that succeeding generations of Americans should revere that compact and consider those who wrote and adopted the Federal Constitution with such awe and respect. Yet, as we are reminded by an ancient philosopher, what really matters is not the *creation* of a wonderful political system, but the *maintenance* of the constitutional system! "Legislators and would-be founders of any Constitution...," observed Aristotle, "will find that the work of construction is not their only or principal business. The maintenance of the Constitution is the thing which really matters." [17]

Although the preservation of the Federal Republic and of States' Rights should have been ensured forevermore by the successful adoption of our present Federal Constitution, in practical terms the continuance of constitutional government has always required the eternal vigilance of the American people.

---

[13] Samuel B. Pettengill, *Jefferson: The Forgotten Man*, America's Future, Inc., New York, 1938, quoted on p. 198.

[14] *Ibid.*, quoted on p. 194.

[15] *Ibid.*, quoted on p. 187.

[16] Alexander H. Stephens, *A Constitutional View of the Late War Between the States*, Volume 1, Kraus Reprint Co., New York, (orig. pub. in 1868) 1970, quoted on p. 283.

[17] Jack Carney, *Nation of Change: The American Democratic System*, Second Edition, Canfield Press, San Francisco, 1972, quoted on p. 49.

Legal theory alone cannot stop those determined to subvert the Constitution, nor can paper guarantees stop the bullets and bombs of a general government determined to conquer the people by military force. The ink had scarcely dried on the new Constitution of 1787 when it became evident that, to preserve constitutionally limited government in the United States, the friends of constitutional liberty would have to be prepared at all times to rise to its defense.

This fact was all too evident to Thomas Jefferson, who summarized the great threat to our Federal Republic in a letter written to William Short on January 8, 1825:

> Monarchy, to be sure, is now defeated, and they wish it should be forgotten that it was ever advocated....Yet the spirit is not done away. The same party takes now what they deem the next best ground, the consolidation of the government; the giving to the federal member of the government, by unlimited constructions of the Constitution, a control over all the functions of the States, and the concentration of all power ultimately at Washington. [18]

The trend toward centralization received a mighty boost as a direct consequence of the horribly cruel and politically tragic War Between the States, which witnessed the military conquest of a number of sovereign States. As Supreme Court Justice Salmon P. Chase could later assert with supreme arrogance, "State sovereignty died at Appomattox." [19] Following this wickedly immoral assertion that a supreme National Government had been established by Military Dictatorship on the ruins of once-sovereign States, the American people witnessed the alarming growth of their general government. A radical Congress quickly arose, proclaiming that it could pass laws to bind the peoples of the several States in all cases whatsoever. The arrogant federal Supreme Court haughtily asserted that the Constitution was whatever it said it was. An imperial Presidency royally laid claim to all powers, including the powers to declare war and to dictate to all nations on the planet. And a vast and complex socialistic bureaucracy was reared to regulate and control every aspect of the lives of the American people.

When we look upon our present Leviathan State, we cannot help but to marvel at the utter unconstitutionality of virtually every act of the Government of the United States. Indeed, to many patriots, the question is no longer what form of tyranny may we expect *in the future* from centralization and consolidation. In the opinion of many observers, the only question is

---

[18] Richard S. Poppen (ed.), *Thomas Jefferson*, St. Louis, 1904, p. 147.
[19] James Ronald Kennedy and Walter Donald Kennedy, *The South Was Right!*, Pelican Publishing Company, Gretna, 1994, quoted on p. 219.

when Americans will awaken to discover that tyranny is already upon them.

It is, of course, undeniable that years of advancing consolidation of authority and centralization of power has propelled us far down the road to despotism. Yet, it is also undeniably true that the States of the Union still survive and that the Federal Constitution still lives. It only remains for the American people to rise up and demand in thunder tones that it be enforced, and that the Federal Government be restored to its proper, constitutional limits.

Although the challenge confronting the champions of liberty and constitutionally limited government is truly great, victory is not beyond reach. It is cause for encouragement to dwell upon the fact that liberty is derived from the *laws of nature*, as a gift from God. As such, it requires no effort to bestow liberty upon any civilization – were it not for the deliberate interventions of mankind to prevent the enjoyment of freedom, liberty would exist as a *natural* blessing throughout the world. Tyranny, on the other hand, is not natural, but is man-made. As such, it requires the *continuous* intervention and active efforts of men to keep liberty from reappearing wherever it has been suppressed. Even after tyranny has been long established, a perpetual effort is required to sustain it, for without continuous sustenance tyranny will succumb to liberty.

In making these observations, we are merely stating the well-established principles of the natural order. It is a fixed law of nature that all things will return to their natural state, unless mankind intervenes to prevent and impede this natural current. Weeds perpetually seek to overcome even the best-tended gardens, and mighty oak trees have been known to push their way through the thickest concrete sidewalks. And, if given enough time, the earth will literally bury man-made homes and cities to such an extent that the standard tools of the archaeologist are the pick and the shovel.

What is true in the physical realm is also true in the political realm. Unnatural political systems can be sustained only by continued and repeated efforts of despots to maintain themselves in power. History is replete with illustrations of tyrants who have attempted to deprive civilizations of their natural freedom by chopping down the Tree of Liberty, only to discover that new Trees of Liberty would spring forth from its seeds. Hence, dictators have found that they must rely on *standing* armies to maintain their authority, for it has been necessary for them to conquer and subdue a civilization, not once, but repeatedly. Even the socialistic regulations and draconian rules of a bureaucratic Welfare State cannot be maintained without continuously expanded efforts and augmentation of authority. It comes as no surprise, therefore, to discover that, within the Interstate Commerce Commission alone, there are more than *one trillion rules* affecting commerce, and the number continues to grow!

In the United States of America, individual liberty, States' Rights, State sovereignty, republican government, and the federal system are all *natural* consequences of American civilization. It required no effort on the part of the Founding Fathers to establish the sovereign States, for they existed naturally, and all that was required on their part was to establish a political system based on these naturally existing American States. Since the time of the War Between the States, however, the concerted efforts of scheming politicians have been employed in an attempt to impose an unnatural supreme National Government on the American people. To maintain this unnatural political system, it has been necessary to rear an army of meddlesome bureaucrats to watch over the resisting people, to enact countless rules and regulations to dominate their lives, and to resort to military force when resistance has been especially strong. Sovereign States may have been conquered in the War Between the States, but their *continued bondage* today results, not from that event of more than one hundred and forty years ago, but from the *current* actions of our Federal Government.

From these observations, the champions of constitutional liberty may derive some hope for the future of the Republic. Yet, while victory is still possible, we must soberly and realistically acknowledge our limitations. Time is clearly working against those who seek to restore constitutional government to the United States. Like a sinking ship, which becomes more difficult to save the more it fills with water, no civilization can endure forever when it is robbed of its most basic freedoms. The ruins of the great civilizations of the past stand as stark reminders that, when all hope for constitutional reformation has past, the doom of all is at hand.

The great challenge we face is significantly magnified by the fact that vast numbers of American citizens have been converted by the Federal Government into wards of the state, both economically and emotionally. To many of our people, the very idea of freedom and its corresponding rugged individualism are frightening thoughts, for they have been convinced that they cannot live without the guiding hand of Big Government. Like the hero of George Orwell's novel, *1984*, large numbers of Americans have been persuaded to love Big Brother. But as Benjamin Franklin once noted, those who are willing to sell their freedom for security will end up with neither liberty nor security.

Already, there are important signposts signaling the bankruptcy of the ignoble Welfare State. For a growing numbers of Americans, the great American Dream has already faded into a distant memory, and prospects of a comfortable retirement in old age steadily become dimmer. The cost of medical care has skyrocketed, inflation is destroying savings, job security no longer exists, disastrous racial and sexual policies have split the people into warring camps, and affirmative action has destroyed all semblance of fairness. American civilization is clearly in decline, a fact that no one will deny. As a consequence, all now agree that major reformation is a stark necessity and that, unless serious reforms are undertaken, the United States of America cannot be saved. The only real question is whether we shall attempt to save ourselves by patching up the unconstitutional political system that has resulted in our distresses, or whether we shall demand the restoration of the system mandated by the Constitution.

The great challenge confronting the modern champions of constitutionally limited government in the United States of America is clearly far greater than that faced by our Founding Fathers to provide us with a political system founded upon the pure and pristine principles of federalism and the sovereignty of the peoples of the States. Unless the American people are equal to the task before them, States' Rights and individual liberty will perish forever in the on-rushing tide of centralization. And should we allow the remaining vestiges of constitutional government to be sacrificed on the altar of a supreme National Government, tyranny – by whatever name we choose to call it – will become inevitable, and the destiny of American civilization will be sealed forever.

Appendix A

The Declaration of Independence

The Unanimous Declaration of the Thirteen United States of America

When, in the course of human events, it becomes necessary for one people to dissolve the political bands which have connected them with another, and to assume among the powers of the earth, the separate and equal station to which the Laws of Nature and of nature's God entitle them, a decent respect to the opinions of mankind requires that they should declare the causes which impel them to the separation.

We hold these truths to be self-evident, that all men are created equal, that they are endowed by their Creator with certain unalienable rights, that among these are life, liberty and the pursuit of happiness. That to secure these rights, governments are instituted among men, deriving their just powers from the consent of the governed. That whenever any form of government becomes destructive to these ends, it is the right of the people to alter or to abolish it, and to institute new government, laying its foundation on such principles and organizing its powers in such form, as to them shall seem most likely to effect their safety and happiness. Prudence, indeed, will dictate that governments long established should not be changed for light and transient causes; and accordingly all experience hath shown that mankind are more disposed to suffer, while evils are sufferable, than to right themselves by abolishing the forms to which they are accustomed. But when a long train of abuses and usurpations, pursuing invariably the same object evinces a design to reduce them under absolute despotism, it is their right, it is their duty, to throw off such government, and to provide new guards for their future security. – Such has been the patient sufferance of these colonies; and such is now the necessity which constrains them to alter their former systems of government. The history of the present King of Great Britain is a history of repeated injuries and usurpations, all having in direct object the establishment of an absolute tyranny over these States. To prove this, let facts be submitted to a candid world.

He has refused his assent to laws, the most wholesome and necessary for the public good.

He has forbidden his Governors to pass laws of immediate and pressing importance, unless suspended in their operation till his assent should be obtained; and when so suspended, he has utterly neglected to attend to them.

He has refused to pass other laws for the accommodation of large districts of people, unless those people would relinquish the right of representation in the legislature, a right inestimable to them and formidable to tyrants only.

He has called together legislative bodies at places unusual, uncomfortable, and distant from the depository of their public records, for the sole purpose of fatiguing them into compliance with his measures.

He has dissolved representative houses repeatedly, for opposing with manly firmness his invasions on the rights of the people.

He has refused for a long time, after such dissolutions, to cause others to be elected; whereby the legislative powers, incapable of annihilation, have returned to the people at large for their exercise; the State remaining in the meantime exposed to all the dangers of invasion from without, and convulsions within.

He has endeavored to prevent the population of these States; for that purpose obstructing the laws for naturalization of foreigners; refusing to pass others to encourage their migration hither, and raising the conditions of new appropriations of lands.

He has obstructed the administration of justice, by refusing his assent to laws for establishing judiciary powers.

He has made judges dependent on his will alone, for the tenure of their offices, and the amount and payment of their salaries.

He has erected a multitude of new offices, and sent hither swarms of officers to harass our people, and eat out their substance.

He has kept among us, in times of peace, standing armies without the consent of our legislature.

He has affected to render the military independent of and superior to civil power.

He has combined with others to subject us to a jurisdiction foreign to our constitution, and unacknowledged by our laws; giving his assent to their acts of pretended legislation:

For quartering large bodies of armed troops among us:

For protecting them, by mock trial, from punishment for any murders which they should commit on the inhabitants of these States:

For cutting off our trade with all parts of the world:

For imposing taxes on us without our consent:

For depriving us in many cases, of the benefits of trial by jury:

For transporting us beyond seas to be tried for pretended offenses:

For abolishing the free system of English laws in a neighboring province, establishing therein an arbitrary government, and enlarging its boundaries so as to render it at once an example and fit instrument for introducing the same absolute rule in these colonies:

For taking away our charters, abolishing our most valuable laws, and altering fundamentally the forms of our governments:

For suspending our own legislatures, and declaring themselves invested with power to legislate for us in all cases whatsoever.

He has abdicated government here, by declaring us out of his protection and waging war against us.

He has plundered our seas, ravaged our coasts, burned our towns, and destroyed the lives of our people.

He is at this time transporting large armies of foreign mercenaries to complete the works of death, desolation and tyranny, already begun with circumstances of cruelty and perfidy scarcely paralleled in the most barbarous ages, and totally unworthy of the head of a civilized nation.

He has constrained our fellow citizens taken captive on the high seas to bear arms against their country, to become the executioners of their friends and brethren, or to fall themselves by their hands.

He has excited domestic insurrections amongst us, and has endeavored to bring on the inhabitants of our frontiers, the merciless Indian savages, whose known rule of warfare, is undistinguished destruction of all ages, sexes and conditions.

In every stage of these oppressions we have petitioned for redress in the most humble terms: our repeated petitions have been answered only by repeated injury. A prince, whose character is thus marked by every act which may define a tyrant, is unfit to be the ruler of a free people.

Nor have we been wanting in attention to our British brethren. We have warned them from time to time of attempts by their legislature to extend an unwarrantable jurisdiction over us. We have reminded them of the circumstances of our emigration and settlement here. We have appealed to their native justice and magnanimity, and we have conjured them by the ties of our common kindred to disavow these usurpations, which, would inevitably interrupt our connections and correspondence. We must, therefore, acquiesce in the necessity, which denounces our separation, and hold them, as we hold the rest of mankind, enemies in war, in peace friends.

We, therefore, the representatives of the United States of America, in General Congress, assembled, appealing to the Supreme Judge of the world for the rectitude of our intentions, do, in the name, and by the authority of the good people of these colonies, solemnly publish and declare, that these United Colonies are, and of right ought to be free and independent States; that they are absolved from all allegiance to the British Crown, and that all political connection between them and the State of Great Britain, is and ought to be totally dissolved; and that as free and independent States, they have full power to levy war, conclude peace, contract alliances, establish commerce, and to do all other acts and things which independent States may of right do. And for the support of this Declaration, with a firm reliance on the protection of Divine Providence, we mutually pledge to each other our lives, our fortunes and our sacred honor.

John Hancock
Button Gwinnett
Lyman Hall
Geo. Walton
Wm. Hooper
Joseph Hewes
John Penn
Edward Rutledge
Thos. Heyward, Junr.
Thomas Lynch, Junr.
Arthur Middleton
Samuel Chase
Wm. Paca
Thos. Stone
Charles Carroll of Carrollton
George Wythe
Richard Henry Lee
Th. Jefferson

Benja. Harrison
Thos. Nelson, Jr.
Francis Lightfoot Lee
Carter Braxton
Robt. Morris
Benjamin Rush
Benja. Franklin
John Morton
Geo. Clymer
Jas. Smith
Geo. Taylor
James Wilson
Geo. Ross
Caesar Rodney
Geo. Read
Tho. Mckean
Wm. Floyd
Phil. Livingston
Frans. Lewis
Lewis Morris

Richd. Stockton
Jno. Witherspoon
Fras. Hopkinson
John Hart
Abra. Clark
Josiah Bartlett
Wm. Whipple
Saml. Adams
John Adams
Robt. Treat Paine
Elbridge Gerry
Step. Hopkins
William Ellery
Roger Sherman
Samuel Huntington
Wm. Williams
Oliver Wolcott
Matthew Thornton

Appendix B
The Articles of Confederation

Preamble

To all to whom these Presents shall come, we the undersigned Delegates of the States affixed to our Names send greeting.

Articles of Confederation and perpetual Union between the States of New Hampshire, Massachusetts-bay Rhode Island and Providence Plantations, Connecticut, New York, New Jersey, Pennsylvania, Delaware, Maryland, Virginia, North Carolina, South Carolina and Georgia.

Article I

The Stile of this Confederacy shall be "The United States of America."

Article II

Each State retains its sovereignty, freedom, and independence, and every power, jurisdiction, and right, which is not by this Confederation expressly delegated to the United States, in Congress assembled.

Article III

The said States hereby severally enter into a firm league of friendship with each other, for their common defense, the security of their liberties, and their mutual and general welfare, binding themselves to assist each other, against all force offered to, or attacks made upon them, or any of them, on account of religion, sovereignty, trade, or any other pretense whatever.

Article IV

The better to secure and perpetuate mutual friendship and intercourse among the people of the different States in this Union, the free inhabitants of each of these States, paupers, vagabonds, and fugitives from justice excepted, shall be entitled to all privileges and immunities of free citizens in the several

States; and the people of each State shall free ingress and regress to and from any other State, and shall enjoy therein all the privileges of trade and commerce, subject to the same duties, impositions, and restrictions as the inhabitants thereof respectively, provided that such restrictions shall not extend so far as to prevent the removal of property imported into any State, to any other State, of which the owner is an inhabitant; provided also that no imposition, duties or restriction shall be laid by any State, on the property of the United States, or either of them.

If any person guilty of, or charged with, treason, felony, or other high misdemeanor in any State, shall flee from justice, and be found in any of the United States, he shall, upon demand of the Governor or executive power of the State from which he fled, be delivered up and removed to the State having jurisdiction of his offense.

Full faith and credit shall be given in each of these States to the records, acts, and judicial proceedings of the courts and magistrates of every other State.

Article V

For the most convenient management of the general interests of the United States, delegates shall be annually appointed in such manner as the legislatures of each State shall direct, to meet in Congress on the first Monday in November, in every year, with a power reserved to each State to recall its delegates, or any of them, at any time within the year, and to send others in their stead for the remainder of the year.

No State shall be represented in Congress by less than two, nor more than seven members; and no person shall be capable of being a delegate for more than three years in any term of six years; nor shall any person, being a delegate, be capable of holding any office under the United States, for which he, or another for his benefit, receives any salary, fees or emolument of any kind.

Each State shall maintain its own delegates in a meeting of the States, and while they act as members of the committee of the States.

In determining questions in the United States in Congress assembled, each State shall have one vote.

Freedom of speech and debate in Congress shall not be impeached or questioned in any court or place out of Congress, and the members of Congress shall be protected in their persons from arrests or imprisonments, during the time of their going to and from, and attendance on Congress, except for treason, felony, or breach of the peace.

Article VI

No State, without the consent of the United States in Congress assembled, shall send any embassy to, or receive any embassy from, or enter into any conference, agreement, alliance or treaty with any King, Prince or State; nor shall any person holding any office of profit or trust under the United States, or any of them, accept any present, emolument, office or title of any kind whatever from any King, Prince or foreign State; nor shall the United States in Congress assembled, or any of them, grant any title of nobility.

No two or more States shall enter into any treaty, confederation or alliance whatever between them, without the consent of the United States in Congress assembled, specifying accurately the purposes for which the same is to be entered into, and how long it shall continue.

No State shall lay any imposts or duties, which may interfere with any stipulations in treaties, entered into by the United States in Congress assembled, with any King, Prince or State, in pursuance of any treaties already proposed by Congress, to the courts of France and Spain.

No vessel of war shall be kept up in time of peace by any State, except such number only, as shall be deemed necessary by the United States in Congress assembled, for the defense of such State, or its trade; nor shall any body of forces be kept up by any State in time of peace, except such number only, as in the judgment of the United States in Congress assembled, shall be deemed requisite to garrison the forts necessary for the defense of such State; but every State shall always keep up a well-regulated and disciplined militia, sufficiently armed and accoutered, and shall provide and constantly have ready for use, in public stores, a due number of field pieces and tents, and a proper quantity of arms, ammunition and camp equipage.

No State shall engage in any war without the consent of the United States in Congress assembled, unless such State be actually invaded by enemies, or shall have received certain advice of a resolution being formed by some nation of Indians to invade such State, and the danger is so imminent as not to admit of a delay till the United States in Congress assembled can be consulted; nor shall any State grant commissions to any ships or vessels of war, nor letters of marque or reprisal, except it be after a declaration of war by the United States in Congress assembled, and then only against the Kingdom or State and the subjects thereof, against which war has been so declared, and under such regulations as shall be established by the United States in Congress assembled, unless such State be infested by pirates, in which case vessels of war may be fitted out for that occasion, and kept so long as the danger shall continue, or until the United States in Congress assembled shall determine otherwise.

Article VII

When land forces are raised by any State for the common defense, all officers of or under the rank of colonel, shall be appointed by the legislature of each State respectively, by whom such forces shall be raised, or in such manner as such State shall direct, and all vacancies shall be filled up by the State which first made the appointment.

Article VIII

All charges of war, and all other expenses that shall be incurred for the common defense or general welfare, and allowed by the United States in Congress assembled, shall be defrayed out of a common treasury, which shall be supplied by the several States in proportion to the value of all land within each State, granted or surveyed for any person, as such land and the buildings and improvements thereon shall be estimated according to such mode as the United States in Congress assembled, shall from time to time direct and appoint.

The taxes for paying that proportion shall be laid and levied by the authority and direction of the legislatures of the several States within the time agreed upon by the United States in Congress assembled.

Article IX

The United States in Congress assembled, shall have the sole and exclusive right and power of determining on peace and war, except in the cases mentioned in the sixth article – of sending and receiving ambassadors – entering into treaties and alliances, provided that no treaty of commerce shall be made whereby the legislative power of the respective States shall be restrained from imposing such imposts and duties on foreigners, as their own people are subjected to, or from prohibiting the exportation or importation of any species of goods or commodities whatsoever – of establishing rules for deciding in all cases, what captures on land or water shall be legal, and in what manner prizes taken by land or naval forces in the service of the United States shall be divided or appropriated – of granting letters of marque and reprisal in times of peace – appointing courts for the trial of piracies and felonies committed on the high seas and establishing courts for receiving and determining finally appeals in all cases of captures, provided that no member of Congress shall be appointed a judge of any of the said courts.

The United States in Congress assembled shall also be the last resort on appeal in all disputes and differences now subsisting or that hereafter may arise between two or more States concerning boundary, jurisdiction or any other causes whatever; which authority shall always be exercised in the manner following. Whenever the legislative or executive authority or lawful agent of any State in controversy with another shall present a petition to Congress stating the matter in question and praying for a hearing, notice thereof shall be given by order of Congress to the legislative or executive authority of the other State in controversy, and a day assigned for the appearance of the parties by their lawful agents, who shall then be directed to appoint by joint consent, commissioners or judges to constitute a court for hearing and determining the matter in question: but if they cannot agree, Congress shall name three persons out of each of the United States, and from the list of such persons each party shall alternately strike out one, the petitioners beginning, until the number shall be reduced to thirteen; and from that number not less than seven, nor more than nine names as Congress shall direct, shall in the presence of Congress be drawn out by lot, and the persons whose names shall be so drawn or any five of them, shall be commissioners or judges, to hear and finally determine the controversy, so always as a major part of the judges who shall hear the cause shall agree in the determination: and if either party shall neglect to attend at the day appointed, without showing reasons, which Congress shall judge sufficient, or being present shall refuse to strike, the Congress shall proceed to nominate three persons out of each State, and the secretary of Congress shall strike in behalf of such party absent or refusing; and the judgment and sentence of the court to be appointed, in the manner before prescribed, shall be final and conclusive; and if any of the parties shall refuse to submit to the authority of such court, or to appear or defend their claim or cause, the court shall nevertheless proceed to pronounce sentence, or judgment, which shall in like manner be final and decisive, the judgment or sentence and other proceedings being in either case transmitted to Congress, and lodged among the acts of Congress for the security of the parties concerned: provided that every commissioner, before he sits in judgment, shall take an oath to be administered by one of the judges of the supreme or superior court of the State, where the cause shall be tried, "well and truly to hear and determine the matter in question, according to the best of his judgment, without favor, affection or hope of reward": provided also, that no State shall be deprived of territory for the benefit of the United States.

All controversies concerning the private right of soil claimed under different grants of two or more States, whose jurisdictions as they may respect such lands, and the States which passed such grants are adjusted, the said grants or either of them being at the same time claimed to have originated antecedent to such settlement of jurisdiction, shall on the petition of either party to the Congress of the United States, be finally determined as near as may be in the same manner as is before prescribed for deciding disputes respecting territorial jurisdiction between different States.

The United States in Congress assembled shall also have the sole and exclusive right and power of regulating the alloy and value of coin struck by their own authority, or by that of the respective States – fixing the standards of weights and measures throughout the United States – regulating the trade and managing all affairs with the Indians, not members of any of the States, provided that the legislative right of any State within its own limits be not infringed or violated – establishing or regulating post offices from one State to another, throughout all the United States, and exacting such postage on the papers passing through the same as may be requisite to defray the expenses of the said office – appointing all officers of the land forces, in the service of the United States, excepting regimental officers – appointing all the officers of the naval forces, and commissioning all officers whatever in the service of the United States – making rules for the government and regulation of the said land and naval forces, and directing their operations.

The United States in Congress assembled shall have authority to appoint a committee, to sit in the recess of Congress, to be denominated "A Committee of the States," and to consist of one delegate from each State; and to appoint such other committees and civil officers as may be necessary for managing the general affairs of the United States under their direction – to appoint one of their members to preside, provided that no person be allowed to serve in the office of President more than one year in any term of three years; to ascertain the necessary sums of money to be raised for the service of the United States, and to appropriate and apply the same for defraying the public expenses – to borrow money, or emit bills on the credit of the United States, transmitting every half-year to the respective States an account of the sums of money so borrowed or emitted – to build and equip a navy – to agree upon the number of land forces, and to make requisitions from each State for its quota, in proportion to the number of white inhabitants in such State; which requisition shall be binding, and thereupon the legislature of each State shall appoint the regimental officers, raise the men and cloath, arm and equip them in a solid-like manner, at the expense of the United States; and the officers and men so cloathed, armed and equipped shall march to the place appointed, and within the time agreed on by the United States in Congress assembled. But if the United States in Congress assembled shall, on consideration of circumstances judge proper that any State should not raise men, or should raise a smaller number of men than the quota thereof, such extra number shall be raised, officered, cloathed, armed and equipped in the same manner as the quota of each State, unless the legislature of such State shall judge that such extra number cannot be safely spread out in the same, in which case they shall raise, officer, cloath, arm and equip as many of such extra number as they judge can be safely spared. And the officers and men so cloathed, armed, and equipped, shall march to the place appointed, and within the time agreed on by the United States in Congress assembled.

The United States in Congress assembled shall never engage in a war, nor grant letters of marque or reprisal in time of peace, nor enter into any treaties or alliances, nor coin money, nor regulate the value thereof, nor ascertain the sums and expenses necessary for the defense and welfare of the United States, or any of them, nor emit bills, nor borrow money on the credit of the United States, nor appropriate money, nor agree upon the number of vessels of war, to be built or purchased, or the number of land or sea forces to be raised, nor appoint a commander in chief of the army or navy, unless nine States assent to the same: nor shall a question on any other point, except for adjourning from day to day be determined, unless by the votes of the majority of the United States in Congress assembled.

The Congress of the United States shall have power to adjourn to any time within the year, and to any place within the United States, so that no period of adjournment be for a longer duration than the space of six months, and shall publish the journal of their proceedings monthly, except such parts thereof relating to treaties, alliances or military operations, as in their judgment require secrecy; and the yeas and nays of the delegates of each State on any question shall be entered on the journal, when it is desired by any delegates of a State, or any of them, at his or their request shall be furnished with a transcript of the said journal, except such parts as are above excepted, to lay before the legislatures of the several States.

Article X

The Committee of the States, or any nine of them, shall be authorized to execute, in the recess of Congress, such of the powers of Congress as the United States in Congress assembled, by the consent of the nine States, shall from time to time think expedient to vest them with; provided that no power be delegated to the said Committee, for the exercise of which, by the Articles of Confederation, the voice of nine States in the Congress of the United States assembled be requisite.

Article XI

Canada acceding to this Confederation, and adjoining in the measures of the United States, shall be admitted into, and entitled to all the advantages of this Union; but no other colony shall be admitted into the same, unless such admission be agreed to by nine States.

Article XII

All bills of credit emitted, monies borrowed, and debts contracted by, or under the authority of Congress, before the assembling of the United States, in pursuance of the present Confederation, shall be deemed and considered as a charge against the United States, for payment and satisfaction whereof the said United States, and the public faith are hereby solemnly pledged.

Article XIII

Every State shall abide by the determination of the United States in Congress assembled, on all questions which by this Confederation are submitted to them. And the Articles of this Confederation shall be inviolably observed by every State, and the Union shall be perpetual; nor shall any alteration at any time hereafter be made in any of them; unless such alteration be agreed to in a Congress of the United States, and be afterwards confirmed by the legislatures of every State.

And Whereas it hath pleased the Great Governor of the World to incline the hearts of the legislatures we respectively represent in Congress, to approve of, and to authorize us to ratify the said Articles of Confederation and perpetual Union. Know Ye that we the undersigned delegates, by virtue of the power and authority to us given for that purpose, do by these presents, in the name and in behalf of our respective constituents, fully and entirely ratify and confirm each and every of the said Articles of Confederation and perpetual Union, and all and singular the matters and things therein contained: And we do further solemnly plight and engage the faith of our respective constituents, that they shall abide by the determinations of the United States in Congress assembled, on all questions, which by the said Confederation are submitted to them. And that the Articles thereof shall be inviolably observed by the States we respectively represent, and that the Union shall be perpetual.

In Witness whereof we have hereunto set our hands in Congress. Done at Philadelphia in the State of Pennsylvania the ninth day of July in the Year of our Lord One Thousand Seven Hundred and Seventy-Eight, and in the Third Year of the independence of America.

On the part and behalf of the State of New Hampshire:
Josiah Bartlett
John Wentworth Junr.
August 8th 1778

On the part and behalf of The State of Massachusetts Bay:
John Hancock
Francis Dana
Samuel Adams
James Lovell
Elbridge Gerry
Samuel Holten

On the part and behalf of the State of Rhode Island and Providence
Plantations:
William Ellery
John Collins
Henry Marchant

On the part and behalf of the State of Connecticut:
Roger Sherman
Titus Hosmer
Samuel Huntington
Andrew Adams
Oliver Wolcott

On the Part and Behalf of the State of New York:
James Duane
Wm Duer
Francis Lewis
Gouv Morris

On the Part and in Behalf of the State of New Jersey, November 26, 1778.
Jno Witherspoon
Nathaniel Scudder

On the part and behalf of the State of Pennsylvania:
Robt Morris
William Clingan
Daniel Roberdeau

Joseph Reed
John Bayard Smith
22nd July 1778

On the part and behalf of the State of Delaware:
Tho Mckean February 12, 1779
John Dickinson May 5th 1779
Nicholas Van Dyke

On the part and behalf of the State of Maryland:
John Hanson March 1 1781
Daniel Carroll Do

On the Part and Behalf of the State of Virginia:
Richard Henry Lee
Jno Harvie
John Banister
Francis Lightfoot Lee
Thomas Adams

On the part and Behalf of the State of No Carolina:
John Penn July 21St 1778
Corns Harnett
Jno Williams

On the part and behalf of the State of South Carolina:
Henry Laurens
Richd Hutson
William Henry Drayton
Thos Heyward Junr
Jno Mathews

On the part and behalf of the State of Georgia:
Jno Walton 24th July 1778
Edwd Telfair
Edwd Langworthy

Appendix C

The Constitution of the United States

Preamble

We the People of the United States, in Order to form a more perfect Union, establish Justice, insure domestic Tranquility, provide for the common defence, promote the general Welfare, and secure the Blessings of Liberty to ourselves and our Posterity, do ordain and establish this Constitution for the United States of America.

Article I

Section 1

All legislative Powers herein granted shall be vested in a Congress of the United States, which shall consist of a Senate and House of Representatives.

Section 2

[Clause 1] The House of Representatives shall be composed of Members chosen every second Year by the People of the several States, and the Electors in each State shall have the Qualifications requisite for Electors of the most numerous Branch of the State Legislature.

[Clause 2] No Person shall be a Representative who shall not have attained to the Age of twenty five Years, and been seven Years a Citizen of the United States, and who shall not, when elected, be an Inhabitant of that State in which he shall be chosen.

[Clause 3] Representatives and direct Taxes shall be apportioned among the several States which may be included within this Union, according to their respective Numbers, which shall be determined by adding to the whole Number of free Persons, including those bound to Service for a Term of Years, and excluding Indians not taxed, three fifths of all other Persons. [*The part of this Clause relating to the mode of apportionment of representatives among the several States has been affected by Section 2 of amendment XIV, and as to taxes on incomes without apportionment by amendment XVI.*] The actual

Enumeration shall be made within three Years after the first Meeting of the Congress of the United States, and within every subsequent Term of ten Years, in such Manner as they shall by Law direct. The Number of Representatives shall not exceed one for every thirty Thousand, but each State shall have at Least one Representative; and until such enumeration shall be made, the State of New Hampshire shall be entitled to chuse three, Massachusetts eight, Rhode-Island and Providence Plantations one, Connecticut five, New-York six, New Jersey four, Pennsylvania eight, Delaware one, Maryland six, Virginia ten, North Carolina five, South Carolina five, and Georgia three.

[Clause 4] When vacancies happen in the Representation from any State, the Executive Authority thereof shall issue Writs of Election to fill such Vacancies.

[Clause 5] The House of Representatives shall chuse their Speaker and other Officers; and shall have the sole Power of Impeachment.

Section 3

[Clause 1] The Senate of the United States shall be composed of two Senators from each State, chosen by the Legislature thereof, for six Years; and each Senator shall have one Vote. [*This Clause has been affected by Clause 1 of Amendment XVII.*]

[Clause 2] Immediately after they shall be assembled in Consequence of the first Election, they shall be divided as equally as may be into three Classes. The Seats of the Senators of the first Class shall be vacated at the Expiration of the second Year, of the second Class at the Expiration of the fourth Year, and of the third Class at the Expiration of the sixth Year, so that one third may be chosen every second Year; and if Vacancies happen by Resignation, or otherwise, during the Recess of the Legislature of any State, the Executive thereof may make temporary Appointments until the next Meeting of the Legislature, which shall then fill such Vacancies. [*This Clause has been affected by Clause 2 of Amendment XVIII.*]

[Clause 3] No Person shall be a Senator who shall not have attained to the Age of thirty Years, and been nine Years a Citizen of the United States, and who shall not, when elected, be an Inhabitant of that State for which he shall be chosen.

[Clause 4] The Vice President of the United States shall be President of the Senate, but shall have no Vote, unless they be equally divided.

[Clause 5] The Senate shall chuse their other Officers, and also a President pro tempore, in the Absence of the Vice President, or when he shall exercise the Office of President of the United States.

[Clause 6] The Senate shall have the sole Power to try all Impeachments. When sitting for that Purpose, they shall be on Oath or Affirmation. When the President of the United States is tried, the Chief Justice shall preside: And no Person shall be convicted without the Concurrence of two thirds of the Members present.

[Clause 7] Judgment in Cases of Impeachment shall not extend further than to removal from Office, and disqualification to hold and enjoy any Office of honor, Trust or Profit under the United States: but the Party convicted shall nevertheless be liable and subject to Indictment, Trial, Judgment and Punishment, according to Law.

Section 4

[Clause 1] The Times, Places and Manner of holding Elections for Senators and Representatives, shall be prescribed in each State by the Legislature thereof; but the Congress may at any time by Law make or alter such Regulations, except as to the Places of chusing Senators.

[Clause 2] The Congress shall assemble at least once in every Year, and such Meeting shall be on the first Monday in December, unless they shall by Law appoint a different Day. [*This Clause has been affected by Amendment XX.*]

Section 5

[Clause 1] Each House shall be the Judge of the Elections, Returns and Qualifications of its own Members, and a Majority of each shall constitute a Quorum to do Business; but a smaller Number may adjourn from day to day, and may be authorized to compel the Attendance of absent Members, in such Manner, and under such Penalties as each House may provide.

[Clause 2] Each House may determine the Rules of its Proceedings, punish its Members for disorderly Behaviour, and, with the Concurrence of two thirds, expel a Member.

[Clause 3] Each House shall keep a Journal of its Proceedings, and from time to time publish the same, excepting such Parts as may in their Judgment require Secrecy; and the Yeas and Nays of the Members of either House on any question shall, at the Desire of one fifth of those Present, be entered on the Journal.

[Clause 4] Neither House, during the Session of Congress, shall, without the Consent of the other, adjourn for more than three days, nor to any other Place than that in which the two Houses shall be sitting.

Section 6

[Clause 1] The Senators and Representatives shall receive a Compensation for their Services, to be ascertained by Law, and paid out of the Treasury of the United States. [*This Clause has been affected by Amendment XXVII.*] They shall in all Cases, except Treason, Felony and Breach of the Peace, be privileged from Arrest during their Attendance at the Session of their respective Houses, and in going to and returning from the same; and for any Speech or Debate in either House, they shall not be questioned in any other Place.

[Clause 2] No Senator or Representative shall, during the Time for which he was elected, be appointed to any civil Office under the Authority of the United States, which shall have been created, or the Emoluments whereof shall have been increased during such time; and no Person holding any Office under the United States, shall be a Member of either House during his Continuance in Office.

Section 7

[Clause 1] All Bills for raising Revenue shall originate in the House of Representatives; but the Senate may propose or concur with Amendments as on other Bills.

[Clause 2] Every Bill which shall have passed the House of Representatives and the Senate, shall, before it become a Law, be presented to the President of the United States; If he approve he shall sign it, but if not he shall return it, with his Objections to that House in which it shall have originated, who shall enter the Objections at large on their Journal, and proceed to reconsider it. If after such Reconsideration two thirds of that House shall agree to pass the Bill, it shall be sent, together with the Objections, to the other House, by which it shall likewise be reconsidered, and if approved by two thirds of that House, it shall become a Law. But in all such Cases the Votes of both Houses shall be determined by yeas and Nays, and the Names of the Persons voting for and against the Bill shall be entered on the Journal of each House respectively. If any Bill shall not be returned by the President within ten Days (Sundays excepted) after it shall have been presented to him, the Same shall be a Law, in like Manner as if he had signed it, unless the Congress by their Adjournment prevent its Return, in which Case it shall not be a Law.

[Clause 3] Every Order, Resolution, or Vote to which the Concurrence of the Senate and House of Representatives may be necessary (except on a question of Adjournment) shall be presented to the President of the United States; and before the Same shall take Effect, shall be approved by him, or being disapproved by him, shall be repassed by two thirds of the Senate and House of Representatives, according to the Rules and Limitations prescribed in the Case of a Bill.

Section 8

[Clause 1] The Congress shall have Power To lay and collect Taxes, Duties, Imposts and Excises, to pay the Debts and provide for the common Defence and general Welfare of the United States; but all Duties, Imposts and Excises shall be uniform throughout the United States;

[Clause 2] To borrow Money on the credit of the United States;

[Clause 3] To regulate Commerce with foreign Nations, and among the several States, and with the Indian Tribes;

[Clause 4] To establish an uniform Rule of Naturalization, and uniform Laws on the subject of Bankruptcies throughout the United States;

[Clause 5] To coin Money, regulate the Value thereof, and of foreign Coin, and fix the Standard of Weights and Measures;

[Clause 6] To provide for the Punishment of counterfeiting the Securities and current Coin of the United States;

[Clause 7] To establish Post Offices and post Roads;

[Clause 8] To promote the Progress of Science and useful Arts, by securing for limited Times to Authors and Inventors the exclusive Right to their respective Writings and Discoveries;

[Clause 9] To constitute Tribunals inferior to the Supreme Court;

[Clause 10] To define and punish Piracies and Felonies committed on the high Seas, and Offences against the Law of Nations;

[Clause 11] To declare War, grant Letters of Marque and Reprisal, and make Rules concerning Captures on Land and Water;

[Clause 12] To raise and support Armies, but no Appropriation of Money to that Use shall be for a longer Term than two Years;

[Clause 13] To provide and maintain a Navy;

[Clause 14] To make Rules for the Government and Regulation of the land and naval Forces;

[Clause 15] To provide for calling forth the Militia to execute the Laws of the Union, suppress Insurrections and repel Invasions;

[Clause 16] To provide for organizing, arming, and disciplining, the Militia, and for governing such Part of them as may be employed in the Service of the United States, reserving to the States respectively, the Appointment of the Officers, and the Authority of training the Militia according to the discipline prescribed by Congress;

[Clause 17] To exercise exclusive Legislation in all Cases whatsoever, over such District (not exceeding ten Miles square) as may, by Cession of particular States, and the Acceptance of Congress, become the Seat of the Government of the United States, and to exercise like Authority over all Places purchased by the Consent of the Legislature of the State in which the Same shall be, for the Erection of Forts, Magazines, Arsenals, dock-Yards, and other needful Buildings; – And

[Clause 18] To make all Laws which shall be necessary and proper for carrying into Execution the foregoing Powers, and all other Powers vested by this Constitution in the Government of the United States, or in any Department or Officer thereof.

Section 9

[Clause 1] The Migration or Importation of such Persons as any of the States now existing shall think proper to admit, shall not be prohibited by the Congress prior to the Year one thousand eight hundred and eight, but a Tax or duty may be imposed on such Importation, not exceeding ten dollars for each Person.

[Clause 2] The Privilege of the Writ of Habeas Corpus shall not be suspended, unless when in Cases of Rebellion or Invasion the public Safety may require it.

[Clause 3] No Bill of Attainder or ex post facto Law shall be passed.

[Clause 4] No Capitation, or other direct, Tax shall be laid, unless in Proportion to the Census or Enumeration herein before directed to be taken. [*This Clause has been affected by Amendment XVI.*]

[Clause 5] No Tax or Duty shall be laid on Articles exported from any State.

[Clause 6] No Preference shall be given by any Regulation of Commerce or Revenue to the Ports of one State over those of another: nor shall Vessels bound to, or from, one State, be obliged to enter, clear, or pay Duties in another.

[Clause 7] No Money shall be drawn from the Treasury, but in Consequence of Appropriations made by Law; and a regular Statement and Account of the Receipts and Expenditures of all public Money shall be published from time to time.

[Clause 8] No Title of Nobility shall be granted by the United States: And no Person holding any Office of Profit or Trust under them, shall, without the Consent of the Congress, accept of any present, Emolument, Office, or Title, of any kind whatever, from any King, Prince, or foreign State.

Section 10

[Clause 1] No State shall enter into any Treaty, Alliance, or Confederation; grant Letters of Marque and Reprisal; coin Money; emit Bills of Credit; make any Thing but gold and silver Coin a Tender in Payment of Debts; pass any Bill of Attainder, ex post facto Law, or Law impairing the Obligation of Contracts, or grant any Title of Nobility.

[Clause 2] No State shall, without the Consent of the Congress, lay any Imposts or Duties on Imports or Exports, except what may be absolutely necessary for executing its inspection Laws: and the net Produce of all Duties and Imposts, laid by any State on Imports or Exports, shall be for the Use of the Treasury of the United States; and all such Laws shall be subject to the Revision and Controul of the Congress.

[Clause 3] No State shall, without the Consent of Congress, lay any Duty of Tonnage, keep Troops, or Ships of War in time of Peace, enter into any Agreement or Compact with another State, or with a foreign Power, or engage in War, unless actually invaded, or in such imminent Danger as will not admit of delay.

Article II

Section 1

[Clause 1] The executive Power shall be vested in a President of the United States of America. He shall hold his Office during the Term of four Years, and, together with the Vice President, chosen for the same Term, be elected, as follows

[Clause 2] Each State shall appoint, in such Manner as the Legislature thereof may direct, a Number of Electors, equal to the whole Number of Senators and Representatives to which the State may be entitled in the Congress: but no Senator or Representative, or Person holding an Office of Trust or Profit under the United States, shall be appointed an Elector.

[Clause 3] The Electors shall meet in their respective States, and vote by Ballot for two Persons, of whom one at least shall not be an Inhabitant of the same State with themselves. And they shall make a List of all the Persons voted for, and of the Number of Votes for each; which List they shall sign and certify, and transmit sealed to the Seat of the Government of the United States, directed to the President of the Senate. The President of the Senate shall, in the Presence of the Senate and House of Representatives, open all the Certificates, and the Votes shall then be counted. The Person having the greatest Number of Votes shall be the President, if such Number be a Majority of the whole Number of Electors appointed; and if there be more than one who have such Majority, and have an equal Number of Votes, then the House of Representatives shall immediately chuse by Ballot one of them for President; and if no Person have a Majority, then from the five highest on the List the said House shall in like Manner chuse the President. But in chusing the President, the Votes shall be taken by States, the Representation from each State having one Vote; A quorum for this Purpose shall consist of a Member or Members from two thirds of the States, and a Majority of all the States shall be necessary to a Choice. In every Case, after the Choice of the President, the Person having the greatest Number of Votes of the Electors shall be the Vice President. But if there should remain two or more who have equal Votes, the Senate shall chuse from them by Ballot the Vice President. [*This Clause has been superseded by Amendment XII.*]

[Clause 4] The Congress may determine the Time of chusing the Electors, and the Day on which they shall give their Votes; which Day shall be the same throughout the United States.

[Clause 5] No Person except a natural born Citizen, or a Citizen of the United States, at the time of the Adoption of this Constitution, shall be eligible to the Office of President; neither shall any Person be eligible to that Office who shall not have attained to the Age of thirty five Years, and been fourteen Years a Resident within the United States.

[Clause 6] In Case of the Removal of the President from Office, or of his Death, Resignation, or Inability to discharge the Powers and Duties of the said Office, the Same shall devolve on the Vice President, and the Congress may by Law provide for the Case of Removal, Death, Resignation or Inability, both of the President and Vice President, declaring what Officer shall then act as President, and such Officer shall act accordingly, until the Disability be removed, or a President shall be elected. [*This Clause has been affected by Amendment XXV.*]

[Clause 7] The President shall, at stated Times, receive for his Services, a Compensation, which shall neither be increased nor diminished during the Period for which he shall have been elected, and he shall not receive within that Period any other Emolument from the United States, or any of them.

[Clause 8] Before he enter on the Execution of his Office, he shall take the following Oath or Affirmation: – "I do solemnly swear (or affirm) that I will faithfully execute the Office of President of the United States, and will to the best of my Ability, preserve, protect and defend the Constitution of the United States."

Section 2

[Clause 1] The President shall be Commander in Chief of the Army and Navy of the United States, and of the Militia of the several States, when called into the actual Service of the United States; he may require the Opinion, in writing, of the principal Officer in each of the executive Departments, upon any Subject relating to the Duties of their respective Offices, and he shall have Power to grant Reprieves and Pardons for Offences against the United States, except in Cases of Impeachment.

[Clause 2] He shall have Power, by and with the Advice and Consent of the Senate, to make Treaties, provided two thirds of the Senators present concur; and he shall nominate, and by and with the Advice and Consent of the Senate, shall appoint Ambassadors, other public Ministers and Consuls, Judges of the Supreme Court, and all other Officers of the United States, whose Appointments are not herein otherwise provided for, and which shall be established by Law: but the Congress may by Law vest the Appointment of such inferior Officers, as they think proper, in the President alone, in the Courts of Law, or in the Heads of Departments.

[Clause 3] The President shall have Power to fill up all Vacancies that may happen during the Recess of the Senate, by granting Commissions which shall expire at the End of their next Session.

Section 3

He shall from time to time give to the Congress Information of the State of the Union, and recommend to their Consideration such Measures as he shall judge necessary and expedient; he may, on extraordinary Occasions, convene both Houses, or either of them, and in Case of Disagreement between them, with Respect to the Time of Adjournment, he may adjourn them to such Time as he shall think proper; he shall receive Ambassadors and other public Ministers; he shall take Care that the Laws be faithfully executed, and shall Commission all the Officers of the United States.

Section 4

The President, Vice President and all civil Officers of the United States, shall be removed from Office on Impeachment for, and Conviction of, Treason, Bribery, or other high Crimes and Misdemeanors.

Article III

Section 1

The judicial Power of the United States, shall be vested in one Supreme Court, and in such inferior Courts as the Congress may from time to time ordain and establish. The Judges, both of the supreme and inferior Courts, shall hold their Offices during good Behaviour, and shall, at stated Times, receive for their Services, a Compensation, which shall not be diminished during their Continuance in Office.

Section 2

[Clause 1] The judicial Power shall extend to all Cases, in Law and Equity, arising under this Constitution, the Laws of the United States, and Treaties made, or which shall be made, under their Authority; – to all Cases affecting Ambassadors, other public Ministers and Consuls; – to all Cases of admiralty and maritime Jurisdiction; – to Controversies to which the United States shall be a Party; – to Controversies between two or more States; – between a State and Citizens of another State; – between Citizens of different States, – between Citizens of the same State claiming Lands under Grants of different States, and between a State, or the Citizens thereof, and foreign States, Citizens or Subjects. [*This Clause has been affected by Amendment XI.*]

[Clause 2] In all Cases affecting Ambassadors, other public Ministers and Consuls, and those in which a State shall be Party, the Supreme Court shall have original Jurisdiction. In all the other Cases before mentioned, the Supreme Court shall have appellate Jurisdiction, both as to Law and Fact, with such Exceptions, and under such Regulations as the Congress shall make.

[Clause 3] The Trial of all Crimes, except in Cases of Impeachment, shall be by Jury; and such Trial shall be held in the State where the said Crimes shall have been committed; but when not committed within any State, the Trial shall be at such Place or Places as the Congress may by Law have directed.

Section 3

[Clause 1] Treason against the United States, shall consist only in levying War against them, or in adhering to their Enemies, giving them Aid and Comfort. No Person shall be convicted of Treason unless on the Testimony of two Witnesses to the same overt Act, or on Confession in open Court.

[Clause 2] The Congress shall have Power to declare the Punishment of Treason, but no Attainder of Treason shall work Corruption of Blood, or Forfeiture except during the Life of the Person attainted.

Article IV

Section 1

Full Faith and Credit shall be given in each State to the public Acts, Records, and judicial Proceedings of every other State. And the Congress may by general Laws prescribe the Manner in which such Acts, Records and Proceedings shall be proved, and the Effect thereof.

Section 2

[Clause 1] The Citizens of each State shall be entitled to all Privileges and Immunities of Citizens in the several States.

[Clause 2] A Person charged in any State with Treason, Felony, or other Crime, who shall flee from Justice, and be found in another State, shall on Demand of the executive Authority of the State from which he fled, be delivered up, to be removed to the State having Jurisdiction of the Crime.

[Clause 3] No Person held to Service or Labour in one State, under the Laws thereof, escaping into another, shall, in Consequence of any Law or Regulation therein, be discharged from such Service or Labour, but shall be delivered up on Claim of the Party to whom such Service or Labour may be due. [*This Clause has been affected by Amendment XIII.*]

Section 3

[Clause 1] New States may be admitted by the Congress into this Union; but no new State shall be formed or erected within the Jurisdiction of any other State; nor any State be formed by the Junction of two or more States, or Parts of States, without the Consent of the Legislatures of the States concerned as well as of the Congress.

[Clause 2] The Congress shall have Power to dispose of and make all needful Rules and Regulations respecting the Territory or other Property belonging to the United States; and nothing in this Constitution shall be so construed as to Prejudice any Claims of the United States, or of any particular State.

Section 4

The United States shall guarantee to every State in this Union a Republican Form of Government, and shall protect each of them against Invasion; and on Application of the Legislature, or of the Executive (when the Legislature cannot be convened) against domestic Violence.

Article V

The Congress, whenever two thirds of both Houses shall deem it necessary, shall propose Amendments to this Constitution, or, on the Application of the Legislatures of two thirds of the several States, shall call a Convention for proposing Amendments, which, in either Case, shall be valid to all Intents and Purposes, as Part of this Constitution, when ratified by the Legislatures of three fourths of the several States, or by Conventions in three fourths thereof, as the one or the other Mode of Ratification may be proposed by the Congress; Provided that no Amendment which may be made prior to the Year One thousand eight hundred and eight shall in any Manner affect the first and fourth Clauses in the Ninth Section of the first Article; and that no State, without its Consent, shall be deprived of its equal Suffrage in the Senate.

Article VI

[Clause 1] All Debts contracted and Engagements entered into, before the Adoption of this Constitution, shall be as valid against the United States under this Constitution, as under the Confederation.

[Clause 2] This Constitution, and the Laws of the United States which shall be made in Pursuance thereof; and all Treaties made, or which shall be made, under the Authority of the United States, shall be the supreme Law of the Land; and the Judges in every State shall be bound thereby, any Thing in the Constitution or Laws of any State to the Contrary notwithstanding.

[Clause 3] The Senators and Representatives before mentioned, and the Members of the several State Legislatures, and all executive and judicial Officers, both of the United States and of the several States, shall be bound by Oath or Affirmation, to support this Constitution; but no religious Test shall ever be required as a Qualification to any Office or public Trust under the United States.

Article VII

The Ratification of the Conventions of nine States, shall be sufficient for the Establishment of this Constitution between the States so ratifying the Same.

Done in Convention by the Unanimous Consent of the States present the Seventeenth Day of September in the Year of our Lord one thousand seven hundred and Eighty seven and of the Independence of the United States of America the Twelfth In witness whereof We have hereunto subscribed our Names,

GO WASHINGTON--Presidt. and deputy from Virginia

Delaware
Geo: Read
Gunning Bedford jun
John Dickinson
Richard Bassett
Jaco: Broom

Maryland
James MCHenry
Dan of ST ThoS. Jenifer
DanL Carroll.

Virginia
John Blair--
James Madison Jr.
North Carolina
WM Blount
RichD. Dobbs Spaight.
Hu Williamson

South Carolina
J. Rutledge
Charles 1ACotesworth Pinckney
Charles Pinckney
Pierce Butler.

Georgia

William Few
Abr Baldwin

New Hampshire
John Langdon
Nicholas Gilman

Massachusetts
Nathaniel Gorham
Rufus King

Connecticut
Wm. SamL. Johnson
Roger Sherman

New York
Alexander Hamilton

New Jersey
Wil: Livingston
David Brearley.
WM. Paterson.
Jona: Dayton

Pennsylvania
B Franklin
Thomas Mifflin
RobT Morris
Geo. Clymer
ThoS. FitzSimons
Jared Ingersoll
James Wilson.
Gouv Morris

Attest William Jackson Secretary

Amendment I

Congress shall make no law respecting an establishment of religion, or prohibiting the free exercise thereof; or abridging the freedom of speech, or of the press; or the right of the people peaceably to assemble, and to petition the Government for a redress of grievances.

Amendment II

A well regulated Militia, being necessary to the security of a free State, the right of the people to keep and bear Arms, shall not be infringed.

Amendment III

No Soldier shall, in time of peace be quartered in any house, without the consent of the Owner, nor in time of war, but in a manner to be prescribed by law.

Amendment IV

The right of the people to be secure in their persons, houses, papers, and effects, against unreasonable searches and seizures, shall not be violated, and no Warrants shall issue, but upon probable cause, supported by Oath or affirmation, and particularly describing the place to be searched, and the persons or things to be seized.

Amendment V

No person shall be held to answer for a capital, or otherwise infamous crime, unless on a presentment or indictment of a Grand Jury, except in cases arising in the land or naval forces, or in the Militia, when in actual service in time of War or public danger; nor shall any person be subject for the same offence to be twice put in jeopardy of life or limb; nor shall be compelled in any criminal case to be a witness against himself, nor be deprived of life, liberty, or property, without due process of law; nor shall private property be taken for public use, without just compensation.

Amendment VI

In all criminal prosecutions, the accused shall enjoy the right to a speedy and public trial, by an impartial jury of the State and district wherein the crime shall have been committed, which district shall have been previously ascertained by law, and to be informed of the nature and cause of the accusation; to be confronted with the witnesses against him; to have compulsory process for obtaining witnesses in his favor, and to have the Assistance of Counsel for his defence.

Amendment VII

In Suits at common law, where the value in controversy shall exceed twenty dollars, the right of trial by jury shall be preserved, and no fact tried by a jury, shall be otherwise re-examined in any Court of the United States, than according to the rules of the common law.

Amendment VIII

Excessive bail shall not be required, nor excessive fines imposed, nor cruel and unusual punishments inflicted.

Amendment IX

The enumeration in the Constitution, of certain rights, shall not be construed to deny or disparage others retained by the people.

Amendment X

The powers not delegated to the United States by the Constitution, nor prohibited by it to the States, are reserved to the States respectively, or to the people.

Amendment XI

The Judicial power of the United States shall not be construed to extend to any suit in law or equity, commenced or prosecuted against one of the United States by Citizens of another State, or by Citizens or Subjects of any Foreign State.

Amendment XII

The Electors shall meet in their respective States, and vote by ballot for

President and Vice-President, one of whom, at least, shall not be an inhabitant of the same State with themselves; they shall name in their ballots the person voted for as President, and in distinct ballots the person voted for as Vice-President, and they shall make distinct lists of all persons voted for as President, and of all persons voted for as Vice-President, and of the number of votes for each, which lists they shall sign and certify, and transmit sealed to the seat of the government of the United States, directed to the President of the Senate; –The President of the Senate shall, in the presence of the Senate and House of Representatives, open all the certificates and the votes shall then be counted; –The person having the greatest number of votes for President, shall be the President, if such number be a majority of the whole number of Electors appointed; and if no person have such majority, then from the persons having the highest numbers not exceeding three on the list of those voted for as President, the House of Representatives shall choose immediately, by ballot, the President. But in choosing the President, the votes shall be taken by States, the representation from each State having one vote; a quorum for this purpose shall consist of a member or members from two-thirds of the States, and a majority of all the States shall be necessary to a choice. And if the House of Representatives shall not choose a President whenever the right of choice shall devolve upon them, before the fourth day of March next following, then the Vice-President shall act as President, as in the case of the death or other constitutional disability of the President. [*This sentence has been superseded by section 3 of Amendment XX*] – The person having the greatest number of votes as Vice-President, shall be the Vice-President, if such number be a majority of the whole number of Electors appointed, and if no person have a majority, then from the two highest numbers on the list, the Senate shall choose the Vice-President; a quorum for the purpose shall consist of two-thirds of the whole number of Senators, and a majority of the whole number shall be necessary to a choice. But no person constitutionally ineligible to the office of President shall be eligible to that of Vice-President of the United States.

Amendment XIII

Section 1. Neither slavery nor involuntary servitude, except as a punishment for crime whereof the party shall have been duly convicted, shall exist within the United States, or any place subject to their jurisdiction.

Section 2. Congress shall have power to enforce this article by appropriate legislation.

Amendment XIV
[*Not Lawfully Ratified*]

Section 1. All persons born or naturalized in the United States, and subject to the jurisdiction thereof, are citizens of the United States and of the State wherein they reside. No State shall make or enforce any law which shall abridge the privileges or immunities of citizens of the United States; nor shall any State deprive any person of life, liberty, or property, without due process of law; nor deny to any person within its jurisdiction the equal protection of the laws.

Section 2. Representatives shall be apportioned among the several States according to their respective numbers, counting the whole number of persons in each State, excluding Indians not taxed. But when the right to vote at any election for the choice of electors for President and Vice President of the United States, Representatives in Congress, the Executive and Judicial officers of a State, or the members of the Legislature thereof, is denied to any of the male inhabitants of such State, being twenty-one years of age, [*See amendment XIX and section 1 of amendment XXVI.*] and citizens of the United States, or in any way abridged, except for participation in rebellion, or other crime, the basis of representation therein shall be reduced in the proportion which the number of such male citizens shall bear to the whole number of male citizens twenty-one years of age in such State.

Section 3. No person shall be a Senator or Representative in Congress, or elector of President and Vice President, or hold any office, civil or military, under the United States, or under any State, who, having previously taken an oath, as a member of Congress, or as an officer of the United States, or as a member of any State legislature, or as an executive or judicial officer of any State, to support the Constitution of the United States, shall have engaged in insurrection or rebellion against the same, or given aid or comfort to the enemies thereof. But Congress may by a vote of two-thirds of each House, remove such disability.

Section 4. The validity of the public debt of the United States, authorized by law, including debts incurred for payment of pensions and bounties for services in suppressing insurrection or rebellion, shall not be questioned. But neither the United States nor any State shall assume or pay any debt or obligation incurred in aid of insurrection or rebellion against the United States, or any claim for the loss or emancipation of any slave; but all such debts, obligations and claims shall be held illegal and void.

Section 5. The Congress shall have power to enforce, by appropriate legislation, the provisions of this article.

Amendment XV

Section 1. The right of citizens of the United States to vote shall not be denied or abridged by the United States or by any State on account of race, color, or previous condition of servitude.

Section 2. The Congress shall have power to enforce this article by appropriate legislation.

Amendment XVI

The Congress shall have power to lay and collect taxes on incomes, from whatever source derived, without apportionment among the several States, and without regard to any census or enumeration.

Amendment XVII

The Senate of the United States shall be composed of two Senators from each State, elected by the people thereof, for six years; and each Senator shall have one vote. The electors in each State shall have the qualifications requisite for electors of the most numerous branch of the State legislatures.

When vacancies happen in the representation of any State in the Senate, the executive authority of such State shall issue writs of election to fill such vacancies: Provided, That the legislature of any State may empower the executive thereof to make temporary appointments until the people fill the vacancies by election as the legislature may direct.

This amendment shall not be so construed as to affect the election or term of any Senator chosen before it becomes valid as part of the Constitution.

Amendment XVIII
[Repealed by Section 1 of Amendment XXI.]

Section 1. After one year from the ratification of this article the manufacture, sale, or transportation of intoxicating liquors within, the importation thereof into, or the exportation thereof from the United States and all territory subject to the jurisdiction thereof for beverage purposes is hereby prohibited.

Section. 2. The Congress and the several States shall have concurrent power to enforce this article by appropriate legislation.

Section. 3. This article shall be inoperative unless it shall have been ratified as an amendment to the Constitution by the legislatures of the several States, as provided in the Constitution, within seven years from the date of the submission hereof to the States by the Congress.

Amendment XIX

The right of citizens of the United States to vote shall not be denied or abridged by the United States or by any State on account of sex.

Congress shall have power to enforce this article by appropriate legislation.

Amendment XX

Section 1. The terms of the President and Vice President shall end at noon on the 20th day of January, and the terms of Senators and Representatives at noon on the 3d day of January, of the years in which such terms would have ended if this article had not been ratified; and the terms of their successors shall then begin.

Section. 2. The Congress shall assemble at least once in every year, and such meeting shall begin at noon on the 3d day of January, unless they shall by law appoint a different day.

Section. 3. If, at the time fixed for the beginning of the term of the President, the President elect shall have died, the Vice President elect shall become President. If a President shall not have been chosen before the time fixed for the beginning of his term, or if the President elect shall have failed to qualify, then the Vice President elect shall act as President until a President shall have qualified; and the Congress may by law provide for the case wherein neither a President elect nor a Vice President elect shall have qualified, declaring who shall then act as President, or the manner in which one who is to act shall be selected, and such person shall act accordingly until a President or Vice President shall have qualified.

Section. 4. The Congress may by law provide for the case of the death of any of the persons from whom the House of Representatives may choose a President whenever the right of choice shall have devolved upon them, and for the case of the death of any of the persons from whom the Senate may choose a Vice President whenever the right of choice shall have devolved upon them.

Section. 5. Sections 1 and 2 shall take effect on the 15th day of October following the ratification of this article.

Section. 6. This article shall be inoperative unless it shall have been ratified as an amendment to the Constitution by the legislatures of three-fourths of the several States within seven years from the date of its submission.

Amendment XXI

Section 1. The eighteenth article of amendment to the Constitution of the United States is hereby repealed.

Section 2. The transportation or importation into any State, Territory, or possession of the United States for delivery or use therein of intoxicating liquors, in violation of the laws thereof, is hereby prohibited.

Section 3. This article shall be inoperative unless it shall have been ratified as an amendment to the Constitution by conventions in the several States, as provided in the Constitution, within seven years from the date of the submission hereof to the States by the Congress.

Amendment XXII

Section 1. No person shall be elected to the office of the President more than twice, and no person who has held the office of President, or acted as President, for more than two years of a term to which some other person was elected President shall be elected to the office of the President more than once. But this article shall not apply to any person holding the office of President when this article was proposed by the Congress, and shall not prevent any person who may be holding the office of President, or acting as President, during the term within which this article becomes operative from holding the office of President or acting as President during the remainder of such term.

Section 2. This article shall be inoperative unless it shall have been ratified as an amendment to the Constitution by the legislatures of three-fourths of the several states within seven years from the date of its submission to the states by the Congress.

Amendment XXIII

Section 1. The District constituting the seat of government of the United States shall appoint in such manner as the Congress may direct:

A number of electors of President and Vice President equal to the whole number of Senators and Representatives in Congress to which the District would be entitled if it were a state, but in no event more than the least populous State; they shall be in addition to those appointed by the States, but they shall be considered, for the purposes of the election of President and Vice President, to be electors appointed by a State; and they shall meet in the District and perform such duties as provided by the twelfth article of amendment.

Section 2. The Congress shall have power to enforce this article by appropriate legislation.

Amendment XXIV

Section 1. The right of citizens of the United States to vote in any primary or other election for President or Vice President, for electors for President or Vice President, or for Senator or Representative in Congress, shall not be denied or abridged by the United States or any state by reason of failure to pay any poll tax or other tax.

Section 2. The Congress shall have power to enforce this article by appropriate legislation.

Amendment XXV

Section 1. In case of the removal of the President from office or of his death or resignation, the Vice President shall become President.

Section 2. Whenever there is a vacancy in the office of the Vice President, the President shall nominate a Vice President who shall take office upon confirmation by a majority vote of both Houses of Congress.

Section 3. Whenever the President transmits to the President pro tempore of the Senate and the Speaker of the House of Representatives his written declaration that he is unable to discharge the powers and duties of his office, and until he transmits to them a written declaration to the contrary, such powers and duties shall be discharged by the Vice President as Acting President.

Section 4. Whenever the Vice President and a majority of either the principal officers of the executive departments or of such other body as Congress may by law provide, transmit to the President pro tempore of the Senate and the Speaker of the House of Representatives their written declaration that the President is unable to discharge the powers and duties of his office, the Vice President shall immediately assume the powers and duties of the office as Acting President.

Thereafter, when the President transmits to the President pro tempore of the Senate and the Speaker of the House of Representatives his written declaration that no inability exists, he shall resume the powers and duties of his office unless the Vice President and a majority of either the principal officers of the executive department or of such other body as Congress may by law provide, transmit within four days to the President pro tempore of the Senate and the Speaker of the House of Representatives their written declaration that the President is unable to discharge the powers and duties of his office. Thereupon Congress shall decide the issue, assembling within forty-eight hours for that purpose if not in session. If the Congress, within twenty-one days after receipt of the latter written declaration, or, if Congress is not in session, within twenty-one days after Congress is required to assemble, determines by two-thirds vote of both Houses that the President is unable to discharge the powers and duties of his office, the Vice President shall continue to discharge the same as Acting President; otherwise, the President shall resume the powers and duties of his office.

Amendment XXVI

Section 1. The right of citizens of the United States, who are 18 years of age or older, to vote, shall not be denied or abridged by the United States or any State on account of age.

Section 2. The Congress shall have the power to enforce this article by appropriate legislation.

Amendment XXVII

No law varying the compensation for the services of the Senators and Representatives shall take effect until an election of Representatives shall have intervened.

Index

Made in the USA